Ethical Justice

Ethical Justice

Applied Issues for Criminal Justice Students and Professionals

Brent E. Turvey
Stan Crowder

Amsterdam ▪ Boston ▪ Heidelberg ▪ London ▪ New York ▪ Oxford ▪ Paris
San Diego ▪ San Francisco ▪ Singapore ▪ Sydney ▪ Tokyo

Academic Press is an imprint of Elsevier

Academic Press is an imprint of Elsevier
The Boulevard, Langford Lane, Kidlington, Oxford, OX5 1GB
225 Wyman Street, Waltham, MA 02451, USA

First published 2013

British Library Cataloguing in Publication Data
A catalogue record for this book is available from the British Library

Library of Congress Cataloging-in-Publication Data
A catalog record for this book is available from the Library of Congress

ISBN: 978-0-12-404597-2

For information on all Academic Press publications
visit our website at store.elsevier.com

Working together
to grow libraries in
developing countries

www.elsevier.com • www.bookaid.org

Contents

Preface
True North

Brent E. Turvey and Stan Crowder

In higher education, Criminal Justice, Justice Studies, and Justice Administration departments (CJ/JS/JA) are distinct from neighboring social science
programs in a number of significant ways. First, they tend to be vocational
in nature, as opposed to being oriented towards scholarship and scientific
research. They offer to prepare students for a career in one of the four major
pillars of the modern criminal justice system: *law enforcement, forensic services,*
the *judiciary,* and *corrections* (Reid, 2003; Turvey and Petherick, 2010).[1] Second, this vocational orientation attracts a particular set of students that are less
interested in the merits of scholarship than in meeting the requirements of
government employment – a reality that has actually caused some to question
the validity of having such programs at university (Morn, 1995). Third, they are
often managed by full-time PhD-level social scientists, while an adjunct staff of
variably educated criminal justice practitioners (e.g., police officers, crime lab
personnel, prosecutors, corrections officers) can be found teaching the applied
subjects. Under these conditions, scholars and practitioners alike are involved
in the administration of CJ/JS/JA programs, and are key to navigating students
down a career path that is likely to involve government service – whether they
fully appreciate it or not.

As we will learn throughout this text, success on such a path requires understanding that the pillars of the criminal justice system are dependent on the
good conduct and character of their members. Further, the penalties for misconduct and dishonesty by criminal justice professionals can be as public as they
are severe. Students hoping for employment in the justice system must therefore
be able to achieve and maintain the trust of the court in order to be allowed the
privilege of providing sworn reports and testimony. They must also understand

---

[1]Despite the public perception that the forensic sciences are necessarily the result of a hard scientific
background comprised of biology and chemistry, many forensic science programs in the United States
are operated from within schools of criminology, criminal justice, or justice studies. Only some are pure
science programs with a hard science entry requirement. Additionally, the conflation and development
of the forensic science within law enforcement are fraught with ethical peril. The consequences of this
reality are explored further in later sections of this text.

that there is no branch of the criminal justice system where this requirement can be avoided, as every task performed is ultimately done in service of, and under the scrutiny of, an agent of the court. This remains true whether tasks relate to the investigation of a criminal charge, the examination of evidence, the administration of a legal proceeding, or the execution of a sentence.

As a result of this trustworthy character requirement, consideration of a professional life in criminal justice work begins at the student level (Stephens, 2006). CJ/JS/JA students must be made aware that employers in the justice system carefully screen the background of all applicants and candidates for what may be referred to as employment disqualifiers. Disqualifiers are past and present activities or affiliations that evidence, or even appear to evidence, criminality, a propensity for dishonesty, or poor character (see discussions in Stephens, 2006; California Crime Laboratory Review Task Force, 2009). They include:

- Illegal drug use.
- Abuse of prescription medications.
- Alcohol abuse.
- Gambling addictions.
- Criminal arrests and convictions.
- Commission of undetected crimes.
- Extensive history of traffic violations.
- Gang affiliations.
- Affiliations with known criminals.
- Mental disorders.
- Pervasive financial problems.
- Falsification of any of the above.
- Failure to disclose any of the above.
- Failure of a pre-employment polygraph examination.

The importance of a particular disqualifier with respect to employability varies from agency to agency. That is to say, there is latitude afforded by some agencies – especially when the pool of viable candidates is limited by geography and pay-scales. This is not necessarily a good thing: the more professional the government agency and the higher the security clearances of its operational employees, the less likely they are to overlook the disqualifiers mentioned. The opposite is also true.

In this text, we take the position that criminal justice educators comprise a fifth necessary pillar of the criminal justice system. That is to say, there exists a responsibility on the part of criminal justice educators with respect to ethics. Not every student that enters and completes a given CJ/JS/JA program can necessarily survive the employment screening process that will eventually confront them. Such students must be made aware of this reality. Students that can navigate this process successfully must also be professionally groomed, both socially and ethically, for the weight and consequences of the work that they will be required to do (Saltzman, 1986; Grant, 2002). To meet these responsibilities, criminal justice educators must be knowledgeable and up front with their students regarding the importance of having, developing, and maintaining ethical character throughout the direction of their professional lives. They must know the direction of true North on their own professional ethical compass, and be capable of guiding their students towards it in both word and deed (Saltzman, 1986). This is how students learn and pretending otherwise is professionally irresponsible.

While criminal justice educators have an obligation to understand and model professional ethical behavior, providing this vital fifth pillar, many are marginal at best (presently and historically; see Regoli and Miracle, 1980). In fact, many confuse their personal moral values with what are meant to be professional ethics while failing to understand the differences between them. As a consequence, they are often incapable of modeling professional ethical behavior. This is certainly transmitted to their students (Saltzman, 1986). When this happens, students graduate having accumulated any number of employment disqualifiers without knowing it and without the real-world tools to navigate the complex ethical landscape that awaits them.

A pervasive ethical shortfall from classroom to courtroom, which will be demonstrated and discussed throughout this text, results in fewer qualified candidates for employment in the justice system. It also contributes to higher turnover rates resulting from job dissatisfaction and misconduct. However, and perhaps most importantly, this shortfall ensures lower quality professionals, and service, with respect to the criminal justice system overall. Such an outcome can hardly be acceptable.

The purpose of this applied text on ethics for criminal justice students and professionals is to help identify the major ethical dilemmas that will be encountered as they work with and within the pillars of the justice system— not the theoretical or the abstract, but rather those predictable controversies that will confront them from the moment they first decide to take a class that might eventually lead them to apply for a job. As such, it is best conceived as a map to a minefield based on the combined experiences of the authors and contributors. It will provide readers with the makings of a compass for professional action and consequence, and serve as a valued reference when they are trapped between competing dogmas, wills, and self-interests.

References

California Crime Laboratory Review Task Force. An Examination of Forensic Science in California. Sacramento, CA: State of California; 2009, Office of the Attorney General, November; url: http://ag.ca.gov/publications/crime_labs_report.pdf.

Grant J., 2002. Ethics and law enforcement. FBI Law Enforcement Bulletin 11–4; December.

Morn F., 1995. Academic Politics and the History of Criminal Justice Education. Westport, CT: Greenwood Press.

Reid S., 2003. Crime and Criminology. tenth ed. Boston, MA: McGraw-Hill.

Regoli R, Miracle A., 1980. Professionalism Among Criminal Justice Educators, Joint Commission on Criminology and Criminal Justice Education and Standards. Washington, DC: US Department of Justice.

Saltzman L., 1986. The feasibility of teaching professionalism in criminal justice. Teaching Sociology 14(October):263–5.

Stephens N., 2006. Law enforcement ethics do not begin when you pin on the badge. FBI Law Enforcement Bulletin 22–3; November.

Turvey B, Petherick W., 2010. An introduction to forensic criminology. In: Turvey B, Petherick W, Ferguson C, editors. Forensic Criminology. San Diego, CA: Elsevier.

About the Authors

Brent E. Turvey, PhD

Brent E. Turvey received a BS from Portland State University in Psychology, with an emphasis on forensic psychology, and an additional BS in History. He went on to receive his MS in Forensic Science after studying from the University of New Haven. He has also earned his PhD in Criminology from Bond University.

Since 1996, Brent has consulted with many organizations, attorneys, and law enforcement agencies in the United States, Australia, Scotland, China, Canada, Barbados, Singapore, Korea, and Mexico on a range of rapes, homicides, and serial/multiple rape death cases as a forensic scientist and criminal profiler. In August of 2002, he was invited by the Chinese People's Police Security University (CPPSU) in Beijing to lecture before groups of detectives at the Beijing, Wuhan, Hanzou, and Shanghai police bureaus. In 2005, he was invited back to China to lecture at the CPPSU and to the police in Beijing and Xian – after the translation of the second edition of his text (*Criminal Profiling: An Introduction to Behavioral Evidence Analysis*) into Chinese for the university. In 2007, he was invited to lecture at the First Behavioral Sciences Conference at the Home Team (Police) Academy in Singapore, where he also provided training to their behavioral science unit. In 2010, he examined a series of sexual homicides for the Solicitor General of the Crown Office and Procurator Fiscal Service in Edinburgh, Scotland. In 2013, he became the sponsor for the Criminal Profiling and Behavioral Analysis Unit of the Forensic Laboratory in Ciudad Juarez in Chihuahua, Mexico.

Brent has been court qualified as an expert in the areas of criminal profiling, victimology, crime scene investigation, sex crimes investigation, false reports, crime scene analysis, forensic science, and crime reconstruction in many courts and jurisdictions (state and federal) around the United States, in both civil and criminal matters – most often in capital murder cases.

Brent has published in numerous peer-reviewed journals and is the author of *Criminal Profiling: An Introduction to Behavioral Evidence Analysis*, first, second, third, and fourth editions (1999, 2002, 2008, and 2011) and *Forensic Fraud* (2013). He is also a co-author of *Rape Investigation Handbook*, first and second editions (2004 and 2011); *Crime Reconstruction*, first and second editions (2007 and 2011), *Forensic Victimology* (2009), and *Forensic Criminology* (2010) – all with Academic/Elsevier Science.

Brent is currently a board member of the International Association of Forensic Criminologists/Academy of Behavioral Profiling; a full partner, forensic scientist, criminal profiler, and instructor with Forensic Solutions, LLC; and an Adjunct Professor of Sociology Justice Studies at Oklahoma City University. He can be contacted at: bturvey@forensic-science.com.

Stan Crowder, PhD

Stan Crowder is a retired US Army Military Police Colonel, and holds a PhD, an MBA, and a BS. During his military career, Stan served in numerous positions including: MP Commander, Chief of Investigations for the Inspector General of Georgia, Counter-drug Commander, Battalion Commander, and Chief of Personnel. He served 7 years as a civilian police officer. He teaches at Kennesaw State University, Kennesaw, Georgia, where he has been teaching since 1999 and was selected as the 2007 recipient of the Betty Siegel teaching award.

Stan is currently the President of the International Association of Forensic Criminologists/Academy of Behavioral Profiling. He can be contacted at: scrowder@kennesaw.edu.

W. Jerry Chisum, BS

William "Jerry" Chisum, now retired from teaching and active government service, started criminalistics practice in 1960. He studied under Dr Paul L. Kirk at the University of California at Berkeley where he received a Bachelor's degree in Chemistry. He worked in San Bernardino and then set up the Kern County Laboratory in Bakersfield. After joining the California Department of Justice, he took a leave of absence (1971–1973) to work at Stanford Research Institute.

Jerry has always been interested crime scene evidence and has developed numerous methods of crime reconstruction. He is a co-author of the text *Crime Reconstruction* with Brent Turvey, and has published numerous other chapters and monographs on related subjects. His teaching has been international in scope. He taught as a part-time Professor at the California State University, Sacramento for 4 years. He instructed with Joe Rynearson for over 25 years in various locations in California, Idaho, Indiana, Illinois, New Mexico, Washington, DC, and Nevada.

Jerry has been president of the California Association of Criminalists three times. He served as President of the American Society of Crime Lab Directors and as President of the Stanislaus County Peace Officers Association. He has also served as Vice-President of the International Association of Forensic Criminologists/Academy of Behavioral Profiling. Although now retired from government service, Jerry still is active in case consultation and accepts cases from throughout the United States. He can be contacted at: wjchisum@surewest.net.

Craig M. Cooley, JD

Craig M. Cooley served as a Staff Attorney with the Innocence Project in New York City for 5 years, where he represented indigent inmates from across the United States trying to prove their innocence with DNA testing. Mr Cooley obtained DNA testing for several of his clients that ultimately exonerated 10 innocent prisoners. Prior to joining the Innocence Project, Mr Cooley served as an Assistant Federal Defender in Las Vegas, Nevada where he represented Nevada death row inmates pursing federal habeas relief.

Prior to attending law school, Mr Cooley received his graduate degree in Forensic Science from the University of New Haven and his undergraduate degree from the University of Pittsburgh. During law school, Mr Cooley served as an Investigator with the Office of the State Appellate Defenders, Death Penalty Trial Assistance Division in Chicago, Illinois, where he provided assistance on several cases affected by Governor George Ryan's 2003 pardons and commutations.

A graduate of Northwestern School of Law, Mr Cooley has served as an Adjunct Professor of Law at St John's School of Law, Hofstra School of Law, and Cardozo School of Law. His scholarship includes articles in *Stanford Law & Policy Review, Indiana Law Journal, George Mason University Civil Rights Law Journal, New England Law Review,* and other law journals and reviews. He can be contacted at: craig.m.cooley@gmail.com.

Michael McGrath, MD

Michael McGrath, MD, is a Board Certified Forensic Psychiatrist, licensed in the State of New York. He is a Clinical Associate Professor in the Department of Psychiatry, University of Rochester School of Medicine and Dentistry, Rochester, NY, and Medical Director and Chair, Department of Behavioral Health, Unity Health System, Rochester, NY.

Dr McGrath divides his time among administrative, clinical, research, and teaching activities. His areas of expertise include forensic psychiatry and criminal profiling. He has lectured on three continents, and is a Founding Member and past President of the International Association of Forensic Criminologists/Academy of Behavioral Profiling. He can be contacted at: mmcgrath@profiling.org.

Shawn Mikulay, PhD

Dr Shawn Mikulay is a Professor of Psychology at Elgin Community College in Elgin, Illinois where he teaches coursework in general, forensic, developmental, and experimental psychology, human sexuality, and criminal profiling. Dr Mikulay has been with Elgin Community College since 1995.

Dr Mikulay received his Doctorate of Philosophy in Psychology from Northern Illinois University (1998). He received his Master of Arts in Psychology (1995) and Master of Science in Industrial Management (1996). During graduate school, he taught as an adjunct instructor at Concordia University, Kishwaukee College, Waubonsee Community College, and Elgin Community College. His research has been published in *Genetic, Social, & General Psychology Monographs, Educational & Psychological Measurement*, and the *Journal of Organizational Behavior*.

Dr Mikulay's areas of research and expertise include workplace deviance, forensic victimology, behavioral analysis, offender modus operandi, and offender signature behavior. He is currently the Vice-President of the International Association of Forensic Criminologists/Academy of Behavioral Profiling. He can be contacted at: smikulay@forensic-science.com.

Ronald Miller, MS

Ron Miller holds a Bachelor of Forensic Science from the University of California at Berkeley, where he studied under Dr Paul L. Kirk and Dr John I. Thornton. He also holds a Master in Public Service, a Master in Clinical Mental Health, and is a Licensed Marriage and Family Therapist. He loved "working the street" as a police officer and as a crime scene investigator, detective, and Explosive Ordnance Disposal (EOD) team member in the 1970s and 1980s in the San Francisco Bay Area. He left law enforcement due to a vision disorder and it was then that he sought his graduate education.

Ron found himself continuing to work in the judicial arena doing mental health evaluations and treatment for the courts and critical incident debriefings for public safety and industry. Eventually, he shifted his focus to felony investigations, specializing in homicides, death penalty mitigation investigations, and post-conviction appellate work in state and federal courts as a licensed private investigator in the Pacific Northwest. He can be contacted at: rjmiller@behavioralforensics.com.

Detective John O. Savino, NYPD (retired 2007)

John Savino joined the New York City Police Department (NYPD) on 26 January 1982, and was promoted to detective in 1989. In a career that spanned 25 years, Detective Savino became one of the best sex crime investigators New York City had to offer. His career spanned all aspects of law enforcement, beginning with a short assignment as a uniformed police officer and his quick advancement to the Organized Crime Control Bureau in 1986. Detective Savino began developing his investigative skills while assigned to the Manhattan North Narcotics Division. His assignment to the narcotics division helped develop his ability and skills to interact with people from all walks of life. His experiences as an "undercover" officer helped develop his ability to gain the confidence and trust of the individuals he purchased narcotics from, and would later use those skills when interviewing victims and suspects during the thousands of investigations he was involved in.

For the last 18 years of his career with the NYPD, he was assigned to the Manhattan Special Victims Squad where he investigated reports of sexual assault and child abuse occurring in the Borough of Manhattan. While assigned to the special victims squad, he rose to the prestigious rank of First-Grade detective. Detective Savino has investigated thousands of reports of rape and sexual assault, and investigated some of the most notorious and heinous sex crimes Manhattan has ever seen.

Detective Savino was chosen to rewrite the policy used for investigating sexual assaults by the NYPD and was tasked with creating a training manual for newly assigned detectives to the Manhattan Special Victims Squad. During his assignment with the Manhattan Special Victims Squad, Detective Savino began lecturing at training classes held for rape advocates and emergency room personnel after he saw a need to bridge the gap between medical personnel and the police. He also created training material and provided training for uniformed officers and first responders on the proper response to a sexual assault, how to interact with a sexual assault victim, and how to preserve a crime scene properly.

In 2000, Detective Savino was the first detective in New York State to participate in the "John Doe" DNA indictment of a DNA profile for a suspect responsible for at least 16 sexual assaults since 1997, dubbed the "East Side rapist" by the New York City press. Detective Savino had been the lead investigator for many successful serial rape and pattern sexual assault investigations, and had conducted lectures for the New York State Police on proper procedures when investigating a serial rape case or pattern sex offender.

In September 2001, after the World Trade Center tragedy, Detective Savino, along with an elite group of detectives, was assigned temporarily to the

New York City morgue for several months and assigned the difficult task of attempting to identify victims of the World Trade Center disaster. His skills, dedication, and attention to details carried over to this assignment and led to the identification of numerous victims of the tragedy.

Since retiring in 2007, Detective Savino has continued his career in law enforcement, and is now conducting complex financial and fraud investigations for a large state agency in Florida.

Angela Torres, PhD, ABPP (Forensic)

Angela Torres majored in Psychology at the University of California at Berkeley. She then went on to complete her Doctorate in Clinical Psychology with a forensic focus at Sam Houston State University in Huntsville, Texas. After course work, she was a Pre-Doctoral Intern at the Federal Medical Center in Rochester, Minnesota. She then went on to become a Post-Doctoral Fellow in Forensic Psychology at Central State Hospital in Petersburg, Virginia. She is Board Certified in Forensic Psychology by the American Board of Professional Psychology.

Dr Torres is currently Chief Forensic Coordinator at the Central State Hospital for the Virginia Department of Behavioral Health and Development Services. Her specialties and research areas include: sex offender risk assessment, gender/sexuality/cultural issues, malingering, and general forensic assessment.

CHAPTER 1

Ethics in the Criminal Justice Professions

Stan Crowder and Brent E. Turvey

Legislative enactment has never been, and never will be, a panacea for moral turpitude. It is absurd, and stupid as well, to think that fines and jail sentences can change the character of an individual.

August Vollmer (1971, p. 81)

Key Terms

Academia The pillar of the criminal justice system comprised of those criminal justice researchers and educators working in colleges, universities, academics, and institutions around the world.

Adversarial system A "jurisprudential network of laws, rules and procedures characterized by opposing parties who contend against each other for a result favorable to themselves. In such a system, the judge acts as an independent magistrate rather than prosecutor; distinguished from an inquisitorial system" (Black, 1990, p. 53).

Corrections The pillar of the criminal justice system that deals with the probation, incarceration, management, rehabilitation, treatment, parole, and in extreme cases the execution of convicted criminals.

Criminal justice system The network of government and private agencies intended to manage accused and convicted criminals.

Due process The preservation of federal and state constitutional rights; the rights of citizens as described in these constitutions may not be violated or taken away without strict adherence to the law.

Ethical dilemma A type of ethical issue that arises when the available choices and obligations in a specific situation do not allow for an ethical outcome.

Ethics The specific institutional rules of conduct constructed from morality and other elements of character (e.g., motivation, libido, courage, loyalty, integrity, and empathy); they are, consequently, the result of reflection and deliberation (Ethics Across the Curricula Committee, 2007).

Forensic services The pillar of the criminal justice system that deals with the examination and interpretation of evidence – physical, behavioral, and testimonial alike (Turvey and Petherick, 2010).

Judiciary The pillar of the criminal justice system that deals with the adjudication or criminal defendants to include exoneration, punishment, treatment, and efforts to reform.

Justice Fair and impartial treatment during the resolution of conflict.

Law enforcement The pillar of the criminal justice system that deals with reported crime.

Legal justice The result of forging the rights of individuals with the government's corresponding duty to ensure and protect those rights.

CONTENTS

Ethical Justice. http://dx.doi.org/10.1016/B978-0-12-404597-2.00001-2

Moral dilemma Exists when available choices and obligations do not allow for moral outcomes.

Morality A significant contributor to the development of ethics and is most commonly associated with individual feelings or beliefs regarding actions.

Professional ethics The specific ideals, principles, values, and constraints imposed on practitioners by the mandates of their profession and workplace.

The purpose of this textbook is to provide an instructional guide for any criminal justice student or professional that needs help identifying, understanding, or resolving ethical issues and dilemmas. To accomplish this, it is necessary to examine the five interdependent pillars of the criminal justice system: academia, law enforcement, forensic services, the courts, and corrections. No matter where in this foundation a professional finds employment, they will depend on or work directly with those within the other supporting pillars. Readers will therefore come to understand the necessity of the different roles and ethical obligations held by each pillar with respect to ensuring that justice is ultimately being served.

In this chapter, readers will be introduced to the basic concepts necessary for understanding and contextualizing each of the chapters that follow: the concepts of ethics and justice will be defined; the mandates of legal justice will be spelled out; the pillars of the criminal justice system will be distinguished from each other; and the value of ethics to both the criminal justice system and individual professionals will be explained.

ETHICS DEFINED

There is a great deal of confusion with respect to ethics in the justice system – including what they actually are, how they should be derived, and their relationship to morality. This occurs when those discussing professional ethics inappropriately conflate philosophy and religion when attempting to understand or explain fundamental issues. For example, the criminal justice literature is rife with publications treating personal morality, religious dogma, and professional ethics as though they are interchangeable constructs. Although often treated as synonymous in common usage, they are quite different.

Ethics and Morality

In philosophy, *ethics* involves the study of individual or group character, which is comprised of many different elements, including variably developed morality, ideals, values, and virtues (Thornton, 2012).[1] *Morality*, a significant

---

[1] *Ideals* are concepts of perfection that may be aspired to but not achieved in reality (e.g., justice, purity, and wisdom). *Values* are those objects, traits, or ideas that are judged to be significant or important, often regardless of morality (e.g., beauty, money, and intelligence). *Virtues* are those actions and choices that are considered moral, useful, or otherwise desirable (e.g., chastity, patience, fidelity, and humility). These terms are not mutually exclusive, as one can value an ideal or a virtue.

contributor to the development of ethics, is most commonly associated with individual feelings or beliefs regarding actions. This is to say that morality provides a thematic basis for making judgments as to whether actions or choices are considered right, wrong, good, or bad. *Ethics* are the specific situational rules of conduct constructed from morality and other elements of character (e.g., motivation, libido, courage, loyalty, integrity, and empathy); they are, consequently, the result of reflection and deliberation (Ethics Across the Curricula Committee, 2007). The influence of morality on ethics can be absolute or finite, shifting wildly depending on individual or group dogma.

For example, groups with a variety of different belief systems consider the act of killing another human being immoral. Consequently, a *moral imperative*[2] exists within such groups to refrain from killing of any kind. However, careful deliberation of this imperative, in consideration of related ideals, values, and virtues, has caused some to develop ethical guidelines that permit killing under specific circumstances. In this way killing may be considered generally immoral, but there may also be specific ethical exceptions (e.g., self-defense, time of war, and capital punishment).

At this point, it is crucial to acknowledge that every belief system (e.g., institutional, political, religious, cultural) has its own set of values, morals, and ideals, with its own subsequent ethical canon. Consider that in some cultures women can drive a car, wear revealing clothes, own property, get an education, and marry or date whomever they prefer. In other cultures, such conduct by a woman is considered immoral; in extreme cases it may even be a violation of religious law. This reality provides that there are no truly universal moral imperatives or obligations: even rape and torture are considered by some to be acceptable, depending on the context (e.g., honor killings, time of war). By the same token, there are also no universally held taboos.

Moral Dilemmas

A *moral dilemma* exists when available choices and obligations do not allow for moral outcomes. In such instances, a choice or an action is anticipated or required, and all of the available alternatives violate some moral obligation. Moral dilemmas are not uncommon when organizations and individuals are working to satisfy competing interests, or when personal morals and professional obligations are directly opposed.

An example would be a devout Catholic that marries, has children, and later discovers that their spouse is abusing one of them. According to the Catholic Church, marriage is a sacrament and is indissoluble – therefore, a moral obligation exists to repair a failing marriage, especially when children are involved. However, a

---

[2]A *moral imperative* is anything that is deemed vital or essential to maintaining morality.

moral obligation also exists to protect one's children. Both choices – getting a divorce and remaining with an abusive spouse – are morally unacceptable at best. This moral dilemma is not unique to those with strong religious beliefs and has resulted in some of the most horrific consequences that can be observed in the criminal justice system.

Notably, the phrase "moral dilemma" is used throughout the criminal justice literature by those unaware of its actual meaning. In many works, authors use it when referring to immoral or unethical behavior with severe consequences – to the choice that must made between moral and immoral behavior. The choice that exists between moral and immoral behavior does not involve a genuine dilemma – unless the moral path conflicts with some other moral obligation.

Ethical Dilemmas

An *ethical dilemma* is a type of ethical issue that arises when the available choices and obligations in a specific situation do not allow for an ethical outcome. In such instances, a choice or an action is required and all of the available alternatives violate an explicit ethical principle or guideline. This should not be confused with ignorance of what is ethical or with the discomfort that often comes from having to make difficult ethical decisions. It also bears mentioning that ethical dilemmas are essentially unavoidable when working with others that maintain different moral foundations or ethical obligations, or when serving in multiple roles with diverse obligations.

Ethical dilemmas commonly occur along one of the following themes:

(1) *Truth v. Loyalty*: Choosing between maintaining personal integrity or keeping fidelity pledged to others (e.g., friends, family members, co-workers, employers, and organizations).
(2) *Individual v. Group*: Choosing between the interests of an individual, or a few, and those of a larger community.
(3) *Immediate v. Future*: Choosing between present benefits and those that that are long-term.
(4) *Justice v. Compassion*: Choosing between fair and dispassionate application of consequences and the individual need or warrant for charity.

One example of an ethical dilemma encountered frequently within the criminal justice system involves the necessity of promotion. When a supervisory position (e.g., sergeant or lieutenant) opens in a police agency, the managing supervisor (usually a lieutenant, captain, or chief) has a decision to make: promote based on loyalty; promote based on political promises and necessity; or promote based on integrity, ability, and achievement. Ideally these elements would align themselves in a single candidate making the decision relatively easy. In reality, this does not happen very often – if ever. The ethical choice would seem to be promoting based on integrity, ability, and achievement; however, there can be tremendous external pressure placed on managing supervisors to maintain their loyalty to friends and family, or to fulfill externally mandated diversity quotas, and consequently promote those who have not otherwise earned it. Promoting the unqualified violates any ethical commitments to professionalism and safety; on the other hand, promoting the qualified can result in the violation of ethical obligations to follow orders or remain loyalty. In any profession where diversity hiring is an issue, or where loyalty is considered a sacred and necessary virtue, this dilemma is going to ensue.

It is worth noting that ethical dilemmas are useful in that they can reveal the need for deeper reflection and deliberation about the consequences of our actions – which is how we are meant to develop ethical rules, principles, and guidelines in the first place. In fact, it is the complexity and specificity of an ethical dilemma that will separate it from a general moral dilemma. This is why those with a more penetrating grasp of ethical issues are able to act with greater preparedness than those without and are often able to identify their best course of action with less difficulty. However, this does not make ethical dilemmas any less demanding, distressing, or painful.

Professional Ethics

Professional ethics are the specific ideals, principles, values, and constraints imposed on practitioners by the mandates of their profession and workplace. They are generally expressed as an explicit code of ethical conduct (Davis, 1995). It can be said that a profession without a written, comprehensive, and uncompromising code of ethics is no profession at all, as explained in Kleinig (1996) and Sullivan (1977, p. 280):

> Without question, a code of ethics is essential in a profession.
> Without it, a profession could not exist. Moreover, the rules and
> regulations selected must reach the highest standards. There must
> be no opportunity for compromise. Professional ethics dictates the
> application of such absolutes as "always" and "never."

Professional codes of ethics include three different kinds of directives: ideals, principles, and requirements (Davis, 1995). *Ideals* are professional aspirations and essentially impossible to achieve with perfection or consistency, such as those related to maintaining unsullied character, showing respect, maintaining dignity, or seeking justice. Professionals are expected to try, but they are also allowed to fail so long as it is not part of an intentional subversive effort. *Principles* are specific values or commitments, such as an organizational commitment to a profession, its members, a particular goal, or a particular school of thought; or member commitments to impartiality and integrity. As with ideals, professionals are expected to maintain principles, but they may unintentionally falter without being severely punished – so long as they acknowledge their failings and seek remedy. *Requirements* are mandatory rules and obligations that must be followed to the letter. Far from being an ideal or a principle, a requirement is explicit and cannot be negotiated – such as forbidding members from misrepresenting their credentials or mandatory expulsion for members convicted of a felony charge. Unfortunately, professional codes of ethics are often written in such a fashion as to confuse these directives, making some difficult to interpret, abide, and enforce (Davis, 1995; Kleinig, 1996).

RELATIVE JUSTICE

Justice may be generally defined as fair and impartial treatment during the resolution of conflict. It is, ultimately, an ideal with significant ramifications for citizens and their government alike. Despite this seemingly benign definition, not everyone agrees on how to define what is considered fair and impartial treatment, or its proper administration. It is a "relative value," as explained in Leonard (1971, p. 3):

> Justice, as an ideal, is the keystone in the arch of social control. It occupies the throne in the whole arena of human affairs. Although its role is overwhelming to contemplate, justice does not lend itself readily to definition. It's principal characteristic is flux, with constant reorientation and readjustment to the growth of man and his expanding social horizons.

For some, fair and impartial means moral; as already discussed, this is subjective at best given the variability of morality from person to person. For others, fair and impartial means equal treatment; they believe that everyone should receive the same consideration regardless of their circumstances. Still for others, fair and impartial means that each person gets the justice that they earn, or fail to earn, by their actions. Ultimately, every group, and every person within that group, has his/her own uniquely formed view of what justice is and how it is best achieved.

These differing views have resulted in the ongoing development of multiple and competing models of justice. The most common model of justice is referred to as *retributive* or *corrective*, focusing on the administration of punishments that are proportionate to the nature and severity of any wrongs committed. *Compensatory* and *restorative* models, on the other hand, focus on making victims whole again, and reintegrating offenders back into society. Finally, there is the *distributive* model, which focuses on the equitable distribution of benefits and burdens across all members of society equally.[3] The utility of any approach to justice is measured by the desired outcome, and again this varies from person to person. Those seeking vengeance are unlikely to have use for restorative justice. Similarly, those seeking compensation are unlikely to be satisfied only by offender punishment.

Invariably, conflict and the need for justice cause tension between people with differing views. When they must work to resolve disputes, they can naturally be expected to disagree as to whether and when justice has been served. Often, the only thing unifying them under these circumstances is the rule of law. This necessitates a "formal system of legal and procedural rules and doctrines, according to which it is administered" (Leonard, 1971, p. 3). Hence the need for legal justice.

LEGAL JUSTICE

Legal justice is the result of forging the rights of individuals with the government's corresponding duty to ensure and protect those rights. This is also referred to as due process. Legal justice is intended to be the proper administration of due process and the law, with the fair and impartial treatment of all individuals by agents of the justice system. *Lady Justice*, a Greco-Roman blend of the goddesses of justice, is commonly used to symbolize its ideals. She holds the balanced scales of truth of fairness in her right hand and a double-edged sword in her left that is never sheathed. She is also blindfolded, representing the necessity for ruling dispassionately – without being influenced by personal feelings or political preferences.

Constitutional Rights

The US Constitution contains Amendments that establish the rights of its citizens, the precise meaning of which are a matter of continual public debate and legal re-interpretation. These include, but are in no way limited to, freedom of religion and freedom of the press (First Amendment); the right to "keep and bear arms" (Second Amendment); freedom from "unreasonable searches and seizures" without "probable cause" (Fourth Amendment); the right to adequate legal representation, a "speedy and public trial, by an impartial jury," and to confront of any witness (Sixth Amendment); freedom from "excessive fines" and "cruel and unusual punishments" (Eighth Amendment); and the right to vote (the 15th, 19th, and 26th Amendments).

In addition, the Fifth and 14th Amendments contain what are referred to as due process clauses – in that they specifically guarantee citizens the right to due process. The Fifth Amendment states:

[3]For in depth discussions on the different models or theories of justice, read Sen (2011).

No person shall be held to answer for a capital, or otherwise infamous crime, unless on a presentment or indictment of a Grand Jury, except in cases arising in the land or naval forces, or in the Militia, when in actual service in time of War or public danger; nor shall any person be subject for the same offense to be twice put in jeopardy of life or limb; nor shall be compelled in any criminal case to be a witness against himself, nor be deprived of life, liberty, or property, without due process of law; nor shall private property be taken for public use, without just compensation.

The 14th Amendment further states:

All persons born or naturalized in the United States, and subject to the jurisdiction thereof, are citizens of the United States and of the State wherein they reside. No State shall make or enforce any law which shall abridge the privileges or immunities of citizens of the United States; nor shall any State deprive any person of life, liberty, or property, without due process of law; nor deny to any person within its jurisdiction the equal protection of the laws.

These and other constitutional rights are guaranteed to all citizens. Government is crafted from the citizenry and is intended to serve them by first providing and then protecting these rights, as discussed in Kleinig (1996, p. 14): "the chief end of government is the protection of individual life, liberty, and property.... The right to government protection against invasions of life, liberty, and property has been reinterpreted to include the government securement or provision of what will enable those rights to be enjoyed, supplemented by other social, political, and welfare rights." Any government or government agent that does not provide for and protect the rights of its citizens is in violation of due process.

Due Process

Due process refers to the preservation of federal and state constitutional rights; the rights of citizens as described in these constitutions may not be violated or taken away without strict adherence to the law. It is central to what justice is and means within any legal system. Due process is achieved only when those in the justice system both understand and follow the laws about when and how individual rights can be infringed. When those laws are not followed, individual's rights are infringed and due process is violated. As we will learn, due process violations can result in severe consequences for those responsible.

As explained in Chapman and McConnell (2012), there are two different interpretations of due process (p. 1676):

Some argue that "due process" meant nothing more than judicial procedure. It therefore applied to the courts and, perhaps, to the executive with respect to prosecution and the enforcement of court judgments. Under this reading, due process did not apply to the legislature. Others contend that "due process *of law*" entailed judicial procedure *and* natural law norms such as reasonableness, justice, or fairness

In other words, there are those of the opinion that due process requires simply following the letter of legal procedure as written. Others, however, argue that due process has an underlying set of moral requirements that are equally inviolate. For example, *Black's Law Dictionary* explains that due process requires an underlying theme of fairness (Black, 1990, p. 501): "Embodied in the due process concept are the basic rights of a defendant in criminal proceedings and the requisites for a fair trial."

Regardless of how one interprets the concept of due process, its establishment and interpretation are not the role of the executive branch of government, as explained in Chapman and McConnell (2012, p. 1681):

> The due process and law-of-the-land clauses of the American state and federal constitutions originate in Magna Charta and the English customary constitution. This is uncontroversial. What commentators have underemphasized is that due process has from the beginning been bound up with the division of the authority to deprive subjects of life, liberty, or property between independent political institutions. In modern parlance, due process has always been the insistence that the executive – the branch of government that wields force against the people – deprive persons of rights only in accordance with settled rules independent of executive will, in accordance with a judgment by an independent magistrate.

To be clear, the history of due process suggests that the executive branch (e.g., law enforcement) is meant to have no part in deciding what due process entails – otherwise it will inevitably be unbalanced in their favor. The precise elements of due process, and the rights being protected, must be established by the judiciary, legislated by congress, and then only enforced by the executive.[4]

Due process and its constitutional origins combine to establish a presumptive requirement for those who seek employment in the criminal justice system at any level – to read and understand not only the US Constitution, but also any subsequent legal decisions that affect its interpretation. Any professional that does not fully comprehend or support the US Constitution, along with the individual rights and due process requirements that it provides all citizens, will continually be at odds with the moral and ethical requirements of working in

---

[4]For in depth discussion and analysis, read Chapman and McConnell (2012), which discusses due process as the separation of powers; see also Leonard (1969) for a law enforcement oriented perspective.

the criminal justice system. Failure to take this obligation seriously, or supplanting it with personal notions of morality, has been the source of much avoidable injustice.

Legal justice is the only model of justice that unifies all of the citizens within a given region. This remains true despite whatever personal or professional definitions of justice the citizenry may ascribe to. Its value to a stable society is therefore tremendous. However, it is not an effective substitute for the good character of individuals, as laws and rules of conduct cannot make those with poor character abide (Vollmer, 1971). This lesson will repeat itself throughout this text.

THE PILLARS OF THE CRIMINAL JUSTICE SYSTEM

The *criminal justice system* is the network of government and private agencies intended to manage accused and convicted criminals. It is adversarial in nature. In this section, we will introduce the pillars of the criminal justice system; discuss its adversarial nature and character; and explain the subsequent necessity for clearly defined professional ethics amongst its operatives.

The criminal justice system is frequently described as being composed of "agencies responsible for enforcing criminal laws, including legislatures, police, courts, and corrections" (Reid, 2003, p. 355). A similar portrayal is offered in Sullivan (1977, p. 157): "The general view of criminal justice reflects a system of three separately organized functions: the *police*, the *courts*, and *corrections*. Each has a distinct role, yet they are interrelated." These and similar explanations, while generally accurate and representative of the literature, are prosecution oriented. As such, they fail to account for the full balance of the adversarial requirements necessary for achieving legal justice.

A prosecutorial point of view dominates the criminal justice landscape. Consequently, many texts and courses on the subject have not, historically, acknowledged the value of the many non-law enforcement and non-prosecutorial components of the criminal justice system. In some instances, these elements have been neglected entirely. That is to say, the literature tends to gloss over, or ignore, the necessary roles fulfilled by academia, the defense community, and private or independent forensic examiners working in the criminal justice system. This leaves students uninformed and unprepared.

In reality, the modern criminal justice system consists of the following major interrelated and interdependent pillars: *academia, law enforcement, forensic services, the judiciary*, and *corrections*.

Academia

Academia is the pillar of the criminal justice system comprised of those criminal justice researchers and educators working in colleges, universities, academies, and institutions around the world – anywhere that criminal justice professionals seek information, knowledge, formal education, or specific training. These researchers and educators combine to form a vital support that advises, informs, educates, and trains those employed by or seeking employment within the criminal justice system. At their best, they provide coordinated knowledge and structured learning to those who seek it, often to fit the needs of a particular agency, profession, or community. Although disorganized in many circles, and routinely neglected, this pillar has been and remains essential to the professional development and overall effectiveness of those employed in the criminal justice system (Morn, 1995; Vollmer, 1971).[5]

Law Enforcement

Law enforcement is the pillar of the criminal justice system that deals with reported crime. Law enforcement agencies are intended to enforce the law – to ensure that citizens act lawfully and to investigate the nature and extent of unlawful acts (Vollmer, 1971). In this capacity they serve as "peace officers," preventing or deterring crime and generally working to keep the peace (see, generally, Kleinig, 1996). However, they are also obligated to investigate any criminal complaints and establish the events that actually caused it to made in the first place (Savino and Turvey, 2011). When the agents of law enforcement believe a crime has been committed, they are obligated to investigate, identify and arrest available suspects. In some cases this will also involve the recognition, collection, storage, and transportation of physical evidence by crime scene investigators. As explained in Sullivan (1977, p. 149):

> It is the job of the police to enforce the law. Thus, officers must remember that they are primarily fact-finders for their department and have no authority or control over the judicial or legislative branches of government. If the police effectively enforce the law, they have done all that is expected.

Law enforcement officers and investigators work for government agencies as dictated by jurisdiction and statute, to include federal, state, county, and municipal (e.g., city, village) authorities, and are supported by a variety of civilian personnel in various administrative and specialist capacities.[6]

---

[5]These and other related issues will be discussed more fully in Part 1: "Academia."
[6]These and other related issues will be discussed more fully in Part 2: "Law Enforcement."

Forensic Services

A number of essential *forensic services* form the pillar of the criminal justice system that deals with the examination and interpretation of evidence – physical, behavioral, and testimonial etc. (Turvey and Petherick, 2010). Government-employed analysts, technicians, criminalists, pathologists, and forensic mental health experts perform a wide variety of forensic services on behalf of the state, generally for the police and prosecution. In the United States, however, there is also a community of privately employed independent forensic examiners. These private sector professionals are regularly engaged to perform examinations for the prosecution and the defense alike. When utilized, they allow for the necessary counterbalance required by an adversarial system.

The availability of forensic science, technology, and expertise is a sore issue within the justice system, as these are scarce resources at best. In most jurisdictions, private labs are limited or non-existent. Consequently, attorneys on both sides may be forced by geographic and budgetary constraints to rely on variably qualified government-employed analysts for the bulk of examinations and interpretations. Such circumstances are rife with ethical dilemmas. It is also fair to say that the lack of available government services, private practitioners, and related funds for either has caused serious case backlogs, delays, and even miscarriages of justice.[7]

The Judiciary

The *judiciary* is the pillar of the criminal justice system that deals with the adjudication of criminal defendants, to include exoneration, punishment, treatment and efforts to reform. As explained in *Black's Law Dictionary* (Black, 1990) it is the role of the judiciary to "interpret, construe, apply, and generally administer and enforce the laws" (p. 847). A short list of those involved in the judiciary includes government prosecutors and public defenders, private defense attorneys, magistrates, judges, investigators for the prosecution, investigators for the defense, investigators for the court, paralegals, court reporters, court clerks, bailiffs, and the juries (drawn from the local citizenry). Each has a specific duty that is explicitly decreed and governed by the law – perversions of which result in violations of due process.[8]

Corrections

Corrections is the pillar of the criminal justice system that deals with the probation, incarceration, management, rehabilitation, treatment, parole, and in extreme cases the execution of convicted criminals. Many law enforcement

---

[7]These and other related issues will be discussed more fully in Part 3: "Forensic Services."
[8]These and other related issues will be discussed more fully in Part 4: "The Courts."

agencies and courthouses have on-site jail facilities to enable short-term incarceration of offenders involved in lesser crimes, or to accommodate the local court appointments of felons "visiting" from other correctional institutions. However, federal, state, and county penitentiaries are designed to accommodate the long-term sentences of convicted felons. Additionally, there are hospitals outside of correctional institutions that have forensic units providing court mandated mental evaluations, treatment, and defendant residency. Some of these institutions are government owned and operated (county, state, and federal), whereas others are privately contracted.

A short list of those professionals involved in corrections includes probation officers, corrections officers, corrections investigators, corrections counselors, parole officers, intelligence officers, social workers, forensic psychologists, forensic psychiatrists, and the members of various parole boards.[9]

THE CHARACTER OF AN ADVERSARIAL SYSTEM

In an *adversarial system*, criminal defendants are entitled to an adequate defense and due process of law, while the burden of proving guilt is on the state or government (i.e., the prosecution). Such systems are grounded firmly in the principle that defendants are presumed innocent until proven guilty. Consequently, there are always at least two sides in each criminal dispute: a prosecution representing the government and its citizens, and a defense representing the accused. As defined in *Black's Law Dictionary* (Black, 1990, p. 53):

> [An adversary system is a] jurisprudential network of laws, rules and
> procedures characterized by opposing parties who contend against
> each other for a result favorable to themselves. In such a system,
> the judge acts as an independent magistrate rather than prosecutor;
> distinguished from an inquisitorial system.

Ultimately, each side of this legal dispute works to convince a judge or a jury that its position is the most correct – ostensibly within a set of specific rules for conduct. In other words, each side must avoid conduct that is illegal or unethical when making their case.

The Prosecution

In the United States, attorneys for the prosecution work exclusively for the government at the city, county, state, or federal level. They are charged with seeking the truth regarding criminal matters on behalf of the citizenry, and work the benefit of law enforcement resources and personnel from both state and federal agencies. Unfortunately, prosecutors are often elected, appointed,

---

[9]Ethical issues in corrections will be discussed more fully in Part 5: "Corrections."

promoted, or otherwise advanced based on political considerations or their conviction rate. This can cause some to be less interested in "truth seeking" and more interested in what they can prove in court to obtain a politically desirable legal outcome.[10]

The state has the greater burden of proof and must prove a defendant's guilt beyond a *reasonable doubt*. This means that before a defendant can be found guilty of any crime, the state must prove every element of that crime and also that the defendant was the person responsible. The reasonable doubt standard is the matter of much law and debate, the ethical application of which will be discussed throughout Part 4 of this work: "The Courts."

The Defense

Attorneys for the defense are not necessarily interested in the truth, but rather are ethically bound to zealously advocate for the best interests of the accused – their client. Some defense attorneys work for the government as county, state, or federal public defenders, while others work in private practice. Defendants with the financial means may hire a private attorney. However, doing so can be prohibitively expensive. Indigent defendants, being unable to afford private counsel, are represented by a public defender. In states or counties without a dedicated public defender system, the court appoints legal representatives to indigent defendants from a list of available local attorneys, referred to as "appointed counsel." The defense rarely enjoys the same resources, experts, and funding available to prosecutors.[11]

The defense is not required to prove innocence in an adversarial justice system. In fact, the defense is not required to prove or disprove anything. The defense need only demonstrate that there is a reasonable doubt with respect to the prosecution's theories in order to prevail. The limited burden of proof required by the defense is founded in the right to be presumed innocent until convicted in a court of law. The fact that a person has been arrested and put on trial may not be considered as evidence of guilt, despite any personal beliefs to the contrary.[12]

---

[10]These and other related issues will be discussed more fully in Chapter 9: "Ethical Issues for Criminal Prosecutors."

[11]These and other related issues will be discussed more fully in Chapter 10: "Ethical Issues for Criminal Defense Attorneys."

[12]In *Taylor v. Kentucky* (1978), a robbery trial, a prosecutor argued in his closing statement that the accused's "status as a defendant tended to establish his guilt." The US Supreme Court disagreed, explaining that this kind of prejudicial statement, in the absence of clear instructions from the trial court about the necessity of the presumption of innocence, was a violation of due process. Consequently, this case was overturned (despite being first upheld in by the Kentucky Court of Appeals).

If convicted of a serious felony, a defendant is further entitled to state and federal appeals that can be based on demonstrable errors and misconduct during trial; ineffective assistance by defense counsel; lack of evidence sufficient to support a conviction; newly discovered evidence; and actual innocence. It is fair to say that any professional that does not abide these defense entitlements causes harm to the justice system by participating in it on any level – and should, in good faith, seek employment elsewhere.

THE VALUE OF PROFESSIONAL ETHICS IN THE CRIMINAL JUSTICE SYSTEM

Legal justice, as we have shown, requires professionals operating at the highest level of awareness, integrity, and accountability. Professional ethics help to provide the mechanism for all of these. Therefore, the value of professional ethics to the criminal justice system cannot be overstated. It may even be argued that without sincere professional ethics there can be no legal justice.

As discussed in the Preface,[13] the criminal justice system has a trustworthy character requirement. This requirement exists because all of the tasks performed in every branch of the criminal justice system are ultimately in service of, and under the scrutiny of, an agent of the court. Every professional report and statement that is generated will eventually be considered by the judiciary, or its agents, as legal decisions are being made. Routinely, these must also be made under penalty of perjury. Work product from all criminal justice professionals must therefore meet the high standards of integrity that the court requires, without exaggeration or omission.

A strong measure of professional character and integrity is found in the quality of one's professional code of ethics. This includes not only what it provides and prohibits, but also whether it is enforced. A worthy code of professional ethics accomplishes the following: it defines acceptable behavior and responsibilities; it clarifies group values, promotes them, and allows for their evaluation; it enables the recognition of unethical behavior by others and establishes penalties; and ultimately helps to nurture professional identity (Gannett, 2009). Having a strong code of ethics is not enough, however. To be of service to the profession, it must also be enforced. Those violating the code must be sanctioned without prejudice and, in serious cases, expelled.

The willingness to submit oneself to such a code of professional ethics is evidence of professional competence, reliability, accountability, and overall trustworthiness. It signals these traits to the court, to fellow professionals, and to the public, acting as a promise or guarantee that the mandates of legal justice

---

[13]If the reader has not yet read the Preface, now would be the time.

are understood and are ultimately being served. In other words, it lets others know that one can be trusted to act honestly and professionally. On that note, the failure to submit oneself to such a code of professional ethics, or to enforce it, should make clear the absence of overall professionalism and the absence of a specific commitment to the mandates of legal justice.

To sum, the value of professional ethics to the criminal justice system is in their ability to assure that competent professionals, acting with honesty and integrity, are hard at work administering legal justice; and that incompetent or corrupt professionals are not.

THE VALUE OF PROFESSIONAL ETHICS TO CRIMINAL JUSTICE PRACTITIONERS

The tremendous social and judicial importance of professional ethics aside, there are also significant benefits for the individual criminal justice practitioner. These include, but are certainly not limited to *employability, preparedness, trustworthiness, resistance to serious corruption*, and *protection*. A discussion of these specific benefits is useful.

Employability

Professionals that submit to a worthy code of professional ethics, and follow it, are employable in the criminal justice system – more so than others. First, they are going to be more able to survive the initial application process, in which criminal justice employers carefully screen the background of all applicants and candidates for disqualifiers (discussed in both the Preface and Chapter 2: "Ethical Issues for Students of Criminal Justice"). Second, they are going to be more capable of sustaining employment during internal investigations, audits or evaluations of their conduct throughout their tenure. Third, their conduct is going to more ably survive the scrutiny of external evaluations and investigations, especially those related to court proceedings.

Preparedness

Criminal justice practitioners that submit to a worthy code of professional ethics, and follow it, are more prepared to identify, understand, and manage ethical issues and dilemmas as they arise. It will help identify relevant ethical issues in advance, allowing anticipation and time for planning. It will also offer a specific course of action for avoiding unethical behavior – by stressing both what is required and what is forbidden.

Ultimately, a good code of professional ethics acts as a series of warning lights that flash when there is pressure building from a foreseeable ethical issue or dilemma. It further provides the corresponding solution, like a switch next to a red indicator light on a boiler that activates a safety valve. An ethical issue arises (increasing ethical pressure); the corresponding red warning lights start flashing next to the relevant ethical guideline; and the safety valve can be activated to release pressure – preventing a professional explosion that can destroy reputations and careers. Without such a safety mechanism in place, even the most honest criminal justice practitioners can find themselves in the exploded rubble of an ethical issue without any knowledge that they were ever in danger to begin with.

Trustworthiness

Beyond the value of individual trustworthiness to the criminal justice system in general, criminal justice practitioners that submit to a worthy code of professional ethics, and follow it, will be more trusted by their co-workers (e.g., supervisors, colleagues, and subordinates). They may not make as many friends in the workplace, if any, and they may not even be well liked. However, they will generally have professional credibility, along with professional respect, among those that they work with. They will also likely be sought out for advice when ethical issues arise between competing interests in their agencies.

Resistance to Serious Corruption

Criminal justice practitioners that submit to a worthy code of professional ethics, and follow it, develop a greater resistance to more serious forms of corruption. Employment in the criminal justice system provides individuals with the training, opportunity, and often the authority to engage in corruption on a variety of levels, all which requires a high level of personal integrity to evade. Once any professional violates their ethical integrity, perhaps even in lock step with the other unethical members of their agency, the potential for future and more severe forms of corruption is increased. This remains true no matter how small the initial misdeed or enticement. Corruption is a small seed that takes root and grows only where integrity does not.

Protection

Criminal justice practitioners that submit to a worthy code of professional ethics, and follow it, are better protected from the negative consequences of unethical behavior.[14] These include loss of promotions, loss of wages, loss of certifications, and other administrative sanctions; loss of professional reputation; susceptibility to blackmail; termination of employment; civil liability; and criminal prosecution. Treating these kinds of consequences as remote

---

[14]As explained in Gannett (2009), in a discussion regarding the importance of maintaining clearly defined professional ethics in the forensic sciences (p. 28): "Even the most cynical student of forensic ethics might find value in this reason: to protect one's posterior. If you are asked to do something inappropriate by a requester or a boss, being able to point to a professional code that supports your refusal to comply grants far more weight to your refusal."

or perhaps negligible is a terrible mistake, as they are both probable and devastating.

In order to appreciate the value of this kind of protection, the criminal justice practitioner must look past the immediate benefits and rewards that can come from lying, breaking the rules, or even violating the law, and into the future. They must consider the consequences that can be incurred from even the slightest misconduct if and when it is made known to all. They must ask themselves, how would I explain this if under investigation or in court and under oath – as this is likely to happen at some point.

It is important for those seeking work in the criminal justice system to understand that the potential for being accused of a crime, arrested, or convicted is dramatically increased should they meet with success. This is because of the legal consequences of the work that is being done and the hostile scrutiny that generally accompanies it. Successful employment in the criminal justice system means being accused of misconduct, being asked to inform on co-workers, and being named in lawsuits on a regular basis, and as a matter of course. As the professional stands almost entirely alone under the pall of such miserable circumstances, the best shield is a clearly defined professional ethics, a reputation for abiding integrity, and a willingness to be honest when mistakes have been made.

SUMMARY

The criminal justice system is comprised of multiple interrelated pillars fashioned to support the ideals of legal justice. Legal justice is the result of forging the rights of individuals with the government's corresponding duty to ensure and protect those rights – referred to as due process. These constitutional entitlements cannot be given and protected without the abiding commitment of those professionals working in the criminal justice system. Consequently, such professionals must submit themselves to the ethical principles of the criminal justice system and evidence persistent integrity in their character. This is accomplished with the help of a worthy code of professional ethics that signals competence, reliability, accountability, and overall trustworthiness – when properly administered.

Questions

1. List the five interdependent pillars of the criminal justice system.
2. Explain the difference between an *ethical dilemma* and a *moral dilemma*.
3. *Professional codes* include three different types of directives. What are they?
4. *Retributive* or *corrective* models of justice focus on making victims whole again and reintegrating offenders back into society. True or False?

5. Which pillar of the criminal justice system interprets, construes, applies, and generally administers and enforces the laws?
6. List three benefits of professional ethics for the criminal justice practitioner.

References

Black, H.C., 1990. Black's Law Dictionary, sixth ed. West Publishing, St Paul, MN.

Chapman, N., McConnell, M., 2012. Due process as separation of powers. Yale Law Journal 121 (7), 1672–1807.

Davis, M., 1995. Code of ethics. In: Bailey, W. (Ed.), The Encyclopedia of Police Science, second ed. Garland, New York.

Ethics Across the Curricula Committee, 2007. Ethics 101: A Common Ethics Language for Dialogue. DePaul University, Institute for Business & Professional Ethics, Chicago, IL, url: http://commerce.depaul.edu/ethics/docs/EthicsManual.pdf.

Gannett, C., 2009. I don't need no stinkin' ethics code! CAC News, Second Quarter, pp.23–28.

Kleinig, J., 1996. The Ethics of Policing. Cambridge University Press, New York.

Leonard, V.A., 1969. The Police, The Judiciary, and the Criminal. Charles C. Thomas, Springfield, IL.

Morn, F., 1995. Academic Politics and the History of Criminal Justice Education. Greenwood Press, Westport, CT.

Reid, S., 2003. Crime and Criminology, tenth ed. McGraw-Hill, Boston, MA.

Savino, J., Turvey, B., 2011. Rape Investigation Handbook, second ed. Elsevier, San Diego, CA.

Sen, A., 2011. The Idea of Justice. Belknap Press, Boston, MA.

Sullivan, J., 1977. Introduction to Police Science, third ed. McGraw-Hill, New York.

Taylor v. Kentucky, 1978. US Supreme Court. 436 US 478, No. 77–5549.

Thornton, J., 2012. Crime reconstruction: ethos and ethics. In: Chisum, W.J., Turvey, B. (Eds.), Crime Reconstruction, second ed. Elsevier, San Diego, CA.

Turvey, B., Petherick, W., 2010. An introduction to forensic criminology. In: Turvey, B., Petherick, W., Ferguson, C. (Eds.), Forensic Criminology, Elsevier, San Diego, CA.

Vollmer, A., 1971. The Police and Modern Society. Patterson Smith, Montclair, NJ.

CHAPTER 2

Ethical Issues for Students of Criminal Justice

Stan Crowder, Shawn Mikulay and Brent E. Turvey

Key Terms

Academic misconduct A specific type of student misconduct, referring to any action that is intended to create an unfair academic advantage for oneself or that unfairly impacts the advantages of other members in the academic community.

Cheating Any dishonest behavior that is intended to secure an unfair advantage – especially during an examination or an assessment of some kind.

Consent The act of giving permission with an awareness of the consequences.

Date and information fabrication "Making up data or results and recording or reporting them" (Office of Research Integrity, 2009, p. 5).

Direct plagiarism The exact reproduction of published work without any attribution of its original source.

Dishonesty Any deliberate misrepresentation of fact by an act or an omission.

Employment disqualifiers Are past and present activities or affiliations that evidence, or even appear to evidence, criminality, a propensity for dishonesty, or poor character.

Hazing A particular kind of initiation ritual that involves physical pain or mental distress coupled with humiliating, intimidating, and demeaning treatment.

Inappropriate relationships Any relationships that cause or promote ethical dilemmas.

Paraphrasing A form of plagiarism that involves reproducing the work of others while changing the precise language of the original source only slightly and then failing to acknowledge the original source.

Plagiarism Involves the use of intellectual property (e.g., words, constructs, inventions, or ideas) without proper acknowledgement, giving others the false impression that it is original work (Office of Research Integrity, 2009).

Plagiarism of authorship Involves placing one's own name on the completed work of another without significant alteration.

Self-plagiarism (a.k.a "double dipping") The practice of submitting the same work product or one that is only slightly altered, to satisfy the requirements of multiple separate courses.

Sexual coercion The psychological, emotional, chemical, or physical manipulation of one person by another for sexual purposes – and can occur in an otherwise consenting relationship.

Sexual misconduct Any sexually oriented behavior that violates established codes of conduct.

Stalking Repeated and persistent unwanted communication or contact that creates fear in the target (Morgan and Kavanaugh, 2011).

Student code of honor (a.k.a student code of ethics or student code of conduct) A mandate that spells out the values, virtues, and behaviors that are expected of all confirmed registrants and their guests.

CONTENTS

21

Ethical Justice. http://dx.doi.org/10.1016/B978-0-12-404597-2.00002-4

Student misconduct Any violation of institutional rules, regulations, or codes of conduct by a student.

Theft or damage of intellectual property Intentionally stealing or destroying the work of another.

No matter the place of study – be it a college, university, or training academy – students of Criminal Justice, Justice Studies, and Justice Administration (CJ/JS/JA) will be confronted with ethical issues and dilemmas. They are unavoidable. More to the point, they cannot be ignored without consequence.

When confronted with an ethical issue, it is of course important for students to understand and follow related institutionally mandated guidelines for ethical conduct and conflict resolution. That is, if there are any and if they provide adequate coverage. However, this advice is incomplete at best and perhaps more than a little misleading.

Satisfactory outcomes from following established policies and procedures are rare, and helpful advice is equally scarce. In truth, the majority of those people encountered by students suffering from genuine ethical pains will seek to maintain a selfish disinterest towards them – if not also a physical distance. Realistically, and under the best circumstances, the ethical student will have the ignorance and apathy of fellow students, instructors, and administrators as adversaries. Some explanation is necessary.

New to the realities of professionalism, fellow students are generally going to be ignorant of related ethical issues and consequences. They will be inexperienced with taking their choices seriously and identifying any related mistakes; and they will have been insulated from adult consequences by virtue of having been, until a recently, a minor. This insulation, along with extreme parental interference, can nurture an attitude of indifference that is unnaturally extended by immediately entering higher education. The classroom environment can enable the delusion that they are still children and that they may behave without consequence. These realities can conspire to breed misunderstanding and apathy towards the importance of behaving either professionally or ethically.

Instructors are often no better, many of whom provide little by way of professional example or guidance. This can be caused by too much time spent in academia or without the benefit of experiencing the severity of consequences in the criminal justice arena; it can be caused by fear, resulting from policy-bred hypersensitivity towards giving students advice or communicating with them on matters unrelated to the classroom; it can be caused by extreme self-involvement, resulting from professional narcissism or from being overwhelmed by everyday responsibilities outside of the workplace (e.g., relationships, children, financial difficulties); and it can also be caused by burn out. Good instructors that are willing to take the time to provide helpful advice and set an appropriate professional example are the exception, not the rule.

Administrators and student–faculty liaisons are meant to be a point of contact for all things confusing, distressing, or harmful to the student. In reality, they often act as a blockade. Many have mastered the art of talking (or frightening) students out of lodging formal complaints and of negotiating the damage that can be incurred by their employers when students do. Less interested in the harm that has or will be suffered by the student, those working for educational institutions may have or may perceive an obligation to protect the reputations of their employer and any co-workers by mitigating liability. Such attitudes, which are prevalent, make student concerns secondary and can leave them essentially without an advocate at all.

As a consequence of these combined realities, the CJ/JS/JA student must research and understand the fluid ethical requirements of the criminal justice system, as well as the specific codes of conduct where they attend classes. They must further be capable of navigating the murky water surrounding those that have not done either and be alert to others with self-interested priorities. Often, they must do all of this alone. It is the purpose of this chapter to help students map these issues out and provide sound direction where possible.

EMPLOYMENT SCREENING

As explained in Chapter 1: "Ethics in the Criminal Justice Professions," there is a trustworthy character requirement for employment in the criminal justice system that spans all branches. This is owing to the general need for maintaining the faith of the court and its agents, found in the anticipation of sworn statements and testimony that are a regular feature of most criminal justice professions. Under these circumstances, the liability for hiring and retaining candidates of low character (or quality) is simply too high for most agencies to bear. Consequently, employers within or servicing the criminal justice system make it a point to screen applicants carefully (Bopp and Schultz, 1972; Sullivan, 1977; Kleinig, 1996; Stout, 2011).[1]

In simple terms, any evidence of poor character is an obstacle to getting hired by a professional agency. CJ/JS/JA students need to come to terms with this sooner rather than later. In doing so, they must also examine their past and

---

[1]As will be discussed throughout this text, there are many criminal justice employers that fail to adequately screen their applicants. As a consequence, ethical co-workers within these agencies suffer, victims suffer, justice is subverted, and liability is incurred. Qualified students of good character would do well to steer clear of any employer with low professional standards – as they are likely to suffer a high turnover rate and continuous scandal.

present choices, to determine the extent to which they are capable of surviving a hiring process focused on their character. If they fail in their sincerity, then a sincere examination will happen at the direction of others with far less sympathy. Professional life in the criminal justice system therefore begins at the student level (Stephens, 2006). Anyone that thinks or suggests otherwise is uninformed.

General Disqualifiers

Employment disqualifiers are past and present activities or affiliations that evidence, or even appear to evidence, criminality, a propensity for dishonesty, or poor character (see discussions in California Crime Laboratory Review Task Force, 2009; Stephens, 2006). In the criminal justice system, they can include:

- Illegal drug use.
- Abuse of prescription medications.
- Alcohol abuse.
- Gambling addictions.
- Criminal arrests and convictions.
- Commission of undetected crimes.
- Extensive history of traffic violations.
- Gang affiliations.
- Affiliations with known criminals.
- Mental disorders.
- Pervasive financial problems.
- Falsification of any of the above.
- Failure to disclose any of the above.
- Failure of a pre-employment polygraph examination.

The importance of a particular disqualifier with respect to employability varies from agency to agency. That is to say there is latitude afforded by some agencies – especially when the pool of viable candidates is limited by geography and pay-scales. This is not necessarily a good thing: the more professional the government agency and the higher the security clearances of its operational employees, the less likely they are to overlook the disqualifiers mentioned. The opposite is also true.

Typical Background Investigations

Professional criminal justice agencies have an ethical obligation to maintain high standards for employment, in order to ensure that justice is being managed with the utmost integrity (Bopp and Schultz, 1972; Hansen and Culley, 1973; Kleinig, 1996; Shane, 2010; Stout, 2011; Sullivan, 1995; Vollmer, 1971). This generally accomplished with a thorough background investigation, as explained in Sullivan (1995, p. 50): "Failure to inquire into all of a candidate's past may result in the employment of a person who may bring discredit and embarrassment to a department. Employment investigators believe that it is much better to be thorough than sorry." As suggested by the disqualifiers listed in the previous section, and apart from physical or mental fitness, the following are typical background investigations aimed at ethical concerns that criminal justice employers may require:

- *Resume and application verification.* Most government agencies have very strict and thorough application policies. If the applicant provides false information during this process it will likely result in non-hiring. If the applicant provides false information during this process that is found out after employment has already bee secured, this can result in termination. In some instances, it can also result in criminal charges.
- *Criminal history.* Most agencies in the criminal justice professions perform criminal background checks of some fashion on applicants. In addition, those charged with law enforcement responsibilities take fingerprints and run them against available criminal databases. Even attorneys and private investigators are required, in most states, to disclose any criminal history and matters of "moral turpitude" before they can be licensed to practice (moral turpitude is discussed in the next section). However, these background checks are not always reliable, immediate, or comprehensive. If an applicant fails to disclose criminal or other relevant history, this and any other relevant omission can result in termination of employment and revocation of any related licensure – even if discovered by a delinquent investigation performed years after the fact.
- *Moral fitness.* Those applying for work in the criminal justice system may be required to submit to, and maintain, standards of moral fitness that are dictated by their eventual employer. In point of fact, many agencies assert morals clauses that must be signed as a standard part of any employment contract. Violations of *moral turpitude*, generally defined as "conduct that is considered contrary to community standards of justice, honesty or good morals," involves vague and sometimes antiquated standards that have caused many legal scholars to declare the concept unhelpful and open to abuse (Holper, 2011). Regardless, employers and supervisors set their own standards for moral turpitude, penalizing and discharging the unfaithful as they see fit. When considering whether to apply for a job in the criminal justice system, students should bear this is mind and learn specific particular moral standards that they may be expected to emulate.

- *Financial history.* Students with too much debt, bad credit history, or a history of poor financial decisions are less likely to be hired than those without. This is in no small part owing to the belief that poor decisions regarding finances, along with high debt, can make for a risky hire with respect to potential corruptibility. Consequently, criminal justice agencies are known for screening such applicants to varying degrees.
- *Known associates.* Applicants are often judged based on whom they choose to associate with – and may even be required to disclose extensive lists of friends, family, and past co-workers. Many agencies have rigid policies about associating with known felons, for example. Students are therefore admonished to choose their friends and other associates with care.
- *Polygraph examination.* In order to test the veracity of information provided during the application process, many employers in the criminal justice system require candidates to submit to a polygraph examination. These typically involve questions about prior employment, including the reasons behind resignations and terminations; whether there was a history of theft from past employers; extensive questions about individual crimes that may have been committed, or drug and alcohol use; questions about past relationships; and questions about traffic violations.

Straightforward awareness of employment disqualifiers, as well as the kinds of investigations traditionally performed on those applying for work in the criminal justice system, is crucial. First, it lets students know whether employment is a realistic possibility, given their background and overall fitness. Second, it helps students to plan a more professional path through the educational process. Finally, it makes the consequences of unethical choices and misconduct clear.

STUDENT CODES OF HONOR, ETHICS, AND CONDUCT

Notions of professionalism, and acceptable professional conduct, start in the classroom. These are transmitted directly to the student by written institutional codes of conduct, the consequences suffered by their classmates for violations, and most importantly through what is taught and modeled by their instructors.[3] These influences conspire to shape the student's professional and ethical character, instructing them on behavior that is expected, permissible, and intolerable. In this section, the nature and role of student codes will be discussed.

---

[3]Instructor ethics and obligations will be discussed in Chapter 3: "Criminal Justice Educators: Ethical Issues in Teaching."

Every educational institution, whether a local trade school, training academy, community college, or university, has its own code of conduct for registered students. Referred to variously as a *student code of honor*, *student code of ethics*, or a *student code of conduct*, these mandates spell out the values, virtues, and behaviors that are expected of all confirmed registrants and their guests. Their overall purpose is to nurture and protect an institution's essential missions. They usually include provisions for a safe and secure environment for students and staff. They also generally provide for student rights, and require that staff and students respect each other in that regard. Some codes are lengthy and explicit, while are others are general and vague.

Although often inclusive of legal concerns, student codes of conduct are not specifically intended to manage unlawful conduct. Local criminal statutes already exist for that purpose. Rather, student codes are first intended to help cultivate and manage student character as a whole. Second, they give the institution domain and recourse when a victimized student does not pursue criminal charges or a civil remedy.

Student codes are also not universal or interchangeable, as each institution has its own particular foundations, missions, and moral agenda. For example, private institutions with religious orientations may have strict policies against homosexuality, premarital sex, smoking, or the otherwise legal consumption of alcohol – made part of any student agreement that is signed as a condition of enrollment (for a useful discussion, see Sanders, 2011). Public institutions, on the other hand, may have specific rules regarding the establishment of sexual consent between students and are known for banning students of all ages from consuming alcohol anywhere on campus. Whatever the case may be, students have an obligation to read and understand any code of conduct that they have agreed to abide as part of their enrollment. Furthermore, they have a duty to seek clarification on any issue that raises a question, concern, or doubt before it becomes a problem.

At this point it should be clear that confusing, contradictory, weak, or unenforced student codes of conduct have no value to those who take them seriously. In fact, the only thing that is guaranteed by an ineffective code is negligence and liability. It is therefore the responsibility of every educational institution to ensure that their respective student code is clear, consistent, and enforced without bias.

STUDENT MISCONDUCT

Student misconduct is generally defined as any violation of institutional rules, regulations, or codes of conduct by a student. Generally, it can be boiled down to four basic prohibitions: do not lie, do not cheat, do not steal, and do not harm. In this section behaviors that are explicitly prohibited include those involving dishonesty; academic misconduct; hazing; indecency; inappropriate sexual behavior; improper relationships between staff and students; illegal possession or use of drugs and alcohol; stalking; threats and harassment; interfering with staff or students; violence; and any conduct that might constitute a criminal offense. Depending on the severity, student misconduct may result in the issuance of a warning, a probationary period, or a suspension. In extreme cases, students that are found to have engaged in misconduct are expelled.

Most institutions also maintain a general policy against dishonesty in any formal context, be it in communications with staff, on classroom assignments, or during an administrative inquiry. For those that are unaware, *dishonesty* is any deliberate misrepresentation of fact by an act or an omission. It generally involves wanting others to believe something that is untrue or wanting to keep others from having information that there is some obligation to report. For example, it is dishonest for a student to report on their resume that they have graduated from college when in fact they have not. It is equally dishonest for the same student to refrain from making a correction when introduced to others as a college graduate.

Policies against dishonesty act as a blanket prohibition, promoting academic responsibility and ethical integrity while helping to safeguard truth, respect, and fairness in all aspects of academic life.

ACADEMIC MISCONDUCT

Academic misconduct is a specific type of student misconduct, referring to any action that is intended to create an unfair academic advantage for oneself or that unfairly impacts the advantages of other members in the academic community. This includes a wide variety of things that may be explicitly or implicitly spelled out by institutional rules, regulations, or codes of conduct. Common examples include cheating, plagiarism, fabrication of information or data, theft or damage of intellectual property, and faking illnesses, family emergencies, or victimization. Academic misconduct evidences an overall lack of ethics and in some cases it may also reflect criminality.

Cheating

Cheating refers to any dishonest behavior that is intended to secure an unfair advantage – especially during an examination or an assessment of some kind. For example, as explained in University of California at Berkeley (2012):

> Cheating is defined as fraud, deceit, or dishonesty in an academic assignment, or using or attempting to use materials, or assisting others in using materials that are prohibited or inappropriate in the context of the academic assignment in question, such as:
>
> - Copying or attempting to copy from others during an exam or on an assignment.

- Communicating answers with another person during an exam.
- Preprogramming a calculator to contain answers or other unauthorized information for exams.
- Using unauthorized materials, prepared answers, written notes, or concealed information during an exam.
- Allowing others to do an assignment or portion of an assignment for you, including the use of a commercial term-paper service.
- Submission of the same assignment for more than one course without prior approval of all the instructors involved.
- Collaborating on an exam or assignment with any other person without prior approval from the instructor.
- Taking an exam for another person or having someone take an exam for you.

Current research confirms that cheating is on the rise (Jones, 2011). This is in part due to the fact that methods for cheating, and related technology, are widely available via the Internet. As discussed in Jones (2011, p. 142): "Within the past few years, high-tech cheating is gradually replacing the simple cut-and-paste cheating. Students have become more tech savvy, and online instructional cheating videos, detailing clever methods to cheat, are populating the Internet daily." It is also due to the ability of students to rapidly access, copy, and share information via small wireless Internet devices – most commonly by using a cell phone (e.g., see the student cheating scandal in New York reported in Bennett, 2012).

Plagiarism

Plagiarism, regarded as a particular type of cheating, is among the most common forms of academic misconduct. Essentially, it involves the use of intellectual property (e.g., words, constructs, inventions, or ideas) without proper acknowledgment, giving others the false impression that it is original work (Office of Research Integrity, 2009). A good working definition can be found in Elsevier (2012): "Plagiarism is the passing off of another's work as one's own. In its simplest form, plagiarism may be verbatim copying, but paraphrasing of text, tables, figures or even ideas without proper citation also constitutes an infringement."[4]

ETHICAL DISPOSITION

Cheating is unethical because it is dishonest, misrepresents accomplishment and ability, and suggests an overall disinterest in doing the work required to meet academic objectives.

---

[4]Elsevier is the publisher of this textbook, as well as numerous other publications and professional journals.

Although a straightforward concept, plagiarism is defined and treated differently by every institution. It is therefore useful to mention a few of its many different manifestations, some of which were mentioned in the previous section.

- *Plagiarism of authorship* involves placing one's own name on the completed work of another without significant alteration (if any). An example would be purchasing a research paper online and submitting it for course credit as one's own original work.
- *Direct plagiarism* involves the exact reproduction of published work without any attribution of its original source. An example would be the absence of internal references and quotations around language that has been reproduced verbatim from another source.
- *Paraphrasing* is a form of plagiarism that involves reproducing the work of others while changing the precise language of the original source only slightly and then failing to acknowledge the original source.
- *Self-plagiarism (a.k.a. "double dipping")* refers to the practice of submitting the same work product (e.g., a research paper or project) or one that is only slightly altered, to satisfy the requirements of multiple separate courses.[5] This provides the illusion that more work has been completed in order to satisfy university requirements for assignments or publication.

Each of these manifestations of plagiarism involves a deliberate attempt to mislead others as to the authorship and originality of words, constructs, inventions, or ideas. However, some institutions have more rigid plagiarism guidelines; academic sloppiness or laziness can evidence sufficient recklessness and negligence to incur a violation. For example, some institutions do not require the intent to deceive, only improper or incomplete citation. Others forbid the use of any quotations or ideas referenced from secondary sources; this requires students to research and confirm any quoted material or idea from its primary source.[6] Whatever the precise institutional requirements, students are admonished to seek them out and abide accordingly.

ETHICAL DISPOSITION

Plagiarism is unethical because it is dishonest; it misrepresents the amount of time and effort that was put into research and writing; and it subsequently misrepresents research and writing ability. It also suggests an overall disinterest, or an inability, with respect to the research and writing that is required to complete assigned work.

---

[5]Ironically, this practice, considered highly unethical among scientific researchers, is rampant in the literature. It will be discussed further in Chapter 3. "Criminal Justice Educators: Ethical Issues in Teaching."
[6]This requirement has the virtue of revealing bad and erroneous scholarship. Certainly the authors have found this to be true, as many scholars have published and referenced erroneous data and conclusions in many areas of criminology. These errors have been folded into the literature, have been further transmitted from one generation to the next, and continue to flourish when primary sources are ignored.

Crowder's Comments

Policy v. Reality

Ironically, the first time that I encountered plagiarism, I was an adjunct professor teaching my first criminal justice ethics course. I even didn't know that this student's research paper was plagiarized until I typed a line from it into a search engine and the whole article came up from another source – almost word for word. At that point, I suspected that I would probably have to give her an "F" on the assignment because of my limited understanding of University policy. But here's the thing – there is a difference between policy and the reality of implementing that policy. That difference is politics – for any number of reasons, there are students that get treated differently by those with the burden of command and I was probably concerned that this might be one of those. But mostly, I knew that I didn't know everything about University policy. And I wanted to have my bases covered in case the student challenged my decision. So, essentially lacking the confidence to make this potentially messy political decision on my own, I got in touch with my department chair and laid it all out for her. She advised me that not only should the student flunk the assignment, but that she should also flunk the whole course. I couldn't have agreed more. Knowing that I had that kind of strong ethical support within my academic chain of command was immediately gratifying, and also crucial to my professional development.

Fabrication of Information or Data

Data and information fabrication refers to "making up data or results and recording or reporting them" (Office of Research Integrity, 2009, p. 5). This definition can be presumed to include the invention of any relevant aspect of an academic assignment, such as phony references, fake interviews, and contrived observations. While this practice invariably takes less time than actual scholarship and results in findings that are aligned perfectly with the student's needs, it is also dishonest. It should not need to be explained that results based on non-existent information and data are themselves a contrivance, no matter how expedient or desirable. Learning to avoid this practice as a student will prevent much professional bias and distress later on down the road.

ETHICAL DISPOSITION

Falsifying data or any other information in relation to scholarship is unethical at face value because it is dishonest. Like plagiarism, it misrepresents the amount of time and effort that was put into research; and it subsequently misrepresents research ability and ingenuity. It also has the potential to poison the well of professional literature in related subject areas, as it may be referenced or actually used in practice by others. The real-world consequences of falsification vary: if fabricated research results are relied on by the court as evidence, it can result in a miscarriages of justice; if the results are relied upon by those in the medical community, it can result in patient harm or death.

CASE EXAMPLE

Bengü Sezen, PhD

Bengü Sezen, PhD, a former graduate student in the Department of Chemistry at Columbia University: "engaged in misconduct in science in research funded by National Institute of General Medical Sciences (NIGMS), National Institutes of Health (NIH), grant R01 GM60326 ... based on evidence that she knowingly and intentionally falsified and fabricated, and in one instance plagiarized, data reported in three (3) papers and her doctoral thesis" (Office of Research Integrity, 2011a, p. 7). After suffering multiple investigations for fraud, Ms Sezen fled the country to study elsewhere. Ultimately, many of her co-authored publications were withdrawn from the literature and Columbia University revoked her PhD.[7]

---

[7]*A more complete discussion of the "Saga of Bengü Sezen," and those involved, is found in Stemwedel (2011).*

Turvey's Comments

Running It Down, Every Time

As an undergrad in the early 1990s, before the Internet was widely available, I developed the habit of running down and reading (and confirming) the primary sources in every reference that I used for every research paper that I wrote. This was something that was beaten into me by my history professors, all of whom really knew their stuff. By the time I graduated, I had stacks and stacks of photocopied articles across every subject I'd taken as testament to many long days and late nights spent at the library. It's a habit that served me well in grad school, then as an instructor at University, and as a forensic examiner. Whenever a student submits a research paper, I run down all of the references to make sure that each says what the student says it did. I do the same thing with the forensic reports that I am asked to examine. After a while, you develop a clearer picture of the literature that is out there, and this is a good thing for an instructor to have, regardless. What I've learned is, there are a lot of sloppy students and researchers, throwing references that they hope nobody checks into a pile at the end of their works. In some cases, they are deliberately misrepresenting what a particular study found or supports. In others, they are actually confused enough to believe that this is what scholarship consists of. Whichever the case, I'm known for pointing out reference errors to an entire class when students give oral presentations, so that everyone can benefit from the mistake. I've found that once a student learns from public pain that they can't fake or fudge their references in my subjects, it's a habit that they leave behind – at least in my classes. If they take that lesson out into the world, so much the better.

Theft or Damage of Intellectual Property

The *theft or damage of intellectual property* involves intentionally stealing or destroying the work of another. Excerpted from University of California at Berkeley (2012), examples include:

- Sabotaging or stealing another person's assignment, book, paper, notes, experiment, project, electronic hardware or software.
- Improper access to, or electronically interfering with, the property of another person or the University via computer or other means.
- Obtaining a copy of an exam or assignment prior to its approved release by the instructor.

When involving theft without sabotage, this may be the first step towards plagiarism or it may simply be an effort to disadvantage a fellow student by preventing them from completing an assignment. This outcome may also be incidental to the theft of a computer, cell phone, external hard drive, camera, or some other electronic storage device. Such thefts are among the most common at educational institutions and codes related to this specific kind of misconduct spell out the severity of consequences to all concerned in the digital age.

ETHICAL DISPOSITION

Theft or damage of intellectual property is unethical because it involves stealing and harm to others. It can also misrepresent one's knowledge, skills, and abilities – to say nothing of taking credit for someone else's effort and ingenuity. The consequences essentially salt the earth for the victim, preventing their hard work from appearing original if they are able to take credit at all. As an indicator, this kind of behavior reflects ethical failure across the board to the point of evidencing a criminal disposition.

CASE EXAMPLE

Vipul Bhrigu, PhD

Vipul Bhrigu, PhD, a former post-doctoral fellow with the University of Michigan Medical School: "engaged in research misconduct in research funded by National Cancer Institute (NCI), National Institutes of Health (NIH), grant R01 CA098730-05" and "knowingly and intentionally tampered with research materials, and switched the labels on culture dishes ... to cause false results to be reported in the research record" (Office of Research Integrity, 2011b, p. 6). He also "tampered with laboratory research materials by adding ethanol to his colleague's cell culture media, with the deliberate intent to effectuate the death of growing cells, which caused false results to be reported in the research record" (Office of Research Integrity, 2011b, pp. 6–7). When the campus police became involved, Dr Bhrigu lied to them about his role and took no responsibility for what he had done. He ultimately came clean, however, when he was informed that his tampering activities in the lab had been recorded by video surveillance (Office of Research Integrity, 2011b).[8] Dr Bhrigu has reported that his actions were the result of what he perceived as internal pressure for results, combined with bad moral judgment.

---

[8]*A more complete discussion of this case, and those involved, along with the surveillance video, is found in Maher (2011).*

Faking Illnesses, Family Emergencies, or Victimization

Whether confronted with unfinished assignments, exams that have not been studied for, poor grades, or just a really bad hangover, it is not uncommon for students to fabricate illnesses, emergencies, or victimity of some kind. As early as grade school, students learn that any one of these circumstances may be invoked as sufficient reason to deflect or avoid academic responsibilities

(Turvey and Petherick, 2009). Inventions range from a temporary sickness and dead relatives, all the way to the perpetration of a complex fraud involving chronic illness.

ETHICAL DISPOSITION

False reports are unethical because they are, again, dishonest. However, they also have a strong potential with respect to wasting resources and harming others. As an indicator, this kind of behavior reflects an absence of ethical reasoning. More than that, however, it reflects a willingness to commit what may be a criminal act, causing harm to others, in order to achieve desired outcomes.

CASE EXAMPLE

Alexandra "Lexi" Pennell

Consider the case of Lexi Pennell, a student at Central Connecticut State University, as reported in Jow (2012):

A Central Connecticut State University student has been arrested and suspended from attending any state university campus for five years for fabricating antigay notes against herself, according to CBS Connecticut.

Lexi Pennell, 19, confessed to police that she had written the notes after a hidden camera installed outside her dorm room captured her sliding a note under her own door on April 5, according to the arrest warrant (PDF).

She was arrested May 9 on charges of tampering with or fabricating physical evidence, falsely reporting an incident, interfering with an officer and making a false statement to police.

In early March, Pennell reported finding gay slurs written on a dry-erase board outside her room as well as on papers attached to and slipped under her door.

Hundreds of CCSU students held a rally March 13 against hate crimes and to show their support for Pennell.

In a letter to her roommate, Pennell said she fabricated the notes because she feared her friends and her girlfriend were slipping away, and she continued to write them for the attention.

The evidence tampering charges stem from the fact that Ms Pennell unplugged area surveillance camera equipment to prevent it from recording properly, initially concealing her involvement in writing and planting the harassing statements and notes.

It other cases, students have been known to make false reports of crime to avoid academic deadlines and responsibilities. These false reports often begin as a small lie to avoid small consequences or gain sympathy from others (Savino and Turvey, 2011). However, they can snowball into a complex and unsupportable narrative when repeated to friends, family, and classmates who involve the authorities.

CASE EXAMPLE

Kelsey L. Hoffman

Consider the unfortunate case of Kelsey Hoffman, a student at the University of Iowa. She was ultimately charged with making a misdemeanor false report after a night of drinking led to regret – and a cover story that went too far, as reported in Serino (2012):

> A 21-year-old University of Iowa student was arrested Friday for alleging a report of her own kidnapping, which an extensive investigation uncovered was made up, police said.
>
> Authorities said they used police and Iowa Dept. of Public Safety resources to investigate the alleged kidnapping of Kelsey L. Hoffman, of Fort Dodge, who reported on Sept. 23 she was snatched from behind at her apartment on Iowa Avenue and awoke hours later at a parking ramp.
>
> In what police called an "extensive and intense investigation," they learned Hoffman had gone out drinking the night before and that she continued with her tale because "things had gone too far to come out with the truth," she told police.
>
> Hoffman told police she became unconscious and was dragged away from her building, but claimed to remember nothing after she was grabbed. During a final interview, police said Hoffman told her roommate she had been attacked, causing her roommate to call 9-1-1 when officers quickly responded.

Additionally, seasoned educators will also no doubt attest to the fact that student visits to campus health service clinics can predictably double or triple at the end of every semester. This occurs as students go in search of a medical note excusing them from class and related assignment deadlines or examinations. Failing to get what they need in person, sincere malingerers have the option of purchasing fake doctor's notes online, at any number of enterprising websites. Although ranging in quality, these bogus medical excuses and permissions can be extremely convincing to the instructor or institution demanding a show of proof.

In recognition of this problem, some educational institutions have adopted specific policies against providing false or misleading information, or making false reports of crime, emergencies, or harassment of any kind. For example, consider the "False Information" section of the University of Delaware's *Code of Conduct*, which dictates broadly that "a student shall not provide false or misleading information" to any University staff. It then goes on to explain that (University of Delaware, 2011):

Specific violations of this standard include, but are not limited to:

- Making a false or misleading oral or written statement to any University official or faculty member (including, but not limited to, application for admission, financial aid, residency classification or participation in any special programs sponsored by the University) when the student knew or should have known the statement was false;

- Making a false or misleading oral or written statement that misrepresents the character, qualifications, or reputation of another;
- Falsely reporting a safety hazard (including but not limited to, a fire, explosive or incendiary device) by any means including by activating an emergency phone on campus when no emergency actually exists;
- Falsely reporting a crime or a violation of this Code of Conduct; or
- Possessing or displaying any form of false identification or any identification not one's own.

These kinds of provisions acknowledge the problem of false reporting by students, and also provide a mechanism for handling them internally in order to penalize dishonesty and limit institutional liability. Some go a bit further and explain how such conduct may also be a violation of criminal law and civil defamation statutes. Spelling it out like that sends perhaps the clearest message. Conversely, educational institutions that ignore the reality of false reporting to staff, and make no provision for it in student codes, all but encourage their students to lie to get by.

INAPPROPRIATE RELATIONSHIPS

Inappropriate relationships are defined in this text as any relationships that cause or promote ethical dilemmas. With respect to students, this includes any relationship with an instructor that exists outside of the established boundaries of traditional student–faculty roles. Sometimes these relationships are social; sometimes they involve employment of the student by the instructor; and sometimes they are romantic or sexual. To be clear, a student–faculty relationship becomes inappropriate when either sacrifices their ethical principles or obligations to maintain the relationship. Although it may be possible for students to engage in appropriate social and employment relationships with faculty members, so long as clear boundaries are defined and observed, this is generally not the case when intimate behavior is involved.

Although legally considered adults, students in higher education tend to be emotionally immature and unfamiliar with the politics of adult sexuality. This is generally accompanied by inexperience with the complex political "ramifications of an intimate personal relationship with a superior" (Barbella, 2010, p. 44). As a consequence of these and other related factors, personal relationships between students and staff are problematic and generally inappropriate.[9]

---

[9]This section takes the perspective of the ethical student and their responsibilities. This same issue will be covered from the instructor's perspective in Chapter 3: "Criminal Justice Educators: Ethical Issues in Teaching."

First, younger students are easy prey for staff members with a penchant for dating those taking their courses. They can be easily overwhelmed, impressed, trustful, and even manipulated by the power and charisma that some staff members appear to have. Student exploitation is therefore a serious concern and ethical students should be ever mindful of the possibility.

Second, staff members that are emotionally involved with their students are in a continuous ethical bind with respect to perceived expectations, grading, and opportunities that are unavailable to those without the same intimate access. The fact is that students who develop personal relationships with their professors often get the best advice, marks, and internships. All of this may have been achieved without high-quality academic effort or any academic effort at all.[10] In extreme cases, instructors have been known to ignore all ethical obligations and institutional policies by doing their students' homework, giving them high marks for work that has not been done, or putting students' names on publications where participation was minimal, if it occurred at all. In any case, the ethical student will want to avoid conduct that places their instructors in situations where they feel compelled to show the student favor for something other than scholarship – and they will not seek credit for what they have not accomplished.

Third, even when staff members are able to resist the temptation to favor those students that they have a relationship with, such relationships can create the appearance of favoritism if not the genuine article. Regardless of the truth, those observing such a relationship from the outside will likely assume the worst. This can result in resentment and complaints about the relationship from other students and staff. The ethical will not want to harm their own reputation, or that of their instructor, by encouraging such judgments.

Finally, there can be severe fallout from student–faculty relationships when they end. This can range anywhere from heated verbal disagreements in the workplace to formal complaints of harassment and coercion. From the student perspective, this can include all manner of negative consequences to their academic career, including but not limited to:

- Low or failing grades when competent work has been completed.
- Inability to receive recommendations for work or graduate school.
- Informal false allegations of misconduct, resulting in harm to perceptions of student character and their ability to cultivate other academic relationships.
- Formal false allegations of misconduct, resulting in academic sanctions.

---

[10]Ironically, from the perspective of the unethical student, this will sound like a list of reasons to seek out a sexual relationship with an instructor.

- Retaliation in the form of public disclosure of private or intimate information.
- Retaliation in the form of stalking and harassment of the student by unstable faculty members that feel jilted or otherwise "wronged."

It is useful to note that many scholars agree, as do many courts, that any relationship between a superior and a subordinate contains some element of coercion because of the inherent power imbalance, as discussed in Barbella (2010, p. 45):

> A close personal friendship or a romantic and/or sexual relationship with a professor can significantly complicate this inherent unequal balance of power. Issues of favoritism can arise, especially if other students know about the relationship. When frictions occur in a friendship or a romantic relationship ends, a professor may allow those feelings to affect his/her professional judgment. As education professionals, professors should be given the benefit of the doubt that they can be trusted to remain fair and professional regardless of their feelings for one another or their personal interactions. However, it only takes the appearance of unfair treatment or impropriety for conflict to surface.

In other words, students, like other subordinates, do not really enjoy the full benefit of free will when responding to requests or pressure from their superiors, as there is always going to be an element of fear regarding potential negative consequences.

As a result of these issues, and more, many educational institutions have adopted non-fraternization policies, forbidding students and staff from engaging in romantic or sexual relationships – at least at the undergraduate level. This is despite the fact that such sexual relationships are frequent (Bellas and Gosset, 2001). Consider the policy at Yale University, which incorporates a number of the concerns already mentioned (Yale University, 2012):

> The integrity of the teacher–student relationship is the foundation of the University's educational mission. This relationship vests considerable trust in the teacher, who, in turn, bears authority and accountability as a mentor, educator, and evaluator. The unequal institutional power inherent in this relationship heightens the vulnerability of the student and the potential for coercion. The pedagogical relationship between teacher and student must be protected from influences or activities that can interfere with learning and personal development. Whenever a teacher is or in the future might reasonably become responsible for teaching, advising, or directly supervising a student, a sexual relationship between them

is inappropriate and must be avoided. In addition to creating the potential for coercion, any such relationship jeopardizes the integrity of the educational process by creating a conflict of interest and may impair the learning environment for other students. Finally, such situations may expose the University and the teacher to liability for violation of laws against sexual harassment and sex discrimination. Therefore, teachers (see below) must avoid sexual relationships with students over whom they have or might reasonably expect to have direct pedagogical or supervisory responsibilities, regardless of whether the relationship is consensual. Conversely, a teacher must not directly supervise any student with whom he or she has a sexual relationship.

Undergraduate students are particularly vulnerable to the unequal institutional power inherent in the teacher–student relationship and the potential for coercion, because of their age and relative lack of maturity. Therefore, no teacher shall have a sexual or amorous relationship with any undergraduate student, regardless of whether the teacher currently exercises or expects to have any pedagogical or supervisory responsibilities over that student.

As this implies, the ethical student must come to understand the importance of developing healthy professional relationships with their instructors, based on mutual respect and academic pursuit. They must also understand their role as student and not engage in any behavior that violates the high standards that professionals in the criminal justice system will expect them to meet. This requires awareness that some faculty members abuse their positions of authority to encourage their students into inappropriate and even sexual relationships. It also requires a realistic acknowledgement of the ethical issues that will arise from pursuing a consensual involvement even when it is permitted.

Ethical students will therefore make all of their decisions with an understanding of the negative consequences discussed in this section and refrain from relationships that might incur them. They will do this regardless of any immediate rewards or benefit, with a mind towards prevention. In this way, they will better maintain an academic record that reflects professionalism and integrity.

DRUGS AND ALCOHOL

Alcohol and drugs are fixtures of campus life in higher education. Opportunities to engage in the illegal use and abuse of both will continuously present themselves. For some students, this will be a welcome distraction, as they are less interested in attending classes than they are in the freedom that being away from home affords them. For others, these opportunities will come amidst all manner of stress and pressure that they are seeking to alleviate. Then there are those students who exploit every opportunity that these circumstances create; they either provide drugs and alcohol to their fellow students or they troll student gatherings for those that are already under the influence. The ethical student will seek to avoid falling into any of these predictable traps, following the law and related student codes.

Most institutions of higher education have strict policies against the possession, use, sale, or distribution of alcohol and non-prescription drugs on campus. Other institutions extend their authority further by making any of the following off-campus misconduct a violation of student code:

- Illegal or excessive consumption of alcohol and other drugs.
- Furnishing alcohol and other drugs to minors.
- Driving under the influence of alcohol and other drugs.

Policies such as these provide educational institutions with valuable tools for identifying at—risk students and expelling those behaving in an irresponsible or predatory fashion.

Apart from being a violation of student code and possibly the law, alcohol and drug abuse accomplish three things with certainty:

(1) This kind of behavior makes it easy to get into inappropriate, illegal, and dangerous situations, as they tend to impair the senses, lower inhibition, and reduce the ability to exercise good judgment.
(2) This kind of behavior makes it difficult to recognize, and get out of, inappropriate, illegal, and dangerous situations for the very same reasons.
(3) Those abusing alcohol and drugs can be certain that professionals, and prospective employers, will view them not as potential colleagues but rather as liabilities to be avoided.

There is something else, however, something specific to students of criminal justice. As already mentioned, unlike those in neighboring academic programs, students of criminal justice must anticipate being hooked up to a polygraph and asked about their history of alcohol and drug use. They will be asked about their social drinking habits and their prescription medications; they will be asked about every single time they recall taking a non-prescription drug; and they will be asked about any related arrests and convictions. If they do not disclose everything, and they are found to be deceptive during these standard background investigations, they will not get hired by the majority of criminal justice employers. Regardless of what the student has been told, illegal drug use of any kind, admitted or not, will generally bar them from getting hired by a professional law enforcement agency. This is especially true at the federal level.

Crowder's Comments

It Just Isn't Worth It

Alcohol abuse is behind just about every bad thing that happens in the criminal justice system, whether it's traffic accidents, domestic violence, or sexual assault. I'm not saying you can't have a drink if you are of legal age. You just shouldn't do it on campus or with people you don't know. And if you do have a few drinks with friends, stay put or have one of them drive you home. If a CJ student gets a DUI or worse, that's it. You're done. You need to start looking for a new career. Sure there are a few agencies that make exceptions, but trust me: you do not want to work for them. It just isn't worth it.

HAZING

Hazing is a reference to a particular kind of initiation ritual that involves physical pain or mental distress coupled with humiliating, intimidating, and demeaning treatment. It is, in essence, bullying and harassment with rules that can be steeped in tradition or arbitrarily cruel. Although often associated with sororities, fraternities, and sports teams, hazing is used by many different kinds of groups to invest new members – especially those in educational or training environments. It is also often promoted, tolerated, or simply ignored by staff members. As explained in Allen and Madden (2008), which reported the findings of a nationwide college survey of hazing and hazing related issues (p. 2):

- 55% of college students involved in clubs, teams, and organizations experience hazing.
- Hazing occurs in, but extends beyond, varsity athletics and Greek-letter organizations, and includes behaviors that are abusive, dangerous, and potentially illegal.
- Alcohol consumption, humiliation, isolation, sleep deprivation, and sex acts are hazing practices common across types of student groups.
- There are public aspects to student hazing including: 25% of coaches or organization advisors were aware of the group's hazing behaviors; 25% of the behaviors occurred on-campus in a public space; in 25% of hazing experiences, alumni were present; and students talk with peers (48%, 41%) or family (26%) about their hazing experiences.
- In more than half of the hazing incidents, a member of the offending group posts pictures on a public web space.
- More students perceive positive rather than negative outcomes of hazing.
- In 95% of the cases where students identified their experience as hazing, they did not report the events to campus officials.
- Students recognize hazing as part of the campus culture; 69% of students who belonged to a student activity reported they were aware of hazing activities occurring in student organizations other than their own.

- Students report limited exposure to hazing prevention efforts that extend beyond a "hazing is not tolerated" approach.
- 47% of students come to college having experienced hazing.
- Nine out of 10 students who have experienced hazing behavior in college do not consider themselves to have been hazed.

They also found that hazing commonly involved the following: sleep deprivation, servitude, cross-dressing, being tied up or confined to small places, drinking large amounts of alcohol, and performing sex acts in groups, with persons of the same gender or on other members of the group.[11]

Significantly, participants engage in hazing activities willingly. They believe that their suffering will earn them the respect and loyalty of the group. They also tend to look back at their experiences with favor and even pride – both for having endured and administered hazing rituals with others.

Most educational institutions forbid hazing in any form, out of concern for student safety and legal liability. Consider the student code adopted by Florida International University (FIU), which is fairly representative (Florida International University, 2008):

> Hazing is a violation of the FIU Student Code of Conduct. Hazing is defined as any group or individual action or activity that inflicts or intends to inflict physical or mental harm or discomfort or which may demean, disgrace, or degrade any person, regardless of location, intent, or consent of participant(s). Hazing includes, but is not limited to forced consumption of any food, alcohol, controlled substances, drugs, or any other substance, forced physical activity, deprivation of food or sleep, physical abuse of any nature, and verbal abuse, including yelling or demands.

These types of student codes, and the laws that make hazing illegal across most of the United States, have been put in place because of the consequences that can result from the extreme behavior involved. These consequences include long-term emotional and psychological damage, physical injury, and even death (Allen and Madden, 2008).

ETHICAL DISPOSITION

Hazing is unethical because it involves causing intentional harm to another – despite the long-term psychological and emotional harm it causes, and the potential legal consequences to those involved.

---

[11]In the authors' experience, hazing also involves extreme forms of physical punishment, tattooing, and even branding.

CASE EXAMPLE

Robert Champion

Consider the tragic case of Robert Champion, a drum major at Florida A&M University (FAMU) who was beaten to death by his band mates in a continuous hail of fists and drumsticks. The beating, part of an established hazing ritual for band members, took place on a bus while the driver stood outside. As reported in Suggs (2012):

> The family of Robert Champion, the drum major who died in November after a beating aboard a band bus, added the HBCU to the list of targets in a wrongful death lawsuit. And FAMU's president, James Ammons, resigned.
>
> The school has been under intense pressure ever since Champion died after a band performance at a football game in Orlando. In their lawsuit, Champion's parents, who live in Decatur, charge that school officials put the money to be earned from band performances ahead of students' safety, despite growing evidence that hazing was rampant ....
>
> In their lawsuit, an amendment to one filed earlier against the bus company, Robert and Pamela Champion said FAMU officials didn't take enough action to stop hazing throughout the lauded band program.
>
> In the 33-page document, the parents, who live in Decatur, said school administrators knew about the Marching 100's history of hazing. Even so, the suit says, the school did not act on a key recommendation to suspend the band just days prior to Champion's death.
>
> Champion and the band were in Orlando on Nov. 19 for the Florida Classic, which pitted FAMU's football team against Bethune-Cookman University.
>
> Days before the game, former band director Julian White – who quietly retired in May – suspended scores of band members for hazing. According to the lawsuit, on Nov. 16, three days before Champion's death, FAMU Dean of Students Henry Kirby "proposed imposing an immediate long-term suspension of the FAMU Band to combat the egregious hazing."
>
> "FAMU refused to suspend the FAMU Band prior to the Florida Classic, as suggested by Dean Kirby, due to the public notoriety and financial gain of participating in events during the three-day Florida Classic Weekend," the document claims.
>
> Kirby's recommendation "shows that they knew or should have known the climate of hazing and violence was escalating," Chestnut said ....
>
> Police and several witnesses say Champion was beaten to death as part of a hazing or pledging ritual. Some band members told police he welcomed the beating in order to earn the respect he would need to become head drum major next season.
>
> In more than 1,500 pages of transcripts and 49 audio recordings released in May by Florida prosecutors, several band members who witnessed the ritual described an evening of terror and chaos aboard the notorious Bus C. On that bus, which carried the band's percussionists, hazing reportedly was a custom, and fists, feet, drumsticks and straps were the tools.
>
> Champion's death put a spotlight on hazing at the school and led to the suspension of the band until at least the 2012–13 academic year. Eleven of Champion's band mates – including four from metro Atlanta – are charged with third-degree felony hazing. The Atlantans are Jonathan Boyce, 24, Shawn Turner, 26, Aaron Golson, 19, and Lasherry Codner, 20. Two other students face misdemeanor charges.

Those who participated in the killing are reported as saying that while they, and even Champion, were conflicted about the violent hazing ritual, they believed it was necessary to gain the respect of other band members. More to the point, they have also reported that those who refused participate in hazing rituals could expect to be isolated and alienated from the band (Hudak and Balona, 2012). The criminal and civil consequences of Mr Champion's death are still unfolding as of this writing.

STALKING

Stalking involves repeated and persistent unwanted communication or contact that creates fear in the target (Morgan and Kavanaugh, 2011). For those that may be unaware of their behavior, and what it can appear like to others, a list of common stalking behaviors includes (Black *et al.*, 2011, p. 29):

- Unwanted phone calls, voice or text messages, hang-ups.
- Unwanted emails, instant messages, messages through social media.
- Unwanted cards, letters, flowers, or presents.
- Watching or following from a distance, spying with a listening device, camera, or global positioning system (GPS).
- Approaching or showing up in places such as the victim's home, workplace, or school when it was unwanted.
- Leaving strange or potentially threatening items for the victim to find.
- Sneaking into victim's home or car and doing things to scare the victim or let the victim know the perpetrator had been there.

It is useful to note that stalking behaviors often begin as small or seemingly innocent gestures, but can quickly accelerate to inappropriate and frightening schemes.

Stalking is most commonly reported by females and often involves a former intimate partner (Morgan, 2010). However, any related statistics or statistical perceptions suffer from tremendous gender bias. Like rape or domestic violence, males are known to underreport being victims of stalking for fear that they will not be taken seriously, that they might appear weak, or that the stalking will actually get worse in retaliation. So while it is easy to be dismissive of male stalking victims, it is important to consider the hidden numbers.

On the college campus, stalking is routinely perpetrated by emotionally immature and unstable students against classmates and instructors alike. As reported in Morgan (2009, p. 109):

> College campuses are filled with students at a very vulnerable stage of development [Fromme *et al.*, 2008]. These students may be away from home for the first time, may be trying to attend school and work full-time, and on many commuter campuses, may be attending school full-time, working full-time, and caring for children. The pressure for all students to attain a college degree has become more intense. It may be that students who attend commuter campuses are even more stressed than those on residential campuses, increasing the dangers to faculty who teach on those campuses.

In this context, stalking may be viewed as a symptom of other student problems, pressures, or stresses – as a failed coping mechanism or evidence of severe mental disturbance. However, most higher education staff members are not properly trained to recognize students in crisis or suffering from mental health issues. Consequently, clear patterns of stalking behavior are often misunderstood, dismissed, and ignored, even when reported by colleagues. This reality has a chilling effect on perceptions of safety in the learning environment (Morgan, 2009, p. 110):

> … the classroom is much like a community, with students participating in both individual and group roles and seeking support and encouragement from their instructor as well as their peers. In order for such a classroom to succeed, it seems evident that the professor must be able to feel safe in the community of students.
>
> Unfortunately for students, however, every professor interviewed directly identified changes in their willingness to interact with students. These changes varied from changes in the syllabus – more rules, more structure, and fewer opportunities for students to interact with the faculty member outside of the classroom – to increasing the difficulty level for students in contacting the professor by no longer providing a home telephone number, to preventing student access to the faculty member's office without supervision. Faculty members who were able to do so reported decreasing their exposure to students by refusing to teach particular classes or even particular populations of students (students from a particular major or students at a particular academic level, such as undergraduates). These changes may decrease student choices in terms of courses and may decrease the community cohesiveness in the classroom ….
>
> As a result of their experiences with stalking, many faculty reported a change in how they viewed colleagues, administrators, and the general climate of the university. Almost every faculty member attempted at some point to communicate their concerns about the student stalking to a colleague (67%) or an administrator (58%). In 62% of these cases, the faculty member reported a lack of concern, disbelief, or recommendations to "let it go and not cause any trouble." Both male and female faculty reported that frequently other colleagues viewed the professor as the instigator of problems or that the professor should be flattered by the student's interest. In these cases, the stalker was perceived by other faculty and, at times, by administrators, as having a "crush" on the faculty member. Since students are almost always of legal age, the perception of many was that as long as the student was no longer in the professor's class, there was no problem with the professor and student dating. Conceptualizing stalking behaviors as simply dating attempts was frustrating and humiliating for the professor involved.

In two cases, the student stalker sought out colleagues of the professor to try and help convince the faculty member to date the student, and the colleagues did so.

The realities discussed in the passage reflect gender bias, as well as conceptual ignorance, with respect to the seriousness and ultimate management of stalking behaviors. Most see stalking as something other than what it is and prefer to avoid the problems that reporting or responding to reports can incur.

ETHICAL DISPOSITION

Stalking is unethical because of the emotional distress and psychological harm that it causes others, the lack of boundaries it demonstrates, and the criminal behavior that is often involved. Students have an ethical obligation to refrain from these kinds of behaviors, respect the boundaries of others, and to report any student or staff member that does not. This means treating such misconduct as a crime and reporting it to the authorities (e.g., campus police). Failure to do so prevents the authorities from taking steps to protect victims, encourages the stalker, and conceals the number of victims that may be involved (many stalkers have a long history of inappropriate behavior).

SEXUAL MISCONDUCT

Sexual misconduct may be defined as any sexually oriented behavior that violates established codes of conduct. However, every educational institution defines it differently. Some definitions are exhaustive and detailed; others are short and generic. Some, however, fail to define it at all.

For instance, the student codes at Elgin Community College and Arizona State University deem it sufficient to prohibit sexual assault or sexual abuse on institutional premises or at related functions (Arizona State University, 2012; Elgin Community College, 2012). However, neither defines these terms or offers any further detail about related prohibitions. Students and faculty are left to interpret these concepts, and any alleged violations, using either legal statutes or their own personal definitions.

On the other end of the spectrum, the student code at the University of California at Berkeley takes great pains to provide clear and comprehensive prohibitions related to its established sense of sexual misconduct. It specifically defines violations related to sexual assault, sexual battery, statutory rape, and sexual harassment (University of California at Berkeley, 2010). The code also delves into the issue of consent, and explains, "a current or previous dating relationship is not sufficient to constitute consent" (University of California at Berkeley, 2010).

Consent

A major factor in the consideration of whether or not there has been sexual misconduct is the issue of consent. *Consent* refers to the act of giving permission with an awareness of the consequences. In some instances a potential victim is able, but unwilling, to give consent for sexual contact. In such cases, a potential victim has communicated their disinterest in sexual activity, either by direct verbal refusal or a continuing failure to respond to sexual advances. In other instances, the potential victim is willing, but unable, to give consent. This occurs when the potential victim is too young or is otherwise impaired by drugs, alcohol, fear or some mental defect (see, generally, Savino and Turvey, 2011).

Some educational institutions have very strict and unforgiving policies regarding consent, while others have none. The ethical student will make themselves aware of these policies and conform to them carefully. They will also refrain from any conduct that places them into a position where their intentions might appear less than honorable. Consequently, in every sexual encounter, the ethical student will make their intentions known, withdraw when declined, and verify any permissions that are given (for a useful discussion, see, generally, Anderson, 2005).

Sexual Coercion

Many educational instructions have policies that prohibit any form of sexual coercion. A short explanation is therefore necessary. *Sexual coercion* refers to the psychological, emotional, chemical or physical manipulation of one person by another for sexual purposes – and can occur in an otherwise consenting relationship. This includes (Goetz and Shackleford, 2009, p. 226) "withholding benefits, threatening relationship defection, and manipulating their partners by reminding them of their 'obligation' to have sex (e.g., 'If you love me, you'll have sex with me')." As a result, student victims may perceive very real physical, emotional, economic, academic, or social consequences should they fail to acquiesce.

Sexual coercion occurs in intimate relationships, but can also be committed by employers, guardianships, police officers, and instructors. Anyone in a position to impose sanctions or take away benefits may use the threat of doing so to engage in sexual coercion. The consequences can include emotional harm, civil liability, and in some case criminal charges. In other words, not all instances of sexual coercion will involve a crime, but they can reach or cross that threshold without great difficulty.

CASE EXAMPLE

Austin Scott and Desiree Minder

Consider the case of Austin Scott (an African-American football player) and Desiree Minder, two students at Pennsylvania State University (PSU). It involves questions of both consent and coercion. On 5 October 2007, they engaged in sexual activity at his apartment on the University campus. After this encounter, Mr Scott was arrested for rape and related charges. However, 6 months later, the district attorney decided to drop all charges because it was ruled by the court that a prior unrelated accusation of rape by Ms Minder (which resulted in a different defendant's acquittal) could be introduced as evidence at Mr Scott's trial. Mr Scott subsequently filed a civil rights lawsuit against all parties involved, including the district attorney's office, the PSU police department, PSU as a whole, and his accuser, Desiree Minder.

Taken entirely from the appellate decision in *Scott v. Marshall et al.* (2011):

> In the early morning hours of October 5, 2007, Minder was with some friends in two bars in State College, Pennsylvania, where Penn State is located. They were first at Tony's Big Easy, where Minder had a couple of mixed drinks made with vodka, leaving her a little intoxicated. (Doc. 69–3 Minder Dep., CM/ECF p. 9). They then went to The Saloon, where she ordered some mixed drinks, again made with vodka. (*Id.*, CM/ECF p. 91). During this time, Scott and Minder exchanged text messages, with Minder texting while she was at The Saloon, "Come get me." (Doc. 65–9, defendant Rodgers' police report, CM/ECF p. 12).
>
> When Scott arrived, Minder met him outside and guided him downstairs to the bar, which was in the basement. (Doc. 69–3, Minder Dep., CM/ECF p. 13). Scott finished her drink for her, (*Id.*), and they left, at around 2:00 a.m., according to one police report. (Doc. 65–8, defendant Cover police report, CM/ECF p. 3). As they were walking in the direction of Scott's apartment, Minder, according to Scott, made the decision to go to his place. (Doc. 69–2, Scott Dep., CM/ECF p. 7). According to

Minder, she "agreed to go back to his house," although her "first choice" would have been to go to her own house, but she "was drunk," and he "offered to let [her] crash" at his place, so she "said okay." (Doc. 69–3, Minder Dep., CM/ECF p. 14).

As they were walking to Scott's apartment, Minder told Scott she wanted him "to respect" her. At that time, according to Scott, she conveyed to him, either directly or indirectly, that she did not want to have sex that night. (Doc. 69–2, Scott Dep., CM/ECF p. 7). When they arrived at the apartment, they went directly to his bedroom. (Doc. 60, Minder's statement of facts ¶ 14). On the bed, they started out on their backs, and then moved to lying on their right sides, with Minder's back to Scott's front. (Doc. 69–2, Scott Dep., CM/ECF p. 8). They lay cuddled like this for some thirty minutes, talking about family, when Minder began "thrusting her butt into [Scott's] pelvic area." (*Id.*, CM/ECF pp. 8–9). Scott began "to reciprocate," moving his hand down her leg to her vagina. She pulled him on top of her, and they both started taking off her pants. (*Id.*, CM/ECF p.12). Minder pulled his arm to signal him to get on top of her. (*Id.*). They had sex. (*Id.*, CM/ECF p. 13). Afterwards, Minder stayed at the apartment for about thirty minutes. Scott thought they were both trying to sleep, but Minder said she could not sleep there, that she needed to go home. (*Id.*, CM/ECF pp. 16–17). She gave him a hug and kiss, they started talking again, she gave him another hug and a kiss, and then she left. (*Id.*, CM/ECF p. 17).

While she was there, Minder never said anything to indicate she had changed her mind about having sex that night, Scott never asked her if she had changed her mind, nor did he ask her to have sex. (*Id.*, CM/ECF pp. 10–11). However, when she pushed up against him with her butt, he took that "as a hint that she wanted some kind of response." (*Id.*, CM/ECF p. 10).

Minder never said no at anytime, and he never punched her anywhere on her body, and not in the kidney. (*Id.*, CM/ECF pp. 14, 19).

After leaving Scott's apartment, Minder called a friend, (doc. 60, Minder's statement of facts ¶ 30), who met her on the street with some other friends. (*Id.*, ¶ 31). At about 4:16 a.m., the Penn State police were called. (Doc. 64, Penn State defendants' statement of material facts ¶ 14). Defendants Cover and Miller were sent to investigate. (*Id.*, ¶ 15). Minder told Cover that Scott had raped her. (Doc. 65–8, Cover's Incident Report Supplement, CM/ECF p. 2). She also told him, "It happened to me again," stating that she had been raped two years earlier. (*Id.*).

Cover and Miller took Minder to the hospital. (Doc. 64, Penn State defendants' statement of material facts ¶ 17). Minder was interviewed by a registered nurse. According to Cover's report, he was there for the interview and Minder repeated that she had been raped. (Doc. 65–8, Cover's Incident Report Supplement, CM/ECF pp. 3–4). She also said during the interview that she had fallen asleep on the bed still fully clothed. She awoke with Scott on top of her. Her jeans had been removed. She told Scott, "No, Please stop." She attempted to move and turn away, but Scott punched her in the kidney area, then placed his fingers and then his penis into her vagina. She went along with it because she was afraid Scott would hurt her. (Doc. 65–8, Cover's Incident Report Supplement, CM/ECF pp. 3–4).

Cover left and the nurse performed a physical examination of Minder. Minder complained of pain in her right flank and vaginal area. (Doc. 64, Penn State defendants' statement of material facts ¶ 21). On physical examination, the nurse found "reddened areas, including in her neck, upper left shoulder and the middle of her

back. Minder also had two ecchymotic areas in her left side flank area in which she had a great deal of tenderness. In addition, Minder had several reddened areas on her front upper right shoulder, her chest and between her breasts.

There was another area of ecchymosis on Minder's right thigh." (*Id.*, ¶ 22). There were other physical signs in the genital area. (*Id.*, ¶ 23).

Defendant Brooks arrived at the hospital at around 6:35 a.m. (*Id.*, ¶ 20). Brooks spoke to one of Minder's friends who met Minder that morning after she left the apartment. This friend reported that Minder was hyperventilating and hysterical and complaining of pain in her back. (*Id.*, ¶ 24). Brooks took copies of the notes of the sexual assault exam and the medical records. She asked Minder to come to the police station and discuss the incident in more detail. Minder agreed. (*Id.*, ¶ 25).

In the meantime, at about 6:18 a.m., defendants Sowerby and Vile contacted District Attorney Madeira to tell him about the reported crime. The three made plans to attempt a consensual phone call between Minder and Scott and to obtain a search warrant for Scott's apartment. (*Id.*, ¶ 26). "At approximately 7:45 a.m., District Attorney Madeira and Assistant District Attorney Lance Marshall arrived at Penn State police services. After their arrival, a meeting was held attended by Madeira, Marshall, Sowerby, Brooks, Cover, Miller, Rodgers, Vile and Shelow. At this meeting, it was decided that Minder would be consensualized and that she would attempt to make phone contact with Scott." (*Id.*, ¶ 27).

This meeting ended at about 8:20 a.m. Madeira and Marshall met with Minder about the investigative plan. (*Id.*, ¶¶ 28 and 29). A consensualized phone conversation took place between Minder and Scott. After the conversation, by way of some text messages, they agreed to meet at the Hentzel Union Building (HUB) at noon. This was a pretext for

Continued

CASE EXAMPLE *CONTINUED*

the Penn State police to meet personally with Scott about Minder's allegations. (*Id.*, ¶ 30).

At about 12:40 p.m., Sowerby and Rodgers met Scott at the HUB. Scott talked with them and confirmed that he and Minder had met at The Saloon; that they did not know each other that well; that before the night in question, he had only "hung out" with her once, lunch at a pizza shop; that "while Minder agreed to stay at his place for the night, she told him not to get the wrong impression and that she wanted him to respect her"; that they had sex; and that "it had been clear to him earlier in the evening that Minder did not want to have sex with him." (*Id.*, ¶ 34).

Vile prepared a search warrant application for Scott's apartment, completing it around 11:15 a.m. The affidavit was then approved both by ADA Marshall and ADA Karen Kuebler.

A search warrant was obtained at approximately 11:30 a.m. from the Centre County Court of Common Pleas. (*Id.*, ¶ 32). Scott's apartment was searched in the afternoon. (*Id.*, ¶ 36). "After they conducted their part of the investigation on October 5, 2007 regarding the alleged assault by Scott, Officers Cover, Miller and Vile had very little further involvement in the investigation." (*Id.*, ¶ 37).

"On October 7, 2007, Minder met at the Penn State police station with ADA Marshall and Officer Brooks. Marshall reviewed with Minder the court process. Marshall then left, and Brooks again did a detailed interview of Minder as to the specifics of the sexual assault and the events leading up to that assault. Upon the conclusion of that interview, Marshall returned to the interview room to meet with Minder. He advised Minder that he would be in touch with her once the District Attorney's office and representatives of Penn State police services met on October 11, 2007, to discuss the case further." (*Id.*, ¶ 38).

"During her discussions with Officer Brooks, Minder told Brooks that she had been

assaulted at a previous college, that she had been through the criminal process and that it had not ended favorably toward her. Minder also told ADA Marshall about the outcome." (*Id.*, ¶ 39). "On October 8, 2007, Officer Brooks met with Minder at the police station to take photographs of her injuries as they appeared at that time. Minder still had redness in her back in the area of her kidney, corresponding to the area where she said Scott had punched her. Minder related that her arms were still sore and that she continued to have pain in her back." (*Id.*, ¶ 40).

"On October 9, 2007, Officer Brooks conducted an interview of Nancy Waring, a friend of Minder's who was with her on the evening of October 4, 2007. Waring was asked about the events prior to Minder going to the Saloon. She was also questioned as to anything Minder had told her about the sexual assault. Waring's statements as to what Minder told her about the assault were consistent with the statements Minder had given to Brooks." (*Id.*, ¶ 41).

"In October 2007, it was the policy and practice of Penn State police services that felony charges would not be brought against a suspect without the approval of the office of the Centre County District Attorney." (*Id.*, ¶ 42).

"On October 11, 2007, a meeting was held at Penn State police services to decide whether to move forward with bringing charges against Austin Scott." The meeting was attended by Madeira, Marshall, Sowerby, Shelow, Brooks and Cover. (*Id.*, ¶¶ 43 and 44). "Marshall led the discussion and did the majority of the talking" at the meeting, which dealt with whether charges should be brought. (*Id.*, ¶ 45). At the conclusion of the meeting, "it was unanimously determined that criminal charges would be filed against Austin Scott. Madeira and Marshall concurred with the decision to file charges, including the filing of felony charges." (*Id.*, ¶ 46).

On the morning of October 12, 2007, defendant Brooks forwarded drafts of the criminal complaint and affidavit of probable cause to Marshall for his review and comment. Marshall made suggestions on the charges and the Affidavit of Probable Cause before the charges were filed. (*Id.*, ¶¶ 47 and 48). Rodgers and Brooks signed the criminal complaint requesting the arrest warrant and its supporting probable-cause affidavit. The complaint was filed the same day. It charged Scott with: (1) rape under 18 Pa. Con. Stat. Ann. § 3121(a)(1) (West 2011), a felony of the first degree; (2) sexual assault under 18 Pa. Con. Stat. Ann. § 3124.1 (West 2000), a felony of the second degree; (3) aggravated indecent assault under 18 Pa. Con. Stat. Ann. § 3125(1)), a felony of the second degree; (4) aggravated indecent assault under 18 Pa. Con. Stat. Ann. § 3125(2), a felony of the first degree; (5) indecent assault under 18 Pa. Con. Stat. Ann. § 3126(a)(1) (West Supp. 2011), a misdemeanor of the second degree; (6) indecent assault under 18 Pa. Con. Stat. Ann. § 3126(a)(2) (West Supp. 2011), a misdemeanor of the second degree; and (7) simple assault under 18 Pa. Con. Stat. Ann. § 2701(a)(1) (West Supp. 2011), a misdemeanor of the second degree.

On October 12, 2007, Scott was arrested. Arrangements were made in advance to release him immediately on bail. (*Id.*, ¶ 50 and response thereto). Scott was not detained, nor was he committed to jail. He simply went through the booking process and was immediately released. (Doc. 65–27, Scott Dep., CM/ECF p. 12).

On October 27, 2007, a preliminary hearing was held before a Pennsylvania magisterial district judge. (Doc. 64, the Penn State defendants' statement of material facts ¶ 52). Two witnesses testified, Desiree Minder, and the nurse who examined her at the hospital. At the close of the hearing, the Commonwealth withdrew the two charges of aggravated indecent assault.

As to all other charges, the magisterial district judge found that there was sufficient evidence to go to trial. (*Id.*, ¶ 53). In a pretrial motion with the trial court, Scott challenged the sufficiency of the evidence. On April 15, 2008, the trial court rejected that argument. (*Id.*, ¶¶ 54 and 55).

On April 18, 2008, District Attorney Madeira moved to dismiss the case, stating that "[i]n light of the trial judge's ruling on the admissibility of evidence, the Commonwealth's case is substantially handicapped, and there is no reasonably likelihood that the Commonwealth can meet its burden of proof." (Doc. 65–28, CM/ECF p. 2). This decision was made without consulting Minder. (Doc. 60–4, Brooks Dep., CM/ECF pp. 13–14). The court granted the motion. (Doc. 65–28, CM/ECF p. 2).

The district attorney was referring to the trial court's apparent ruling that Scott could enter into evidence at trial that in a prior criminal proceeding in which Minder was also the complaining witness the defendant had been acquitted of a charge of rape.

As noted, Minder told Cover that she had been raped before when he was the responding officer on the morning of October 5, 2007. Cover did not ask Minder anything about this prior incident, either the facts, who was involved, or the outcome. (Doc. 72, Pl.'s counter-statement of facts ¶ 5). Penn State has a policy on investigating sexual assaults. This policy essentially limits the first officer responding to a sexual assault to investigating the assault itself and to assisting the victim in obtaining psychological and medical care. (Doc. 65–18, the Penn State Policy).

Defendant Brooks was the "primary contact" with Minder. (Doc. 72, Pl.'s counter-statement of facts ¶ 5). As Brooks put it, she knew "this was going to be a high media case," and that she "had a victim that [she] needed to know was strong enough and ready to move forward with such a sensitive case." (*Id.*, ¶ 7). Brooks also knew that Minder had been through the criminal process before

Continued

CASE EXAMPLE *CONTINUED*

and it had not been favorable to her, that it was hard on her family and her relationship with her parents, and that it was a very negative experience for her. (*Id.*, ¶ 8). Brooks did not investigate the previous criminal case until April 2008 when requested to do so by Marshall. (*Id.*, ¶ 9, and Doc. 73–7, Brooks Dep., pp. 10–11). The minutes from a prosecution meeting held on April 4, 2008, indicate that "Def. will potentially have the Detective from the previous assault testify" and that "transcripts, criminal complaints, etc, need to be obtained from previous incident so that the Prosecution can be prepared." (Doc. 69–6, CM/ECF p. 39).

It should also be noted the Mr Scott was kicked off of the Penn State football team as a result of Ms Minder's allegation and his later arrest. This, he asserts, caused irreparable harm to his professional football career (Hall, 2011).

Mr Scott's civil rights lawsuit was dismissed entirely by the court in summary judgment. He subsequently filed an appeal of the court's decision, which also failed. However, this case serves to illustrate that the issue of consent and coercion can be blurred by context (e.g., alcohol) and character (e.g. prior history of failed rape allegations) – which can fatally alter its trajectory through the criminal and civil justice systems. In the end, neither the criminal complainant (Ms Minder) nor the criminal defendant (Mr Scott) received the justice that they were seeking and both were harmed in the process.

The ethical student will read and learn institutional policies related to sexual coercion at their place of study. They will refrain from conduct that is coercive in nature. They will also report any observed instances, whether it involves students, faculty members, or both.

ONLINE NETWORKING

With the rise and proliferation of the Internet, there has also been the corresponding development of online social media websites intended to facilitate information sharing and networking (e.g., Facebook, Twitter, MySpace, YouTube, LinkedIn, Plaxo, Instagram, Google+, and Pinterest). These websites enable and promote connections between individuals based on all manner of relationships, employment backgrounds, and personal interests. They also provide those in one's designated circle of friends or associates with variably detailed information regarding one's education, employers, and living circumstances. In some instances, they can also provide a fully archived and easily accessible personal timeline, with up-to-the-minute information regarding location, activity, and those one is with.

Students have a responsibility to understand that these virtual websites create a virtual presence that will be taken seriously by others and can result in very real consequences – regardless of any stated intentions.

In addition, any virtual presence, whether via a website, a blog, or an online discussion list, may be archived forever. This can be done by the hosting website itself, by third-party web archiving sites such as the *WayBackMachine* (see www.archive.org), or by interested third parties who archive it for their own purposes. This includes any text, photos, and even videos. For the modern student, it means that the Internet has become a permanent repository of all publicly shared activities (successes and failures alike) with no expiration date and no forgiveness.

The student must come to appreciate that any level of virtual presence enables others to monitor, track, and share whatever information is provided. The scrupulous and unscrupulous alike will sift through their posts and pictures for hours at a time ("creeping"); they will also put together details and connections that are beyond what was intended for public consumption. "Creepers" will include fellow students, instructors, co-workers, and future employers. Any virtual presence, therefore, invites intrusions into privacy and may unintentionally provide a powerful means for those intent on stalking and harassment.

Ultimately, the ethical student will understand the need to conduct him- or herself online in the same ethical fashion as they would in person. There is, to be clear, no discernible difference between the two worlds. This means protecting one's reputation and character, respecting the rights of others, and maintaining appropriate boundaries to ensure privacy and safety.

Institutional Policies
While some educational institutions have definitive policies regarding social media and related student misconduct, others are woefully behind in their understanding and consideration of virtual behavior. They may or may not take it seriously. Whichever is the case, students should expect to be held accountable for their online activities and associations. Like any other form of behavior, online speech and other activities can be regulated and used against the student depending on the relative morality and will of the educational institution concerned.

For example, in 2005, Cameron Walker was expelled from Fisher College in Boston, Massachusetts for violating their policies against "verbal, written, graphic, or electronic abuse, harassment, coercion, or intimidation of an individual" (Woo, 2005). The first case of its kind, Mr Walker's misconduct involved joining a Facebook group that sought the termination of a campus police officer that was said to be harassing students – and making a comment in support of termination. The Chief of Police for the campus was directly involved with that decision and was apparently more concerned with student speech than allegations of misconduct against one of his officers. Similarly, Kiah Zabel was threatened with eviction from her dorm at Rochester College for posting a picture on her Facebook page that stated "Out ... Proud ... Lesbian;" the Dean of the College stated that this behavior was inconsistent with the Christian heritage of the school and was also disruptive to other students that took offense (O'Reilly, 2012).

The attempt to regulate online speech and activity includes any behavior that would be considered a violation of the student code – not just lifestyle choices or political views. For example, Tony Harris, a 19-year-old sophomore at Calvin College in Grand Rapids, Michigan, was expelled for posting derogatory slurs and explicit sexual comments on his Facebook page in reference to his ex-girlfriend subsequent to their break-up (Reens, 2009).

In addition to controlling the student's behavior, many educational institutions seek to control online associations as well – particularly where staff is concerned. Some have policies forbidding staff and students from networking outside of the classroom or sanctioned institutional functions, often in response to specific past instances of misconduct. Others have no policies in place at all, allowing virtual relationships between staff and students to exist and develop unchecked. The authors would note that there is no student code or institutional policy that can regulate unethical behavior into oblivion; unethical students and instructors alike will find the means to exploit one another. However, a student that networks with their instructors via social media of any kind increases the ability of those that are unethical to identify and exploit vulnerabilities.

Background and Monitoring

Many prospective employers, law enforcement agencies, and even judges are using the Internet and social networking sites to compile information and evidence. Prospective employers are seeking background information that applicants may have left out, for one reason or another. In some cases, they may even require that applicants surrender their usernames and passwords as a condition of employment. Law enforcement agencies are known for using these same sources to gather suspect evidence, or for monitoring the activities of suspects and suspect groups.[12] The courts have also taken note of the serious consequences of online behavior. Upon request, some judges have agreed that both parties involved in legal actions (e.g., divorce cases, custody disputes, and defamation suits) surrender their usernames and passwords to each other – to prevent one party from bad-mouthing the other, witness tampering, and further defamation (see, generally, Locker, 2011).

---

[12]Sometimes this is conducted legally and sometimes it is not. Fore example, the NYPD has been found conducting online surveillance of, among others, Muslim student groups at Universities in New Jersey, including Rutgers (Goldman and Apuzzo, 2012).

CASE EXAMPLE

Ryan Mills

Consider the case of 21-year-old Ryan Mills, a student at the University of North Carolina-Wilmington. He and Peyton Strickland, a student from Cape Fear Community College, were jointly suspected of theft. As a result of photos posted on his Facebook page that were discovered by police, Mr Mills was considered armed and dangerous. This caused law enforcement to send a SWAT team when serving their search warrant on Mr Strickland at his home. Tragedy resulted, as reported in Locke (2006):

Ryan Mills knows the cost of posting a photo that unsettled police.

Mills, 21, posed on Facebook with friends and high-powered guns. A deputy sheriff ended up shooting to death Mills' friend Peyton Strickland, an 18-year-old college student from Durham, during a botched raid in December in Wilmington. A grand jury decided last week that the deputy, who said he expected heavily armed resistance based on the Facebook picture, should not be indicted for fatally shooting an unarmed Strickland through the door.

University of North Carolina-Wilmington police and sheriff's deputies had gone to the Wilmington home of Strickland, a student at Cape Fear Community College, looking for a PlayStation 3 video game machine they suspected he and Mills stole.

Police feared that the guns pictured with Mills were in Strickland's house. Christopher Long, the deputy who shot Strickland, carried a .45-caliber submachine gun, a .45-caliber pistol, two extra pistol magazines, two extra sub gun magazines, a gas mask, a knife and a flash bang grenade, according to court records.

Long fired through the front door after mistaking the sound of a battering ram hitting the door for the blast of a gun.

"If I had even thought once that [the photo] could be misconstrued, or even worse, used against me or my friends by the people who are supposed to be protecting human life, I would have removed them," Mills said Friday, speaking publicly about the photo for the first time.

Two years ago, Mills tried out his new digital camera by snapping pictures of himself and his buddies posing with a friend's gun collection.

They spent the day target shooting, then goofed around at the licensed gun owner's house in Pittsboro, posing like tough guys with the unloaded rifles and handguns. In the photos, Mills is smirking; another friend is grinning.

Mills thought the photos were cool and posted a few to his Facebook profile. They joined a collage of pictures of college parties and beach trips.

An affidavit by Long filed as part of the grand jury proceedings last week shows just how much stock police put in Mills' Facebook photo.

Long said the mission that night was expected to be "extraordinarily dangerous." He described Mills' photo as "intimidating" and "hostile."

Long's team, he said in the affidavit, had been briefed that the "AR-15 firearms that we had seen in the photos and which were believed to be in the residence were capable of penetrating our body armor."

Mills said he can't believe officers made such a leap.

"Anyone looking closely at the facial expressions in the photo can tell it is just guys goofing on the guns," Mills said.

It is not clear why officers thought those guns would be in Strickland's house. Strickland is not in the photo. Mills did not live with Strickland. He lived in a townhouse three miles away; the address appeared in a campus directory.

Police found nothing but an unloaded hunting rifle and shotgun in Strickland's room at the other end of his house, said his father, Don Strickland of Durham. Peyton Strickland was a licensed hunter.

The lesson in this case is that criminal suspects (whether a student or not; whether guilty or not) are judged by the content of their social networking sites, as well as the content maintained by friends and associates.

Consequences

The consequences for engaging in unethical behavior and misconduct in the virtual world are both immediate and long term. As suggested by the examples provided, they can include immediate academic sanction, suspension, and expulsion. This is separate from any related criminal and civil liability. They can also involve immediate harm outside of academia: harm to one's character, and physical harm to oneself and others in extreme cases.

Given the durable nature of the data that is archived in the virtual world, consequences for online activities and affiliations may also be delayed, but no less harmful. Prospective employers can search online databases that store information going back not months or years, but decades (e.g., alternate or conflicting resumes, inflammatory postings, compromising photos, bad choices, and uncharged criminal activity). The Internet does not forget, and anything that is available online about an individual and their choices is fair game – whether it is fair or not.[13]

SPECIAL ISSUES FOR GRADUATE STUDENTS

Graduate students occupy a special rung in the ladder that is higher education. They are not entirely professionals, but they are not merely students either. While still in need of guidance and mentoring, the more capable among them may be asked to participate in professional activities. This includes opportunities to teach, conduct research, publish, and participate in grant projects. Under the right circumstances, any of these involvements should be welcomed by the graduate student as a chance to learn, grow, and demonstrate capability in relation to their field. However, there are ethical issues to consider.

Teaching

Owing to their immediate availability, graduate students may be asked to teach undergraduate courses at their place of study. Ethical or not, this practice is commonplace at educational institutions around the world. However, it is problematic at best.

First, there is an inherent covenant in all models of education requiring that the person teaching knows more than the students they are entrusted with. It demands that they be capable of preparing students for the next

---

[13]There are many private companies that will, for a fee, conduct extensive online background investigations related to criminal matters, civil matters, and pre-employment screening – to include social networking activity (e.g., Social Intelligence Corp., Sterling InfoSystems Inc.). One of the authors (Turvey) has experience using related services for conducting background checks of expert witnesses, which is commonplace in the world of litigation.

level of coursework required to complete their studies. When this is not the case, and the person teaching the class cannot adequately meet these requirements, this covenant is broken. Therefore, graduate students have an ethical responsibility to refuse any teaching assignment that they feel is beyond their capabilities – because the university is generally too busy counting enrollments to concern itself with the quality of available graduate instructors that will naturally refresh every few years.

Second, most institutes of higher education operate under the requirement that instructors must have at least one advanced degree before they can be allowed teach and assess student learning. By definition, most graduate students fail to meet this requirement given that they are in pursuit of an advanced degree. However, educational institutions circumvent this requirement by listing more qualified faculty as the instructor of record, while making one or more graduate students conduct the majority if not all of the lectures and assessments. This practice may or may not be ethically bankrupt, depending on state requirements and graduate student teaching capabilities.

Third, undergraduate students are paying tuition fees with the expectation of being taught by qualified faculty – some with an eye to receiving recommendations for graduate school or future employment. The failure to provide these students with access to fully qualified faculty with respect to teaching and recommendations is an educational disservice. Students should not have to pay the same tuition for teaching that is substandard or that will not result in the same opportunities for internships or recommendations.[14] In any case, instructors have an ethical obligation to make the limits of their education, training, and experience clear to their students – to avoid misrepresentation and any related misunderstanding.

Unaccredited Writing or Research

Graduate students are often given the opportunity to engage in research and writing projects for their mentors. Generally, this is a good thing and arguably a consideration when applying to a graduate program in the first place. However, some faculty members have no problem taking advantage of their graduate students, and may ask them to do research or complete writing assignments without giving them appropriate credit, if any. Worse, they may require that graduate students list them as co-authors on publications where they have

---

[14]The ethical problems that result from using grad students to teach undergraduate courses are compounded by institutional failures to make instructor qualifications clear prior to student enrollment. It is the experience of the authors that undergraduate students are often unaware of the fact that they are or were being taught by grad students at key points in their academic careers. Many have suggested that they would be less likely to enroll in courses (or at colleges) where this reality was communicated in advance.

made no significant contribution. Either is unethical, and may be considered fraud. As explained in Krimsky (2007, p. 450):

> Ghost authorship occurs when the person whose name appears on the publication was not involved either in doing the research, framing the ideas behind the article, or in writing the article. Alternatively, it can occur when an individual who has made substantial contributions to the manuscript is not named as an author or whose contributions are not cited in the acknowledgments.

This is also referred to as "gift authorship" (Jones, 2003, p. 245) or in some cases as "by-line corruption."

Ghost authorship and gift authorship are among the most serious academic abuses that can be inflicted on a graduate student. One deprives them of the ability to receive credit for the work they have done, while the other minimizes their contributions to a work that was in fact entirely their own. Mentors that would in engage in either practice do harm not only to their students, but to the literature as well. Authorship impacts public perceptions of integrity and credibility, while also contributing to individual promotions, bonuses, and pay-raises. Perversions of the byline are akin to claiming title and ownership of property that one has no claim to. Consequently, a failure to be honest about authorship, and a propensity to corrupt the byline, is a form of fraud (Jones, 2003; Krimsky, 2007; Street *et al.*, 2010).

Reporting Fraud

Graduate students working for an educational institution generally have an obligation to report known instances of fraud. This is especially true when their work is done as part of a research grant – as the government has strict rules about research fraud. For example, the US government requires any organization that receives government funding to have policies and procedures in place for the reporting, investigation, and identification and any questionable research practices. As mandated in Office of Research Integrity (2009, p. 4):

> All institutions receiving research funds from Public Health Service (PHS) agencies must have on file an assurance form with the Office of Research Integrity (Office of Research Integrity). This assurance is to ensure that the institution has in place policies and procedures for dealing with allegations of research misconduct, has provided Office of Research Integrity with contact information for its assurance official, and will submit an annual report to Office of Research Integrity identifying any activity from the previous year requiring inquiries and investigations into allegations of possible research misconduct involving research supported by PHS funds.

Failure to report known instances of fraud can result in academic suspension, expulsion, and even degree revocation. In cases involving government grants, it can result in the termination of the grant, as well as blacklisting for any future grant projects. In extreme cases, it can also result in civil and criminal liability.

SUMMARY

Students of criminal justice have before them an endless series of choices that will define their character. Thoughtful and sober control of their ethical compass is immediately important to their professional career, as all of their conduct is open to scrutiny by future employers. This is truer in the criminal justice professions than any other, given the moral fitness requirement.

The first line of defense for the ethical student is learning the values and ethical requirements of their educational institution. If they cannot abide these requirements, they should seek their education elsewhere. If they have questions regarding specific prohibitions, they are encouraged to ask about them before they become a problem.

The ethical student will not violate any law or code of conduct they have agreed to; they will avoid inappropriate relationships; they will avoid any situations that might cause others to violate the law or institutional codes of conduct; and they will conduct themselves professionally at all times – even in the virtual world. When asked to do something that is unethical, they will decline; when they observe something that is unethical, they will report it. The ethical student recognizes that every choice they make has a consequence and that if they fail to make the best ethical choices their career options will be limited.

Questions

1. List five examples of employment disqualifiers in the criminal justice system.
2. Define *academic misconduct*. Provide two examples.
3. List and define three forms of *plagiarism*.
4. Define *hazing*. Why is hazing unethical? Explain.
5. *Stalking* often involves a former intimate partner. True or False?
6. Define *sexual misconduct*. What is the major factor in the consideration of whether or not there has been sexual misconduct?

References

Allen, E., Madden, M., 2008. Hazing in view: college students at risk. The University of Maine, College of Education and Human Development, url: http://www.hazingstudy.org/publications/hazing_in_view_web.pdf.

Anderson, M.J., 2005. Negotiating sex. Southern California Law Review 78, 1401–1438.

Arizona State University, 2012. Student code of conduct 5-30. Arizona State University website, url: http://deanofstudents.ariona.edu/studentcode.

Bellas, M., Gosset, J., 2001. Love or the "lecherous professor": consensual sexual relationships between professors and students. Sociological Quarterly 42 (4), 529–558.

Bennett, C., 2012. Stuyvesant HS students to take exams again in wake of cheating scandal. New York Post, July 9; url: http://www.nypost.com/p/news/local/manhattan/stuyvesant_cheating_students_will_HglAlADvsPM14hCycvvnXJ.

Black, M.C., Basile, K.C., Breiding, M.J., Smith, S.G., Walters, M.L., Merrick, M.T., Chen, J., Stevens, M.R., 2011. The National Intimate Partner and Sexual Violence Survey (NISVS): 2010 Summary Report. National Center for Injury Prevention and Control, Centers for Disease Control and Prevention, Atlanta, GA.

Barbella, L., 2010. Hot for teacher: the ethics and intricacies of student–professor relationships. Sexuality & Culture 14, 44–48.

Bopp, W., Schultz, D., 1972. Principles of American Law Enforcement and Criminal Justice. Charles C. Thomas, Springfield, IL.

California Crime Laboratory Review Task Force, 2009. An Examination of Forensic Science in California. State of California, Office of the Attorney General, Sacramento, CA, November; url: http://ag.ca.gov/publications/crime_labs_report.pdf.

Elgin Community College, 2012. Student code of conduct 4-402. Elgin Community College website, url: www.elgin.edu/codeofconduct.

Elsevier, 2012. A question of ethics: plagiarism and ethical infringement in publishing. Elsevier website, url: http://www.elsevier.com/wps/find/reviewershome.reviewers/ru_issue2a.

Florida International University, 2008. 'Hazing,' student conduct and conflict resolution. Florida International University website, url: http://www2.fiu.edu/~sccr/hazing.html.

Goldman, A., Apuzzo, M., 2012. Confused 911 caller outs NYPD spying in NJ: apartment located near college campus was rented by NYPD officer under false name, July 25; url: http://www.msnbc.msn.com/id/48317809/ns/us_news/#.UBbZII7d2WQ.

Goetz, A., Shackleford, T., 2009. Sexual coercion in intimate relationships: a comparative analysis of the effects of women's infidelity and men's dominance and control. Archives of Sexual Behavior 38, 226–234.

Hall, P., 2011. Judge tosses Austin Scott lawsuit over rape charges. The Morning Call, July 12; url: http://articles.mcall.com/2011-07-12/news/mc-austin-scott-penn-state-lawsuit-di20110712_1_desiree-minder-district-attorney-michael-madeira-sexual-assault-charges.

Hansen, D., Culley, T., 1973. The Police Training Officer. Chares C. Thomas, Springfield, IL.

Holper, M., 2011. The new moral turpitude test. Brooklyn Law Review 76 (4), 1241–1307.

Hudak, S., Balona, D., 2012. Defendant, champion friend: hazing was all about earning 'respect'. Orlando Journal Sentinel, July 19.

Jones, D., 2011. Academic dishonesty: are more students cheating? Business Communication Quarterly 74 (2), 141–150.

Jones, A., 2003. Can authorship policies help prevent scientific misconduct? What role for scientific societies? Science and Engineering Ethics 9 (2), 243–256.

Jow, L., 2012. Connecticut student arrested for fabricating antigay notes. The Advocate, July 2; url: http://www.advocate.com/society/education/2012/07/02/connecticut-student-arrested-fabricating-antigay-notes.

Kleinig, J., 1996. The Ethics of Policing. Cambridge University Press, New York.

Krimsky, S., 2007. Defining scientific misconduct: when conflict-of-interest is a factor in scientific misconduct. Medicine and Law 26, 447–463.

Locke, M., 2006. Police increasingly use Myspace-like sites as investigation tool. The News-Observer, December 17; url: http://www.newsobserver.com/2006/12/17/81538/how-raid-went-wrong-and-young.html.

Locker, M., 2011. Judge orders divorced couple to swap Facebook passwords: getting a divorce? Be careful what you post. Time Magazine, November 14; url: http://newsfeed.time.com/2011/11/14/judge-orders-divorced-couple-to-swap-facebook-passwords/.

Maher, B., 2011. Lab sabotage deemed research misconduct (with exclusive surveillance video). Nature News Blog, April 27; url: http://blogs.nature.com/news/2011/04/lab_sabotage_deemed_research_m_1.html.

Morgan, R., 2009. Student stalking of faculty: impact and prevalence. The Journal of the Scholarship of Teaching and Learning 9 (2), 98–116.

Morgan, R., 2010. Students stalking faculty: real and imagined relationships. Sexuality & Culture 14, 5–16.

Morgan, R., Kavanaugh, K., 2011. Student stalking of faculty: results of a nationwide survey. College Student Journal 45 (3), 512–523.

O'Reilly, S., 2012. Rochester College student threatened with expulsion from dorm after coming out … on Facebook. Campus Progress, March 15; url: http://campusprogress.org/articles/rochester_college_student_threatened_with_expulsion_from_dorm_after_co/.

Office of Research Integrity, 2009. The Office of Research Integrity Annual Report 2009. US Department of Health and Human Services, Washington, DC, url: http://ori.hhs.gov/documents/annual_reports/ori_annual_report_2009.pdf.

Office of Research Integrity, 2011a. Case Summaries. Office of Research Integrity Newsletter 19 (2), 6–7.

Office of Research Integrity, 2011b. Case Summaries. Office of Research Integrity Newsletter 19 (3), 6–8.

Reens, N., 2009. Calvin College expels student accused of writing derogatory Facebook message. MLive, February 12; url: http://www.mlive.com/news/grand-rapids/index.ssf/2009/02/calvin_college_expels_student.html.

Sanders, E., 2011. The secret sex lives of SPU students. The Stranger, March 29; url: http://www.thestranger.com/seattle/the-secret-sex-lives-of-spu-students/Content?oid=7435772.

Savino, J., Turvey, B., 2011. Rape Investigation Handbook, second ed. Elsevier, San Diego, CA.

Scott v. Marshall, et al., 2011. US District Court. Civil No. 4: CV-09–1989, WL 2682819, July 11 .

Serino, K., 2012. UI student charged after fabricating her own kidnapping. Eastern Iowa News Now, January 14; url: http://easterniowanewsnow.com/2012/01/14/ui-student-charged-after-fabricating-her-own-kidnapping/.

Shane, J., 2010. Performance management in police agencies: a conceptual framework. Policing: An International Journal of Police Strategies and Management 33 (1), 6–29.

Stemwedel, J., 2011. What about Dalibor Sames? The Bengü Sezen fraud and the responsibilities of the PI in the training of new scientists. Scientific American Blog, August 29; url: http://blogs.scientificamerican.com/doing-good-science/2011/08/29/what-about-dalibor-sames-the-bengu-sezen-fraud-and-the-responsibilities-of-the-pi-in-the-training-of-new-scientists/.

Stephens, N., 2006. Law enforcement ethics do not begin when you pin on the badge. FBI Law Enforcement Bulletin, November, pp. 22–23.

Stout, B., 2011. Ethics and academic integrity in police education. Policing 5 (4), 300–309.

Street, J., Rogers, W., Israel, M., Braunack-Mayer, A., 2010. Credit where credit is due? Regulation, research integrity and the attribution of authorship in the health sciences. Social Science & Medicine 70, 1458–1465.

Suggs, E., 2012. Ammons out at FAMU; champion family files lawsuit. The Atlanta Journal-Constitution, July 11.

Turvey, B., Petherick, W., 2009. Forensic Victimology. Elsevier, San Diego, CA.

Sullivan, J., 1977. Introduction to Police Science, third ed. McGraw-Hill, New York.

University of California at Berkeley, 2010. The Berkeley Campus Student Policy and procedures regarding sexual assault and rape. University of California at Berkeley website, url: http://ccac.berkeley.edu/assault.shtml.

University of California at Berkeley, 2012. Student code of conduct violations. University of California at Berkeley website, url: http://campuslife.berkeley.edu/conduct/faculty-staff/violations.

University of Delaware, 2011. Student guide to university policies. Student Code of Conduct, University of Delaware website, url: http://www.udel.edu/stuguide/11-12/code.html.

Vollmer, A., 1971. The Police and Modern Society. Patterson Smith, Montclair, NJ.

Woo, S., 2005. The Facebook: not just for students. The Brown Daily Herald, November 2; url: http://www.browndailyherald.com/2.12231/the-facebook-not-just-for-students-1.1679665.

Yale University, 2012. Policy on teacher–student consensual relations. University Policy Statements, Yale University website, url: http://yalecollege.yale.edu/content/university-policy-statements-0#3.

CHAPTER 3

Criminal Justice Educators: Ethical Issues in Teaching

Stan Crowder, Shawn Mikulay and Brent E. Turvey

Key Terms

Capability Possessing adequate resources for completing a particular task or serving in a particular appointment.

Competence Possession of the knowledge, skills, and abilities required in order to do something effectively.

Scholarship A broad term that refers to academic study or achievement.

Criminal justice educators are not all cut from the same cloth. They are an interdisciplinary lot, drawn from the ranks of the forensic sciences, law enforcement, corrections, the legal community, the behavioral sciences, and academia. This professional diversity, characterized by academics and practitioners alike, is a necessary reflection of those that must band together in order for the criminal justice system to be effectively informed.

Criminal justice educators are employed by colleges and universities. Some are full-time faculty, holding PhDs and perhaps even tenure. Others work part-time, serving as adjunct faculty, with lots of professional experience but less formal education.

No matter where they come from, or where they work, criminal justice educators share a common set of ethical responsibilities towards their employers, colleagues, students, and the fiats of scholarship. The purpose of this chapter is to discuss the nature of these responsibilities, and help those concerned understand whether and when there may be an ethical obligation that needs attending. It will also offer some insight into the consequences of related decisions that have been made by other educators.

THE ROLE OF THE CRIMINAL JUSTICE EDUCATOR

The criminal justice educator is, ultimately, a professional guide. They are charged with ushering their students towards professionalism, letting them

Ethical Justice. http://dx.doi.org/10.1016/B978-0-12-404597-2.00003-6

know what to expect and how to behave, all the while explaining the rules that must be followed. Among the first professionals that any student is likely to encounter, the criminal justice educator has an obligation to ensure that their example is worthy of imitation – because it will be remembered and it will be imitated.

An important part of this obligation involves providing students with essential knowledge. This means giving students information that they do not have and advancing any practical understanding of what they already know using carefully developed assessments. However, educating is also much more than that.

Educating a student requires modeling professional behavior, supporting the cause of justice, and anticipating the evolution of knowledge. It also requires adherence to the three Cs: Capability, Competence and Confidentiality. A discussion of each is provided.

Modeling Happens

By choosing to be a criminal justice educator, one also chooses to be a professional role model. This happens regardless of any intent. If you teach, many of your students will very likely repeat what you say, adopt your values, and mimic your actions – inside and outside of the classroom. For example, if you show a lack of enthusiasm for either professionalism or the subject matter, your students will reduce their enthusiasm accordingly to follow. If you act with integrity and avoid conflicts of interest, your students will take notice and follow. If you value experience over scholarship, your students will put down their books and follow. Such is the reality of leadership.

Students will follow because instructors provide them with what is often the first and most authoritative example of what it means to be a professional. Instructors serve as a proxy for actual mentorship until the student finds their way to guidance that is more formal and specific. Students will follow and in following they will be led either towards or away from their best professional selves.

Acknowledging this reality, and the responsibility that gives it weight, helps the criminal justice educator anticipate and manage the impact of their influence on those that they teach (Nadelson, 2007).

Modeling Justice

No matter their professional orientation, or their personal feelings, the criminal justice educator has an obligation to model an ethic that is in fact justice oriented (Wood and Hilton, 2012). This involves presenting material and making decisions in a way that is characterized by the acknowledgement of individual rights and an overall fairness in protecting them. It also involves knowing, understanding, and following any relevant rules for conduct – legal and institutional alike. As explained in Wood and Hilton (2012, p. 201):

> … from an ethic of justice perspective, college leaders have a responsibility to learn, understand, and abide by rules, codes, and procedures. As a result, when leaders encounter ethical dilemmas, they may consider several questions that may aid in constructing or considering alternatives from an ethic-of-justice standpoint: What are the rules, codes, policies, and procedures relevant to this dilemma?

The criminal justice educator also has an obligation to understand and explain that the justice system works best when the professionals involved behave ethically and are treated as though they have equal value. Fairness is not achieved by ignoring individual rights or by allowing the dominance of one group over others. For instance, educators from law enforcement have an obligation to acknowledge the role and value of the defense community, while also acknowledging the reality of police corruption. Defense attorneys and defense investigators alike are a required feature of the justice system, meant to ensure fairness and justice in the face of what can be overwhelming or corrupted state resources. Similarly, educators from the academic and legal communities have an obligation to acknowledge the role and value of law enforcement with respect to keeping the peace, investigating crime, and apprehending criminals.

The ethical criminal justice educator will of course understand and explain the intended value of the many professional groups involved in the justice system, as well as their own. However, they will also remember to balance this by acknowledging when and how professional failures have occurred. This will help create a safe and reality-based learning environment in which the student can choose their own professional path with integrity. Students must not be herded or professionally bullied by their instructors as though there is only one morally correct way to serve the cause of justice, as this is contrary to the existence of the justice system's many parts.

If the criminal justice educator is incapable of modeling lawfulness and justice in the way that they act and teach, then they will do their students a disservice. They will provide a view that is too narrow or provide an example that betrays the rules of their chosen profession. The result will be students that are uninformed, unaware, and ultimately unprepared. In no way is this an acceptable dispatch of the educator's charge – not to their students and not with respect to the defects that will be bred into the professional community as a result.

The Evolution of Knowledge

Knowledge evolves with time. What is accepted today about the psychology of criminals, the best methods for criminal investigation and evidence testing, and even the law, will be different 10 years from now. This is how it should be. Research continues, technologies emerge and advance, methodologies are refined, and the law (and its interpretation) evolves. These realities demand that the criminal justice educator know and provide knowledge that is up to date. Therefore, the criminal justice educator is either a constant student of the changes brought by the professional tide or irrelevant to the profession within a decade.

Since knowledge evolves, there is also a corresponding obligation to provide students with the ability to critically evaluate, and faithfully integrate or refute, anything new that washes ashore. They need to be taught how to gauge the reliability, validity, and utility of that which is novel. This enables their professional growth and development beyond the classroom. Without such tools, the student graduates with a limited base of knowledge and information – and then they shortly become irrelevant for failing to adapt (or failing to recognize the need to adapt).

Consequently, teaching without also imparting a critique-oriented ethic contributes little to a student's longevity. Such academic negligence all but ensures that what has been learned cannot be refined or built upon and that what is new cannot be properly evaluated for future use. In fact, it may be argued that teaching this ability is what distinguishes education from training.[1]

Capability

Capability refers to possessing adequate resources for completing a particular task or serving in a particular appointment. With respect to being a criminal justice educator, this means professional competence (discussed in the next section); knowledge of effective teaching strategies; a professional disposition that engenders respect and encourages learning; and the support of, or connections with, the criminal justice community. Such capabilities allow for the effective delivery of the most up-to-date information to the classroom, the ability to provide applied knowledge from the non-academic world when necessary (e.g., guest lecturers), and networking to facilitate student internship possibilities. It also translates into the perceived community value of any recommendations written by the educator for students seeking further educational opportunities, an internship, or employment.

However, capability also refers to more basic issues that can be missed by institutions that employ criminal justice educators without background checks or ongoing assessment. Consider, for example, the policy for "Dismissal for

---

[1]To be clear, there is nothing negligent about giving training so long as it is clearly presented as such, and not represented as something with a more complete critical and theoretical foundation.

Cause and Termination" at the University of Colorado (University of Colorado, 2012):

> The Laws of the Regents establish a provision for the dismissal of faculty members on the grounds of demonstrable profession incompetence, neglect of duty, insubordination, conviction of a felony, or any offense involving moral turpitude upon a plea or a verdict of guilty or following a plea of *nolo contendere*, or sexual harassment, or other conduct which falls below minimum standards of profession integrity.

Although every educational institution is different, this policy reflects what is possible in the current academic workplace. Institutions maintaining less stringent employment guidelines certainly do exist, but they do so while encouraging less professional integrity amongst the staff. Consider, specifically, the following issues:

Criminal Backgrounds

The employment of an educator with a criminal background is essentially corrosive to the goals of any criminal justice program:

- Convicted criminals provide students with a poor example to follow, sending the wrong message about acceptable character and conduct in the criminal justice community.
- They work against the creation of a safe working and teaching environment – often causing apprehension and fear amongst students and staff.
- They create enhanced institutional liability should any future harm come to students or staff.
- They generally cannot provide internship opportunities or letters of recommendation with any value to their students.

Given that criminal justice programs are preparing students for work in the criminal justice system, and require its support, it is counterintuitive that a convicted criminal should work as an educator in such a program – although using criminals as guest lecturers can be quite instructive, providing cautionary tales and insight into the criminal justice system from a criminal's perspective.

CASE EXAMPLE

Cecil Fore, III

Consider the case of Cecil Fore, III, a tenured professor at the University of Georgia. He was fired for concealing information about his criminal history during the hiring process. As reported in Shearer (2008):

Cecil Fore III, an associate professor of communication science and special education in the UGA College of Education, had been at UGA since 2001, said university spokesman Tom Jackson.

Continued

CASE EXAMPLE *CONTINUED*

UGA's Legal Affairs Office got a tip Tuesday about Fore's conviction and confirmed that the tip was accurate, Jackson said. University officials fired Fore today, he said.

Fore served a three-year prison sentence in Alabama in the early 1990s for sexual molestation of students under his care, Jackson said.

The university's grounds for firing Fore is not for his conviction, but for providing false information when he was hired. New UGA employees are asked if they have ever been convicted of a felony, and Fore said on an application form that he had not, Jackson said.

Fore, who received tenure last year, is legally entitled to a tenure revocation hearing if he desires one, Jackson said.

New employees at UGA and the state's 34 other public colleges and universities are subject to background checks, but the background check policy was not in effect when Fore was hired, Jackson said.

As mentioned, the new policy at the University of Georgia is that all new faculty, and any of those staff who are promoted to positions of trust, must now submit to a thorough background check. Fore was hired in 2001 and received tenure before this policy was adopted.

Mental Defects

As the result of mental disorders, medication, or physical injury (e.g., brain injury), some criminal justice instructors become incapable of effecting their teaching duties. In other circumstances, an instructor's mental condition can make them unstable to the point where campus safety is a legitimate issue. The criminal justice educator has a responsibility towards their students, to recognize if and when this is this case, and then take corrective action. If unable due to cognitive deficits associated with mental impairment, then their employers have a corresponding responsibility to remove them from teaching duties until such time as they are determined safe and capable.

CASE EXAMPLE

Anthony Chase

Consider Anthony Chase, formerly a tenured professor of law at Nova Southeastern University's Shepard Broad Law Center. He was fired in 2010 for concerns over his "mental derangement." As of this writing, he is suing for reinstatement, back-pay, and damages, as reported in Sloan (2012):

According to Chase's complaint, he began teaching at the school in 1979 and was tenured in 1985, although the school said in its response that he was tenured in 1984. He was placed on administrative leave on Oct. 7, 2010, after

several colleagues reported that he had made statements involving a gun and what they took as threats of violence.

The school fired Chase by letter on Dec. 8, 2010, according to the complaint. Administrators cited several e-mails Chase had sent, including one to a fellow law professor complaining of his treatment by the facilities management staff. It read in part, "I have acquired a large Beretta hand gun and I take

CASE EXAMPLE *CONTINUED*

my 'how to shoot' course Tuesday or Thursday of the week," according to the complaint.

In a separate e-mail chain, several law professors questioned Chase about whether he was serious about obtaining and using a gun, and expressed hope that he was not. Chase replied that he had a registered Beretta 8000 and a license to own it, the complaint says. In an e-mail sent three days before he was placed on administrative leave, according to the complaint, Chase wrote that he was removing items from his office at night. "Just trying to avoid being shot," he continued. "I can shoot pretty good from the windows into the parking lot."

[Chase's attorney, William] Amlong said that administrators had misconstrued the messages. That last comment, for example, was a joke referencing a seminar Chase had attended in which lead FBI investigator on the Beltway Sniper case said he would zig zag through the parking lot on the way to his car as a safety precaution, the complaint says.

Nova security officers searched Chase's office and truck on the day he was placed on administrative leave but found no gun, according to the complaint, and administrators barred him from campus. In reality, according to the complaint, Chase never actually owned a gun.

Chase alleges that university officials perceived him to be "mentally deranged enough to engage in a campus shooting rampage." That perception was not based on his actions, since a search turned up no

gun and he lacked a concealed-carry permit, the complaint argues. Still, administrators perceived that Chase had a mental disability and fired him on that basis in violation of the ADA, it reads.

Additionally, Nova breached Chase's contract for lifetime employment under the tenure system, the complaint says.

In its response, Nova denied that it had violated the ADA or other state and federal laws. "Defendant asserts that the employment actions taken with respect to plaintiff do not violate applicable employment laws; rather, such actions were based on facts other than unlawful discrimination and were taken for legitimate, non-discriminatory reasons," the school argued.

In this complaint, however, Chase denies that administrators believed he actually suffered a physical or mental impairment.

In another discovery fight, Seltzer on May 29 denied Nova's motion to compel Chase to turn over medical records from his psychiatrist. Chase's attorney argued that those records are protected under the psychotherapist–patient privilege.

Former Professor Chase's filed his lawsuit in 2011 and it is ongoing. Of note is the fact that Mr Chase had actually been under psychiatrists care and knowing whether he was taking any medication during the timeframe under review would certainly be relevant to understanding his mental state. Despite the court's denial of the motion to turn those records over, that information could still come out during depositions of the psychiatrist, colleagues, or from the Plaintiff himself.

Competence

Competence is defined by possession of the knowledge, skills, and abilities required in order to do something effectively. It is best demonstrated with extensive research, practice or experience marked by repeated success at achieving a desired aim. Additionally, as explained in Kruger and Dunning (1999), the requirements for achieving competence are essentially the same as those necessary for evaluating competence (p. 1121):

> [W]hen people are incompetent in the strategies they adopt to achieve success and satisfaction, they suffer a dual burden: Not only do they reach erroneous conclusions and make unfortunate choices, but their incompetence robs them of the ability to realize it. Instead … they are left with the mistaken impression that they are doing just fine.

This means that competence is demonstrated by the ability to successfully recognize error in one's own work as well as that of others.

It is not unreasonable to expect that the criminal justice educator be competent in the subjects that they are assigned to teach. This is, in fact, a presumptive threshold requirement for any teacher of any subject. If an instructor is put in front of students, those students should be safe to assume that the instructor knows what they are talking about. Therefore, educational institutions have an ethical obligation to screen potential instructors with diligence and to employ only those that are competent. The incompetent, it must be remembered, necessarily lack the ability to meet their own ethical obligation to refrain from teaching. They can also be very difficult to terminate.

Turvey's Comments

Guests and Grads

It is not uncommon for criminal justice instructors to augment their lectures with guest speakers and graduate students. Like a police detective to talk about what it actually means to do interviews and interrogations or a defense attorney to talk about their experience with prosecutorial misconduct. Or like having a grad student present a lecture on some relevant aspect of their dissertation. This exposes students to those working real-world, and to real-world issues, as well as providing them with access to the most up to date research.

However, some instructors are known for stacking their courses with guest speakers from start to finish. Worse, some institutions allow grad students to teach an entire subject having just taken it themselves the year prior – with no other relevant education, training, or experience. Such practices violate the covenant that exists between a student and their educational institution, wherein they presume they will be taught by the qualified and competent.

Confidentiality

Instructors frequently learn details regarding the private lives of their students. Disclosures of private information occur in many ways: in class, when students speak of their life experiences or seek to explain absences; during the enrollment process, as documentation is reviewed prior to student acceptance into a program; and from other staff members relating their own student experiences. Often, however, the most sensitive disclosures occur before and after class, as students approach trusted instructors in search of personal advice. This includes information about medical history, mental health history, personal tragedies, sexual activity/dating history, victimization, and of course academic achievement (or lack thereof). With this information comes the responsibility to know whether and when to share it with others.

Mikulay's Note

It's not that student classroom utterances can never be repeated, but clear consideration should be given to evaluating the pedagogical value of the information. When a student recounts their personal experiences with childhood abuse and recovered memories, that anecdote can be of clear and evident educational value for future students. But many times, the student will make statements of this sort with the distorted belief that the classroom is somehow protected by an implicit privacy agreement and that their words will never leave the room. An ethical educator needs to err on the side of protecting the student from their own public disclosures. If the story of the abuse and memory can be sanitized and redacted, then a case could be made for recounting an account told by "a previous student." In the event that the essential details of the story point to an individual regardless of efforts to disguise the person in the story, it is probably best to accept that the material should be taught without the tale. Imagine teaching future students with the amended story; will they say "That's sounds like what happened to my friend, Mike" or will they say "Oh, you're talking about Mike."

Each learning institution has specific policies and procedures related to student confidentiality. Generally speaking, instructors are often forbidden from sharing sensitive student information with other staff members or students, facing serious administrative penalties should they do so. Consequently, instructors are best served by first learning the policies that govern their conduct regarding students and student information as a function of their employment.

Family Education Rights and Privacy Act

FERPA, short for the Family Education Rights and Privacy Act of 1974 (US Public Law 93-579), is also referred to as the Buckley Amendment. This Federal law generally provides that student records, and any information they contain, are confidential and not subject to disclosure except upon written permission by the student or their parents (if they claim the student as a dependent for tax purposes). As explained in Mayers *et al.* (2010, p. 19):

> [FERPA] places statutory restrictions on public educational institutions from disclosing certain types of information contained in students' educational records. The first section of the act prohibits any education institution from adopting policies that would prohibit or result in a denial of student access to his/her educational records. The second section of the act forbids educational institutions from enacting policies or permitting practices which would allow the release of student records without consent of the student or the student's parents.

Some have taken this to mean that students have a Federally guaranteed right with respect to privacy regarding their student record and other sensitive student information. This is not the case at all.

In *Gonzaga University v. Jane Doe* (2002), the US Supreme Court made it clear that:

> FERPA's confidentiality provisions create no rights enforceable under §1983. The provisions entirely lack the sort of individually focused rights-creating language that is critical. FERPA's provisions speak only to the Secretary, directing that "[n]o funds shall be made available" to any "educational ... institution" which has a prohibited "policy or practice," §1232g(b)(1).

In other words, FERPA creates a responsibility on the part of educational institutions to set specific policies regarding the protection and disclosure of student records. However, the institution gets to decide how stringent those policies are (e.g., who gets access and under what conditions). As explained in Mayers *et al.* (2010, p. 26): "Since the statute itself does not define who has an legitimate educational interest, each individual educational institution must, in policy, provide a framework to address this issue, so its employees are clear on who does and who does not have authorization to possess or disclose confidential student records."

In addition, FERPA does not set down a clear mandate with respect to what constitutes a formal student record. This means that educational institutions must also decide this issue for themselves. For example, a state college in one part of the country may consider homework assignments, grade-books and emails to be part of the overall student record, and therefore protected from disclosure under FERPA; a private university in another part of the country may consider the student record to be comprised of only final grades and transcripts – allowing disclosure of everything else.

In short, FERPA was only ever intended to protect student records from improper disclosure, not to guarantee an overall student right to privacy. The disclosure of sensitive or private information by an educator is therefore not prohibited by Federal law, unless it is part of what is considered to be the student record and it is disclosed outside of what is considered a "legitimate educational interest." As these are concepts defined by each individual educational institution, and not students or the law, students currently have little recourse to protect what they may consider to be private information from being disseminated (Mayers *et al.*, 2010).

Exceptions to Disclosure

Many educational institutions maintain the necessary exceptions to sharing or disclosing otherwise confidential or sensitive student information that can include:

(1) The information is shared with other staff or professionals out of concern for student safety or well-being.

(2) The information is shared with other staff as part of a discussion regarding student assessments or other legitimate educational interests.

(3) The information has already been shared by the student in a public fashion – such as a disclosure in class or in social media.

The authors of this work recommend that educators avoid sharing sensitive student information of any kind without the student's explicit consent – unless either of the first two exception criteria above have been met. In the age of email this should not be difficult to obtain. If neither of the first two exception criteria have been met, then there is a very real question about the legitimacy of sharing student information at all, outside of a formal request from a third party. Ultimately, this will help dampen harmful tendencies towards gossip, protect students and instructors from miscommunication, and remind instructors that all students should be treated with the respect afforded any other adult.

ETHICAL RESPONSIBILITIES

Criminal justice educators have the same ethical responsibilities as any other professional in higher education. These responsibilities are a function of the trust and authority afforded to them by their employers, scholarship, colleagues, and students. Failure to recognize and attend these ethical responsibilities often stems from a lack of professional commitment and development, and perhaps even apathy. As provided in the "Statement on professional ethics" provided by the American Association of University Professors[2] (American Association of University Professors, 2009):

> Professors, guided by a deep conviction of the worth and dignity of the advancement of knowledge, recognize the special responsibilities placed upon them. Their primary responsibility to their subject is to seek and to state the truth as they see it. To this end professors devote their energies to developing and improving their scholarly competence. They accept the obligation to exercise critical self-discipline and judgment in using, extending, and transmitting knowledge. They practice intellectual honesty. Although professors may follow subsidiary interests, these interests must never seriously hamper or compromise their freedom of inquiry.

The convictions mentioned in this excerpt speak to an abiding professional fidelity – wherein the educator must be devoted to competence, scholarship,

---

[2] While the authors by no means agree with every position and publication of the American Association of University Professors, many of those set forth in their "Statement of professional ethics" are met with great accord.

and honesty in order to be worthy of being entrusted with the academic and professional development of their students. Some of this has already been hinted at or discussed in this chapter, but more specific discussion is necessary.

To Employers

In most learning environments, the criminal justice educator is first and foremost an employee. They will have been hired by a particular agency or institution to perform teaching duties, for a single subject, for a limited duration, in part-time capacity, or as part of a tenure track position. In doing so, they will also have been required to provide relevant (and accurate) information about their background and to sign an employment contract of some sort. This contract, along with institutional policies and procedures, furnishes the instructor with a set of rules for acceptable conduct.

If the explicit policies, rules or guidelines of any institution are unacceptable to an instructor at the outset, then they should seek employment elsewhere. If they become unacceptable subsequent to hiring, then the instructor must conduct themselves in a professional fashion while making their concerns clear. As explained by the American Association of University Professors (2009):

> As members of an academic institution, professors seek above all to be effective teachers and scholars. Although professors observe the stated regulations of the institution, provided the regulations do not contravene academic freedom, they maintain their right to criticize and seek revision. Professors give due regard to their paramount responsibilities within their institution in determining the amount and character of work done outside it. When considering the interruption or termination of their service, professors recognize the effect of their decision upon the program of the institution and give due notice of their intentions.

In other words, if the explicit policies or rules of an institution become unacceptable subsequent to employment, educators must consider the impact of simply walking away from their responsibilities before doing so. When that kind of decision is made, it should be done so thoughtfully and with sufficient prior notice so as not to harm students.

To Scholarship and Professionalism

Scholarship is a broad term that refers to academic study or achievement. Criminal justice educators have an ethical responsibility to promote, if not also participate in, scholarly efforts with respect to their students and colleagues. Otherwise they are just giving training and taking no responsibility for their own professional development, let alone that of the community they are serving.

Scholarship requires the cultivation of integrity. This means that educators may not falsify, misrepresent, or withhold any methodology, information or findings with respect to their research efforts. Nor can they conceal any relationships or direct sponsorship that might suggest the appearance of bias in their work. In short, scholarship demands professional transparency in order to allow for peer review – because science demands proofs and does not rely on trust. The honest scholar invites peer review; the honest scholar does not shun or hamper it (see, generally, National Academy of Sciences, 2002).

The commitment to scholarship and professionalism can also include participation in relevant professional organizations with professional membership requirements and prescribed codes of ethical conduct. Such organizations, so long as they are not merely networking organizations that let anyone in without proper screening, can provide an important second line of ethical guidance and defense. This is necessary because there can and will be issues that arise during the course of a professional career that lack sufficient clarity or coverage in the educator's employment contract and related policies and procedures. A professional organization provides external authority on such matters. Its mandates, by which all active members are bound, can be used to guide individual decision making and to educate employers when necessary.

Perhaps the greatest threat to scholarship and professionalism is indifference; indifference to cheating, plagiarism, competence, and integrity, in general (see, generally, Rosenberg, 2011). This starts with the instructor and then infects the classroom. Professional apathy is therefore to be avoided – requiring an unwavering commitment to scholarship and professionalism in both word and deed.

To Colleagues

Criminal justice educators may find themselves at odds with other faculty members. This often occurs because criminal justice educators, many of whom are practitioners, view scholars as too theoretical and therefore under-informed by real-world issues. Similarly, those outside of criminal justice, to include those sociologists and theoretical criminologists that teach alongside them, tend to view criminal justice educators as lacking scholarship and academic rigor. Each views the other with professional disdain, which can create an environment lacking communication, to say nothing of basic professionalism.

Colleagues have an ethical obligation towards each other with respect to communication, privacy, and tolerance. This means refraining from acts of inappropriate disclosure to students, biased decision making, general hostility, threatening behavior, or harassment in any context. However, colleagues must also respect each other's points of view. Opinions can and will vary, as reasonable people can and will disagree.

This is different, however, from matters of law, policy violation, or safety. If a colleague is violating the law or an explicit policy, or is behaving in a fashion that might cause students or staff to be harmed, another ethical obligation exists. That obligation is to report such conduct to the appropriate authorities. In some cases this will be a supervisor; in others it might be the campus police. The ethical criminal justice educator owes nothing to a colleague that is betraying the law, their institution, or their students. They must report all misconduct with indifference, even when it is assured that nothing will come of it so that a record can be made. Failure to report misconduct, or misreporting it, makes one a party to it.

To Students

Not all students choose to act ethically and that choice is determined by a number of factors. These factors include individual moral development, knowledge of academic codes of conduct (along with fear of the consequences for being caught), and student–faculty interactions (Nadelson, 2007; see also Chapter 2: "Ethical Issues for Students of Criminal Justice"). Given that educators play a significant role in this choice, they are ethically obligated to create a safe learning environment, promote academic honesty and learning, and to respond quickly to instances of suspected academic misconduct (Nadelson, 2007). As explained by the American Association of University Professors (2009):

> As teachers, professors encourage the free pursuit of learning in their students. They hold before them the best scholarly and ethical standards of their discipline. Professors demonstrate respect for students as individuals and adhere to their proper roles as intellectual guides and counselors. Professors make every reasonable effort to foster honest academic conduct and to ensure that their evaluations of students reflect each student's true merit. They respect the confidential nature of the relationship between professor and student. They avoid any exploitation, harassment, or discriminatory treatment of students. They acknowledge significant academic or scholarly assistance from them. They protect their academic freedom.

Consider also the advice of Starratt (2004, p. 3), arguing that:

> The work of educational leadership should be simultaneously intellectual and moral; an activity characterized by a blend of human, professional, and civic concerns; a work of cultivating an environment for learning that is humanly fulfilling and socially responsible. In cultivating that environment, moral educational leaders enact the foundational responsibilities of responsibility, authenticity, and presence – the same virtues that should characterize students' learning.

Instead of getting what they need, too many students suffer from what can only be described as academic neglect. They are too often taught by burnt-out instructors who are themselves overworked and consequently overwhelmed by personal and professional commitments. Such students are not being professionally cultivated; rather, they are viewed as distractions. Or worse, they are viewed as a commodity for which none take responsibility.

Student–Faculty Relationships

As discussed in Chapter 2, there are all manner of student–faculty relationships. Those relationships based on respect, like the student–mentor relationship, are ideal. Those that deprive the students of respect, knowledge, or the appropriate credit for work that has been done are not. This is because, under even the best circumstances with the most mature students, there are small matters with big ethical ramifications that will arise, as explained in Schwartz (2011, p. 363):

> Determining and maintaining interpersonal boundaries with students is an ever-present yet rarely discussed element of teaching graduate students. Where to meet students for advising appointments, how much to self-disclose in the classroom, and whether to collaborate with students on community projects – these are typical of the challenges that graduate school faculty encounter regularly as classroom teachers, and program, thesis, and practicum advisors.

Even with grad students, then, criminal justice educators need to attend to ethical concerns. Ultimately, the best student–faculty relationships are based on clearly defined, deliberately expressed, and mutually understood professional boundaries (Schwartz, 2011). This requires the ethical educator to anticipate related ethical dilemmas as best they are able and to discuss them openly with each student concerned. In this way, they show students the same respect that should be afforded other adults, which is the perfect way to start any professional relationship.

In the worst cases, however, student–faculty relationships can be openly exploitative – as discussed in Chapter 2. These involve students exploiting faculty members for professional or academic advantage, or faculty members exploiting their students. In either circumstance, someone is being manipulated or taken advantage of – and the victim, often a willing participant, may or may not be fully aware of, or willing to admit, their ultimate exposure.[3]

Student–Faculty Sex

Sexual relationships between students and faculty, or any non-familial relationships that betray emotional considerations for that matter, are ill-advised for

---

[3] The authors have experienced that naiveté and wishful thinking about the cost and harm of an inappropriate relationship can be found among students and faculty alike.

all of the reasons discussed in Chapter 2. Educational institutions have been slow to come around. However, they began to develop policies that govern and even prohibit these kinds of relationships when the US Supreme Court ruled, in the mid-1990s, that they could be held financially liable for sexual harassment (Endelmen and Briquelet, 2012). This is because relationships between students and faculty, involving a superior and subordinate, often go bad – resulting in bad feelings. These bad feelings, regardless of their origin, can now result in litigation.

For example, in 2003, the University of California began the academic year with policy banning "romantic or sexual" relationships between students and faculty (Rimer, 2003):

> The university has long had a strict sexual harassment policy. With its new rules, it has joined a small but growing number of colleges that have taken the extra step of trying to regulate those relationships that, at least at the outset, both parties seem to want....
>
> The new policies, at Duke, the University of California and elsewhere, arise out of a range of concerns, including the ethics and conflicts of interests involved in such relationships. Gayle Binion, a professor of political science who helped negotiate the adoption of the new policy at the University of California, said her primary concern was ensuring that faculty members did not cross "normal professional relationship boundaries," the same sort of boundaries that have long been clearly established between doctors and their patients, she said.
>
> As other supporters of the policy do, she questions if relationships between faculty members and students they supervise, recommend for graduate school or jobs, or otherwise evaluate can ever be truly consensual.
>
> "It's not just about power," Professor Binion said. "It's about the asymmetry of the life situation. For faculty members, they have relationships, they break up, their lives go on. They're established. For students, these things can have dramatic repercussions. We're saying the faculty member has to be the one to take responsibility. You can't just say the student says it was O.K."
>
> At several schools, including William and Mary and Ohio Wesleyan, the policies were prompted by highly publicized incidents involving sexual relationships between professors and students.
>
> At the University of California, such a policy was already under discussion when the dean of the university's Boalt Hall School of Law at Berkeley, John Dwyer, resigned after a student accused him of sexual harassment. Mr. Dwyer, who was not married at the time, said that he had had one consensual encounter with the student – whom he did not teach or supervise – and that his actions represented "a serious error in judgment."

Later, Yale University followed suit, adopting a similar no tolerance attitude towards students having relationships with faculty members. This was done, it was explained, to address the inherent imbalance of power that exists in all such relationships, regardless of any adult consent, as reported in Bass (2010):

> After more than a quarter century of debate, Yale faculty members are now barred from sexual relationships with undergraduates – not just their own students, but any Yale undergrads ....
>
> An imbalance of power forms the rationale for treating Yale College students differently from their older counterparts. Undergrads, the revised handbook says, "are particularly vulnerable to the unequal institutional power inherent in the teacher–student relationship and the potential for coercion, because of their age and relative lack of maturity."

As seasoned educators will attest, the unfortunate reality is that there are a great many students who want to have inappropriate relationships with their professors and a great many professors that want precisely the same thing. When either prevails, it is bad for everyone concerned – students, faculty, and institutions alike. It is therefore the responsibility of colleagues and institutional leadership (e.g., departmental chairs, deans, provosts, chancellors) to ensure that the predators among them are properly reported, documented, and dispatched.

Consider the following Case Example of Bethune-Cookman University and the "Nigerian Mafia."

CASE EXAMPLE

Bethune-Cookman University and the "Nigerian Mafia"

In May of 2009, citing overwhelming evidence that included the statements of students and faculty members, Bethune-Cookman University in Florida terminated four of its professors in the School of Social Sciences for cause related to sexual misconduct. A year later, the American Association of University Professors released a report condemning these terminations, and others, for lack of evidence and violations of institutional due process (see American Association of University Professors, 2010). This in turn prompted Bethune-Cookman University to release the report of its internal investigation, conducted by the NAACP's principal attorney in Florida, in the capacity of the Florida State Conference of Branches' Special Counsel for Civil Rights (Honig, 2010, pp. 2–4)*:

> The University responded [to numerous faculty complaints of sexual misconduct] by

conducting interviews with approximately 20 faculty members. Statements in some of these interviews implicated four faculty members in the School of Social Sciences: Professor #1 and three faculty members – Professor #2, Professor #3 and Professor #4 (collectively referred to as the "four professors"). The faculty interviews further alleged that:

- The four professors had publicly identified themselves as the "Nigerian Mafia" (several faculty members remembered the four professors joking about this in a faculty meeting and at other public functions);
- The four professors had an off-campus apartment where they took female students

Continued

CASE EXAMPLE *CONTINUED*

to have sex; one or more of the four professors would take nude photos of the female students at the apartment and threaten to release the photos on Facebook if the students revealed their improper actions to the University's administration;

■ A faculty member in the School of Social Sciences, who reported a student's complaint that Professor #3 had attempted to rape her at the referenced off-campus apartment, was called to testify at a hearing, conducted by the University's former administration. The complainant was not advised of the outcome of the hearing.

■ The Social Sciences faculty members further revealed that there was an aura of intimidation by the four professors. The faculty members told the investigators that they were afraid to speak further about the situation in the School of Social Sciences for fear of retaliation. The faculty member who reported the alleged rape, and was called as a witness at the University hearing, stated that she did in fact suffer retaliation because she was not given adequate courses to maintain a full load and was intimidated from seeking opportunities for promotion.

In addition to the above faculty interviews:

■ A Social Sciences student confided in her Philosophy professor that Professor #2 had continued to harass her sexually. She stated that this incident occurred in her classes with him in front of the other students as well as at clubs where Professor #2 would grab at her and ask her to go with him. The student also alleged that Professor #2 had asked her for sex and offered her an "A" in exchange for sex. The student felt so intimidated and harassed that she left [Bethune-Cookman University] and planned not to return. Upon speaking to her mother, she decided to return to [Bethune-Cookman University] and confront the sexual harassment.

■ The Daytona Beach Police Department was called in by Dr. Reed to interview the above student. Based on her allegations, the Police Department suggested using a wire to record the conversations of Professor #2 when he next approached the student. Dr. Reed called the student's mother for her approval, and she agreed. A date was set for the police wire of the student but before the launch, the student informed the police that Professor #2 found out their plan from another female student who said she was having sex with Professor #1 and did not see anything wrong with having sex with the professors. Due to a concern for the student's safety and Professor #2's verbal insults the prior evening letting the student know that he was aware of the police's plan, the police cancelled their plans.

■ Another Social Sciences' student sent an email to Dr. Reed expressing concerns, including: "… I am concerned about the complaints about the professor in our department/school who is having inappropriate relations with students. I would like to know what is going to be done about it and about the other professors/instructors who are exhibiting this type or other types of behavior that are harmful to the learning of our students. Many students are skeptical to come forward with their complaints because they feel that it will affect their grades or hinder their matriculation. But I have heard enough about this particular professor and others who are not doing their jobs and hurting students."

■ The University's Vice President for Assessment conducted a survey of the students in the School of Social Sciences. The survey revealed that the students felt there was a problem with sexual harassment in their School and the written comments made general references to allegations of sexual harassment and specific reference to Professor #2.

CASE EXAMPLE *CONTINUED*

- The Director of Human Resources reviewed the personnel file on Professor #2 and reported that a female student had filed a claim of sexual harassment against Professor #2 in 2005. This student's allegations are consistent with the types of unwarranted sexual advances and conduct alleged by the above-referenced Social Sciences student.
- Based on the comments in a senior exit survey, which alleged sexual misconduct by the four professors, Dr. Hiram Powell, the Associate Vice President for Academic Affairs conducted interviews with each professor. Dr. Powell stated that the survey identified them as participating in the sexual harassment of students. Each denied the allegations although Professor #4 admitted that he would invite the top student in his class (which he admitted was always a female student) for dinner at the apartment. Professor #4 was asked if he invited anyone else to attend the dinner and he said no. Dr. Powell advised the four professors that they should discontinue the practice of inviting female students to their apartment without a female faculty member in attendance.
- In total, seven women students, the targets of sexual harassment, revealed that various of the four professors pressured them to trade sex for grades. One of the seven women students reported receiving sexually explicit text messages and an email with depictions of sexual photographs from Professor #2. This same student also reported being accosted by him at an off-campus venue. Another reported demeaning, sexually explicit jokes told during class.
- Based on the above, the University suspended the four professors in May 2009, pending a review.
- Upon review of all relevant data and evidence, the University's outside counsel recommended that the University terminate the four professors based on the allegations of sexual misconduct and their violation of the University's Mission Statement, Statement of Academic Integrity and the Faculty Contract. The four professors were informed of their termination shortly thereafter and they appealed this decision.

As of this writing, these terminations are still being litigated in civil court. This case, however, demonstrates almost every kind of improper sexual relationship between students and faculty. It also demonstrates the fall-out that can result, even when there is consent.

Bethune-Cookman University is a well-known African-American university; all four of the professors that were terminated, were African-American, although not all of them were actually from Nigeria.

It bears noting that zero-tolerance policies can never eradicate feelings of true love that develop between faculty members and mature students, as those who are mature and ethical can wait until they are no longer in a relationship that might require or give the appearance of ethical compromise. Rather, they are intended to provide a mechanism for identifying and removing those individuals who routinely exercise bad judgment, and who constantly compromise themselves and others. This includes the staff member who procures a new student girlfriend (or three) every couple of years and treats the classroom as though it is a feature of their own personalized dating service. It also includes the student who charms a new professor (or three) each semester, in order to get them to do their assessments or lay the foundation for a sexual harassment complaint should someone confront them about it.

Ultimately, from the criminal justice educator's perspective, avoiding such relationships is about protecting oneself from liability and it is about ensuring that the hard work of serious students is not overlooked or discounted in favor of those that have inappropriately curried favor. It is about ensuring that fairness prevails and that everyone feels safe to learn in order to advance the profession. If the criminal justice educator finds that personal considerations are taking a front seat to these fundamentals, then this is call for a top to bottom re-evaluation of priorities, as professional downfall is near.

SOCIAL MEDIA

Social media has exploded over the last decade (e.g., Facebook, LinkedIn, Twitter, and Reddit). It has increased the means by which educators connect and interact with their students. It has also increased the mechanisms by which educators can voice personal and professional opinions, as well as express personal lifestyle choices. Each of these is fraught with ethical peril.

Connecting with Students

Social media offers a great many opportunities for students to network with their professors and other potential mentors. As discussed in Chapter 2, this can be a good thing. However, it is only as good as the character of either.

More invasive forms of social media, such a Facebook and Twitter, increase the risk that students will learn too much about the private lives of their professors. This can cause students to lose respect for them as role models. This risk is especially high for those educators whose personal lives are in chaos or disrepair, or for those who are less than professional in the way they conduct themselves off-campus.

Similarly, more invasive forms of social media increase the risk that professors will learn too much about the private lives of their students. Potentially, it allows them to know who a student is dating, what they did on their weekend (and with whom), how drunk they got, what they wear on the beach (or do not), who is currently mad at them (and why), and what their personal plans are for the immediate future (e.g., going to a party with other students to get wasted; getting stoned alone in their dorm room; going to a bar to pick up drunk chicks). It also allows them the ability to "creep" through student photos and timelines for the same information as far back as the student has archived it – years in many cases. Depending on the intended use of this information, such a level of passive intimacy in the context of the student–faculty relationship may not be appropriate.

Freedom of Speech

While the criminal justice educator enjoys the same constitutionally guaranteed freedom of speech as any other citizen, there are limits. These limits exist as a function of their employment contracts. Some educational institutions do not mind if their employees are openly critical of colleagues, supervisors, or institutional policies. Others have strict prohibitions about discussing such things in public. In addition, speech that is hateful, prejudiced, or threatening; that incites violence or criminality; or that fails the vague institutional standards of morality can result in sanctions or termination. The same is true of speech that violates the privacy of students as dictated by institutional policies.

Consequently, freedom of speech and social media are uncomfortable bedfellows in the world of academia, as more and more professors are being sanctioned or terminated for what it is learned by others that they have expressed online.

PROPOSED ETHICAL GUIDELINES FOR CRIMINAL JUSTICE INSTRUCTORS

The following guidelines are offered as a friendly suggestion, to protect the ethical criminal justice educator from false accusations and liability, as well as from the appearance of impropriety in the eyes of others. They also help to create clear professional boundaries and deter students with an exploitative intent. For the unethical criminal justice educator, the authors would suggest that every guideline and recommendation that has ever been written has been ignored by the lazy and the selfish – we expect the same here:

(1) Never ask a student for a date.
(2) Never meet with a student alone.
(3) If you meet with a student in your office, keep the door open at all times.
(4) If you meet with the student off campus, do so in public and in a manner that makes boundaries clear.
(5) Be cautious about accepting gifts from students to help to avoid the appearance of favoritism.
(6) Avoid giving out your home address or phone number.
(7) Communicate with students using staff email; document all conversations with an email.
(8) Award grades fairly and based on performance only.
(9) Never grade assessments while drugged or intoxicated.
(10) Never inflate a grade out of pity or a belief that the student could have done better.
(11) Be suspicious if a student has had more than three relatives die in a semester.
(12) Be knowledgeable, and remain current, in your areas of teaching.
(13) Be capable of teaching.
(14) Be capable of admitting errors and fixing mistakes; students learn a great deal from this.

(15) Never use the teaching materials of others without clear citation, reference, or acknowledgement.

(16) Never complete a student's assessments for them.

(17) Never meet students at your home.

(18) Never press a student into employment outside of school.

(19) Students are not friends; they are future colleagues. Treat them as such.

(20) Report the misconduct of any colleague to the proper authorities, in writing, regardless of personal feelings.

The ethical educator will note that those who have a problem with these suggestions are likely accustomed to dating their students, exploiting them, or they are interested in protecting friends and colleagues that are.

SUMMARY

Criminal justice educators share a common set of ethical responsibilities towards their employers, colleagues, students, and fiats of scholarship. They are a professional guide, charged with ushering their student towards professionalism, letting them know what to expect and how to behave, all the while explaining the rules that must be followed. Educating a student requires modeling professional behavior, supporting the cause of justice, and anticipating the evolution of knowledge. It also requires the adherence to capability, competence, and confidentiality.

Questions

1. Educating students requires adherence to the "three Cs." List them.

2. Explain the issues associated with the employment of an educator with a criminal background.

3. Criminal justice educators have an ethical responsibility to promote scholarly efforts with respect to their students and colleagues. True or False?

4. The criminal justice educator has an obligation to model an ethic that is justice oriented. Explain.

5. List three examples of ethical guidelines for criminal justice educators.

References

American Association of University Professors, 2009. Statement on professional ethics. American Association of University Professors, Washington, DC, url: http://www.aaup.org/AAUP/pubsres/policydocs/contents/statementonprofessionalethics.htm.

American Association of University Professors, 2010. Academic freedom and tenure: Bethune-Cookman University. American Association of University Professors, Washington, DC, url: http://www.aaup.org/NR/rdonlyres/086B24EA-4F28-4A67-A934-D4512ABAB493/0/BethCook.pdf.

Bass, C., 2010. University bans faculty–student sex. Yale Alumni Magazine, March/April.

Endelmen, S., Briquelet, K., 2012. CUNY mulls ban on professor–student relationships. New York Post, March 11.

Gonzaga University v. Jane Doe, 2002. US Supreme Court. 536 US 273, No. 01-679, 143 Wash. 2d 687, 24 P.3d 390, reversed and remanded.

Honig, D., 2010. Faculty–student sexual harassment case study. Bethune-Cookman University, Daytona Beach, FL, June 30; url: http://www.cookman.edu/documents/acad_docs/FinalHonigReportBCUCS063010.pdf.

Kruger, J., Dunning, D., 1999. Unskilled and unaware of it: how difficulties in recognizing one's own incompetence lead to inflated self-assessments. J. Pers. Soc. Psychol. 77 (6), 121–134.

Mayers, R., Mawer, W., Price, M., Denny, J., 2010. Family education rights and privacy act: who has an educational need to know? Mustang Journal of Law & Legal Studies 1, 19–26.

Nadelson, S., 2007. Academic misconduct by university students: faculty perceptions and responses. Plagiary: Cross-Disciplinary Studies in Plagiarism, Fabrication, and Falsification 2, 67–76.

National Academy of Sciences, 2002. Integrity in Scientific Research: Creating an Environment That Promotes Responsible Conduct. National Research Council of the National Academies Committee on Assessing Integrity in Research Environments, National Academies Press, Washington, DC, url: www.nap.edu/catalog/10430.html.

Rimer, S., 2003. Love on campus: trying to set rules for the emotions. New York Times, October 1.

Rosenberg, M., 2011. Principled autonomy and plagiarism. Journal of Academic Ethics 9, 61–69.

Schwartz, H., 2011. From the classroom to the coffee shop: graduate students and professors effectively navigate interpersonal boundaries. International Journal of Teaching and Learning in Higher Education 23 (3), 363–372.

Shearer, L., 2008. UGA prof fired, lied about molestation conviction. Athens Banner-Herald, October 23.

Sloan, K., 2012. Nova Law wins round with professor fired over gun fears. The National Law Journal, June 26.

Starratt, R.J., 2004. Ethical Leadership. Jossey-Bass, San Francisco, CA.

University of Colorado, 2012. Nonreappointment, termination, suspension, dismissal and resignation. Regents of the University of Colorado, University of Colorado website, url: https://www.cu.edu/content/nonreappointment-termination-suspension-dismissal-and-resignation.

Wood, J., Hilton, A., 2012. Five ethical paradigms for community college leaders: toward constructing and considering alternative courses of action in ethical decision making. Community College Review 40 (3), 196–214.

CHAPTER 4

Criminology Research: Theory Testing and Publishing

Michael McGrath

Key Terms

Bias Prejudice in favor of, or against, something. Generally used to suggest an unfair advantage or disadvantage.

Circular reasoning Using data to prove something that was used to develop the hypothesis; a proof that essential restates the question.

Falsification Refers to subjecting a theory to repeated attacks in order to disprove it – testing it against the case facts or alternative theories.

Logical fallacies Errors in reasoning that essentially deceived those whom they are intended to convince. They are brought about by the acceptance of faulty premises, bias, ignorance, and intellectual laziness.

Overgeneralization Making general statements to a broad population based on insufficient data.

Peer review The process of subjecting an author's work, research, or ideas to the scrutiny of others who are experts in the same field.

Reliability A test is reliable if it consistently yields the same result within whatever margin or error we are willing to accept.

Scientific method A way to investigative how or why something works, or how something happened, through the development of hypotheses and subsequent attempts at falsification through testing and other accepted means.

Validity In reference to testing, when the results are reliable and accurate.

Adherence to ethical guidelines is important in conducting research and scholarly publishing as the end-user relies on the integrity of such products in conducting further research, using the research in forming professional opinions, and possibly relying on the research when testifying under oath in a court of law. Ethical guidelines for research and publishing are numerous and the purpose of this chapter is not to give a definitive list of such guidelines. Readers can refer to an organization such as the Committee On Publication Ethics (http://publicationethics.org/resources/guidelines) for detailed information in this area. Likewise, the National Institutes of Health list research ethical guidelines (available at http://www.niehs.nih.gov/research/resources/bioethics/whatis/) for those conducting research. Subjects that trend through any discussion of ethics in research and scholarly publication include objectivity, honesty, and openness.

Ethical Justice. http://dx.doi.org/10.1016/B978-0-12-404597-2.00004-8

THE SCIENTIFIC METHOD

The scientific method is a way of ensuring the results one obtains when researching something are both valid and reliable. Quite simply, it is a method of devising a theory regarding something, collecting data relevant to the theory, and a way to systematically test the theory to see if it is "correct." The method of testing is called falsification (Popper, 2002). It may seem odd, but one is not trying to prove one's theory is true, but rather trying to prove it is false. The method allows for the fact that a researcher can be wrong, yet think they are right. It allows for discarding a theory when a better one comes along to explain things. For example, when astronomers made observations of the movement of heavenly bodies, they developed theories to explain this. At first the theory/belief was that the Sun orbited around the Earth. When scientists questioned this as new observations were made, it was necessary to eventually discard this theory in favor of a theory that better fit the observed facts and allowed for prediction of events, such as eclipses. Sir Isaac Newton invented a branch of mathematics (calculus) to research the motion of bodies. His theories worked quite well until the subatomic realm was discovered where so-called Newtonian physics no longer was up to the task and Quantum Mechanics was developed. Scientists are still hard at work trying to reconcile the two. Whoever does will be sure to win a Nobel Prize or two.

But what is science? There are several similar definitions given in *Webster's Dictionary* (Webster's, 1996, p. 1716). The first describes science as a branch of knowledge or study that deals with a body of facts or truths that is systematically arranged and showing the operation of general laws. Mathematics or physics would be an example of this. The second definition is that science is systematic knowledge of the physical or material world acquired through observation and experimentation. Here is introduced the idea that we can learn from studying phenomena and performing experiments to validate theories we develop from our observations, although the term *theory* is not mentioned. An additional definition is that science is systematized knowledge in general or knowledge gained by systematized study. This allows for the possibility of calling something a science that is essentially a descriptive listing. Surprisingly, *Webster's Dictionary* gives as synonyms for science: art, technique, method, discipline. While these terms could describe parts of a science, on their own they do not equal science.

In the behavioral sciences we are at a disadvantage because what we try to measure may be very difficult to quantify and subject to observer bias that is difficult to defend against. Bias can creep in at the conceptual stage, at the data collection stage, and at the interpretation stage. While bias, as well as other study flaws, is potentially present in any scientific endeavor, the behavioral and social sciences appear to be at greater risk.

RELIABILITY AND VALIDITY

Two important research terms are *validity* and *reliability*. A test is reliable if it consistently yields the same result within whatever margin of error we are willing to accept. For example, we could label a scale reliable if we have a rock and every time we weigh the rock the scale shows the same weight, say 4.5 pounds. To find out if the scale (or rather the weights it gives) is valid, though, we would check the weight of the rock on a scale that we know to be accurate. If such testing gave the same weight, we would decide the weights the first scale gives are valid. However, if the known (accurate) scale gives a weight of 4.2 pounds we would not consider the first scale as giving valid weights, unless we were willing to accept a difference of 0.3 pounds error. The takeaway message is that no matter how reliable something is scientifically, if it does not possess validity, it is worthless. This, for example, is a major problem with the FBI *Organized–Disorganized* paradigm used in criminal profiling. FBI-style criminal profiles (now called *Criminal Investigative Analysis*) rely on observations that led to theories (e.g., that a disorganized crime scene tells us this and an organized crime scene tells us that) that have never been shown to have any validity. However, that has not stopped publication related to the paradigm. Although further study was identified as a need in the original Organized–Disorganized study, it appears none was ever undertaken by the original researchers. A 2004 study by Canter *et al.* has been very helpful in showing the lack of validity of the model (Canter *et al.*, 2004). The *Battered Woman Syndrome* and *Rape Trauma Syndrome* suffer from similar problems with reliability and validity (McGrath, 2008).

PEER REVIEW

The concept of peer review is that research submitted for publication should be critiqued and that research not meeting acceptable standards should be kept from publication. Some think that peer review only occurs prior to publication, when in fact that is only the beginning. Peer review continues upon publication when a broader audience of professionals has the ability to read, digest, and assess the information presented in a journal article or text. Peer review can be in the form of letters to the editor, rebuttal articles, and other avenues.

Peer review can even be review by one's friends and known colleagues; often an effective venue of constructive or destructive criticism, assuming bias is curtailed. Most peer review is, however, by (for want of a better word) strangers. Some researchers take reasonable questions regarding methodology and tools as a personal affront, frustrating the openness necessary for peer review and possible attempts at replication of findings, etc. To ignore the legitimate questions of others is inappropriate and thwarts the scientific method.

Responsibilities of Authors

According to King (2001), "Important ethical concerns to consider while writing a manuscript include etiquette, fraudulent publication, plagiarism, duplicate publication, authorship, and potential for conflict of interest."

Authors of academic works have responsibilities. It is important that their audience can rely on what they have written and that it accurately portrays their research, which they should strive to make reliable and valid. There are many examples of publishers' descriptions of these responsibilities. One list, from Elsevier, can be found at: http://www.academypublisher.com/ethics.html. While these lists are generally found in relation to journal articles, they apply to all scholarly publications. Below are some relevant issues taken from the Elsevier website:

Duties of Authors
Reporting standards
Authors of reports of original research should present an accurate account of the work performed as well as an objective discussion of its significance. Underlying data should be represented accurately in the paper. A paper should contain sufficient detail and references to permit others to replicate the work. ....

Data access and retention
Authors may be asked to provide the raw data in connection with a paper for editorial review, and should be prepared to provide public access to such data (consistent with the [Association of Learned and Professional Society Publishers (ALPSP)/International Association of Scientific, Technical & Medical Publishers (STM)] Statement on Data and Databases), if practicable, and should in any event be prepared to retain such data for a reasonable time after publication.

Originality and plagiarism
The authors should ensure that they have written entirely original works, and if the authors have used the work and/or words of others, that this has been appropriately cited or quoted. Plagiarism takes many forms, from 'passing off' another's paper as the author's own paper, to copying or paraphrasing substantial parts of another's paper (without attribution), to claiming results from research conducted by others. ....

Multiple, redundant or concurrent publication
An author should not in general publish manuscripts describing essentially the same research in more than one journal or primary publication. ....

Acknowledgement of sources
Proper acknowledgment of the work of others must always be given. ....

Authorship of the paper
Authorship should be limited to those who have made a significant contribution to the conception, design, execution, or interpretation of the reported study. All those who have made significant contributions should be listed as co-authors. Where there are others who have participated in certain substantive aspects of the research project, they should be acknowledged or listed as contributors. ....

LOGICAL FALLACIES

It is incumbent on researchers and authors to recognize and avoid logical fallacies. Such fallacies are numerous and beyond the scope of this chapter to mention, let alone describe them all.

- *Circular reasoning.* Using data to prove something that was used to develop the hypothesis; a proof that essentially restates the question. An example would be: "There is no such thing as a false confession, because innocent people do not confess to crimes they did not commit."
- *Overgeneralization.* Making generalizations to a broad population based on insufficient data.

CASE EXAMPLES

Lack of Validity/Overgeneralization
In the early years of criminal profiling FBI special agents honing the craft began observing what they felt were collections of things at crime scenes. They formulated the idea that there were essentially two types of crime scene (hence offenders) – an organized crime scene and a disorganized crime scene. An organized crime scene might be one where the offender planned the assault and brought a weapon which he/she took with him/her when leaving the scene. The disorganized crime scene would be one where the offender acted impulsively and used something he/she found at the scene as a weapon to commit an assault of some kind. It was further speculated that if a profiler could determine which type of crime scene was present, he/she could determine characteristics of the offender that might aide an investigation. Armed with this hypothesis, in the early to mid-1980s the agents of the FBI criminal profiling unit began visiting prisons when possible to try and interview serial killers using a questionnaire that had been developed.

The profilers joined forces with some academics to try and to test the organized-disorganized paradigm empirically. They applied for and received a National Institute of Justice (NIJ) grant that funded the study from 1982 to 1985 (Burgess and Ressler, 1985). The population studied consisted of

36 sexual murderers who were willing to speak to FBI agents. The 36 were responsible for 118 crimes studied. This was a convenience sample, with no reason to believe it was representative of sexual murderers, serial murderers, or even murderers in general. Also, there was no control group of any kind. There is no way of knowing whether the study population was truthful throughout their interviews. The design of the study was poor. Study population data was missing from most items assessed. For example, subjects did not answer[1] anywhere from 7% to 22% or more of the questions for many items For illustration, note the following in relation to some items related to "Actions during the offense:"

Actions during the offense	Organized/disorganized
Planned v. sudden	86% (81) v. 44% (8)
Violence to achieve sex	28% (68) v. 86% (7)
Restraints	49% (97) v. 10% (21)
Weapon left at scene	19% (67) v. 69% (16)
Sex acts committed	76% (85) v. 46% (13)
Sadistic acts committed	32% (97) v. 43% (21)
Masochistic acts	15% (97) v. 0% (21)

The numbers in parentheses are the *n* for the organized and disorganized groups. However, these do not add up to 118, the number of crimes studied. The reason is that data is missing, as noted. How significant is this? Take "Planned v. sudden," where 25% of the study subjects are not accounted for (118 − (81 + 8)). For "Weapon left at scene," (118 − (67 + 16)) data on 30% of the study population is not available. The study is rife with this kind of problem. Adding to the problems, of the 36 study subjects, 22 were identified as organized, nine as disorganized, and five as a "mixed" type. These five mixed types (14% of the sample) were then "forced" into either the organized or disorganized group, resulting in 24 organized offenders (97 victims) and 12 disorganized offenders (21 victims). No explanation was given of how this "forcing" was accomplished. The study is often referred to as the "FBI serial killer" study, but in fact only 29 of those interviewed had killed more than one person. Among the 29, there is no breakdown of the number of murders each committed, as to a range or a median.

The study, though, confidently states (Burgess and Ressler, 1985, p. 29): "Based on data available at the crime scene, there are significant differences between the organized and disorganized offenders." Then it is taken back: "However,

---

[1]Missing data was due to: incomplete records; conflicting responses; offender unwillingness to respond to questions.

it should be noted that there are *no* [emphasis in original] situations where the organized and disorganized offenders are mutually exclusive. That is, both types of murderers are capable of all types of behavior." Peer review conducted by the NIJ was very negative. Reviewing the Ted Bundy case, Nobile (1989) stated: "the Justice Department rejected the study for government publication after outside reviewers flayed its statistics and methodology." The study was then published as: *Sexual Homicide: Patterns and Motives* (Ressler *et al.*, 1988). Although the actual study itself (Burgess and Ressler, 1985) had notable disclaimers, these were nowhere to be found in *Sexual Homicide: Patterns and Motives*. Although (Burgess and Ressler, 1985, p. 24) the NIJ grant is mentioned, the significant problems identified during peer review are ignored. For example, in the study (Burgess and Ressler, 1985): p. 24, "Our study was an exploratory one."; p. 32, "It is imperative that this be viewed as demonstrating only that profiling is an objective possibility.," "The study does *not* [emphasis in original] establish that profiling can, in fact, be done, or that if it were done, it would be successful." and "Instead, we show that further study of profiling is, indeed, reasonable and appropriate." What we have are very important disclaimers that never made it past the original study. The study required further study that never occurred, yet the paradigm has never been truly abandoned and for years its product has been offered to law enforcement and even in court. The qualitative findings of the study were presented in a special issue of the *FBI Law Enforcement Bulletin (LEB)* published in August 1985 (Burgess *et al.*, 1985). Aside from the disclaimer that the study was exploratory, no investigator in the reading audience would have understood the limited and flawed basis for the organized–disorganized paradigm presented.

Authorship/Simultaneous Publication

When the second edition of the *Crime Classification Manual* (CCM2) (Douglas *et al.*, 2006) was published this author was surprised to find changes in authorship of two chapters that had been in the first edition. Further, it was discovered that the two chapters in question had been published previously without attribution at the time of the first edition of the *Crime Classification Manual* (CCM) (Burgess *et al.*, 1992). Essentially, the facts are that:

(1) In *CCM2* Ms Corinne Munn is no longer listed as co-author with John Douglas for the chapter "Modus operandi and the signature aspects of violent crime," as she was in the first edition.
(2) Ms Lauren Douglas is now listed as co-author of that chapter with John Douglas. There is no explanation offered for the change. Any changes to the chapter are minimal; in fact, the vast majority of the chapter is word-for-word the same as the original, with no new cases or illustrating material.

(3) A second chapter in *CCM2* is titled "The detection of staging, undoing, and personation at the crime scene," again listing John Douglas and Ms Lauren Douglas as co-authors. This chapter is analogous to "The detection of staging and personation at the crime scene" authored by John Douglas and Ms Munn in the original *CCM*. Other than insertion of a few brief extra case examples and a two-paragraph section (Courtroom Implications) near the end of the chapter, one would be hard pressed to describe the chapter as meaningfully revised. Knowing that the vast majority of the chapter had been written by others (John Douglas and Corrine Munn), at best Ms Douglas would deserve a contributor status.

(4) There is no explanation offered as to why Ms Munn no longer appears as an co-author to "The detection of staging and personation at the crime scene" in *CCM2*.

The issue raised here is attribution of authorship, as Ms Munn is no longer listed as a co-author and a new co-author has appeared with either no significant change to a chapter from the previous version or changes that would more appropriately warrant a contributor status.

In the original *CCM* the two chapters in question do not indicate any prior publication. There is no attribution in either *CCM* or *CCM2* to a prior published work. Yet, the two chapters were published in *LEB* in February 1992 as: "Violent crime scene analysis: modus operandi, signature, and staging" (Douglas and Munn, 1992). It is not clear whether technically it was published first in *LEB* or *CCM*. In either case, though, one should have mentioned publication in the other.

In reviewing the *LEB* article (Douglas and Munn, 1992) it was noted that the two chapters in *CCM* noted above contained heavy borrowing from the paper (at times verbatim, at other times with minimal changes such as tense or insertion or deletion of a word or words) without attribution. The bibliographies at the end of *CCM* and *CCM2* were reviewed, but there is no listing of the *LEB* article. If one relies to any significant extent on a work and it was not directly cited in the text, at a minimum it should at least be listed in the bibliography.

Some examples will be listed to illustrate the content of the article and chapters in question. The February 1992 *LEB* article by Douglas and Munn ("Violent crime scene analysis: modus operandi, signature, and staging") will be referred to as VCSA. The two chapters by Douglas and Munn published in 1992 in the *CCM* will be referred to as MO ("Modus operandi and the signature aspects of violent crime") and DSUP ("The detection of staging, undoing, and personation at the crime scene").

The *LEB* article VSCA can be divided into two parts. From the beginning of the article to the end of the subsection titled IMPORTANCE OF OFFENDER

SIGNATURE (pp. 1–6) would be part one and this part was incorporated into MO in CCM, while the remaining part of VSCA (pp. 6–10) was incorporated into DSUP.

Example A
LEB-VSCA (p. 2):

> The victim's response also significantly influences the evolution of the M.O. If a rapist has problems controlling a victim, he will modify the M.O. to accommodate resistance. He may use duct tape, other ligatures, or a weapon on the victim. Or, he may blitz the victim and immediately incapacitate her. If such measures are ineffective, he may resort to greater violence or he may kill the victim. Thus, offenders continually reshape their M.O. to meet the demands of the crime.

CCM-MO (p. 260):

> The victim's response can significantly influence the evolution of an MO. If the rapist has problems controlling a victim, he will modify the MO to accommodate resistance. He may bring duct tape or other ligatures, he may use a weapon on the victim, or he may blitz-attack the victim and immediately incapacitate her. If such measures are ineffective, he may resort to greater violence or kill the victim. Thus, the MO will evolve to meet the demands of the crime.

CCM2-MO (p. 21):

> In violent crimes, victims' responses can significantly influence the evolution of an offender's MO. If a rapist has problems controlling a victim, he will modify his MO to accommodate and overcome resistance. He may bring duct tape or other ligatures, he may use a weapon, or he may blitz-attack the victim and immediately incapacitate her. If such measures are ineffective, he may resort to greater violence, including killing the victim.

Example B
LEB-VSCA (p. 3):

> For example, a rapist demonstrates his signature by engaging in acts of domination, manipulation, or control during the verbal, physical, or sexual phase of the assault. The use of exceptionally vulgar or abusive language, or preparing a script for the victim to repeat, represents a verbal signature. When the rapist prepares a script for a victim, he dictates a particular verbal response from her, such as "Tell me how much you enjoy sex with me," or "Tell me how good I am."

CCM-MO (p. 261):

> A rapist demonstrates his signature by engaging in acts of domination, manipulation, or control during the verbal, physical, and/or sexual phase of the assault. Exceptionally vulgar and/or abusive language or scripting represents a verbal signature. When the offender scripts a victim, he dictates a particular verbal response from her (e.g., "Tell me how much you enjoy sex with me," or "Tell me how good I am").

CCM2-MO (p. 21):

> For example, a rapist may demonstrate part of his signature by engaging in acts of domination, manipulation, or control during the verbal, physical, or sexual phase of the assault. Exceptionally vulgar or abusive language or scripting is a verbal signature. When the offender scripts a victim, he demands a particular verbal response from her (for example, "Tell me how much you enjoy sex with me," or "Tell me how good I am").

Example C
LEB-VSCA (p. 6):

> In 1984, Vasquez pled guilty to the murder of a 34-year-old Arlington, Virginia, woman. The woman had been sexually assaulted and died of ligature strangulation. The killer left her lying face down with her hands tied behind her back. He used unique knots and excessive binding with the ligatures, and a lead came from the wrists to the neck over the left shoulder. The body was openly displayed so that discovery offered significant shock value.

CCM-MO (p. 267):

> In 1984 Vasquez pled guilty to the murder of a thirty-two-year-old Arlington, Virginia, woman. The woman had been sexually assaulted and died of ligature strangulation. The killer left her lying face down with her hands tied behind her back. He had used unique knots and excessive binding with the ligatures, and a lead came from the wrists to the neck over the left shoulder. The body was openly displayed so that discovery would offer significant shock value.

CCM2-MO (p. 29):

> In 1984 David Vasquez pleaded guilty to the murder of a thirty-two-year old Arlington, Virginia, woman. The woman had been sexually assaulted and died of ligature strangulation. The killer left her lying

face down with her hands tied behind her back. He had used unique knots and excessive binding with the ligatures, and a lead came from the wrists to the neck over the left shoulder. The body was openly displayed so that discovery offered significant shock value.

Example D

LEB-VSCA (p. 6):

The offender spent considerable time at the crime scene. He made extensive preparations to bind the victim, allowing him to control her easily. His needs dictated that he move her around the house, exerting total domination over her. It appeared that he even took her into the bathroom and made her brush her teeth. None of this behavior was necessary to perpetrate the crime; the offender felt compelled to act out this ritual.

CCM-MO (p. 267):

The offender had spent an excessive amount of time at the crime scene. He had made extensive preparations to bind the victim, allowing him to control her easily. His needs dictated that he move her around the house, exerting total domination over her. It appeared he had even taken her into the bathroom and made her brush her teeth. None of this behavior was necessary to perpetrate the crime; the offender had felt compelled to act out this ritual.

CCM2-MO (p. 29):

The offender had spent an excessive amount of time at the crime scene. He had made extensive preparations to bind the victim, allowing him to control her easily. His needs dictated that he move her around the house, exerting total domination of her. It appeared he had even taken her into the bathroom and had made her brush her teeth. None of this behavior was necessary to perpetrate the crime; the offender felt compelled to act out this ritual.

Many more examples of borrowing from *LEB*-VSCA can be found in *CCM*-MO and *CCM2*-MO.

Example E

LEB-VSCA (p. 7):

Principally, staging takes place for two reasons--to direct the investigation away from the most logical suspect or to protect the victim or victim's family. It is the offender who attempts to redirect the investigation. This offender does not just happen to come upon a victim, but is someone who almost always has some kind of association or relationship with the victim. This person, when in contact with law enforcement, will attempt to steer the investigation away from himself, usually by being overly cooperative or extremely distraught. Therefore, investigators should never eliminate a suspect who displays such distinctive behavior.

CCM-DSUP (pp. 251–252):

There are two reasons someone employs staging: to redirect the investigation away from the most logical suspect or to protect the victim or victim's family. When a crime is staged, the responsible person is not someone who just happens upon the victim. It is almost always someone who had some kind of association or relationship with the victim. This offender will further attempt to steer the investigation away from him by his conduct when in contact with law enforcement. Thus, investigators should never eliminate a suspect solely on the grounds of that person's overly cooperative or distraught behavior.

CCM2-DSUP (pp. 34–35):

There are two reasons that someone employs staging: to redirect the investigation away from the most logical suspect or to protect the victim or victim's family. When a crime is staged, the responsible person is not someone who just happens upon the victim. It is usually someone who had some kind of association or relationship with the victim. This offender will further attempt to steer the investigation away from him by his conduct when in contact with law enforcement. Thus, investigators should never eliminate a suspect solely on the grounds of that person's overly cooperative or distraught behavior.

Example F

LEB-VSCA (p. 7):

Finally, at some crime scenes, investigators must discern if the scene is truly disorganized or if the offender staged it to appear careless and haphazard. This determination not only helps to direct the analysis to the underlying motive but also helps to shape the offender profile. However, recognition of staging, especially with a shrewd offender, can be difficult. Investigators must examine all factors of the crime if they suspect it has been staged. This is when forensics, victimology, and minute crime scene details become critical to determine if staging occurred.

CCM-DSUP (p. 252):

> Finally, the investigator should discern whether a crime scene is truly disorganized or whether the offender staged it to appear careless and haphazard. This determination not only helps to direct the analysis to the underlying motive, but also helps to shape the offender profile. However, the recognition of staging, especially with a shrewd offender, can be difficult. The investigator must scrutinize all factors of the crime if there is reason to believe it has been staged. Forensics, victimology, and minute crime scene details become critical to the detection of staging.

CCM2-DSUP (pp. 36–37):

> Finally, the investigator should discern whether a crime scene is truly disorganized or whether the offender staged it to appear careless and haphazard. This determination not only helps to direct the analysis to the underlying motive, but also helps to shape the offender profile. However, the recognition of staging, especially with a shrewd offender, can be difficult. The investigator must scrutinize all factors of the crime if there is reason to believe it has been staged. Forensics, victimology, and minute crime scene details become critical to the detection of staging.

Example G

LEB-VSCA (p. 9):

> Sexual and domestic homicides usually demonstrate forensic findings of a close-range, personal assault. The victim, not money or property, is the primary focus of the offender. However, this type of offender will often attempt to stage a sexual or domestic homicide that appears to be motivated by personal gain. This does not imply that personal assaults never happen while a property crime is being committed, but usually these offenders prefer quick, clean kills that reduce the time spent at the scene.

CCM-DSUP (pp. 254–255):

> Sexual and domestic homicides will demonstrate forensic findings of this type: a close-range, personal assault. The victim (not money or goods) is the *primary* [emphasis in original] focus of the offender. This type of offender will often attempt to stage a sexual or domestic homicide to appear motivated by criminal enterprise. This does not imply that personal-type assaults never happen during the commission of a property crime, but usually the criminal enterprise offender prefers a quick, clean kill that reduces his time at the scene.

CCM2-DSUP (p. 39):

> Sexual and domestic homicides demonstrate forensic findings of this type: a close-range, personalized assault. The victim (not money or goods) is the primary focus of the offender. This type of offender often attempts to stage a sexual or domestic homicide to appear motivated by criminal enterprise. This does not imply that personal-type assaults never happen during the commission of a property crime, but usually the criminal enterprise offender prefers a quick, clean kill that reduces time at the scene.

Example H

LEB-VSCA (p. 9):

> Forensic red flags are also raised when there are discrepancies between witness/survivor accounts and forensics results. For example, in one case, an estranged wife found her husband in the tub with the water running. Initially, it appeared as if he slipped and struck his head on a bathroom fixture, which resulted in his death by drowning. However, toxicological reports from the autopsy showed a high level of valium in the victim's blood. Also, the autopsy revealed several concentrated areas of injury or impact points on the head, as if the victim struck his head more than once. Subsequently, investigators learned that the wife had been with the victim on the evening of his death. She later confessed that she laced his dinner salad with valium, and when he passed out, she let three men into the house. These men had been hired by the wife to kill the victim and to make it look like an accident.

CCM-DSUP (p. 255):

> Other discrepancies may arise when the account of a witness/survivor conflicts with forensic findings. In one case, an estranged wife found her husband, a professional golfer, dead in the bathroom tub with the water running. Initially, it appeared as if the golfer slipped in the tub, struck his head on a bathroom fixture, and drowned. However, the autopsy began to raise suspicion. Toxicology reports revealed a high level of Valium in the victim's bloodstream at the time of death. The autopsy also revealed several concentrated areas of injury or impact points on the head, as if the victim struck his head more than once. Later, investigators learned the wife had been with him the night of his death. The wife later confessed that she had made dinner for her husband and had laced his salad with Valium. After her husband passed out, she let three

men she had hired into the house to kill him and make the death look accidental.

CCM2-DSUP (p. 39):

> Other discrepancies may arise when the account of a witness or survivor conflicts with forensic findings. In one case, an estranged wife found her husband, a professional golfer, dead in the bathroom tub with the water running. Initially it appeared as if the golfer had slipped in the tub, struck his head on the bathroom fixture, and drowned. However, the autopsy began to raise suspicion. Toxicology reports revealed a high level of Valium in the victim's bloodstream at the time of death. The autopsy also revealed several concentrated areas of injury or impact points on the head, as if the victim struck his head more than once. Later, investigators learned the wife had been with him the night of his death. The wife later confessed that she had made dinner for her husband and had laced his salad with Valium. After her husband passed out, she let three men she hired into the house to kill him and make the death look accidental.

Many more examples of borrowing from VSCA can be found in DSUP.

Summary of Concerns

(1) Significant portions of two chapters in the original *CCM* were taken from a *LEB* article published before, after, or simultaneously with the *CCM*, without attribution to either publication. Both the article and the two chapters in the *CCM* were co-authored by John Douglas and Corrine Munn.
(2) The two chapters in question were authored by John Douglas and Corrine Munn in the first edition of *CCM*, but Ms Munn has been removed as co-author and replaced by Ms Lauren Douglas in the *CCM2*.
(3) The two chapters are not significantly revised from the *CCM* to the *CCM2*, except that one chapter has some additional material that might qualify for contributor status if written by the new co-author.
(4) There is no explanation in *CCM2* as to why Corrine Munn was removed as co-author of the two chapters.

Efforts were made to bring these issues to the attention of John Douglas, as well as other editors of the *CCM2* in February of 2009. Dr Ann Burgess was kind enough to reply, but was unable to shed light on the issues. Dr Douglas would be expected to be familiar with academic publishing issues as he holds a doctorate in education. An email was forwarded in 2009 to the Wiley (publisher of *CCM* and *CCM2*) Ethics Department (see http://www.wiley.com/bw/publicationethics) with no response to date.

SUMMARY

Maintaining expected standards in research and academic publishing is important to further and protect scientific endeavors. Adherence to ethical guidelines is important in conducting research and scholarly publishing as the end-user relies on the integrity of such products in conducting further research, using the research in forming professional opinions, and possibly relying on the research when testifying under oath and in a court of law.

Questions

1. What is the cornerstone of the *scientific method*? Explain.
2. Explain the difference between *reliability and validity.*
3. Define *logical fallacies.* Provide two examples.
4. *Peer review* must occur prior to publication. True or False?
5. List three duties of authors/researchers.

References

Burgess, A., Ressler, R., 1985. Final Report: Sexual Homicide Crime Scenes and Patterns of Criminal Behavior, NIJ Grant 82-IJ-CX-0065. National Institute of Justice, Rockville, MD, abstract, url: https://www.ncjrs.gov/App/Publications/abstract.aspx?ID=98230.

Burgess, A., Ressler, R., Douglas, J.E., D'Agostino, R.B., 1985. Crime scene and profile characteristics of organized and disorganized murderers. FBI Law Enforcement Bulletin 54 (8), 18–25.

Burgess, A.N., Burgess, A.W., Douglas, J., Ressler, R. (Eds.), 1992. Crime Classification Manual, Lexington Books, New York.

Douglas, J.E., Munn, C., 1992. Violent crime scene analysis: modus operandi, signature, and staging. FBI Law Enforcement Bulletin 61 (2), 1–10.

Douglas, J.E., Burgess, A.W., Burgess, A.G., Ressler, R.K. (Eds.), 2006. Crime Classification Manual, second ed. Jossey-Bass, San Francisco, CA.

Canter, D., Alison, L.J., Alison, E., Wentink, N., 2004. The organized/disorganized typology of serial murder: myth or model? Psychology, Public Policy and Law 10, 293–320.

King, C.R., 2001. Ethical issues in writing and publishing. Oncology Nursing Society, url: http://www.ons.org/Publications/CJON/AuthorInfo/WritingSupp/Ethics, last accessed 12 October 2012.

McGrath, M., 2008. Psychological aspects of victimology. In: Petherick, W., Turvey, B. (Eds.), Forensic Victimology, Elsevier, San Diego, CA, pp. 229–264.

Nobile, P., 1989. The making of a monster. Playboy, July.

Popper, K., 2002. The Logic of Scientific Discovery. Routledge, New York.

Ressler, R.K., Burgess, A.W., Douglas, J.E., 1988. Sexual Homicide: Patterns and Motives. Lexington Books, New York.

Webster's, 2001. Webster's Encyclopedic Unabridged Dictionary of the English Language. Thunder Bay Press, Berkeley, CA.

CHAPTER 5

Ethical Issues in Police Administration

Stan Crowder and Brent E. Turvey

Key Terms

Administrative investigations Fact-finding inquiries conducted by an agency or government regarding its own management and performance, generally in relation to internal violations of policy and procedure.

Enforcement-oriented policing An approach to policing where there is a clear separation between members of an agency or department and the citizens they police.

Garrity Rule Refers to the US Supreme Court's decision in *Garrity v. New Jersey* (1967). It provides that during an administrative investigation, a police officer or other public employee may be compelled to provide statements under threat of discipline or discharge, but those statements may not be used to prosecute him/her criminally.

Intelligence-oriented policing An approach to policing that is driven by gathering intelligence and analyzing it for crime patterns and trends.

Law enforcement The branch of the criminal justice system that is legally commissioned to respond to crime (Sullivan, 1997; Kappeler, 2006; Turvey and Petherick, 2010).

Leadership A set of traits and abilities that compel others to follow.

Peacekeeper-oriented policing An approach to policing where officers are often integrated with the community they serve, viewing themselves as an important part of it.

Police administration The control and operation of law enforcement agencies, and the subsequent discharge of policies that keep the peace, increase public safety, and prevent crime.

Police administration refers to the control and operation of law enforcement agencies, and the subsequent discharge of policies that keep the peace, increase public safety, and prevent crime. From a command perspective, police administration involves setting agency policy and making operational decisions that best achieve the aforementioned goals without violating the law or the public trust. From a human resources perspective, police administration involves making ethical and lawful decisions related to the hiring, management, retention, discipline, and termination of law enforcement personnel. All of this requires accountability, both internal and external.

This chapter examines the primary ethical issues relevant to law enforcement command, human resources, and related mechanisms for accountability in turn. It closes with a discussion of issues related to transparency.

THE ROLE OF LAW ENFORCEMENT

Before we discuss the major ethical issues that exist relative to law enforcement administration, it is first necessary to explain what law enforcement is. *Law*

103

Ethical Justice. http://dx.doi.org/10.1016/B978-0-12-404597-2.00005-X

enforcement is the branch of the criminal justice system that is legally commissioned to respond to crime (Sullivan, 1977; Kappeler, 2006; Turvey and Petherick, 2010). It is composed of various municipal, state, and federal agencies that are required, by law, to develop strategies and deploy personnel within an established jurisdiction that (Bopp and Schultz, 1972):

- Facilitate the prevention of crime.
- Respond to criminal complaints.
- Investigate unsolved crime.
- Arrest suspected criminals.
- Recover stolen property.

Specific obligations and duties vary, as a function of individual agency policy as well as local statute (see, generally, Bopp and Schultz, 1972; Hansen and Culley, 1973; Kleinig, 1996; Kappeler, 2006; Vaughn *et al.*, 2001).

Law enforcement agents are generally responsible for keeping the peace, protecting the citizenry, and representing justice (Kleinig, 1996; Kappeler, 2006; Wolfe and Piquero, 2011). These virtues, and related principles, are often a feature of the sworn oaths or pledges that officers must take when receiving their police credentials. They generally relate to maintaining professional integrity, protecting citizens and property, faithfully enforcing the laws of their state, and upholding the US Constitution (Bopp and Schultz, 1972; Kleinig, 1996; Shane, 2010; International Association of Chiefs of Police, 2011; Stout, 2011). Specific values, missions, or creeds can be found on the backside of an officer's credentials, on the side of an officer's patrol car, or on their department's website.

MODELS OF POLICING

There are several approaches to policing, each of which reflects differing agency values and understandings of crime. These include those that are *enforcement* oriented, *peacekeeping* oriented, and *intelligence* oriented. Many agencies will be a mix of these models, depending on who is leading (or failing to lead) at any given moment in time. The values discussed bear directly on the professional ethics that each model purports to uphold.

Enforcement-Oriented Policing

In metropolitan areas, it is not uncommon for law enforcement officers in big agencies to view themselves as *enforcers* – either as a function of their training or culture. In this *enforcement approach* to policing, there is a clear separation between members of an agency or department and the citizens they police, almost like an occupying force. Generally, the relationship is authoritarian; officers sit in their patrol cars and wait for crime to occur; policing is largely reactionary, concerned with responding to 911 calls; citations and arrests are the first tool in the kit; and the consequences for legal violations are dispensed without compassion. This model also involves zero trust of the citizenry, if not an open "Us *v.* Them" mentality. This is particularly common in areas where there are a high number of complaints against the police; officers tend to seek out their own company to avoid the conflicts that arise from having to defend endless or highly publicized instances of police misconduct (Kleinig, 1996; discussed shortly). As a result, those working for law enforcement tend to have no other contact with the community while in uniform and therefore no other impressions or relationships develop. This enforcement model can intensify public animosity among those citizens that have contact with the justice system, because the focus is on the letter of the law and not necessarily the immediate needs of citizens or the community (i.e., justice).

Peacekeeper-Oriented Policing

In more rural areas with smaller agencies, it is not uncommon for those in law enforcement to view themselves more as *peace officers*. In the *peacekeeper approach* to policing, akin to so-called community-oriented models, officers are often found to be integrated with the community they serve, viewing themselves as an important part of it. They do not seek to occupy and control their jurisdiction as much as they seek to maintain a sense of order and fairness. In doing so, they mingle freely with citizens, get to know them, try to identify potential problems before 911 needs to be called, and respond to specific complaints with a high degree of accountability.

Generally, the peacekeeper relationship is more liberal: police encourage citizens to work out their differences amicably, except in more extreme cases; they rely on citizens to provide them with tips and information regarding serious crime; and the enforcement of the law is more compassionate. Notable exceptions include domestic violence, drug-related offenses, and felony matters.[1] For this to work, community trust between law enforcement and citizens is crucial. Ideally, this enforcement model can result in better communication, less animosity, and greater cooperation with respect to those being policed, as the focus is on justice as opposed to simply following the narrow rule of law.

Intelligence-Oriented Policing

In agencies with more educated officers and better technology at their disposal, it is possible to engage in policing that is driven by gathering intelligence and analyzing it for crime patterns and trends. Used by the enforcement-oriented

---

[1]These are discussed in Chapter 6: "Ethical Issues for Police Officers and Criminal Investigators," under the section "Police Discretion and Selective Enforcement."

and peacekeepers alike, this involves an emphasis on trying to understand the causes of crime, on sharing that information, on developing prevention strategies, and on reducing the amount of crime that is occurring. This approach to policing is credited, largely, to the efforts of former commissioner William Bratton of the New York City Police Department, in response to problems that he identified during the mid-1990s (Weisburd *et al.*, 2004, p. 2):

> At the outset, Bratton and his administration's analysis of the NYPD's problems revealed several deficiencies that have long been identified as forms of bureaucratic dysfunction (Merton 1940). First, the organization lacked a sense of the importance of its fundamental crime control mission. Second, because the NYPD was not setting high enough expectations about what its officers could do and accomplish, a lot less was getting done than was possible. Third, too many police managers had become moribund and were content to continue doing things the way they had always been done rather than exploring new theories and studies for promising strategies to reduce crime and improve the quality of life in neighborhoods. Fourth, the department was beset with archaic, unproductive organizational structures that did more to promote red tape and turf battles than to facilitate teamwork to use scarce resources effectively. As a result, operational commanders were "handcuffed" by headquarters and lacked authority to customize crime control to their precincts' individual needs. Finally, the department was "flying blind." It lacked timely, accurate information about crime and public safety problems as they were emerging; had little capacity to identify crime patterns; and had difficulty tracking how its own resources were being used. Since middle managers were not in the habit of monitoring these processes, they served as a weak link in the chain of internal accountability between top brass and street-level, police employees.
>
> Bratton used a "textbook" approach to deal with these problems, following the major prescriptions offered by organizational development experts to accomplish organizational change (Beer 1980). He brought in outsiders to obtain a candid diagnosis of the organization's strengths and weaknesses. He incorporated both top-down and bottom-up processes to implement change (Silverman 1996). He sought and obtained early indicators of the success of the change efforts and sought ways to reinforce the individual efforts of his precinct commanders and the rank-and-file by using both incentives and disincentives (Bratton 1996).

Generally, this model of policing is more transparent and informed. It also results in more professional and tactical policing efforts that have a greater impact on responding to, and reducing, specific crime trends (Maples, 1999).

Additionally, those in charge are able to quantify their work and progress to civilian bosses and the public. This in turn can engender trust and respect, which is vital to effective long term policing efforts. Conversely, this approach makes it painfully clear when those in command are failing at their duties.

COMMAND

From a command perspective, police administration involves setting agency policy and making operational decisions that best achieve the goals of police administration without violating the law or the public trust. This includes knowing the law, adopting lawful and ethical departmental policies, enforcing those policies, and setting a clear professional example for subordinates to follow. In short, it requires ethical and professional leadership from an ethical and professional leader.

Leadership

Leadership, which is distinct from management or supervision, describes a set of traits and abilities that compel others to follow. Leaders set an example that will be emulated by others, as described in Wyatt-Nichol and Franks (2009, p. 41): "Leadership by example is important because subordinates pay attention to the actions of leaders and model their own behavior accordingly." In law enforcement, good leadership requires:

- Good and trustworthy character.
- Explicit knowledge of the law.
- Explicit knowledge of agency functions and operations.
- The ability to set effective agency policy.
- The ability to create effective budgets and build consensus.
- The ability to inspire pride and loyalty among subordinates.
- The ability to accurately assess the strengths and weaknesses of subordinates and situations.
- The personal strength to harness the abilities of others in such a fashion as to guide an agency towards success in its endeavors.
- The ability to survive and succeed despite constant political divisiveness.

It must be made clear that not everyone is capable of learning to become an effective leader. Moreover, being placed in command by promotion or circumstance does not automatically provide one with the qualities or abilities necessary to lead effectively. Consequently, those who find themselves in a leadership role while also lacking the qualities above are also likely to find themselves in professional jeopardy – in one form or another. Additionally, it is not uncommon for exceptional leaders to be undone by failings of varying intensity that are exposed and exploited by political adversaries. Examples will be provided throughout this section.

Professional Integrity

Command officers have a responsibility to develop a culture that nurtures those values which reflect professional and ethical integrity. This is because the majority of police employees learn their professional ethics from co-workers and supervisors, as explained in Fitch (2011, pp. 20–21):

> Most officers enter law enforcement with minimal experience in the field or in handling the moral dilemmas that officers typically encounter. They learn how to perform their jobs, as well as recognize the organizational norms, values, and culture, from their peers and supervisors. While supervisors provide direct, formal reinforcement, officers' peers offer friendship and informal rewards that, in many cases, hold greater influence than official recognition from the agency. Also, police often spend considerable time socializing with other officers, both on and off the job. This sense of community drives officers to adopt the behaviors, values, and attitudes of the group in order to gain acceptance.
>
> Because behavior results from consequences, law enforcement officers learn about acceptable and unacceptable practices through a consistent, timely, and meaningful system of reward and punishment. Officers likely will repeat behaviors that lead to reinforcing outcomes, while they rarely will duplicate behaviors that lead to punishment ....

As a consequence of this reality, and in comportment with *Social Learning Theory*, a local law enforcement community is ultimately a function of the values and ethics modeled, re-enforced, and mandated by those in command.[2] If those in command seek to hire, retain, or defend those of low character, this sets the bar low for everyone within their agency. Moreover, it has been shown that ethical dilution predisposed towards loyalty over integrity can cause those in any group to shift their moral principles in order to adapt and survive within it (Leidner and Castano, 2012). Only through higher recruitment standards, careful applicant screening, consistent operational standards and discipline, and realistic ethics training is a culture of integrity preserved (Wyatt-Nichol and Franks, 2009).

It cannot be disputed that those in positions of command have an unmitigated obligation to provide clear ethical guidance and mandates for those under their supervision. Failing to do so, they may even incur civil liability, as explained in Wyatt-Nichol and Franks (2009, p. 40):

---

[2]*Social Learning Theory* holds that "peer associations, attitudes, reinforcement, and modeling are predictors of delinquency and crime in general," because these things are shaped by culture and environment (Chappell and Piquero, 2004, p. 89); see also Wolfe and Piquero (2011).

Ethics training is essential for law enforcement personnel due to the nature of the position and the potential for liability. As public servants, law enforcement officers are held to a higher standard – when officers behave unethically, it is a violation of the public trust and damages the image of law enforcement everywhere. Numerous civil lawsuits have been filed against police agencies as the result of unethical conduct (Trautman 2000). The U.S. Supreme Court ruled in *City of Canton, Ohio v. Harris*, 489 U.S. 378 (1989), that cities can be held liable when it is demonstrated that failure to provide training is a factor that resulted in the violation of a citizen's constitutional rights. Many professionals and organizations in the law enforcement community hold that ethics training bridges the gap between written policies and actual behavior by introducing or reinforcing rules and expectations of behavior. Ethics instruction exposes officers to ethical dilemmas and scenarios through training prior to "hitting the streets" or moving up in rank.

Unfortunately, this obligation is often ignored by command culture. Those working in law enforcement become aware of this reality from the moment they apply to the agency until the day they resign or retire. They can observe that recruiting officers routinely cozy up to the most attractive female cadets and may even begin "dating" them; training officers with the most seniority procure for themselves the most physically desirable probationary officers; supervisory officers often "date" multiple subordinates as they matriculate through their chain of command, having their pick of applicants and personnel – sometimes in exchange for choice assignments or promotions; and command officers routinely select the most attractive female assistants or drivers.

Worse, command officers are often appointed based on political considerations, with little thought given to actual qualifications. Those in law enforcement can attest that it is not uncommon for a supervisor to lack any knowledge or experience of the job being done by those under their supervision. Such circumstances can lead to further *nepotism* by appointment, which breeds a cultural of favoritism and incompetence from the top down.[3] When a department is this badly led and managed, it can takes years, even generations, to fix – and only under the leadership of one that is willing to be hated by the existing command structure for doing so.

To summarize, it is understood that new hires will generally have had little exposure to the ethical dilemmas faced in law enforcement; it is understood that culture and environment shape beliefs, attitudes, and values; and it is understood that those in command influence culture and environment greatly. Therefore,

---

[3]*Nepotism* is the practice of giving jobs, or showing favor, towards friends and relatives.

the professional ethics and overall integrity of a law enforcement community must be built from the top down. This requires serious and informed efforts to instruct employees regarding the ethical dilemmas that they will be confronted with, and clear agency policies with respect to handling them that are consistently enforced. It also requires zero tolerance for nepotism.

CASE EXAMPLE

Former Chief Ralph L. Godbee, Detroit Police Department

According to published reports (Lewis, 2012), then Detroit Police Chief Ralph Godbee, also a minister, was estranged from his wife for about a year and filing for divorce when a sex scandal broke. Chief Godbee had been dating a married subordinate, Officer Angelica Robinson, from the Internal Affairs Division (IAD). This affair had been going on since 2008, according to Officer Robinson's attorney.

In the last week of September 2012, Officer Robinson had learned that Chief Godbee was attending a law enforcement conference in San Diego with another woman. Officer Robinson became emotionally distraught and began posting the details of her inappropriate relationship with Chief Godbee on her Twitter account. This ultimately included a photo with the barrel of her departmental issue handgun, a 9-mm Glock, in her mouth (Figures 5.1 and 5.2) (Lacey, 2012).

Officer Robinson was quickly relieved of her firearm and submitted for a mental health evaluation; subsequently, her gun was returned, and she returned to duty; however, she was reassigned from IAD.

As result of these and related revelations, Chief Godbee was suspended by Detroit Mayor Dave Bing for 30 days, pending an internal investigation. Mayor Bing's office made it clear that the Human Resources Department would investigate all of the administrative allegations against the Chief thoroughly. However, upon being suspended, Chief Godbee immediately resigned. This is a common tactic for those in law enforcement under investigation, as it effectively ends all administrative investigations by the police department.[4] As reported in Burns (2012):

> "Once the chief has resigned and retired, there is no further need for us to investigate," said Bob Warfield, a spokesman for Bing. "He is no longer a member of the Detroit Police Department."

However, not all of the investigations into former Chief Godbee were ended by his resignation, as so often is the case in other municipalities. Instead, the matter was handed over to the Office of the Chief Investigator – the investigative arm of the Detroit Police Commission, comprised of citizens and former members of law enforcement – which is separate from the Detroit Police Department (Burns, 2012). As of this writing, administrative and criminal charges are being considered.

It bears mentioning that former Chief Godbee took over the Detroit Police Department from former Chief Warren Evans. Former Chief Evans was fired by Mayor Dave Bing in 2010 for misconduct, including an inappropriate relationship with now Lieutenant Monique Patterson (White, 2012). Lieutenant Patterson has a history violent outbursts and problems with self-control, resulting in departmental discipline on at least four different occasions (Lewis, 2010). She was retained despite this record and despite her other inappropriate sexual relationship – with the newly appointed Chief Godbee, as reported in Hunter and Ferretti (2012):

> The alleged affair [between Godbee and Robinson] is the latest sex scandal to embroil the department in two years. Godbee's predecessor, Warren Evans, stepped down in 2010 after reports surfaced he had a relationship with Lt. Monique Patterson. Then, when Godbee was named interim chief, text messages surfaced showing he also had an affair with Patterson, who currently is in charge of the Police Department's Sex Crimes Unit.
>
> Mark Zausmer, an attorney who formerly represented Evans, said it was shocking when Godbee was appointed chief.
>
> Zausmer at the time provided former Deputy Mayor Saul Green with a string of sexually-charged text messages that documented the exchange between Godbee and Patterson.
>
> "Somebody could have read those text messages and concluded that Mr. Godbee was

using his office in an inappropriate way; and Warren, on the other hand, was pressured to resign when he didn't use his office in an inappropriate way," he said.

Zausmer said Evans made the administration aware of his relationship with Patterson and was given permission to continue the relationship. Later, he was forced to resign.

"Warren did nothing wrong and was forced out. Godbee did everything wrong and was promoted. It made no sense then and it makes no sense now," he said.

Godbee's departure adds insult to injury as officers are already dealing with a pay cut, new 12-hour shift configuration and "skyrocketing" crime rate, Detroit Police Officers Association President Joe Duncan said

"The scandal alone would be horrible in the best of times; irrespective of where we are today," Duncan said Monday. "Morale is at the lowest ever."

It should also be noted that Lieutenant Patterson has given media interviews in which she fully acknowledges that she had a sexual relationship with former Chief Godbee, with the expectation being that she would receive a promotion. As reported in LeDuff (2012), based on his interview with Lieutenant Patterson:

I got a call from Lieutenant Monique Patterson, the cop caught in the love triangle between former chief Warren Evans and Ralph Godbee two years ago. She said she had some text messages showing that she had sex with Godbee in exchange for a promotion.

One text message from Godbee to Patterson said, "I want you, I think you, I breathe you, I taste you, I smell you, need I go on?"

Another text message from Godbee to Patterson read, "I need a face to face so you can see that I say what I say because I'm in LOVE WITH YOU!"

Yet another text message from Godbee to Patterson said, "I can meet you by 8'ish. Can you have everything set up where you can just let me know the room #?"

A text message from Patterson to Godbee read, "I hate that all we have discussed (transfer, etc.) nothing has occurred. Nothing seems hopeful to me at this point. Nothing."

Then a text message from Godbee to Patterson said, "You will learn over time that my word is my bond!" This is clearly more than sex between consenting adults. It's an abuse of power. The police department has been turned into a brothel ....

"Are you a tramp?" I asked.

"People can call me whatever. It's fine, you know. If my behavior two years ago earned me that title then, then okay. That was in 2009. It's a new day. I have a new life, and the department needs a new chief."

As of this writing, Lieutenant Patterson remains the Commander of the Detroit Police Department Domestic Violence Unit.

The specifics of related cases, involving one of the largest law enforcement agencies in the United States, are still unfolding. However, they serve as an important reality check regarding the dangers and ethical pitfalls of engaging in sexual relationships with subordinates; of trading sex for promotions; of retaining personnel with serious character deficiencies; and of the ultimate consequences with respect to cost, culture, and department morale.

---

[4]It also serves to protect the officer's pension, which is more often the primary motivation.

Politics

The authors have observed that, on average, the majority of police chiefs serve between 3 and 5 years. If their tenure does not end with scandal (e.g., a hasty resignation or an outright termination), it ends with them finding better pay at a larger department. Sometimes, almost inexplicably, it ends with both. Generally, bad outcomes for a chief are predictably related to one of three things,

FIGURE 5.1
After learning that Chief Ralph Godbee was attending a law enforcement conference with another woman, Officer Angelica Robinson disclosed the details of her affair with him on Twitter and then posted a photo of herself with her service revolver in her mouth.

FIGURE 5.2
Chief Ralph Godbee.

often occurring all at once: political discord, abuse of power offenses (e.g., misappropriation of funds, resources, and personnel), and sexual misconduct.

A *chief of police* is usually an "at will" or "exempt" employee, meaning they do not have a traditional employment contract and can be fired at any time, for any reason (and conversely they can leave at any time, for any reason). This is inherently problematic because they are most often hired by politicians that are seeking to serve interests and agendas generally unrelated to police administration. *Chief of police* is therefore a political position, subordinate to the mercurial needs of those that have the power to both hinder and terminate them.

A chief also has the authority to make other "at will" appointments in their chain of command. If they appoint command staff based on friendships, loyalties, and favors owed, then this spells disaster for the department from the top down, as previously mentioned. If they appoint based on ability, then they risk making serious enemies within their own department – enemies that invariably know their weaknesses and secrets.

Creating such enemies is a constant problem for any chief of police. This is because there are always those in the political realm seeking to identify and confederate with the current chief's in-house enemies, in order to help orchestrate the chief's demise. Such political operatives are any of those that disagree with the current chief's personal choices, policies, or politics, or who simply want the job for themselves.

Under such adverse employment conditions, the extent to which a chief of police or command officer is scrutinized and held accountable is generally a function of their ability to maneuver favorably within complex or hostile political environments. If they make friends in high places, they can often get away with a lot. If they make enemies, there will be investigations and allegations. This is enough to get them suspended and then terminated given the generally tenuous conditions of their employment. Consequently, the best course for avoiding this kind of ethical conflict is to take command positions only when qualified, and subordinate only to those who are themselves professional and ethical – or to avoid command positions entirely, as many in law enforcement choose to.

HUMAN RESOURCES

At the human resources level, law enforcement agencies are responsible for hiring and retaining only those employees that have demonstrated a commitment to the agency's moral and ethical agenda. Failing to do so essentially prevents the development or sustenance of an ethical culture. Law enforcement is therefore best served by the employment of only the highest quality applicants (Vollmer, 1971; Brennan *et al.*, 2009). This requires that they "strive to recruit,

CASE EXAMPLE

Former Chief Steve MacKinnon, Santa Paula Police Department, California

According to published reports, Steve MacKinnon was hired as the Chief of Police in Santa Paula, California in 2005. As part of his employment package, the letter from the city offering him the job stated: "A City vehicle will be provided for your personal use as well as use in the performance of your duties" (Cohn, 2012). He took the job over from Bob Gonzalez, who retired and became Mayor of Santa Paula – and one of MacKinnon's civilian bosses.

In January of 2012, City Manager Jaime Fontes hired a private investigator to look into irregularities with Chief MacKinnon's use of his City vehicle, at a cost of around $15 000 (Scheibe, 2012). Apparently, there were concerns over trips that the Chief had taken to Arizona between 4 April 2010 and 28 December 2011, and related charges to the City for fuel. Subsequent to this investigation, the Chief was placed on leave by the City Manager in April of 2012 (Cohn, 2012). This led to heated City Council meeting in, as reported in Cohn (2012):

> The vast majority of speakers Monday night addressed how the city has blossomed on MacKinnon's watch. The crime rate has fallen, civic engagement has grown and business has flourished, MacKinnon supporters attested. The investigation is a waste of taxpayers' money and could have been handled internally, many of the speakers said.
>
> "I'm greatly concerned about the response of both the City Council and city manager. You were obviously caught unaware about a concern or question about the use of a car by the chief," said Mary Ann Krause, former mayor of Santa Paula, who was also interviewed by the investigator about the chief's car use. "That's understandable, but over the couple of years the city manager has been here, he has had the opportunity to meet the department heads and he should have done personnel reviews during that time to be familiar with the terms of his chief department heads' terms of employment."
>
> Mayor Bob Gonzalez, who retired as police chief in 2005, attempted to cut off Krause by saying he had mistakenly allowed the previous speakers five minutes to address the Council and it would now be shortened to three minutes.

> The crowd booed Gonzales, and Krause continued to say that any attempt to show the community that MacKinnon has not been doing his job is not going to be accepted by the community because "They know he is pulling shifts during the night in order to avoid paying overtime …. They respect the work he is doing very much and are very glad that someone is finally getting the work done in Santa Paula."
>
> "I've never seen a leader as energetic, as creative, as hard working as Chief MacKinnon," said Betsy Blanchard Chess. "The real Santa Paula is better than this. Please stop what appears to be a tawdry little witch hunt, and reinstate the chief."
>
> Two speakers during the hour-long public comment period supported the city manager's decision to place MacKinnon on leave. Andrew Castaneda said there is likely more to the investigation than the public is aware of and encouraged the Council not to give in to the "mob mentality" of MacKinnon supporters.
>
> Resident Larry Sagely, speaking for what he called "the silent majority," complimented the city manager on doing his job and said, "I know you all (Council members) have had to deal with problems created by former city managers, former City Council and mayor. I know that many of you, in the whole time you've been here, have had to straighten out that mess."
>
> Sagely added that perhaps Fontes is in the line of fire because he is Latino. "Could there be a degree of racism going on here?" he asked. The crowd jeered, and Sagely exited City Hall.

Chief MacKinnon was fired by the City Manager the very next month, as reported in Scheibe (2012):

> In his June 6 letter to MacKinnon, Fontes said MacKinnon had driven about 19,000 miles in two city vehicles for 23 trips to Arizona.
>
> He also said one of the vehicles broke down during a return trip from Arizona in December 2011 and that MacKinnon sought

CASE EXAMPLE *CONTINUED*

and got the city to reimburse him for about $300 in repair costs to the vehicle.

Fontes acknowledged in the letter that a job offer letter sent to MacKinnon in 2005 granted the chief of police personal use of a city vehicle.

However, Fontes said "it is evident to me that 'personal use' was not meant to include frequent, unauthorized, out-of-state trips taken for purely personal reasons." Fontes said MacKinnon claimed former Santa Paula City Manager Wally Bobkiewicz, who hired MacKinnon, had OK'd the extended personal use of the vehicle.

Fontes wrote that "even assuming that is true, you never advised me that you were using the city vehicle for these purposes …. Instead, you mistakenly assumed that I knew of, and authorized, your frequent personal trips to Arizona in a city vehicle," he wrote. "Placing 19,000 miles on a city vehicle for personal reasons constitutes waste of city property and using city resources for personal convenience," Fontes wrote. "I find your conduct to be inconsistent with city rules and incompatible with my management beliefs, and directions and policy. "Your conduct reflect(s) poorly upon the city." ….

Fontes said the city estimates that MacKinnon logged 112.5 hours of lost work time, which he said totaled $11,561.53. He said MacKinnon told him he consistently worked more than 40 hours a week and applied those extra hours to the time he took off. By doing so, he said MacKinnon was using a "flextime" practice to take time off without "formally recording or applying leave time." Fontes said

that as an "exempt" employee, MacKinnon was not entitled to practice flextime, under city rules. He added that MacKinnon had "exhibited a pattern of conduct and misjudgment that is incompatible with city management's purposes and policies." ….

However, MacKinnon's lawyer Ron Bamieh said the actions against MacKinnon were an indication that Santa Paula "continues to be a rudderless ship, which apparently cannot tolerate professionalism and success." He said MacKinnon was Santa Paula's most successful chief of police in recent history, "and unfortunately for some it exposed the poor job performance of the former heads of that agency." ….

Bamieh said in this week's release that an investigation has been launched on behalf of MacKinnon that centers on "suspected financial malfeasance" by some city staff members, City Council members and the former chief of police, Robert Gonzales, who now is the city's mayor.

An investigation into the allegations made against former Chief MacKinnon by city officials, conducted by the Ventura County District Attorney's Office, failed to uncover sufficient evidence to press any criminal charges (Harris, 2012).

This case demonstrates the extreme consequences of political tensions and rivalries when they exist between those in city government and the Office of the Chief of Police. Those in city government have both the resources and the authority to find, and in some cases even create, grounds for termination. The Chief, being an "at will" employee, can be evaluated and terminated based on almost any criteria, regardless of any successes at duties related to police administration. Consequently, they investigate those in government at their own peril and risk exposing themselves to scrutiny that is generally unwelcome when they do.

hire, and train only those who demonstrate strong moral values before they enter the academy" (Fitch, 2011, p. 1) in order to "create a culture of ethics within their agency" (p. 4).

Unfortunately, the hiring and retention practices of many law enforcement agencies suggest that there is an internal tolerance for varying levels of overt criminality in the culture.[5] That is to say, being convicted of a crime does not always result in prohibition from law enforcement employment. Nor is termination automatic when an officer is arrested, convicted of crime, or is proved to have given false testimony (Spector, 2008).

First, it is important to acknowledge that many police agencies openly acknowledge the fact that they hire recruits with criminal records; however, most claim to avoid hiring those with felony convictions.

Consider the State of Georgia. Approximately one-third of police recruits in the city of Atlanta have criminal records and more than half have admitted to drug use. As reported in Eberly (2008):

> More than one-third of recent Atlanta Police Academy graduates have been arrested or cited for a crime, according to a review of their job applications. The arrests ranged from minor offenses such as shoplifting to violent charges including assault. More than one-third of the officers had been rejected by other law enforcement agencies, and more than half of the recruits admitted using marijuana.

A further investigation of State records revealed 1384 Officers with arrests and convictions for serious offenses that also remained certified to practice law enforcement with the Georgia Peace Officer Standards and Training Council (POST); many were still on active duty with police agencies (Moore, 2008). Law enforcement spokespersons in Atlanta cited shrinking budgets and fierce competition with other police agencies for the need to relax hiring standards, but also rationalized that it was common for many law enforcement agencies to hire applicants with misdemeanor convictions (Eberly, 2008).

Consider also the City of Milwaukee, Wisconsin. Currently, the City of Milwaukee Police Department allows the hiring of candidates with up to four misdemeanor convictions and two drunken driving offenses (Wooten, 2007). However, in responding to a Freedom of Information Act (FOIA) request, the city refused to release the exact number of officers with criminal convictions, saying that such an effort would be too burdensome (Wooten, 2007). Despite a promise to make this data publicly available, the Milwaukee Fire and Police Commission has yet to do so (Barton, 2011).

Second, many police agencies find ways to retain officers convicted of violent crimes, as opposed to firing them outright.

Consider the fallout since *United States v. Hayes* (2009). This litigation arose from Federal legislation enacted in 1996: Possession of Firearm After Conviction of Misdemeanor Crime of Domestic Violence, 18 USC §922(g)(9).

---

[5]Portions of this section have been adapted from Turvey (2012).

> As of September 30, 1996, it is illegal to possess a firearm after conviction of a misdemeanor crime of domestic violence. This prohibition applies to persons convicted of such misdemeanors at any time, even if the conviction occurred prior to the new law's effective date. A qualifying misdemeanor domestic violence crime must have as an element the use or attempted use of physical force or the threatened use of a deadly weapon.

Since 1999, some law enforcement employed defendants have attempted to get around the consequences of Federal legislation by pleading "down to a plain simple assault not *called* domestic violence" (Rider, 2010). They have done so when charged with offenses that might cause them to lose their right to carry a firearm and subsequently any job that requires the ability to do so as a condition of employment. A simple assault, for example, is a criminal charge without the predicate "domestic" descriptor.

Additionally, a percentage of law enforcement officers, and other government employees, faced the possibility of retroactively losing their guns and jobs in the resulting fallout from the 1996 legislation. These were individuals that had been convicted of violent offenses against their intimate partners, but not subsequently terminated by their law enforcement employers (May, 2005). Immediate reaction to this legislation by those in the law enforcement community included claims that it was unfair, as reported in Rodriquez (1997):

> A new federal law that makes it illegal for anyone convicted of domestic violence to carry a gun is threatening the jobs of dozens of police officers around the country.
>   Officers in Texas, Colorado, California, Minnesota and Michigan have been re-assigned or put on administrative leave as a result of their past arrests. The numbers are growing, and those affected are claiming the law is unfair and even unconstitutional.

Others in law enforcement have expressed gratitude that the existence of convicted domestic violence offenders among the ranks of law enforcement has been made an issue by the new legislation, considering such violations a firing offense (Davidow and Teichroeb, 2003).

In any case, *Hayes*, a ruling by the US Supreme Court, closes any perceptual loophole: it holds that a domestic relationship need not be a consideration in the specific criminal conviction; only the actual relationship between the victim and the offender matters. If anyone is convicted of any crime that involves violence against a domestic partner, whether it is a misdemeanor or a felony, they are banned from carrying a firearm by Federal law. If one's profession requires carrying a firearm, then one must find other employment if so convicted.

Consider the actions of the New Haven Police Department in the recent case of Police Officer Sam Streater, as reported in Kaempffer (2009). In this case out of Connecticut, Officer Streater was arrested and convicted of soliciting a known prostitute, Vanessa DiVerniero, by paying her $20 to have sex with him in his car while off duty. He was caught by a police sting operation being run in the neighborhood and made false statements to his fellow officers about his activities during the investigation. Although he was suspended without pay for 2 weeks, he was not terminated. The New Haven Police Department made it clear that this is typical of how they handle such offenses, even when they involve law enforcement personnel (Kaempffer, 2009).

Consider the Los Angeles County Sheriff's Office, which employed a more creative solution when sworn personnel engaged in criminal activity: they were sent to work in the Los Angeles County Jail. As explained in Leonard and Faturechi (2011): "For years, the department transferred problem deputies to the system's lockups as a way of keeping them from the public. Other deputies were allowed to remain working in the jails after being convicted of crimes or found guilty of serious misconduct." This included deputies with convictions related to fraud, loan sharking, death threats, assault, beating inmates, smuggling contraband into the jail, and falsified reports (Leonard and Faturechi, 2011).

Consider the circumstances surrounding the eventual downfall of former East St Louis police chief Michael Baxton, which came to a head in early 2012. As reported in Pistor (2012):

> Michael Baxton Sr abruptly resigned Wednesday and pleaded guilty Thursday in federal court of two felonies after being snared in an FBI sting. He was caught stealing four expensive Xbox 360 game systems in an undercover investigation of corruption in the neighboring community of Alorton, where he was police chief until late last year ....
>
> Baxton, 49, has served in the past on the Centreville, Washington Park and Brooklyn departments, and was once chief in Brooklyn. He was hired as East St. Louis chief in 2007, beginning a rocky period marked by criticism of his hiring of officers with criminal records and handling of homicide investigations. He resigned in February 2009 and worked as a private investigator.
>
> In May, 2011, he was hired to be Alorton police chief to replace Robert L. Cummings, who pleaded guilty of federal tax crimes. Baxton lost that job in October 2011, when the Illinois Law Enforcement Training and Standards Board revoked his police license over felony theft and burglary convictions in Madison County in 1982. Baxton sued and the following month a St. Clair County judge reinstated his credentials after finding that the criminal record had been expunged in 1989.
>
> On Nov. 30, he was rehired in East St. Louis.

Despite his criminal convictions and history of hiring convicted criminals to serve as law enforcement officers, former Chief Baxton still enjoys the strong support of local politicians, judges, and the East St Louis Police Department (Pistor, 2012).

Consider also the case of Chicago Police Officer Thomas P. Nash. As reported in Novak and Fusco (2012):

> In January 2002, in a case that somehow remained out of the public eye, a Cook County grand jury indicted him for theft and perjury – 31 counts in all – for collecting disability pay from the city's police pension fund while also getting a paycheck from the sheriff's office. Nash – the son of a crooked cop who'd gone to federal prison – pleaded guilty to a single misdemeanor count of theft to avoid prison.

The then Police Superintendent Philip Cline moved to fire Nash 8 years ago. But the Chicago Police Board said no, instead suspending Nash for 10 months, then returning him to the city payroll.

Officer Nash currently does desk duty, taking non-emergency reports for the Chicago Police Department, while earning more than $86 000 a year.

Finally, consider the high-profile case of Ross Mirkarimi, the Sheriff of San Francisco. He was convicted of a domestic violence offense involving his wife, a Venezuelan actress; however, he did not resign from office and even announced plans to run for re-election (Elias, 2012). In a case that is still unfolding, the civilian Mayor of San Francisco was forced to suspended Sheriff Mirkarimi while administrative charges are being pursued in order to facilitate his termination.

A tradition of hiring and retaining those with a criminal background, and failing to terminate members convicted of a crime subsequent to hiring, suggests some tolerance for criminality within the culture of law enforcement. This practice, often a violation of policy and the law, undermines the overall credibility of law enforcement agencies and the reputations of all those they employ. Some law enforcement agencies agree, as reported in Barton (2011):

> An officer who has been convicted of a crime can be rendered useless as a prosecution witness – especially if dishonesty is involved, said Kenosha County Assistant District Attorney Richard Ginkowski, who once worked as a police officer in Iowa. The defense can use that information to cast doubt on the cop's testimony.
>
> "If an officer is caught lying, that dilutes their credibility in other cases and makes them less effective as an officer," he said. "That's a significant concern."
>
> That's one reason departments in many other states, including Illinois, preclude people convicted of certain misdemeanors – generally involving deception, drugs and abusive behavior – from carrying a badge and a gun.
>
> "It's just overwhelming how people in communities really do believe law enforcement officers have to be held to this standard," said Kevin

McClain, executive director of the Illinois Law Enforcement Training and Standards Board. "People feel that police officers should be models in society."

Not only are people convicted of those types of crimes barred from being hired as Illinois officers – working officers who are convicted of those crimes are automatically decertified under state law, which means they immediately lose their jobs and can't be rehired, McClain said. Any officer who fails to notify the state of a conviction – either during the application process or after hiring – can be charged with a felony.

It bears acknowledging that there is also hypocrisy in the practice of policing the citizenry with convicted criminals. First, it violates the ideal of personal integrity that is held up as a necessary hiring mandate within the law enforcement literature. Second, it betrays the public trust. Finally, it contributes to the decay of agency culture and ethics, as it sends the message to all subordinates that breaking the law is no big deal.

ACCOUNTABILITY

Law enforcement employees must tell the truth and uphold the law. Therefore, professional law enforcement agencies adhere strictly to the principle of accountability. They also promote the notion that every supervisor is responsible for the ethical conduct of their subordinates. Supervisors, no matter high up the chain they have climbed, have a duty to set an example that is competent and ethical, and to enact policies aimed at preventing, identifying, and punishing both incompetence and misconduct. In furtherance, they must assert the appropriate safeguards and sanction those responsible for wrong-doing. Without this kind of oversight, professional integrity dissolves and is replaced by the inevitability of corruption. Corruption is a foreseeable outcome within law enforcement; if unchecked by the actions and examples of supervisors, then they are complicit in any resulting scandal (Mollen, 1994; Cancino and Enriquez, 2004; Turvey, 2012)[6].

Unprofessional law enforcement groups prize agency loyalty over individual honesty and integrity. They may even make "loyalty" a part of the agency creed. Loyalty can be a misplaced value, as it breeds hostility, and alienation, between the police and any community they intend to serve (Mollen, 1994; Cancino and Enriquez, 2004). It also encourages corruption, given that the price of

---

[6]As will be discussed in Chapter 6: "Ethical Issues for Police Officers and Criminal Investigators," law enforcement officers that are allowed to act as though they are above the law can develop an entitled personality. This starts with speeding when they do not need to, running red lights just because they can, and accepting gratuities from the public despite departmental policies against them. Without accountability and consequence, such personalities and attitudes are all but guaranteed, and can lead down a path to much more serious forms of corruption.

agency loyalty under corrupt or inept supervision must be the surrender of individual honesty and, by extension, professional integrity.

Accountability in law enforcement starts with the judicious use of administrative investigations, with a full awareness of *Garrity*.

Administrative Investigations and *Garrity*

Administrative investigations are fact-finding inquiries conducted by an agency or government regarding its own management and performance. Such investigations are authorized as a routine matter, as the result of suspected infractions of policies, complaints to the agency, or by the general concerns of a person in authority. They involve an investigation into an event or circumstance, and are in many cases a required safeguard in the normal course of ethical police work. Examples include:

- Employee background.
- Employee character and fitness.
- Promotions and pay raises.
- Employee or departmental performance reviews.
- Employee or departmental audits.
- Employee safety.
- Officer-involved shootings.
- Violations of agency policies, rules, or protocols.
- Professional misconduct.
- Harassment or discrimination (e.g., sexual harassment or racial bias).
- Property misuse/damage/theft.
- Threatening, intimidating, or violent behavior.
- Potential criminal activity involving agency personnel or resources (e.g., theft or drug use).

These circumstances and related violations are non-criminal for the most part, and may result in disciplinary actions such as suspension, demotion, financial sanctions, and even dismissal. However, the circumstances can also be procedural – in relation to promotions, pay raises, transfers, or in response to a particular yet general concern. In such cases, administrative investigations are a necessary step intended to help secure favorable outcomes.

If an administrative investigation confirms the likelihood or the existence of criminal activity, then a separate criminal investigation must be requested by the appropriate law enforcement agency. However, if this occurs within a law enforcement agency in the United States, a controversial protection is engaged, referred to as the *Garrity Rule*. ⟶ Exam

The *Garrity Rule* refers to the US Supreme Court's decision in *Garrity v. New Jersey* (1967). It provides that during an administrative investigation, a police officer or other public employee may be compelled to provide statements under threat of discipline or discharge, but those statements may not be used to prosecute him or her criminally. As explained in Clymer (2001, pp. 1314–1321):

Police departments routinely conduct noncriminal, administrative investigations into allegations of police misconduct to determine whether discipline is warranted. As part of those investigations, investigators often interview the suspect officer or officers along with witness officers. In cases in which alleged misconduct may result in criminal charges, suspect officers have a valid basis for asserting their Fifth Amendment privilege and refusing to answer questions on the ground that their statements may incriminate them. To promote thorough investigations, and perhaps to avoid the unseemly spectacle of officers refusing to cooperate with their own departments, regulations, state statutes, and departmental policies often require that police officers, whether suspects or witnesses, answer questions that investigators pose. Refusal to do so can result in discipline, including job loss.

In a series of cases decided from 1967 to 1977, the Supreme Court confronted states' use of economic sanctions – job termination, loss of pension benefits or political office, disbarment from legal practice, and ineligibility for state contracts – to compel cooperation in criminal and noncriminal investigations. In all but one of these "so-called 'penalty' cases," public employees and officials, contractors, and others refused to waive immunity or answer questions and later contested the resulting economic sanctions. *Garrity v. New Jersey* arrived in the Supreme Court in a different posture. In *Garrity*, the employees, most of whom were police officers, answered the questions, thus avoiding the threatened economic sanctions, and challenged the state's subsequent use of their answers in criminal prosecutions. *Garrity*, unlike the other penalty cases, presented the question whether compelled statements were admissible in criminal prosecutions.

Edward Garrity, the Chief of Police for the New Jersey Borough of Bellmawr, other police officers, and a court clerk were suspected of fixing traffic tickets. The Supreme Court of New Jersey ordered the state Attorney General to conduct an investigation into the alleged misconduct and report his findings. A deputy attorney general questioned the suspects. A state statute required that they answer questions or lose their jobs and pensions. Before conducting the interrogation, the deputy attorney general told each interviewee that his answers could be used in state criminal proceedings and that "if he refused to answer he would be subject to removal from office." The interviewees answered the questions posed to them. Later, local prosecutors brought criminal charges and introduced into evidence at trial the statements that the defendants had made to the deputy attorney general. After their convictions, the defendants appealed, claiming that the use of their compelled statements violated their constitutional rights. New Jersey courts rejected those claims. But, in a five-to-four decision, the United States Supreme Court reversed, holding the admission of the compelled statements unconstitutional. The Court offered two explanations: The statements were inadmissible under the Due Process Clause as coerced confessions, and the state's threat to fire the police officers unless they gave statements was an unconstitutional condition.

In a later case, the Court offered a different rationale for the result in *Garrity*: The police officers' compelled statements were analogous to immunized testimony and thus inadmissible under the Fifth Amendment privilege. Many lower courts have followed suit, describing *Garrity* as a case involving the privilege and compelled statements as "immunized." ....

The *Garrity* protection ... enables states to compel statements from public employees by threatening job termination but bars use of the statements in later criminal prosecutions. Accordingly, when the deputy attorney general threatened *Garrity* and the others with loss of their jobs, he granted them de facto use immunity in exchange for their answers. Although *Garrity* and the others did not first assert the privilege, an action typically required to trigger its protection, the Court since has concluded that when assertion itself would be penalized, as was the case in *Garrity*, the protection is self-executing.

Opponents of the *Garrity Rule* argue that it essentially immunizes corrupt law enforcement officers by operating "as a trap for investigators and prosecutors who fail either to take steps to minimize exposure to compelled statements or to prepare to disprove taint." Further, the rule "can serve as a tool for unscrupulous internal affairs investigators who seek to undermine criminal prosecutions by disseminating compelled statements and treacherous police witnesses who allege that they are tainted in order to avoid giving prosecution testimony" (Clymer, 2001, p. 1382).

Professional law enforcement agencies conduct administrative investigations of their personnel with full appreciation of Garrity and bring in an outside agency to conduct a separate investigation should criminal offenses be suspected. In this way, separate investigations are conducted by separate investigators preventing administrative evidence from being used improperly. Law enforcement agencies that fail with respect to understanding the consequences of ignoring *Garrity* do so at their own peril. They can be sued by corrupt cops that have been improperly terminated, and in some instances may even be forced to give them their jobs back.

Internal Affairs

Law enforcement officers generally pride themselves as being "the good guys." They also pride themselves in working hard to get the "bad guys" off the street. This notion forms the core of law enforcement identity and provides foundational rationalizations for many of the values asserted within law enforcement culture (Harris, 2000).

In stark contrast to this identity, professional law enforcement agencies also maintain a division or unit that is tasked with the investigation of its own members for suspected crimes and misconduct. While the functions of such units are essentially the same, they may be referred to by different names, such as the *Internal Affairs Division (IAD)*, the *Internal Investigation Division (IID)*, or the *Office of Police Integrity (OPI)*. As discussed in Middleton-Hope (2003, p. 177):

> Generally, within a police service, the professional standards section (PSS), also known as internal affairs, is responsible for managing the intake of complaints regarding both the conduct of sworn officers and, more broadly, police service policy and procedures. Members of the PSS deal directly with complainants, assign matters for alternative dispute resolution, and investigate improper and criminal conduct of sworn officers. PSS members also draft documentation for formal disciplinary hearings and senior executive review. Their mandate is to provide for the resolution of complaints. ... the PSS investigates firearms discharges, serious injury, death, or attempted suicides that occur during in-custody detention, and complaints alleging racial discrimination ....

Whatever the designation, internal affairs is responsible for investigating any allegations made against members of the agency; for tracking the types of allegations that are made; and for identifying any patterns of misconduct associated with a particular employee, group, or command. Some agencies go so far as to release this information to the public via press release and the official agency website, to facilitate transparency and accountability. This cuts sharply against the image that most law enforcement officers would prefer the general public to perceive, as it both acknowledges and publicizes the reality of the criminal cop.

Consequently, law enforcement culture as a whole does not tend to view the efforts of IAD favorably, abhorring its very existence. This is also because of the politicized nature of such units, as explained in Cancino and Enriquez (2004, p. 333):

> ... administrative oversight is perhaps the most common way departments respond to the regulation of officers' behavior. However, police reformers have failed to understand that administrative oversight (e.g. internal affairs, standard operating procedures) is a

source of loose compliance and a powerful reinforcement regarding cultural norms of secrecy and solidarity (Perez, 1994). Crank (1998, p. 65) posits that police typically view department policies as "organizational bullshit." The administration is viewed by officers as an operational nuisance and ineffective when needed.

This is consistent with perceptions reported in Chemerinsky (2005, pp. 556–567):

> ... officers experience the LAPD's discipline system as an arbitrary, demeaning system of entrapments that burns whistleblowers, fails to stop the big abuses ... and yet assiduously prosecutes officers for "micro-infractions."
> ... The degree of rank and file alienation from the LAPD's system is compounded by the politicized control that command staff exert over Internal Affairs and the documented disparity between the lenient discipline applied to infractions by command staff and the relatively harsh punishment of rank and file for minor infractions.

The harsh punishments for minor infractions may stem from that fact that many IAD investigations are initiated internally, by fellow officers that are jealous or overly competitive. Add to this the fact that IAD investigators are evaluated just like any other detective – based on cases made during a given time period. If they put in the time to conduct an investigation, without a charge being made, they may feel that this reflects poorly on their ability and employment prospects. As a result, they may feel pressure to make a big case out of a minor violation when major allegations do not pan out.

Owing to such negative views, not every law enforcement agency has the equivalent of an IAD. They may simply designate officers to conduct such investigations as needed. This is not an acceptable practice, as it does not provide even the appearance of taking complaints of police misconduct seriously. Failure to designate an IAD, with a proper leader, command structure, authority, and cultural disposition, ensures that the most available and least experienced/qualified individuals will be put in charge of such investigations. Consequently, they will also lack the knowledge, confidence, and character to seek the truth in all matters and assert their findings for just resolution. Moreover, IAD complaints should not be "investigated within the division where the officer serves" (Chemerinsky, 2005, p. 603). Such investigations must be as impartial as possible, and beyond the influence of local politics or commanders with an agenda.

In some jurisdictions, especially those with less than 100 employees, IAD responsibilities are outsourced to sister or state agencies. This is a preferable solution, so long as those involved are not compromised by prior relationships or shared interests with those under investigation.

In communities where there has been a complete breakdown of trust between law enforcement and the community; where there is an established history of law enforcement misconduct and abuse of power; and where law enforcement has shown to be essentially ineffective at policing its own, external civilian oversight of internal affairs duties may be mandated. Or there may be a civilian complaint review board that is in charge of deciding disciplinary matters for minor infractions (those that do not warrant termination).

Integrity Testing

Professional law enforcement agencies employ a variety of screening tools to asses officer integrity. Usually conducted by Internal Affairs, they include, but are not limited to:

- *Anonymous radio runs*, in which a call is put out that there are drugs or cash underneath a vehicle or in another unsecured location. In such cases, IAD knows exactly how much is there and monitors the actions of responding officers closely. This includes whether it actually gets reported, whether proper weights and amounts are recorded, and attendance to proper vouchering protocols (e.g., evidence submission).
- *Conspicuous placement of drugs, cash, or pornography in a crime scene.* This is just what it sounds like and involves IAD monitoring the scene closely to see whether any responding officers take the "bait" without reporting it.
- *Sting operation.* IAD rents a hotel room or an apartment and then officers are sent there to serve a warrant or buy drugs. The entire operation is monitored by IAD from start to finish. This includes proper service of any warrants, proper vouchering of any cash, drugs, or valuables, and truth and accuracy in report writing about how items of evidence were found and who found them.[7]
- *Personal use of department issue cell phone.* Most officers are given a department issue cell phone that is not to be used for personal calls. If they make or receive personal calls, to be kept at a minimum, it is generally required that they serve notice and make arrangements to compensate the department, especially when the calls are made on duty. Commonly, IAD will call an officer in for an interview, on the record, and ask whether their department issue phone has been used for personal calls. If the officer says no, IAD presents them with the phone bill which invariably shows personal calls and the officer may be terminated on the spot. If they say yes, IAD will present them with the same phone bill and ask that they arrange for making compensation – generally without penalty.

---

[7]It is not unheard of for multiple officers involved in a drug bust to falsify their reports and vouchers, to make it appear as though one officer collected and vouchered all of the evidence when in fact multiple officers were involved. This is done to avoid having multiple officers go to court. It is also a crime.

- *Arrest and debrief of prostitutes.* IAD investigators have been known to detain prostitutes and then bring them in for questioning, to establish whether anyone claiming to be a police officer has been shaking them down for cash, drugs, or sex under threat of arrest.

These integrity tests are intended to provide officers with the opportunity to spontaneously demonstrate their character to the department, without any ability to plan ahead or change their normal routine. Sometimes these tests are random and cast a wide net in the search for corruption; but generally they are much more focused. They are, for the most part, brought to bear in response to fairly predictable circumstances:

- An officer has received a pattern of complaints that were founded, but did not result in termination.
- An officer has received a pattern of complaints that were unfounded.
- An anonymous complaint has been made against an officer by someone (often within the department) who does not want to be identified as a whistleblower.
- An officer has received a serious complaint for which there is no direct evidence.
- An officer has fallen out of favor with their department.
- An officer is approaching the date of their retirement.

False Statements, Reports, and Testimony

As reported in McClurg (1999, p. 394): "many police officers have come to believe that lying is a necessary and justifiable component of their jobs. 'Doing God's work' is how one officer defended the practice of falsification for the purpose of apprehending and convicting criminals." In fact, false statements, reports, and testimony are so common in law enforcement culture that police training officers actually developed their own term for what would eventually be required in the courtroom: "testilying" (Mollen, 1994; McClurg, 1999).[8] As provided by the research presented in Dorfman (1999, p. 457): "Judges, prosecutors and defense attorneys report that police perjury is commonplace, and even police officers themselves concede that lying is a regular feature of the life of a cop."

This kind of criminal misconduct occurs in all manner of contexts related to the work of law enforcement officers, whether it is a falsified timesheet related to overtime, sick days, or firearms qualification (e.g., Aseltine, 2011; Boyd, 2011; Litz, 2011); a false statement in a report or affidavit about directly observing a suspect drop drugs, weapons, or other contraband (referred to as "dropsy"

---

[8]This section has been adapted from Turvey (2012).

evidence; Cloud, 1996; Dorfman, 1999; McClurg 1999; Capers, 2008); false testimony about finding evidence on a suspect when it was actually planted (referred to as "flaking;" Dorfman, 1999; see also the scandal involving the NYPD Brooklyn Narcotics Squad with respect to "flaking" innocent suspects with no criminal record in order to boost arrests for overtime, chronicled in Jarrett, 2011; Stelloh, 2011; Yaniv, 2011); or false testimony in a pretrial hearing, or before a Grand Jury, about the results of forensic testing to help obtain an indictment prior to actually seeing the results (Smith, 2008).

Professional law enforcement agencies have a zero-tolerance policy for lying in any form. This means that they immediately terminate any officer that is determined to have made false statements, or to have given false evidence, in the course of dispatching their sworn duties. This is because their sworn oath almost always forbids it, and those who lie to investigators and the court cannot be trusted to give evidence – which is a central function of law enforcement. As explained in Noble (2003, p. 101): "In law enforcement, there are no second chances when it comes to the integrity of our officers and ourselves. In law enforcement, malicious deceptive conduct is untenable and cannot be tolerated at any level in the organization."

Sexual Harassment → Still happens

Law enforcement culture is often characterized by a military hierarchy and mindset, involving "a maximum use of force even in minor situations, use of heavy, sophisticated gear and equipment, a threatening and hostile demeanor toward the public, and a siege mentality in which the police dehumanize the citizens into enemies in a war which must be won at all costs" (Benson, 2001, p. 687); hypermasculinity; and intense pressure not to be perceived as feminine or homosexual (Harris, 2000).

As a consequence of these cultural traits, the sexual harassment of female officers is always a potential concern and homosexual officers often hide their sexual orientation out of fear, to avoid harassment and discrimination (Hassell and Brandl, 2009). In some instances, complaints related to these issues are ignored or swept under the rug by supervisors and city officials. In others, they can result in serious departmental consequences and civil liability.

For example, consider the case of former Spirit Lake police officer Crystal Sudol. She worked for that agency for less than a year, from March to November of 2011. In early 2012, former Officer Sudol filed a sexual harassment lawsuit against Chief Pat Lawless and the department. The lawsuit alleges that "Sudol endured sexual harassment both verbal and physical from Chief Lawless during her time working at the department. In the claim Sudol says the Chief 'created a hostile working environment for females and did batter and assault Sudol'" (Wohlenhaus, 2012). As reported in Utehs (2012):

Sudol worked as a police trainee and was required to ride in a police car with Lawless. Sudol says Lawless made sexual comments about her and other women while they were together.

Sudol also claims the chief touched her inappropriately while making her try on multiple bullet proof vests. The notice says Sudol brought her concerns to Mayor Todd Clary but says Clary and Lawless are friends.

The documents say, "Clary negligently investigated the matter and negligently failed to take swift and appropriate remedial action."

Subsequent to the filing of Sudol's lawsuit, Chief Lawless was suspended and then resigned (5 months later); two of his officers were disciplined; and former Chief Lawless was placed under investigation by neighboring Post Falls Police – for allegations of child abuse. Further still, another alleged victim from the Spirit Lake police came forth to corroborate former Officer Sudol's complaint that Chief Lawless created a "hostile work environment," performed "lewd actions" in public, and did both while in uniform (Wohlenhaus, 2012). That individual is represented by the same attorney as former Officer Sudol. Regardless of the merits of the ongoing lawsuit, the consequences to all concerned have already been serious.

Professional law enforcement agencies have a zero-tolerance policy for sexual harassment and intimidation of any kind. They understand that "the job" can be rife with sexually explicit context, but expect their employees to behave with the utmost respect towards each other just the same. In many instances this is a leadership issue: hostile work environments are created by hostile or dismissive leaders and the opposite is also true.

Use of Force

In the United States, police officers are issued both firearms and non-lethal weapons (e.g., pepper-spray, batons, and Tasers) by their respective law enforcement agencies. These are intended to provide the officer with different options for self-defense and when acting in defense of citizens (Broome, 2011). Consequently, these agencies have a legal and ethical obligation to provide adequate training to their personnel regarding the safe and lawful use of force.

For the majority of law enforcement officers, weapons training begins at the academy and continues with mandated intervals of re-qualification throughout their career. They are required to be knowledgeable and proficient with respect to weapon safety, maintenance, accuracy, and the applicable law. They must not be allowed to carry or use a weapon on which they have not been appropriately qualified. Once qualified, they are better prepared to use their varied arsenal in response to an array of threats, without unnecessary escalation or loss of life.

From a legal perspective, police use of force is addressed in *Tennessee v. Garner* (1985), which asserts that lethal force:

> … may not be used unless necessary to prevent the escape [of a fleeing suspect] and the officer has probable cause to believe that the suspect poses a significant threat of death or serious physical injury to the officer or others … the extent of the intrusion on the suspect's rights under [the Fourth] Amendment must be balanced against the governmental interests in effective law enforcement. This balancing process demonstrates that, notwithstanding probable cause to seize a suspect, an officer may not always do so by killing him. The use of deadly force to prevent the escape of all felony suspects, whatever the circumstances, is constitutionally unreasonable.

Garner does not explicitly tell law enforcement what their use of force policies must be in total, only what they must include and cannot allow. Law enforcement officers may not indiscriminately shoot suspected felons to prevent them from fleeing; and "the officer must *reasonably believe* that deadly force is necessary to stop or mitigate the violent threat to him or herself, or to others" (Broome, 2011, p. 140).

Individual law enforcement agencies have the responsibility to develop their own use of force policies in alignment with existing state and federal laws. In reality, however, these policies are constantly evolving with changes in law, leadership, and public perception.

Consider also the recent changes imposed on the Portland Police Bureau, made in response to an investigation by the US Department of Justice which determined that its officers were engaging in a "pattern and practice" of excessive force against those suffering from mental illness, as reported in Bernstein (2012):

> **A new "Application of Force" policy** specifically directs officers to recognize that people in mental health crisis may require a "specialized response" to ensure confrontations are resolved with as little reliance on force as possible.
>
>   …
>
>   It added language that says officers, when considering what to do in a confrontation with a person experiencing mental illness or emotional crisis, "must recognize and reasonably balance society's significant interest in providing care for that person." Officers must also describe their "[sic] de-escalation and force decisions in a report.
>   **Under a draft revision of the bureau's Deadly Physical Force policy**, officers involved in shootings would be required to provide an "on-scene interview" to a detective, after given a reasonable chance to confer with a lawyer or union official. They'll be expected to provide

an overview of what occurred, describing in general what threat prompted their use of force, where they were standing, the direction they fired at, their backdrop, if there were injuries, witnesses and the boundaries of the scene.

But a full, immediate sit-down interview remains voluntary. The union contract permits officers involved in such critical incidents to wait 48 hours before they're questioned.

Yet once detectives do conduct a full interview of the officer, an internal affairs investigator must be present, the draft says.

…

The draft policy on Taser use does not restrict the number of stun gun cycles an officer may fire at a single person, as federal authorities had urged. But it says, "members should evaluate their force options and give strong consideration to other force options, if the Taser is not effective after two" cycles on the same person.

Officers must give a warning before using a Taser, unless it would put someone at risk. It also says officers should consider a person's current mental health condition as a factor in deciding whether to use a Taser.

…

Police may only fire the stun gun's probes in response to "active aggression or active resistance", and defines active resistance as "physically evasive movements to defeat an officer's attempt at control, which could include "verbally signaling" an intention to resist arrest.

Yet, the draft also says officers can use the Taser to take a person into custody when the person "makes or is a credible threat to engage in physical resistance' [sic] that is likely to create a risk of injury to the officer or others.

The draft no longer allows the Taser be used against a fleeing suspect unless that person presents an immediate threat of physical injury.

Such policies are meant to act as a guide for the ethical officer trying to make good decisions in bad situations, not as a hammer to punish the conscientious. When officers are acting in good faith, with competent training, under clear policies and consistent leadership, following agency policy is therefore not generally a problem.

However, when officers act recklessly, and give false or misleading information during mandatory post-shooting investigations, this can get them fired even when no criminal charges are involved. Consider the case of former Austin Police Officer Chris Allen, as reported in Smith (2012):

On Dec. 5, 2011, Allen, a seven-year veteran, and probationary officer Justin Cummings responded to a call to assist Travis County

Sheriff's deputies who were pursuing Todd Michael Zurovetz who was allegedly driving a stolen car. With the [Travis County Sheriff's Office] in pursuit, Zurovetz reportedly led the officers on a high-speed chase before abandoning the car on Aspen Creek Parkway, a tree-lined residential neighborhood just west of Brodie Lane.

Instead of surrendering, Zurovetz broke into a home (the homeowners fled the house on foot) and stole the keys to another car, which he backed out the driveway and attempted to drive away in. Zurovetz ended up crashing that car, however, after Allen fired 14 rounds at him, striking him in the shoulder, side and wrist. Zurovetz reportedly tried again to flee, but was eventually taken into custody.

Although the grand jury cleared Allen of any criminal wrongdoing in connection with the incident, [Cheif Art] Acevedo found that Allen acted "negligently and recklessly" in a way that posed a "great safety risk to other officers and citizens."

According to a disciplinary memo, when Allen showed up at the Aspen Creek address he failed to check in with other officers and when the homeowners fled from their house, telling Allen that Zurovetz was inside, Allen gave the wrong address (3708 Leadville) over the police radio. When Zurovetz ultimately appeared, backing the newly-stolen car out of the driveway, Allen failed to follow his training for "high risk" approaches and "without communicating his intent" approached the car, raised his gun and, as Zurovetz drove away, fired four rounds through the driver side window. When Zurovetz kept driving, Allen pulled off another 10 shots while running down the block behind the car, Acevedo wrote.

To make matters worse, Acevedo wrote, Allen's statements to police investigating the incident "were not supported by the evidence and in many aspects were contradicted by the evidence." Indeed, Allen apparently said first that he backed away from the car as it pulled down the drive and then later that the vehicle was coming toward him, which is what prompted him to fire his weapon. Moreover, Allen told investigators that he didn't recall running down the street while firing his gun. All of the "potential risks" – not only to civilians, but also to other officers who could've caught a stray bullet – "should have been weighed by Officer Allen in his decision to continue firing at the vehicle as it drove away," Acevedo wrote. "That Officer Allen could not even remember running down the street and firing his weapon 10 additional times without being shown the video of him doing so is deeply disturbing to me."

Professional law enforcement agencies take their responsibilities with respect to weapons very seriously: officers are well trained on the safe use of the weapons they employ; officers are scrupulously educated about what the law allows and requires with respect to the use of deadly force; and agencies provide officers with clear use of force policies that do not violate the law or the Constitution of the United States. Failing at any of these, an agency risks harming the innocent, depriving suspects of their civil rights, and exposing itself, and its officers, to severe liability.

Law enforcement accountability is taken very serious in some jurisdictions. For example, in some jurisdictions, the department or the state puts out a monthly discipline report (e.g., NYPD), or an ethics bulletin (e.g., Oregon Department of Public Safety – Board on Public Safety Standards and Training). These include the names of, or information related to, officers that have been disciplined or terminated for ethics violations, as well as any relevant circumstances. Such public notices serve to alert active law enforcement employees regarding the seriousness of ethics violations, in addition to serving the public need for agency transparency.

TRANSPARENCY: POLICE POLICIES, THE PUBLIC, AND THE MEDIA

Currently, law enforcement transparency is greater than ever before, owing to five convergent and equally important influences. These are agency policies, crime statistics, personal cell phone technology, social media, and press scrutiny (Forst, 2008).

CRLEA → Standards, its a voluntary program.

Law Enforcement Policies

Many law enforcement agencies have developed strict policies related to the surveillance and recording of officer activity, both inside departments and out with the public at large. This includes the deployment of security cameras throughout police stations and in detention areas; dash-cams in patrol vehicles with audio capability; personal digital recorders carried by patrol officers, used to record the time and script of any contact with the public; and the mandatory recording (e.g., audio and video) of every interview that is conducted – witness, complainant, suspect alike. Such policies and technologies are used by professional law enforcement agencies to protect both citizens and officers, as complaints of officer misconduct can be quickly verified or refuted by referencing these recordings.

This kind of documentation, the cost of which is small compared to the liability that it can prevent, only benefits the lawful and ethical. Therefore, failure to engage in, preserve, or turn over such documentation is generally an indication that the agency involved lacks faith in its officers or agents, at least on some level. Specifically, it suggests that there are things going on that the agency does not want the public, or the justice system, to be aware of. This is because all such documentation is discoverable as evidence in both criminal and civil matters. It may also be subject to FOIA requests from interested citizens and media agencies.

Consider the following case, reported in Brown (2011), involving misconduct by four officers and false accusations of drug possession with the intent to distribute:

> Clermont Police Officer Cecil Garrett was fired this week and three other officers were reprimanded, after an investigation into a May 11 arrest concluded Garrett falsely charged a teenager with possession of cocaine with intent to distribute.
>
> "To terminate any employee is a serious matter, but for an officer to falsify a document or be untruthful about an arrest is a serious infraction," Clermont Police Chief Steve Graham said Friday. "It's one thing if an officer makes a mistake, but to knowingly charge a defendant with a serious crime that you know didn't occur, that's different."
>
> According to an Internal Affairs Investigation memo summarizing the incident leading up to Garrett's termination, a complaint regarding the arrest was filed by the 19-year-old boy's uncle, a retired 30-year detective for the Orange County Sheriff's Office.
>
> "The complaint alleged that the probable cause affidavit and police report completed by Officer Garrett was not correct and that the video from the in-car police camera, obtained by the defendant's lawyer, showed that the defendant was not in the possession of cocaine with intent to distribute as charged, and that the video clearly showed the charges as outlined in the police report were false," the memo reads. "Furthermore, the Florida Department of Law Enforcement Lab report showed that the illegal substance, of which the defendant was charged with possessing, was not cocaine but a form of aspirin packaged to look like cocaine."
>
> According to information in Garrett's original arrest report, he stopped the teen driving a friend's car for having a defective tail light. The car was occupied by the driver and three other people.
>
> Garrett initiated the stop on eastbound State Road 50 and the defendant pulled into a Staples parking lot. Garrett's report said he saw five bags of "cocaine" fall from the teen's lap, but the dash camera tape showed the bags were thrown from the left rear passenger side of the car by a passenger sitting behind the driver's seat.
>
> According to information provided by the police department, Garrett said he based the arrest on "probable cause" and not the tape.

The officer viewed the tape, but "chose to ignore the evidence on the video" the investigation showed. Furthermore, officers Dennis Hall and Marc Thompson watched it and expressed their concerns to Garrett about the charges, but he held steadfast with his probable cause affidavit.

Garrett's negligent actions, the investigation concluded, caused the defendant to be wrongly charged with a false and serious charge. The officer was terminated based on violations including untruthfulness, conduct unbecoming a member of the department, unlawful conduct offenses in falsifying an official record or document, and job knowledge and performance.

This case involves clear officer misconduct that would not have been uncovered but for the "dash-cam" video, and the efforts of defense counsel to make sure it was examined. It is clear, based on the circumstances reported, why the officer felt compelled to give false evidence – he needed to strengthen the weak legal foundations of the evidence in the case (Kleinig, 1996). However, as made clear by his chief, there are no circumstances that justify falsification of a police report to fit a desired outcome.

Crime Statistics

The release of crime-related statistics is one of the ways that law enforcement agencies purport to be transparent. They provide the number of complaints, arrests, victims, and suspects (along with other limited details) to the federal government, to the media, and often via their departmental website.[9] In exchange, they may continue to qualify for Federal funding and they let the public know how well they are handling the volume of crime in their jurisdiction.

Most major metropolitan police departments are under significant pressure to keep crime statistics low and provide the community with a sense of security, even if it means manipulating their crime data. Data manipulation occurs in a variety of ways. They include downgrading the crime to a lesser offense; misclassifying the crime to conceal all of the crimes involves (e.g., classifying a rape-robbery as only a robbery); and unfounding complaints – deciding that they are false or baseless without the benefit of an investigation. When these are not an option, police may even actively discourage certain victims from filing a complaint, especially in cases of domestic violence, assault, or sex crimes (Savino and Turvey, 2011).

---

[9]Police agencies that wish to qualify for federal funding are required to submit their crime data to FBI's Uniformed Crime Report (UCR) program. Each year, the FBI compiles and publishes UCR crime data in a report called *Crime in the United States*. Not every police agency reports its crime statistics.

For example, consider the crime data scandal in Milwaukee, Wisconsin, as reported in Poston (2012a):

> When Milwaukee Police Chief Edward Flynn touted the city's fourth-straight year of falling crime in February, hundreds of beatings, stabbings and child abuse cases were missing from the count, a *Journal Sentinel* investigation has found.
>
> More than 500 incidents since 2009 were misreported to the FBI as minor assaults and not included in the city's violent crime rate, the investigation found. That tally is based on a review of cases that resulted in charges – only about one-fifth of all reported crimes.
>
> Yet the misreported cases found in 2011 alone are enough that Flynn would have been announcing a 1.1% increase in violent crime in February, instead of a 2.3% decline from the reported 2010 numbers, which also include errors.
>
> Missing, for example, was the case of Crystal L. Mitchell, 21, who last May grabbed a 9-inch serrated steak knife during an argument with her uncle, stabbed him in his thigh and slashed his arm.
>
> And the case of John F. Sanford, 57, who in December bound his 6-year-old stepson's arms and legs, covered his mouth with duct tape and struck him some 90 times with a belt, later telling him: "I was trying to make you (expletive) on yourself." A doctor at Children's Hospital found cuts and bruises all over the boy's body.
>
> Based on FBI reporting guidelines, both should have been classified as aggravated assaults, the city's most common violent crime. Instead, they were reported as simple assaults, a category reserved for shoving matches and slaps to the face.
>
> … FBI crime experts reviewed these and dozens of other incidents and confirmed that they should have been labeled as aggravated assaults. In addition to the more than 500 misreported incidents, the investigation found at least 800 more that fit the same pattern but could not be confirmed through available public records ….
>
> The misclassified crimes included cases where perpetrators threatened to kill victims; stabbed or cut them with knives; and beat them with canes, crowbars and hammers.
>
> Nearly one-third of the assault cases identified by the *Journal Sentinel* involved the abuse of children – most were struck in the head with belts and electrical cords, causing cuts, bloody eardrums and black eyes.
>
> Instead of accurately reporting the weapons used as firearms, knives or blunt objects, the department reported them to the state and FBI in a way that avoided triggering scrutiny by those who review the numbers.

As a result of this and other scandals within the Milwaukee Police Department, including an FBI civil rights investigation into the agency's internal handling of an in-custody death, community leaders have organized to call for Chief Flynn's resignation (Poston, 2012b).[10]

Brady v. Maryland

Brady v. Maryland (1963) is a Supreme Court ruling requiring the timely disclosure of potentially exculpatory evidence to the defense by the prosecution.[11] This includes reports and notes from both law enforcement agencies (Noble, 2003) and government crime labs (Gershman, 2006). It also includes material that might impeach credibility of state witnesses, to include police officers, police experts, and any forensic personnel. As explained in Lisko (2011, pp. 12–13):

> As a result of the 1963 U.S. Supreme Court decision regarding *Brady*, prosecutors are required to provide all exculpatory information about their witnesses to defense attorneys prior to trial. Subsequent U.S. Supreme Court decisions in *Giglio v. U.S.* and *U.S. v Agurs* further expanded the duty of prosecutors to provide this information to defense attorneys prior to trial, even if no prior request was made. However, the court's decision in *Kyles v. Whitley* has had the most significant impact on law enforcement agencies. It requires prosecutors to learn about any favorable information to the defendant that is known to others who are acting on behalf of the government, including information about police officers. This duty also extends to information about police officers contained in internal affairs files. But if prosecutors are unaware of that information or evidence, subsequent disclosures to defense attorneys can never occur. The result can be devastating for prosecutors, victims of crime, and law enforcement agencies.
>
> Take for example, the recent revelation by the San Francisco, California, Police Department in May 2010, in which the names of more than 135 police officers with potential *Brady* problems were disclosed to the prosecutor's office. The problem was discovered after the chief of police asked a staff member to evaluate a disciplinary case for potential *Brady* policy problems. As the staff member stared blankly back at the chief, the only response was,

---

[10]As reported in Poston (2012b), police video shows that in July 2011, robbery suspect Derek Williams was arrested, placed in a patrol car, and died over the course of 8 minutes – all the while gasping for air and pleading for help from officers. An internal investigation involved a review of the video and a determination that officers did nothing wrong. The cause of death was initially ruled to be "natural causes" by the medical examiner; however, this was changed to "homicide" when the police video was released to the press and made public.

[11]This issue will be covered in greater detail in Chapter 9: "Ethical Issues for Criminal Prosecutors," in reference to prosecutorial misconduct.

"We don't have one of those." Recognizing the potential of the problem that he discovered, the chief immediately contacted the prosecutor's office. To his surprise, he learned that the prosecutor's office did not have a policy to track or disclose *Brady* information to attorneys representing criminal defendants. Does this sound familiar?

As a result of its disclosure, the San Francisco Police Department jeopardized hundreds of felony and misdemeanor cases, both waiting trial and those in which defendants have been convicted …

Regrettably, the San Francisco Police Department is not alone in this problem. Law enforcement agencies across the United States have faced similar problems.

- The Tulsa, Oklahoma, Police Department announced in July 2010 a "no-tolerance-for-lying policy" after seven police officers were charged in federal court with perjury and corruption. As a result of those charges, 11 criminal suspects were either released from jail or had their cases dismissed.
- In 2009, Dallas, Texas, prosecutors were faced with the possibility that dozens of criminal convictions dating back 15 years might be reversed after the discovery of a 1994 conviction for lying by the arresting officer. The officer had been fired for lying to internal investigators and causing false information to be placed in an arrest report. He was later reinstated by an administrative law judge but the police department failed to notify the prosecutor's office.
- Prosecutors in Seattle, Washington, were forced to establish their own list of officers with *Brady* problems because the local police departments failed to do so. The problem came to light after a 2007 memo from a senior prosecutor directed attorneys to track officers that had credibility problems. The names of 11 officers were immediately added to the list.
- By 2007, Maricopa County, Arizona, prosecutors had compiled a list of 328 names of police officers that were placed on their *Brady* list, indicating that they may not be eligible to testify in court. The problem was highlighted during the internal investigation of a Gilbert, Arizona, police officer who was accused of lying about conducting a records check of an arrestee.
- In Boston, Massachusetts, an investigation by the local newspaper in 2005 uncovered 19 cases in which officers were convicted of lying in official investigations, under oath, or in police reports. However, only two officers were fired for their actions ….

Like the problems in San Francisco, most of these problems were discovered after a single critical incident or court case in which an officer's past conduct was questioned. Unfortunately, all of them could have been prevented if the law enforcement agency had a policy to routinely disclose *Brady* information to prosecutors.

Professional law enforcement agencies have clear and strict policies regarding compliance with *Brady*. They not only train their officers regarding the importance of disclosing *Brady* material, they also develop experience with efficiently preparing discovery packages for the defense in order to maintain openness and accountability. Moreover, they do not tolerate employees who alter or suppress police evidence and records in order to avoid compliance with lawful *Brady* requests (which need not actually be requested, but rather must be provided as a matter of course). Consequently, in professional law enforcement agencies, officers that intentionally lose evidence in their desk (e.g., interview recordings, physical evidence, or tips regarding alternate suspects) will find that they may also lose their job. Agencies that tolerate this kind of conduct will generally wind up paying for it later when they are sued – in which case officers and commanders alike can wind up on the wrong end of a pink slip.

Personal Cell Phone Technology and Social Media

The proliferation of personal use cell phones over the past two decades, and related technology, has changed the way we interact with each other forever. This includes our interactions with authority figures, as almost every cell phone has the capability to record audio, take high-quality still photographs, and capture video. In addition, most cell phone users are connected directly to the Internet, to their preferred social media platform, and therefore to the rest of the world (e.g., Facebook, YouTube, and Twitter). This means that any interaction with law enforcement can be documented or recorded via civilian cell phone and posted globally as it happens.

Police officers, being public figures, generally forfeit their privacy when interacting with the public. The same is not true for private citizens, however. Preserving this right to privacy is a matter of agency policy, and often the law. As a consequence, law enforcement employees that violate the privacy of citizens by posting the details of, and photos related to, the performance their law enforcement duties can find themselves severely disciplined, if not fired.

Many departments have policies that can be used to regulate the use of social media by employees. However, few have specific policies that address officer conduct, or privacy, while online. Consider the following case examples, involving police officers, their online social media activity, and departmental responses to misconduct:

CASE EXAMPLE

Deputy Daniel Ray Carter Jr, Hampton Sheriff's Department

In 2009, Deputy Daniel Ray Carter Jr, and five of his co-workers, were fired by their boss, the Sheriff of Hampton, Virginia. They were fired for clicking "like" on the Facebook page of the Sheriff's rival in an upcoming election. Former Deputy Carter felt that this violated his right to free speech and sued for wrongful termination; in 2012 the court ruled against him (Gross, 2012):

> Free-speech advocates argue that the "like" should have been clearly protected by Carter's right to freedom of expression. But a U.S. District Court judge in Virginia ruled differently saying, in effect, that free-speech protections don't kick in when someone doesn't actually say something.
>
> "Liking a Facebook page is insufficient speech to merit constitutional protection," Judge Raymond A. Jackson wrote in his May ruling, because it doesn't "involve actual statements."

While the court gets up to speed regarding the Internet, what it is, and the various forms of technological expression that constitute speech, officers like former Deputy Carter may continue to be sanctioned for what they do and do not "like" on Facebook.

CASE EXAMPLE

Officer Michael McClatchy, Pickens Police Department

On September 3, 2012, Officer Michael McClatchy of the Pickens Police Department gave South Carolina Clemson Tigers head coach Dabo Swinney a speeding ticket. He then posted about the experience online, suggesting that coach Swinney appeared to expect special treatment because of his local popularity. As reported in DeCelles (2012):

> A spokesman for the city of Pickens said that McClatchy was fired for spending an hour and a half posting on a University of South Carolina message board on a police department computer while on duty. However, McClatchy's lawyer and South Carolina trustee Chuck Allen said that there are no city policies that regulates the use of the Internet for active-duty police officers.

While his former employers insist that he was fired for spending time online while at work engaging in personal activity, former Officer McClatchy disagrees. He contends that he was fired for doing his job, based on pressure from city officials, and for not letting coach Swinney out of the ticket.

What these cases demonstrate is the need for police agencies to develop and enforce clear policies with respect to the appropriate use of social media by employees. Currently this is not happening and there is a lot of confusion. Ultimately, active police personnel are perhaps best served by avoiding online activity altogether, given the historical use of social media as a means for impulsive venting, the intense scrutiny that can be levied against departmental employees, the ability of departments to restrict and penalize employee speech, and the court's ignorance of social media and how it works.

CASE EXAMPLE

Melissa Walthall, Mesquite, Texas

In 2012, Melissa Walthall of Mesquite, Texas was arrested for re-posting Facebook photos of an undercover officer online, identifying him and his job to the public. As reported in Newcomb (2012):

> A Texas woman is facing a felony retaliation charge after she allegedly posted a photograph of an undercover narcotics officer on Facebook and identified his job.
>
> Melissa Walthall, 30, told Mesquite police she saw the photograph on a flyer three weeks earlier and posted it because her friend was upset with the officer's testimony on drug charges, according to a federal affidavit.
>
> On Oct. 7, one of Walthall's friends told police a photograph of a man appeared in her newsfeed and was labeled "Undercover Mesquite Narcotics" with the caption "Anyone know this b****." Investigators checked Walthall's Facebook page and issued a warrant for her arrest on harassment charges after they deemed her post a "viable threat to that officer's safety," the affidavit stated.
>
> Walthall refused to identify her friend. However a computer search led police to George Pickens.
>
> Pickens, 34, told investigators he and his brother, Bobby Stedham, began researching the undercover officer online and found his Facebook page and photograph. They used the photo to make flyers featuring the officer with

the intent to display them "like garage sale signs," according to the affidavit.

> "It's a very dangerous situation," said Kevin Lawrence, executive director of the Texas Municipal Police Association. "If you're trying to infiltrate a cartel, a drug ring, a gang, one of the keys is people have to believe you're not an officer. Anything that hints at tying you to law enforcement is very dangerous," he said.
>
> Stedham, 26, has also been charged with retaliation. Pickens faces drugs and weapons charges after authorities found 28.6 grams of methamphetamine in his room and an unregistered, sawed-off shotgun.
>
> Lawrence said his group advises members of law enforcement to be very cautious about social media, if they must use it at all. "There are too many opportunities for bad things to happen in exchange for very little up side," he said. "But the fact the officer shouldn't have had a Facebook doesn't excuse her [Walthall] either."

It is unclear how this or similar cases might play out, given that the officer testified in open court, identified himself on the public record, and that he identified himself on Facebook with his own photos. Unless Ms Walthall made specific threats, or her acts can be construed as particularly threatening, it seems the prosecution may be on shaky legal ground. This does not change the very real dangers, however, for undercover officers that choose to identify themselves on social media.

Press Scrutiny

In concert with social media, the press has and continues to be a powerful tool for ensuring the degree of law enforcement transparency that society currently enjoys. This includes investigative reporting on television, in the print media (e.g., newspapers and magazines), and even in the blogosphere. Without the pressure to release information, the ability to make organized and directed FOIA requests, and the public attention that results from media scrutiny, the public would know much less than they do about what law enforcement is doing (or failing to do). Consequently, public opinions would be less informed and matter less to law enforcement decision makers. Press scrutiny, ultimately, provides a level of accountability without which law enforcement has historically been able to avoid both consequences and reform when confronted with its own misconduct.

SUMMARY

This chapter examines the primary ethical issues relevant to law enforcement command, human resources, and related mechanisms for accountability. From a command perspective, police administration involves setting agency policy and making operational decisions that best achieve the aforementioned goals without violating the law or the public trust. This includes knowing the law, adopting lawful and ethical departmental policies, enforcing those policies, and setting a clear professional example for subordinates to follow. From a human resources perspective, police administration involves making ethical and lawful decisions relating to the hiring, management, retention, discipline, and termination of law enforcement personnel. All of this requires accountability, both internal and external.

Questions

1. List three different approaches to policing.
2. What is an administrative investigation? Provide two examples.
3. Explain the significance of the Supreme Court ruling in *Brady v. Maryland* (1963).
4. List three examples of screening tools that can be used to assess officer integrity. Explain why integrity tests are used.
5. Explain the importance of crime statistics.

References

Aseltine, P., 2011. Captain of human services police charged with falsifying records concerning vacation time & firearms qualification. Press Release, State of New Jersey, Office of the Attorney General, May 17; url: http://www.nj.gov/oag/newsreleases11/pr20110517b.html.

Barton, G., 2011. Officers' criminal records are tough to track. Milwaukee Journal-Sentinel, October 29.

Benson, R., 2001. Changing police culture: the *sine qua non* of reform. Loyola of Los Angeles Law Review 34 (January), 681–690.

Bernstein, M., 2012. Portland Police chief's draft policy changes on use of force embrace some DOJ reforms, not others. The Oregonian, October 18; url: http://www.oregonlive.com/portland/index.ssf/2012/10/portland_police_chief_mike_ree_10.html.

Bopp, W., Schultz, D., 1972. Principles of American Law Enforcement and Criminal Justice. Charles C. Thomas, Springfield, IL.

Boyd, D., 2011. Fort Worth detective fired, accused of falsifying time sheets. Ft Worth Star-Telegram, September 30.

Brady v. Maryland, 1963. US Supreme Court, 373 US 83.

Brennan, A., Rostow, C., Davis, R., Hill, B., 2009. An investigation of biographical information as a predictor of employment termination among law enforcement officers. Journal of Police and Criminal Psychology 24, 108–112.

Broome, R., 2011. An empathetic psychological perspective of police deadly force training. Journal of Phenomenological Psychology 42, 137–156.

Brown, R., 2011. Cops fired for lying. The Daily Commercial, November 5; url: http://www.daily-commercial.com/110511policefired.

Cancino, J., Enriquez, R., 2004. A qualitative analysis of officer peer retaliation. Policing: An International Journal of Police Strategies and Management 27 (3), 320–340.

Capers, B., 2008. Crime, legitimacy, and testilying. Indiana Law Journal 83 (Summer), 835–880.

Chappell, A., Piquero, A., 2004. Applying social learning theory to police misconduct. Deviant Behavior 25, 89–108.

Chemerinsky, E., 2005. An independent analysis of the Los Angeles Police Department's Board of Inquiry report on the Rampart Scandal. Loyola of Los Angeles Law Review 34, 545–657.

Cloud, M., 1996. Judges, 'testilying', and the constitution. Southern California Law Review 69 (May), 1341–1387.

Clymer, S., 2001. Compelled statements from police officers and Garrity immunity. New York University Law Review 76, 1309–1382.

Cohn, S., 2012. Santa Paula investigation of police chief completed. VC Reporter, May 10; url: http://www.vcreporter.com/cms/story/detail/santa_paula_investigation_of_police_chief_completed/9802/.

Davidow, J., Teichroeb, R., 2003. Cops who abuse their wives rarely pay the price. Seattle Post-Intelligencer, July 23.

DeCelles, K., 2012. Dabo Swinney ticket led to firing, says police officer. SB Nation, September 27; url: http://www.sbnation.com/college-football/2012/9/27/3419428/dabo-swinney-speeding-police-officer-fired.

Dorfman, D., 1999. Proving the lie: litigating police credibility. American Journal of Criminal Law 26, 455–503.

Eberly, T., 2008. One-third of Ga. officer recruits have police records. The Atlanta Journal-Constitution, October 12.

Elias, P., 2012. SF mayor suspends sheriff, seeks removal. San Jose Mercury News, March 21.

Fitch, B., 2011. Focus on ethics: rethinking ethics in law enforcement. FBI Law Enforcement Bulletin, October.

Forst, B., 2008. Improving police effectiveness and transparency: national information needs on law enforcement. Bureau of Justice Statistics Data User's Workshop, Washington, DC, February 12.

Garrity v. New Jersey, 1967. US Supreme Court, No. 13, 385 US 493, January 16.

Gershman, B., 2006. Reflections on Brady v. Maryland. South Texas Law Review 47 (Summer), 685–728.

Gross, D., 2012. Virginia deputy fights his firing over a Facebook 'like'. CNN, August 13; url: http://www.cnn.com/2012/08/10/tech/social-media/deputy-fired-facebook-like/index.html.

Hansen, D., Culley, T., 1973. The Police Training Officer. Chares C. Thomas, Springfield, IL.

Harris, A., 2000. Gender, violence, race, and criminal justice. Stanford Law Review 52 (4), 777–807.

Harris, M., 2012. Prosecutors won't file charge against former Santa Paula Police Chief. VC Star, August 15; url: http://m.vcstar.com/news/2012/aug/15/prosecutors-decline-to-charge-former-santa-paula/.

Hassell, K., Brandl, S., 2009. An examination of the workplace experiences of police patrol officers: the role of race, sex, and sexual orientation. Police Quarterly 12 (4), 408–430.

Hunter, G., Ferretti, C., 2012. Detroit Police Chief Godbee retires amid alleged sex scandal. Detroit News, October 9; url: http://www.detroitnews.com/article/20121009/METRO01/210090358/1409/METRO/Detroit-Police-Chief-Godbee-retires-amid-alleged-sex-scandal.

International Association of Chiefs of Police, 2011. What is the law enforcement oath of honor? The International Association of Chiefs of Police website, url: http://www.theiacp.org/PoliceServices/ExecutiveServices/ProfessionalAssistance/Ethics/WhatistheLawEnforcementOathofHonor/tabid/150/Default.aspx.

Jarrett, T., 2011. Judge blasts NYPD, convicts rogue detective. The Brooklyn Ink, November 1; url: http://thebrooklynink.com/2011/11/01/34082-judge-blastsnypd-convicts-rogue-detective/.

Kaempffer, W., 2009. Sullied city cop given special probation. New Haven Register, February 3.

Kappeler, V., 2006. Critical Issues in Police Civil Liability, fouth ed. Waveland Press, Long Grove, IL.

Kleinig, J., 1996. The Ethics of Policing. Cambridge University Press, New York.

Lacey, E., 2012. Detroit Police Chief Ralph Godbee's retirement in wake of sex scandal generates anger, frustration. Michigan Live, October 8; url: http://www.mlive.com/news/detroit/index.ssf/2012/10/detroit_police_chief_ralph_god_8.html.

LeDuff, C., 2012. Will Godbee resign? Bing to hold Monday news conference. Fox News Channel 2, October 8; url: http://www.myfoxdetroit.com/story/19750499/officer-says-she-has-proof-she-traded-sex-with-godbee-for-promotion.

Leidner, B., Castano, E., 2012. Morality shifting in the context of intergroup violence. European Journal of Social Psychology 42, 82–91.

Leonard, J., Faturechi, R., 2011. Sheriff's Department used jail duty to punish deputies. The Los Angeles Times, November 12.

Lewis, L., 2010. Former Detroit Police Chief's girlfriend has a history of being a hot head. ABC Action News 7, July 30; url: http://www.wxyz.com/dpp/news/local_news/former-detroit-police-chief's-girlfriend-has-a-history-of-being-a-hot-head.

Lewis, L., 2012. Detroit Police Chief Ralph Godbee suspended amid sex scandal allegations. ABC Action News 7, October 2; url: http://www.wxyz.com/dpp/news/region/detroit/sex-scandal-brewing-at-the-highest-levels-of-detroit-police-department.

Lisko, R., 2011. Agency policies imperative to disclose *Brady v. Maryland* material to prosecutors. The Police Chief 78 (February), 12–13.

Litz, S., 2011. Miami Beach ATV crash probe uncovers lies, false timesheets. NBC-Miami, October 13; url: http://www.nbcmiami.com/news/Miami-Beach-ATVCrash-Probe-Uncovers-Lies-131629663.html.

Maples, J., 1999. The Crime Fighter. Doubleday, New York.

May, L.D., 2005. The backfiring of the domestic violence firearms bans. Columbia Journal of Gender and the Law 14 (1), 1–35.

McClurg, A., 1999. Good cop, bad cop: using cognitive dissonance theory to reduce police lying. UC Davis Law Review 32 (Winter), 389–453.

Middleton-Hope, J., 2003. Misconduct among previously experienced officers: issues in the recruitment and hiring of gypsy cops. Saint Louis University Public Law Review 22, 173–183.

Mollen, M., 1994. Commission to Investigate Allegations of Police Corruption and the Anti-Corruption Procedures of the Police Department. Commission Report, The City of New York.

Moore, J., 2008. Channel 2 finds nearly 1,400 certified officers with criminal records. Action News 2, December 8; url: http://www.wsbtv.com/videos/news/channel-2-finds-nearly-1400-certified-officers/vCLXw/.

Newcomb, A., 2012. Woman charged with felony after posting undercover cop's picture on Facebook. ABC News, October 15; url: http://abcnews.go.com/US/woman-charged-felony-posting-undercover-cops-picture-facebook/story?id=17483006#.UH9TErTd2WQ.

Noble, J., 2003. Police officer truthfulness and the *Brady* decision. The Police Chief 70 (10), 92–101.

Novak, T., Fusco, C., 2012. Chicago cop who pleaded guilty in disability scam still on force. Chicago Sun-Times, October 15.

Pistor, N., 2012. Former East St. Louis police chief admits theft. St. Louis Today, January 20.

Poston, B., 2012a. Hundreds of assault cases misreported by Milwaukee Police Department. Milwaukee Journal-Sentinel, May 22.

Poston, B., 2012b. Group calls for Milwaukee police chief's firing. Milwaukee Journal-Sentinel, May 22.

Rider, R., 2010. *United States v. Hayes*: retroactive removal of your ability to be a police officer. Officer.com, url: http://www.officer.com/article/10232309/unitedstates-v-hayes.

Rodriquez, R., 1997. Some police say domestic violence law a threat to their jobs. CNN, January 6; url: http://www.cnn.com/US/9701/06/domestic.abuse.cops/.

Savino, J., Turvey, B., 2011. Rape Investigation Handbook, second ed. Elsevier, San Diego, CA.

Scheibe, J., 2012. Police chief fired in Santa Paula. VC Star, June 7; url: http://www.vcstar.com/news/2012/jun/07/police-chief-fired-in-santa-paula/.

Shane, J., 2010. Performance management in police agencies: a conceptual framework. Policing: An International Journal of Police Strategies and Management 33 (1), 6–29.

Smith, J., 2012. Austin officer fired for shooting at fleeing suspect. The Austin Chronicle, October 16.

Smith, T., 2008. Police provided false testimony in rape case: judge considers dismissal of indictment against Marsalis. Idaho Mountain Express, December 3.

Spector, E., 2008. Should police officers who lie be terminated as a matter of public policy? The Police Chief 75 (4), 10.

Stelloh, T., 2011. Detective is found guilty of planting drugs. New York Times, November 2; url: http://www.nytimes.com/2011/11/02/nyregion/brooklyn-detectiveconvicted-of-planting-drugs-on-innocent-people.html.

Stout, B., 2011. Ethics and academic integrity in police education. Policing 5 (4), 300–309.

Sullivan, J., 1977. Introduction to Police Science, third ed. McGraw-Hill, New York.

Tennessee v. Garner, 1985. US Supreme Court, 471 US 1.

Turvey, B., 2012. Forensic fraud: evaluating law enforcement and forensic science cultures in the context of examiner misconduct. *Doctoral Dissertation* Bond University Library, Robina, Queensland.

Turvey, B., Petherick, W., 2010. An introduction to forensic criminology. In: Turvey, B., Petherick, W., Ferguson, C. (Eds.), Forensic Criminology, Elsevier, San Diego, CA.

United States v. Hayes, 2009. US Supreme Court, No. 07–608, February 24.

Utehs, K., 2012. Spirit Lake Police Chief accused of sexual harassment. KREM.com, July 6.

Vaughn, M., Cooper, T., del Carmen, R., 2001. Assessing legal liabilities in law enforcement: police chief's views. Crime and Delinquency 47 (1), 3–27.

Vollmer, A., 1971. The Police and Modern Society. Patterson Smith, Montclair, NJ.

Weisburd, D., Mastrofski, S., Greenspan, R., Willis, J., 2004. The Growth of Compstat in American Policing. NIJ Grant No. 97-IJ-CX-007. The Police Foundation, Washington, DC.

White, E., 2012. Detroit chief steps down amid sex probe. Associated Press, October 8; url: http://www.policeone.com/chiefs-sheriffs/articles/6005947-Detroit-chief-steps-down-amid-sex-probe/.

Wohlenhaus, D., 2012. Spirit Lake woman says she & her sons endured sexual comments & gestures from police chief. KHQ Channel 6 News, July 10.

Wolfe, S., Piquero, A., 2011. Organizational justice and police misconduct. Criminal Justice and Behavior 38 (4), 332–353.

Wooten, B., 2007. Milwaukee police, city won't tell public how many officers have criminal convictions. Front Page Milwaukee, February 12.

Wyatt-Nichol, H., Franks, G., 2009. Ethics training in law enforcement agencies. Public Integrity 12 (1), 39–50.

Yaniv, O., 2011. Judge shocked by 'cowboy culture' of cops. New York Daily News, November 1; url: http://articles.nydailynews.com/2011-11-01/news/30348008_1_narcotics-cops-plant-drugs-cowboy-culture.

CHAPTER 6

Ethical Issues for Police Officers and Criminal Investigators

Stan Crowder, John O. Savino and Brent E. Turvey

Key Terms

Coercion The use of force, threats, or intimidation to gain someone's compliance.

Conduct unbecoming A charge used by police agencies to discipline its officers for any behavior that violates department rules and virtues.

Confession A voluntary statement, written or recorded, by a criminal suspect that acknowledges guilt for a particular crime.

Duty of care The professional and legal obligation to be competent custodians of any victims that are encountered; any criminal investigations that are initiated; and any evidence that supports or refutes allegations of criminal activity against accused suspects.

Entrapment A general term that refers to law enforcement inducing a person to commit criminal acts, specifically one that they would not have otherwise been likely to commit (Hughes, 2004).

False confession An admission of guilt that is untrue, often involuntary, made under duress, and as the result of coercion.

Inculpatory statement A voluntary statement, written or recorded, by a criminal suspect, acknowledging a particular decision or activity associated with a crime.

Mandatory arrest laws Requires law enforcement to make an arrest at the scene if there is probable cause that a crime has been committed.

Mere suspicion A level of confidence that is sometimes considered a gut feeling, or a hunch, that leads the individual to question a particular circumstance.

Noble cause corruption Corrupt or illegal acts committed by law enforcement in order to secure or maintain an arrest or conviction, or some other worthy end (Caldero and Crank, 2004; Martinelli, 2006; Crank et al., 2007; Porter and Warrender, 2009).

Patrol officers Uniformed police assigned to move in a pattern within designated areas of a community (a.k.a. "beats") by foot, horse, bicycle, motorcycle, or more commonly a marked patrol car.

Probable cause A reasonable belief that an individual has, is, or will commit a crime.

Racial profiling Discrimination against an ethical racial group based on the presumption that all members share criminal traits or tendencies (Reynolds, 2007; Pitt, 2011).

Reasonable suspicion A level of confidence that is intended to describe facts and circumstances that may lead an officer to believe that a person will be involved in a crime, or was involved in a crime.

Search and seizure laws The laws surrounding police authority to stop and search persons and their property for evidence related to a crime, as long as they have probable cause to believe that a crime has occurred and that the person being stopped is the one responsible.

147

Ethical Justice. http://dx.doi.org/10.1016/B978-0-12-404597-2.00006-1

Selective enforcement The arbitrary punishment of certain individuals or groups for legal violations or crimes, rather than the equal punishment of all known offenders.

Law enforcement responders working in the field are routinely confronted by
ethical challenges that are very different from those experienced by their commanders or by those working in an administrative capacity. Physically and phil-
osophically separated from the operational decisions faced by administrators,
those on patrol or conducting investigations work directly with the public.
Their encounters routinely occur in full public view, often during moments of
stress and crisis, and are suffused with differing levels of ethical strain.

In this chapter, we will explore the more common ethical issues that are
confronted by those on patrol, and also by those conducting criminal investigations. This will be preceded by establishing police duty of care and the
requisite professional ethos ("character") for responding officers. While each
agency differs with respect to specific duties and codes of conduct, there are
universal law enforcement concerns which transcend jurisdiction.

What becomes clear when considering misconduct and consequences across
agencies is that each has its own level of professionalism and tolerance. In
less professional agencies, a history of serious misconduct and even criminal convictions among sworn officers can be the norm. In more professional agencies, sworn officers are held to the strictest codes of conduct. It
all depends on the quality of leadership, resulting agency culture, and the
ready pool of available cadets to replace those that have retired, transferred,
or been terminated.

DUTY OF CARE

The investigation of reported crime is the statutory and jurisdictional province of various local, state, and federal law enforcement agencies. The specific
agencies responding to a criminal complaint, and ultimately in charge, depend
on which laws have been reported to be broken and where. Crimes reported
in the city generally belong to municipal police (e.g., city, borough, village, or
township); crimes reported outside city limits generally belong to the county
sheriff; and the state police bureaus are in charge of the highways, investigations
of fraud related to state licensure and services (e.g., Medicaid and welfare),
coordination of multijurisdictional cases, and providing resources to local
agencies upon request (these responsibilities vary from state to state). Federal
law enforcement agencies (e.g., the FBI, the Bureau of Alcohol, Tobacco, Firearms, and Explosives (B-ATF), and the US Marshals) become involved when
federal crimes are suspected or alleged (e.g., terrorism, organized crime, trafficking, civil rights violations, and tax evasion), or when a crime occurs in a
federal building or on federal land (e.g., a federal prison, a Native American

reservation, or a National Park).[1] Whichever agency takes charge of a criminal complaint, they alone have the legal authority to respond, interview witnesses and suspects, collect evidence, or make arrests.

A responding law enforcement agency has a *duty of care*. This refers to the professional and legal obligation to be competent custodians of any victims that are encountered; any criminal investigations that are initiated; and any evidence that supports or refutes allegations of criminal activity against accused suspects. Very often this is a matter of local state or local statute, wherein law enforcement officers are not allowed to turn a blind eye to crime and must respond to protect life and property, and very often it is made part of the formal oath they take when being sworn in.[2] If an agency, or its officers and investigators, do not hold or perceive a professional duty of care to their community, then they are not fit to serve it.

The primary responsibilities of law enforcement, when responding to a criminal complaint, include:

(1) Protect themselves; call for back-up when needed.
(2) Establish who is involved.
(3) Ensure that everyone involved is safe.
(4) Get medical assistance for those that need it.
(5) Determine what happened.
(6) Establish who made the complaint and what it is about.
(7) Identify any witnesses.
(8) Seek out, identify, collect, and protect any physical evidence.
(9) Ensure the objective forensic examination of all relevant evidence.
(10) Determine whether or not a crime has taken place.
(11) Identify any criminal suspects.
(12) Establish whether probable cause exists for an arrest.
(13) Arrest any criminal perpetrators.

These tactical issues also reflect an ethical responsibility. Investigators may not assume what happened based on the statements of one party, whether responding to a domestic situation or an alleged sexual assault. They may not assume that any crime has actually occurred until the facts have been established. They

---

[1]For example, despite film and television depictions of the FBI, that organization does not have jurisdiction over homicides or sex crimes – unless they occur on federal property. FBI agents are, as a consequence, largely inexperienced with these kinds of investigations. However, their services are free to law enforcement, which is why smaller agencies contact them for investigative support (e.g., photocopies, manpower, advanced investigative resources and technology, and media contacts).
[2]It bears noting that the US Supreme Court has twice held that the government, including police agencies, do not normally "have a federal constitutional duty to protect citizens from third parties" (Unkelbach, 2006).

must be sufficiently educated to understand what the elements of each crime are and the what probable cause is. They must also impartially place the cuffs on anyone they determine has broken the law. For example, as explained in Bryden and Lengnick (1997, pp. 1230–1231):

> As with all crimes, the police decide whether a reported rape actually occurred, and attempt to determine who committed it. If they want the case to go forward, they "found" the complaint and transmit the file to the prosecutor's office …. The police must investigate, a task that cannot easily be combined with offering the emotional support that the victim needs. The detective presumably wishes to avoid an injustice to a wrongly accused individual. In addition, for reasons of professional pride, he does his best to avoid looking naive by falling for a story that turns out to be false. Experienced investigators also know that many rape complainants ultimately decline to press charges, sometimes to the dismay of a detective who has worked hard to build a case.

Meeting these responsibilities is best accomplished with a thorough, diligent, and comprehensive investigation. By comprehensive investigation, the authors mean a detailed review of the complainant and their statements; the careful consideration of witness and suspect statements; and the diligent collection and examination of any physical evidence. All of this must be attended prior to making final determinations regarding whether a crime has been committed and whether probable cause exists to arrest any suspects.

Too often, the police do not comprehend the needs of a criminal investigation, let alone probable cause, and the responsibilities mentioned are implemented in reverse. This is to say that suspects are often arrested first and investigations happen later, if at all. This is backward and may result in the creation of bias, missed suspects and evidence, and then doubt when the results of the investigation begin to point away from the person that was initially arrested. Investigators have a duty to refrain from becoming invested in their suspects to the point where they consider making an arrest before a sufficient (or any) investigation has been undertaken. Failure to proceed with the investigation first, and ensure that any arrests are a natural result of that process, can lead to a miscarriage of justice (e.g., a failed prosecution of the factually guilty or a successful prosecution of the factually innocent).

BREAKING THE LAW TO UPHOLD IT

In order to do their work, it is understood that law enforcement needs to violate some of the rules and laws that the rest of us must abide, including those related to traffic ordinances, privacy, firearms possession/use, property seizure, the use of coercive force, and the use of lethal force (Bopp and Schultz, 1972; Kleinig, 1996; Leonard, 1969; Chappell and Piquero, 2004; Brennan *et al.*, 2009; Marche, 2009).

In other words, the police must sometimes break the law in order to uphold it. They are therefore exempt from numerous legal conventions (prescribed by specific circumstances) and enjoy the privilege of exercising authority over regular citizens, under the aegis that they are engaged in an official capacity (Kleinig, 1996; Waddington, 1999; Chappell and Piquero, 2004; Brennan *et al.*, 2009).

This means that those employed by law enforcement agencies are required to walk a fine line while discharging their duties. On one hand, they must strive to represent law and justice to the community through honest, fair, and professional conduct. On the other hand, they are uniquely permitted to break laws that regular citizens are required to uphold. As explained in Waddington (1999, p. 287): "The notion that the police possess a distinctive occupation subculture … derives from the discovery that police work is rarely guided by legal precepts … police officers exercise extensive discretion in how they enforce the law." Ideally, this requires the ability to exercise discretion without a great deal of direct supervision while consistently refusing endless opportunities to engage in graft and corruption (Kleinig, 1996; Hickman *et al.*, 2001; Seron *et al.*, 2004; Chappell and Piquero, 2004; Klockars *et al.*, 2000; Westmarland, 2005). Exercising the proper discretion under these conditions is key to maintaining public confidence in law enforcement integrity (this concept is discussed more extensively, later in this chapter, in the section titled "Police Discretion and Selective Enforcement").

NOBLE CAUSE CORRUPTION

Law enforcement culture is defined by the belief that theirs is a noble cause. A feature of this belief is that a war is currently being waged against particular evils or societal ills (e.g., drugs, terrorism, gang violence) and that those working for law enforcement are on the only good or moral side of the conflict. By extension, anyone not working with or supporting law enforcement is on the wrong side of the conflict, protecting or perhaps even practicing evil.

Commitment to this noble cause means a commitment to preventing illegal activity and apprehending criminal offenders, also referred to as "getting bad guys off the street" (Caldero and Crank, 2004, p. 29). As described in Garcia (2005, p. 68):

> The officer is expected to seek out situations where crimes can be detected and criminals apprehended. Accordingly, the good officer holds to the noble cause of fighting crime and helping the victim … and to an image of being adventurous and brave …. The good officer must carry a gun and handcuffs and "charge the tower" at the sight of crime. However, in the process of becoming a good officer and internalizing police culture, the good officer also becomes cynical and distrusting of the citizens he or she polices ….

Dedication to the noble cause both inspires the values of law enforcement culture and acts as justification for individual officer decisions (Crank *et al.*, 2007).

Noble cause corruption, as it is termed, refers to corrupt or illegal acts committed by law enforcement in order to secure or maintain an arrest or conviction, or some other worthy end (Caldero and Crank, 2004; Martinelli, 2006; Crank *et al.*, 2007; Porter and Warrender, 2009). It reflects dilemmas faced by law enforcement agents in which they must (Crank *et al.*, 2007, p. 105) "select between competing ethics. They either selected the legal means, playing by society's rules even if sometimes that meant letting dangerous offenders go free, or they sought a good end: they acted to prevent truly dangerous offenders from committing additional crimes, however that end was accomplished."

The justification for noble cause corruption stems from the siege mentality of law enforcement officers who believe either they are at war or that their cause is particularly righteous. This is a learned belief system, and the corresponding illegal behavior must be culturally reinforced and molded through experience within the group culture (Sunhara, 2004). When law enforcement culture reinforces a model of ends justifying the means, noble cause corruption becomes the norm that every "good" officer or agent aspires to. This in turn mandates acceptance of and reliance upon what has been referred to as the "Blue Wall of Silence" for both individual and organizational survival.

POLICE RESPONDER ETHOS: "WE DON'T DO THAT HERE"

Ethical law enforcement responders do not usually spend time thinking about ethics. For them, ethics are a straightforward proposition; they understand that there are black and white rules of conduct with no shades of gray. In fact, their decision to behave professionally and ethically is not usually a decision at all, but rather a permanent feature of their character. They know their duty, they carry it out, and they do their best to ignore temptation by identifying and refusing inducements to misconduct. Anything else would be a violation of their professional identity.

What they think about during a response are the tactical concerns: what is waiting for them at the other end of the call; is anyone hurt; do they have the equipment they need to handle the call in their vehicle; is there a suspect at large and are they armed; and do they need to notify any other agencies or units to respond and give assistance?

As a result of this ethical disposition towards doing their job competently, and also doing the right thing, unethical and lazy members of their command will not want to associate with them. Unethical and lazy responders do not want to risk the exposure and they do not want to be called out for not doing what they are supposed to. Consequently, birds of a feather tend to flock together with respect to professionalism and ethics.

The greatest concern for the ethical responder is a new partner – and whether they will need to be broken of bad habits picked up elsewhere. Fortunately, it is relatively easy to spot the lazy and the unethical while on the job. One only need listen to their gripes and watch where they focus their attention.

The unethical responder has a very particular mindset when answering a call. They are thinking about what is in it for them: if the call involves a theft from an electronics store, they are thinking about whether there are security cameras on site and what they might be able help themselves to; if the call involves a domestic dispute, they are hoping that it also involves an attractive member of the opposite sex so that they can step in as the protector and maybe initiate a sexual relationship; if the call involves drugs, they are hoping there is cash and a stash that they can skim while nobody is looking; and if there is an unattended death, they are wondering whether they might be able to lift any prescription medications, or whether there will be a $20 referral fee for calling the right funeral home. Every call is viewed as an opportunity to act in self-interest and those that cannot be exploited in some way are treated without enthusiasm, as an annoyance.

Retired NYPD Sex Crimes Detective John Savino (Savino and Turvey, 2011) related the following example to the authors. Detective Savino was working with a detective newly assigned to the Special Victim Squad. The new detective had transferred in from narcotics. They were investigating a rape complaint and identified a suspect inside of an apartment. They used a ruse to get the suspect to come out of his apartment, at which point they arrested him (they did not have a search warrant for the home and therefore they could not forcibly enter the residence to arrest him; this was a probable cause arrest only). While the suspect was being searched and cuffed, the new detective from narcotics entered the residence several times to conduct searches; he went through drawers and even turned over couch cushions but did not appear to retrieve anything. Detective Savino noted this behavior.

Back at the station, while processing the suspect and writing up the arrest, Detective Savino confronted the his new co-worker and asked: "What were you doing in the residence?" The new detective's response was: "I was, you know, looking for a gun." Detective Savino asked: "Was there a gun reported in the complaint?" The officer responded, "No. But in narcotics that's we do. We enter and search for stuff. These guys have guns a lot the time." Detective Savino, having spent many years in narcotics, knew this to be true, as narcotics detectives operated under a completely different set of operational conditions and legal authorities. Oftentimes, when executing narcotics arrest warrants on apartment buildings, the residents would actually flee, leaving their doors wide open, and the resulting searches for drugs, cash, and guns would utterly destroy the interior. Not so in sex crimes.

Concerned that the new detective was bringing in bad habits from his old unit, and that the new detective was also likely testing the legal and ethical boundaries of his position within the Special Victim Squad, Detective Savino took him aside for an education. Detective Savino explained:

> I know that in narcotics things are very fast and loose. I know that you've been trained to think a certain way and just enter a premises after making an arrest – search for whatever. But we don't do that here. We follow the law and our cases don't get tossed because we couldn't wait for the right piece of paper. So whatever that was, it can't happen again; not with me. We don't do that here.

This turned out to be an important teaching moment for the new detective, and he adjusted his attitude and conduct accordingly. His choice was simple: meet the expectations of the unit's culture or leave. He stayed, learned, and did the right thing from then on.

PATROL OFFICERS

Patrol officers are those uniformed police assigned to move in a pattern within designated areas of a community (a.k.a. "beats") by foot, horse, bicycle, motorcycle, or, more commonly, a marked patrol car. Their presence and activities are intended to serve a number of important functions:

(1) Police visibility is intended to be a crime deterrent, although opinions are mixed on whether, when, and where this is actually effective. For example, some research suggests that targeted and random patrols are the most effective because of their unpredictability (Weisburd and Eck, 2004).

(2) Police presence is essential for maintaining public order and related public perceptions of response availability.

(3) Patrol officers are best situated to identify unreported crime, accidents, hazardous situations, and lack of compliance with local statutes. Patrol officers often serve as *ad hoc* investigators of criminal complaints, specifically those that will not be assigned to a detective. It is interesting to note that one way to gauge the effectiveness of a detective unit is to assess whether it is closing more cases than patrol.

(4) Patrol officers provide security for crime scenes, and assist with the arrest and transport criminal suspects from those scenes when necessary.

(5) Patrol officers are the eyes and ears of effective investigative units: they can facilitate the identification and location of witnesses, suspects and other persons of interest; they know where the crime "hot spots" are at, who has been arrested for what, and who the repeat offenders are; and they are best situated to share this information across different shifts and with pertinent speciality units throughout the day.

While executing these duties, patrol officers encounter many situations that are rife with ethical strain. Additionally, they may become so used to breaking the law in order to uphold it that they are able rationalize certain violations – even when motivated entirely by personal gain. Consider the following issues and circumstances, each of which has led to the resignation or termination of patrol officers subsequent to related legal and departmental violations.

Improper Use of Databases

Most law enforcement employees have rapid accessibility to information that the general public does not, as explained in Berkow (2004): "Police departments have access to national databases of the National Crime Information Center (NCIC) and the National Law Enforcement Telecommunication System (NLETS) and many other systems such as their state motor vehicle records, criminal warrant records, and wanted information." Patrol officers in particular have this information at their fingertips, through terminals in their vehicles, or a quick call to a sympathetic dispatcher.

When logging in to restricted government databases, personnel are generally required to use a secure password and make a record of the ongoing case that their query is associated with. In other words, they must have a legitimate "need to know" that is attached to an official investigation. However, it is not common for those who use such systems to develop or learn techniques for making unlawful queries appear legitimate within it.

Subsequently, law enforcement employees frequently access government databases for personal reasons under false pretenses. For example, out of Michigan, Elrick (2001) reports:

> Over the past five years, more than 90 Michigan police officers, dispatchers, federal agents and security guards have abused the Law Enforcement Information Network (LEIN), according to a Free Press examination of hundreds of pages of LEIN records and police reports.
> In many cases, abusers turned a valuable crime-fighting tool into a personal search engine for home addresses, for driving records and for criminal files of love interests, colleagues, bosses or rivals.

This is similar to reports out of California, where officers are routinely found guilty of (Cassidy, 2009): "using law enforcement databases to meet women, investigate romantic rivals and keep tabs on ex-girlfriends." This includes abuse of the California Law Enforcement Telecommunications System (CLETS), which connects to the Department of Motor Vehicles (DMV), state, and federal law enforcement databases. Abuse of this system, which is a misdemeanor, is so common that there is actually a "CLETS MISUSE INVESTIGATION REPORTING FORM" included with the "CLETS POLICIES, PRACTICES and PROCEDURES" manual made available to subscribing agencies.

In a more severe case out of Maryland, Delores Culmer, a Montgomery County Police Officer, was charged with drug and fraud-related offenses after using a police computer database. She used the system to help her fiancé, a drug trafficker, keep track of and intimidate his competition (News Release, 2011). She eventually pled guilty to conducting unauthorized warrant checks on her fiancé, a different person who owed a drug related debt to her sister, and to conducting vehicle checks on her fiancé's brother (Castaneda, 2011). As a result of her criminal misconduct, she resigned from law enforcement and was sentenced to 5 months home detention and 2 years probation.

In Minnesota the practice is considered "widespread and pervasive" by authorities. Consider the case of former St Paul Officer Anne Marie Rasmussen. She sued the City of St Paul because so many sworn officers across the state, from chiefs to patrolmen, had accessed her driver's license photo improperly – and for using that DMV database like Facebook. As reported in Roper (2012):

> Police and other public employees in Minnesota have routinely abused their access to the massive state drivers' license database, looking up personal information on citizens thousands of times for their own purposes, records show.
>
> In the last two years, audits have revealed that about 160 individuals, mostly in government agencies, have improperly used Minnesota's Driver and Vehicle Services (DVS) database. Protected under state and federal law, it contains photographs, addresses, driving records, physical descriptions and other details about most Minnesotans.
>
> The database recently drew public attention when a former police officer, in an ongoing civil suit, named more than 140 officers that she has accused of inappropriately accessing her data, in many cases to see her driver's license photo.
>
> A child-support worker in southwest Minnesota logged about 4,000 queries over four months, most of them without an official purpose. An Osseo woman received her boyfriend's DVS driving record and photo in the mail, possibly violating a restraining order, and authorities traced it to a local court employee. A deputy admitted using the database to look up the records of his ex-wife and the pop star Prince ....
>
> Records obtained by the *Star Tribune* show that the consequences for these privacy violations vary widely. Some employees caught snooping in the database have merely gotten reprimands, while others have been fired. Many lose access to the database temporarily. In rare instances, some have been charged with gross misdemeanor criminal offenses ....

Rock County fired Child-Support Officer Janet Patten in May 2011 after she made nearly 4,000 photo queries over four months. The county administrator, Kyle Oldre, said the normal number of searches per month should have been about 50.

"She looked up friends and neighbors and co-workers and workers in other counties," Oldre said. "It was just people she knew. And she spent a ton of time doing it." A criminal investigation did not turn up any nefarious intent, but the county nonetheless sent out at least 3,000 data-breach letters in response to the findings ....

This spring, the Department of Public Safety alerted the public after discovering that a Forest Lake car dealership employee had given his DVS login to a friend in the repossession business. The department estimated that the misuse could affect 3,700 Minnesotans.

Ramsey County Sheriff's Deputy Chris Dugger made nearly 2,000 DVS queries over two years and "many (if not most) were performed while he was off-duty and were clearly not work related," according to a complaint in his personnel file. Dugger admitted searching the records for Prince, friends, his ex-wife, co-workers and "members of the public."

... Two recent court cases have raised allegations that the misuse of the database is commonplace. In a civil suit against about 140 officers and at least 16 jurisdictions for improper access of her file, former Eden Prairie and St Paul police officer Anne Rasmusson's legal team wrote that the "extent of this illegal access appears to be widespread and pervasive throughout departments, and is a custom and practice."

When Minneapolis housing inspections director Tom Deegan, a 37-year city employee, was charged criminally last month for accessing DVS data without a business purpose, his attorney shot back that "over 40 city employees have done the same thing and have not been charged."

Former Officer Rasmussen (Figure 6.1) learned of the improper access to her information from fellow officers who would comment directly to her regarding her DMV photo and how it looked. As reported in Zetter (2012):

[Rasmussen] first became aware that other officers were using the database to look her up when a former police academy colleague mentioned to her in 2009 that he and his partner had used their squad car computer to view her driver's license photo. The guy told her he thought she looked great ....

Later, she heard from a cop she'd briefly met years before who suddenly texted her out of the blue to ask her out. This and other incidents over the years prompted her to contact the state's Department of Public Safety in August 2011 asking if it was possible to

FIGURE 6.1

Former St Paul officer Anne Marie Rasmussen successfully sued the City of St Paul after learning that at least 140 officers in at least 16 jurisdictions across the state of Minnesota had accessed her personal information in a restricted government database to ogle her driver's license photo. She also participated in body sculpting contest with fellow officers at a gym in Lakerville, which apparently fueled interest in looking her up by male co-workers. Formerly referred to as "Bubbles" because of her friendly and outgoing attitude, she retired due to injury and now lives privately in the country.

restrict access to her driver's license file. After telling someone in that department that she'd once heard that fellow officers had been looking up her file, a worker in the office investigated and found that her record had been accessed by cops repeatedly across the state going back to 2007.

Investigators began looking into the matter. One officer told investigators that he'd been out on patrol one day when his supervisor called his cellphone and indicated he should check out Rasmusson's record. When investigators asked why he was told to run her record, the officer replied, "to look at her picture, um, and this had something, I believe the conversation surrounded plastic surgery that she had done."

Another officer who'd looked at Rasmusson's record 13 times over the years indicated he kept looking her up to compare her images to see if "she's got a new look."

In late October 2012, the City of St Paul settled former Officer Rasmussen's privacy violation lawsuit for $665 000, explaining that it would be cheaper than paying out each individual claim made against specific officers (Melo, 2012). The consequences for those officers known to have been involved in the scandal include suspensions, temporary restrictions from the database, and written warnings; as of this writing, others are still being investigated (Zetter, 2012).

Consider also the case of Voorhees Police Officer Jeffrey M. Tyther out of New Jersey. On 9 September 2011, Officer Tyther passed a female driver in his marked police vehicle and waved at her. He did not stop her, speak with her, or witness an infraction. Later that day, he used the restricted State Police NCIC motor vehicle database to look up her license plate number, get her name and contact info, and then friended her on Facebook. When she did not respond to his friend request, he emailed her and identified himself as the officer that had waved at her. She became unnerved, told a co-worker, and police were eventually notified. Officer Tyther was suspended and charged, criminally, with Computer Theft and Violating the Motor Vehicle Record Law (Quinones and Cranmore, 2012).

A pernicious aspect to database-related misconduct is that it can continue even after retirement. Law enforcement agents retire to the private sector, or are terminated, but can continue to access restricted law enforcement databases with unexpired passwords or through their relationships with former co-workers. The ability to achieve this kind of unauthorized access is a major consideration in the hiring of retired law enforcement agents by private security or insurance firms.

To be clear, there is no ethical gray area here. It is illegal and therefore unethical to access restricted government databases for personal reasons or for reasons unrelated to an active investigation. Yet it is done every day by law enforcement officers around the nation – some of who are able to do so while no longer on the job. It is also often clustered with other forms of misconduct, as with the example of Delores Culmer.

Police Discretion and Selective Enforcement

In all reality, law enforcement maintain a great deal of discretion with respect to whether, when, and how they intervene to exercise authority over citizens (Kleinig, 1996). As discussed in Coates *et al.* (2009, p. 400):

> Police use a variety of interventions to moderate behaviour, from passive presence, to low level interventions (such as words of advice), to enforcement action (such as the issuance of an 'on the spot' fine or an arrest). Police officers cherish their right to exercise discretion, to be able to use a range of permissible actions and judicially approved sanctions within the constraints of the law and professional doctrine.

For the poorly trained officer, the exercise of discretion is therefore an ethical quagmire. The problems inherent with exercising discretion are raised in Greenleaf *et al.* (2008, p. 4):

> The exercise of discretion infuses virtually every aspect of law enforcement in the United States. Decisions to intervene in a situation or not, cite, arrest, or not, and to prosecute, or not, are all greatly discretionary. The police are obviously not the sole agents of the criminal justice system with the authority to make discretionary decisions; however, they are the most recognized and their decisions are the most numerous. The decision to make a traffic stop, issue a ticket, or issue a verbal warning, is in the hands of the police officers on the street. The problem is that everything about policing makes the exercise of discretion hard to monitor and control. Most officers operate alone or perhaps with a partner, not under the constant scrutiny of their superiors.

To summarize, police discretion can be found in the following routine decisions confronted by patrol officers:

(1) Whom to pull over for traffic violations.
(2) Whether to issue a citation or a warning during a traffic stop.
(3) Whether to interview a witness or not.
(4) Whether to include certain details in a written report.
(5) Whether and whom to arrest when observing a violation.
(6) Whether and whom to arrest in a dispute.
(7) Whether or not to seize or return items of evidence, or as evidence (e.g., alcohol, cash, cell phones, drugs, and vehicles) from or to their owners.
(8) Whether or not to use force.[3]
(9) Whether or not to use lethal force.
(10) Whether or not to pursue prosecution in certain misdemeanor cases or traffic crimes.

The reality of police discretion suggests that law enforcement perceptions regarding what is happening, and the necessary response, are key. According to the literature, the two most important variables considered by officers in their response are the seriousness of the offense and the protection of the community (Coates *et al.*, 2009). However, perceptions related to these two variables are dynamic and easily influenced by contextual variables that officers might not even be consciously aware of (e.g., suspect age, gender, and race; the officer's personal emotional state; and the officer's personal bias; see Greenleaf *et al.*, 2008). This can result in what is referred to as *selective enforcement*: the

---

[3]See Chapter 5: "Ethical Issues in Police Administration," under "Use of Force."

arbitrary punishment of certain individuals or groups for legal violations or crimes, rather than the equal punishment of all known offenders.

The consequences for failing to exercise proper and just discretion range from loss of public confidence in local authorities, to civil liability and loss of life. Consider the following contexts, where selective enforcement has had a major impact on lives and legislation:

Racial Profiling

With respect to policing, *racial profiling* refers to discrimination against an entire racial group based on the presumption that all members share criminal traits or tendencies (see, generally, Reynolds, 2007; Pitt, 2011; p. 53).

> Prior to September 11, 2001 Japanese immigrants were often denied citizenship during WWII because they were profiled as not being loyal to the United States especially after the attack on Pearl Harbor (Muller 2003). African Americans have been the main targets of many racial profiles, like the "Driving While Black" tactics used by law enforcement (Muller 2003) and Hispanics and Asians questions in "routine" investigations pertaining to drug crimes (Gross & Livingston 2002; Ramierez 2003).

Racial profiling is generally considered a fundamentally flawed, often unlawful, and even an unconstitutional approach to policing. It was, consequently, on track to be eradicated in the United States only a decade ago. That is, until the events of 11 September 2001, as explained in Reynolds (2007, p. 667):

> It is a prevailing belief that most criminal acts, excluding the "intellectual" crimes of CEOs involved in the recent Enron and Martha Stewart fiascos, are typically committed by the poorest, darkest, and newest members of American society.
>
> By the mid-1990s society treated racial profiling by law enforcement as the great taboo. In 2000 eighty percent of Americans surveyed in a Gallup poll stated that they had not only heard of the act of profiling but believed the practice should be stopped. Between January 1999 and September 2001, thirteen states had moved to pass legislation that banned racial profiling or required police departments to collect data on the act. Yet, in the wake of the September 11 terrorist attacks, the consensus of profiling in the nation changed. All nineteen of the hijackers were Arabic men. In no less than "a month [after] the attack, surveys showed that a majority of Americans favored more intensive security checks for Arab and Middle Eastern people."

Racial profiling is self-fulfilling prophecy: if policing efforts focus on a particular racial group, then crime statistics eventually reflect that group's association with violent crime and the efficacy of racial profiling is believed to be confirmed. The consequences of racial profiling include increased racial tension, increased violence from those being profiling, and an overall mistrust of law enforcement (Pitt, 2011). It also hardens any "Us *v.* Them" attitudes held by law enforcement.

Domestic Violence

In cases of reported domestic violence, most states have what are referred to as *mandatory arrest laws*, requiring law enforcement to make an arrest at the scene if there is probable cause that a crime has been committed (e.g., victim injury). This requires them to decide who is the aggressor on the spot, which can in some instances be difficult at best. Mandatory arrest laws exist to prevent law enforcement from making subjective determinations regarding whether to arrest during a domestic violence call. They are meant to counteract officer apathy, abuser likeability, personal relationships, and other personal bias, and to keep these from influencing the decision to arrest the aggressor. They are also meant to prevent the primary aggressor from further injuring or killing the victim once law enforcement leaves. Many states have these kinds of laws (Tarr, 2007); however, awareness among patrol officers can be limited.

The reality is that responding officers maintain broad discretion in domestic violence cases. They can find or create a reason not to arrest if they work hard enough and refrain from investigating too thoroughly. As discussed in Durant (2003):

> Changes in law ... do not necessarily change officers' behavior; studies and anecdotal reports suggest that many officers still do not arrest in response to a report of domestic violence ....
>
> Although most states now mandate or encourage arrest when there is probable cause that a domestic violence incident has occurred, police still retain discretion to determine, under a mandatory regime, when probable cause exists and, under a pro-arrest regime, whether or not to arrest at all.

The decision not to arrest, despite mandatory arrest laws, may have something to do with the bias issues already discussed. However, it may also have to do with law enforcement perceiving a lack of support from prosecutors. For example, the local district attorney may not prosecute domestic violence crimes against police officers with the same zeal for justice as others. According to one study (Brannan 2003): "In San Diego, a national model in domestic violence prosecution, the City Attorney typically prosecutes 92% of referred domestic violence cases, but only 42% of cases where the batterer is a cop."

When a prosecutor cannot or will not put a case on, this often goes right back to the quality of the investigation that was performed. A case that has not been properly investigated and assembled by law enforcement in the first place should not be accepted by the prosecutor's office, as it will invite an alert jury to acquit. It should also be noted that the majority of domestic violence complaints are not assigned a detective, generally resulting in investigations that are conducted entirely by patrol and concluded by the end of a single shift. In such ways, law enforcement has tremendous influence over whether a domestic violence complaint results in an arrest, can be brought to trial, and whether the district attorney will be willing to take it forward.

Prostitution

The law enforcement response to sex trafficking has been, generally, a focus on efforts to arrest the trafficked victims (i.e. prostitutes).[4] As explained in Youth Radio (2010), this is because it is easier than arresting customers or traffickers ("pimps"):

> Though they arrest few pimps and prosecute even fewer, Oakland police say that arresting the girls is a necessary first step toward shutting down sex trafficking. But many children's advocates disagree.
>
> Nola Brantley, who was trafficked as a teenager, now runs MISSSEY, a program that helps girls get out of the sex trade. "The reason why we arrest them is because they are the easiest person to arrest," Brantley says. "It's hard to arrest the johns, and they represent many different facets of society and life. It's hard to arrest the exploiters because of the amount of evidence necessary. So, the easiest person to arrest is the child."
>
> Brantley says these children are not really prostitutes. "Every act of what's called ... 'prostitution' with these children is actually a form of child sexual abuse – and to take it further, child rape," she says. "So I don't think children who are raped should be criminalized, no I don't."
>
> Alameda County Assistant District Attorney Sharmin Bock counters that arresting the girls is actually a way to save them – it gives the county a way to introduce victimized girls to social services. "Having a court involved with a case hanging over your head provides that added incentive to stay in a program, at the end of which a great likelihood exists that you will in fact recognize that you were in fact exploited," she says. And, Bock says, the logistics of going after the men are daunting. "It's very hard to get a hold of those johns. Because by the time you hear about it, they're just a number. It's the child telling you, 'I had sex with 15 different men yesterday.' They're long gone."

---

[4]Portions of this section have been adapted from Savino and Turvey (2011).

As explained in Lodge (2011), when law enforcement arrests the prostitute and does not investigate the flow of money back up to the top, the conditions that create organized trafficking are essentially ignored (p. 1B):

> Theresa Flores, who helps exploited teens at a safe house in Dublin, Ohio, also told members of the Human Trafficking Task Force for the Middle District of Louisiana that children increasingly are victims of the monstrous business.
>
> Worldwide, Flores said, sex slavery pours $32 billion into the pockets of criminals each year .... She said children forced into prostitution sometimes are branded as criminals for their inability to escape the adults who are torturing them. "We're arresting teenagers for this," Flores said. "We're arresting the wrong people." ....
>
> Today, approximately 20,000 sex slaves are brought into the U.S. annually, Flores noted. But more than 3,500 children born in this country go missing or become runaways each day. She said many of those children become sex slaves. Flores said 77 percent of adult prostitutes in this country were trafficked as children.

The result of arresting sex workers can be secondary victimization; they may come to believe that the system does not recognize them as a victim and that their trafficker has both power and immunity. This is especially true when arrests are not part of an overall effort to intervene and provide mental health and social services needed to escape the cycle that they are in.

In extreme cases, however, law enforcement officers themselves are arrested for soliciting prostitution. The cases are unending, and result in suspension, demotion, and termination at more professional agencies (e.g., McCabe, 2011; Visser, 2011; Sudekum, 2012). Law enforcement officers have also been known to approach prostitutes and offer them protection from other pimps, and safety from arrest, in exchange for sex and a cut of their earnings. They have also been known to run, or work as "security" for, illegal brothels in their jurisdiction, as reported in Hauser (2007) :

> A former city police officer admitted on Thursday that he took favors and money from a Queens brothel as part of a protection scheme that helped shut down its competitors. The former officer, Dennis Kim, 31, pleaded guilty in United States District Court in Brooklyn to a federal charge of conspiracy to commit extortion in his capacity as a police officer. The plea enables him to avoid a trial and the prospect of a lengthy jail sentence.
>
> Mr Kim, who resigned from the Police Department on Monday, admitted that he and a partner accepted money from the owners of the brothel, who supplied information that was then used in raids that closed their rivals. Mr Kim also said that his partner would receive sexual services from the brothel's prostitutes for his role in the scheme.

In March 2006, law enforcement authorities arrested Mr Kim and the partner, Jerry Svoronos, now 32, along with the man and woman who ran the brothel. Immigration took into custody 16 women believed to have worked there as prostitutes. The case was one of the city's largest sex-and-bribes protection scandals since more than a dozen officers were implicated a decade ago for protecting a brothel on the West Side of Manhattan ....

Mr Kim's lawyer, Maurice H. Sercarz, said his client had been a capable and aggressive police officer, and now wanted to put the ordeal behind him. "That and a feeling he let down people close to him," Mr Sercarz said ....

The arrests followed a 10-month investigation by the Federal Bureau of Investigation, the Police Department, the United States attorney's office in Brooklyn, and Immigration and Customs Enforcement. According to court documents, the brothel took in more than $1 million a year, and the information supplied by the brothel owners enabled the officers to make career-advancing arrests.

In other jurisdictions, officers have also been found doing such things and running escort services, some involving underaged girls, out of their homes, even with the help of with their wives (see, generally, Abraham, 2012; Callahan, 2012; Hasch, 2011; McKenzie, 2012). For example, consider the case of Lori Vernon-Lee and her husband, Indianapolis Metro Police Officer Jeremy Lee; they reportedly operated a prostitution business for several years. As detailed in Jefferson (2008):

"People would call up and she would hook them up with the call girls for payments at a hotel or at their house," said Johnson County Prosecutor Lance Hamner.

"We're disgusted by his conduct, we're ashamed of him, and I think the thing that the public needs to know is that this investigation started by the work of members of our own agency," said IMPD Chief Michael Spears.

Chief Spears fired probationary officer Lee immediately.

Investigators say a *NUVO* magazine escort ad uncovered the Lees' secret business. Prosecutors say after Lori Vernon-Lee arranged dates at the Cambridge Apartments in Greenwood, where Jeremy Lee sometimes handled the money.

"Lee was actually collecting money from these call girls and sometimes while he was in uniform," said Hamner.

Investigators executed a search warrant at the fired officer's home. They reportedly found a client list and started calling names on the list. Investigators name public safety consultant Jerry McCory among the escort service clients. McCory is charged with patronizing a prostitute.

In other cases, patrol officers have been arrested and convicted for looking the other way and for providing security and transportation of prostitution rings (see, generally, Herman, 2012).

It should go without saying that this kind of misconduct is an illegal abuse of power and therefore unethical. However, there are officers that develop an entitlement-oriented attitude towards those that they police, especially when it comes to cash, drugs, crime victims, and prostitutes. The discretion that they wield becomes currency for personal gain – and they ultimately use their positions of authority to exploit those that they are sworn to police (discussed further in the section "Bribes, Inducements, and Entitlement").

High-Speed Chases ("Hot Pursuit")

High-speed chases involving law enforcement and suspect vehicles pose a significant risk to officer, suspect, and bystander safety. Too often they result in serious injury or death. They can also result in the destruction of property (e.g., vehicles and structures). As a consequence, they also incur departmental litigation from which the police and their related government administrators are not necessarily immune. As explained in Cooley (2006, p. 28):

> Liability arising from pursuits exists in all states with only slight differences in the degree of fault applied to the pursuit, such as whether the officer showed deliberate indifference or reckless disregard. Some states limit liability to cases where the pursuing officer has been involved in a crash or directly caused a collision. However, some states permit a wide variety of lawsuits against the police when they are operating emergency vehicles that cause other drivers to crash, including lawsuits against the police for collisions caused by the fleeing criminal.
>
> The latter category of lawsuit depends on the theory that a fleeing criminal's collision is a foreseeable risk of a pursuit. In other words, if the police action started the pursuit, then the police can and should be able to control the criminal's driving behavior. The logic supporting this theory is questionable at best, and the police attorney must make sure that a jury understands the difficulties an officer realistically faces during a pursuit-one of the most volatile, dangerous, and unpredictable tasks of police work.
>
> The federal courts are the only jurisdictions that essentially bar pursuit lawsuits arising from a fleeing criminal's collision. In *County of Sacramento v. Lewis*, the U.S. Supreme Court held that the federal civil rights act theory does not apply to the usual pursuit lawsuit. The Supreme Court held that in order for an officer to deprive someone of his or her constitutional right of due process, an officer's conduct

during the pursuit must have been so outrageous that it "shocks the conscience."

Therefore, patrol officers must be diligently trained to enforce clearly defined departmental policy with respect to engaging in the "hot pursuit" of any suspect vehicle. This includes deliberately assessing whether the risk of pursuit is worth the threat posed by the individual taking flight. That is to say, they must assess (Kleinig, 1996, p. 118): "(1) the danger posed to the occupant(s) of the pursued vehicle; (2) the danger posed to innocent bystanders and other travelers; and (3) the danger posed to themselves."

Another problem with high-speed chases is that increased stress and adrenaline experienced by officer can result in excessive use of force issues should they actually catch up with the fleeing suspect. These are referred to as "POP" cases (Pissing Off Police"). Should an officer (or a group of officers) with the wrong attitude and temperament catch a fleeing suspect after a long and stressful chase, liability can result – often captured on camera from a news helicopter that officers are not paying attention to.

Consequently, as explained in Kleinig (1996, p. 118): "The decision to pursue … should be based on some reasonably grounded law enforcement, public safety or peacekeeping purpose." This requires clearly defined department policies with an explicit rationale that is taught to every responding officer. Consider the following types of law enforcement policies:

- *No chase.* As the result of multiple or high-profile incidents of high-speed chases gone wrong, ending in loss of life and departmental liability, some police agencies have adopted a strict "no chase" policy. This means that under no circumstances will they give chase should a suspect flee in their vehicle. This is done to avoid accidents, loss of life, damage to property, and related liability. The argument is that suspect and vehicle information can be recorded and the suspect can be picked up later when there is less chance of anyone getting hurt, perhaps even just hours later at their home or place of work.
- *Felony chase.* Some police agencies have adopted a "felony chase" policy. This means that they will only pursue suspects when they have probable cause to believe that a serious felony has been committed or perhaps a reasonable belief that a felony will be avoided by the suspects, immediate capture. This policy is argued to prevent injury, loss of life, and liability resulting from minor traffic infractions, while also acting to protect the community from serious felons. Generally speaking, the patrol officer calls in the chase and supervisors either assist with a pursuit determination or make it for them; this takes the decision out of their hands, and helps prevent on scene bias and emotions from taking over.

- *Mandatory chase.* Some police agencies have adopted a "mandatory chase" policy. This means that they always pursue fleeing suspects, no matter the circumstances. The argument behind this policy is that no officer on the scene or back at the station can know just how dangerous a suspect is. The fact that they are fleeing is reasoned to suggest that they are very dangerous, as they are willing to recklessly put the lives of others in danger with their high-speed driving. Such policies, exercised without discretion, have resulted in much tragedy. This is especially true when seen in concert with poor or low pursuit training.

It also bear mentioning that pursuit policies can differ greatly from county to county. This means that there may be a *mandatory chase* policy in one county, but within minutes the suspect can enter a neighboring county with a *no chase* policy. This will result in suspect escapes, regardless of the professed policies, mission, and values of the initial pursuing agency.

Bribes, Inducements, and Entitlement

While there are many forms of law enforcement corruption, Gottschalk (2011, p. 170) found that the "Blue Wall of Silence" provided the most protection for those officers accepting "gratuities" or using "excessive force." These are among the most tolerated forms of misconduct in law enforcement culture. This is also detailed by research prepared in Chappell and Piquero (2004, p. 90):

> … acceptance of meals and gifts is the most common and most extensive form of police corruption …. Many cities actually allow officers to accept free or discount meals. It is often accepted behavior when it is an act of gratitude toward the police, but sometimes the motive is to buy protection from the police. In other words, some businesses offer free items or services in expectation for quicker response times and extra protection from the police.

Not surprisingly, free coffee, meal discounts, and other small gifts are also the gateway through which otherwise lawful officers are initiated into other corrupt group practices. This can be witnessed on a daily basis in just about every city around the country, at any eatery where multiple police units gather for a break or a meal. For example, both the Denny's and Chik-Fil-A restaurant chains offer a 50% discount to law enforcement for all meals, as do many donut and coffee shops; Denny's actually puts "law enforcement discount" on the receipt. Officers will enter such establishments wearing their uniforms, or show their police radios or badges conspicuously when plainclothed, all of this with the hope, and often the expectation, of receiving a "law enforcement discount." Discounted meals or drinks are actually bribes, enticing officers to show favor, to give special consideration and quicker response times, or merely for the security provided by their continual presence.

Once a police officer gives up their integrity in lockstep with the other members of their command, no matter how small the enticement, the potential for future and more severe forms of corruption is increased. It also provides a motive for looking the other way when something more severe is witnessed involving fellow officers. While seeming minor to some, giving in to these kinds of initial temptations teaches the new officer to become morally and ethically malleable. From a public relations standpoint, accepting gifts and gratuities also reinforces the worst view of the police held by those that are successful with enticements: that the services of law enforcement are partial, or otherwise for sale.

Consider the extreme examples of former DeKalb County Sheriff's Deputy Chief Donald Frank and Lieutenant Willie Durrett, as reported in Rankin (2012):

> The former deputy police chief of DeKalb County declared that "no one should sell their badge" and admitted he'd done just that.
>
> Donald Frank was sentenced Thursday to three years and seven months in prison for conspiring to take bribes from an Atlanta businessman. But before that happened, U.S. District Judge Bill Duffey had plenty to say, and Frank didn't disagree with any of it.
>
> Duffey reminded Frank of the day he took his oath of office and swore to uphold the law. Over the next two decades, as Frank rose through the ranks from sergeant to lieutenant to head of the county's homeland security division and finally to deputy chief, there were many young officers who looked up to Frank as an example, the judge said.
>
> "You were in a unique position to have a positive influence, not only in the police department but in your community," Duffey said. "It's a position you uniquely abused." As he spoke, Duffey looked down at Frank, who was in a wheelchair because of injuries from a motorcycle accident. All the while, Frank kept his gaze on Duffey, never looking away ....
>
> Earlier Thursday, Duffey sentenced businessman Amin Budhwani to 20 months in prison. Budhwani, who owned gas stations and convenience stores, pleaded guilty to bribing Frank and former DeKalb Police Lt Willie Daren Durrett, who will be sentenced Friday. Budhwani wined and dined Frank at fine restaurants and strip clubs, gave him thousands of dollars in payoffs and bankrolled trips to casinos. In return, Frank made threatening calls to Budhwani's mistress at the businessman's behest, strong-armed Budhwani's employees into paying back money they owed, and got DeKalb police to follow one of Budhwani's business partners to make him feel so threatened he'd want to leave the country, prosecutors said.

> Frank, a former U.S. Marine who once headed former DeKalb CEO Vernon Jones' security detail, received leniency for testifying against Durrett at a trial in July. A number of former colleagues, friends and U.S. Rep. Hank Johnson, D-Ga., who first got to know Frank while serving as a DeKalb magistrate judge, wrote letters to Duffey asking for mercy.
>
> Duffey told Frank that his acts will make people wonder whether police officers can be trusted.

This is similar to another example out of Mississippi, in which two patrol officers have plead guilty to taking money for protecting drug shipments, as reported in Hernandez (2012):

> Two former Jackson Police Department patrol officers pleaded guilty to accepting bribes to protect a drug shipment coming into Hawkins Field in Jackson, according to the U.S. Attorney's Office.
>
> Former Officers Monyette Quintel Jefferson, 27, and Terence Dale Jenkins, 25, pleaded guilty Wednesday in federal court to getting paid bribes to protect 100 kilograms of cocaine that was going to be coming in on an airplane to Jackson, federal officials stated.

Both cases demonstrate how bribery can ultimately corrupt in law enforcement, involving both patrol officers and supervisors who look the other way, actively serve as security, or even become enforcers with respect to organized crime. It is a mindset, and an entitlement, that can all start with that first cup of free coffee while on patrol.[5]

Another example of how entitlement can manifest itself is in the application for departmental awards and service medals. Law enforcement culture makes earning these a priority, because they look good on the uniform, they matter in the officer's file and on their "hero sheet," and sometimes they come with a cash reward. In some instances, the officer will apply for an award or a medal before a case has gone to the grand jury – and they might forget or be unaware that all such applications are discoverable to the defense. When they testify before the grand jury later, the case can be utterly blown if both versions of

---

[5]This brings to mind the case of Lieutenant Major Garvin of the Daytona Beach Police department. Lieutenant Garvin was fired in 2008 after an internal affairs investigation determined that he had threatened to delay future response times to a local Starbucks when employees there refused to make his specialty coffee for free; Lieutenant Garvin reportedly visited the coffee shop multiple times each shift, often cutting in front of paying customers, as that location offers free regular coffee to law enforcement. Lieutenant Garvon was re-instated in 2010 subsequent to an appeal. However, he was investigated again that same year after parking his vehicle in a handicapped spot at "Disney's Wide World of Sports;" instead of a handicapped placard, he placed his law enforcement picture ID and badge in the windshield (Hijek, 2010).

events do not line up. In some cases, the officer may have embellished details in one or both accounts to achieve a particular end. This is why such applications should not be made until a case has gone to the grand jury and testimony is firmly on the record.

Conduct Unbecoming

Conduct unbecoming is a charge used by police agencies to discipline its officers for any behavior that violates departmental rules and virtues. It is levied when instances of misconduct fall outside of explicit written policies and codes of behavior. As explained in Martinelli (2007, p. 41): "The officer's perceived deviant behavior usually does not fit perfectly into an agency's rules and regulations, so administrators charge the offending officer with conduct unbecoming. It is used as a catch-all charge." Ultimately, conduct unbecoming is imposed against officers for moral failures and inappropriate behavior that reflects poorly on the agency's public image while on duty. For example, many police agencies have strict policies against employees having sex while on duty – evidencing just how prevalent this is.

Conduct unbecoming is also used to sanction certain inappropriate off-duty public conduct, such as public alcohol abuse, affiliation with criminals and criminal activity, and inappropriate sexual relationships or activity. As explained further in Martinelli (2007, p. 42):

> Courts have struggled to balance an organization's public image and its need to foster an orderly and dutiful force with an officer's individual right to privacy while off duty. Over the years, costly litigation has still not provided clear-cut guidelines for agencies to follow.
>
> For example, one court upheld an officer's three-day suspension for engaging in a "whipped cream race" with other officers while off duty, licking whipped cream off of a dancer's torso. A federal court upheld the termination of an officer for an act of adultery in a public park while off duty, because such acts could jeopardize a department's effectiveness. The U.S. Supreme Court declined to hear the appeal of an officer who was denied promotion because of his affair with the spouse of a fellow officer.
>
> Discipline was appropriate where there existed a nexus between the diminished effectiveness of an organization's service and an officer's videotaping his sexual activities with three women without their consent. Appellate courts have sustained the termination of officers for off-duty "kinky sex" with prostitutes, for consorting with prostitutes even though there was no payment of monies for sexual services, and for being at an after-hours club, engaging in promiscuous relations with known prostitutes. In these cases, the agencies successfully argued there was a rational basis between the proscribed

conduct and the discipline meted out. As long as police have a valid "state objective" (i.e., the need to foster a professional force through accountability and maintenance of public image), reasonable disciplinary measures can be used to seek officer compliance in off-duty privacy situations.

Consider also the case of former Officer Bert Lopez of the New Mexico State Police, which involved both public departmental image and perceptions of accountability. In 2011, Officer Lopez was caught on a surveillance camera having sex with a woman on the hood of a car, in public, while in uniform (Figure 6.2). Still images were forwarded to the State Police for investigation and Officer Lopez was placed on leave for 3 weeks; initially, internal affairs investigators claimed that there was no crime in part because there were no witnesses making any formal complaints regarding specific misconduct. A few days after taking this position regarding the incident, and subsequent to the story and

FIGURE 6.2
Officer Bert Lopez of the New Mexico State Police was fired in 2011 for conduct unbecoming an officer, including having sex in public, while on duty, and wearing his uniform.

related images going viral, police officials confirmed that Officer Lopez had been fired (Grammer, 2011).

While termination in this case may seem unfair to some, the consequences of this incident have had far-reaching consequences, even into the courtroom. In September 2011, former Officer Lopez was called as a prosecution witness in a drunken driving case; the reporting officer is usually the only witness in such cases. In court, the defendant, a married woman, testified that Officer Lopez told her that she made his patrol car smell good during the vehicle stop. She also testified that he eventually propositioned her. She was ultimately acquitted by the jury of driving while intoxicated (DWI), who claimed that their decision was based on the dash-cam video and the defendant's apparent lack of intoxication (Vela, 2011).

Consider also the case of La Vergne police officer Nick Walters out of Tennessee, who showed self-interest, insensitivity, and bad judgment in his conduct toward at least one victim of domestic violence, as reported in Gebbia (2010):

> Seven text messages in 40 minutes cost a La Vergne police officer his job. Investigators said it was the content of those texts and who he was sending him to that got him fired.
>
> Officials said they were flirtatious some even sexually charged, and the La Vergne police chief said they crossed the line when he realized they were being sent on the job to a woman this officer met on a call for help.
>
> "It really shocked me to be honest with you," said Mayor Ronnie Erwin.
>
> Both he and the police chief were surprised and disappointed to learn what officer Nick Walters texted while on the job.
>
> "I was surprised that he would do something like that," said Chief Ted Boyd.
>
> "I don't understand what he was thinking and why he would think this is alright," said Erwin.
>
> The messages were sent to a woman he just met while responding to a domestic violence dispute. Documented on the woman's phone and in his personnel file, it shows the texts started flirtatiously just after 1 a.m.
>
> Walters typed: "Hey, this might be kind of forward but your beautiful and I hope it all works out for you … it's officer Walters by the way."
>
> The woman's response: "Well thank u but I'm not feeling very beautiful right now."
>
> Chief Boyd said what he texted next is when Walters crossed the line, telling the woman how he wanted to use his handcuffs, but not to make an arrest.

The message read: "Well putting you in handcuffs would be nice haha sorry that was dirty haha … I would only put you in hand cuffs if you wanted it."

"When you are sent out to a house – you have a job to do, nothing else. It's not a dating service. It's for you to do your job," said Erwin. While the sexually charged texts aren't illegal, the chief said Walters broke the code of conduct and trust of the public and they had no choice but to let him go.

"That is something we are not going to tolerate, being out here in the street working and while you are working make these inappropriate text messages or anything else that might happen," said Boyd.

Apparently this isn't his first time Walters abused the buttons on his phone. His personnel file shows another woman, a coworker at the department, had a similar incident with a similar text about handcuffs months ago.

Boyd said the decision to fire Walters was an easy one and reminder to the others that victims call police for help, not to be hit on. "That is something we are not going to tolerate," said Boyd.

Chief Boyd said that when he approached Walters about the texts he did admit to sending them and knew that it was wrong. He did apologize, but Chief Boyd said it was too late to change the situation.

Officials said the woman and her husband have hired a lawyer and may pursue legal action against the officer.

Fortunately, in this case, there was a prior reported instance of misconduct against Officer Walters that made the decision to terminate him straightforward. This was not a momentary lapse in judgment, but rather part of a pattern of sexually inappropriate behavior while on the job. Had his co-worker not reported the prior incident of texting, former Officer Walters might have received different treatment from his supervisors. Not every complaint results in definitive action, but they can lay the necessary foundation for something definitive in the future.

Carrying and Responding Off-Duty

Some agencies require officers to carry their firearms, their police identification, and maintain response readiness even while off-duty. Others do not or have no clear policies in place. In any case, subsequent to the terrorist attacks perpetrated on 11 September 2001, the law enforcement community has been encouraged by Federal legislation to carry and respond, no matter where they are or what they are doing, as explained in Bulzomi (2011).

On July 22, 2004, President George W. Bush signed into law H.R. 218, the Law Enforcement officers Safety Act (LEOSA), which created a general nationwide recognition that the public is better served by allowing law enforcement officers to carry their firearms outside of their jurisdictions whether they are on or off duty. The theory behind LEOSA already was recognized among a number of states. That is, law enforcement officers retain their identity, training, experience, and dedication to the safety and welfare of the community regardless of whether they are on duty in their employer's jurisdiction, going home to another community, or merely traveling for leisure purposes. However, the act creates a limited privilege to carry concealed weapons for law enforcement officers, not a right to bear arms.

This law, and related policies, increase the chances for police-on-police encounters where accidents and fatalities can result, especially when sufficient training is not afforded to officers, and proper identification procedures are not followed. As detailed in Spawn (2010, p. 24):

The issue of police-on-police shootings has been brought to the forefront in New York following three recent fatal shootings:

- On May 28, 2009, off-duty New York City Police Department (NYPD) Officer Omar Edwards was shot and killed by another officer as Edwards was in foot pursuit of a suspect who had broken into Edwards's car.
- On January 25, 2008, off-duty Mt Vernon, New York, Police Department Officer Christopher Ridley was shot and killed by officers from another department while Ridley was holding a suspect.
- In 2006, off-duty NYPD Officer Eric Hernandez was shot and killed by an on-duty officer after attempting to apprehend suspects who had attacked him.

However, there are also many examples of cases where crimes in progress have been effectively thwarted and lives saved due to the intervention of well-trained off-duty officers. To avoid tragedy in such situations, it is necessary for agencies to have clear policies regarding off-duty officer responses to crime; to provide consistent training in relation to those policies; and for officers to follow those police and that training with care and deliberation.

CRIMINAL INVESTIGATORS

In response to a criminal complaint, law enforcement agencies have a legal obligation to investigate, establish the facts, and determine whether a crime has actually been committed (Bopp and Schultz, 1972; Kappeler, 2006; Sexual Assault Task Force, 2009; Savino and Turvey, 2011). When their agents believe that a crime has been committed, they also have a related obligation to identify and apprehend any suspects (Bopp and Schultz, 1972; Kleinig, 1996). As explained in Sullivan (1977, p. 149): "It is the job of the police to enforce the law. Thus, officers must remember that they are primarily fact-finders for their department and have no authority or control over the judicial or legislative branches of government."

Common ethical issues faced by criminal investigators involve or are related to the use of confidential informants (CIs), problems with search and seizure, concerns over entrapment, the use of deception, the possibility of inducing a false confession, and the temptation to falsify evidence. Each of these will be discussed in turn, save falsifying evidence, which was discussed in Chapter 5: "Ethical Issues in Police Administration."

The Use of CIs

A good detective will tell you that they are only as good as their CIs. As discussed in Leson (2012, p. 398):

> Modern law enforcement agencies focus their use of informants on ferreting out individual criminals. Informants permeate every level of the criminal justice system, particularly in the investigation of drug crimes. Indeed, the U.S. government's "War on Drugs" increased the use of informants in the prosecution of drug crimes. Professor Alexandra Natapoff explains that "approximately one-third of criminal offenders are under the influence of drugs at the time of their offenses, while as many as 80 percent of inmates have a history of substance abuse." These offenders have information and contacts that make them ideal informants. Informants are "irreplaceable" in the context of "the investigation of narcotics, prostitution, and other vice crimes, because inside information is often necessary for police to learn about their occurrence."

Some informants are regular citizens in possession of useful connections or information. However, the majority of CIs are themselves criminals; their information is paid for in cash or in consideration for looking the other way with regards to known criminal activity (e.g., police discretion with respect to arresting the informant for prostitution or possession of controlled substances). This is, in fact, how a good investigator develops informants – by catching them in the act and trading their discretion for information related to more serious criminal activity.

There are, in reality, different kinds of informants, as explained in Leson (2012, pp. 397–398):

> There are several categories of informants. Some are paid by the police for their cooperation. Others are voluntary, sharing information with

police out of "feelings of civic duty" or for other various reasons. The third category … is composed of offenders trading cooperation in exchange for leniency. Professor Michael Rich calls this subcategory "coerced informants" because the government claims to have sufficient evidence for a conviction. Most active informants are coerced informants.

Coerced informants are subject to intense pressures to cooperate. For instance, an offender's uncertainty is highest immediately following arrest. This "mak[es] her most likely to agree to cooperate at that time." When the individual does not readily offer information, "the most powerful motivational tool available to the police or prosecutor is the fear of criminal charges and a long prison sentence." The promise of leniency, sometimes vague and uncertain, can be enough to "flip" an offender.

Critics often overlook the issue of coercion, instead focusing on the inherent unreliability of information generated by informants.

There is also a great distinction between the CI and the "street snitch." The most important is that a formal agreement exists between the CI and the investigator, with clear rules and expectations. The investigator takes responsibility for the CI, their future conduct, and with managing the terms of their agreement. With a street snitch, they provide information to the investigator and then they are gone.

CIs are an important investigative resource because of their direct access to the world of crime and criminals. This is something that is denied the traditional detective, unless they are working undercover. However, because of the CI's involvement in criminal activity, they can also become a tremendous liability, as explained in Lieberman (2007, p. 62):

Confidential informants are crucial to many law enforcement investigations and are especially essential in the field of narcotics investigations. Informants can provide specific information that is simply not available from other sources. However, the informants are often criminals themselves; if not properly managed, they can render a law enforcement investigation useless, destroy an agency's credibility, and even endanger officers' lives.

Additionally, CIs that are paid for their services, and are allowed to continue to do things like use drugs or engage in prostitution, are essentially using departmental funds to further their criminal activities. If the CIs are responsible for children and use narcotics, then they are essentially using departmental funds to further create a neglectful environment. Those who agree to use CIs under these circumstances must be aware of such issues, and be prepared to answer questions about them honestly when asked by supervisors or the courts.[6] They must also be prepared to deal with it emotionally, when things go wrong.

Consider the development of *Rachel's Law* in the State of Florida, as described in Leson (2012, p. 406):

> In March of 2008, police received a tip from a confidential informant regarding Rachel Hoffman's involvement in drug activity. Police searched her trash and found a ledger with names and amounts of money. In April, police searched Hoffman's apartment. They found 151.7 grams of marijuana, six ecstasy pills, and other drug paraphernalia. Police did not take Hoffman to jail or notify the prosecutor's office about the drugs. Instead, Hoffman – in a drug treatment program at the time – agreed to assist the police.
>
> On May seventh, the police gave Hoffman thirteen thousand dollars and sent her on a controlled drug buy to purchase both drugs and weapons. She approached two suspected criminals, who then unexpectedly changed the meeting plan and directed her to a remote location not under police surveillance. At this point, the police lost contact with Hoffman. They found her body two days later.

As a result of Rachel Hoffman's (Figure 6.3) murder while being coerced to act on behalf of law enforcement, her parents lobbied for the creation of what became known as *Rachel's Law*, described in Leson (2012, p. 408):

> The original version of the bill included a provision concerning the use of informants in substance abuse programs. It specified that a confidential informant participating in a court-ordered substance abuse treatment program could not be an informant without the permission of a supervising circuit judge. It also required potential informants participating in voluntary substance abuse treatment programs to receive express approval of a state attorney before accepting. The state attorney would have had to consult with treatment providers to discuss whether working as an informant would jeopardize an individual's success in the program.
>
> The final version of the bill, however, allows law enforcement agencies to "establish policies and procedures to assess the suitability of using a person as a confidential informant by considering" eight factors. One of these factors is "[w]hether the person is a substance abuser or has a history of substance abuse or is in a court-supervised

---

[6]See also the case of *Washington v. Gary Benn*, involving prosecutorial misconduct related to a CI, detailed in Chapter 9: "Ethical Issues for Criminal Prosecutors."

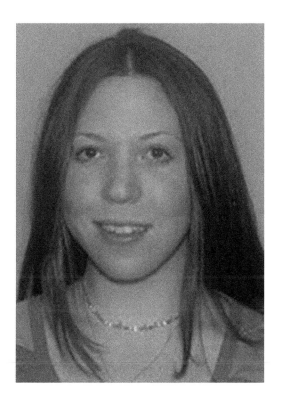

FIGURE 6.3

Rachel Hoffman was coerced by law enforcement to work as a CI. She was killed by two suspected criminals when law enforcement lost contact with her during a so-called "controlled" drug buy. Her murder was the impetus for *Rachel's Law* in the State of Florida.

drug treatment program ...." This provision lacks the original bill's express concern with the success of the informant's treatment.

Professional law enforcement agencies actually have very strict rules about the use of CIs (e.g., NYPD, Florida Department of Law Enforcement). First, there must be a written contract specifying the terms of the CI's assistance, where and how they must meet investigators, and how long until the terms of the contract are satisfied (often in exchange for sentence reduction). Second, they are usually required to meet with CIs with at least one witness. Also, the CI is generally prohibited from engaging in further criminal activity.

Regardless of state law or agency policy, the ethical use of CIs has some additional basic requirements, adapted from Lieberman (2007):

(1) The investigator's relationship with the CI must be professional, not personal, with clear boundaries.

(2) The investigator should not engage in a sexual or romantic relationship with the CI, as this blurs professional lines, compromises the investigator's objectivity, and increases the potential for gullibility, to say nothing of destroying the investigator's courtroom credibility.

(3) The investigator should not visit the CI in their home or provide means for the CI to access them at their own home, as this blurs professional lines.

(4) The investigator must not be gullible and must be aware of the CI's alternate motives for giving genuine or even false information.

(5) The investigator should seek to corroborate all information provided by the CI with an alternate source before taking definitive action.

(6) The investigator should pay the informant with departmental funds in a manner that is carefully documented for later administrative and court purposes; the investigator should not reimburse the CI with seized cash, drugs, or other valuables.

(7) The investigator should not promise anything that is impossible or illegal, such as the reduction or elimination of criminal charges; these must be arranged with the proper legal authorities responsible for making such plea bargains.

(8) The investigator should carefully document all information and activities related to the CI, to document the professional nature of the relationship for later administrative and court purposes.

For example, Montgomery County Sheriff's Deputy Steve Gardiner was fired in 2010 for sleeping with one of his CIs and then lying to his department about it. As reported in Page (2010):

> "It is my policy to terminate immediately any deputy who isn't truthful," Sheriff Phil Plummer said Wednesday. "Steve (Gardiner) is a good officer, but I will not tolerate untruthfulness."
>
> Gardiner, 37, a 15-year veteran, had spent the past two years in the sheriff's organized crime unit assigned to a Drug Enforcement Administration task force. When the allegations came to light, Plummer said he immediately transferred Gardiner to the road patrol until the investigation was complete. Gardiner was fired Oct. 27.
>
> Investigators said Gardiner began a sexual relationship with the sheriff's office informant in spring 2009. He used his "covert identification" to rent motel rooms and his duty car to "take her on dates."
>
> When asked, Gardiner said the relationship ended in summer 2009. Investigators found evidence that the couple "engaged in sex ... as late as April 24, 2010."
>
> They found no evidence that he used his police powers for favors with the motels or that they had sex in his sheriff's vehicles. The

sheriff's office gave no details about her beyond that she was a paid informant.

Gardiner and the informant said they met at the sheriff's road patrol headquarters. The informant told investigators she thought Gardiner "attractive." He asked her if she knew a known criminal, and they exchanged phone numbers so she could call him with any information.

The informant said at some time in the next four months, she called Gardiner and they set up a "date." Both told investigators they soon became sexually involved. "The only thing we didn't do was live together," the informant told investigators …

Gardiner also told investigators he used his undercover ID to rent motel rooms and used various undercover vehicles for their dates. He initially told investigators they split in summer 2009.

When presented with motel reservations in his covert name and ID from April, he was unable to explain it. In a second interview, he said he remembered that they had broken up and reconciled for a short period this year ….

Two days before his firing, Gardiner said he had "created a nightmare for himself and his family (and) … how sincerely sorry he is for what he described as a nightmare," according to a pre-disciplinary conference report ….

Maj. Dave Hale, head of operations, wrote in a memo that an investigation "revealed a pattern of repeated infractions of rules, regulations, directives, or orders of the Sheriff's Office over an approximately approximate 18-month time period."

Sheriff Plummer also explained that while former Deputy Gardiner's actions were not illegal, they were unethical and, in his judgment, put other officers at risk.

Given that the courts generally lean in favor of protecting the flow of confidential information, it is imperative that investigators exercise discretion related to CIs with great care (Leonard, 1969) – and document everything thoroughly. If anything happens to the CI, or the CI commits crimes under the direction of investigators, their agency is on the hook and is ultimately going to be held responsible.

Search and Seizure

As already discussed, the professional investigator has a duty to arrest those responsible for the commission of crimes. This requires knowing what constitutes a crime, and whether there is probable cause for a search or an arrest. Unfortunately, many police officers either do not know what probable cause is or only know the rote script to repeat when asked but not what it actually means in practice.

Search and seizure laws are those surrounding police authority to stop and search persons and their property for evidence related to a crime, so long as they have probable cause to believe that a crime has occurred and that the person being stopped is the one responsible. The following discussion regarding the levels of suspicion that must be cleared before probable cause has been achieved is taken directly from Savino and Turvey (2011, pp. 95–98):

PROBABLE CAUSE

Police officers can only make an arrest if they have **probable cause**. Typically it is held that probable cause exists when known facts and circumstances, of a reasonably trustworthy nature, are sufficient to justify a person of reasonable caution or prudence to believe that a crime has been or is being committed by the person being arrested. This definition can vary between different jurisdictions, but is often referred to as the "reasonable man standard."

Probable cause statements in search warrant and arrest applications must detail those facts and circumstances that lead the investigator to reasonably believe that a crime has occurred and the person that they want to arrest is responsible. Those facts must be accurate, and there must also be sufficient detail demonstrating how these facts and circumstances were reliably established. It is not sufficient to simply provide a "hero sheet" (the officer's education, history with the department, and accomplishments), list the charges suspected, maybe the uninvestigated statement of the victim, and hope a judge will sign the warrant on faith. Even if a judge does sign a warrant application without reading it carefully, the case could be lost or reversed at any point in the future when the probable cause is challenged ….

The Fourth Amendment

In order to establish probable cause, it is necessary to understand its Fourth Amendment origins and the different levels of suspicion that lead up to it. The Fourth Amendment to the U.S. Constitution reads: "The right of the people to be secure in their persons, houses, papers, and effects, against unreasonable searches and seizures, shall not be violated, and no Warrants shall issue, but upon probable cause, supported by Oath or affirmation, and particularly describing the place to be searched, and the persons or things to be seized."

In order to search or seize (arrest) an individual, as mentioned in the previous section, the police must demonstrate that they have probable cause. This is the highest level of confidence and is preceded by lesser degrees. Awareness of these standards during an investigation is crucial to the long-term success of any case. Mistakes made in their application may not prevent the initial search and arrest, but they can wreak havoc during pretrial hearings or postconviction appellate reviews. If a jurist determines that the police violated the defendant's Fourth Amendment rights, the charges may be dismissed early on or the case may be overturned subsequent to a successful prosecution as in the previous case example. In order to prevent errors in officer certainty, the following levels of suspicion should be applied to the evidence: *mere suspicion*, *reasonable suspicion*, and then *probable cause*.

Mere Suspicion

This level of confidence is sometimes considered a gut feeling, or a hunch, that leads the individual to question a particular circumstance. Police are usually held to a lower threshold for "mere suspicion" because of their training and experience. At this level, the officer can approach the individual and attempt to engage the subject in a consensual encounter. The individual does not have to speak with the police or even stop for them at this level. They can walk away at any time.

Reasonable Suspicion

This level of confidence is intended to describe facts and circumstances that may lead an officer to believe that a person will be involved in a crime, or was involved in a crime. It is more than a hunch, but less than probable cause. At this level, the police may conduct an investigatory stop. A person may not be arrested based on reasonable suspicion; however, if probable cause develops during an investigatory stop, the officer may arrest the suspect.

As defined earlier, *probable cause* is a reasonable belief that an individual has, is, or will commit a crime. This belief must be based on facts, not a hunch or a suspicion. To determine if there is probable cause, the court must find that a person with reasonable intelligence would believe the same, given the same facts and circumstances. Probable cause requires stronger evidence than reasonable suspicion.

It bears noting that the courts are divided on the issue of whether or not warrantless (probable cause) stops to investigate completed misdemeanors are actually constitutional: some hold that they are not and others hold that they are if they meet the subjective "reasonableness" criterion. Legal scholars are also divided on the matter (Bajaj, 2009). Consequently, every jurisdiction abides by its own legal standard, making it difficult for officers and investigators alike.

The professional investigator must operate with clear departmental search and seizure policies to fall back on – policies that conform with governing statutes. This requires knowledgeable and informed supervisors. They must also have their own working knowledge of the law, and the ladder of suspicion that leads them to "reasonable." Without these, they are going to be continually challenged regarding their stops, arrests, and any information or seizures obtained as a result; those challenges will likely be successful.

The authors have found that the best method for preventing accusations of unlawful search and seizure is to prepare written consent forms that can be administered to suspects on scene. These forms can be used when requesting vehicle searches, property searches, and even when requesting DNA samples. Each form gets signed, dated, and filed with the rest of the paperwork associated with the search. Should there ever be a question regarding lawfulness or good faith, the relevant consent form can be provided to show the suspect's signature, alongside that of the investigator, indicating both knowledge of, and agreement to, investigative activities. Obviously this will not work when the suspect is disagreeable, but it can be a powerful step with respect to showing good faith, building trust, and developing a rapport when used in concert with professionalism and a pleasant demeanor.

Entrapment/Creating Crime

Entrapment is a general term that refers to law enforcement inducing a person to commit criminal acts, specifically one that they would not have otherwise been likely to commit (Hughes, 2004). In some legal jurisdictions, claims of entrapment are a legitimate legal defense against criminal charges. However, entrapment does not apply when it can be shown that the suspect would have committed the crime anyway, by related planning, intent, or a pattern of similar criminal activity.

Similar to entrapment are those cases involving sting operations that induce or facilitate low level or poorly connected criminals to commit more serious crime. One example would include law enforcement investigators encouraging a drug user that sells a few bindles of cocaine to friends to sell them an entire kilo, despite no prior history of moving that kind of weight. Another example would be selling explosives (fake or real) to a suspected terrorist, helping them make a bomb, and then arresting them when it fails to detonate, as recently occurred in a case out of New York (Stebner and Boyle, 2012). In these cases, there may be a tactical advantage to creating a more serious crime and consequences by facilitating criminal activity – such as a greater desire for a plea deal and a willingness to flip on more senior members of an organized criminal enterprise. However, allowing a known criminal to continue in their activity without arresting has it own ethical downside; any crime they commit, and any harm that is caused, falls on the shoulders of investigators.

Consequently, the professional investigator uses this tactic sparingly, and with only the greatest care. They do not use it blindly for political gain, to enhance the status of their case closures unnecessarily, or to make their supervisors look good. They use it to make good cases against specific known targets using those further down the criminal chain of command.

Use of Deception

When agents of law enforcement lack sufficiently reliable evidence to lawfully arrest a prime suspect in a criminal investigation, they tend to focus their efforts on obtaining a confession (Magid, 2001; Thomas, 2007). One means of obtaining a confession is through the use of deception. The courts tend to have a variable yet generally permissive attitude towards the police use of deception to gain inculpatory evidence from criminal suspects – to include undercover work and ploys where false witness statements, false co-conspirator statements, and fabricated evidence are referenced or presented during interrogations (Kassin *et al.*, 2010). Consequently, pretense, trickery, and lies are standard instruments found in many police toolkits.

There are limits set on the acceptable use of deceptive methods, generally established by state laws and departmental policy. However, some criminal justice commentators argue that deception, and outright lying, has become an integral feature of law enforcement culture. One overall view is presented in Slobogin (1997), which offers a continuum of falsity that runs from justifiable to inexcusable (pp. 775–776):

> Many police, like many other people, lie occasionally, and some police, like some other people, lie routinely and pervasively. Police lie to protect innocent victims, as in hostage situations, and they tell "placebo lies" to assure or placate worried citizens. They tell lies to project nonexistent authority, and they lie to suspects in the hopes of gathering evidence of crime. They also lie under oath, to convict the guilty, protect the guilty, or frame the innocent.
>
> Some of these lies are justifiable. Some are reprehensible. Lying under oath is perjury and thus rarely permissible. On the other hand, lying that is necessary to save a life may not only be acceptable but is generally applauded (even if it constitutes perjury). Most types of police lies are of murkier morality, however.

A more chilling perspective on police deception is reported in the research compiled by Dorfman (1999, pp. 460–461):

> Police officers can be expected to omit, redact, and even lie on their police reports, sworn or unsworn; they will conceal or misrepresent to cover up corruption and brutality; they are trained to deceive citizens during investigations as part of good police practice; they will obscure facts, and even lie, to cover up the misconduct of fellow officers. Additionally, command practice and policy gives officers

every incentive to lie to cover for lack of productivity or to aggrandize themselves for recognition and promotion. And yes, police officers will commit perjury in our courts of law.

In any case, it is generally agreed that there must be clearly defined limits set against the use of deception-based police tactics, given the tremendous power that agents of the government wield (Dorfman, 1999; Magid, 2001; Thomas, 2007; Kassin *et al.*, 2010). However, unless there are salient penalties associated with violations of those limits, it seems unlikely that longstanding attitudes towards the use of deception will be changed.

The ethical investigator understands these limits and uses deception judiciously, only when the situation warrants it, and with clearly defined boundaries.[7] They do not lie in court, they do not lie in their reports, and they do not lie to fellow officers – only as a deliberately measured and carefully documented tactic in the course of an investigation. They also know that deception is an option that can have disastrous results. For example, if a suspect or interviewee calls an investigator's bluff or somehow knows they are being deceived, any credibility the investigator had is lost.

Confessions and False Confessions

There are different forms of admission by criminal suspects, to include the confession and the inculpatory statement. A *confession* is a voluntary statement, written or recorded, by a criminal suspect that acknowledges guilt for a particular crime. This is different than an *inculpatory statement*, which is a voluntary statement, written or recorded, by a criminal suspect, acknowledging a particular decision or activity associated with a crime.

A *false confession* is, in fact, not a confession at all. Rather, it is an involuntary statement of guilt made under duress, or as the result of *coercion*. As described in Uphoff (2006, pp. 791–794):

> Most people find it hard to fathom that anyone would confess to a serious crime – like murdering a parent – unless the person actually committed the act. The reality, however, as the case of David Vasquez dramatically illustrates, is that the pressure placed on suspects during custodial interrogations can, and does, produce false confessions.
>
> While investigating the rape and murder of Carolyn Hamm in Arlington, Virginia, the police learned that a man named David Vasquez was seen walking by Hamm's house on the evening of

---

[7]In some jurisdictions, for example, it is legally permissible to present suspects with false evidence and reports in order to spur a confession or inculpatory statement; in others, this conduct by an officer would be considered a crime.

the murder and then again two days later. Vasquez had lived in Hamm's neighborhood but had moved to Manassas, Virginia about eight months earlier. Two Arlington detectives picked up Vasquez in Manassas for questioning and, when he denied being in Arlington on the day of the murder, concluded he had something to hide.

Within thirty minutes of questioning, the detectives were able to convince Vasquez to change his story by falsely telling him that he was seen climbing through Hamm's window and that his fingerprints were found in her house. For Vasquez, a thirty-seven-year-old with a [General Educational Development diploma], who was described as having "'borderline retarded/low normal' intelligence," it was unfathomable that his fingerprints were there.

The detectives pressed the distraught and crying Vasquez by insisting that the only real question was why he was at Hamm's house. Vasquez suggested he might have helped Hamm move something. From there, the police fed Vasquez details of the crime and encouraged him to confirm those details. When his answers did not fit the facts of the case, the detectives yelled at him.

Although during this first interrogation Vasquez admitted to hanging Hamm, by the end of this first session, he denied even being at her home. He stated that he was admitting all this "because you tell me my fingerprints were there." At the end of a second interrogation, Vasquez began to recount a "horrible dream." In that dream, he admitted to the facts that he learned during his first interrogation. The following day, Vasquez gave a shorter version of this dream confession.

Based largely on his three confessions, Vasquez was charged with capital murder, rape, and burglary. To avoid the death penalty, Vasquez ultimately entered an Alford plea to second-degree murder and was sentenced to twenty years on that charge, along with fifteen years for the burglary. Five years later, Vasquez was pardoned when Hamm's real killer was caught following a killing spree.

Few laypeople appreciate the coerciveness of the interrogation process. Many mistakenly believe that the Miranda warnings, including the right to the presence of counsel, offer suspects considerable protection from police overreaching. In practice, however, few defendants request counsel and those that do are rarely allowed to see counsel, at least not until the police have had an opportunity to secure a confession. Police are permitted to lie about incriminating evidence and to bring a variety of psychological pressures to bear to get at the truth. The problem, unfortunately, is that in their zeal to get the truth, law enforcement agents may only get the defendant to acquiesce to the officer's version of events.

As further explained in Gohara (2006), any "confession" can be rendered involuntary by the unethical behavior of investigators (pp. 805–807):

> Deception, false assurances, and misrepresentations of the availability of independent incriminating evidence by themselves are generally insufficient to establish involuntariness under the federal courts' application of the "totality" test. Rather, federal courts' central inquiry into the impact of a particular interrogation tactic on voluntariness is whether the allegedly coercive tactic overcame the suspect's free will and rational decision-making.
>
> Despite the general paucity of federal case law circumscribing deceptive interrogation techniques, there are a few noteworthy federal decisions sanctioning the use of particular tactics. The Seventh Circuit, for example, held, in the context of a Fourth Amendment consent-to-search claim, that "[a]lthough the law permits the police to pressure and cajole, conceal material facts, and actively mislead, it draws the line at outright fraud, as where police extract a confession in exchange for a false promise to set the defendant free." In so holding, the court drew explicit parallels between law enforcement deception in executing a search and in extracting a confession. The Ninth Circuit held that when detectives coerced a suspect into confessing by falsely telling him that his statement could not be used against him, the resultant statement was involuntary.
>
> Interrogations employing false or fabricated evidence where interrogators have misled suspects to believe that police possessed inculpatory evidence, including physical evidence or accomplices' confessions have generally been held to be voluntary. At least one federal court, however, has held that a confession obtained after police presented fabricated evidence, like that employed in Cayward, was involuntary.
>
> Cayward and its progeny represent an admirable effort by courts to set some limits on the use of deliberate deception to induce suspects to confess.

Just in case it is not clear, *coercion* refers to the use of force, threats, or intimidation to gain someone's compliance. It can be as direct as a threat of physical violence, like pushing someone up against the wall or raising a fist, or it can be indirect, like a baseball bat in the corner of an interrogation room. It can be also be intentional or unintentional, for example, two big detectives interviewing a small teenage girl, alone, with loud voices in a tiny room, combined with what can only be described as the detectives "looming" over her. Maybe one of the detectives says "If you don't confess, we can't help you" or "If you tell us what we want to hear, we can make sure you go down hard for this." The authors have seen these things, and variations, on more than one occasion.

Any statement made by an interviewee under any of these conditions could easily be considered coerced – whether coercion was intended or not.

Research has also shown that the poorly trained (and ultimately unethical) investigator believes that they have a sixth sense regarding suspect guilt and deception, which leads them to improperly believe that the false confessions they achieve are genuine (Kassin *et al.*, 2007). This same research shows other problems contributing to false confessions, such as:

- *Miranda.* The false belief that Miranda warnings are a safeguard sufficiently understood by criminal suspects, or the fact that they may be read by investigators, who in turn misunderstand or simply ignore them.
- *Coercion.* The use of coercive tactics by investigators that presume suspect guilt (e.g., physical isolation while in custody, positive confrontations with evidence, and minimization of deeds and consequences).
- *Time in the box.* Prolonged interrogations, in excess of 6 hours, with "confessions" achieved after a long night of other coercive tactics. In one study (Drizin and Leo, 2004) of 125 false confessions, 34% of interrogations lasted 6–12 hours and 39% lasted 12–24 hours, with a mean of 16.3 hours.
- *Recording the confession.* Many police investigators do not record the entirety of the interview or interrogation process; rather they record or document only the final confession (e.g., video, audio, and in writing).

Additionally, the unethical or biased investigator approaches the interview with the wrong mindset. They believe the suspect is guilty. As a consequence, they do not believe the suspect is telling the truth until they get a confession; everything else is viewed as a lie and treated with hostility.

During interviews and interrogations, the ethical investigator has an open mind. If anything, they are looking to exclude the suspect – and failing to find a way to exclude them they will build a more reliable case should the suspect actually be guilty of a crime. They also make certain to provide suspects with the following:

- An environment free of coercive elements and language.
- Water.
- Food.
- Regular bathroom breaks.
- A conspicuous mechanism for recording the entire interaction with the suspect, to include any inculpatory statements or confessions.
- A cigarette only as a reward.
- An attorney if requested.

Ethical investigators also understand that anything achieved after more than 3 hours is probably not going to be a reliable statement – but something else entirely.[8] They are also acutely aware of the fact that, if they are good enough, they can get anyone to confess to just about anything given enough time.

SUMMARY

This chapter explores the more common ethical issues that are confronted by those on patrol, and also by those conducting criminal investigations. However, before these issues are explored, one must understand that a responding law enforcement agency has a duty of care, referring to the professional and legal obligation to be competent custodians of any victims that are encountered; any criminal investigations that are initiated; and any evidence that supports or refutes allegations of criminal activity against accused suspects.

Patrol officers, while executing duties, encounter many situations that are rife with ethical strain. These situations include, but are not limited to, the improper use of databases; police discretion and selective enforcement; high speed chases; carrying and responding off-duty; conduct unbecoming; bribes, inducements, and entitlement.

Similarly, common ethical issues faced by criminal investigators include or are related to the use of confidential informants; problems with search and seizure; concerns over entrapment; the use of deception; the possibility of inducing a false confession; and the temptation to falsify evidence.

Questions

1. List 5 primary responsibilities of law enforcement when responding to a criminal complaint.
2. List 2 ethical issues that may be encountered by *patrol officers* while executing duties. Explain.
3. List and define the levels of suspicion that should be applied to evidence to prevent errors in officer certainty.
4. Why do *mandatory arrest laws* exist? Explain.
5. Define the term *false confession*. List 3 factors that contribute to false confessions.

References

Abraham, H., 2012. Former city cop back in court on prostitution charges. CBS Pittsburgh, August 17; url: http://pittsburgh.cbslocal.com/2012/08/17/former-city-cop-back-in-court-on-prostitution-charges/.

Bajaj, S., 2009. Policing the Fourth Amendment: the constitutionality of warrantless investigatory stops for past misdemeanors. Columbia Law Review 109, 309–349.

---

[8]This excludes any time spent letting the suspect make initial false statements that then require follow-up and confrontation, in order to get the suspect to the point where they are telling the truth – which can take over an hour in some cases.

Berkow, M., 2004. Homeland security: the internal terrorists. The Police Chief 71, June; url: http://www.policechiefmagazine.org/magazine/index.cfm?fuseaction=display_arch&article_id=319&issue_id=62004.

Bopp, W., Schultz, D., 1972. Principles of American Law Enforcement and Criminal Justice. Charles C. Thomas, Springfield, IL.

Brannan, T., 2003. Domestic violence in police families. Purple Berets, June http://www.purpleberets.org/violence_police_families.html.

Brennan, A., Rostow, C., Davis, R., Hill, B., 2009. An investigation of biographical information as a predictor of employment termination among law enforcement officers. Journal of Police and Criminal Psychology 24, 108–112.

Bryden, D., Lengnick, S., 1997. Rape in the criminal justice system. Journal of Criminal Law and Criminology 87, 1194–1384, (Summer).

Bulzomi, M., 2011. Off-duty officers and firearms. FBI Law Enforcement Bulletin 80 (1), url: http://www.fbi.gov/stats-services/publications/law-enforcement-bulletin/january2011/off_duty_firearms.

Caldero, M., Crank, J., 2004. Police Ethics: The Corruption of Noble Cause. Anderson, Cincinnati, OH.

Callahan, J., 2012. Memphis police officer arrested on sex trafficking charge. Memphis Commercial Appeal, September 18; url: http://www.knoxnews.com/news/2012/sep/18/memphis-police-officer-arrested-on-sex-charge/.

Cassidy, J., 2009. Police officer accused of misusing database. Orange County Register, August 14.

Castaneda, R., 2011. Ex-Montgomery officer accused of helping drug ring admits unlawful computer checks. Washington Post, April 27.

Chappell, A., Piquero, A., 2004. Applying social learning theory to police misconduct. Deviant Behavior 25, 89–108.

Coates, S., Kautt, P., Mueller-Johnson, K., 2009. Penalty notices for disorder: influences on police decision making. Journal of Experimental Criminology 5 (4), 399–428.

Cooley, A., 2006. Police pursuit and high-speed driving lawsuits. The Police Chief 73 (10), 26, 28–30, 32–33 and 35.

Crank, J., Flaherty, D., Giacomazzi, A., 2007. The noble cause: an empirical assessment. Journal of Criminal Justice 35, 103–116.

Dorfman, D., 1999. Proving the Lie: litigating police credibility. American Journal of Criminal Law 26, 455–503.

Drizin, S., Leo, R., 2004. The problem of false confessions in the post-DNA world. North Carolina Law Review 82, 891–1007.

Durant, C., 2003. When to arrest: what influences police determination to arrest when there is a report of domestic violence? Southern California Review of Law and Women's Studies 12, 301–340, (Spring).

Elrick, M., 2001. Cops tap database to harass, intimidate: misuse among police frequent, say some, but punishments rare. Detroit Free Press, July 31.

Garcia, V., 2005. Constructing the 'other' within police culture: an analysis of a deviant unit within the police organization. Police Practice and Research 6 (1), 65–80.

Gebbia, K., 2010. La Vergne officer fired over inappropriate texts. News Channel 5, September 23; url: http://www.newschannel5.com/Global/story.asp?S=13208729.

Gohara, M., 2006. A lie for a lie: false confessions and the case for reconsidering the legality of deceptive interrogation techniques. Fordham Urban Law Journal 33 (3), 791–842.

Gottschalk, P., 2011. Management challenges in law enforcement: the case of police misconduct and crime. International Journal of Law and Management 53 (3), 169–181.

Grammer, G., 2011. State cop gets ax over sex scandal. The New Mexican, September 2; url: http://www.santafenewmexican.com/localnews/State-police-fire-cop-in-sex-tape#.UJX86bTd2WQ.

Greenleaf, R., Skogan, W., Lurigio, A., 2008. Traffic stops in the Pacific Northwest: competing hypotheses about racial disparity. Journal of Ethnicity in Criminal Justice 6 (1), 3–22.

Hasch, M., 2011. Pittsburgh officer linked with prostitution, drug operation. TribLive, August 30; url: http://triblive.com/x/pittsburghtrib/news/s_754134.html#axzz2BHoN4dUL.

Hauser, C., 2007. Officer admits he helped thwart a brothel's rivals. New York Times, December 28.

Herman, H., 2012. Prostitution ringleader sentenced in sex assault. Reading Eagle, October 19; url: http://readingeagle.com/article.aspx?id=422131.

Hernandez, R., 2012. Two Mississippi cops plead guilty to accepting bribes to protect cocaine deals. Ventura County Star, October 18; url: http://blogs.venturacountystar.com/the_court_reporter/2012/10/two-mississippi-cops-plead-guilty-to-accepting-bribes-to-protect-cocaine-deals.html.

Hickman, M.J., Piquero, A.R., Lawton, B.A., Greene, J.R., 2001. Applying Tittle's control balance theory to police deviance. Policing 24 (4), 497–519.

Hijeck, B., 2010. Cop in free coffee flap under investigation again. Sun Sentinel, May 7; url: http://weblogs.sun-sentinel.com/news/specials/weirdflorida/blog/2010/05/officer_in_free_coffee_flap_un.html.

Hughes, P., 2004. What's wrong with entrapment? Southern Journal of Philosophy 42 (1), 45–60.

Jefferson, S., 2008. Officer accused in prostitution ring turns himself in. WTHR, Channel 13, July 3; url: http://www.wthr.com/global/story.asp?s=8615573.

Kappeler, V., 2006. Critical Issues in Police Civil Liability, fourth ed. Waveland Press, Long Grove, IL.

Kassin, S., Leo, R., Meissner, C., Richman, K., Colwell, L., Leach, A., La Fon, D., 2007. Police interviewing and interrogation: a self-report survey of police practices and beliefs. Law and Human Behavior 31, 381–400, (August).

Kassin, S., Drizin, S., Grisso, T., Gudjonsson, G., Leo, R., Redlich, A., 2010. Police-induced confessions: risk factors and recommendations. Law and Human Behavior 34, 3–38.

Kleinig, J., 1996. The Ethics of Policing. Cambridge University Press, New York.

Klockars, C., Ivkovic, S., Harver, W., Haberfeld, M., 2000. The measurement of police integrity. US Department of Justice, Office of Justice Programs, National Institute of Justice NCJ 181465.

Leonard, V., 1969. The Police, The Judiciary, and the Criminal. Charles C. Thomas, Springfield, IL.

Leson, I., 2012. Toward efficacy and equity in law enforcement: "Rachel's Law" and the protection of drug informants. Boston College Journal of Law and Social Justice 32 (2), 391–419.

Lieberman, B., 2007. Ethical issues in the use of confidential informants for narcotic operations. The Police Chief 74 (6), pp. 62 and 64–66.

Lodge, B., 2011. Escaped victim, officials target sex slavery in state. Baton Rouge Advocate, 1B, January 27.

Magid, L., 2001. Deceptive police interrogation practices: how far is too far? Michigan Law Review 99, 1168–1210, (March).

Martinelli, T., 2006. Unconstitutional policing: the ethical challenges in dealing with noble cause corruption. The Police Chief 73 (10), 148, 150, 152–154 and 156.

Martinelli, T., 2007. Minimizing risk by defining off-duty police misconduct. The Police Chief 74 (6), 40–45.

McCabe, F., 2011. Henderson lieutenant demoted after prostitution arrest. Las Vegas Review-Journal, April 7; url: http://www.lvrj.com/news/henderson-lieutenant-demoted-after-prostitution-arrest-119425119.html.

McKenzie, K., 2012. Arrests of Memphis officers spotlight major, minor missteps. Memphis Commercial Appeal, October 7; url: http://www.commercialappeal.com/news/2012/oct/07/arrests-of-memphis-officers-spotlight-major/.

Melo, F., 2012. Former St. Paul cop agrees to $665K to settle privacy claims. Twin Cities Pioneer Press, October 17; url: http://www.twincities.com/localnews/ci_21786600/st-paul-council-consider-385-000-settlement-eden.

News Release, 2011. Maryland police officer charged with drug trafficking conspiracy and computer fraud: she allegedly used her police powers to access law enforcement databases to obtain information concerning a co-conspirator and his drug associates. US Immigration and Customs Enforcement, March 16; url: http://www.ice.gov/news/releases/.

Page, D., 2010. Sheriff's deputy fired for sleeping with informant, lying about it. Daytona Daily News, November 11; url: http://www.daytondailynews.com/news/news/local/sheriffs-deputy-fired-for-sleeping-with-informant-/nNJdF/.

Pitt, C., 2011. U.S. patriot act and racial profiling: are there consequences of discrimination. Michigan Sociological Review 25, 53–69, (Fall).

Porter, L.E., Warrender, C., 2009. A multivariate model of police deviance: examining the nature of corruption, crime and misconduct. Policing and Society 19 (1), 79–99.

Quinones, T., Cranmore, C., 2012. Voorhees cop charged with using police database to 'friend' driver on Facebook. CBS Philly, July 25; url: http://philadelphia.cbslocal.com/2012/07/25/voorhees-police-officer-charged-with-misusing-police-powers-for-personal-reasons/.

Rankin, B., 2012. Former top DeKalb County cop gets prison for bribery. Atlanta Journal-Constitution, October 25; url: http://www.ajc.com/news/news/local/former-top-dekalb-county-cop-gets-prison-for-bribe/nSndb/.

Reynolds, A., 2007. So you think a woman can't carry out a suicide bombing? Terrorism, homeland security, and gender profiling: legal discrimination for national security. William and Mary Journal of Women and the Law 13 (24), 667–699.

Roper, E., 2012. Misuse of Minnesota drivers' records is relatively common. Star Tribune, October 14; url: http://www.startribune.com/local/174052311.html.

Savino, J., Turvey, B., 2011. Rape Investigation Handbook, second ed. Elsevier, San Diego, CA.

Seron, C., Pereira, J., Kovath, J., 2004. Judging police misconduct: "Street-level" versus professional policing. Law and Society Review 38 (4), 665–710.

Sexual Assault Task Force, 2009. False reports and case unfounding. Attorney General's Sexual Assault Task Force, State of Oregon, Position Paper, January 22.

Slobogin, C., 1997. Deceit, pretext, and trickery: investigative lies by the police. Oregon Law Review 76, 775–816, (Winter).

Spawn, M., 2010. Officer safety during police-on-police encounters. The Police Chief 77 (4), 24–30.

Stebner, B., Boyle, L., 2012. Federal Reserve 'bomber' plotted to kill Obama: Foreign student, 21, who 'tried to blow up Manhattan bank with 1,000lb car bomb planned to take out President.' Daily Mail, October 17; url: http://www.dailymail.co.uk/news/article-2219268/New-York-terror-plot-Man-attempted-blow-Federal-Reserve-Bank-New-York-1-000-pound-bomb.html.

Sudekum, M., 2012. Jeffrey Holmes, police officer, pleads not guilty to having sex with women in exchange for not arresting them. The Huffington Post, July 3; url: http://www.huffingtonpost.com/2012/07/04/jeffrey-holmes-police-officer-not-guilty-sex-women-arrest_n_1648691.html.

Sullivan, J., 1977. Introduction to Police Science, third ed. McGraw-Hill, , New York.

Sunhara, D.F., 2004. A social-psychological model of unethical and unprofessional police behaviour. Canadian Review of Policing Research 1, December 16; url: http://crpr.icaap.org/index.php/crpr/issue/view/1.

Tarr, N., 2007. Employment and economic security for victims of domestic abuse. Southern California Review of Law and Social Justice 16, 371–427, (Spring).

Thomas, G., 2007. Regulating police deception during interrogation. Texas Tech Law Review 39, 1293–1319, (Summer).

Unkelbach, L., 2006. Supreme Court refuses to expand Section 1983 liability: no federal constitutional duty to enforce a restraining order. The Police Chief 73 (5), url: http://www.policechiefmagazine.org/magazine/index.cfm?fuseaction=display_arch&article_id=889&issue_id=52006.

Uphoff, R., 2006. Convicting the innocent: aberration or systemic problem? Wisconsin Law Review, 739–842, url: http://hosted.law.wisc.edu/lawreview/issues/2006-2/uphoff.pdf.

Vela, V., 2011. SF DA plans to continue using ex-state cop as prosecution witness. Albuquerque Journal, September 11; url: http://www.abqjournal.com/main/2011/09/09/abqnewsseeker/updated-sf-da-plans-to-continue-using-ex-state-cop-as-prosecution-witness.html.

Visser, S., 2011. Former deputy convicted of killing pimp. The Atlanta Journal-Constitution, February 2.

Waddington, P., 1999. Police (canteen) sub-culture: an appreciation. British Journal of Criminology 39 (2), 287–309.

Weisburd, D., Eck, J., 2004. What can police do to reduce crime, disorder, and fear? The Annals of the American Academy of Political and Social Science 593 (1), 42–65.

Youth Radio, 2010. Arresting youth in sex trafficking raises debate. NPR.org, December 7; url: http://www.npr.org/2010/12/07/131757175/arresting-youth-in-sex-trafficking-raises-debate.

Zetter, K., 2012. Cops trolled driver's license database for pic of hot colleague. Wired Magazine, February 23; url: http://www.wired.com/threatlevel/2012/02/cop-database-abuse/.

CHAPTER 7

Ethical Issues in Crime Lab Administration

W. Jerry Chisum and Brent E. Turvey

Key Terms

NAS Report Presents the findings of a Congressionally funded system-wide investigation and review of the forensic science disciplines and related crime lab practice.

Quality control Monitoring and evaluating the environment, methods, and work-product for scientific integrity.

Scientific integrity Refers to consistency with the scientific method and established scientific guidelines, as well as the absence of corruption by other influences.

Scientist "Someone who possesses an academic and clinical understanding of the scientific method, and the analytical dexterity to construct experiments that will generate the empirical reality that science mandates" (Chisum and Turvey, 2011).

The current debate over the crime lab crisis in the United States demonstrates the need for more informed management and honest leadership in the forensic science community. To begin with, too many vested in the current broken system deny that such a crisis even exists.[1] This is found in the publications and interviews of crime lab supervisors who erroneously assert that the occurrence of error and misconduct in forensic science is only a minor problem, rarely evident (e.g., Pyrek, 2005; Fisher, 2012). Supervisory law enforcement authorities, in response to accusations of fraud and error, are known for similar assertions – dismissively suggesting that problems are isolated to a "few rogue practitioners" or "bad apples" (Chemerinsky, 2005; Budowle, 2007; Collins and Jarvis, 2007; Pyrek, 2007; Thompson, 2009; Taylor, 2011; Taylor and Doyle, 2011). This popular view is also reported in Thompson (2009, p. 1028): "According to the standard account, the problem is limited to 'a few bad apples', and the solution follows from that analysis – the bad apples need to be identified and either re-trained or replaced."

This is a useful position for a crime lab manager to take, as it protects the reputations of lab employees and the overall image of the institution under fire; at the same time, it requires no further action, investigation, or responsibility on anyone's part. However, it is a position that misinforms the public because

---

[1]See the *NAS Report* (National Academy of Sciences, 2009b) for a discussion on precisely how and why the current system, which has changed little since its publication, is broken. See also the discussion regarding the *NAS Report* in Chapter 8: "Ethical Issues in Forensic Examination."

Ethical Justice. http://dx.doi.org/10.1016/B978-0-12-404597-2.00007-3

it is incorrect (Cooley, 2004; Garrett and Neufeld, 2009; Thompson, 2009). As established in research by Turvey (2013), problems in crime laboratories around the United States are cultural, systemic, and widespread. In terms of specific consequences to the criminal justice system, Turvey (2013) found that (p. 189):

> The actions of the 100 forensic examiners in the present study resulted in at least the following consequences, conservatively: 42,042 cases reviewed for potential by forensic laboratory employers; 5,443 criminal cases dismissed or overturned; and 9 forensic laboratories closed, either temporarily or permanently. In addition, 38% ($n = 38$) of fraudulent examiners were terminated, and 32% ($n = 32$) eventually resigned. These findings evidence a significant impact with respect to expenses necessarily related to reviewing cases and hiring/training new employees incurred by employers; a significant impact on the financial cost and credibility to the justice system related to cases that must be overturned and perhaps retried; a significant impact on forensic services as laboratory caseloads must be shifted due to suspensions, terminations, and closures; and a significant impact on the financial cost to those individuals, agencies, and governments that incur civil liability.

This same research also revealed that when examiner fraud was identified, the forensic offender was not always terminated. In fact, many fraudulent forensic examiners were actually retained as crime lab employees without significant consequence, described in Turvey (2013, p. 188): "37% ($n = 37$) of the fraudulent examiners in the present study were initially retained by their respective employers without severe consequences despite their misconduct; of these, the weightiest involved examiners being reassigned or temporarily suspended." While this percentage also means that 63% of fraudulent examiners were forced to resign or terminated outright, it is still problematic. Forensic fraud is intolerable and ultimately corrosive in every aspect. The termination rate of those committing acts of fraud should therefore be 100% – and none should be able to secure employment in the forensic sciences elsewhere by simply moving to another region.

For example, consider the case of Ann Marie Gordon, a forensic toxicologist and section manager for the Washington State Toxicology Laboratory (also see Case Example in Chapter 14: "The Role of Professional Organizations in Criminal Justice"). She was accused of faking drug test certifications in multiple cases; these are sworn documents intended for the court. She resigned on 20 July 2007, only a few days after the investigation into her misconduct was initiated (Johnson and Lathrop, 2007). Her fraudulent acts were confirmed in a three-judge-panel decision granting an "Order of Suppression" across multiple criminal cases (Washington v. Amach et al., 2008) – at least 100 of her cases were ultimately dismissed. In 2008, the Office of the Medical Examiner for the County of San Francisco hired Ms Gordon as a forensic toxicologist. She worked in that system for 2 years, testifying under oath, before her history of fraud in Washington State was made known to local prosecutors and defense attorneys (Van Der Beken, 2010). She has since asserted her Fifth Amendment right to remain silent and not self-incriminate in subsequent court proceedings. She remains a member of the American Academy of Forensic Sciences (AAFS) in good standing and as recently as 2011 hosted the annual meeting for The International Association of Forensic Toxicologists (TIAFT) in San Francisco, where she apparently enjoys the continued support of her peers (Verstraete, 2011).

In the 2 years subsequent to the original study performed by Turvey (2011–2012), things in the forensic science community have not improved. Actually, they have got worse. More fraud and error were revealed, more forensic laboratories were closed, and at least 12 experienced major crises associated with: "cultural alignment with law enforcement … poor or negligent leadership; decreased budgets; ignorance of science and scientific integrity; lack of transparency and accountability; and institutional tendencies toward sweeping things under the rug" (Turvey, 2013, pp. 252–253). Unfortunately this trend has continued into 2013 and shows no signs of relenting any time soon.

In this chapter, the authors intend to take a realistic view of crime lab management and administration, in order to ferret out the most significant ethical issues as we have experienced them. It will focus on the obligations and responsibilities of those in supervisory roles, with respect to management, culture, maintenance, and personnel issues. We take the position that culture is a key factor in the ethical development of forensic personnel and the subsequent community of professionals. Specifics regarding ethical conduct as it relates to forensic examinations will be discussed in Chapter 8: "Ethical Issues in Forensic Examination."

LABORATORY MANAGEMENT

In 2009, the National Academy of Sciences Committee on Science, Engineering, and Public Policy report *Strengthening Forensic Science in the United States: A Path Forward* (the *NAS Report*; National Academy of Sciences, 2009b) presented the findings of a Congressionally funded system-wide investigation and review of the forensic science disciplines and related crime lab practice. Implicit in these findings is the assumption that running a crime lab is a scientific endeavor. Certainly, those crime lab employees who testify in court want everyone to believe this is the case, as this adds credibility to their findings and any related opinions.

This reality dictates that the only appropriate supervisors, managers, or directors in a crime lab are *scientists*.[2] Only a scientist understands what science is and requires; only a scientist can competently evaluate the methods and work-product of other scientists; and therefore only a scientist is capable of gaining the consensus and respect needed to effectively lead or provide oversight to a scientific endeavor. They must have time on the line, doing the work they are meant to be supervising or managing. Anyone else, with any other kind of background or mission, is generally ignorant and ultimately ineffective at the task of scientific laboratory oversight.[3]

However, many crime labs are managed or supervised by administrators without a scientific background. Worse, some are under the direction of law enforcement administrators. If a group of scientists are operating under the direction or oversight of someone holding a rank (e.g., a sergeant, captain, major, or special agent), this is red flag for cultural conflict, as will be discussed in the next section.

In short, the laboratory must be managed by a scientist, and it must employ scientists, in order to fulfill the requirements of a scientific endeavor. Scientists do not carry guns, they do not carry handcuffs, and they do not arrest people. Further still, they do not wear a badge while examining evidence or testifying in court. Their mission is that of objective evidence examination and interpretation. There can be nothing else to strain or bias their purpose.

Law enforcement agencies often disagree and some tend to prefer that the crime labs within their agencies remain under the direct supervision of someone that can be trusted to keep the scientists in line – someone that wears a uniform.

For example, consider the St Paul Police Crime Lab in Minnesota. In 2012, chronic and systemic problems at the lab were exposed during courtroom testimony. The circumstances, which had developed while the lab was under the direction of a police sergeant, were reported in Xiong (2013):

> Sgt. Shay Shackle oversaw the lab from 2001 until last July, when courtroom testimony revealed that lab staff did not follow basic scientific procedures in its drug testing. Independent audits later revealed a host of problems, including poorly maintained testing instruments, unscientific language in reports and deficient skills among staff.

---

[2]A scientist is "someone who possesses an academic and clinical understanding of the scientific method, and the analytical dexterity to construct experiments that will generate the empirical reality that science mandates" (Chisum and Turvey, 2011). This generally involves at least a 4-year science degree, if not a graduate education in the sciences.

[3]In addition to a scientific background, a crime lab director may also benefit from a business or management degree of some kind, but the scientific credentials are a must.

This revelation resulted in the removal of Sergeant Shackle from his position as lab director, the suspension of all drug testing at the lab, and an external audit. The audit found that things at the lab, and subsequent failures, were even worse than initially believed, as reported in Baran (2013):

> The failures include sloppy documentation, dirty equipment, faulty techniques and ignorance of basic scientific procedures, according to reports released Thursday, Lab employees even used Wikipedia as a "technical reference" in at least one drug case.
>
> Consultants found lab employees mistakenly classified at least one-third of all fingerprints as unidentifiable and destroyed them. Case files "were largely unintelligible," consultants found. The lab lacked any clean area designated for the review and collection of DNA evidence. The lab stored crime scene photos on a computer that anyone could access without a password. Conditions at the lab violated federal safety and health requirements.

However, when the auditors advised that the crime lab would be best served by the direction of a civilian scientist, the police union (i.e., the St Paul Police Federation) responded critically. Of key concern was that sworn police officers in the lab, including those who conduct fingerprint examinations and accident reconstructions, should not be required to serve beneath a civilian. According to the Federation's attorney, Chris Wachtler: "Sworn officers should not be reporting to civilians" (Xiong, 2013).

The City of St Paul countered this position with an explanation for the decision that would seem reasonable to most, reported in Xiong (2013):

> "We have an excellent police department ... but they're not forensic scientists," said city labor relations manager, Jason Schmidt. "To me, it would be irresponsible for the city to ignore what the experts recommended we do."
>
> ... The city is seeking accreditation for the police lab. Schmidt said the city can't earn accreditation without a forensic scientist overseeing the lab. "The city is really just trying to put the right people in the right positions," he said.

As of this writing, the position of director for the St Paul Police Crime Lab remains unfilled and there is no firm agreement on what the precise qualifications should be.

Consider also retired Chief Deputy Rick Perez, hired as the Canton-Stark County Crime Lab director in the early days of February 2013. A former police officer, he has no formal scientific or even business management education, as reported in Rink (2013a):

The city lowered the job qualifications for the director of the Canton-Stark County Crime Lab and then hand-picked a retired county sheriff's investigator for the post without advertising the vacancy. Rick Perez was hired this week and will make $70,848 annually, about $12,500 less than the lab's previous director.

Based on a job description dated Jan. 14, Perez does not meet the education qualifications, which include having a bachelor's degree in chemistry, forensic science or business management. Perez, 57, retired Jan. 1 from the Stark County Sheriff's Department where he was the chief deputy. As such, he will be able to collect his state pension while also getting a paycheck from the city. So-called "double-dipping" is legal but often criticized.

He replaces Robert E. Budgake, who was among 30 city employees fired last year for retiring and then improperly being rehired to the same position.

Safety Director Thomas Ream and Police Chief Bruce Lawver defended the hiring, saying they're confident Perez's 37 years in law enforcement qualify him. They also recognize that Perez's lack of education and technical background prohibit him from performing some duties. "He may not be able to run the DNA himself," Lawver said, "but that's why we have technicians."

"We checked with the national accreditation folks as far as some of the qualities," Ream said. "There were thoughts that some level of scientific expertise was necessary. ... We felt a strong management background serves the crime lab appropriately."

The Canton Civil Service Commission declassified the job on Jan. 25 at the request of the administration. The crime lab director now serves at the behest of the mayor, safety director and police chief, and does not have civil service protection. The move also allowed the administration to bypass the job posting requirements.

Less than a week after this story was published, Mr Perez was asked to resign by the Mayor, under pressure from local area law enforcement agencies that did not want their evidence being examined under such poorly conceived managerial conditions. Pressure also came from the City Council, who were apparently left in the dark about Perez's qualifications, as reported in Rink (2013b):

Canton-Stark County Crime Lab Director Rick Perez resigned at the urging of Mayor William J. Healy II on Monday, a week after being hand-picked for the job ....

Healy also said he was unaware that Safety Director Thomas Ream lowered the required qualifications on a job description for the director's post .... "When this scenario came to my attention, there were things I was not aware of," Healy said. "... This isn't necessarily

about Rick Perez. This is about the process, and I don't think the
process was handled appropriately. We are trying to fix that. Most
importantly, the process immediately created integrity and credibility
problems for the entire (lab). We can't have that. Not in the city of
Canton and not in Stark County."

Healy said he supported the hiring of Perez initially because of
his lengthy law-enforcement career. However, the process was not
transparent, he said. He took responsibility for the situation ....

Marlboro Township Police Chief Ron Devies sent a letter to the crime
lab asking it to return evidence from about a dozen cases. Devies
plans to send the evidence to the Bureau of Criminal Identification and
Investigation in Richfield.

"I have to question the political back-room antics that led to this
new direction of 'leadership' and the qualifications the new 'director'
has," Devies wrote. "The Marlboro Police Department wishes to have
no part in this questionable decision stemming from the good ole
boy networking of politics. I suspect whatever the reason was, ethics
certainly was not a talking point."

Alliance Police Chief Scott Griffith said Monday his department had
been considering such a move for about a month, and that the hiring of
Perez raised additional concerns.

Members of North Canton City Council and Mayor David Held also
questioned the decision at their Monday meeting. Councilman Doug
Foltz proposed that council pass a resolution calling on the city of
Canton to restore the original job qualifications ....

Ream said last week that the city wanted someone to serve in a
managerial role, rather than possessing a scientific and technical
background. Ream defended the hiring by saying that the city and county
are fortunate to have someone with Perez's law enforcement experience.

However, the American Society of Crime Lab Directors/Lab
Accreditation Board "strongly recommends" that lab directors,
especially for highly scientific backgrounds, possess a degree in
criminalistics, natural sciences or a closely related field.

In March 2013, in the wake of this scandal, Canton Safety Director Thomas
Ream resigned from his post. Around the same time, criminalist Michelle
Foster, the quality control manager for the Canton-Stark County Crime Lab,
accepted a job as the lab's new director.

LABORATORY CULTURE

Crime lab managers and directors have an ethical obligation to create and nurture a culture of science in order to best serve their scientific mission, as well as

the needs of employees. The National Academy of Sciences observes that a culture of science exists as a function of both individual and institutional integrity.[4] This begins with the institutional obligation to create an environment where ethical scientific practice is encouraged and protected, and misconduct is not tolerated (National Academy of Sciences, 2002, p. 26):

> The human contribution to the research environment is greatly shaped by each individual's professional integrity, which in turn is influenced by the individual's educational background and cultural and ethical upbringing. These result in values and attitudes that contribute to the formation of the individual's identity, unique personality traits, and ethical decision-making abilities. Because each researcher brings unique qualities to the research environment, the constants must come from the environment itself. Research institutions should consistently and effectively provide training and education, policies and procedures, and tools and support systems. Institutional expectations should be unambiguous, and the consequences of each individual's conduct or misconduct should be clear.

The *NAS Report* further describes scientific culture as being comprised of honorable values and standards similar to those expected from lawful citizens in everyday life (National Academy of Sciences, 2009a, p. 3):

> Research is based on the same ethical values that apply in everyday life, including honesty, fairness, objectivity, openness, trustworthiness, and respect for others.
>
>   A "scientific standard" refers to the application of these values in the context of research. Examples are openness in sharing research materials, fairness in reviewing grant proposals, respect for one's colleagues and students, and honesty in reporting research results.

This is consistent with the *NAS Report* (National Academy of Sciences, 2009b), which characterizes the culture of science as rewarding humility, openness, and criticism as it strives to refine itself through self-correction (p. 125):

> The methods and culture of scientific research enable it to be a self-correcting enterprise. Because researchers are, by definition, creating new understanding, they must be as cautious as possible before asserting a new "truth." Also, because researchers are working at a frontier, few others may have the knowledge to catch and correct any errors they make. Thus, science has had to develop means of revisiting provisional results and revealing errors before they are widely used. The processes of peer review, publication, collegial interactions

---

[4]This section is adapted from writing originally prepared for Turvey (2013).

(e.g., sharing at conferences), and the involvement of graduate students (who are expected to question as they learn) all support this need. Science is characterized also by a culture that encourages and rewards critical questioning of past results and of colleagues. Most technologies benefit from a solid research foundation in academia and ample opportunity for peer-to-peer stimulation and critical assessment, review and critique through conferences, seminars, publishing, and more. These elements provide a rich set of paths through which new ideas and skepticism can travel and opportunities for scientists to step away from their day-to-day work and take a longer-term view. The scientific culture encourages cautious, precise statements and discourages statements that go beyond established facts; it is acceptable for colleagues to challenge one another, even if the challenger is more junior.

The self-correction required for science to prevail can only come in an environment that embraces critical thinking and skepticism. As explained in Brookfield (1987), critical thinking requires strict adherence to logical analysis, and the discipline to scrutinize the strengths, weaknesses, and overall rationality of all arguments and assertions. It also requires (p. 6) "continual questioning of assumptions;" (p. 8) "challenging the importance of context;" (p. 9) "imagining and exploring alternatives" and "reflective skepticism;" and (pp. 11–12) "the ability to distinguish bias from reason and fact from opinion." Critical thinking necessitates doubt and proof, no matter the source of data or the strength of assertions about the integrity of findings. This means that scientists are prohibited from blindly accepting what they are told by anyone. The importance of this scientific norm was echoed recently in Gardenier (2011), which explains that (p. 3):

> Analytic methodology cannot be divorced from the data. Both must be specifically congruent in structure, relevance, and assumptions. Even more important than any measure of confidence or significance in the output is the logic that the conclusions follow from the data ….
>
> Scientists may mistakenly consider it an ethical obligation to accept data from colleagues or superiors for statistical analysis without detailed attention to all of the considerations above. That is incorrect. Without data integrity, it is impossible to achieve research integrity.

This advisory is universally applicable to any context where a scientist is being asked to assume the integrity of information they are provided from any source: such assumptions are impermissible. *Scientific integrity*[5] must be earned at all junctures and not presumed. When weaknesses exist, they must be

---

[5]*Scientific integrity* refers to consistency with the scientific method and established scientific guidelines, as well as the absence of corruption by other influences.

acknowledged, considered, and then reported as a function of limits set against interpretation.

Scientific understanding is also regenerative – constantly evolving as new information is developed and assimilated. Consequently, the caution and humility advised for responsibly exploring "new truth" requires acceptance that there is no such thing as absolute scientific certainty (Botkin, 2011). The scientist must therefore show an appreciation for exploring the limitations of their findings and inferences. They must also accept the need for clearly expressing those limitations to others and for admitting that any scientific findings "are not absolute truths or immutable facts" (Inman and Rudin, 1999, p. 164).

From all of this discussion, a consistent pattern of core scientific obligations associated with the establishment of scientific integrity is evident. As suggested by the National Academy of Sciences, these are appropriately divided into requisite values and practices associated with either the individual scientist or their institution/employer. This acknowledges the reality that every scientist has their own variable personality, education, abilities, and professional identity; and that: "Since each individual researcher brings unique qualities to the research environment, the constants must come from the environment itself" (National Academy of Sciences, 2002, p. 4).

Based on this literature, fundamental institutional obligations to ethical scientific culture would include at least the following:

- The employment of only qualified individuals, with ethical and professional character.
- To provide mentorship and leadership that emulates and promotes scientific literacy and professional integrity.
- To provide clearly stated practice standards and ethical guidelines.
- To provide opportunities for ongoing collaboration, education and training.
- To encourage peer review and self correcting enterprise.
- To provide *quality control*.[6]
- To maintain transparency regarding institutional conflicts of interest.
- To assert zero pressure on employees to produce results favoring the institution.
- To levy promotions and pay raises based on scientific competence, not outcomes favorable to the institution.
- To maintain zero tolerance for misconduct, with all allegations to be properly investigated.

---

[6]In this context, *quality control* may be defined as monitoring and evaluating the environment, methods, and work-product for scientific integrity.

- To provide protection for whistleblowers – zero tolerance for negative consequences or reprisal during the investigation of whistleblower complaints.
- To avoid reckless disregard for maintaining scientific integrity.

While these obligations are not the set limit of what an ethical scientific culture requires, they are generally accepted as the basic starting point for building and preserving scientific integrity.

ALIGNMENT WITH LAW ENFORCEMENT

The vast majority of forensic scientists are employed directly by police agencies or by crime labs associated with law enforcement and the prosecution (Peterson and Hickman, 2005; Thornton and Peterson, 2007). However, a conflict exists because, as explained in Thornton and Peterson (2007, p. 2): "[m]ost forensic examinations are conducted in government-funded laboratories, usually located within law enforcement agencies, and typically for the purpose of building a case for the prosecution." The *NAS Report* (National Academy of Sciences, 2009b) warns us further that (pp. 183–184):

> ... [t]he majority of forensic science laboratories are administered by law enforcement agencies, such as police departments, where the laboratory administrator reports to the head of the agency. This system leads to significant concerns related to the independence of the laboratory and its budget "as well as" cultural pressures caused by the different missions of scientific laboratories vis-à-vis law enforcement agencies.

In other words, law enforcement and scientific cultures are incompatible, for at least the following reasons, as described in Turvey (2013, pp. 109–110):

> ... there is almost complete direct conflict between the reality of one and the needs of the other. Law enforcement culture promulgates a noble cause belief system that tolerates corruption at variable levels depending on localized leadership and norms; alternatively, scientific integrity demands zero tolerance for misconduct of any kind. Law enforcement culture is authoritative and coercive, training officers to take charge, solve problems, and maintain control on a continuum of force that includes handcuffs and firearms; alternatively, scientific integrity demands that examiners achieve results through empirical research and analytical logic while embracing overall fairness, without the use of threats or coercion of any kind. Law enforcement culture is essentially masculine and aggressive in its approach to problem solving; alternatively, scientific integrity demands conservative humility and the consideration of alternatives. Law enforcement culture rewards members for unwavering group loyalty and solidarity

regardless of the circumstances; alternatively, scientific integrity demands that the findings of others be questioned, to the point of skepticism being a scientific virtue. Law enforcement culture embraces the use of differing levels of deception as a means to an end, lawful and otherwise; alternatively, scientific integrity demands honesty at all levels of reporting. Law enforcement culture instills an "Us versus Them" mentality in its members, creating a sense of isolation from the community and hostility toward outsiders; alternatively, scientific integrity requires examiners to welcome peer review and external inquiry as a necessary part of any validation process. Law enforcement culture is marked by an overall secrecy, or "code of silence," with respect to the errors and misconduct of its membership; those who break this code are punished and in extreme cases ostracized. Scientific integrity mandates transparency of all methodology, including errors, as well as the reporting of any and all misconduct; those who report misconduct, referred to as "whistleblowers," are theoretically entitled to absolute protection without sanction.

This research finding comports with the *NAS Report*, which explains that forensic science and law enforcement are culturally incompatible, with separate missions in the justice system. Therefore, publicly funded crime labs should be "independent of or autonomous within law enforcement agencies" (National Academy of Sciences, 2009b, p. 184). Otherwise forensic examiners may adopt the attitudes and belief systems of their law enforcement employers; those that are able to resist may feel pressure to comport their findings and related testimony to law enforcement needs out of a sense of self-preservation or as the result of subconscious bias (Risinger *et al.*, 2002; Giannelli, 2010; Turvey, 2013).[7]

It is the opinion of the authors that a crime lab is best situated as one of the following, with respect to budget and oversight:

- As an independent department or entity within the government, subordinate to the city or county administrator.
- As a city, county, or state department of laboratories, with its own organizational budget and structure, but sharing certain facilities and equipment. For instance, it could share a building with a department of public health and also share quality control services related to the maintenance of instrumentation.
- As a division of the court.
- As a department within a university.

[7]See the section "Institutional Pressure and Observer Effects" in Chapter 8: "Ethical Issues in Forensic Examination."

It bears mentioning that the goal is to relieve scientists of the political tension that occurs between competing law enforcement agencies and the prosecution, as the scientific community already has enough if its own tension to worry about without inheriting the politics of others (Turvey, 2013). This causes role strain, as will be discussed in Chapter 9: "Ethical Issues for Criminal Prosecutors." These proposed structures are therefore better suited to allow crime labs the autonomy required for developing and sustaining a more independent, impartial, and ethical scientific culture, because they help take the scientist from beneath the boot of those with external political agendas.

MAINTAINING THE CRIME LAB

Crime lab managers and directors have an ethical obligation to provide employees with adequate workspace and storage. They also have a related obligation to keep both workspace and storage areas safe, secure, clean, and free from contaminates and infestation. These continue to be problems suffered within many crime labs, as already suggested by the example of the St Paul Police Crime Lab in Minnesota at the beginning of this chapter.

Consider, specifically, that evidence storage is a subject avoided by lab employees testifying under oath, especially when there are chain of custody concerns. This is because it is often the source of extreme angst. Commonly, crime labs do not have enough space to examine or store the evidence they receive. They may not even have sufficient or qualified personnel available to keep it inventoried properly. Deficiencies in these area can be disastrous, resulting in evidence lost or destroyed, and in some cases dismissed.

Take, for example, the circumstances uncovered at the Houston Police Department (HPD) crime lab. The problems identified in the HPD lab system are representative of chronic, system-wide laboratory failure. Apart from their many other issues, the HPD crime lab has suffered from evidence storage nightmares that range from evidence overcrowding to incompetent storage practices and even to rats. According to the independent investigator's report (the following are selected outtakes from Bromwich, 2005):

> In March 2002, Mr. Bolding estimated that there were 19,500 sexual assault kits received by HPD that had never been processed, some dating as far back as 1980 [53]. During our tours of the Property Room, we were struck by the number of unprocessed rape kits currently being stored in the Property Room's freezers [54]. The Property Room is located at 1103 Goliad Street and is comprised of two main areas. One area houses central receiving; the evidence tracking system; the administrative area; file storage; a vault for high value evidence; and

property storage areas for firearms, knives, digital equipment, and small item evidence. Although this area is air-conditioned, it remains susceptible to high heat and humidity.

The second, and much larger, component of the Property Room consists of a large, single-floor warehouse and an annexed three-story warehouse, known as the Volker Building. Most of this area has shelving containing evidence and property stored in bins and boxes, as well as tools, bicycles, and other large items of evidence. We observed that some of the boxes stored in this area are marked with biohazard labels. This area is not air-conditioned and is subject to extreme heat and humidity. The floors are dirty and dusty. Currently, the area lacks space for the storage of additional property [60]. This area also houses two walk-in freezers containing sexual assault kits and other biological evidence [61].

The Property Room facility has two major deficiencies as a property storage facility – (1) inadequate storage space and (2) lack of humidity and temperature control. In addition, the facility has had major ongoing maintenance problems over the last 15 years, which have included roof leaks, faulty electrical wiring and lighting, inoperable elevators, asbestos concerns, and the need for new windows and doors. Managers of the Property Room have documented these major facility issues.

The roof at 1103 Goliad Street was repaired in 2004, but many of the other problems with the facility still exist. Even if repairs are made to the present facility, it may not be adequate for the proper storage and handling of evidence due to the lack of temperature and humidity control and inadequate storage space ....

Beginning in the early 1980s, the Property Room allowed various divisions of HPD to store items on the third floor of the Volker Building. The items stored on the third floor were considered to be under the control of the divisions that deposited the items and were not logged or inventoried by the Property Room. The Crime Lab was one of the divisions that stored items on the third floor of the Volker Building. The items stored by the Crime Lab included evidence as well as nonevidentiary items, such as excess office furniture. The evidence was stored in envelopes and boxes placed inside larger white boxes, which were stacked against a wall and under several windows.

In the 1980s and 1990s, the Volker Building's roof was in poor condition and experienced leaks. Rainwater leaked through the windows and roof, damaging some of the evidence stored by the Crime Lab. In addition, rats were present on the third floor, and they ate through a number of envelopes and boxes containing evidence.

In early 2000, the Property Room began to run out of space to store the evidence in its custody. Divisions storing property on the third floor of the Volker Building were asked to remove their property to free up space. When Crime Lab personnel came to the Property Room to remove the Lab's property, they took the contents of the damaged white boxes of evidence and placed the items in 283 new, large cardboard boxes. Each of the 283 boxes contained multiple pieces of evidence from multiple cases. Some boxes contained evidence from as many as 100 cases. The evidence dated from the 1960s to the early 1990s.

Once the evidence had been placed into the 283 boxes, Crime Lab personnel tagged the boxes to transfer custody to the Property Room so that the boxes could remain there. In doing so, the Crime Lab personnel identified each box by the incident number related to only one of the many items of evidence contained in each box, which misleadingly suggested that each box contained evidence related to only a single case. In fact, each box contained evidence relating to many cases. At some point, two of the 283 boxes were checked out of the Property Room by Crime Lab personnel. The pieces of evidence contained in these two boxes were individually tagged as individual pieces of evidence, and checked back into the Property Room. Thus, these two boxes ceased being part of the original 283-box collection.

On September 21, 2000, the Property Room received a routine destruction order to dispose of certain evidence. The evidence subject to the order was contained in one of the 281 remaining boxes. Coincidentally, the incident number related to the evidence subject to the destruction order was the incident number that happened to be listed on the outside of the box. Because the Property Room personnel believed, based on the box's label, that the box contained evidence related only to the one incident identified in the destruction order, Property Room personnel destroyed all of the box's contents. Subsequently, it was determined that this box contained evidence from 33 cases in addition to the one case identified on the box label.

In November 2003, the remaining 280 boxes were moved from the Property Room to a section of the 24th floor of the HPD headquarters, located at 1200 Travis Street, to protect the evidence from further degradation. On August 1, 2004, the Inspections Division began cataloguing and tagging the evidence contained the original 283 boxes of evidence. Approximately 8000 individual evidentiary items have been identified in the boxes. We will continue reviewing this area, and we will provide additional information regarding Project 280 in future reports ....

The storage of biological evidence has been an ongoing problem for the Property Room. The primary issue is the lack of sufficient temperature-controlled space for the storage of such materials. Prior to 1998, the Property Room stored sexual assault kits and other bodily fluid evidence in a freezer for a period of 18 months. After 18 months, the evidence was moved to air-conditioned areas within the Property Room for long-term storage. By 1998, the Property Room was running out of space in the freezers as well as the air-conditioned storage area. In March 1998, the head of the Property Room, Ron Cobb, asked Mr. Bolding if it was necessary to provide air-conditioned storage for this evidence after the initial 18-month period of storage in the freezer. In a March 18, 1998, memorandum to the captain of HPD's Homicide Division, Mr. Cobb relayed the response he had received from Mr. Bolding: "[T]here is NO need to provide air-conditioned storage for any type of body fluid evidence after the original freezer period of 18 months. [Mr. Bolding] related that he has taken evidence that was stored on the third floor of this building (which reaches extremely high temperatures in the summer), and has achieved successful DNA testing."

On April 1, 1998, in reliance on the information received from Mr. Bolding, Property Room personnel began relocating sexual assault kits and other biological evidence to general property storage areas. The general property storage areas are not air-conditioned and, therefore, are subject to high humidity and temperatures. Both of the Property Room's freezers are overloaded and additional storage space is needed. Some biological evidence is commingled with other general evidence and stored in the general property room storage areas. This practice raises serious concerns about proper storage of biological evidence.[62] HPD has advised us that it expects delivery very soon of an additional freezer, which has been on order for several months, to the Property Room.

53. In a letter to Council Member Shelley Sekula-Gibbs, M.D., dated May 22, 2002, Chief Bradford stated that "current estimates indicate that there are 7200 sexual assault cases dating back to 1992 with usable DNA evidence at HPD which have not been processed."

54. The Property Room freezer currently contains 2233 rape kits, most of which (2116) date from the period 2000 to present. Of the kits in the Property Room freezer, 112 are from the 1990s and 5 predate 1990. Approximately 7886 sexual assault kits are being stored at HPD headquarters at 1200 Travis Street. In sum, HPD is currently storing over 10,000 sexual assault kits.

60. HPD is attempting to address overcrowding in the Property Room by storing evidence at the 1200 Travis Street building and

exploring the alternative of auctioning items through the Web site www.propertyroom.com.

61. During a tour of the Property Room, one freezer appeared not to be maintaining the proper temperature, and we observed a considerable amount of water on the floor around the freezer. HPD advised us that the freezer was subsequently inspected and that it did not malfunction. HPD has suggested that the water we observed may have been attributable to condensation.

62. For example, in May 2004, water caused damage to 10 to 12 boxes of evidence due to a roof leak. Nine of these boxes contained clothing with possible biological evidence. The wet clothing was removed and hung to dry before being checked back into the Property Room.

The physical storage problems allowed to persist at the HPD Crime Lab are a model of both forensic negligence and forensic incompetence. Under such conditions, the integrity of the evidence cannot be assured nor can forensic examiners testify about related findings with any verifiable certainty. Such conditions are an utter affront to scientific integrity, and the fact that HPD crime lab employees were not forthcoming about them in prior testimony speaks to a lack of scientific training and/or cultural pressures from within to keep quiet about it.

Crime lab managers and supervisors have an ethical obligation to refrain from allowing or forcing their analysts to work under these kinds of conditions, and to ensure that they are documented and rectified immediately. Certainly they have an additional obligation to ensure that examiners are forthcoming about the impact of such conditions on the reliability of related evidence testing. This means disclosing adverse evidence examination and storage conditions to supervisors and requesting agencies, and making it clear that test results might be affected.[8]

LABORATORY ACCREDITATION

The *NAS Report* recommends, "laboratory accreditation and individual certification of forensic science professionals should be mandatory, and all forensic science professionals should have access to a certification process" (National Academy of Sciences, 2009b, p. 25). This is because laboratory accreditation and examiner certification are currently voluntary. The practice of forensic science does not generally require examiner certification – although some labs do have

---

[8]Failure to create such documentation is generally used to suggest managerial and supervisory negligence, when things are finally brought to light, when cases are being overturned, and when the media gets involved.

in-house mechanisms for such things. The *NAS Report* argues that external accreditation and certification are necessary for ensuring that scientific standards are being met, providing an extra layer of professional accountability.

Certainly this can be true, and a benefit of laboratory accreditation is the reality of external audits, accountability to established protocols, and some external oversight.

However, the primary accrediting agency associated with forensic science laboratories is the American Society of Crime Lab Directors – Laboratory Accreditation Board (ASCLD-LAB). ASCLD-LAB rarely revokes the accreditation of labs employing fraudulent examiners or those labs demonstrating repeated negligence. In fact, ASCLD-LAB generally prefers not to suspend or revoke laboratory accreditation. This was explained by then Chair Don Wycoff when defending the decision not to suspend the accreditation of the FBI crime lab subsequent to the Brandon Mayfield scandal, which admittedly involved a systemic problem with the way the fingerprint examinations were being performed at the time (Wycoff, 2005, p. 39):

> The suspension of a laboratory's accreditation, without complete review of facts, does little to support a laboratory that must immediately deal with QA issues and, in fact, shows that ASCLD/LAB really does not abide with its stated objective of trying to improve the quality of service to the criminal justice system. Had ASCLD/LAB's first response been to suspend accreditation, the right to due process would have been violated.
>
> … Because the ASCLD/LAB accreditation program is voluntary and our goal is to encourage every forensic laboratory to subject its operation to the scrutiny of accreditation, the process discussed above is routinely carried out in a confidential manner.

It is relevant to note that despite numerous such scandals over the past decade, the FBI crime lab has never had its ASCLD-LAB accreditation suspended or revoked. As Mr Wycoff explains, the mission of ASCLD-LAB is to "support a laboratory" through voluntary accreditation (presumably, the logic is that if labs fear losing accreditation, they are less likely to pay the costs associated with achieving and maintaining it). This is not to say that suspension or revocation never happens, but that it is rare, even when forensic fraud is involved.

It is also of note that ASCLD, the parent organization of ASCLD-LAB, does not expel members that have been determined by the court to have committed fraud. This is certainly true in the instance of Dr Barry Logan, the 2013 President of the American Academy of Forensic Sciences, who was forced to resign as director of the Washington State Patrol Crime Lab (see Case Example in

Chapter 14: "The Role of Professional Organizations in Criminal Justice"). Dr Logan is currently the director of National Medical Services, a large private toxicology lab that is accredited by ASCLD-LAB, and he is also currently a member of ASCLD in good standing. This circumstance certainly does not bode well for the ethics of either organization.

Of additional concern, research published in Turvey (2013) found that:

(1) If a forensic laboratory is accredited, fraudulent examiners are significantly more likely to exaggerate, embellish, lie about, or otherwise misrepresent results (e.g., to maintain their proficiencies).
(2) Laboratory accreditation is significantly correlated to increased falsification of only one kind of physical evidence: DNA. Other types of fraud occur within accredited labs without significant correlation.
(3) Accredited laboratories are significantly less likely to impose severe consequences on fraudulent examiners.

All of this combines to suggest that while laboratory accreditation sounds like a good thing, with the potential to be a powerful force with respect to much needed forensic reform, the current context suffers and leaves much to be desired.

PERSONNEL

In order to preserve the integrity of the crime lab, and to avoid the moral corrosion of laboratory employees, managers and directors have an ethical obligation to hire and retain only qualified scientists of good character and ethics. This requires the following:

(1) Crime lab applicants must have at least an undergraduate scientific education.
(2) Crime labs must engage in a comprehensive vetting process prior to hiring any new personnel. This must include the verification of every aspect of the prospective employee's resume, from acquiring official college transcripts and reviewing educational qualifications, to direct verification of any certifications and publications.
(3) Crime lab applicants must be required to submit to a thorough criminal background investigation – in and out of state.
(4) Crime lab applicants must be required to submit to a medical and mental health evaluation, to screen for those with a history of mental disturbance (and related medication), substance abuse, and addiction. This is common practice for most law enforcement agencies.
(5) Crime labs should adopt a zero-tolerance policy with respect to substance abuse and require all employees to refrain from illegal drug use as part of their employment contracts. As an adjunct, employers should require all

forensic examiners to submit to random on the spot drug testing without pre-notification of any kind.

Additional personnel issues are described below, related to examiner competence, quality control, research and publication, courtroom testimony, and disciplinary action.

Competence

As with any profession, forensic examiners have an ethical obligation to practice only within their areas of knowledge and established competence. The incompetent or ignorant examiner is a threat to forensic science and to the mission of justice it intends to serve. Crime lab managers and directors, therefore, have an ethical obligation to ensure that their employees are competent. This is accomplished with ongoing opportunities for training and education, as well as with blind proficiency testing. If an examiner fails their proficiencies, they must be taken off of casework until the problem is identified and corrected.

Supervisors that knowingly leave incompetent examiners on the line, examining evidence, violate the covenant of scientific integrity. They also risk faulty forensics leaving their lab and contributing to wrongful convictions. The recognition and reining in of incompetent examiners is one of the most important functions of the crime lab supervisor.

Quality Control

The *NAS Report* recommends that forensic laboratories develop and adopt quality assurance and control procedures. It explains that "quality control procedures should be designed to identify mistakes, fraud, and bias; confirm the continued validity and reliability of standard operating procedures and protocols; ensure that best practices are being followed; and correct procedures and protocols that are found to need improvement" (National Academy of Sciences, 2009b, p. 26). This because current quality assurance and control procedures are inconsistently attended or entirely absent in the majority of forensic laboratories in the United States.

This recommendation by the *NAS Report* acknowledges that mistakes, bias, and fraud are not intentionally screened for, let alone identified and managed, in the majority of forensic laboratories. Such inaction, again, violates the covenant of scientific integrity. It also, again, risks faulty forensics leaving the crime lab and contributing to wrongful convictions.

Research and Publication

Laboratory directors and supervisors have an obligation to encourage their forensic examiners to conduct research, publish in respected journals, and participate in professional conferences. This contributes to the examiner's professional development, and to the betterment of the laboratory community as a whole. It also supports the overall mission of quality science in the service of justice.

Failure to support these endeavors is a common shortcoming. In fact, some laboratory managers support these efforts preferentially, as a reward to those they like or are sleeping with. When the lab manager or director is constantly "conferencing" with their in-house paramour, this creates subordinate hostility and an environment that is toxic to scientific integrity.[9]

Equally problematic, some laboratory directors and supervisors require that subordinates list them as a co-author on any publications that are written, and any papers that are presented, during the subordinate's employment. This highly unethical practice is referred to as "gift authorship" (Jones, 2003, p. 245) or in some cases as "by-line corruption."[10] It is wrong at university and it is wrong in the professional world. Papers belong to those who wrote them. Although common practice, requiring that a student or subordinate list a supervisor as a co-author when they have done nothing to earn it is both academic and scientific fraud.

Courtroom Testimony

Laboratory directors and supervisors have an obligation to ensure that forensic examiners are able to testify competently and consistently as a necessary adjunct to their casework. To accomplish this, they must listen to their subordinates testify whenever possible, in order to evaluate the quality of both the delivery and the science involved. This will allow them to give specific feedback that the examiner can use to become better in their future testimonial efforts.

The crime lab should also maintain an archive of examiner testimony. This can serve at least three important ends:

(1) Archives of examiner testimony can be used for training purposes, so that new examiners can learn what to expect and how to answer difficult or tricky questions.
(2) They can help examiners refresh their memory on cases where some testimony has already been given – if there is a significant delay between hearing testimony and a trial, or if the case comes back on appeal years later.

---

[9]One of the authors (Chisum) experienced this problem in a California police crime lab, in a county just north of Los Angeles. It was poor leadership, set a bad professional example, and was caustic to everyone working there. It was therefore a key factor in the author's decision to leave the lab for a more ethical work environment.

[10]See discussions of *gift authorship* in Chapter 2: "Ethical Issues for Students of Criminal Justice" and Chapter 8: "Ethical Issues in Forensic Examination".

(3) These archives can be used by supervisors to identify any false or misleading testimony that may have been given, in order that the appropriate corrective action might be taken.

It is also important for forensic examiners to understand that it is unethical, improper, and potentially illegal to testify about cases that they did not work. If they did not perform the examination, they may not testify about it. They may, however, testify regarding subsequent interpretations, but they cannot vouch for the nature and quality of what was done with the evidence in the lab, or its disposition.

This issue is discussed further in Chapter 8: "Ethical Issues in Forensic Examination," with respect to the US Supreme Court's ruling in *Melendez-Diaz v. Massachusetts* (2009).

Disciplinary Action

Laboratory directors and supervisors have an obligation to impartially investigate any and all complaints regarding laboratory personnel, and to levy the appropriate sanctions when these complaints are founded. This can mean a letter of sanction in an employee's personnel file for violating lab policy; it can mean suspension without pay; or it can mean termination for dry-labbing results. However, any disciplinary action must be the result of a thorough and impartial investigation.

It is important that crime labs adopt a zero-tolerance policy for drug abuse, resume fraud, tampering with the evidence and related documentation, fabrication of laboratory results, general dishonesty, and giving intentionally false testimony. Currently, this is not the case. As already mentioned, fraudulent and otherwise dishonest examiners are retained in a large percentage of instances – to protect a friend, a colleague, or the reputation of an agency. This is toxic to scientific integrity and corrosive to existing, otherwise honest, personnel who are compelled to look the other way along with management.

If laboratory directors and supervisors do not fulfill their ethical obligation to protect the culture and character of the lab by requiring subordinate honesty and penalizing everything else, then they can expect laboratory culture and character to suffer exponentially.

SUMMARY

This chapter takes a realistic view of crime lab management and administration, in order to ferret out the most significant ethical issues as the authors have experienced them. It focuses on the obligations and responsibilities of those in supervisory roles, with respect to management, culture, maintenance, and personnel issues. The authors take the position that culture is a key factor in the ethical development of forensic personnel and the subsequent community of professionals.

Questions

1. Explain the significance of the *NAS Report*.
2. Define *scientific integrity*.
3. Explain why law enforcement and scientific cultures are incompatible.
4. The practice of forensic science requires examiner certification. True or False?
5. Describe three ethical issues related to crime lab personnel.

References

Baran, M., 2013. Troubled St Paul crime lab problems even worse than first thought, probe reveals. Minnesota Public Radio, February 14; url: http://minnesota.publicradio.org/display/web/2013/02/14/news/saint-paul-crime-lab-major-errors-found.

Botkin, D., 2011. Absolute certainty is not scientific. The Wall Street Journal, December 2.

Bromwich, M.R., 2005. Third Report of the Independent Investigator for the Houston Police Department Crime Laboratory and Property Room. Fried, Frank, Harris, Shriver and Jacobson LLP, Washington, DC June 30.

Brookfield, S., 1987. Developing Critical Thinkers. Jossey-Bass, San Francisco, CA.

Budowle, B., 2007. Forensic science: issues and direction. Presentation to the National Academy of Sciences Committee on Identifying the Needs of the Forensic Science Community, June 5; url: http://sites.nationalacademies.org/PGA/stl/forensic_science/.

Chemerinsky, E., 2005. An independent analysis of the Los Angeles Police Department's Board of Inquiry report on the Rampart Scandal. Loyola of Los Angeles Law Review 34, 545–657.

Chisum, W.J., Turvey, B., 2011. Crime Reconstruction, second ed. Elsevier, San Diego, CA.

Collins, J., Jarvis, J., 2007. Blame the judicial system for wrongful convictions, not crime laboratories. Crime Lab Report, June 1; url: http://www.crimelabreport.com/our_analysis/dontblame.htm.

Cooley, C.M., 2004. Reforming the forensic community to avert the ultimate injustice. Stanford Law and Policy Review 15, 381–446.

Fisher, B., 2012. Ethics in the crime laboratory and in crime scene investigations. In: Upshaw-Downs, J.C., Swienton, A. (Eds.), Ethics in Forensic Science, Elsevier, San Diego, CA.

Gardenier, J., 2011. Data integrity is earned, not given. Office of Research Integrity Newsletter 19 (3), 3.

Garrett, B., Neufeld, P., 2009. Invalid forensic science testimony and wrongful convictions. Virginia Law Review 95 (1), 1–97.

Giannelli, P., 2010. Independent crime laboratories: the problem of motivational and cognitive bias. Utah Law Review 2, 247–266.

Inman, K., Rudin, N., 1999. Principle and Practice of Criminalistics: The Profession of Forensic Science. CRC Press, Boca Raton, FL.

Johnson, T., Lathrop, D., 2007. State lab manager quits after she's accused of signing false statements. Seattle Post Intelligencer, July 31.

Jones, A., 2003. Can authorship policies help prevent scientific misconduct? What role for scientific societies? Science and Engineering Ethics 9 (2), 243–256.

Melendez-Diaz v. Massachusetts, 2009. US Supreme Court, No. 07-591, June 25.

National Academy of Sciences, 2002. Integrity in Scientific Research: Creating an Environment That Promotes Responsible Conduct, National Academy of Sciences Committee on Assessing Integrity in Research Environments. National Academies Press, Washington, DC.

National Academy of Sciences, 2009a. On Being a Scientist: A Guide to Responsible Conduct in Research, third ed. National Academies Press, Washington, DC National Academy of Sciences Committee on Science, Engineering, and Public Policy.

National Academy of Sciences, 2009b. Strengthening Forensic Science in the United States: A Path Forward, National Academy of Sciences Committee on Identifying the Needs of the Forensic Sciences Community. National Academies Press, Washington, DC.

Peterson, J., Hickman, M., 2005. Census of Publicly Funded Forensic Crime Laboratories, 2002. US Department of Justice, Office of Justice Programs, Bureau of Justice Statistics Bulletin, NCJ 207205, Washington, DC.

Pyrek, K., 2007. Forensic Science Under Siege. Academic Press, Boston, MA.

Rink, M., 2013a. Rick Perez will be new crime lab director. Canton Repository, February 7; url: http://www.cantonrep.com/news/x1433780796/Rick-Perez-will-be-new-crime-lab-director.

Rink, M., 2013b. Rick Perez out as crime lab director. Canton Repository, February 11; url: http://www.cantonrep.com/news/x1959339983/Rick-Perez-is-out.

Risinger, D.M., Saks, M.J., Thompson, W.C., Rosenthal, R., 2002. The Daubert/Kumho implications of observer effects in forensic science: hidden problems of expectation and suggestion. California Law Review 90 (1), 1–56.

Taylor, M., 2011. Beyond missteps, military crime lab roils with discontent. McClatchy Newspapers, June 26.

Taylor, M., Doyle, M., 2011. More errors surface at military crime labs as Senate seeks inquiry. McClatchy Newspapers, May 15.

Thompson, W., 2009. Beyond bad apples: analyzing the role of forensic science in wrongful convictions. Southwestern University Law Review 37, 1027–1050.

Thornton, J., Peterson, J., 2007. The general assumptions and rationale of forensic identification. In: Faigman, D., Kaye, D., Saks, M., Sanders, J. (Eds.), Modern Scientific Evidence: The Law and Science of Expert Testimony, vol. 1. West Publishing, St Paul, MN.

Turvey, B., 2013. Forensic Fraud. Elsevier, San Diego, CA.

Van Der Beken, J., 2010. Problems of S.F. toxicologist not disclosed. San Francisco Chronicle, May 26; url: http://www.sfgate.com/bayarea/article/Problems-of-S-F-toxicologist-not-disclosed-3263652.php.

Verstraete, A., 2011. President's message. The International Association of Forensic Toxicologists, October 21; url: http://www.tiaft.org/president_message.

Washington v. Amach, et al., 2008. District Court of King County, Case No. C00627921 *et al.*, decided January 30.

Wycoff, D., 2005. An open letter from ASCLD/LAB to forensic science organizations. CAC News, 39, First Quarter.

Xiong, C., 2013. No agreement on St Paul crime lab manager. Star Tribune, March 12; url: http://www.startribune.com/local/east/197462871.html.

CHAPTER 8

Ethical Issues in Forensic Examination

W. Jerry Chisum and Brent E. Turvey

Key Terms

Brady v. Maryland A legal ruling from the US Supreme Court that holds, "the suppression by the prosecution of evidence favorable to an accused upon request violates due process where the evidence is material either to guilt or to punishment, irrespective of the good faith or bad faith of the prosecution." It requires timely disclosure of exculpatory evidence by the prosecution to the defense.

Contingency fee agreements Agreements in which experts are paid based on outcomes, which arguably guarantee findings or testimony favorable to their employer.

Dissemblers Examiners who exaggerate, embellish, lie about, or otherwise misrepresent findings.

Forensic examiner Any professional who examines and interprets physical evidence with the expectation of courtroom testimony.

Forensic fraud Occurs when forensic examiners provide sworn testimony, opinions, or documents (e.g., affidavits, reports, or professional resumes) bound for court that contain deceptive or misleading information, findings, opinions, or conclusions, deliberately offered in order to secure an unfair or unlawful gain.

Ghost authorship "Ghost authorship occurs when the person whose name appears on the publication was not involved either in doing the research, framing the ideas behind the articles, or in writing the article. Alternatively, it can occur when an individual who has made substantial contributions to the manuscript is not named as an author or whose contributions are not cited in the acknowledgements" (Krimsky, 2007, p. 450).

Hired guns Private forensic experts who will testify to any opinion for a fee.

NAS Report Presents the findings of a Congressionally funded system-wide investigation and review of the forensic science disciplines and related crime lab practice.

Observer effects Any form of bias that occurs when the results of a forensic examination are distorted or influenced by the context (e.g., environment, culture) and mental state of the forensic scientist, to include subconscious expectations and desires.

Perjury The act of lying or making verifiably false statements on a material matter under oath or affirmation in a court of law or in any sworn statements in writing (Black, 1990).

Pseudoexperts Examiners who fabricate or misrepresent their credentials.

Role strain Provides that individual strain increases when "demands associated with one role interfere directly with one's ability to satisfy the demands of another role" (Hecht, 201, p. 112).

Scientific integrity A level of trustworthiness that must be earned and must not be assumed (National Academy of Sciences, 2002, 2009a; Jette, 2005; Gardenier, 2011).

Simulators Examiners who physically manipulate physical evidence or related forensic testing.

Ultimate facts "Facts which are necessary to determine issues in cases, as distinguished from evidentiary facts supporting them" (Black, 1990).

Ultimate issue The legal question before the trier of fact (i.e., the judge or the jury).

Ethical Justice. http://dx.doi.org/10.1016/B978-0-12-404597-2.00008-5

Ultimate Issue Doctrine Holds that witnesses are prohibited "from giving an opinion on the ultimate issues in the case. The rationale underpinning the ultimate issue rule is that expert opinion should not be permitted to invade the province of the jury" (Moenssens *et al.*, 1995, p. 75).

When there is a criminal complaint, law enforcement investigators are responsible for conducting a criminal investigation.[1] As discussed in prior chapters, this involves gathering evidence of all kinds, interviewing witnesses, and developing potential suspects. This helps them to determine what happened; to determine whether or not a crime has actually taken place; to eliminate suspects; and to identify and arrest criminal perpetrators (Kappeler, 2006; Sexual Assault Task Force, 2009). To assist with this effort, it is necessary to examine the physical evidence.

The term *forensic examiner* generally refers to any professional who examines and interprets physical evidence with the expectation of courtroom testimony. These professionals are responsible for the *scientific investigation* that takes place as a part of the overall criminal investigation. Forensic examiners are expected to analyze evidence in a scientific manner, to interpret the results objectively, and to report their findings faithfully (Chisum and Turvey, 2011).

Forensic examiners exist across a broad spectrum of professions, including (but not limited to): criminalists, forensic pathologists, forensic toxicologists, firearm and tool mark examiners, forensic odontologists, crime reconstructionists, criminal profilers, and forensic mental health practitioners.

The purpose of this chapter is to explore the primary ethical issues that confront forensic examiners in their casework and subsequent testimony. We will open with a discussion of role and traits of the forensic examiner. This will be followed by a discussion of the *NAS Report* – the congressionally funded investigation of the forensic science community (National Academy of Sciences, 2009b). The *NAS Report* will be used to contextualize the remaining sections on examiner bias and observer effects; inducements to commit forensic fraud; and issues with report writing and testimony. This chapter will close with a proposed code of professional ethics for the forensic examiner.

THE ROLE OF THE FORENSIC EXAMINER

As prior and subsequent chapters make abundantly clear, the decision makers in the justice system (e.g., investigators, attorneys, judges, and juries) are required to make inquiries into, and theorize about, the facts surrounding criminal cases. In doing so, they get close to the information, evidence, and

[1]This chapter has been adapted, in part, from Chisum and Turvey (2011), as well as relevant sections from Turvey (2013).

witnesses, often becoming vested (even entrenched) in their notions of what happened and who is ultimately responsible. The emotional attachment to uninformed ideas and mistaken beliefs is a predictable aspect of the investigative process that requires a consistent filter.

Forensic examiners, whether employed by the prosecution or the defense, are intended to serve as an objective filtration system. They employ the physical evidence as a tool to sift out case theories that can be either supported or refuted and report this faithfully to the aforementioned decision makers. The first onus of the forensic examiner, then, is to dispassionately establish the objective facts of a case as determined by a scientific examination of the evidence. It is not to seek out evidence that supports the theories of a particular institution, employer, or side. A forensic examiner works to establish the scientific facts and their contextual meaning with no investment in the outcome. Their job is the education of investigators, attorneys, courts, and juries with these findings, not advocacy for or against the guilt of any suspect or defendant.

Forensic examiners are not intended to be decision makers in the criminal justice system – despite some misinformed fictional portrayals to the contrary. They do not decide guilt or innocence; they do not rule on the admissibility of evidence in court proceedings; and they do not generally have the authority to make arrests or take life. This is intentional, as the goals of the forensic examiner with respect to explaining the strengths and limits of the evidence must remain ideologically separate from such extraneous efforts to maintain any semblance of impartiality.

TRAITS OF THE ETHICAL FORENSIC EXAMINER

Ethical forensic examiners have a fundamental scientific obligation to develop, maintain, and demonstrate impartiality; to acquire knowledge of scientific methodology; and to demonstrate the employment of scientific methodology in their work. Additionally, there is the corresponding need for maintaining transparency so that others will be able to review and validate any findings that are offered – to ensure the integrity of any facts and evidence relied upon. These are the traits essential to any scientist. They are also those necessary for achieving and maintaining what is referred to as *scientific integrity* – a level of trustworthiness that must be earned and must not be assumed (National Academy of Sciences, 2002, 2009a; Jette, 2005; Gardenier, 2011). Useful instructions for the forensic examiner are found in Kennedy and Kennedy (1972, p. 4):

> To be objective, an inquirer should be prepared to accept and record whatever facts he may encounter. He must not let personal feelings affect what he sees or hears. Although he does not need to like the nature of the information, he must be willing to investigate it. When

such an investigation is begun, it must be carried through with a degree of skepticism. Skepticism does not imply cynicism or a distrust of the world. It only suggests that the [forensic examiner] must be prepared to distinguish truth from the opinion or inclinations of others.

Good science is therefore not about making friends, pleasing supervisors, or trusting colleagues. Scientific integrity requires doubt, skepticism, and the willingness to question.

However, forensic examiners differ from other scientists in the likelihood that they will be called upon to testify in legal proceedings about the results of their work. Subsequently, they will be asked to explain how their findings were derived and what they mean. As explained in Thornton and Peterson (2007, p. 4):

What then, of the forensic scientist? The single feature that distinguishes forensic scientists from any other scientist is the expectation that they will appear in court and testify to their findings and offer an opinion as to the significance of those findings. The forensic scientist will, or should, testify not only to what things are, but to what things mean.

This provides that a forensic examiner does not just test or examine evidence and then record the results; they are meant to explore, understand, and explain its significance under oath. The defining quality of a forensic examiner is the possibility that they will be called upon to present their findings, under penalty of perjury, in a court of law.

Consequently, the *anticipation of sworn expert testimony* and the *offering of sworn expert testimony* are distinctive traits possessed by the forensic examiner. The ability to provide sworn expert testimony being integral to forensic examinations, a *trustworthy character* requirement is also presumptively invoked. As mentioned throughout this text, this is true for the majority of those working in the criminal justice system. For example, the State Attorney General's "California Crime Laboratory Review Task Force" describes the necessity of employment disqualifiers related to criminal history and character (California Crime Laboratory Review Task Force, 2009, p. 25):

... the Task Force recognizes that background checks are necessary because of the sensitive and critical role criminalists play in the criminal justice system. Mistakes or lack of professional standards by forensics professionals can lead, in a worst-case scenario, to wrongful convictions. The Task Force suggests that candidates, as well as those still in college who wish to become forensic scientists, be better informed that any association with criminal activity or lack of personal responsibility could preclude them from future employment in a crime lab.

Forensic examiners of every kind, like members of law enforcement, must achieve and maintain the trust of the court in order to be allowed the privilege of giving sworn testimony. This includes avoiding activities or affiliations that evidence criminality, a propensity for dishonesty, or poor character – whether past or present. If it can be shown that a forensic examiner cannot be taken at their word, or that they have a propensity for criminal activity or affiliation, then the court may exclude that examiner's testimony. Ultimately, a forensic examiner that cannot be trusted to testify in court has no value to the criminal justice system.

THE *NAS REPORT*

In 2009, the National Academy of Sciences Committee on Science, Engineering, and Public Policy report *Strengthening Forensic Science in the United States: A Path Forward* (the *NAS Report*; National Academy of Sciences, 2009b) presented the findings of a Congressionally funded system-wide investigation and review of forensic science disciplines and crime laboratory practice. It was initiated by Congress in response to the endless publication of critical legal reviews regarding the bias and lack of science in forensic practice; the ongoing occurrence of highly publicized forensic frauds, blunders, and crime lab scandals nationwide; and the ever-increasing number of DNA exonerations sourced back to flawed or misleading forensic evidence documented by groups such as the Innocence Project. The *NAS Report* represents the first major effort to investigate the forensic science community by actual scientists – and to recommend related reforms.

The *NAS Report* provides the following conclusions, among many, in relation to individual forensic examiners and their ethical obligations:

(1) Forensic science and law enforcement are culturally incompatible, with separate missions in the justice system. Therefore, publicly funded crime labs should be "independent of or autonomous within law enforcement agencies" (p. 184). Specifically the *NAS Report* recommends that "To improve the scientific bases of forensic science examinations and to maximize independence from or autonomy within the law enforcement community, Congress should authorize and appropriate incentive funds to the National Institute of Forensic Science (NIFS) for allocation to state and local jurisdictions for the purpose of removing all public forensic laboratories and facilities from the administrative control of law enforcement agencies or prosecutors' offices" (p. 24).
(2) The majority of the forensic science community lacks standardized terminology and report writing requirements. This results in forensic reporting that is unclear and in many cases incomplete.

(3) Many forensic examiners perform examinations and testify regarding subsequent findings with an inappropriately high degree of certainty. The *NAS Report* states: "research is needed to address issues of accuracy, reliability, and validity in the forensic science disciplines" (p. 22).

(4) The *NAS Report* recommends empirical research into the frequency and nature of examiner bias and error, in order to "develop standard operating procedures (that will lay the foundation for model protocols) to minimize, to the greatest extent reasonably possible, potential bias and sources of human error in forensic practice" (p. 24). This because there is an overall dearth of scientific research into examiner bias and error in forensic practice.

(5) Currently, there is no uniform code of ethics across forensic science disciplines. The *NAS Report* recommends that the NIFS "should establish a national code of ethics for all forensic science disciplines and encourage individual societies to incorporate this national code as part of their professional code of ethics. Additionally, NIFS should explore mechanisms of enforcement for those forensic scientists who commit serious ethical violations" (p. 26). These are because existing professional codes of ethics are non-existent, inadequate or selectively enforced within the majority of forensic science organizations.

(6) In order to practice forensic science competently, the forensic examiners must first be educated and trained as scientists. As explained in the *NAS Report* (pp. 26–27):

> Forensic science examiners need to understand the principles, practices, and contexts of scientific methodology, as well as the distinctive features of their specialty. Ideally, training should move beyond apprentice-like transmittal of practices to education based on scientifically valid principles. In addition to the practical experience and learning acquired during an internship, a trainee should acquire rigorous interdisciplinary education and training in the scientific areas that constitute the basis for the particular forensic discipline and instruction on how to document and report the analysis. A trainee also should have working knowledge of basic quantitative calculations, including statistics and probability, as needed for the applicable discipline.

These findings and recommendations are essential to an honest discussion of ethical issues encountered by the forensic examiner. They also represent important admissions, providing context that might otherwise be missed by those unaware of the absence of science found in current forensic practice. To summarize, many forensic examiners lack a scientific education or background; there has been little or no research into examiner bias and error; forensic examiners lack consistent ethical guidelines, practice standards, and terminology; and, as a result, too many forensic examiners testify about their findings with an inappropriately high degree of certainty. All of this generally occurs under the improper influence of law enforcement culture, resulting in examiner strain.

EXAMINER BIAS AND ROLE STRAIN

While forensic examiners must seek to serve the court and its agents as impartial educators, they must also understand the law and respect its adversarial nature in order to survive its crucibles. Thornton and Peterson (2007) describe the forensic examiner as a "handmaiden of the law," while recognizing the potential for conflict between the goals of science and criminal justice system (p. 4): "Forensic science is science exercised on behalf of the law in the just resolution of conflict. It is therefore expected to be the handmaiden of the law, but at the same time this expectation may very well be the marina from which is launched the tension that exists between the two disciplines." The criminal justice system necessarily sets two legal sides against each other and objective forensic examiners are not meant to take up the cause of either. In fact, their only theoretical value to the legal process is scientific objectivity.

Forensic examiners are ostensibly employed because of their oath to advocate for the evidence and its dispassionate scientific interpretation – nothing more. They must be capable of demonstrating that they have no emotional, professional, or financial stake in the outcome of legal proceedings. In other words, they cannot be paid to guarantee findings or testimony favorable to their employer, nor can their advancement or pay be connected to the success of one party over another.[2] *Contingency fee agreements*, as these are called in the private sector, are utterly forbidden (Siegal, 2012). Ironically, many government crime labs consider things that evidence similar improper relationships, focus, or mindsets (e.g., maintaining strong relationships with police and prosecutors, testing evidence that leads to an arrest, and providing testimony that facilitates a conviction) when evaluating forensic examiners for advancement, pay raises, and awards of merit (which can include a cash bonus).

Picking Sides; Picking Evidence

Science, whether practiced in a forensic culture or not, must be honest and unbiased in its methods and reporting, as explained in Steneck (2007, p. xi): "[scientists] who report their work honestly, accurately, efficiently, and

---

[2]This is separate from being compensated for time spent performing analysis, writing reports, and giving testimony.

objectively are on the right road when it comes to responsible conduct. Any-one who is dishonest, knowingly reports inaccurate results, wastes funds, or allows personal bias to influence scientific findings is not." When scientists become biased, and step outside of their objective role to craft, withhold or distort relevant findings in an effort to help a particular side, justice is per-verted. The problem is that the nature of the adversarial process can pressure even well-intentioned forensic scientists to forget this. Some have become utter partisans, inappropriately choosing to identify their practice with one side over another.

Cops in Lab Coats

On the prosecution side, the phrase that has been used to describe this occur-rence is "cops in lab coats" – those in police laboratories who try to make their results match their agency's case against the accused. According to Dr Elizabeth Johnson, a private forensic DNA analyst, formerly DNA Section Chief for the Harris County, Texas, Medical Examiner's office (Leung, 2009):

> "[Most people] think it's absolute and black and white and infallible," says Johnson. "But it is not. The testing has to be performed correctly in the first place and interpreted correctly in the second place."
>
> Johnson, who used to be director of a different lab in Houston, showed 60 Minutes II how evidence can be tampered with or contaminated …. Her theory is that it had more to do with a problem that's found in many cities when crime labs are located in police departments and analysts can feel pressured to be "cops in lab coats" – trying to make the science match the police department's case.
>
> "Too much of the time the police or the detectives come in and they submit evidence and they stand around and visit for a while and start telling chemists their version of what happened in the crime," says Johnson. "That's a dangerous situation."

This problem is also described in James and Nordby (2003, p. 4): "While crime laboratory scientists may pride themselves as being 'independent finders of fact', most operate under police jurisdiction or administration, and many scientists, perhaps unconsciously, develop the attitude that they work exclu-sively for the police or prosecutor."

This context creates a secretive and confirmatory environment in which foren-sic scientists are rewarded, often directly, through promotions, bonuses, or let-ters of appreciation, for their certainty and for their assistance with successful prosecutions. As discussed in Saks (1998, pp. 1092–1094):

> No other fields are as closely affiliated with a single side of litigation as forensic science is to criminal prosecution. Police crime laboratories

were not begun in order to provide science for police and courts, but as a public relations device. Even today, few of the personnel of crime laboratories have scientific training beyond the undergraduate level, and some not even that. Crime laboratories generate very little research, which to a scientist means they are not doing science, and to a lawyer should say at least that little progress is being made. At best, they apply science, but even that often is not the case. Progress might come from their colleagues in industrial or academic departments. But there are no industrial uses of what forensic identification scientists do. And the number of university programs to train forensic scientists can be counted on one's fingers. The maldistribution of forensic scientists so favors the prosecution that the defense has little access to any, which prevents the adversary process from working, as intended, to expose error. The institutional setting of forensic science promotes habits of thought that more closely resemble the thinking of litigators than of scientists. While science pursues knowledge through disconfirmation, prosecutions are won by confirmatory proofs. This confirmatory bias dominates the thinking of most forensic scientists. Where science advances by open discussion and debate, forensic science has been infected by the litigator's preference for secrecy. Tests of the proficiency of crime laboratories are conducted anonymously, kept secret, and are not routinely published. It is ironic that while studies of the effectiveness and accuracy of so many professional enterprises are available in published literature, the same is not true of a field whose sole purpose is to do some of the public's most public business.

In short, courts and lawyers and the criminal justice establishment within which the forensic identification sciences exist are in all probability the major cause of the arrested development of forensic identification science. The norms of science and of scientific institutions have been too faint and distant an influence on forensic science.

The same concern is echoed in the findings of the *NAS Report* discussed previously.

Such attitudes, and bias, are perpetuated by a slough of popular television shows and docudramas in which forensic scientists are portrayed as part of the law enforcement team, and sometimes the whole affair, wielding science like a badge to push suspects into confessions and even make arrests. This powerful imagery, given an air of authenticity by consulting law enforcement officers and police scientists whose names roll in the credits, contradicts everything that good forensic science is about.

Hired Guns

On the defense side of the courtroom, there are private forensic experts who will testify to any opinion, rightly labeled by some as "hired guns" or "whores of the court." These unscrupulous individuals will offer sworn testimony that helps the defense regardless of whether their "interpretations" contradict the evidence or established science, ignore ethical standards of practice, or conflict directly with opinions they have previously given under oath. They are often motivated by money and ego. However, money is less likely to be a major consideration for the criminal defense expert, as the prosecution is generally able to pay significantly more for private forensic examinations and expert loyalty.[3]

In all reality, good defense attorneys will not hire those forensic examiners with a reputation for favoring one side over the other, primarily because the examiners are so easy to identify and expose in front of a jury. Defense partisanship also cuts down on expert referrals significantly, which are the lifeblood of the private forensic examiner. So while hired guns for the defense do exist, they are far less frequent than those willing to commit forensic fraud on behalf of the prosecution (Turvey, 2013).[4]

Cherry-Picking

Even when the forensic examiner does maintain an aura of impartiality, their lack of control over the evidence may cause them to contribute a biased result. Unless they attend the crime scene, and observe which items of evidence are collected and which items are left behind, they will be limited to receiving and analyzing only that which has been provided to them. This evidence will have been cherry-picked from the scene by those in charge of collection efforts and laboratory submissions. In other words, the evidence provided to the forensic examiner is often selected from the crime scene by a police investigator in support of a particular theory or by a prosecutor looking for a conviction. Under these conditions, a forensic examiner employed by the state is given carefully chosen evidence with a specific request for a specific analysis; rarely is there full knowledge or disclosure of everything that was collected or left behind, let alone a comprehensive reconstruction effort (Chisum and Turvey, 2011).

The ethical forensic examiner understands this limitation, seeks to ameliorate it when possible, and works to explain its impact on subsequent findings.

---

[3]See Chapter 9: "Ethical Issues for Criminal Prosecutors" for discussion regarding "extraordinary expenditure by the prosecution" to secure expert testimony in the section "Almost Unlimited Funding." The defense is most commonly underfunded, unless the defendant has great personal wealth and can afford to retain private attorneys and experts at their own expense.

[4]The general concept of forensic fraud is discussed later in this chapter.

Role Strain

The objective mandates of good science are frequently in direct conflict with the needs of investigators, the desires of attorneys, and even the rule of law as decided by various courts. This conflict creates often unbearable strain in the role that forensic scientists intend to serve. The constant shifting of roles and the collision of multiple-role expectations can cause what sociologists refer to as *role strain*. As explained in Kennedy and Kennedy (1972, p. 16), role strain is a reference to the "difficulties and contradictions inherent in one's role." Specifically, it provides that individual strain increases when "demands associated with one role interfere directly with one's ability to satisfy the demands of another role" (Hecht, 2001, p. 112).

In an employment context, employee role obligations are prescribed by institutional policy and supervisory instruction; however, these can be contradicted or even contravened by directives from multiple supervisors, work overload, and pressure from workmates to conform with adverse cultural norms (Pettigrew, 1968). Individuals experiencing role strain continually bargain with themselves regarding which of their competing role demands to satisfy and tend to seek out options that reduce or alleviate the anxiety that it causes.

If directly employed by the government, agency policy and politics will ensure further tension for the forensic examiner. As discussed in Thornton (1983, pp. 86–88):

> Basic conflicts that influence the practice of forensic science become apparent at the interface of law and science. Law and science on occasion have conflicting goals, each having developed in response to different social and attitudes and intellectual needs. The goal of law is the just resolution of human conflict, while the goal of science traditionally has been cast, although perhaps too smugly, as the search for "truth." Certainly there is nothing intrinsically dichotomous in the pursuit of these goals; the court or jury strive in good faith to determine the truth in a given situation as a way to resolve conflicts. But proof is viewed somewhat differently by law and science, as is the application of logic and the perception of societal values.

Numerous writers have commented on these incompatibilities, including Glanville Williams in *Proof of Guilt* (1958):

> The principles of [the legal system] are not the product of scientific observation, but embody a system of values. These values do not necessarily have to be changed with the march of knowledge of the material world .... The rule conferring upon an accused the right not to be questioned ... may be a good or a bad rule, [but it] has certainly not been made better or worse by the invention of printing or the aeroplane.

How, then, do these differences between law and science lead to abuse of forensic science? They do simply because all the players want to win and are likely to use any ethical means at their disposal to do so. The attorneys in a case are aligned with only one side, and it is entirely appropriate under the adversary system for them to advocate a particular point of view, even without full and fair disclosure of all relevant facts. Subject only to the rules of evidence, the rules of procedure, and the Code of Professional Responsibility, attorneys are free to manipulate scientific evidence to maximize the opportunity for their side to prevail. Not only is behavior of this sort countenanced by the law, it is the ethical responsibility of counsel to attempt to do so.

In some government agencies, "the culture of group loyalty and protection is powerful" and attitudes develop where "loyalty to [co-workers] – even corrupt ones – exceeds loyalty to the [agency] and to the law" (Mollen, 1994, p. 5). As these conflicting rules, values, and circumstances compound, strain draws and weakens even the most honorable practitioners.

For example, in forensic laboratories, pressure to achieve quantity over quality can be applied in order to reduce backlogs despite staff or of budgetary short-falls. This may cause some examiners to cut corners, ignore protocols, and then conceal what has not been done. Additionally, some law enforcement agencies have been caught pressuring their scientists to report findings that are in accordance with suspect theories, and some law enforcement-employed scientists perceive pressure to avoid the appearance of helping the defense.

CASE EXAMPLE

Lynn Scamahorn, Forensic Scientist, Indiana State Police Crime Lab – Evansville

David Camm, a former Indiana State Police Trooper, was arrested for killing his wife, Kimberly, 35; son, Bradley, 7; and daughter, Jill, 5. He was tried and convicted for all three murders in March of 2002. In 2004, however, the Indiana Court of Appeals overturned these convictions. He was charged and tried again in 2006.

Lynn Scamahorn is a Forensic Scientist and DNA criminalist with the Indiana State Police Evansville Regional Laboratory. In February of 2006, she took the stand for the prosecution in the second trial of David Camm. Under oath, she broke down in tears and recounted being pressured during the first trial to change her findings, specifically that: "former Floyd County Prosecutor Stan Faith cursed and shouted at her and threatened to charge her with obstruction of justice if she wouldn't testify as he expected" (Zion-Hershberg, 2006). As further reported in Zion-Hershberg (2006):

> Scamahorn said that during a break in her testimony in the first trial, Faith took her to his office and closed the door.
>
> She said she believes he wanted to influence her to testify that she had found Camm's DNA on the sweat shirt ... "I felt that was something I could not say," Scamahorn said, adding that the evidence she found on the sweat shirt didn't support that conclusion ....
>
> Scamahorn said yesterday that Faith was asking her about DNA evidence that was

actually inconclusive and might have contained DNA from several people, including Camm. But she couldn't determine whose it was, Scamahorn said. "He wanted me to say David Camm was on the sweat shirt, but I couldn't," Scamahorn said.

Faith also wanted her to say more about unidentified bodily fluids on another piece of evidence than was supported by her tests, Scamahorn said.

She said she has felt no pressure to influence her testimony from Owen or from Keith Henderson, the current Floyd County prosecutor. "It has been more of a team effort," Scamahorn said.

She also said ... that she told Faith he could talk with her immediate supervisor if he felt she was testifying improperly. But Faith said he would contact a colonel in the state police several ranks above her supervisor, Scamahorn said. She said she took it "as a threat" to her continued employment.

In a telephone interview, Faith denied threatening Scamahorn in any way. He said he recalled his conversation with her during a break in the first trial. But, he said, they were discussing her reluctance to say that a bodily fluid found on some of the evidence was that of an unknown female.

In a letter of complaint to her supervisor (F. Joseph Vetter, First Sergeant and Manager of the Indiana State Police Evansville Regional Laboratory), written only a few days after her testimony in the first trial, Lynn Scamahorn provided specific details regarding the pressure applied by the prosecutor's office (Scamahorn, 2002):

On Friday February 8, 2002 at a break, Mr Faith called me into his office. There were no witnesses as it was only Mr Faith and myself. Questioning was now on defense cross and recross stage. Mr Faith shut the door to his office and began yelling at me very loudly using foul language. I felt it was totally inappropriate behavior and it was extremely unsettling to me due to the fact that I had to go back on the stand after break. Mr Faith was upset at the fact that he wanted me to state that a stain was identified as vaginal secretions or saliva. To which (on the stand) I said that it could be. Mr Faith was not satisfied with this answer. He said how could I let the defense lead me allover the place and when he (Mr Faith) questioned me that I tried to second guess him and was so "damned literal". Mr Faith stated that he felt I was being biased. Mr Faith also wanted me to make a statement that David Camm could be included on the sweatshirt and the DNA types clearly do not include David Camm and I felt this is not something that could be stated. I told Mr Faith that I could not make a statement of identity for vaginal secretions or saliva due to the fact that there is not an identifying test for these types of stains. To which Mr Faith replied that I was being "told how to testify" and this was a "Class D Obstruction of Justice". I told Mr Faith that he was welcome to contact my supervisor at Indianapolis ISP Laboratory, Paul Misner and discuss this. Mr Faith said he would not call Indianapolis, he would call Brackman. Mr Faith stated that he would open his own laboratory and his analyst could "say whatever they wanted". I told Mr Faith that if he felt I was being biased then I apologized but restated that I could not testify to the things he wanted me to. He then said "They have been horrible to you ever this". At this point I excused myself to the restroom to be able to go back on the stand. After coming out of the restroom, I asked Detective Sean Clemons from Sellersburg district to sit with me so that Mr Faith would be less likely to yell at me again.

It is important to note that the forensic examiner in this case reported overt pressure and threats from an external law enforcement agency (the Floyd County Prosecutor's office) to change DNA interpretations mid-trial. This is the very definition of role strain. However, she had the character to ignore these threats and testified in accordance with the evidence, as she perceived it. She also filed an immediate notification of these threats with her own police laboratory manager in order to make a record of the prosecutor's misconduct.

When examiner roles and expectations are in direct and irrefutable conflict, forensic examiners must decide which duty is primary and which set of rules they are going to follow. Theoretically, science should win out: after all, objectivity and skepticism are what give them value to the criminal justice system. In reality, however, acting objectively and skeptically comes at a cost. It can end friendships, it can earn one the derision of colleagues or supervisors, it can hamper promotions and pay raises, it can bring unwanted attention to individual errors and failings, and it can even get one fired. Role strain blurs matters further and weakens the resolve to conduct oneself impartially.

Institutional Pressure and Observer Effects[5]

As cognitive psychologists have documented, tested, and proven repeatedly, "[T]he scientific observer [is] an imperfectly calibrated instrument" (Rosenthal, 1966, p. 3). Imperfections stem from the fact that subtle forms of bias, whether conscious or unconscious, can easily contaminate what appears outwardly to be an objective undertaking. These distortions are caused by, among other things, *observer effects*. This particular form of bias is present when results of a forensic examination are distorted by the context and mental state of the forensic scientist, to include their employment culture, their subconscious expectations, and their personal desires.

Identifying Observer Effects

Identifying and curtailing observer effects are considerable tasks when one takes into account the forensic science community's affiliation with law enforcement and the prosecution. Specifically, this association has created an atmosphere in which an unsettling number of forensic professionals have all but abandoned objectivity and become partial to the prosecution's objectives, goals, and philosophies (Turvey, 2013). They may even go so far as to regard their alignment with law enforcement as virtuous, noble, and heroic. Such partisanship is a distortion of any scientific identity.

As Professor D. Michael Risinger and colleagues explained in their groundbreaking law review article on observer effects in forensic science, many different forms of observer effects exist (2009, p. 9): "At the most general level, observer effects are errors of apprehension, recording, recall, computation, or interpretation that result from some trait or state of the observer." These covert biases are more concerning than deliberate fraud and misconduct because they are often misperceived, or even thought of as beneficial, and therefore tend to go undetected. As discussed in the *NAS Report* (2009a, p. 122):

> Human judgment is subject to many different types of bias, because
> we unconsciously pick up cues from our environment and factor them

---

[5]This section is adapted from Cooley and Turvey (2011).

in an unstated way into our mental analyses. Those mental analyses might also be affected by unwarranted assumptions and a degree of overconfidence that we do not even recognize in ourselves. Such cognitive biases are not the result of character flaws; instead, they are common features of decision-making, and they cannot be willed away. A familiar example is how the common desire to please others (or avoid conflict) can skew one's judgment if co-workers or supervisors suggest that they are hoping for, or have reached, a particular outcome. Science takes great pains to avoid biases by using strict protocols to minimize their effects.

In order to blunt the impact of observer effects, forensic examiners must be aware that they exist and can significantly influence their analyses and results. Once recognized, they can also be studied and understood; once understood, they can be addressed and even mitigated. In fact, just about every other scientific endeavor accepts the need to blunt examiner bias and observer effects as a given. Put simply, "[s]ensitivity to the problems of observer effects has become integral to the modern scientific method" (Risinger *et al.*, 2002, p. 6).

Mitigating Observer Effects

The ethical forensic examiner has an obligation to mitigate observer effects, to the extent possible. As Risinger and colleagues (2002) explain, the notion that observer effects can be willed away is unfounded (p. 51):

> Every field that has considered the problem has concluded that it cannot be solved merely by trying to will it away. When everyone from Nobel prize winners to average citizens, who informally subject themselves to homemade "blind taste tests," take steps to make sure their judgments are not distorted by extraneous context information, then it is hard to conceive of what it is that makes forensic scientists think they are immune from the same effects.

Neglect and misunderstanding regarding observer effects have prevented, and continue to prevent, the forensic community from developing procedures that could minimize their impact. With no preventative measures in operation, these imperceptible effects thrive in an environment that provides two powerful ingredients for the distillation of subconscious examiner influence – ambiguity and expectation. As a result of ignorance and inaction, even the most neutral forensic scientists may offer conclusions that are imprecise, erroneous, or misleading, even when achieved through validated forensic techniques (Saks, 2003).

To mitigate subconscious bias, the forensic science community must use the same checks and balances already adopted in other scientific communities. The first check is awareness: forensic scientists have a duty to understand which of these influences may persist in their environment, and to adjust their professional manner and practices to guard against them when possible. This begins with admitting their existence and becoming more than just literate on the subject.

Second, they must be capable of identifying and filtering information that is irrelevant to their examinations. Too much of the wrong kind of information, like emotional content from investigators, can bias the way that a forensic examiner perceives and interprets the evidence he or she is provided. However, forensic examiners are regularly put into situations in which they are privy to information that can easily cultivate conscious or unconscious expectations. The most common expectation developed is that a suspect or defendant must be guilty of something, if not the crime they are accused of.

A competent forensic examiner should be able to create a list of the kinds of information that might bias or influence their analysis, and then whether and how it might be filtered. Then they can develop strategies to shield themselves from it. The inability or unwillingness of any forensic examiner to perform this task suggests that they have become lost in the geography of observer effects and are unable to distinguish what they do as an objective form of forensic analysis with an articulable methodology.

Third, evidence line-ups should be used when appropriate, particularly within the identification sciences. In an evidence line-up, multiple samplings are presented to the forensic examiner. However, some samples are "foils." Forensic examiners would be blind to which samples constitute the foils and which samples constitute the true questioned evidence. For instance (Risinger *et al.*, 2002, p. 48):

> [A] firearms examiner might be presented with a crime scene bullet and five questioned bullets labeled merely "A" through "E." Four of those bullets will have been prepared for examination by having been fired through the same make and model of firearm as the crime scene bullet and the suspect's bullet had been. The task for the examiner would then be to choose which, if any, of the questioned bullets was fired through the same weapon as the crime scene bullet had been.

As discussed already, many forensic examinations are currently the equivalent of eyewitness identification show-ups. In both situations, only one suspect or sample is presented to the examiner; because of the selective nature of this process and the often high rate of past identifications that have been positive, the environment works to reinforce the expectation of a match. Evidence line-ups would serve to help resolve this particular influence and may even help to identify biased examiners who are unaware that they are being unduly influenced.

Finally, forensic examiners should be insulated from law enforcement culture. As already mentioned, among the findings in the *NAS Report* was the resolution that a true scientific culture cannot develop or even exist subordinate to a law enforcement agency. The *NAS Report* explains that the resulting conflicts are fiscal, organizational, and cultural, resulting in the wrong kind of examiner pressure (National Academy of Sciences, 2009b, pp. 23–24):

> Scientific and medical assessment conducted in forensic investigations should be independent of law enforcement efforts either to prosecute criminal suspects or even to determine whether a criminal act has indeed been committed. Administratively, this means that forensic scientists should function independently of law enforcement administrators. The best science is conducted in a scientific setting as opposed to a law enforcement setting. Because forensic scientists often are driven in their work by a need to answer a particular question related to the issues of a particular case, they sometimes face pressure to sacrifice appropriate methodology for the sake of expediency.

Pressure to achieve results is nothing new in scientific endeavor; however, the context is quite different for the forensic examiner. As already discussed, the forensic examiner is often working in law enforcement culture that is at odds with, and even hostile towards, their scientific mandate. The primary objectives of law enforcement agencies are to investigate, identify, prosecute, and convict the guilty. Too often this involves a narrow mindset of building cases against suspects – not working to eliminate the innocent. Conducting casework in a pro-prosecution environment, where a suspect's guilt is both suspected and even anticipated, it is easy to see how and why some forensic scientists can subconsciously develop certain pre-examination expectations that may influence their results.

ETHICAL ISSUES IN REPORT WRITING

Forensic examiners are hired to analyze the evidence and objectively report findings, no matter the outcome. Regardless of the side that employs them, the ethical forensic examiner will prefer to give clients the "bad" news before anyone else does – to realistically educate them regarding the nature and the strengths of prevailing case theories in light of the opposition's legal arguments. This may be done verbally, with a written report, in formal interviews and sworn depositions, and finally in the form of courtroom testimony. At each step, there are ethical issues and obligations that must be attended.

Due Process and *Brady v. Maryland*

Scientists employed by the prosecution have a very specific burden with respect to their findings and what is referred to as due process. The Fifth and 14th Amendments to the US Constitution provide that the government may not deprive its citizens of "life, liberty, or property without due process of law." This provision is essentially a fairness requirement. Ideally, citizens may only be tried and punished for crimes alleged by the state under the most impartial and unprejudiced conditions. Any condition or treatment that tends to bias a judge, jury, or the process as a whole in favor of the state is considered a violation of due process.

In accordance with due process, the US Supreme Court's ruling *Brady v. Maryland* (1963) and its legal progeny mandate that forensic scientists must facilitate equal access to the evidence, subsequent forensic tests, and related results. A more complete discussion of this standard is found in Chapter 9: "Ethical Issues for Criminal Prosecutors." Suffice it to say that anything found by the police, state's forensic examiners, or prosecutor's office must be turned over or made available to the defense if it might have an exculpatory value. This includes an array of evidence, including information and reports related to every one of the forensic examinations conducted by the state.

Writing It Down

Forensic examiners have an ethical responsibility to ensure that all examinations and results are wholly and effectively communicated to the intended recipients, including investigators, attorneys, and the court (Gannett, 2011). There is no better mechanism than writing it down, which is perhaps the most accepted form of professional communication. This requires the forensic scientist to be competent at the task of intelligible writing. After all, the goal of a forensic examination report is to relay findings in a clear and logical manner. This cannot be achieved with imprecise, sloppy, or poorly crafted writing. It is therefore the duty of the forensic examiner to learn not only the science and skills associated with their work, but also how to write without making basic errors in grammar and logic.

The suggestion that report writing has a particular value when rendering forensic conclusions is not at all new. Dr Hans Gross wrote, for example, of the critical role that forensic examination reports play in both investigative and forensic contexts. Specifically, he wrote that just looking at evidence and forming opinions are only the beginning. He argued that there is utility in reducing one's opinions to the form of a report, in order to identify problems with the logic used to develop theories (Gross, 1906, p. 439):

> So long as one only looks on the scene, it is impossible, whatever the care, time, and attention bestowed, to detect all the details, and especially note the incongruities: but these strike us at once when we set ourselves to describe the picture on paper as exactly and clearly as possible ….

The authors agree that the act of preparing opinions in a written format, gathering references, forming supportive argumentation, and rendering deliberately crafted conclusions is a valuable step in the analytical process. It allows errors and omissions in any of these areas to be realized, and helps identify breaks in the logic of misinformed interpretations.

Report writing is also intended to help the forensic examiner abide with the mandates of good science, due process, and *Brady*. Specifically, scientists employed by the government must conduct forensic examinations in such a way as to be transparent in their methods and findings. As explained in National Academy of Sciences (2009b, pp. 21–22):

> As a general matter, laboratory reports generated as the result of a scientific analysis should be complete and thorough. They should contain, at minimum, "methods and materials," "procedures," "results," "conclusions," and, as appropriate, sources and magnitudes of uncertainty in the procedures and conclusions (e.g., levels of confidence). Some forensic science laboratory reports meet this standard of reporting, but many do not. Some reports contain only identifying and agency information, a brief description of the evidence being submitted, a brief description of the types of analysis requested, and a short statement of the results (e.g., "the greenish, brown plant material in item #1 was identified as marijuana"), and they include no mention of methods or any discussion of measurement uncertainties.
>
> … although appropriate standards exist, they are not always followed. Forensic reports, and any courtroom testimony stemming from them, must include clear characterizations of the limitations of the analyses, including measures of uncertainty in reported results and associated estimated probabilities where possible.

A written report that abides by these guidelines also serves a secondary and often more valuable function. It provides the forensic examiner with a record of the examination that should be sufficient to refresh their recollection from the stand should their memory of any pertinent specifics falter – when asked about them years later as is often the case.

Reporting Obligations of the Defense Examiner

When working for the state, forensic scientists are required to make written reports of any examinations or tests performed on the evidence, as well as subsequent findings. They are also required to preserve any photographs, drawings, or bench notes that are generated. This is in accordance with the legal rules of discovery and *Brady v. Maryland* (1963).

However, the rules of discovery ("disclosure") are not the same on both sides of the courtroom. Those who work privately for defense attorneys are bound by the attorney–client privilege. They may subsequently be asked by their clients to refrain from writing a report of their findings, for any number of legitimate reasons.[6] The forensic examiner should weigh this request carefully, as they are entitled to decline and write a report anyway.

In some cases, the forensic examiner may agree to refrain from making a written report of findings, to help maintain the state's burden of proof and to preserve the defendant's right to conduct their own investigation without fear of penalty. However, they should take scrupulous notes of their examinations – to document their work. These notes can be shared with the court and opposing counsel upon request to demonstrate the soundness of methodology and related opinions. They can also serve to assist with courtroom testimony, in place of a comprehensive report, should this be required.

Inconclusive Is a Result

A common *Brady* violation, often committed out of nothing more than ignorance, is related to the forensic practice of reporting, or failing to report, "inconclusive" results. There are forensic practitioners employed by the government, from fingerprint analysts to DNA technicians, who erroneously believe that inconclusive or indeterminate findings are not an actual result. Therefore, they feel justified in withholding the existence of such examinations or tests and any related outcomes. The consequence of this thinking is that there is no mention of any such findings in their reports and nothing about it gets disclosed to the defense.

Consider the discussion and the examples provided in Giannelli and McMunigal (2007, pp. 1515–1516):

> a. Timing of Disclosure
>
>   Brady is a trial right, not a pretrial disclosure rule. Nevertheless, exculpatory evidence must be disclosed in time for defense counsel to make use of it. Here, as with the discovery rules discussed above, delayed disclosure may place a defendant in an untenable position. In *Ex parte Mowbray*, [943 S.W.2d 461 (Tex. Crim. App. 1996)] a murder case, the prosecutor used a blood spatter expert to refute the defense suicide theory. According to the prosecutor, his case "depended upon" this evidence. Prior to trial, the prosecution retained another expert, Herbert MacDonell, considered the premier expert in the field. After reviewing the crime scene, the physical evidence and the photographs, MacDonell concluded months before trial that "it was more probable than not that the deceased died from a suicide rather than a homicide." Yet the defense did not receive his written report until ten days before

---

[6]The ethical obligations of the criminal defense attorney are discussed more thoroughly in Chapter 10: "Ethical Issues for Criminal Defense Attorneys."

trial and then only after the trial judge threatened sanctions. MacDonell never testified. The court wrote ... State's counsel early on recognized the potential lethal effect of MacDonell's testimony on their theory of the case, and beginning in November and continuing until May they engaged in a deliberate course of conduct to keep MacDonell's findings and opinions from Applicant's counsel until the last days before trial. Even then they caused Applicant's counsel to believe MacDonell would be a witness and available for cross-examination.

b. "Exculpatory" Requirement

Brady does not apply unless the evidence is exculpatory. Consequently, labeling a laboratory report as inconclusive may relieve the prosecution of the disclosure requirement. For example, in one case an inconclusive handwriting report "was not exculpatory, but merely not inculpatory." [*United States v. Hauff*, 473 F.2d 1350, 1354 (7th Cir. 1973)] Similarly, a report showing that hair from a rape defendant was not found at the scene of the crime was deemed a "neutral" report. [*Norris v. Slayton*, 540 F.2d 1241, 1243–44 (4th Cir. 1976)] However, as one court correctly understood, [S]uch a characterization [as neutral] often has little meaning; evidence such as this may, because of its neutrality, tend to be favorable to the accused. While it does not by any means establish his absence from the scene of the crime, it does demonstrate that a number of factors which could link the defendant to the crime do not. [*Patler v. Slayton*, 503 F.2d 472, 479 (4th Cir. 1974)] Similarly, in *Bell v. Coughlin*, [820 F. Supp. 780, 786–87 (S.D.N.Y. 1993)] the prosecution failed to turn over FBI ballistics test results to the defense. The lab positively matched a cartridge shell (B3) to the .45 caliber pistol but reported that no conclusion could be reached with respect to the two bullets (J/R2 and J/R4) in its possession. Thus, although the results of the FBI tests may be characterized as mixed, they clearly contained exculpatory material.

In a forensic context, the practice of selecting which results to disclose is dishonest and may be referred to as another form of cherry-picking: selectively reporting (and thereby emphasizing) only desired results or information rather than the entirety of examinations performed and results achieved. Those employed by the state have an ethical obligation to refrain from such partisan practices. Specifically, the cherry-picking of results violates due process because:

(1) The concealment of any examination performed on any item of evidence represents a break in the chain of custody. This is especially important to those third parties involved in reviewing subsequent reports (i.e., judges, juries, attorneys, and independent forensic examiners). The defense in particular has a right to know of every individual who handled an item of evidence, what he or she did with it or to it and where, and in what order.

(2) The execution of any examination on an item of evidence has a potential impact on its volume and quality (destruction, consumption, contamination, etc.). The nature of any impact on the evidence must be made clear to the police, court, and all of the attorneys involved in a case.

(3) The failure to notify the police, court, or attorneys involved in a case regarding the existence of inconclusive examinations assists with concealing the causes behind such results. This can include errors in examination procedure, problems with the evidence itself, or individual examiner proficiency. Unless the cause of an inconclusive result has been unequivocally established, the impact on the interpretation of any subsequent or related results is unknown and potentially limiting.

(4) The failure to investigate and report the cause of inconclusive results potentially conceals the error rate and/or the individual examiner proficiency rate related to a particular test. If these are unknown, then the scientific reliability of that test is not known. This may in turn create a false illusion of competence and proficiency in the mind of forensic examiners, their superiors, and the court.

To be clear, inconclusive findings are a result, just not one that is expected or necessarily desired.

Specifically, inconclusive findings are relevant to the reconstruction of a crime, the nature and extent of examinations performed, the evidence they were performed on, the quality of any testing, the competency of the examiner, and any legal proceedings that hinge upon the weight that a judge or jury attributes to that evidence.

Additionally, inconclusive means different things under different circumstances. It may suggest an error in testing methodology, an inadequate sample or control, or it may reflect a poorly trained examiner miscommunicating their findings. Unless such findings are disclosed to the defense and they are allowed to conduct their own private consideration, the cause of the inconclusive will remain unknown to the court. The failure to disclose inconclusive results is therefore a violation of due process.

Ghost Authorship

As explained in Krimsky (2007, p. 450):

Ghost authorship occurs when the person whose name appears on the publication was not involved either in doing the research, framing the ideas behind the article, or in writing the article. Alternatively, it can occur when an individual who has made substantial contributions to

the manuscript is not named as an author or whose contributions are
not cited in the acknowledgments.

This practice is also referred to by some as "gift authorship" (Jones, 2003, p. 245). Essentially, it involves hiding who did the actual work by giving credit that has not been earned.

Ghost authorship, or gift authorship, is generally considered to be a form of scientific misconduct. In some cases, the authorship of a report may be concealed or obscured to improperly bolster the credentials of an inept examiner; in others, it may be done to hide the work of an examiner with a problematic background or insufficient credentials. In either circumstance, the result is the same: those who read the report are left with a false impression of who did the work and are deprived of the means to critically evaluate its source.

Some crime labs have a long history of such practices. Federal agencies have, for example, engaged in the practice of preparing forensic laboratory reports such that it is unclear who actually performed examinations and who wrote the report. In these instances, reports were drafted by a particular unit or section without a specific name attached to them. Another, more common, practice has been to prepare forensic laboratory reports with everyone's name on them: multiple supervisors, multiple analysts, and multiple peer reviewers.

Either practice would allow a crime lab to send just about any forensic examiner that is available from the section that generated the report to satisfy the ever-changing need for required courtroom testimony. When the lab does not send the actual examiner who performed the actual testing and wrote the actual report to testify, then the accused is usually out of luck. There can be no meaningful inquiry into the nature, quality, and competence of the forensic testing under such conditions. The available examiner can only testify to generalities and could honestly deny any direct knowledge of the testing involved in the given case.

Pre-trial evidentiary hearings can be even worse. Prior to trial, some legal jurisdictions have allowed police officers or detectives to bring crime lab reports to the stand and explain their meaning in the absence of testimony from a crime lab scientist. In these cases, oversimplification, misinterpretation, and misrepresentation of scientific findings by law enforcement officers become not just possible, but likely.

Such practices favor the prosecution heavily. They have also allowed government crime labs to put their best foot forward and law enforcement agents to inappropriately co-pilot scientific testimony. However, the advent of the US

Supreme Court's ruling in *Melendez-Diaz* has made such practices impermissible. *Melendez-Diaz v. Massachusetts* (2009) provides that if a lab analyst performed evidentiary analysis and wrote a report of findings, then they alone may offer it as evidence against the accused in a legal proceeding. As reported in Liptak (2009):

> Crime laboratory reports may not be used against criminal defendants at trial unless the analysts responsible for creating them give testimony and subject themselves to cross-examination, the Supreme Court ruled Thursday in a 5-to-4 decision.
>
> The ruling was an extension of a 2004 decision that breathed new life into the Sixth Amendment's confrontation clause, which gives a criminal defendant the right "to be confronted with the witnesses against him."
>
> ...
>
> Noting that 500 employees of the Federal Bureau of Investigation laboratory in Quantico, Va., conduct more than a million scientific tests each year, Justice Kennedy wrote, "The court's decision means that before any of those million tests reaches a jury, at least one of the laboratory's analysts must board a plane, find his/her way to an unfamiliar courthouse and sit there waiting to read aloud notes made months ago."
>
> Justice Antonin Scalia, writing for the majority, scoffed at those "back-of-the-envelope calculations."
>
> In any event, he added, the court is not entitled to ignore even an unwise constitutional command for reasons of convenience.
>
> "The confrontation clause may make the prosecution of criminals more burdensome, but that is equally true of the right to trial by jury and the privilege against self–incrimination," Justice Scalia wrote.
>
> "The sky will not fall after today's decision," he added.
>
> But that is not how prosecutors saw it. "It's a train wreck," Scott Burns, the executive director of the National District Attorneys Association, said of the decision.
>
> "To now require that criminalists in offices and labs that are already burdened and in states where budgets are already being cut back," Mr Burns said, "to travel to courtrooms and wait to say that cocaine is cocaine – we're still kind of reeling from this decision."
>
> ...
>
> The decision came in the wake of a wave of scandals at crime laboratories that included hundreds of tainted cases in Michigan, Texas and West Virginia. William C. Thompson, a professor of

criminology at the University of California, Irvine, said those scandals proved that live testimony from analysts was needed to explore potential shortcomings in laboratory reports.

"The person can be interrogated about the process, about the meaning of the document," Professor Thompson said. "The lab report itself cannot be interrogated to establish the strengths and limitations of the analysis."

...

Cross-examination of witnesses, Justice Scalia wrote, "is designed to weed out not only the fraudulent analyst, but the incompetent one as well." He added that the Constitution would require allowing defendants to confront witnesses even if "all analysts always possessed the scientific acumen of Mme Curie and the veracity of Mother Teresa."

Again, this ruling means that only those who did the work and wrote the report can show up to testify about it in court. Otherwise, their reports are not admissible as evidence. It also means that examiners should expect to be more thoroughly grilled about their precise roles in case examinations and whether they are capable of testifying about the relevant forensic testing issues at hand.

ETHICAL ISSUES IN EXPERT TESTIMONY

The ethical forensic examiner will refrain from making any false or misleading statements, especially when giving sworn testimony. This includes testimony regarding education, training, experience, and credentials. It also includes testimony regarding the occurrence of examination and testing, the results of examination and testing, and the meaning of those results.

Perhaps the most comprehensive and instructive code of ethics for the forensic examiner has been developed by the California Association of Criminalists. With respect to courtroom presentation, the California Association of Criminalists holds that the forensic examiner has professional and scientific obligations which extend beyond the requirements of law (California Association of Criminalists, 2010):

A. The expert witness is one who has substantially greater knowledge of a given subject or science than has the average person. An expert opinion is properly defined as "the formal opinion of an expert." Ordinary opinion consists of one's thoughts or beliefs on matters, generally unsupported by detailed analysis of the subject under consideration. Expert opinion is also defined as the considered opinion of an expert, or a formal Judgment. It is to be understood that an "expert opinion" is an opinion derived only from a formal consideration of a subject within the expert's knowledge and experience.

B. The ethical expert does not take advantage of the privilege to express opinions by offering opinions on matters within his or her field of qualification to which he or she has not given formal consideration.

C. Regardless of legal definitions, the criminalist will realize that there are degrees of certainty represented under the single term of "expert opinion." He or she will not take advantage of the general privilege to assign greater significance to an interpretation than is justified by the available data.

D. Where circumstances indicate it to be proper, the expert will not hesitate to indicate that, while he or she has an opinion, derived of study, and judgment within their field, the opinion may lack the certainty of other opinions he or she might offer. By this or other means, the expert takes care to leave no false impressions in the minds of the jurors or the court.

E. In all respects, the criminalist will avoid the use of terms, and opinions which will be assigned greater weight than are due them. Where an opinion requires qualification or explanation, it is not only proper but incumbent upon the witness to offer such qualification.

F. The expert witness should keep in mind that the lay juror is apt to assign greater or less significance to ordinary words of a scientist than to the same words when used by a lay witness. The criminalist, therefore, will avoid such terms as may be misconstrued or misunderstood.

G. It is not the object of the criminalist's appearance in court to present only that evidence which supports the view of the side to which he or she is employed. The criminalist has a moral obligation to see to it that the court understands the evidence as it exists and to present it in an impartial manner.

H. The criminalist will not by implication, knowingly or intentionally, assist the contestants in a case through such tactics as will implant a false impression in the minds of the jury.

I. The criminalist, testifying as an expert witness, will make every effort to use understandable language while presenting explanations and demonstrations in order that the jury will obtain a true and valid concept of the testimony. The use of unclear, misleading, circuitous, or ambiguous language with a view of confusing an issue in the minds of the court or jury is unethical.

J. The criminalist will answer all questions in a clear, straight-forward manner and will refuse to extend his or her responses beyond their field of competence.

K. Where the expert must prepare photographs or offer oral "background information" to the jury in respect to a specific type of analytic method, this information shall be reliable and valid, typifying the usual or normal basis for the method. The instructional material shall be of a level that will provide the jury with a proper basis for evaluating the subsequent evidence presentations, and not such as would provide them with a lower standard than the science demands.

L. Any and all photographic displays shall be made according to acceptable practice, and shall not be intentionally altered or distorted with a view to misleading court or jury.

M. By way of conveying information to the court, it is appropriate that any of a variety of demonstrative materials and methods be utilized by the expert witness. Such methods and materials shall not, however, be unduly sensational.

This portion of the California Association of Criminalists Code of Ethics spells out the obligations of the forensic examiner in a fairly straightforward manner. It describes the practice of forensic science as a profession, with a moral obligation that goes beyond the instructions of the court, or the requests of attorneys. It also holds partisanship and legal trickery in contempt of good science. The authors concur.

The Ultimate Issue

The *ultimate issue* is the legal question before the trier of fact (i.e., the judge or the jury). As explained in *Black's Law Dictionary* (Black, 1990), the ultimate issue is "That question which must finally be answered as, for example, the defendant's negligence is the ultimate issue in a personal injury action." The ultimate issue relates to legal findings of guilt, innocence, or, in civil matters, liability. The ultimate issue is meant to be determined by the trier of fact based on consideration of the *ultimate facts*, defined in Black (1990) as "facts which are necessary to determine issues in cases, as distinguished from evidentiary facts supporting them." The judge decides what the ultimate facts of a case are, based on their deductions and good judgment as they relate to the evidentiary facts. This is why forensic science and the law are often found at cross-purposes: scientific facts and legal facts are not the same thing.

The history of case law that prohibits forensic experts from intruding on the ultimate issue by directly answering these kinds of questions for the judge or jury is referred to as the *Ultimate Issue Doctrine*. This holds that witnesses are prohibited "from giving an opinion on the ultimate issue is the case. The rationale underpinning the ultimate issue rule is that expert opinion should not be permitted to invade the province of the jury" (Moenssens *et al.*, 1995, p. 75).

However, forensic examiners routinely render scientific findings or opinions within their respective fields that bear closely or directly on the ultimate issue. As explained in Moenssens *et al.* (1995, p. 76):

> The problem regarding the ultimate issue limitation is simply that in complex cases involving issues beyond the abilities of a layman, a jury may need an expert's opinion on the ultimate issue in order to reach a fair verdict. Opinion on the issues of identity [i.e., DNA, fingerprint comparison, etc.], value, insanity, and intoxication, for instance, all border on what would be considered ultimate fact issues, yet they are generally held admissible.

Forensic practitioners should, of course, be able and willing to educate the court as to scientific opinions related to and bordering on the ultimate issue, but they must fully acknowledge their limitations. As scientific fact and legal truth do not abide by the same standards, forensic practitioners are necessarily barred from intruding on the ultimate issue when it involves a purely legal determination or subject matter that is beyond their area of expertise. The reasons for this are fairly straightforward: forensic practitioners are not generally experts at rendering legal conclusions within the complex considerations of regional statutes and case law that binds the average jurist; and, while they may hold opinions on many issues, not all of these are necessarily expert opinions. If the ultimate issue relates to a question that is within the practitioner's area of expertise, then it is disingenuous for the court to bar the forensic practitioner from giving related testimony. However, this assumes that both the court and the practitioner are being careful to delineate the nature and scope of that expertise. This is not always the case.

Some examples may be useful:

- A *psychiatrist* may be asked to give an opinion on the ultimate issue of competency or sanity in a pre-trial hearing. As the interpretation of either is a question of mental character, this is properly within certain kinds of psychiatric and even psychological expertise. In such cases the ultimate issue of guilt is either conceded or irrelevant to the proceedings.
- A *DNA criminalist* may be asked to give testimony regarding the nature and probability of a particular DNA "match" at trial. He or she may then be asked a follow-up question regarding the identity of the

contributor of a particular DNA sample. These are properly within their area of expertise – assuming that the criminalist has sufficient education and training in probabilities and statistics. However, asking them to opine regarding the guilt or innocence of a particular person based on these findings would intrude on the ultimate issue in an improper fashion.

- An *expert on sexual assault* or *sexual assault investigation* may be asked to give testimony on the existence of injuries related to sexual assault, or false reports of sexual assault, and related indicia. Then they may be asked whether or not the case at hand involves evidence that is consistent with a sexual assault or false report.

The expert has both a legal and ethical obligation to refrain from delving into issues of ultimate legal guilt or innocence. They must stick with the scientific facts and make clear that no legal conclusions are being drawn. This is analogous to a forensic pathologist testifying as to cause and manner of death – determining cause as a gunshot wound and manner as homicide (which is a crime, and subsequently an ultimate issue) – without naming the person responsible.

Perjury

Perjury is a criminal charge. It is the act of lying or making verifiably false statements on a material matter under oath or affirmation in a court of law or in any sworn statements in writing (Black, 1990). A violation of specific criminal statutes, it is not sufficient for a statement to be false to meet the threshold of perjury; it must be an intentionally false statement regarding a material fact – a fact relevant to the case at hand. Consequently, not all lies under oath are considered perjury.

For example, in Title 18 of the US Code of Laws, §1621 "General Perjury" provides that perjury involves a person:

> ... having taken an oath before a competent tribunal, officer, or person, in any case in which a law of the United States authorizes an oath to be administered, that he will testify, declare, depose, or certify truly, or that any written testimony, declaration, deposition, or certificate by him subscribed, is true, willfully and contrary to such oath states or subscribes any material matter which he does not believe to be true.

As it stands, not all intentionally false statements made under oath by a forensic examiner are considered perjury – nor are all forensic examiners who give false testimony under oath charged with a crime. The decision to bring such charges is made at the discretion of the District Attorney's Office in the jurisdiction where the false testimony occurred.

CASE EXAMPLE

Kathleen Lundy, Forensic Scientist, FBI Crime Laboratory

Kathleen Lundy held a BS in metallurgy and was employed as a forensic scientist by the FBI Crime Laboratory; as part of her work, she would routinely testify that bullets or bullet fragments associated with a crime were chemically and "analytically indistinguishable," or "consistent with," boxes of ammunition found in the possession of law enforcement suspects (*Ragland v. Commonwealth of Kentucky*, 2006). The chemical test that she used in these cases is referred to as comparative bullet lead analysis (CBLA). As described in Giannelli (2007, pp. 199–200):

> In *Ragland v. Commonwealth*, a Kentucky murder case, Lundy got herself in trouble while testifying at a pretrial admissibility hearing. She stated that the elemental composition of a .243 caliber bullet fragment removed from the victim's body was "analytically indistinguishable" from bullets found at the home of the defendant's parents. Lundy further testified that the Winchester Company purchased its bullet lead in block form prior to 1996 and then remelted it at its manufacturing plant.
>
> During cross-examination at trial, however, Lundy admitted that she knew prior to the hearing that Winchester had purchased its lead in billet form in 1994. This was not a minor point. Millions more bullets could have the same "source" if they were last melted by a secondary smelter instead of by Winchester. Lundy subsequently admitted to her superiors that she had lied, and on June 17, 2003, she pleaded guilty to testifying falsely and was sentenced to a suspended ninety-day jail sentence and a $250 fine.

Further detail regarding the circumstances of Ms Lundy's false testimony, and the pressure she was under, was reported in Solomon (2003):

> FBI lab scientist Kathleen Lundy, an expert witness in murder trials who performs chemical comparisons of lead bullets, was indicted by Kentucky authorities earlier this year on a charge of misdemeanor false swearing after

she acknowledged she knowingly gave false testimony in a 2002 pretrial hearing for a murder suspect.

> Lundy informed her FBI superiors of the false testimony a couple of months after it occurred. By that time she had corrected her pretrial testimony at the trial and had been questioned about it by defense lawyers. Federal authorities decided not to prosecute her, but Kentucky prosecutors brought the misdemeanor charge.
>
> In memos and a sworn affidavit, Lundy stated she had an opportunity to correct her erroneous testimony at the hearing, but didn't. "I had to admit it was worse than being evasive or not correcting the record. It was simply not telling the truth," Lundy wrote in a memo to a superior. "I cannot explain why I made the original error in my testimony … nor why, knowing that the testimony was false, I failed to correct it at the time," Lundy wrote in a subsequent sworn affidavit. "I was stressed out by this case and work in general."
>
> Lundy also said she was increasingly concerned that a former lab colleague, retired metallurgist William Tobin, was beginning to appear as a defense witness in cases and openly questioning the FBI's science on gun lead. "These challenges affected me a great deal, perhaps more than they should have. I also felt that there was ineffective support from the FBI to meet the challenges," Lundy wrote.

While Kathleen Lundy pleaded guilty to false swearing and lost her job at the FBI crime laboratory, she had already testified as prosecution expert in CBLA in more than 100 cases. As of this writing, those cases have all come under review and at least three convictions secured with her testimony have been overturned.

Ultimately, subsequent to being declared junk science by the National Academies of Science in 2004 (National Academy of Sciences, 2004), the FBI acquiesced and put an end to all CBLA casework in their lab.

FORENSIC FRAUD

Forensic fraud occurs when forensic examiners provide sworn testimony, opinions, or documents (e.g., affidavits, reports, or professional resumes) bound for court that contain deceptive or misleading information, findings, opinions, or conclusions, deliberately offered in order to secure an unfair or unlawful gain. As with the case of Kathleen Lundy mentioned in the prior section, it involves intentionally unethical behavior.

As discussed at length in Turvey (2013), forensic fraud is no small problem for the justice system. It results in the conviction of innocents, destroys careers, and create immense financial liability for law enforcement agencies, individual examiners, and the municipalities that employ them. It also creates incalculable expense for the justice system in general. Forensic fraud is therefore not something to be disregarded, minimized, or otherwise ignored. It is a serious concern that requires the close attention of any professional community intersecting with the forensic sciences.

The Research

Much of the research into forensic fraud has come as a consequence to the work conducted by the Innocence Project in New York. It has revealed that some forensic examiners have no concern for professional ethics whatsoever, and are content to behave in an unethical manner. Consider the following research efforts stemming from their cases:

In a study of 86 DNA exoneration cases, Saks and Koehler (2005) reported the following frequency data: forensic testing errors in 63%, police misconduct in 44%, prosecutorial misconduct in 28%, and false or misleading testimony by forensic experts in 27%.

In a broader study of 340 exonerations between 1989 and 2003, 196 of which did not involve DNA evidence, Gross *et al.* (2005) found the following: "In 5 [1.5%] of the exonerations that we have studied there are reports of perjury by police officers. In an additional 24 [7%] we have similar information on perjury by forensic scientists testifying for the government" (p. 19).

Lastly, in the first published study of scientific testimony by prosecution experts in cases where the defendant was eventually exonerated, Garrett and Neufeld (2009) reviewed the transcripts from 137 trials. They found that (pp. 1–2):

> … in the bulk of these trials of innocent defendants – 82 cases or 60% – forensic analysts called by the prosecution provided invalid testimony at trial – that is, testimony with conclusions misstating empirical data or wholly unsupported by empirical data. This was not the testimony of a mere handful of analysts: this set of trials included invalid testimony

by 72 forensic analysts called by the prosecution and employed by 52 laboratories, practices, or hospitals from 25 states. Unfortunately, the adversarial process largely failed to police this invalid testimony. Defense counsel rarely cross-examined analysts concerning invalid testimony and rarely obtained experts of their own. In the few cases in which invalid forensic science was challenged, judges seldom provided relief.

Examining trial testimony did not reveal the entire picture, however. Garrett and Neufeld discovered, after evaluating "post-conviction review, investigations, or civil discovery" (p. 14), that 13 (10%) of the 137 cases also involved withheld exculpatory evidence. This included three cases that did not involve invalid testimony. Consequently, 85 (63%) of the 137 cases under review involved either invalid scientific testimony or the withholding of exculpatory evidence.

A Fraud Typology

Adapted from, and consistent with, typologies provided in Babbage (1830), National Academy of Sciences (2002), Office of Research Integrity (2009), and Turvey (2003), forensic examiners can be cross-categorized as having used one or more of three general approaches to committing fraud, referred to as *Simulators*, *Dissemblers*, and *Pseudoexperts* (Turvey, 2013).

- *Simulators* are those examiners who physically manipulate physical evidence or related forensic testing.[7] This means that they physically fabricate, tamper with, or destroy evidence. As the name suggests, they are trying to create the appearance that something happened when it did not or to create the appearance that nothing happened at all when in fact it did. This approach to fraud also describes those examiners engaging in evidence suppression by concealing its existence (e.g., hide it in a desk drawer, hide it on the evidence shelf, remove it from the evidence log).
- *Dissemblers* are those examiners who exaggerate, embellish, lie about, or otherwise misrepresent findings.[8] They are not tampering with the evidence; they are simply not telling the truth about it. *Dissemblers* exist on a continuum from those who lie outright about the significance of examination results to those who intentionally present a biased or incomplete view.
- *Pseudoexperts* are those examiners who fabricate or misrepresent their credentials. They are also referred to as fakes, phonies, charlatans, and mountebanks.[9] Pseudoexperts exist on a continuum of severity as well, from those with valid credentials who misrepresent a credential or an affiliation, to those with no valid credentials at all.

---

[7]Also referred to as *forging* (Babbage, 1830) or *fabrication* (Office of Research Integrity, 2009b).
[8]Also referred to as *trimming* and *cooking* (Babbage, 1830) or *falsification* (Office of Research Integrity, 2009b).
[9]Also referred to as *falsifying credentials* (Office of Research Integrity, 2009b).

Original research regarding forensic fraud was published in Turvey (2013); it analyzed data collected from 100 forensic examiners in the United States that had committed fraud related to the examination of physical evidence between 2000 and 2010. This research also employed the typology above and reported the following major findings with respect to fraudulent forensic examiners:

- 23% ($n = 23$) of the forensic examiners in this study were determined to have a history of addiction, 21% ($n = 21$) a history of fraud, and 17% ($n = 17$) a history of other criminal convictions.
- 27% ($n = 27$) of forensic examiners in this study were found to have been lying about some or all of their education, training, and experience. They were subsequently classified as pseudoexperts.
- 82% ($n = 82$) of the forensic examiners in this study were determined to be involved in an ongoing pattern of fraud within their agency, often involving multiple examiners, prior to discovery. In context, this finding generally points towards the contribution of systemic and cultural factors.
- 78% ($n = 78$) of the forensic examiners in this study were employed directly by law enforcement agencies. This finding supports the assertion that those working on behalf of the police and the prosecution (though not necessarily the government in general) are responsible for a substantial amount, if not the majority, of the known cases of forensic fraud.
- 37% ($n = 37$) of the fraudulent examiners in the present study were initially retained by their respective employers without severe consequences despite their misconduct; of these, the weightiest involved examiners that were reassigned or temporarily suspended.

The typology and these research findings are offered in the hope that the ethical forensic examiner will be more able, and not fail in their obligation, to identify and report the unethical behavior and misconduct of others. This ethical obligation, and its ramifications, will be discussed more thoroughly in Chapter 15: "Whistleblowers in the Criminal Justice System."

A PROPOSED ETHICAL CANON

In 2010, the authors invited the renowned Dr John Thornton, a practicing criminalist and a former Professor of Forensic Science at the University of California at Berkeley, to develop a simple professional canon of ethics to which the forensic examiner could adhere. It was published in Thornton (2011) and bears our attention as we close this discussion:

The Professional Canon of Ethics for the Reconstructionist

One simple device that may assist the crime reconstructionist in maintenance of a proper professional stance against external pressure is a printed statement of ethical behavior posted conspicuously in his or her office. A consulting reconstructionist could have it posted on his/her Web site. This may read something along the lines of the following.

1. As a practicing crime reconstructionist, I pledge to apply the principles of science and logic and to follow the truth courageously wherever it may lead.
2. As a practicing crime reconstructionist, I acknowledge that the scientific spirit must be inquiring, progressive, logical, and unbiased.
3. I will never knowingly allow a false impression to be planted in the mind of anyone availing themselves of my services.
4. As a practicing crime reconstructionist, it is not my purpose to present only that evidence which supports the view of one side. I have a moral and professional responsibility to ensure that everyone concerned understands the evidence as it exists and to present it in an impartial manner.
5. The practice of crime reconstruction has a single professional demand – correctness. It has a single ethical demand – truthfulness. To these I commit myself, totally and irrevocably.
6. The exigencies of a particular case will not cause me to depart from the professionalism that I am required to exercise.

The authors commit to utter agreement with this ethical canon and urge others to do the same in their respective forensic practices. We would add the caveat that the ethical forensic examiner has an additional obligation to the profession, to identify unethical behavior and other forms of misconduct whenever it is observed, and to report it to the appropriate authority whenever possible. When this duty is not attended, the profession suffers as does the criminal justice system and society as a whole.[10]

SUMMARY

The term forensic examiner generally refers to any professional who examines and interprets physical evidence with the expectation of courtroom testimony. This chapter explores the primary ethical issues that confront forensic examiners in their casework and subsequent testimony. These issues include examiner bias and observer effects, inducements to commit forensic fraud, and issues with report writing and testimony.

---

[10]The mechanics and consequences of reporting unethical behavior will be discussed in Chapter 14: "Professional Organizations in the Criminal Justice System" and Chapter 15: "Whistleblowers in the Criminal Justice System.

Questions

1. The role of a *forensic examiner* is to seek out evidence that support the theories of a particular institution, employer, or side. True or False?
2. "[T]he scientific observer [is] an imperfectly calibrated instrument" (Rosenthal, 1996, p. 3). Explain this quote.
3. Define *observer effects*. Explain how a forensic examiner can mitigate observer effects.
4. Forensic examiners are not required to report "inconclusive" results. True or False? Explain.
5. Explain the difference between the *ultimate issue* and *ultimate facts*.
6. List and define the three general approaches to committing fraud.

References

Babbage, C., 1830. Reflections on the Decline of Science in England, and on Some of its Causes. B. Fellowes, London.

Black, H.C., 1990. Black's Law Dictionary, sixth ed. West Publishing, St Paul, MN.

Brady v. Maryland, 1963. US Supreme Court, 373 US 83, Case No. 490.

California Association of Criminalists, 2010. Code of Ethics of the California Association of Criminalists. CAC Website, April 24; url: http://www.cacnews.org/membership/California%20 Association%20of%20Criminalists%20Code%20of%20Ethics%202010.pdf.

California Crime Laboratory Review Task Force, 2009. An Examination of Forensic Science in California. State of California, Office of the Attorney General, California Crime Laboratory Review Task Force, Sacramento, CA, November; url: http://ag.ca.gov/publications/crime_labs_report.pdf.

Chisum, W.J., Turvey, B., 2011. Crime Reconstruction, second ed. Elsevier, San Diego, CA.

Cooley, C., Turvey, B., 2011. Observer effects and examiner bias: psychological influences on the forensic examiner. In: Chisum, W.J., Turvey, B. (Eds.), Crime Reconstruction, second ed. Elsevier, San Diego, CA.

Gannett, C., 2011. Ethical dilemmas. CAC News, First Quarter, pp. 25–32.

Gardenier, J., 2011. Data integrity is earned, not given. Office of Research Integrity Newsletter 19 (3), 3.

Garrett, B., Neufeld, P., 2009. Invalid forensic science testimony and wrongful convictions. Virginia Law Review 95 (1), 1–97.

Giannelli, P., 2007. Wrongful convictions and forensic science: the need to regulate crime labs. North Carolina Law Review 86, 163–236.

Giannelli, P., McMunigal, K., 2007. Prosecutors, ethics, and expert witnesses. Fordham Law Review 76, 1493–1537, (December).

Gross, H., 1906. Criminal Investigation. G. Ramasawmy Chetty & Co, Madras.

Gross, S., Jacoby, K., Matheson, D., Montgomery, N., Patil, S., 2005. Exonerations in the United States, 1989 through 2003. Journal of Criminal Law and Criminology 95, 523–559, (Winter).

Hecht, L., 2001. Role conflict and role overload: different concepts, different consequences. Sociological Inquiry 71 (1), 111–121.

James, S., Nordby, J., 2003. Forensic Science: An Introduction to Scientific and Investigative Techniques. CRC Press, Boca Raton, FL.

Jette, A., 2005. Without scientific integrity, there can be no evidence base. Physical Therapy 85 (1), 1122–1123.

Jones, A., 2003. Can authorship policies help prevent scientific misconduct? What role for scientific societies? Science and Engineering Ethics 9 (2), 243–256.

Kappeler, V., 2006. Critical Issues in Police Civil Liability, fourth ed. Waveland Press, Long Grove, IL.

Kennedy, D.B., Kennedy, B., 1972. Applied Sociology for Police. Charles C. Thomas, Springfield, IL.

Krimsky, S., 2007. Defining scientific misconduct: when conflict-of-interest is a factor in scientific misconduct. Medicine and Law 26, 447–463.

Leung, R., 2009. DNA testing: foolproof? CBS News, February 11; url: http://www.cbsnews.com/2100-500164_162-555723.html.

Liptak, A., 2009. Justices rule lab analysts must testify on results. New York Times, June 25.

Melendez-Diaz v. Massachusetts, 2009. US Supreme Court, No. 07–591, June 25.

Moenssens, A., Starrs, J., Henderson, C., Inbau, F., 1995. Scientific Evidence in Civil and Criminal Cases, fourth ed. Foundation Press, New York.

Mollen, M., 1994. Commission Report, City of New York. Commission to Investigate Allegations of Police Corruption and the Anti-Corruption Procedures of the Police Department July 7.

National Academy of Sciences, 2002. Integrity in Scientific Research: Creating an Environment That Promotes Responsible Conduct, National Academy of Sciences Committee on Assessing Integrity in Research Environments. National Academies Press, Washington, DC.

National Academy of Sciences, 2004. Forensic Analysis Weighing Bullet Lead Evidence, National Academy of Sciences Committee on Scientific Assessment of Bullet Lead Elemental Composition Comparison. National Academies Press, Washington, DC.

National Academy of Sciences, 2009a. On Being a Scientist: A Guide to Responsible Conduct in Research, third ed. National Academies Press, Washington, DC National Academy of Sciences Committee on Science, Engineering, and Public Policy.

National Academy of Sciences, 2009b. Strengthening Forensic Science in the United States: A Path Forward, National Academy of Sciences Committee on Identifying the Needs of the Forensic Sciences Community. National Academies Press, Washington, DC.

Office of Research Integrity, 2009. The Office of Research Integrity Annual Report 2009. US Department of Health and Human Services, Washington, DC, url: http://ori.hhs.gov/documents/annual_reports/ori_annual_report_2009.pdf.

Pettigrew, A., 1968. Inter-group conflict and role strain. Journal of Management Studies 5 (2), 205–218.

Ragland v. Commonwealth of Kentucky, 2006. Supreme Court of Kentucky, No. 2002-SC-0388-MR, 2003-SC-0084-TG, 191 S.W.3d 569, March 23.

Ridolfi, K., Possley, M., 2010. Preventable Error: A Report on Prosecutorial Misconduct in California 1997–2009. Northern California Innocence Project at Santa Clara University School of Law, Santa Clara, CA.

Risinger, D.M., Saks, M.J., Thompson, W.C., Rosenthal, R., 2002. The Daubert/Kumho implications of observer effects in forensic science: hidden problems of expectation and suggestion. California Law Review 90 (1), 1–56.

Rosenthal, R., 1966. Experimenter Effects in Behavioral Research. Appleton-Century-Crofts, New York.

Saks, M., 1998. Merlin and Solomon: lessons from the law's formative encounters with forensic identification science. Hastings Law Journal 49, 1069–1081, (April).

Saks, M.J., 2003. Book review: Ethics in Forensic Science: Professional standards for the practice of criminalistics. Jurimetrics 43 (3), 359–363.

Saks, M., Koehler, J., 2005. The coming paradigm shift in forensic identification science. Science 309 (5736), 892–895.

Solomon, J., 2003. New allegations target two FBI crime-lab scientists. Seattle Times, April 16; url: http://community.seattletimes.nwsource.com/archive/?date=20030416&slug=fbilab16.

Savino, J., Turvey, B., 2011. Rape Investigation Handbook, second ed. Elsevier, San Diego, CA.

Sexual Assault Task Force, 2009. False reports and case unfounding. Attorney General's Sexual Assault Task Force, State of Oregon, Position Paper January 22.

Scamahorn, L., 2002. Letter to F. Joseph Vetter, First Sergeant, Manager, Evansville Regional Laboratory, Subject "Floyd County Prosecutor". dated February 11.

Siegal, J., 2012. General forensic ethical dilemmas. In: Upshaw-Downs, J.C., Swienton, A. (Eds.), Ethics in Forensic Science, Elsevier, San Diego, CA.

Steneck, N., 2007. Introduction to the Responsible Conduct of Research. revised edition Office of Research Integrity, Washington, DC.

Thornton, J., Peterson, J., 2007. The general assumptions and rationale of forensic identification. In: Faigman, D., Kaye, D., Saks, M., Sanders, J. (Eds.), Modern Scientific Evidence: The Law and Science of Expert Testimony, vol. 1. West Publishing, St Paul, MN.

Thornton, J.I., 1983. Uses and abuses of forensic science. In: Thomas, W. (Ed.), Science and Law: An Essential Alliance, Westview Press, Boulder, CO.

Turvey, B., 2013. Forensic Fraud. Elsevier, San Diego, CA.

Williams, G., 1958. The Proof of Guilt: A Study of the English Criminal Trial. Stevens & Sons, London.

Zion-Hershberg, B., 2006. Analyst felt pressured in Camm's first trial. The Evansville Courier-Journal, February 1.

CHAPTER 9

Ethical Issues for Criminal Prosecutors

Ronald Miller and Brent E. Turvey

Key Terms

Brady v. Maryland A legal ruling from the US Supreme Court that holds, "the suppression by the prosecution of evidence favorable to an accused upon request violates due process where the evidence is material either to guilt or to punishment, irrespective of the good faith or bad faith of the prosecution." It requires timely disclosure of exculpatory evidence by the prosecution to the defense.

City/Municipal Attorneys Elected or appointed officials, serving to represent and advise local governments (e.g., assemblies, boards, administrators, and department heads in villages, townships, and cities) in criminal prosecutions, civil disputes, and other legal matters.

Conflict of interest Occurs when a person or an agency has competing loyalties, or loyalties that are at odds, because of their need to satisfy multiple roles, duties, or obligations.

District Attorneys (DAs) Elected officials that operate at the borough or country level to represent local government in the prosecution of criminal defendants.

Doyle Error As held in *Doyle v. Ohio* (1976), "after an arrested person is formally advised by an officer of the law that he has a right to remain silent, the unfairness occurs when the prosecution, in the presence of the jury, is allowed to undertake impeachment on the basis of what may be the exercise of that right."

Grand jury Used to determine whether or not there is probable cause to believe that specific crimes have been committed by those named in any indictment – this instead of relying solely on the discretion of law enforcement.

Harmless error An error that is not egregious enough to require a criminal conviction to be set aside or overturned.

Material witness A witness that has information that is material to a criminal proceeding (the material nature of which is largely at the discretion of the prosecutor).

Material witness warrant Used to detain a witness until their testimony is complete if the prosecutor believes that the witness would not respond to a subpoena to appear.

Overcharging The practice of charging a defendant with every conceivable criminal act committed or with the most serious form of a crime with the steepest penalty.

Probable cause Exists when the known facts and circumstances, of a reasonably trustworthy nature, are sufficient to justify a person of reasonable caution or prudence to believe that a crime has been or is being committed by the person being arrested.

CONTENTS

257

Ethical Justice. http://dx.doi.org/10.1016/B978-0-12-404597-2.00009-7

Prosecutorial misconduct "… the use of deceptive or reprehensible methods to attempt to persuade either the court or the jury" (*California v. Hill*, 1998; *California v. Espinosa*, 1992; *California v. Price*, 1991; *California v. Pitts*, 1990).

US Attorneys Operate at the Federal level, working directly for the US Attorney General and representing the US government.

In collaboration with their law enforcement counterparts, criminal prosecutors are the most powerful and influential agents of the criminal justice system (Gershowitz, 2009). They alone can decide whether to bring charges against criminal suspects before the court; whether a case or particular evidence is presented to a grand jury; who gets called as a credible witness and who gets charged as a co-defendant; whether information and evidence is shared with the defense; whether additional charges are added during trial; and, in the most politicized cases, who gets a plea deal and who faces the death penalty. This broad discretion gives prosecutors an almost absolute power to shape the face of a criminal trial and is backed up by all of the resources available to the State (Gershman, 1993).

It is also not unfair to observe that prosecutorial authority exists in many legal jurisdictions without practicable checks or balances. As described in Gershman (1993, p. 513): "The prosecutor's decision to institute criminal charges is the broadest and least regulated power in American criminal law." Consequently, we must accept that there is an ethical contrast in the character of the prosecutorial community. Some manage their authority towards the cause of justice with extraordinary fairness and legal agility; others willfully engage in what can only be described as extraordinary abuse, holding the criminal justice system "hostage" for personal or political gain (Oppel, 2011).

The purpose of this chapter is to consider the major ethical issues and questions peculiar to criminal prosecutors as they dispatch their duties in the pursuit of justice within the public trust. It will necessarily touch on many forms of *prosecutorial misconduct*, which is "the use of deceptive or reprehensible methods to attempt to persuade either the court or the jury" (see *California v. Hill*, 1998; *California v. Espinosa*, 1992; *California v. Price*, 1991; *California v. Pitts*, 1990). While it is not possible to consider or anticipate every dilemma faced by those empowered to prosecute criminal defendants, the authors will attempt to present a realistic overview that goes beyond what is typically discussed in the idealized or theory-oriented classroom of the past. For organizational purposes, specific ethical considerations are discussed across the following sub headings: *law enforcement, pre-trial, trial*, and *post-conviction*. This is preceded by a review of basic prosecutorial structure and function.

CRIMINAL PROSECUTORS: STRUCTURE AND FUNCTION

Owing to inaccurate media portrayals of criminal investigations and court-room drama, there is a great deal of confusion regarding the role of prosecutors in the criminal justice system. It is therefore necessary to provide a general overview. Although many prosecutorial archetypes exist, there are three primary types of criminal prosecutors in the US: *US Attorneys*, *District Attorneys (DAs)*, and *City/Municipal Attorneys*.

US Attorneys

US Attorneys operate at the Federal level, working directly for the US Attorney General and representing the US government. Appointed by the President of the United States, they are the ranking Federal law enforcement officers and chief criminal litigators for their respective Federal jurisdictions. As explained in Offices of the United States Attorneys (2013):

> There are 93 United States Attorneys stationed throughout the United States, Puerto Rico, the Virgin Islands, Guam, and the Northern Mariana Islands. United States Attorneys are appointed by, and serve at the discretion of, the President of the United States, with the advice and consent of the United States Senate. One United States Attorney is assigned to each of the 94 judicial districts, with the exception of Guam and the Northern Mariana Islands where a single United States Attorney serves in both districts.
>
> Each United States Attorney is the chief federal law enforcement officer of the United States within his or her particular jurisdiction.
>
> United States Attorneys conduct most of the trial work in which the United States is a party. The United States Attorneys have three statutory responsibilities under Title 28, Section 547 of the United States Code:

> - the prosecution of criminal cases brought by the Federal Government;
> - the prosecution and defense of civil cases in which the United States is a party; and
> - the collection of debts owed the Federal Government which are administratively uncollectible.

Cases prosecuted by the US Attorney's Office involve violations of Federal law, including those related to human trafficking, drug trafficking, interstate money laundering and embezzlement, wide-scale fraud, and corruption (Figure 9.1). They also have exclusive jurisdiction to prosecute felonies that occur on non-State and Federal property (e.g., Native American reservations, US-flagged

FIGURE 9.1

In February 2013, US Attorney Sally Yates holds a joint agency press conference at the Richard B. Russell Federal Building in downtown Atlanta, flanked by DeKalb County Sheriff Thomas Brown and Atlanta Police Chief George Turner. She announced the arrest of 10 police officers in different law enforcement agencies for charges related to the protection and transportation of illegal drugs — in essence, for taking money to use their police uniforms, badges, and guns to facilitate drug trafficking at the direction of street gangs. The investigation was a joint FBI and ATF venture which resulted in Federal charges against the corrupt officers (Visser, 2013).

merchant vessels, and national parks); in Federal facilities (e.g., Federal office buildings, US Post Offices and Federal court houses, and Federal prisons); and on US military bases around the world.

Often criticized for taking only politically motivated or high-profile cases to trial in order to maximize publicity, US Attorneys are known for exercising their authority in a way that is guaranteed to make the news. Despite this penchant for media coverage, the US Attorney also handles many other "low-level" federal crimes. These include those related to firearms possession, interstate transport of stolen property, narcotics and immigration violations, and civil rights violations by law enforcement officials.

District Attorneys (DAs)

DAs are elected officials that operate at the borough or county level to represent local government in the prosecution of criminal defendants. This means that they are politicians, beholden to voters with influence over the interpretation of law and its enforcement. It also means that they must face re-election and can be voted out of office by a dissatisfied electorate.

DAs are generally charged with prosecuting felony matters in their respective jurisdictions and may also have a responsibility to prosecute misdemeanors in any *unincorporated*[1] areas. The DA's Office maintains a staff of Assistant District Attorneys (ADAs) to manage their regional caseload. In larger jurisdictions, this includes the creation of specialized prosecutorial units or divisions, to align efforts with their law enforcement counterparts (e.g., capital murder, homicide, sex crimes, juvenile justice, family violence, white collar crimes, hate crimes, and appellate divisions). They may also have a civil division to represent their employing agency (usually at the county level) in defending and bringing civil actions.

Depending upon local statutes, budgets, and jurisdiction, the DA's Office may also employ its own investigators (comprised almost exclusively of retired law enforcement officers) and maintain its own crime laboratory.

City/Municipal Attorneys

City/Municipal Attorneys are elected or appointed officials, serving to represent and advise local governments (e.g., assemblies, boards, administrators, and department heads in villages, townships, and cities) in criminal prosecutions, civil disputes, and other legal matters. These duties generally include the prosecution of criminal defendants for misdemeanor crimes, and the interpretation of contracts, legal statutes, and court decisions for municipal decision makers. Depending on the local population and crime rate, the City Attorney's Office can be limited with respect to its role or it can be heavily involved and diverse.

In smaller jurisdictions with less crime, the City Attorney may be constrained to handling traffic tickets, housing code infractions, or neighborhood zoning violations. This is because the DA's Office would have the time and resources to prosecute both felonies and misdemeanors under such circumstances. In these scenarios, it is typical to find a private attorney working part-time for a city while maintaining their own separate legal practice. This division of "labor" between City Attorneys and DAs may be determined by local court rule or other jurisdictional statutes at the state and local levels.

In larger jurisdictions, the City Attorney may be in charge of handling the many cases of misdemeanor level domestic violence, elder abuse, sexual battery, stalking, child abuse and neglect, child molestation, child pornography, and statutory rape. Other misdemeanor criminal offenses commonly prosecuted by City Attorneys can include: driving under the influence of alcohol and/or drugs, vandalism, graffiti, theft, weapons offenses, prostitution, hate crimes, illegal street racing, reckless driving, hit-and-run, road rage, furnishing alcohol to minors, minors in possession of alcohol, resisting arrest, utility theft, harassing telephone

---

[1]Unincorporated areas are those that are not governed by a local municipal (city) corporation; rather, they are run by another larger entity, such as a borough, county, or state government.

calls, lewd acts in public, vehicular manslaughter, sex crimes, embezzlement, and credit card fraud. In such large jurisdictions, the City Attorney's Office may be structured in a fashion that is similar to the DA's Office – the difference being the severity of the offenses prosecuted along with municipal code violators.

The Mission

The criminal prosecutor's mission should be a straightforward one: the just prosecution of criminal defendants. The key concept is *just* – as in fair, impartial, and honest. In an unequivocal testament to this fundamental responsibility towards justice "prosecutors take an oath of office swearing to uphold the law, and every prosecutor is expected to conform her personal ethical code to the baseline ethical code that is established by law" (Cummings, 2010, p. 2147). If local statutes make it unclear, this mandate for prosecutorial honesty and fairness can be found in rulings made by the US Supreme Court. An early example is the language provided in *Berger v. United States* (1935):

> The United States Attorney is the representative not of an ordinary party to a controversy, but of a sovereignty whose obligation to govern impartially is as compelling as its obligation to govern at all; and whose interest, therefore, in a criminal prosecution is not that it shall win a case, but that justice shall be done. As such, he is in a peculiar and very definite sense the servant of the law, the twofold aim of which is that guilt shall not escape or innocence suffer. He may prosecute with earnestness and vigor – indeed, he should do so. But, while he may strike hard blows, he is not at liberty to strike foul ones. It is as much his duty to refrain from improper methods calculated to produce a wrongful conviction as it is to use every legitimate means to bring about a just one.

Ultimately, as explained in Gershman (1993), the prosecutor is a "gatekeeper of justice" and is expected to "engage in a rigorous moral dialogue in the context of factual, political, experiential, and ethical considerations … to make and give effect to the kinds of bedrock value judgments that underlie our system of justice – that the objective of convicting guilty persons is outweighed by the objective of ensuring that innocent persons are not punished" (p. 522).

Consider, for example, the "Mission Statement" of the Los Angeles County DA's Office in California (Los Angeles County District Attorney's Office, 2012):

> The District Attorney of Los Angeles, as a constitutional officer and the public prosecutor acting on behalf of the people, is vested with the independent power to conduct prosecutions for public offenses, to detect crime and to investigate criminal activity. The District Attorney advises the Grand Jury in its investigations. By law, the District Attorney sponsors and participates in programs to improve the administration of justice.

The District Attorney fulfills these responsibilities through the efforts of the employees of the Office of the District Attorney. Each employee of the District Attorney's Office shall adopt the highest standards of ethical behavior and professionalism. Each employee, moreover, is integral to achieving the mission of the Office and shares the District Attorney's obligation to enhance the fundamental right of the people of Los Angeles County to a safe and just society. At all times, the mission of the District Attorney's Office shall be carried out in a fair, evenhanded and compassionate manner.

This mission statement is generally consistent with those proclaimed by county prosecutors and DAs all over the United States. Emphasis is placed on crime detection, criminal investigation, and just prosecutions – along with the promise that high ethical standards will be maintained with respect to "behavior and professionalism."

These notions align with the Standards set forth by the American Bar Association (ABA), which outlines the function of the prosecutor in clear terms as a seeker of truth, an advocate of justice, and a mechanism for reforms and remediations. As detailed by the ABA (American Bar Association, 1993, p. 4):

Standard 3- 1.2 The Function of the Prosecutor

(a) The office of prosecutor is charged with responsibility for prosecutions in its jurisdiction.
(b) The prosecutor is an administrator of justice, an advocate, and an officer of the court; the prosecutor must exercise sound discretion in the performance of his or her functions.
(c) The duty of the prosecutor is to seek justice, not merely to convict.
(d) It is an important function of the prosecutor to seek to reform and improve the administration of criminal justice. When inadequacies or injustices in the substantive or procedural law come to the prosecutor's attention, he or she should stimulate efforts for remedial action.
(e) It is the duty of the prosecutor to know and be guided by the standards of professional conduct as defined by applicable professional traditions, ethical codes, and law in the prosecutor's jurisdiction.

However, as discussed in prior chapters, the concept of justice varies dependent upon regional law, culture, and even personally held beliefs. So while this standard creates the appearance of uniformity among members of the ABA, it does not result in (or even reflect) universally held beliefs regarding ethical practice and professional conduct.

In theory, then, the criminal prosecutor's mission is one of assuring *just* investigations and providing *just* prosecutions. Should either of these fail, it falls on the prosecutor to figure it out, make amends, and take steps to keep it from happening again. It is a hopeful theory.

The reality, explored in this chapter, is that criminal prosecutors of every kind serve in highly politicized positions where they are judged not based on their ability to achieve justice, but rather on their conviction rate. In other words, they are retained and promoted based primarily on how often they win in court, and their ability to achieve convictions serves as a proxy for professional competence. It is a political rubric, not one that is oriented towards justice.

Ultimately, this measure of success challenges the prosecutor to be true to the mission of justice; the institutional and often personal desire to win in court can overcome their need to serve "broader obligations." Those duties are eloquently described by David Sklansky, Professor of Law at the University of California at Berkeley (2009):

> American prosecutors play two roles. On the one hand they are officers of the court, charged with seeing to it that the guilty are convicted and the innocent acquitted. On the other hand, prosecutors are participants in an adversary system of adjudication. They are expected to field one side of a courtroom battle. If they lack zeal, the system fails …. Prosecutors can come to believe too strongly that justice requires the defendant's conviction.
>
> These two roles can pull prosecutors in opposite directions. The habits of combat we encourage in prosecutors, and that they need if they are to succeed in hard-fought cases, can tempt them to be less than painstaking about their broader set of obligations – the requirements imposed on them, for example, to disclose all potentially exculpatory information to the defense.
>
> Prosecutors can come to believe too strongly that justice requires the defendant's conviction. Once that happens, it is easy for them to convince themselves that, say, a bit of awkward information isn't "really" exculpatory, or that it shouldn't really count as "evidence," or that, for some other reason, it shouldn't be disclosed.
>
> The danger arises not only because of the two roles prosecutors play, but because they shuttle back and forth between the courtroom and the world of law enforcement. In one they are constantly reminded of their status as officers of the court; in the other, they work closely with police officers and government investigators, whom they often admire.
>
> The divided roles and divided allegiances of prosecutors create constant pressures to step over the line.

A more blunt perspective on the matter was provided by investigative journalist Maurice Possley, formerly of the *Chicago Tribune*, whose ongoing research into wrongful convictions has helped to shape and inform the debate for the next generation (Armstrong and Possley, 1999):

With impunity, prosecutors across the country have violated their oaths and the law, committing the worst kinds of deception in the most serious of cases.

They have prosecuted black men, hiding evidence the real killers were white. They have prosecuted a wife, hiding evidence her husband committed suicide. They have prosecuted parents, hiding evidence their daughter was killed by wild dogs. They do it to win.

They do it because they won't get punished.

The lack of accountability for criminal prosecutors will be touched on throughout this chapter, but is discussed specifically in the final sections.

The ethical criminal prosecutor's mission is the search for truth in the pursuit of justice. They recognize that winning in court is one of many possible just outcomes as the truth is investigated and revealed. They are, in essence, truth seekers that are meant to hold their professional integrity dear, preferring to avoid media celebrity and lose legal contests honestly than to win cases by means of deceit or trickery. The criminal prosecutor without an ethical compass, and without honest professional bearings, seeks only to stage and win legal battles – as this serves not the public trust but their own personal agenda.

Avoiding Conflicts of Interest

A *conflict of interest* occurs when a person or an agency has competing loyalties, or loyalties that are at odds, because of their need to satisfy multiple roles, duties, or obligations. ABA Standards make it clear that conflicts of interest are to be avoided, while also providing explicit guidelines to help prosecutors recognize them (American Bar Association, 1993, pp. 7–8):

(a) A prosecutor should avoid a conflict of interest with respect to his or her official duties.

(b) A prosecutor should not represent a defendant in criminal proceedings in a jurisdiction where he or she is also employed as a prosecutor.

(c) A prosecutor should not, except as law may otherwise expressly permit, participate in a matter in which he or she participated personally and substantially while in private practice or nongovernmental employment unless under applicable law no one is, or by lawful delegation may be, authorized to act in the prosecutor's stead in the matter.

(d) A prosecutor who has formerly represented a client in a matter in private practice should not thereafter use information obtained from that representation to the disadvantage of the former client unless the rules of attorney–client confidentiality do not apply or the information has become generally known.

(e) A prosecutor should not, except as law may otherwise expressly permit, negotiate for private employment with any person who is involved as an accused or as an attorney or agent for an accused in a matter in which the prosecutor is participating personally and substantially.

(f) A prosecutor should not permit his or her professional judgment or obligations to be affected by his or her own political, financial, business, property, or personal interests.

(g) A prosecutor who is related to another lawyer as parent, child, sibling, or spouse should not participate in the prosecution of a person who the prosecutor knows is represented by the other lawyer. Nor should a prosecutor who has a significant personal or financial relationship with another lawyer participate in the prosecution of a person who the prosecutor knows is represented by the other lawyer, unless the prosecutor's supervisor, if any, is informed and approves or unless there is no other prosecutor authorized to act in the prosecutor's stead.

(h) A prosecutor should not recommend the services of particular defense counsel to accused persons or witnesses unless requested by the accused person or witness to make such a recommendation, and should not make a referral that is likely to create a conflict of interest. Nor should a prosecutor comment upon the reputation or abilities of defense counsel to an accused person or witness who is seeking or may seek such counsel's services unless requested by such person.

The ABA also makes it clear that a prosecutor cannot serve two masters effectively; that being a prosecutor is literally a full-time commitment (1993, p. 24):

a) The function of public prosecution requires highly developed professional skills. This objective can best be achieved by promoting continuity of service and broad experience in all phases of the prosecution function.

b) Wherever feasible, the offices of chief prosecutor and staff should be full-time occupations.

In other words, part-time prosecutors (e.g., City Attorneys in small towns) will necessarily fail in their commitment to professional continuity and ethical service because their loyalties are, by definition, divided. They, or their office, may wind up having to prosecute former clients or those associated with them; or at the very least they will not be able to give prosecutorial responsibilities the full weight of their professional attention because of the burden of an additional private caseload. This is even before more complex ethical questions are considered, such as client identity (i.e., whether their client in a given matter is an individual city employee, any number of its governing bodies, or the city as a corporation) and who enjoys the subsequent attorney–client privilege (Thompson, 2012).

Those who work in the criminal justice system are painfully aware of how often this particular ethical covenant is not just violated but openly ignored by criminal prosecutors. Apart from the conundrums brought about by the casual prosecutor (e.g., Swift, 2012), other common conflicts of interest include the prosecutor trying a case before a judge that is also their former law partner; the prosecutor negotiating for a reality TV show, for a book deal, or to sell the movie rights related to a high-profile case they are in the process of trying (Grippando, 2013); or the conflicts inherent in prosecuting a case that involves a friend, (ex-)lover, colleague, staff member, or relative as a defendant, witness, or juror. To be fair, it must be acknowledged that conflicts of interest are unavoidable in even the largest legal communities. Ethical problems arise, however, when prosecutors are aware and yet still fail to serve proper notice and take corrective action.

Increasingly, perhaps given the unforgiving nature of the digital age, bold violations from criminal prosecutors are being unequivocally revealed. Consider the following examples:

- In 2009, Calumet County DA Kenneth Kratz, 50 (Figure 9.2), solicited Stephanie Van Groll, 26, with more than 30 text messages over a 3-day period, including one that read: "Are you the kind of girl that likes secret contact with an older married elected DA … the riskier the better?" and another that read: "I'm serious! I'm the atty. I have the $350,000 house. I have the 6-figure career. You may be the tall, young, hot nymph, but I am the prize!" Conflict of interest? Mr Kratz was prosecuting a domestic violence case against Ms Van Groll's ex-boyfriend – a case in which Ms Van Groll was the victim (Elliot, 2010). Though DA Kratz lost his job, he was not charged with a crime; Van Groll later filed a Federal lawsuit which was settled in 2013.
- A criminal prosecutor for more than 30 years, Douglas Godbee,[2] 59, was fired from the Hawkins County DA's office in Tennessee and disbarred. This occurred because of a sex scandal involving multiple criminal defendants. Ultimately, Mr Godbee pleaded guilty to felony misconduct for his role in trading sex for leniency with females being prosecuted by his office. As a result multiple cases have been revealed, all involving improper *quid pro quo* (sexual favors for lighter sentences) with either defendants or their mothers (Figure 9.3; Bobo, 2012).

---

[2]Not to be confused with former Detroit Police Chief Ralph Godbee, mentioned previously in Chapter 5: "Ethical Issues in Police Administration."

FIGURE 9.2
Republican Prosecutor Ken Kratz sent over 30 text messages intended to initiate a sexual relationship with Stephanie Van Groll, all while he was prosecuting her boyfriend for domestic violence.

FIGURE 9.3
Former prosecutor Doug Godbee lost his job, his law license, and went to jail for his part in trading sex for leniency in criminal cases, most of which involved defendants charged with drug-related crimes.

FIGURE 9.4
Jennifer Mitrick was an ADA in Philadelphia who began dating a shooting victim, also an alleged drug dealer, in a case that she was prosecuting. The case resulted in a mistrial and it was referred to another agency to avoid any further conflicts.

- Jennifer Mitrick, 30, was an ADA with the Philadelphia DA's office (Figure 9.4). As reported in Slobodzian (2011): "Mitrick handled the prosecution of Aquil Johnson, 23, who with Matthew Smith, 21, was charged in 25 September 2008 shooting of Michael Wilson. Wilson, 32, a Jamaican, survived a gunshot wound to the head during an attack in his West Philadelphia home." Ms Mitrick began dating the shooting victim (also an alleged drug dealer) during the trial of Mr Johnson – which resulted in a mistrial. After the mistrial was declared, she came forward to her boss and acknowledged the relationship. She was taken off the case and it was properly transferred to the Attorney General's Office (Slobodzian, 2011).
- At the end of 2011, Clark County DA's Office in Las Vegas, Nevada fired one of their own and then filed ethics charges against her with the State Bar: Lisa Willardson, a prosecutor with the Juvenile Division. The complaint, which arose from her romantic involvement with Family Court Judge Steven Jones, stated that she was fired for "violating the rules of professional conduct for lawyers, including lying in a sworn

affidavit about her relationship with Jones" (German, 2011). One of Ms Willardson's supervisors, Chief Deputy DA Mary Brown, wrote: "In recent months, we have discovered numerous acts of misconduct that bear directly on her fitness to practice law .... In doing so, Ms Willardson undermined the integrity of the legal profession and imperiled the public's confidence in the child welfare system, specifically, and the entire judicial system, generally," (German, 2011). The complaint further alleges that Ms Willardson conspired with Judge Jones to keep their relationship a secret while he presided over some of her cases. Emails detailing the relationship, and steamy text messages, featured strongly as evidence against Ms Willardson, but ultimately the DA's office did not choose to press any criminal charges.[3] In July 2012, 6 months after being fired, Ms Willardson applied for a job with the courts that reports directly to Judge Jones. Judge Jones was also part of the selection committee. This raised more concerns about potential conflicts of interests. In October 2012, Judge Jones was indicted on Federal charges related to "money laundering, mail and wire fraud and engaging in money transactions in criminally derived property" (Ryan, 2012). Then special prosecutors from the state Commission on Judicial Discipline filed a 12-count complaint against Judge Jones for misusing his office (and staff) to help Ms Willardson, both while she was an ADA and while she was being investigated by the Nevada State Bar; he was suspended without pay in November 2012, pending the outcome of these criminal and ethical inquiries (Ryan, 2012).

ETHICAL ISSUES WITH LAW ENFORCEMENT

Criminal prosecutors must rely on the investigative work performed by law enforcement agencies in order to do their job. High-quality investigations are therefore a must. Anything less can still achieve enough inertia to result in a failed prosecution of the factually guilty or a wrongful conviction of the factually innocent. The ethical prosecutor will work hard to prevent either.

When a law enforcement agency refers a case for prosecution, there are three discretionary options available: *prosecute*, *decline prosecution* (e.g., *nolle prosequi*[4]),

---

[3]It is contextually helpful to note that that DA David Rogers resigned in early November 2011, prior to the termination of Ms Willardson – but after his wife Susan Rogers became a newly elected Las Vegas municipal judge (German and Jourdan, 2011). His resignation came 3 years early and he went to work as legal counsel for the local police union.

[4]*Nolle prosequi* is Latin for "we shall no longer prosecute." It means that the prosecution is dropping the case against the defendant altogether.

or *further investigation required*. Regardless of their discretionary authority, prosecutors have an ethical obligation to make this decision based on informed, competent, and unbiased criteria. This means reviewing each case submitted with the utmost attention to detail and kicking back anything that does not meet the highest professional standards.

In smaller jurisdictions burdened by poorly trained or low-quality law enforcement personnel, kicking cases back to the police creates political animosity and even open hostility between agencies. As a direct consequence, prosecutors may lack the confidence to call out inadequate police investigations. In such circumstances, it may actually be easier for them to proceed and fail in front of a judge at a preliminary hearing, or to admit defeat and decline prosecution at the outset. Although a waste of time and resources, going along with law enforcement and "rolling the dice" as it is called enables the shifting of blame for a failed effort from the DA's office to the court. This is further made possible by the absence of local media, without which there is no pressure from public exposure of such dealings.

In larger jurisdictions, red-flagging a case as being inadequately investigated is perhaps more feasible because the prosecutor's office will have greater experience negotiating negative political fallout with the offending department. In addition, they may not care what the fallout is because they likely have and other agencies, other pressures, to worry about. Maintaining a relationship with the police can rank low on the list of prosecutorial priorities, especially if there is a constant media presence, and pressure, keeping tabs on local political gamesmanship.

Regardless, it is the prosecutor's duty to review all charges referred to their office and make the tough calls. If they do not, they will encourage, or at the very least fail to identify and penalize, inadequate investigations. For the ethical prosecutor, the question is not whether a case can win in court by virtue of securing a friendly judge, an emotional or stacked jury, or an apathetic or overwhelmed public defender. The question is whether a case is worthy of taking all the way to trial and whether or not it should be won, based on the quality of all of the available information and evidence. If the answer is no, then the next question should be whether more investigation needs to be done. Often this is the case. Unfortunately, it is fair to observe that a policy of quality and sufficiency is not always the first considerations in the political world of criminal prosecutions.

In order for the ethical prosecutor to exercise their discretion properly, and to assess the quality of the investigation that has been conducted, there are a number of specific legal issues that can serve as litmus tests. While not a comprehensive list of issues, these are the ones most frequently observed by the authors in their respective casework.

Reading the Case File

Owing to an overwhelming caseload or lack of professional organization, it is not uncommon for some prosecutors to proceed all the way to trial before actually studying the details of the cases that they are assigned. They might give the file a cursory once over on the week they are assigned or they might just take a briefing from a detective and not follow up. However, many criminal cases are plead out or dismissed entirely because of deals struck with the prosecutor's office. These realities conspire with the unethical prosecutor to rationalize a general absence of enthusiasm for studying the specifics until a case is actually slated for trial. This means that important time-sensitive details can get missed, witnesses might not get interviewed or checked out, and crucial physical evidence might not get collected, preserved, or tested. When the prosecution is unprepared, and evidence or witnesses are lost to time, the court can punish them by dismissing the case.[5]

Overall Investigative Quality

In reviewing the police case files, the ethical prosecutor has an obligation to check and ensure the quality of any investigation that they intend to rely on in court. In general, this means making sure that nothing is biased, sloppy, or half-hearted – whether it is related to evidence, witnesses, or case theories. In cases of extreme investigative apathy or negligence, the prosecutor's office will take charge of interviews and evidence testing themselves. Their in-house investigators will do everything again (or for the first time), in order to avoid relying on unprofessional or untrustworthy police investigators on the stand.

Warrants and Probable Cause

The ethical prosecutor understands that police officers can only make an arrest, or effect a search, if they have *probable cause* to do so.[6] Typically it is held that probable cause exists when known facts and circumstances, of a reasonably trustworthy nature, are sufficient to justify a person of reasonable caution or prudence to believe that a crime has been or is being committed by the person being arrested. This definition can vary between different jurisdictions, but is often referred to as the "reasonable man standard."

---

[5]It should be mentioned that even when a case is dismissed those released from criminal charges are not undamaged. Frequently, time has been spent in jail (often months, even years), jobs will have been lost, homes foreclosed, reputations ruined, and personal relationships damaged – all while an unread file sits on a desk for months – and usually without recourse.

[6]This section is adapted from Savino and Turvey (2011).

Probable cause statements in search warrant and arrest applications must detail those facts and circumstances that lead the investigator to reasonably believe that a crime has occurred and the person that they want to arrest is responsible. Those facts and circumstances must be accurate, and there must be sufficient detail demonstrating how they have been reliably established. It is not sufficient for officers applying for a warrant to simply provide a "hero sheet" (the officer's education, history with the department, and accomplishments), list the charges suspected, maybe the uninvestigated statement of a victim or witness, and hope a judge will sign off on faith. Even if a judge does sign a warrant application without reading it carefully, the case could be lost or reversed at any point in the future if the probable cause is challenged by an alert DA.

Prosecutors therefore have an obligation to carefully review the basis for each and every warrant that comes across their desk. They must take care to ensure that the elements of the crime have been reliably established by the sworn facts and evidence (e.g., *corpus delicti*[7]) before putting any of it in front a judge with the blessing of their office. If necessary, they must send back or re-investigate anything that is substandard. In this way, they can avoid having to explain or defend substandard investigative work in court later on and the legal setbacks that might result.

Witness Credibility

Criminal prosecutors have an obligation to ensure that any witnesses they intend to put under oath are reliable. This means that witnesses must be of generally good character, and there must be independent corroboration of their statements when possible. Witness statements only become reliable upon investigation and corroboration with the facts and evidence, such as when they align with the physical evidence or contain details that only the offender or someone who witnessed the crime could know. This is something that professional attorneys and investigators understand from years of being burned by liars and DNA testing (Savino and Turvey, 2011). Only the lazy and inexperienced ignore these realities. Examples of statement evidence that should demand further investigation and corroboration include, but are certainly not limited to, those from:

(1) Jailhouse informants.
(2) Multiple jailhouse informants.
(3) Co-conspirators and co-defendants.

---

[7]*Corpus delicti* is Latin for "the body of the crime," referring to those facts and evidence that establish that a crime has actually occurred.

(4) Any witness who only agrees to testify as a result of a *"quid pro quo"* arrangement (e.g., immunity or a plea deal).
(5) Criminals (e.g., criminal competitors, drug dealers, prostitutes, drug addicts).
(6) Persons with a history of criminal activity related to truthfulness and integrity (e.g., fraud, deceptive practices, theft, identity theft).
(7) Persons that have made contradictory or false statements within the context of the investigation.
(8) Complainants with a history of false reporting.
(9) Witnesses with an established history of false testimony.
(10) The mentally infirm (e.g., mentally ill, under the influence of alcohol or other drugs).
(11) Those with ulterior motives against suspects.
(12) Those with any potential criminal culpability in the crime at hand.

In some states, there is specific legislation and case law backing up this ethical obligation, requiring that some witness testimony be corroborated (Elko, 2011) and eyewitness identifications suffer through an admissibility hearing (Weiser, 2011).

When uncorroborated statements come from a witness that is inherently unreliable or duplicitous (e.g., a career informant or convicted criminal), failures to investigate and corroborate are all the more egregious. The lack of an investigation into such statements may even suggest the intentional concealment of potentially contrary evidence. If there are any problems with witness character or corroboration, the prosecutor must disclose them to the defense under the *Brady Rule*, which is discussed in the "Pre-Trial Ethical Issues" section below.

Officer Credibility

Criminal prosecutors that have been burned in court for lack of their own due diligence understand that they must take measures to ensure that it does not happen again. The most professional will maintain a list of law enforcement officers and other government investigators in their jurisdictions that are known to have given false testimony, are known to be under investigation, or are known to be of generally unreliable character. In the District of Columbia, this is a computerized database referred to as a *Lewis List* (*United States v. Bowie*, 1999). In New Hampshire, the Attorney General's Office and DAs in 10 other counties are required to keep and maintain what are referred to as *Laurie Lists* or *Laurie Material* (see *New Hampshire v. Laurie*, 1995). On a national level, the FBI's Office of Professional Responsibility (FBI-OPR) maintains a record of all agents investigated for ethics violations, misconduct, and criminal activity (Will, 2012) (Figure 9.5).[8]

Despite the denials of some, such records are maintained explicitly to prevent law enforcement and other government employees with credibility problems from testifying for the prosecution, and by extension to prevent them from undermining a prosecutor's case.

Knowing the risks of maintaining a formal record of such explosive impeachment material related to active personnel, many agencies circumvent discovery

FIGURE 9.5

Candice M. Will, Assistant Director of the FBI-OPR, sent an email to all employees in October 2012 that detailed ethics violations, professional misconduct, and criminal violations by its employees (including FBI Special Agents). The retention of agents engaged in such misconduct, which is explicitly discussed, would seem to be an outright violation of the agency's motto: Fidelity, Brotherhood, and Integrity. Such information would seem to be required discovery for defense counsel in any pending criminal cases involving agents that have been under investigation, but the nature of the email and its content suggests that this is not standard practice.

---

[8]Candice M. Will, Assistant Director of the FBI-OPR, sent an email to all employees in October 2012 that detailed a litany of ethics violations, professional misconduct, and criminal violations by its employees (including FBI Special Agents) – the vast majority of whom were disciplined internally and retained. It included cases of FBI agents engaged in sexting (sending nude photos to each other), harassment, unauthorized surveillance, domestic violence (some involving the use of firearms), DUIs, solicitation of sex acts from sex workers, improper handling of evidence, disclosure of confidential internal reports and information outside the Bureau (e.g., to defense attorneys and members of the public), lying to investigators, theft, abuse of authority, and fraud (Will, 2012). The email was leaked to CNN and then published in the free press. As described in Zamost and Griffin (2013): "From 2010 to 2012, the FBI disciplined 1,045 employees for a variety of violations …. Eighty-five were fired."

requirements with duplicitous practices designed to seal information away from defense requests. Some agencies will maintain separate personnel files that are not evident to outsiders, under lock and key in the offices of supervisors or internal affairs bureaus and never meant to see the light of day. Other agencies maintain separate investigative files – for instance, they might create a task force that keeps its own investigative records on multiple but related cases. Still others engage in the tried and tested practice of disseminating documents piecemeal, intentionally withholding inflammatory information and providing only that which is explicitly requested.[9] For example, as explained in West (2012):

> New Hampshire has more than 60 law enforcement officers with credibility issues so serious they could jeopardize their ability to testify at trials, but the process tracking them is so secretive it is virtually impossible to identify them or even say for sure exactly how many there are.
>
> When first asked by a reporter, most of the county attorneys refused to provide even the number of those officers in their counties, but did so after consulting with Deputy Attorney General Ann Rice.
>
> Called potential "Laurie" issues, the attorney general and the 10 county attorneys are required to keep lists of law enforcement officers who have lied under oath, committed theft or fraud or other conduct that could affect their truthfulness, according to former Attorney General Peter Heed's 2004 policy.
>
> A judge could ultimately require the officer's confidential personnel information be turned over to the defense. The defense could then use the information in an effort to impeach the officer's credibility.
>
> Rice said her office doesn't keep a complete Laurie list of all such officers statewide as outlined in the Heed memo. Instead, Rice sends out "Laurie letters" to determine whether any of the officers who are to testify have potential Laurie matters in their personnel files.
>
> Rice also said she wasn't aware that the state police department wasn't reporting the two troopers with potential Laurie issues to all 10 counties, which was also directed in the Heed memo. Rice didn't

---

[9]One of the authors (Miller) worked a case involving felony assault with a firearm in which it was learned by defense counsel, mid-trial, that the lead investigator had been suspended by his department for misconduct. The initial disclosure came from a non-law-enforcement source, but was confirmed by the DA when confronted by defense counsel. When confronted with this glaring omission in court, the prosecutor first denied any responsibility for investigating and providing related discovery; in his view, this was the responsibility of the officer's agency. Later, the prosecutor claimed that the officer's suspension was irrelevant because it was unrelated to the case at hand. The judge was not amused. The specific nature of the accusations were not known until a civil tort claim was filed, and then discovered and reported by the media (it was a sexual harassment case). The officer was ultimately terminated.

know how many officers with potential Laurie issues are working in the state.

...

The purpose of the Laurie lists is to make sure the defense can be alerted beforehand if an officer with credibility issues is going to testify. They have no other purpose, she said.

"It was not intended to label some as bad cops or bad police departments," Rice said.

Training is provided to police chiefs, who are supposed to report such officers to prosecutors, Rice said.

"It is a policy," Rice said. "They should be doing it, but there is no penalty for not doing it other than the integrity of the prosecutions."

Former Strafford County Attorney Lincoln Soldati said law enforcement officers and other public officials should be held to a higher standard when it comes to troubling conduct that is buried – and protected by law – in their personnel files.

Soldati, now a Portsmouth defense attorney, remembers one police department years ago that deliberately kept two sets of personnel files to avoid Laurie disclosures.

"There ought to be a different standard for public employees when it comes to the protection of personnel records," Soldati said. "It seems too often the rules are used to protect the institution. The individual not so much."

...

The numbers of police with potential Laurie issues provided by the county attorneys suggest that some keep names on the list longer than others, although they can be removed after 10 years.

Some reported more state troopers than did state police. Since the lists are held in the strictest confidence, there is no way to cross-check the names.

Assistant Safety Commissioner Earl Sweeney said in the future, state police will report to all counties, as outlined in the Heed memo as a result of the Sunday News inquiry.

...

Officers have only potential Laurie issues until a judge decides the conduct is definitely information that should be disclosed. Many of the names on the lists have not been tested by a judge because they haven't been scheduled to testify, prosecutors say.

...

Prosecutors didn't want to repeat the mistakes that led to *State v. Laurie* in 1995, in which the state Supreme Court overturned a murder conviction because information about the credibility of one of the testifying officers, which is considered evidence favorable to the defense, was withheld.

Although it is common for those responsible to turn a blind eye to officer credibility issues, in order to safeguard criminal convictions (see, generally, Ridolfi and Possley, 2010; Turvey, 2013), the failure of the police and prosecution to maintain and disclose this kind of information about its personnel is a violation of constitutional due process, related case law, and often official agency policy.[10]

Credibility of Forensic Evidence and Personnel

Ethical prosecutors have a duty to know the facts of their cases to ensure the timely collection and testing of relevant physical evidence. In some instances, prosecutors can be found searching for, or testing, physical evidence only weeks before and even during trial – looking for something, anything, to corroborate a case theory with no other objective substantiation. In others, there is a conspicuous absence of physical evidence collection or testing, in essence signaling a prosecutorial fear of those results.

The ethical prosecutor does not hide the facts, or the evidence, by refraining from collection and testing efforts. As theirs is in the search for truth and justice, they want answers prior to filing any criminal charges. In other words, they must work to ensure that a thorough investigation has been done prior to suspect arrest and court proceedings, not only as a reaction to the retention of experts by the defense.

CASE EXAMPLE

Kirsten "Blaise" Lobato

This case involves the sexual homicide of a homeless African-American male who was found beaten, sexually mutilated, and covered with garbage in the dumpster enclosure where he regularly slept – on a bank property across the street from the Palms Hotel in Las Vegas. He was at first unidentified, so authorities logged in his body as John "Palms" Doe because of where he found. His real name was Duran Bailey and he was a rapist.

On July 20, Laura Johnson, the juvenile probation officer for Lincoln County, Nevada, contacted detectives. She relayed a tip from Dixie Tienken, a Lincoln County teacher. According to Johnson, Ms Tienken had been contacted by a former student who said that she had cut off the penis of a man who attacked her in Las Vegas. This tip led them to

the former student, Kirstin "Blaise" Lobato. It should be noted that Ms Tienken later testified to being pressured by detectives during her interview to shape her statements toward implicating Ms Lobato.

At Ms Lobato's first trial, police also enlisted Korinda Martin, an inmate at the Clark County Detention Center ("a jailhouse snitch"), with separate convictions for robbery and coercion. Ms Martin testified that Ms Lobato had confessed to her in jail. The jury convicted Ms Lobato, and the district court imposed consecutive 20- to 50-year sentences for first-degree murder with the use of a deadly weapon and a 5- to 15-year sentence for sexual penetration of a dead body.

However, the Nevada Supreme Court heard the case, reviewed the evidence, and reversed the convictions

[10] This is a reference to the *Brady Rule*, which is discussed in the "Pre-Trial Ethical Issues" section below.

CASE EXAMPLE *CONTINUED*

entirely in 2004; they found that Ms Martin lacked any credibility, that she had engaged in other frauds against the court (including forgery of letters on her behalf to the court – evidence that was examined by the police crime lab after Ms Lobato's conviction), and that Ms Lobato was improperly prevented by the judge in her case from impeaching Ms Martin in front of the jury (*Lobato v. Nevada*, 2004).

In preparation for her retrial, Ms Lobato's attorneys hired one of the authors (Turvey) to examine and reconstruct the physical evidence in the case, as the Nevada Supreme Court had already agreed as part of its ruling that "no physical evidence tied Lobato to the homicide" (*Lobato v. Nevada*, 2004). As part of this effort, a long list of items were identified that had never been examined or tested by the state – and some of which had been misplaced. Untested items included the victim's penis (which had been severed), myriad items from the rape kit, and items found on the body (e.g., a bloody paper towel, bloody plastic, and a cigarette butt).

While on the one hand denying the evidentiary value of these items in court before the judge and jury, the prosecution had the Las Vegas Metro Police Crime Lab test them for DNA in hopes of neutralizing the author's testimony. The prosecution was desperate to find any physical evidence

connection between the crime scene and Ms Lobato. At the instruction of the prosecution, DNA tests were being conducted by criminalist Kristina Paulette right up until the time of trial, and during the presentation of the State's case, in September 2006. However, Ms Paulette was not entirely forthcoming about the tests that she was still running for the prosecutor's office even while giving expert testimony for them. These tests ultimately excluded the defendant. Consequently, the defense was forced to called Ms Paulette as their own witness, to explain the entire scope and results of the DNA testing more fully and accurately to the jury. See Figure 9.6.

Ultimately, the second trial resulted in Ms Lobato's conviction for manslaughter despite the absence of any physical evidence connecting her to the crime, clear evidence of other likely suspects, and the absence of any credible witnesses against her. This wrongful conviction, though lacking the urgency of a first degree murder conviction given effectiveness of Ms Lobato's second defense team, is still under appeal.

It is also worth noting that DNA criminalist Kristina Paulette was fired from her job at the Las Vegas Metro Police Crime Lab in 2011 for attempting to conceal mistakes made during DNA testing and then lying about it to supervisors (Duran, 2011).

Ethical prosecutors also have a duty to ensure that the crime laboratories they use are in compliance with scientific practice standards and generally free of scandal. They have a related duty to ensure that the forensic experts they ask to give evidence are competent, unbiased, and credible. Similar to a *Lewis List*, prosecutors often maintain lists of crime labs or forensic personnel in their jurisdictions that are known to be unreliable for any number of reasons. This includes crime labs that have failed to achieve or maintain accreditation; forensic examiners with a history of substance abuse problems, criminal convictions, false testimony, or fraudulent credentials; and forensic examiners that have failed their proficiencies or have been taken off active casework.[11] This information should be automatically shared with defense counsel in every effected case, but often it is not.

[11]For a discussion of these and related issues, see Chapter 7: "Ethical Issues in Crime Lab Administration," Chapter 8: "Ethical Issues in Forensic Examination," and the textbook *Forensic Fraud* (Turvey, 2013).

FIGURE 9.6
Those interested in reading an in-depth account of the wrongful conviction of Kirstin "Blaise" Lobato are encouraged to reference *Kirstin Blaise Lobato's Unreasonable Conviction: Possibility Of Guilt Replaces Proof Beyond A Reasonable Doubt* (Sherrer, 2008).

Unfortunately, some prosecutors are also known for a practice referred to as *expert shopping* (discussed in the next section). In such instances, when they do not get the results or cooperation they want from local or regional government laboratories, they seek a private expert that is prosecution friendly (e.g., a retired law enforcement officer or a former government lab employee who knows how to play ball). This practice is highly unethical for the prosecution, especially when they fail to provide the defense with a record of all of the expert examinations and opinions they went through before getting the one they wanted.

Other unethical practices used to neutralize private forensic experts that might be retained by the defense include *expert poaching* (retaining a potentially damaging expert for a few hours of work with no intention of having them testify, in order to prevent them from being hired by the defense due to an artificially created pre-existing conflict) and *blackballing* (using the weight of the prosecutor's influence to get an expert fired; to block an expert from employment opportunities; to block expert entry into prosecution-controlled professional organizations; or to forbid an expert from being hired by police or prosecutors in a particular region. Blackballing, in particular, is essentially prosecutorial retaliation for an expert's willingness to engage in defense casework and then testifying against any law enforcement experts.[12] As reported in Carpenter (2002): "… expert witnesses testify the way they are paid to testify, and it is almost always the prosecution that has all the money. Some paid experts testify exclusively for the prosecution side, knowing that if they ever testify for the defense, they will be blackballed."

PRE-TRIAL ETHICAL ISSUES

Prior to trail, there are myriad ways for an unethical prosecutor to manipulate the criminal justice system in order to achieve convictions without solid evidence or reliable witnesses. In this section, we will discuss the more common forms of pre-trial misconduct, some of which are not generally known or understood by the public. The authors would like to stress that while not all prosecutors engage in the unethical activities described, it is uncommon to see a case brought to trial without at least one of these issues coming to light. This speaks to a cultural problem that exists because of a lack of consequences.[13] As argued in Carpenter (2002): "there are two harmful dynamics in criminal proceedings – the money paid to expert witnesses and the excessive zeal of some prosecution witnesses, especially police officers."

Almost Unlimited Funding

Owing to the way that criminal prosecutions are funded, many prosecutors have almost unlimited access to financial resources. This allows them to pay for exhaustive investigations into whatever they deem of relevance, as well as for law enforcement–friendly experts that charge a premium for their services. In some instances, the prosecutor's office will have a discretionary coffer built from grant money or their share of crime-related asset forfeitures. In others, they can simply trade on political relationships with those judges in charge of funding approval (too many judges are actually former prosecutors, serving improperly as back-up when the state's case falters). Regardless, prosecutors are generally able to use the state's financial resources without any disclosure process or external accountability.

---

[12] This is a tactic that has long been used by the Pierce County DA's Office in Washington State (see the judicial reprimand in the Gary Benn Case Example, mentioned later in this chapter). When they have been threatened by forensic experts who work for the defense, they have sought to destroy that expert's every opportunity for casework and employment through direct intimidation of employers and professional groups – and have later claimed this misconduct on their part is actually a public service (e.g., Gillie, 1998; Lynn, 2012).

[13] This issue will be discussed at the end of the chapter, in the section titled "Incentivized Misconduct."

Consider the following examples of extraordinary expenditure by the prosecution in order to secure criminal convictions:[14]

(1) Forensic Psychiatrist Park Dietz, MD has testified under oath that the majority of his expert testimony is on behalf of the prosecution (Bolton, 2003). In 2002, Dr Dietz billed the prosecution around $300 000 for his assessment of Andrea Yates regarding her competency to stand trial for the murder of her children (Wood, 2002). Dr Dietz, who employs numerous retired FBI agents with his private company, has admitted under oath that he testifies for the prosecution in the majority of criminal casework.

(2) In 2005, Forensic Psychiatrist Michael Welner, MD, billed the US Attorney's office $500 000 for his assessment of Brian David Mitchell; this was in relation to assessing Mitchell's competency to stand trial for charges related to the kidnapping of Amy Smart (Reavy, 2009). See also Carpenter (2002), reporting: "A fee of $30,000 for a few hours of work is not bad. That is how much Dr. Michael Welner was paid last year to testify for the prosecution in the case of Richard Baumhammers in Pittsburgh."

(3) In 2006, law enforcement bloodstain expert Rod Englert testified that "he expected to receive a total of about $250,000" for his prosecution work in the murder trial of David Camm in Indiana (Zion-Hershberg, 2006). Mr Englert testifies almost exclusively for the prosecution.

What this demonstrates is that the unethical prosecutor is often financially able to "shop" for experts until they find one that will say what is required for a conviction, almost irrespective of cost, in a complete betrayal of their role as a truth-seeker.

Indigent defendants (i.e., those who cannot afford an attorney), in contrast, are not so fortunate. They must beg the court for every nickel intended to provide for investigative assistance or forensic examinations. Even when the court does approve a funding for investigations, forensic experts, or evidence testing, it is not uncommon for judges to later shave defense invoices across the board by as much as 50% in some states.[15] This reality creates a financial penalty against those that chose to do criminal defense work.

---

[14]It is rare for a defense expert to receive funding approval in excess of $50 000. In fact, $30 000 is considered high, even in capital murder cases involving multiple victims and crime scenes. In general, forensic examiners for the defense can get approved by the court for between $5000 and $10 000 to pay for examinations conducted related to murder trials. That is the high end; in cases that do not involve homicide, funding for the defense investigators and experts can be even more scarce.

[15]This includes invoices to the state from appointed defense attorneys, defense investigators, and private forensic examiners – even when there is a pre-approved court order for a specific dollar amount. The judge has final authority on the authorization of, and amount of, requested funding for the defense. They have the ability to increase or decrease a funding request depending upon its merits, but frequently they are under pressure to keep defense budgets low.

Abusing the Grand Jury

Contrary to the mistaken beliefs of some, a *grand jury* is not empaneled to decide a defendant's guilt or innocence – that happens later with a different kind of jury. A grand jury is intended to be investigative in nature, empaneled to determine whether or not someone will be indicted ("charged") for a crime. The grand jury is used to determine whether or not there is probable cause to believe that specific crimes have been committed by those named in any indictment – this is instead of relying solely on the discretion of law enforcement. Theoretically, the grand jury is empowered as an independent investigative body intended to safeguard citizens from unfounded accusations made by police or prosecutors (Hoffmeister, 2008).

The grand jury, however, is a powerful and effective investigative tool for any prosecutor that wields it. It provides them with the authority to subpoena witnesses, compel them to testify under oath, and then to subpoena the production of evidence (e.g., financial records, business records, and health records; Vaira, 1984) – all without criminal charges pending. Its temptations require the ethical prosecutor to serve as an investigator of fact only; their role of advocate for the state against a criminal defendant must be faithfully set aside until the grand jury actually indicts someone (*Zahrey v. Coffey*, 2000). As observed in *United States v. Samango* (1979): "If the grand jury is to accomplish either of its functions, viz., independent determination of probable cause that a crime has been committed and protection of citizens against unfounded prosecutions, limits must be set on the manipulation of grand juries by overzealous prosecutors."

At this point it should be explained that each state has its own rules and requirements for the grand jury. In some states, the use of a grand jury by the prosecutor's office is optional. In others, a grand jury indictment is required for levying specific types of criminal charges. In still others, the grand jury no longer enjoys the power to charge people with crimes (reserving that for the prosecutor's office), but it retains the power to investigate different types of crime and malfeasance. Again, each state is a little different.

Whatever the case, the prosecutor has "vast discretion" to shape and direct the decisions of the grand jury, as explained in Vaira (1984, pp. 1130–1131):

> The prosecutor's role is crucial to the operation of the modem grand jury. The prosecutor decides what subjects the grand jury investigates, and what witnesses and documents to subpoena. He questions the witnesses. He advises the grand jury on the relevance of the evidence, drafts the charges, advises the grand jury on the law, and requests the grand jury to return an indictment. The grand jury cannot return an indictment without the signature of the prosecutor. This power can easily be misused.

In other words, the grand jury is at the mercy of the prosecutor. They alone present the evidence and witnesses most favorable to their desired outcome; they are able to leave out anything that might work against that outcome; and they are not required to show evidence that might be contrary. No judges or DAs are involved prior to deliberations. The grand jury is steered entirely by the evidence, information, and advice of the prosecutor. If the prosecutor gives in to temptation and violates their role as investigator in favor of advocacy, then the facts, and the truth, can become lost.[16]

To be very clear, however, criminal prosecutors do not necessarily have an obligation to tell the whole truth to the grand jury; they can leave out exculpatory evidence and might not be held accountable later on, depending on the temperament of the local appellate court (Johns, 2005; see, generally, *United States v. Samango*, 1979; *United States v. Syling*, 2008).[17]

In this fragile context, evidence and witnesses can be cherry-picked and stacked by the unethical prosecutor. They hold a discretionary authority that is ripe for misconduct by those bent on their own personal or political mission. As described in Gershman (1997, p. 123):

> A prosecutor can influence the reliability and fairness of a criminal trial in three principal ways. First, a prosecutor can prevent access by the fact-finder to relevant and reliable evidence. Second, a prosecutor can present to the fact-finder false, misleading, and irrelevant evidence. Third, a prosecutor can significantly distort the fact-finder's evaluation of the evidence.

Indeed, as acknowledged by the Appellate Court in *Zahrey v. Coffey* (2000), this context subsequently creates a "likelihood that a prosecutor will use the false information before a grand jury to secure an indictment against the defendant, leading to the defendant's arrest and likely prosecution" (Zhang, 2011, p. 2157).

Perhaps the two most common abuses of the grand jury observed by the authors include: seeking the indictment of suspects for crimes in which there is no direct evidence of their involvement or guilt, or perhaps even suppressing evidence of actual innocence, and seeking the dismissal of charges in high profile or politicized cases, such as those involving police officers or politicians

---

[16]Prosecutors can also violate their role as legal advisor to the grand jury and improperly become an unsworn, unchecked witness by: giving personal opinions, discussing facts not introduced already as evidence, and attacking the credibility of any witnesses.

[17]As reported in Johns (2005, p. 67), see also: "*Strickler*, 527 U.S. at 289–96 (finding harmless error where prosecutor failed to disclose exculpatory evidence); *United States v. Williams*, 504 U.S. 36, 45–55 (1992) (holding harmless error where prosecutor engaged in misconduct before the grand jury)."

suspected of crimes. These abuses are not difficult to accomplish when there is no duty for prosecutors to present exculpatory evidence to grand jury, as held in *United States v. Syling* (2008):

> The United States Supreme Court and the Ninth Circuit have ruled that the Government does not have a duty to present exculpatory evidence at grand jury proceedings. In *United States v. Williams,* 504 U.S. 36, 36, 112 S.Ct. 1735, 118 L.Ed.2d 352 (1992), for example, the defendant challenged his indictment on the ground that the prosecutor failed to disclose exculpatory evidence. The Supreme Court ruled that there was no such duty because "requiring the prosecutor to present exculpatory as well as inculpatory evidence would alter the grand jury's historical role, transforming it from an accusatory to an adjudicatory body." *Williams,* 504 U.S. at 51, 112 S.Ct. 1735. The Supreme Court noted, "It is axiomatic that the grand jury sits not to determine guilt or innocence, but to assess whether there is adequate basis for bringing a charge." *Id.* The Supreme Court reversed the district court's dismissal of the indictment because "[i]mposing upon the prosecutor a legal obligation to present exculpatory evidence in his possession would be incompatible with this system."

As an example of selective presentation of the evidence to the grand jury, consider that prosecutors do not generally prefer to arrest, try, and convict police officers – especially those needed as state's witnesses in other cases. It is bad publicity for everyone, and can contaminate any prior criminal cases that rest on that officer's credibility and testimony. Such cases generally result in criminal charges, and are brought to trial, only when media attention is high, when public outcry is great, or when the prosecutor's office has a political investment of some kind.

The quickest way to dump cases, to clear those involved and avoid bad publicity, is to take them to the grand jury. The unethical prosecutor can intentionally present limited and selected evidence – creating the false impression that no crime has been committed or that the officer is not responsible. The next day, the papers will read something like "Grand jury clears officer of charges." Publicly, the prosecutor can claim that they did their best; that the grand jury decided there was not enough evidence; and that the decision was ultimately out of their hands. It creates the illusion that a complete and impartial investigation has been conducted, while nothing could be further from the truth.

So, for example, while grand jury cases involving police shootings of even unarmed citizens are common, criminal indictments against officers are rare (e.g., Naziri, 2011; Freehan, 2013; Long, 2013; Marshall, 2013; Umstead, 2013). Avoiding indictments against city employees also has the added benefit of helping to avoid or at least mitigate municipal liability.[18]

Sometimes, however, despite the secrecy that is intended to conceal a grand jury and its deliberations, and despite the best efforts of a prosecutor to craft a particular outcome, the facts do come to light. This was certainly true in the JonBenet Ramsey case, with respect to the grand jury empaneled by Boulder DA Alex Hunter in the Fall of 1999.

CASE EXAMPLE

JonBenet Ramsey

In 1996, 6-year-old JonBenet Ramsey was found murdered in her home in Boulder, Colorado. Owing to the wealth of the family, the nature of the crime, the age of the victim, and her involvement in pageantry, the case garnered unprecedented media attention and became "high profile." The case was mishandled by law enforcement investigators from day one, and, despite the emergence of numerous suspects, the evidence has never resulted in a trial.

In 1999, Boulder DA Alex Hunter brought the facts and evidence of the case before a grand jury. At the time, subsequent to the conclusion of the grand jury, Hunter held a press conference to inform the public that his office had insufficient evidence or basis to charge anyone for the crime (Figure 9.7).

In 2013, it was confirmed that the grand jury actually returned an indictment against both of JonBenet's parents on charges of child abuse resulting in her death. In what some legal commentators are calling an extraordinary abuse of power, and even a "miscarriage of justice," DA Hunter had refused to sign those indictments back in 1999. He also refused to take the case to trial, arguing at the time that, in his opinion, he would have been unable to secure verdicts against the Ramseys in court. However, legal experts have argued that the DA has a legal obligation to sign grand jury indictments and file criminal charges, regardless of personal feelings – even if he decides later to decline prosecution (Brennan, 2013).

Until this revelation from some of the grand jurors, speaking under condition of anonymity 13 years later, it was presumed that the grand jury convened by DA Hunter had not actually indicted anyone – a presumption that would have continued (Hassan and Bothelo, 2013).

Overcharging

Increasingly tough sentencing guidelines have given prosecutors encouragement to engage in what is already a problematic habit of *overcharging* criminal defendants. Overcharging refers to the all too common practice of charging a defendant with every conceivable criminal act committed or with the most serious form of a crime with the steepest penalty. This is used to coerce the defendant into cutting a deal for fewer charges with less time, with cooperative

---

[18]In recognition of this problem, created by the veil of secrecy that covers such proceedings combined with temptation to engage in prosecutorial abuses, the district attorney in Albuquerque, New Mexico actually suspended the historic practice of sending all police shootings to a grand jury; this because, over the course of 2 years, no grand jury in Albuquerque had ever ruled a police shooting to be unjustified (Krayewski, 2012). However, the DA's office reversed its position a year later (Proctor, 2013).

FIGURE 9.7
Boulder DA Alex Hunter, pictured here on 13 October 1999, in the parking lot of the Boulder County Justice Center. He spoke to reporters and told them that his office did not have enough evidence to arrest or prosecute anyone for the murder of JonBenet Ramsey. However, he failed to mention the fact that the grand jury had actually just indicted both of her parents – and that he was not going to sign off on those charges.

testimony against co-defendants when there are any. In such circumstances, the "deal" is in all likelihood a more realistic approximation of the charges warranted by the facts. As reported in Oppel (2011):

> After decades of new laws to toughen sentencing for criminals, prosecutors have gained greater leverage to extract guilty pleas from defendants and reduce the number of cases that go to trial, often by using the threat of more serious charges with mandatory sentences or other harsher penalties.
>
> Some experts say the process has become coercive in many state and federal jurisdictions, forcing defendants to weigh their options based on the relative risks of facing a judge and jury rather than simple matters of guilt or innocence. In effect, prosecutors are giving defendants more reasons to avoid having their day in court.
>
> "We now have an incredible concentration of power in the hands of prosecutors," said Richard E. Myers II, a former assistant United States attorney who is now an associate professor of law at the University of North Carolina. He said that so much influence now resides with prosecutors that "in the wrong hands, the criminal justice system can be held hostage."
>
> One crucial, if unheralded, effect of this shift is now coming into sharper view, according to academics who study the issue. Growing prosecutorial power is a significant reason that the percentage of felony cases that go to trial has dropped sharply in many places.

Plea bargains have been common for more than a century, but lately they have begun to put the trial system out of business in some courtrooms. By one count, fewer than one in 40 felony cases now make it to trial, according to data from nine states that have published such records since the 1970s, when the ratio was about one in 12. The decline has been even steeper in federal district courts.

...

The decrease in trials has also been a consequence of underfinanced public defense lawyers who can try only a handful of their cases, as well as, prosecutors say, the rise of drug courts and other alternative resolutions.

The overloaded court system has also seen comparatively little expansion in many places, making a huge increase in plea bargains a cheap and easy way to handle a near-tripling in felony cases over the past generation.

The temptation to plead to lesser charges, in order to avoid excessive jail time, is unavoidable for the criminal defendant facing 20 to life. The hope of having a life after incarceration, or the fear of losing it, can overwhelm all reason. It also tempts the innocent, who regularly plead guilty to crimes they did not commit in order to avoid jail time, life in prison, or in some cases the death penalty. Ironically, these false "confessions" are often given at urging of DAs who are unequipped to fight inflated charges, and see a clearer path to a lesser legal victory (see, generally, Garrett, 2010).

Plea Deals and Immunity

As already mentioned, one of the most powerful tools in the prosecutor's arsenal is their authority to grant plea deals or immunity to those involved in criminal enterprise; these are often granted in exchange for testimony favorable to one or more of their cases. As explained in Gershman (1993, p. 529): "The subject of prosecutorial discretion in the charging process is one of the most difficult problems in the administration of criminal justice. The prosecutor is afforded substantial leeway in making charging decisions, and there are few constraints on those decisions." This discretionary authority is easily manipulated by the experienced criminal: they may be induced to point the finger up the criminal ladder, or laterally, to become a state's witness; or they may simply be smart enough to be the first one to cut a deal. It is the experience of the authors that the practice of embracing the first suspect who wants to make a deal in a case with multiple defendants can result in the more egregious criminal getting a lighter sentence; at the same time, their inexperienced co-defendant receives more charges and more jail time despite being less involved.

Plea deals can also be used to bury police and prosecutorial misconduct, as explained in Gershowitz (2009, p. 1061):

> Because most criminal cases are resolved by plea bargains and not subject to appeal, there is often little opportunity to discover prosecutorial misconduct. And in cases when defendants do go to trial, indigent defendants are sometimes represented by underpaid and overworked criminal defense lawyers who lack the time or the ability to recognize and preserve claims of prosecutorial misconduct.

The ethical prosecutor weighs all of these considerations, and more, when entering into a plea deal of any kind with a criminal defendant. Again, they want to reveal the facts, to charge the appropriate defendants with the appropriate crime, and to avoid burying misconduct of any kind.

Witness Harassment and Intimidation

The tremendous authority enjoyed by the prosecution can lead to abuse by means of wielding it as a mechanism for harassment and intimidation of potential witnesses.

As already discussed at length, the prosecutor's office enjoys the exclusive power to grant plea deals and immunity. It can also threaten to take any such deals off the table if a so-called "cooperating witness" does not agree to testify exactly as instructed. For some, this can mean immediate arrest and jail time.

Other means of witness harassment, intimidation, and abuses peculiar to the prosecution include: threats of, or actual deportation of, witnesses from other nations (whether in the country illegally or not); threats of additional criminal charges (whether warranted or not); instructing witnesses not to speak with DAs or investigators; and withholding victim services from those legally entitled to them. It is important to note that many of these abuses occur in collusion with law enforcement.

In some criminal cases, the prosecution is so desperate and out of control that it will jail witnesses who refuse to cooperate – even if they are children – using a *material witness warrant*. A *material witness* is one that has information that is material to a criminal proceeding (the material nature of which is largely at the discretion of the prosecutor). If the prosecutor believes that the witness would not respond to a subpoena to appear, they can petition the court for a material witness warrant and then detain the witness until their testimony is completed. This can result in the ironic circumstance of a criminal posting bond and going free to await trial, while the witness against them sits in jail.[19]

---

[19]For a discussion regarding the abuses of material witness warrants in particular, see Parker (2009).

However, consider the imprisonment of 11-year-old Cierra Hull, related to *Washington v. Guy Rasmussen*, in 1998.[20] As documented for the court in defense motions, the evidence is clear that Pierce County Prosecutor Barbara Corey-Boulet and her office openly harassed multiple defense experts, withheld discovery material, and may have been complicit in evidence tampering. Up to and during the trial, she and her husband Francis were also under investigation for charges stemming from theft and fraud at Francis' former place of work.[21] It is this context that gave rise to Corey-Boulet's decision to jail a child witness – Cierra Hull, an honor student.

Young Ms Hull had originally told investigators that she saw the victim, her friend and neighbor, with Guy Rasmussen on the day that she disappeared. Later, she and her family wanted nothing to do with the case. However, this was a witness that the prosecution desperately needed. Ms Hull's ordeal is described in Hucks (2003):

> Two Pierce County deputy prosecutors say they had no choice in 1998 but to jail an 11-year-old girl as a witness in a murder trial, and Monday asked a judge to dismiss the girl's family lawsuit against them. Prosecutors Barbara Corey-Boulet and Lisa Wagner said Cierra Hull was vital to the case against child rapist and murderer Guy Rasmussen, but hadn't shown up for a required interview.
>
> Also, they said, her grandmother planned to move her out of state and her family had told police they no longer wanted her involved in the trial ....
>
> But attorney Brian Ladenburg, representing Hull's family, said they had been cooperative, and detectives knew by the time they arrested the girl that she simply hadn't had transportation to the missed interview ....

---

[20] One of the authors (Turvey) examined evidence as an expert in this case for the defense. Subsequently, he is intimately familiar with the prosecutorial misconduct that occurred (Gillespie, 1998) having observed and experienced it first hand.

[21] Francis Corey-Boulet ultimately took a plea deal and went to jail – after the conviction of Guy Rasmussen. Subsequently, Barbara Corey-Boulet was not indicted and the investigation into her potential knowledge or complicity in that matter was dropped. As reported in Gillie (1999c): "Superior Court Judge Ronald Kessler ... imposed a three-year, seven-month sentence on Francis Corey-Boulet in the theft of more than $600,000 from a Tacoma medical clinic he managed for nearly eight years. Corey-Boulet pleaded guilty to one first-degree theft and nine second-degree theft charges earlier this summer in a plea bargain with prosecutors, who dropped 75 other charges   Francis Corey-Boulet is the former husband of Pierce County deputy prosecutor Barbara Corey-Boulet. She divorced him last spring, a year after he came under investigation for stealing from the clinic. She since has tried to put legal distance between herself and her former spouse, declaring bankruptcy and avoiding any public show of support for him." Barbara Corey was later dismissed from the prosecutor's office and now works as a DA in private practice.

On May 28, 1998, after Hull didn't show up for a court-ordered pretrial interview with defense lawyers, Corey-Boulet and Wagner – with the blessing of the prosecutor – asked a judge to detain her as a material witness.

Lawyers for the county and the prosecutors say they had hoped the girl would be held for no more than 12 to 18 hours. Detectives arrested Hull at Edison Elementary School the next day, just before she was to be named "student of the month."

But Superior Court Judge Karen Strombom wasn't available that Friday afternoon, so Hull spent the weekend at Remann Hall juvenile jail. "Instead of receiving her student-of-the-month award and being lauded by her peers," Ladenburg said Monday, "she's arrested, thrown in a sheriff's car, taken to Remann Hall for the weekend and then mocked by her peers when she gets out. And she did nothing wrong."

While locked up, Hull was afraid, her lawsuit contends. An older girl spit on her in a fight and she wasn't able to talk to her grandmother as often as she wanted, her lawyer said. And on that Monday, prosecutors let her go and scheduled the interview for later, he said.

Attorneys for the state and county counter that Hull watched television with the guards and received daily visits from her mother. Outside the courtroom Monday, attorneys bickered over whether the girl had been unfairly treated. "She came into court in chains," Ladenburg said. "That's standard procedure" for handling material witnesses, county attorney Dan Hamilton said, noting they feared Hull would flee. "For criminals," Ladenburg shot back.

In an unfortunate decision, Ms Hull's wrongful imprisonment lawsuit was dismissed. Her arrest, detention, and placement in jail were determined to be lawful acts by the civil court, even though the need to put a child in adult jail was clearly not as exigent as prosecutors had led the court to believe. Ultimately, the prosecution of Guy Rasmussen continued unchecked by the trial court, despite evidence of his innocence and evidence of a confession by the victim's mother that the jury was not allowed to consider (Gillie, 1999a, 1999b).

Brady Violations

In the United States, law enforcement agencies, government crime laboratories, and prosecutorial agencies are required by law to comply with a well-known (and often ignored) legal standard passed down from the US Supreme Court in *Brady v. Maryland* (1963).[22] This ruling was intended to spell out the government's duty to provide the defense with equal access to inculpatory

---

[22] This section is adapted from Petherick and Turvey (2010).

evidence, to prevent what is generally referred to as "trial by ambush" and to avoid miscarriages of justice by allowing timely independent investigations of the prosecutor's evidence by the defense. As explained in Gershman (2006, pp. 685–686):

> *Brady*'s holding is familiar to virtually every practitioner of criminal law: "[T]he suppression by the prosecution of evidence favorable to an accused upon request violates due process where the evidence is material either to guilt or to punishment, irrespective of the good faith or bad faith of the prosecution."
>
> This principle, according to the *Brady* Court, reflects our nation's abiding commitment to adversarial justice and fair play toward those persons accused of crimes. As the Court observed: "Society wins not only when the guilty are convicted but when criminal trials are fair; our system of the administration of justice suffers when any accused is treated unfairly." Indeed, by explicitly commanding prosecutors to disclose to defendants facing a criminal trial any favorable evidence that is material to their guilt or punishment, *Brady* launched the modern development of constitutional disclosure requirements.

The high-minded language offered in *Brady* requiring timely disclosure of potentially exculpatory evidence stands in contrast to its interpretation and application. It was intended as a clear standard set forth for reasonable minds to appreciate and follow. However, the adversarial nature of the criminal justice system, and the general lack of accountability for even blatant prosecutorial misconduct, has left *Brady* without the teeth it needs. This was in fact the conclusion offered in Gershman (2006, pp. 727–728):

> Reflecting on the evolution of *Brady v. Maryland*, one is struck by the stark dissonance between the grand expectations of *Brady*, that the adversary system henceforth would be transformed from a "sporting contest" to a genuine search for truth, and the grim reality that criminal litigation continues to operate as a "trial by ambush." The development of the *Brady* rule by the judiciary depicts a gradual erosion of *Brady*: from a prospective obligation on prosecutors to make timely disclosure, to the defense of materially favorable evidence, to a retrospective review by an appellate court into whether the prosecutor's suppression was unduly prejudicial. The erosion of *Brady* has been accompanied by increasing prosecutorial gamesmanship in gambling that violations will not be discovered or, if discovered, will be allowed, and tactics that abet and hide violations. Finally, the absence of any legal or ethical sanctions to make prosecutors accountable for violations produces a system marked by willful abuse of law, cynicism, and the real possibility that innocent persons may be wrongfully

convicted because of the prosecutor's misconduct. Indeed, more than any other rule of criminal procedure, the *Brady* rule has been the most fertile and widespread source of misconduct by prosecutors; and, more than any other rule of constitutional criminal procedure, has exposed the deficiencies in the truth-serving function of the criminal trial.

The original language in *Brady* has been expanded by the Supreme Court to cover any and all potentially exculpatory information in control of the prosecution, the police, and their agents. This includes government-operated crime labs, as well as private labs and private experts contracted into government service. Unfortunately, ignorance regarding *Brady* remains even within these informed circles, as explained in Giannelli and McMunigal (2007, pp. 1517–1518):

> The U.S. Supreme Court has extended *Brady* to cover exculpatory information in the control of the police. Some courts have explicitly included crime labs within the reach of *Brady*. In one case, the Supreme Court of California noted that a laboratory examiner "worked closely" with prosecutors and was part of the investigative team. The court concluded that the "prosecutor thus had the obligation to determine if the lab's files contained any exculpatory evidence, such as the worksheet, and disclose it to petitioner." [*In re: Brown*, 952 p. 2d 715, 719 (Cal. 1998)]
>
> In another case, a court wrote that an experienced crime lab technician "must have known of his legal obligation to disclose exculpatory evidence to the prosecutors, their obligation to pass it along to the defense, and his obligation not to cover up a *Brady* violation by perjuring himself." [*Charles v. City of Boston*, 365 F. Supp. 2d 82, 89 (D. Mass. 2005)] While the expert should have been on notice about perjury, it is less clear that the *Brady* obligation would be known to lab personnel – without the prosecutor tutoring the lab. How often do prosecutors discharge this duty? Many lab examiners have never heard of *Brady*.

The unethical prosecutor, instead of demanding compliance with *Brady* from all agencies, will claim ignorance when the issue is raised by the defense in pre-trial hearings. They may even purposefully delay discovery of such evidence until just before trial – or even during it – to prevent an informed review or response from the defense. They will claim that they cannot provide the defense with evidence and reports that law enforcement and respective crime labs have not first provided to the prosecutor's office. This is of course strictly true, but it becomes an ethical issue when the prosecutor goes out of their way not to ask, and not to investigate, whether exculpatory evidence, reports, or information are being intentionally withheld. The prosecutor has a greater ethical obligation to more thoroughly investigate the cases referred to their office, and to identify any holes in the record (e.g., missing evidence, missing reports, and *Lewis* material), than does the defense. In fact, one might say this is the prosecutor's first responsibility; passing the buck and taking no responsibility for the quality of the police investigation and the physical evidence is indicative of negligence, and it is among the most common forms of prosecutorial misconduct.

Fabricating, Falsifying, and Suppressing Evidence

Prosecutors have been known to fabricate, falsify, and even suppress evidence to make their cases, and then to cover their tracks by falsifying or concealing every other subsequent related record in their control. This is of course an utter affront to *Brady* and related rulings. A review of appellate court rulings indicates that such misconduct is by no means a rare occurrence, and can be found in cases that range from those that seem relatively minor to those that would be considered high profile. Consider the following Case Examples.

CASE EXAMPLE

Former DA Mike NiFong[23]

Duke University Lacrosse team players Reade Seligmann, David Evans, and Collin Finnerty were charged with first-degree kidnapping and first-degree sexual offense after participating in an off-campus team party in March 2006. Ultimately dismissed as false, with the North Carolina Attorney General declaring the accused were "innocent" (CNN, 2007), the allegations in this case made national news, increased racial tensions, and spanned multiple motives on the part of the accuser, including alleged mental instability, avoiding criminal charges, profit, and revenge.

According to the compliant, Crystal Gail Magnum accused members of the Duke Lacrosse Team of dragging her into a bathroom at one their parties, raping her, and shouting racial slurs during an off-campus party in March 2006. However, none of this came to light until after she was arrested the same night for public intoxication. And only days after making the complaint she bragged to co-workers about the possibility of filing civil actions against those involved.

This case had almost every problem imaginable and in the absence of public attention it is possible that the accused players, ultimately cleared of all charges, could have been jailed for a very long time. Consider the context: the accuser was an African-American stripper with a criminal history, an alleged mental health history, and a history of unfounded claims of being gang raped. A vocal segment of the African-American community rallied behind her, initially, and demanded swift justice. Racial tensions were, in some circles, rising. The prosecutor was running for re-election, conspired with forensic personnel to conceal evidence, and openly attacked the defendant in the press. Also, Duke University was found in the unenviable position of having swiftly punished its lacrosse coach and players for crimes that it turns out did not occur.

The following is a timeline of significant events, involving prosecutorial misconduct almost across the board:

- March 13, 2006 – Duke University lacrosse players throw a party at an off-campus house, hiring two strippers.
- March 14 – One of the dancers tells the police she was forced into a bathroom by three men and beaten, raped, and sodomized.
- March 23 – Forty-six of 47 team members comply with judge's order to provide DNA. The sole black member is not tested because the accuser said her attackers were white.
- March 28 – Duke University suspends the lacrosse team from playing.

CASE EXAMPLE *CONTINUED*

- March 29 – DA Mike Nifong refers to members of the lacrosse team "a bunch of hooligans" in the press.
- April 4 – The accuser identifies her attackers in a photo lineup.
- April 5 – Lacrosse coach Mike Pressler is forced to resign. Duke President Richard Brodhead cancels the rest of the season.
- April 10 – DAs announce DNA tests fail to connect any of the players to the accuser.
- April 17 – Grand jury indicts Reade Seligmann and Collin Finnerty on rape and other charges.
- April 25 – Granville County authorities confirm the accuser told police 10 years ago three men raped her when she was 14. None of the men was charged.
- May 15 – Grand jury indicts team co-captain David Evans on rape charges. He calls the allegations "fantastic lies."
- June 5 – Duke University president says team can resume play in 2007 under close monitoring.
- November 7 – DA Mike Nifong wins the election to continue as DA.
- December 15 – Forensic scientist Brian Meehan, lab director of DNA Security, Inc., in an agreement with Nifong, omitted from his report that genetic material from several men – none of them Duke team members – was found in the accuser's underwear and body.[24]
- December 22 – Nifong drops the rape charges, saying the woman is no longer certain whether she was penetrated. The players still face charges of kidnapping and sexual offense.
- December 28 – North Carolina bar files ethics charges against Nifong, accusing him of making misleading and inflammatory comments to the media about the athletes. (He is also later accused of withholding evidence and lying to the court.)
- January 3, 2007 – Duke invites Seligmann and Finnerty to return to school. (They have not returned.) The accuser gives birth. Both sides later say she was not impregnated at the party.
- January 12 – Nifong asks to withdraw from case because of ethics charges.
- January 13 – The North Carolina Attorney General's office begins reviewing the case, not only by going over the case to date, but by conducting an independent investigation, including interviewing witnesses.

- April 10 – The North Carolina Attorney General reports his office's findings. The investigation raised such discrepancies to what the complainant claimed versus the actual evidence that "Based on the significant inconsistencies between the evidence and the various accounts given by the accusing witness, we believe these three individuals are innocent of these charges" (CNN, 2007).

The Attorney General's office investigation was thorough, as noted in the office's April 2007 public statement that included the following (Cooper, 2007):

> During the past 12 weeks, our lawyers and investigators have reviewed the remaining allegations of sexual assault and kidnapping that resulted from a party on March 13, 2006, in Durham, North Carolina. We carefully reviewed the evidence, collected by the Durham County prosecutor's office and the Durham Police Department.
>
> We've also conducted our own interviews and evidence gathering. Our attorneys and SBI agents have interviewed numerous people who were at the party, DNA and other experts, the Durham County district attorney, Durham police officers, defense attorneys, and the accusing witness on several occasions. We have reviewed statements given over the year, photographs, records, and other evidence.
>
> The result of our review and investigation shows clearly that there is insufficient evidence to proceed on any of the charges. Today we are filing notices of dismissal for all charges against Reade Seligmann, Collin Finnerty, and David Evans. The result is that these cases are over, and no more criminal proceedings will occur. We believe that these cases were the result of a tragic rush to accuse and a failure to verify serious allegations. Based on the significant inconsistencies between the evidence and the various accounts given by the accusing witness, we believe these three individuals are innocent of these charges.
>
> Now, we approached this case with the understanding that rape and sexual assault victims often have some inconsistencies in their account of a traumatic event. However, in this case, the inconsistencies were so significant

Continued

CASE EXAMPLE *CONTINUED*

and so contrary to the evidence that we have no credible evidence that an attack occurred in that house on that night.

Now, the prosecuting witness in this case responded to our questions and offered information. She did want to move forward with the prosecution. However, the contradictions in her many versions of what occurred and the conflicts between what she said occurred and other evidence like photographs and phone records, could not be rectified.

Our investigation shows that the eyewitness identification procedures were faulty and unreliable. No DNA confirms the accuser's story. No other witness confirms her story. Other evidence contradicts her story. She contradicts herself ….

Now, in this case, with the weight of the state behind him, the Durham district attorney pushed forward unchecked. There were many points in this case where caution would have served justice better than bravado, and in the rush to condemn a community and a state, lost the ability to see clearly ….

This case shows the enormous consequences of over-reaching by a prosecutor. What has been learned here is that the internal checks on a criminal charge – sworn statements, reasonable grounds, proper suspect photo lineups, and accurate and fair discovery – all are critically important.

Therefore, I propose a law that the North Carolina Supreme Court have the authority to remove a case from a prosecutor in limited circumstances. This would give the courts a new tool to deal with a prosecutor who needs to step away from a case where justice demands.

In June 2007, Mike Nifong, the prosecutor in the Duke University Lacrosse Team rape case, was disbarred for unethical conduct related to his actions in that attempted prosecution. The chairman of the disciplinary committee blamed Nifong's "political ambition," a "self-serving agenda," and "self-deception."

---

[23]This example is taken with only minor revisions from Turvey and McGrath (2011).

[24]It is clear that Brian Meehan, lab director of DNA Security, Inc., made a conscious decision to assist DA Mike Nifong with the job of hiding exculpatory DNA results in this case (see discussion in Mosteller, 2007).

CASE EXAMPLE

Former ADA Danielle M. Muscatello

Consider the misconduct of former ADA Danielle M. Muscatello of Kings County, New York, as reported by the Supreme Court of New York (*In Re: Danielle M. Muscatello*, 2011):

Charge one alleges that the respondent by misrepresenting evidence to the Grand Jury, engaged in: (1) conduct involving dishonesty, fraud, deceit, or misrepresentation, (2) conduct that is prejudicial to the administration of justice, and (2) conduct that adversely reflects on her fitness as lawyer, in violation of Rules

8.4(c), (d) and (h) of the Rules of Professional Conduct (22 NYCRR 1200.0).

The respondent was employed as an Assistant District Attorney with the Office of the District Attorney for Kings County. On November 5, 2009, she was presenting evidence to a Kings County Grand Jury in relation to a defendant who had been arrested on October 18, 2009, for driving while intoxicated. As part of the presentation, she moved into evidence a New York City Police

CASE EXAMPLE *CONTINUED*

Department form known as the Chemical Test Analysis (hereinafter the Form). The Form is an official document that reports, inter alia, the defendant's blood alcohol content at the time the breathalyser test is performed. The police officer who administered the test is required to certify on the Form that its contents are true, accurate, and complete. After moving the Form into evidence, the respondent realized that it was incomplete, in that the space where the number reflecting the defendant's blood alcohol content should have been, was blank. Nonetheless, the respondent told the Grand Jury that the form reflected a blood alcohol content of .08%, a fact she knew from other evidence previously introduced before the Grand Jury.

Charge two alleges that the respondent altered a document that had been entered into evidence before a Grand Jury, thus, violating rules 8.4(c), (d) and (h) of the Rules of Professional Conduct (22 NYCRR 1200.0).

On or about November 12, 2009, the respondent subpoenaed the police officer who had prepared the Form. On that date, knowing that her supervisor was out of the office, the respondent entered and searched that office for the Form. The respondent found the Form in her supervisor's briefcase and removed it. She then directed the police officer to fill in the blank to reflect the defendant's blood alcohol content, and returned the altered Form to her supervisor's briefcase without her supervisor's knowledge.

Based on the evidence adduced and the respondent's admissions, the Special Referee properly sustained the charges. Accordingly, the motion to confirm is granted.

As provided, Ms Muscatello was terminated as an ADA, disbarred, and the court ordered that (*In Re: Danielle M. Muscatello*, 2011):

… during the period of suspension and until such further order of this court, the respondent, Danielle M. Muscatello, admitted as Danielle Marguerite Muscatello, shall desist and refrain from (1) practicing law in any form, either as principal or as agent, clerk, or employee of another, (2) appearing as an attorney or counselor-at-law before any court, Judge, Justice, board, commission, or other public authority, (3) giving to another an opinion as to the law or its application or any advice in relation thereto, and (4) holding herself out in any way as an attorney and counselor-at-law.

However, on 17 October 2012, Ms Muscatello "reinstated as an attorney and counselor-at-law and the Clerk of the Court [was] directed to restore the name of Danielle Marguerite Muscatello to the roll of attorneys and counsel-ors-at-law" (*In the Matter of Danielle M. Muscatello* 2012). She subsequently began the next phase of her legal career as a DA.

CASE EXAMPLE

US Senator Ted Stevens (R-Alaska; 1923–2010)

In October 2008, after a lengthy investigation by the FBI, federal prosecutors were able to convict the longest sitting US Senator, Ted Stevens (Figure 9.8), of charges related to corruption. Senator Stevens, one of the most powerful and influential Senators in history, was found guilty of seven counts of lying on Senate financial disclosure statements. The scandal cost him his seat in the Senate, as only a week after the conviction he lost his bid for re-election by a narrow margin. A former

Continued

CASE EXAMPLE *CONTINUED*

US Attorney himself, Senator Stevens refused to speak with reporters about the verdict, but released a statement alleging prosecutorial misconduct in which he proclaimed: "I will fight this unjust verdict with every ounce of energy I have" (Persky, 2009). In 2010, Mr Stevens died in a plane crash.

However, even before his death, the convictions were unraveling. During the trial, there were significant inconsistencies between FBI reports of witness statements and actual witness testimony. There were also allegations of deals for immunity and witness coaching – from a state's witness. Then a juror disappeared and had to be replaced by an alternate. After the trial, in December 2008, an FBI Agent came forward. This had been his first assignment and he was no longer able to stomach the misconduct of his fellow agents and that of the prosecutors. As reported in Persky (2009):

> On December 2, 2008, FBI Special Agent Chad Joy filed a whistleblower complaint stating that prosecutors tried to hide a witness and intentionally withheld evidence from defense lawyers. Joy further accused a fellow FBI agent of having an inappropriate relationship with [the key state's witness in the case, Bill] Allen.
>
> "The week or so before Christmas, we had round-the-clock litigation over whether Joy's complaint would be made public or not," Cary says. "We took the position that it should all be made public."
>
> According to a transcript of a previously sealed court hearing, Morris of the PIN [Public Integrity] Section argued that Joy's name should not be revealed nor should the complaint be made public. Judge Sullivan ultimately released the complaint to the public with Joy's name redacted. Subsequently, the judge grew increasingly irate when the Justice Department changed its position and said that since the complaint was made public, Joy's name should be revealed. After portions of the complaint were made public, the Justice Department then argued that it would be easier to respond in court filings if all the names were revealed. The Justice Department also said Joy had no whistleblower status, but then it changed its mind on that. In January 2009 Judge Sullivan

made public the details, along with Joy's name. But Judge Sullivan was angry and wanted Mukasey to submit a declaration ....

> Judge Sullivan ordered full discovery on Joy's whistleblower status. The Justice Department then made yet another error – prosecutors only handed the discovery to the judge, not the defense.
>
> "That was a court order. That wasn't a request," Judge Sullivan said at a February 13 hearing. "I didn't ask for them out of the kindness of your hearts .... Isn't the Department of Justice taking court orders seriously these days?"
>
> Judge Sullivan then held Morris, Welch, and Patricia Stemler, chief of the Criminal Division's Appellate Section, in contempt of court for failing to follow the court order to turn over documents.
>
> At this point, the Justice Department removed its prosecutors from the case and assigned a new team, which found additional evidence that had never been handed to the defense.

On 1 April 2009, the newly appointed Attorney General, Eric Holder, asked for the dismissal of all charges against Mr Stevens as a result of additional prior prosecutorial misconduct that was uncovered by the new prosecution team. Judge Sullivan agreed and threw out the convictions. He also took the further step of ordering an investigation to establish the full extent of the misconduct committed by the original prosecutors.

In March 2012, investigator Henry F. Schuelke III (Figure 9.9), a Washington lawyer, presented the results of his inquiry into prosecutorial misconduct in a 500+ page report that "shook the legal community," as reported in Johnson (2012a):

> The report is based on a review of 128,000 documents and interviews with prosecutors and FBI agents on the hot seat.
>
> It details critical failings by the government as it raced to get ready for the 2008 trial: disheveled files; key meetings at which FBI agents never took notes; insufficient management by supervisors at the Justice

CASE EXAMPLE *CONTINUED*

Department's criminal division; and pained egos that led resentful members of the prosecution team to stop talking to each other in the weeks before the case went to a Washington, D.C., jury ....

Finally, the report says, prosecutors should have shared information that might have obliterated [Bill] Allen's credibility: an explosive allegation that Allen had a sexual relationship with a 15-year-old girl and then asked her to lie about it under oath.

According to the Schuelke report, the prosecutorial misconduct in the Stevens case was intentional, but it could not be proved in court beyond a reasonable doubt. He also found that the prosecutorial effort was "permeated by the systematic concealment" of any evidence favorable to the defense.

Two federal prosecutors were eventually punished by the Justice Department for their role in the Ted Stevens case, to include "reckless professional misconduct:" Assistant US Attorney Joseph Bottini, out of Alaska, was suspended for 40 days and Assistant US Attorney James Goeke, out of Washington State, was suspended for 15 days (Johnson, 2012b).

The story was a bit different at the FBI. Special Agent Mary Beth Kepner, Bill Allen's handler, was found to have "hid evidence from the defense, failed to follow FBI protocols, and ... was, in her own words, 'overwhelmed' and 'disorganized' by the case;" leaked grand jury testimony; and also "forged documents and appears to have lied about doing so" (Hopfinger and Coyne, 2012). She was investigated for ethics violations by the FBI-OPR, but remains employed by the FBI. Special Agent Chad Joy, the whistleblower (and Special Agent Kepner's partner), was taken off criminal cases by the FBI in 2009. On 2 January 2010, he felt compelled to resign (Hopfinger and Coyne, 2012).

FIGURE 9.8
The late Senator Ted Stevens loved his home state of Alaska; he loved the outdoors, especially fishing; and he was known by those close to him for unwavering integrity and bipartisan statesmanship. He especially enjoyed fresh Alaskan salmon, shrimp, and King crab. He is pictured on the right holding up a King crab, in support of Alaskan Bering Sea crabbers, during a news conference in Washington on 7 February 1974.

ETHICAL ISSUES DURING TRIAL

Once trial is under way, the ethical landscape changes considerably. There are more professionals involved (e.g., police, courthouse staff, judges, DAs, defense investigators, and witnesses testifying for both sides); each of them has their own ethical burden to bear; and most of them are accountable directly to the

FIGURE 9.9
In March 2012, Henry F. Schuelke, the special investigator appointed by Judge Sullivan, testified before the Senate Judiciary Committee in Washington, DC. He investigated misconduct committed by federal prosecutors against the late Senator Ted Stevens and found that "contest living" – the desire to win a big case – explained the failure to follow the rules in one of the biggest political corruption prosecutions in decades" (Johnson, 2012b).

court, often under oath. As a consequence, getting away with blatant prosecutorial misconduct requires a deliberate intent to conceal it; a prosecutor ignorant of the law and pre-trial judicial rulings; a sleeping or biased judiciary; or the absence of knowledgeable and alert defense counsel. Unfortunately, one or more of these conditions is generally going to exist – and therefore examples of prosecutorial misconduct during trial are easy to find.

In terms of ethical issues, problems arise in court from the kinds of questions prosecutors can and cannot ask; what they can and cannot argue or aver; and evidence that they are not allowed to reference or elicit from witnesses. Case-specific prohibitions will be worked out in advance, in front of the judge, in a series of pre-trial hearings. Otherwise, here are some (not all) of the general rules that apply – and one or more will be broken in just about every criminal trial, often without notice or objection:

- *Improper testimony.* Prosecutors are not allowed to elicit testimony that has been ruled inadmissible in the case at hand by the presiding judge. Even asking the wrong question can be a form of misconduct, regardless of whether there is an answer from the witness.
- *Impeachment for post-arrest silence.* Prosecutors are not allowed to use the fact that a defendant remained silent as evidence of guilt or duplicity. This is referred to as a *Doyle Error.* As held in *Doyle v. Ohio* (1976): "After an

arrested person is formally advised by an officer of the law that he has a right to remain silent, the unfairness occurs when the prosecution, in the presence of the jury, is allowed to undertake impeachment on the basis of what may be the exercise of that right."

- *Witness intimidation.* Prosecutors are not allowed to threaten or intimidate witnesses. This includes threatening witnesses with arrest or threatening them with criminal charges for perjury. These offenses are especially egregious if they occur in court, are observed by other witnesses, or if they prevent the witness from giving testimony.

- *Commenting on the decision not to testify.* When a defendant chooses not to testify on their own behalf, to explain themselves to the jury, prosecutors are not allowed to comment on that fact. Should they do so, it invites the jury to infer, or suggests, that the reason behind this decision is their guilt. In fact, this may not be the case at all and criminal defendants have the right to avoid being subjected to cross-examination.

- *Commenting on the decision to hire an attorney.* It is improper for the prosecutor to suggest that asking for a lawyer or hiring an attorney is evidence of guilt or duplicity, as the right to counsel is a well-established constitutional guarantee.

- *Commenting on the decision to refuse a warrantless search.* It is improper for the prosecutor to suggest that refusing consent for a warrantless search is evidence of guilt or criminal activity, as this is also a constitutional right.

- *Stating personal opinions about guilt.* As held in *California v. Mayfield* (1997): "It is misconduct for a prosecutor to express a personal belief in the defendant's guilt if there is a substantial danger that the jurors will construe the statement as meaning that the belief is based on information or evidence outside the trial record."

- *Witness vouching.* Prosecutors may not give an opinion about the reliability or credibility of an expert witness based on personal opinion or prior dealings. As held in *United States v. Roberts* (9th Cir. 1980), it is even more egregious to suggest that the integrity of the DA's office should be considered in assessing the credibility of prosecution witnesses (e.g., that working for the DA's office gives an expert credibility). This suggests that working for the defense deprives the expert of credibility, or reduces their credibility, in some fashion – which the court should not allow.

- *Disparaging defense counsel.* It is impermissible for the prosecutor to imply, without evidence, that a DA has fabricated evidence or to otherwise malign a DA's character (e.g., they do not care about the truth or that they represent the guilty while telling people that they are actually innocent). For example, they cannot reference the type of clients they tend to represent or whether they were found guilty of criminal charges.

- *Misstating the law.* Misstating the law is a form of misconduct, but it requires bad faith on the part of the prosecutor (*California v. Hill*, 1998).

Most commonly, this mistake arises out ignorance or misunderstanding of the law. However, there is an ethical responsibility to be utterly knowledgeable of any law that is invoked and explained to the court. Often this happens and the prosecutor is simply wrong in their remembrance or interpretation of codes and case law, but nobody in the court corrects them because nobody else has read the motion attached to their argument with sufficient care.

- *Courtroom intoxication or drunkenness.* Those making decisions in court to determine the course of justice and influence its outcome have an ethical obligation to do so while wholly sober. This means that they should not be under the influence of controlled substances, such as illegal drugs or alcohol. Even high doses of prescription medications can be observed to cause problems. Indications of improper courtroom behavior from an impaired officer of the court would include slurred speech, impaired reasoning, sluggishness or stumbling, paranoia, physical aggressiveness, inappropriate yelling or threats, and falling asleep or passing out – all of which has happened in courtrooms around the United States.

CASE EXAMPLE

George H. Dunlap

In 1999, one of the authors (Turvey) testified as an expert during an admissibility hearing in a multiple murder trial (*California v. Louis Peoples*), and was cross-examined by San Joaquin ADA George H. Dunlap. During this questioning, Dunlap was red-faced, inappropriately close, and smelled of alcohol. The author mentioned this to defense counsel at the lunch break and learned that the judge in the case was Dunlap's former law partner. This was apparently why he felt free to hang out up at the bench with the judge during direct examination, and bray and guffaw at the author's responses to defense counsel's questions (opposing counsel is most appropriately seated, and certainly not hanging out with the judge, during the direct examination of opposing counsel's witness).[25] There was also mention of potential problems with drunk driving and wrecked county vehicles. In any case, nothing came of the author's concerns at the time – the judge seemed to have a tolerance for what was happening and it would clearly be a matter for appeal.

However, the journey of George Dunlap taken as a whole is one that defies credulity – it speaks to the collusion of some prosecutors that, like their law enforcement counterparts, work hard to protect their own despite the flouting of professional ethics and a litany of misconduct, as well

as criminality. In 2002, George Dunlap finally suffered what should have been a mortal professional blow, as reported in Hughes-Kirchubel (2002):

> San Joaquin County Deputy District Attorney George Dunlap ... will be placed on leave until District Attorney John Phillips determines whether to discipline him or fire him. Dunlap appeared June 17 as a prosecutor in a hit-and-run and insurance-fraud case in which his former girlfriend, Amelita Manes, is the defendant.
>
> Attorneys must remove themselves from cases in which they have a vested interest or the appearance of a conflict, according to recognized ethical standards.
>
> Since June, district attorney investigators have been probing Dunlap's involvement in the case, asking questions of local attorneys, law enforcement officers and Dunlap.
>
> Phillips said he expected to read a report generated on the investigation Monday. He would not comment on specific details of

CASE EXAMPLE *CONTINUED*

the probe. "George is going to be placed on administrative leave starting Monday morning until I have a chance to fully digest this situation and … decide what action we should take," Phillips said. "It's a personnel deal and I wish I could lay it out."

Less than a month later, DA John Phillips fired Dunlap for cause, as reported in Hughes-Kirchubel (2002), which provides relevant background detail:

On July 29, Phillips placed Dunlap on paid administrative leave more than a month after opening an investigation into whether he violated ethical standards by representing the San Joaquin County District Attorney's Office in a court case involving his ex-girlfriend Amelita Manes.

Manes faces charges of making false statements to an insurance company. Manes' charges stem from a noninjury collision in June 2001, after she and Dunlap left a north Stockton party and Manes' uninsured truck struck a parked car.

It's unclear who was driving, but witnesses said both had been drinking. Phillips said Manes, a former *Record* photographer, later obtained insurance and then tried to claim the accident on the policy.

Deputy district attorneys working in the insurance-fraud unit filed charges against her, and Dunlap appeared for the prosecution on Manes' court case June 17. After court, the pair argued outside the Courthouse. Manes told Stockton police that Dunlap, not she, caused the collision but that she took the blame so "George wouldn't mess up his life," reports said. She later recanted that statement ….

An examination of records stretching back 12 years shows Dunlap remained on the job despite having caused at least three vehicle crashes in which alcohol appears to have played a key role. He has admitted to drunken driving, has cost the county thousands of dollars in repair bills and, according to reports, has lied to authorities investigating the collisions.

Dunlap pleaded guilty to two counts of misdemeanor drunken driving in San Francisco in 1995, where he injured his ex-wife and another driver when he ran a red light at Gough and Oak streets. During the preliminary hearing, the other driver, Tracy Denham, said Dunlap got out of the driver's side of his truck and walked around to the passenger side after the collision. "As I walked past the truck, I hear Mr Dunlap saying, 'The driver ran up Oak Street,'" Denham testified. "And I remember thinking to myself, 'I saw him get out the driver's side.'"

Dunlap's blood-alcohol level was nearly twice the legal limit of 0.08 percent, according to court documents.

In 1999, while he was prosecuting (Louis) Peoples, he crashed a county car, causing more than $5,000 worth of damage. He then lied to the California Highway Patrol officer investigating the collision, saying he had told his supervisor about the crash, according to reports.

Incredibly, having a history of criminal convictions, being fired from his job as a county prosecutor, and lying to police investigators did not stop George Dunlap from gaining employment at another law enforcement agency. He just moved his career out of San Joaquin County. In 2004, he got a job as an investigator with the Santa Cruz County DA's office and then later became one of their prosecutors.

Dunlap's tenure in Santa Cruz did not come to an end until 2008, when the State Bar of California Court finally ordered him "suspended from practicing law …. The San Francisco court found in an Aug. 29 [of 2008] written ruling that George H. Dunlap Jr, 47, had violated four counts of professional conduct while working in the San Joaquin County District Attorney's Office" (Smith, 2008). He had already resigned from the San Joaquin County DA's office a few weeks prior, in anticipation of the Court's ruling. As of this writing, George H. Dunlap's status with the California State Bar is "Not Eligible To Practice Law."[26]

---

[25]*Years later, the author gave a sworn interview regarding this matter for the appellate court.*
[26]*See: The State Bar of California website; George Hall Dunlap Jr – #138896; url: http://members.calbar.ca.gov/fal/Member/Detail/138896.*

Subornation of Perjury

Subsequent to an investigation or an admission, if a criminal prosecutor knows that one of their witnesses intends to give false testimony they cannot put them on the stand. It is not only unethical, it can also be illegal. The specific criminal charges could include Subornation of Perjury and Conspiracy to Subornation of Perjury. According to Federal Law, as described in 18 USC § 1622, "whoever procures another to commit any perjury is guilty of subornation of perjury." The conspiracy charges can be levied if there is evidence of an intent to put on false testimony, even when no false testimony has been given. This particular legal reality may cause the unethical prosecutor to intentionally avoid any investigative action that might tend to uncover evidence related to the reliability of witness statements; in this way, the unethical prosecutor willfully blinds themselves from any knowledge that the witness might be lying when their testimony is helpful.

Additionally, when the prosecutor is aware of perjured testimony, there is an obligation to fix it. As reported in *United States v. LaPage* (2000): "Where the prosecutor knows that his witness has lied, he has a constitutional duty to correct the false impression of the facts."

CASE EXAMPLE

Gary Benn

In 2002, the US Circuit Court of Appeals overturned the State of Washington's cases against Gary Benn for the capital murder of his half-brother, Jack Dethlefsen, and his half-brother's friend, Michael Nelson. In 1988, the victims were found by authorities at Mr Dethlefsen's home after Mr Benn had called 911. Both had been shot once in the chest and once in the back of the head. According to the appellate court ruling (*Benn v. Lambert*, 2002): "The prosecution, however, contended that Benn had planned the killings primarily in order to cover up his participation with the victims in an arson-insurance-fraud scheme. At trial, the prosecution relied heavily on various inculpatory statements that Benn had allegedly made to Roy Patrick, a 'jailhouse informant' who was in Benn's cell block while Benn was awaiting trial, as well as on highly circumstantial evidence relating to the alleged arson."

The Court of Appeals determined that the Pierce County DA's office had withheld information about Mr Patrick's ongoing criminal activity (he was a known jailhouse informant and drug dealer), and had also withheld exculpatory expert findings. As detailed in *Benn v. Lambert* (2002):

The Court of Appeals, Reinhardt, Circuit Judge, held that: (1) prosecution's withholding multiple pieces of critical impeachment evidence that would have seriously undermined credibility of key prosecution witness violated *Brady*; (2) prosecution's withholding experts' findings that fire had accidental origin, which would have undermined prosecution's proffered motive for killings, aggravating circumstance, and premeditation, violated *Brady*; and (3) state court's determinations to contrary were unreasonable application of established Supreme Court law.

As reported in Johnson (2002):

Gary Michael Benn was sentenced to die in 1990 for shooting to death his half-brother and a longtime friend. In his trial, his former cellmate told jurors Benn confessed to the

CASE EXAMPLE *CONTINUED*

murders and was looking for someone to pin it on.

But the cellmate, Roy Patrick, had an admitted habit of lying, according to court papers. He once smuggled shotguns into prison so he could get credit for "finding" them. He stole drugs and cash while working as a police informant.

He even lied about evidence against Benn, claiming he had a videotape of Benn and several other men killing a prostitute and suggesting it was linked to the Green River killings. Patrick was given $150 to produce the tape – before investigators concluded it didn't exist.

The 9th U.S. Circuit Court of Appeals' ruling, which affirmed an earlier decision by U.S. District Judge Franklin Burgess, found that prosecutors should have revealed Patrick's checkered past.

...

Benn's attorneys, David Zuckerman and Suzanne Lee Elliott, agreed.

"I think it tells prosecutors, if you're going to present the testimony of a snitch, you have to reveal just how dirty that snitch is," Zuckerman said.

The court held that prosecutors should have disclosed information about Patrick's recent run-ins with the law, including a police raid that allegedly turned up drug paraphernalia.

Patrick was also arrested for outstanding warrants and called the assistant prosecutor

handling Benn's case, Michael Johnson, "who ensured that he was released without being charged," the judges wrote.

The appellate court went on to describe the misconduct at the Pierce County prosecutor's office with language that is damning, and appropriate, calling it a "textbook example" of the abuse of prosecutorial power (*Benn v. Lambert*, 2002):

> The law and the truth-seeking mission of our criminal justice system, which promise and demand a fair trial whatever the charge, are utterly undermined by such prosecutorial duplicity. Although our Constitution guarantees to a person whose liberty has been placed in jeopardy by the State the right to confront witnesses in order to test their credibility, that right was willfully impaired in this case. By unlawfully withholding patently damaging and damning impeachment evidence, the prosecutor knowingly and willfully prevented Benn from confronting a key witness against him. Such reprehensible conduct shames our judicial system.

Gary Benn was subsequently retried by the State; prosecutors did not seek the death penalty and abandoned their insurance-fraud theory. Mr Benn was convicted a second time, and has since appealed based on the trial court's refusal to admit evidence of bias and incompetence relating to the State's forensic experts, Rod Englert and Michael Grubb (*Washington v. Benn*, 2005).[27]

[27]For a discussion regarding bias, incompetence, and misconduct relating to police bloodstain analyst Rod Englert, and text from the American Academy of Forensic Sciences memo regarding Mr Englert that the trial court in Benn excluded, see Cooley (2011).

Improper Closing Arguments

During closing arguments, prosecutors are known for making impassioned pleas to the jury for a guilty verdict. Sometimes this is because of their own personal convictions about the case and their investment in the outcome; sometimes it is a response to the high-profile nature of a case or its sensational elements; sometimes it is a response to the inherent weaknesses that are evident in the case; and sometimes it is all just theater. Whatever their motives, prosecutors are still admonished to abide by their canons of professional conduct and the rules of admissibility levied by the judge. However, the emotional context of closing arguments can lend itself to crossing those lines.

Consider the following examples of closing arguments that would be considered improper, beyond the types of prosecutorial misconduct already mentioned in this chapter.

Prejudiced or Racist Arguments

Prosecutors are not allowed to appeal to the prejudices of juror or to make racist arguments. For example, they may not comment on the defendant's social background, sexual orientation, or ethnicity. As held in *California v. Simington* (1993): "It is improper for the prosecutor to appeal to the passion and prejudice of the jury in closing argument." For example, the Supreme Court of the United States (SCOTUS) recently (Balko, 2013):

> … scolded a federal prosecutor for a racist comment he made during a drug trial. While questioning the defendant, the prosecutor asked, "You've got African-Americans, you've got Hispanics, you've got a bag full of money. Does that tell you – a light bulb doesn't go off in your head and say, This is a drug deal?" This struck [Justice Sonia] Sotomayor as a wholly inappropriate thing for an Assistant U.S. Attorney to even be thinking, let alone blurting out in open court, in front of a jury. And rightly so. More troubling, as both Sotomayor and United States Court of Appeals for the Fifth Circuit Judge Catharina Hayes point out, is the Justice Department's nonchalance about the comment.

The case – *Bogani Charles Calhoun v. United States* (2012) – was not granted review by the SCOTUS. However, the Justices wanted to make it clear that these sorts of comments are still not acceptable from representatives of the Department of Justice.

Commenting on the Prosecutor's Role

It is not permissible for a prosecutor to assert that their role is that of truth-seeker, in contrast to that of the defense which is not seeking truth, or to suggest that the duty of the prosecution is to uncover the truth, while the defense has no such obligation. For example, consider prosecutor Amy McGowan from Douglas County, Kansas, as reported in Cummings (2013):

> Douglas County prosecutor Amy McGowan has been removed from her cases and assigned to other duties after the Kansas Supreme Court faulted her for trial errors.
>
> McGowan's comments during the closing arguments of several trials from 2007 to 2009 have been questioned by the court in several recent appeals, and last week the court vacated a sentence in a

child-exploitation case because it said McGowan made improper comments during a sentencing hearing.

Douglas County District Attorney Charles Branson said Thursday he had removed McGowan from her caseload of major felony sex crime cases. Instead, McGowan will be assigned as a charging attorney. Branson said McGowan was not available for comment.

The reassignment comes after the court's decision, on Feb. 8, to vacate the 52-month sentence of a Douglas County man convicted of attempted exploitation of a child. The court ruled McGowan made comments during Robert Peterson's sentencing that violated a plea agreement, and sent the case back to district court for sentencing.

Four other cases have been appealed on similar arguments that McGowan made improper comments during closing arguments. All of the trials in those cases occurred between 2007 and 2009 and the appeals came in the past two years. The first court ruling to find fault with the prosecutor's statements came in May 2012, and McGowan stopped using that language then, Branson said.

In two cases, the court found misconduct in McGowan's comments but upheld the convictions. Two others await decisions from the court. In the appeal of Allen Dale Smith, who was sentenced to life in prison for the 2005 slaying of Clarence David Boose near Lecompton, Smith's attorney argued that McGowan made improper comments that prejudiced the jury. McGowan had told the jury that "the truth" would give the victim a verdict against the defendant.

Appeals to the Religion

Prosecutors may not appeal to religious authority, or to biblical obligation, in their closing arguments to the jury (*California v. Harrison*, 2005).

POST-CONVICTION ETHICAL ISSUES

Contrary to popular belief in the general public, a criminal matter is not always settled by the reading of the jury's verdict at the end of a trial. Upon conviction, some criminal matters enter the appellate phase, where the defense has the right to have their case reviewed for errors and impropriety that may have influenced judge or jury in their decisions. This post-conviction review of the trial and the conduct of the prosecutors only happens if the defendant has the funds to file an appeal or if the charges are serious enough to legally require an appellate review by the state.

The majority of prosecutorial misconduct is not uncovered and reported to the court until the case is reviewed on appeal by a fresh set of professional eyes. This can involve a new investigation into the case by the defense. It can even lead to the hiring of private forensic examiners to review evidence either missed by the original defense effort or originally denied with respect to funding by the court. In many cases, it can be said that more attention is given to the facts of a case, and to the conduct of prosecutors, by an appellate defense effort then is afforded by DAs at trial.[28]

Therefore, in the post-conviction interval, the prosecutor has an obligation to remain a stalwart seeker of truth. This does not mean holding fast to their convictions, although it rewards them to do so. Even after a defendant has been convicted, prosecutors have an ethical, and sometimes legal, duty to preserve a copy of both the discovery material provided to the defense and any physical evidence that was collected. They must be open to the examination and testing of newly discovered evidence, have the character to reconsider findings and decisions in the light of any new evidence test results, and be willing to admit mistakes when they have been made.

Some state agencies recognize this obligation and take it very seriously, especially in light of ongoing DNA exonerations by organizations like the Innocence Project in New York (see, generally, Garrett, 2011). To ensure that criminal convictions have been honestly won, some states have set up innocence commissions which are meant to provide an independent external review of cases where actual innocence is claimed. Additionally, some prosecutors have set prosecution integrity units within their offices, to provide an internal review when they believe it is warranted. Yet problems persist with prosecutorial attitudes and culture, as discussed in Martin (2011):

> The issues raised by DNA exonerations have led to an overhaul of the criminal-justice system. Some states now require that evidence be preserved; others require mandatory videotaping of interrogations. Several states, including Illinois, New Jersey and New York, abolished the death penalty largely because of concerns about executing an innocent person. North Carolina, meanwhile, has created an independent commission to review innocence claims. And some prosecutors' offices, including those in New York and Dallas, have created conviction-integrity units.
>
> More often, though, the fate of an inmate with powerful new evidence of innocence still rests with local prosecutors, some of whom have spun creative theories to explain away the exculpatory findings. In Nassau County on Long Island, after DNA evidence showed that the sperm in a 16-year-old murder victim did not come from the man convicted of the crime, prosecutors argued that it must have come from

---

[28]This will be discussed in Chapter 10: "Ethical Issues for Criminal Defense Attorneys."

a consensual lover, even though her mother and best friend insisted she was a virgin. (The unnamed-lover theory has been floated so often that defense lawyers have a derisive term for it: "the unindicted co-ejaculator.") In Florida, after DNA showed that the pubic hairs at the scene of a rape did not belong to the convicted rapist, prosecutors argued that the hairs found on the victim's bed could have come from movers who brought furniture to the bedroom a week or so earlier. "They essentially argued that there were naked movers," said Nina Morrison, a senior staff lawyer at the Innocence Project, a New York-based group that seeks to exonerate wrongfully convicted inmates.

Why prosecutors sometimes fight post-conviction evidence so adamantly depends on each case. Some legitimately believe the new evidence is not exonerating. But legal scholars looking at the issue suggest that prosecutors' concerns about their political future and a culture that values winning over justice also come into play. "They are attached to their convictions," [Brandon Garrett, a law professor at the University of Virginia] says, "and they don't want to see their work called into question."

Few offices have fought post-conviction evidence with as much gusto as the Lake County state's attorney's office, which is coming under increased scrutiny for what defense lawyers and law professors suspect is an alarming number of wrongful convictions. One murder case has unraveled, and several other rape and murder convictions are now being challenged. "They can never admit a mistake," said Kathleen Zellner, a lawyer who is suing Lake County on behalf of a man named Jerry Hobbs, who spent five years in jail for killing his daughter and her friend; he was released last year after sperm found inside one of the girls was linked to a convicted rapist and accused murderer. "They have to solve cases quickly, and if a problem develops or doubt develops about a person's culpability, they feel like they have to press on," she said. "It's a self-defeating philosophy."

The crux of post-conviction review for the prosecution is a willingness to acknowledge the rights of the convicted defendant to have their case reviewed on appeal and their corresponding duty to facilitate that effort in order to avoid wrongful convictions. This means not "losing" or accidentally destroying evidence; not hiding or preventing access to newly discovered evidence; and being open minded to the possibility that mistakes may have been made. Often, it is not prosecution's mistakes that demonstrate serious misconduct, but rather the prosecution's concerted efforts to deny that those mistakes occurred, to hide them from the court, and then to act as though they are unimportant when revealed. Such is not the conduct of the ethical prosecutor.

Incentivized Misconduct

Unfortunately, as shown in this chapter, a lack of professional ethics and even professional misconduct can be incentivized by prosecutorial culture. This includes the mentality associated with winning at any and all costs; receiving promotions and pay raises based on conviction rates; and toxic agency policy with respect to retaining or failing to severely punish prosecutors that engage in ethics violations, misconduct, or criminal acts. In any employment context, a prosecutor becomes what the agency rewards and allows.

However, criminal prosecutors are incentivized to engage in ethical violations and misconduct by the court system as well.

(1) Violations of prosecutorial ethics and prosecutorial misconduct are rarely punished in a meaningful way.
(2) The court often finds that violations of prosecutorial ethics and prosecutorial misconduct amount to *harmless error* (an error that is not egregious enough to require a criminal conviction to be set aside or overturned). This legal determination is often used to improperly suggest that there was no misconduct or that the misconduct was not serious.
(3) The court fails to "to take meaningful action. Courts fail to report prosecutorial misconduct (despite having a statutory obligation to do so), prosecutors deny that it occurred, and the California State Bar almost never disciplines it" (Ridolfi and Possley, 2010, p. 3).

All of this combines to create the presence of incentives, and the absence of disincentives, for not just a lack of prosecutorial ethics, but for engaging in flagrant acts of misconduct, as explained in Cummings (2010, p. 2151):

> By encouraging convictions while condoning the violation of ethics rules, the prosecutorial system sends the implicit message that prosecutors have a moral mandate to procure convictions at all costs. When an institution provides a moral justification for harmful behavior, an individual's "detrimental conduct is made personally and socially acceptable by portraying it as serving socially worthy or moral purposes." This allows people to "act on a moral imperative and preserve their view of themselves as moral agents while inflicting harm on others." This not only reduces self-sanctions but also can even result in feelings of personal pride for actions that would otherwise be immoral.

What this can amount to is a tolerance for achieving convictions by virtue of engaging in criminal acts against the defense – crimes that traditionally go unpunished, as observed in Johns (2005, p. 120):

> Prosecutors who engage in misconduct strike not just hard blows, but criminal blows. Specifically, when a prosecutor violates a person's

due process rights, the violation is a crime. Subornation of perjury is a crime. Tampering with and coercing witnesses is a crime. Using false evidence before a grand jury or court is a crime. Yet the prosecutors who engage in this criminal conduct are not prosecuted, are not disciplined, and are not held liable for their crimes.

In order to rid prosecutorial culture of these elements, there must be clear ethical and professional guidelines developed for criminal prosecutors that are universal; mandated ethics training for all criminal prosecutors; mandated discipline and reporting of prosecutorial misconduct to state bar associations by courts and supervisors – even in cases of so-called harmless error; the internal regulation of the prosecutor's office with mandatory professional and conviction integrity units; and the removal of prosecutorial immunity from civil liability for wrongful convictions (see, generally, Ridolfi and Possley, 2010; Scheck, 2010). Until these reforms manifest, unethical prosecutors will likely continue act in the way that they always have – with tremendous authority, undisciplined by their agencies, and unchecked by the courts.

SUMMARY

In order for the ethical prosecutor to exercise their discretion properly, and to assess the quality of the investigation that has been conducted, attention must be given to the following legal issues: reading the case file; overall investigative quality; warrants and probable cause; witness credibility; officer credibility; and the credibility of forensic evidence and personnel.

Prior to trial, ethical issues include: almost unlimited funding; abusing the grand jury; overcharging criminal defendants; plea deals and immunity; witness harassment and intimidation; *Brady* violations; and fabricating, falsifying, and suppressing evidence. During trial, ethical issues include: the types of questions asked; subornation of perjury; and improper closing arguments.

Post-conviction, prosecutors have an ethical, and sometimes legal, duty to preserve a copy of both the discovery material provided to the defense and any physical evidence that was collected. They must be open to the examination and testing of newly discovered evidence; have the character to reconsider findings and decisions in the light of any new evidence test results; and be willing to admit mistakes when they have been made.

In order to rid prosecutorial culture of unethical behavior, there must be clear ethical and professional guidelines developed for criminal prosecutors that are universal; mandated ethics training for all criminal prosecutors; mandated discipline and reporting of prosecutorial misconduct to state bar associations by courts and supervisors; the internal regulation of the prosecutor's office with mandatory professional and conviction integrity units; and the removal of prosecutorial immunity from civil liability for wrongful convictions.

Questions

1. List the three primary types of criminal prosecutors in the United States.
2. Define *conflict of interest*. Provide three examples.
3. List the discretionary options available when a law enforcement agency refers a case for prosecution.
4. List two pre-trial ethical issues. Explain.
5. List the ethical duties of prosecutors post-conviction.
6. Criminal prosecutors are incentivized to engage in ethical violations and misconduct by the court system. Explain.

References

American Bar Association, 1993. ABA Standards for Criminal Justice: Prosecution Function and Defense Function, third ed. American Bar Association, Washington, DC.

Armstrong, K., Possley, M., 1999. Trial and error, part 1. The Chicago Tribune, January 11; url: http://www.chicagotribune.com/news/watchdog/chi-020103trial1,0, 1561461, full.story.

Balko, R., 2013. Shaming bad prosecutors. The Huffington Post, February 25; url: http://www.huffingtonpost.com/2013/02/25/shaming-bad-prosecutors_n_2760123.html.

Benn v. Lambert, 2002. US Court of Appeals, 9th Circuit, No. 00–99014, February 26.

Berger v. United States, 1935. US Supreme Court, 295 US 78, Case No. 544.

Bobo, J., 2012. Update: Former Hawkins County prosecutor pleads 'no contest', receives two years probation. Kingsport Times-News, October 1; url: http://www.timesnews.net/article/9052334/former-hawkins-county-prosecutor-pleads-no-contest-receives-two-years-probation.

Bogani Charles Calhoun v. United States, 2012. Petition For Writ Of Certiorari To The United States Court of Appeals, 5th Circuit, Appeal Cause No. 11–50605.

Bolton, M., 2003. Expert's stance becomes crucial. The Times-Union, July 2url: http://www.timesunion.com/AspStories/story.asp?storyID=147936&category=REGION&BCCode=&newsdate=7/2/2003.

Brady v. Maryland, 1963. US Supreme Court, 373 US 83, Case No. 490.

Brennan, C., 2013. JonBenet Ramsey grand jury voted to indict parents in 1999, but DA refused to prosecute. Denver Post, January 27; url: http://www.denverpost.com/news/ci_22446410/boulder-grand-jury-voted-indict-ramseys.

California v. Espinosa, 1992. 3 Cal.4th 806, 820.

California v. Harrison, 2005. 35 Cal.4th 208, 247.

California v. Hill, 1998. 17 Cal.4th 800, 819.

California v. Mayfield, 1997. 14 Cal.4th 668, 781–782.

California v. Pitts, 1990. 223 Cal.App.3d 606, 691.

California v. Price, 1991. 1 Cal.4th 324, 447.

California v. Simington, 1993. 19 Cal.App.4th 1374, 1378.

Carpenter, P., 2002. Expert illuminates perjury problem involving experts; there is virtually no accountability. Allentown Morning Call, March 31.

CNN, 2007. N.C. attorney general: Duke players "innocent." CNN http://www.cnn.com/2007/LAW/04/11/cooper.transcript/index.html, April 11.

Cooley, C., 2011. Crime reconstruction: expert testimony and the law. In: Chisum, WJ., Turvey, B. (Eds.), Crime Reconstruction, second ed. Elsevier, San Diego, CA.

Cooper, R., 2007. Press Release. North Carolina Attorney General's Office, April 11.

Cummings, I., 2013. Douglas County prosecutor removed from cases for errors in trials. Lawrence Journal-World, February 14.

Cummings, L., 2010. Can an ethical person by an ethical prosecutor? A social cognitive approach to systemic reform. Cardozo Law Review. vol. 31 (6), 2139–2159.

Doyle v. Ohio, 1976. US Supreme Court 426 US 610, 619, No. 10.

Duran, M., 2011. DNA tech fired after allegedly lying to supervisors. KLAS-Las Vegas, July 13; url; http://www.8newsnow.com/story/15078769/dna-tech-fired-after-allegedly-lying-to-supervisors.

Elko, B., 2011. Law requires corroboration of cellmate's testimony. San Francisco Chronicle, August 3, p. C2.

Elliot, J., 2010. D.A. comes on to abuse victim with lewd texts. Salon.com, September 17; url: http://www.salon.com/2010/09/17/calumet_district_attorney_texts_victim/.

Freehan, J., 2013. Wood County grand jury clears police in October shooting. The Toledo Blade, February 9; url: http://www.toledoblade.com/Courts/2013/02/09/Wood-Coounty-grand-jury-clears-police-in-October-shooting.html.

Garrett, B., 2010. The Substance of false confessions. Stanford Law Review 62 (4), 1051–1119.

Garrett, B., 2011. Convicting the Innocent: Where Criminal Prosecutions Go Wrong. Harvard University Press, Cambridge, MA.

German, J., 2011. Fired prosecutor, tied romantically to judge, faces Bar inquiry. Las Vegas Review-Journal, December 31; url; http://www.lvrj.com/news/fired-prosecutor-tied-romantically-to-judge-faces-bar-inquiry-136471113.html.

German, J., Jourdan, K., 2011. District attorney makes retirement official. Las Vegas Review-Journal, November 1 http://www.lvrj.com/news/roger-makes-retirement-official-133008463.html.

Gershman, B., 1993. A moral standard for the prosecutor's exercise of the charging discretion. Fordham Urban Law Journal 20, 513–530.

Gershman, B., 1997. Trial Error and Misconduct. Lexis Law, Charlottesville, VA.

Gershman, B., 2006. Reflections on *Brady* v. Maryland. South Texas Law Review 47, 685–728, (Summer).

Gershowitz, A., 2009. Prosecutorial shaming: naming attorneys to reduce prosecutorial misconduct. University of California Davis Law Review 42 (4), 1059–1105.

Giannelli, P., McMunigal, K., 2007. Prosecutors, ethics, and expert witnesses. Fordham Law Review 76, 1493–1537, (December).

Gillie, J., 1998. Murder suspect's lawyer assails prosecutors/Allinger case attorney alleges unethical conduct, wants charges dropped. Tacoma News Tribune, July 24.

Gillie, J., 1999a. Late allegation arises in Rasmussen case/lawyers for man found guilty of killing girl raise questions about her mother's role. Tacoma News Tribune, February 17.

Gillie, J., 1999b. Man pleads guilty to attacking woman. Tacoma News Tribune, July 27.

Gillie, J., 1999c. Prosecutor's ex-husband sentenced. Tacoma News Tribune, August 28.

Grippando, J., 2013. Prosecutors and book deals. The National Law Journal, January 28; url: http://www.law.com/jsp/nlj/PubArticleNLJ.jsp?id=1202585689193&Prosecutors_and_book_deals&slreturn=20130117202759.

Hoffmeister, T., 2008. The grand jury legal advisor: resurrecting the grand jury's shield. The Journal of Criminal Law and Criminology 98 (4), 1171–1230.

Hassan, C., Bothelo, G., 2013. Paper: Panel voted in '99 to indict parents of JonBenet Ramsey, DA didn't sign on. CNN, January 28; url: http://www.cnn.com/2013/01/28/justice/colorado-ramsey-indictment/index.html.

Hopfinger, T., Coyne, A., 2012. Why is lead FBI agent in botched Ted Stevens case still employed? Alaska Dispatch, June 6; url: http://www.alaskadispatch.com/article/why-lead-fbi-agent-botched-ted-stevens-case-still-employed.

Hucks, K., 2003. Officials defend jailing of 11-year-old. Tacoma News Tribune, April 22.

Hughes-Kirchubel, L., 2002. S.J. County prosecutor suspended: DA cites conflict of interest. The Stockton Record, July 27; url: http://www.recordnet.com/daily/news/articles/4news072702.html.

In Re: Danielle M. Muscatello, 2011. Supreme Court. Appellate Division, Second Department, New York Grievance Committee for the Second, Eleventh, and Thirteenth Judicial Districts, Attorney Registration No. 4479754, July 5.

In the Matter of Danielle M. Muscatello, 2012. Supreme Court. Appellate Division, Second Department, New York Attorney Registration No. 4479754, October 17.

Johns, M., 2005. Reconsidering absolute prosecutorial immunity. Brigham Young University Law Review 53, 53–149.

Johnson, C., 2012a. Report: prosecutors hid evidence in Ted Stevens case. NPR, March 15; url: http://www.npr.org/2012/03/15/148687717/report-prosecutors-hid-evidence-in-ted-stevens-case.

Johnson, C., 2012b. Prosecutor says a desire to win led to misconduct in Senator Stevens' case. NPR, March 28; url: http://www.npr.org/blogs/thetwo-way/2012/03/28/149557117/prosecutor-says-a-desire-to-win-led-to-misconduct-in-sen-stevens-case.

Johnson, K., 2012b. Prosecutors in botched case against Senator Stevens suspended. USA Today, May 24; url: http://content.usatoday.com/communities/ondeadline/post/2012/05/prosecutors-in-botched-case-against-sen-stevens-suspended/1#.USq3GqXd36U.

Johnson, T., 2002. New trial ordered in slayings where prosecutors hid evidence. Seattle Post-Intelligencer, February 27; url: http://seattlepi.nwsource.com/local/59947_trial27.shtml.

Krayewski, E., 2012. D.A. suspends Grand Jury investigations of police shootings in Albuquerque; no shooting ever ruled unjustified. Reason Magazine, May, 25; url: http://reason.com/blog/2012/05/25/da-suspends-grand-jury-investigations-of.

Lobato v. Nevada, 2004. Supreme Court of Nevada, No. 40370, September 3.

Long, C., 2013. No grand jury indictment in Queens police shooting. ABC News, February 14; url: http://abclocal.go.com/wabc/story?section=news/local/new_york&id=8993207.

Los Angeles County District Attorney's Office, 2012. Office overview. Los Angeles County District Attorney's Office Official Website url: http://da.lacounty.gov/oview.htm. Updated December 11.

Lynn, A., 2012. Prosecutors: public endangered by western psychologist's work. Tacoma News Tribune, February 24; url: http://www.thenewstribune.com/2012/02/25/2041645/prosecutors-public-endangered.html.

Marshall, E., 2013. Grand jury closes case in shooting of Martinsburg woman by police officers. The Mobile Journal-News, February 22; url: http://www.Journal-news.net/page/content.detail/id/591314/Grand-jury-closes-case-in-shooting-of-Martinsburg-woman-by-police-officers.html.

Martin, A., 2011. The prosecution's case against DNA. The New York Times, November 25; url: http://www.nytimes.com/2011/11/27/magazine/dna-evidence-lake-county.html.

Mosteller, R., 2007. The Duke Lacrosse case, innocence, and false identifications: a fundamental failure to "do justice". Fordham University Law Review 76 (3), 1337–1412.

Naziri, J., 2011. Grand jury: no indictment in police shooting of college student. CNN, February 14; url: http://www.cnn.com/2011/CRIME/02/14/new.york.police.shooting/index.html.

New Hampshire v. Carl Laurie, 1995. Supreme Court of New Hampshire, No. 93–459, February 9.

Oppel, R., 2011. Sentencing shift gives new leverage to prosecutors. New York Times, September 25; url: http://www.nytimes.com/2011/09/26/us/tough-sentences-help-prosecutors-push-for-plea-bargains.html.

Offices of the United States Attorneys, 2013. United States Attorneys' Mission Statement. US Department of Justice, US Attorneys' Official Website url: http://www.justice.gov/usao/about/mission.html.

Parker, B., 2009. Abuse of the material witness: suspects detained as witnesses in violation of the Fourth Amendment. The Rutgers Law Record 36, 22–37, (Fall).

Persky, A., 2009. A cautionary tale: the Ted Stevens prosecution. The Washington Lawyer, October; url: http://www.dcbar.org/for_lawyers/resources/publications/washington_lawyer/october_2009/stevens_prosecution.cfm.

Petherick, W., Turvey, B., 2010. Cognitive ethos of the forensic examiner. In: Turvey, B., Petherick, W., Ferguson, C. (Eds.), Forensic Criminology, Elsevier, San Diego, CA.

Proctor, J., 2013. Police shootings return to grand juries. Albuquerque Journal, January 11; url: http://www.abqjournal.com/main/2013/01/11/news/police-shootings-return-to-grand-juries.html.

Reavy, P., 2009. Ed Smart 'appalled' at psychiatrist's testimony. Deseret News, December 5; url: http://www.deseretnews.com/article/705349138/Ed-Smart-appalled-at-psychiatrists-testimony.html.

Ridolfi, K., Possley, M., 2010. Preventable Error: A Report on Prosecutorial Misconduct in California 1997–2009. Northern California Innocence Project at Santa Clara University School of Law, Santa Clara, CA.

Ryan, C., 2012. Indicted family court judge hit with new complaints. The Las Vegas Sun, December 21; url: http://www.lasvegassun.com/news/2012/dec/21/judicial-disciplinary-commission-brings-charges-ag/.

Savino, J., Turvey, B., 2011. Rape Investigation Handbook, second ed. CA Elsevier, San Diego.

Scheck, B., 2010. Professional and conviction integrity programs: why we need them, why they will work, and models for creating them. Cardozo Law Review 31 (6), 2215–2256.

Sherrer, H., 2008. Kirstin Blaise Lobato's Unreasonable Conviction: Possibility Of Guilt Replaces Proof Beyond A Reasonable Doubt. The Justice Institute, Seattle, WA.

Sklansky, D., 2009. When prosecutors step over the line: divided roles and allegiances. The New York Times, April 1; url: http://roomfordebate.blogs.nytimes.com/2009/04/01/when-prosecutors-step-over-the-line/.

Slobodzian, J., 2011. Conflict-of-interest removal of prosecutor confirmed. Philadelphia Inquirer, May 21; url: http://articles.philly.com/2011-05-21/news/29568802_1_retrial-state-prosecutor-first-trial.

Smith, S., 2008. State Bar Court suspends ex-S.J. prosecutor. The Stockton Record, September 3.

Swift, J., 2012. Conflict of interest finding for former East Haven town attorney. New Haven Register, August 8; url: http://www.nhregister.com/articles/2012/08/08/news/metro/doc5021e00dda4ca201833748.txt?viewmode=fullstory.

Thompson, C., 2012. Some ethical conundrums for city and county attorneys. Handouts and materials from the 2012 The Missouri Municipal League (MMAA) Summer Seminarurl: http://c.ymcdn.com/sites/www.mocities.com/resource/resmgr/mmaa_handouts/imla_ethics.pdf. pp. 1–16.

Turvey, B., 2013. Forensic Fraud. Elsevier Science, San Diego, CA.

Turvey, B., McGrath, M., 2011. False allegations of sexual assault. In: Savino, J., Turvey, B. (Eds.), Rape Investigation Handbook, second ed. Elsevier, San Diego, CA.

Umstead, M., 2013. Grand jury: no further investigation against officers in woman's fatal shooting. Herald Mail, February 20; Url: http://articles.herald-mail.com/2013-02-20/news/37207177_1_ douglas-charles-butler-review-of-police-shootings-officer-shot.

United States v. Bowie, 1999. US Court of Appeals, District of Columbia, Nos. 98–3146, 99–3027, December 21.

United States v. LaPage, 2000. 231 F.3d 488–492.

United States v. Roberts, 9th Cir. 1980. 618 F.2d 530, 536–537.

United States v. Samango, 1979. US Court of Appeals, Ninth Circuit, 607 F.2d 877, C.A.Hawaii, December 13.

United States v. Syling, 2008. US District Court, D. Hawai'i, Cr. No. 07–00406 SOM, April 11.

Vaira, P., 1984. The role of the prosecutor inside the grand jury room: where is the foul line? The Journal of Criminal Law and Criminology 75 (4), 1129–1148.

Visser, S., 2013. 10 metro police officers face corruption charges. The Atlanta Journal-Constitution, February 12; url: http://www.ajc.com/news/news/10-metro-police-officers-face-corruption-charges/nWM4j/.

Washington v. Benn, 2005. State of Washington, Court of Appeals, Division 2, Case No. 31122–4-II, November 15.

Weiser, B., 2011. In New Jersey, rules are changed on witness IDs. New York Times, August 24.

West, N., 2012. Officers on list for honesty concerns. New Hampshire Sunday News, October 6.

Will, C., 2012. Email to "FBI_ALL_EMPLOYEES, " subject line: "OPRS QUARTERLY ALL EMPLOYEE E-MAIL" FBI Office of Professional Responsibility. October 1.

Wood, P., 2002. Expert testimony comes with steep cost. The News Gazette, December 6; url: http://www.news-gazette.com/story.cfm?Number=12831.

Zahrey v. Coffey, 2000. 221 F.3d 342, 354 (2d Cir. 2000).

Zamost, S., Griffin, D., 2013. FBI battling 'rash of sexting' among its employees. CNN, February 22; url: http://www.cnn.com/2013/02/21/us/fbi-misbehavior.

Zhang, V., 2011. Throwing the defendant into the snake pit: applying a state-created danger analysis to prosecutorial fabrication of evidence. Boston University Law Review 91 (6), 2131–2165.

Zion-Hershberg, B., 2006. Camm lawyer challenges witness' credibility. The Courier-Journal, February 6; url: http://www.courier-journal.com/apps/pbcs.dll/article?AID=/20060206/ NEWS02/60206010.

CHAPTER 10

Ethical Issues for Criminal Defense Attorneys

Craig Cooley and Brent E. Turvey

Key Terms

Appointed counsel Private defense attorneys appointed by the court to represent indigent defendants, often at a fixed or hourly rate.

Attorney–client privilege Legal entitlement to privacy intended to facilitate truthful communication and fully informed advocacy by a defendant's legal advisors.

Conflict of interest Occurs when a person or an agency has competing or incongruent loyalties, because of their need to satisfy multiple roles, duties, or obligations.

Criminal defense attorney Serves as the legal representative and advocate for the criminal defendant.

Ineffective assistance of counsel Refers to defense attorney conduct that undermines the proper functioning of the adversarial process to the extent that the trial cannot be relied on as having produced a just result (*Strickland v. Washington*, 1984).

Legal aid attorneys Those who volunteer to represent or assist indigent criminal defendants, usually as part of a non-profit organization (e.g., a legal aid society).

Presumption of innocence The premise that all criminal defendants are considered innocent until proven guilty and that the burden of proving criminal guilt rests entirely on the government.

Principle of confidentiality "A fundamental principle in the client–lawyer relationship is that, in the absence of the client's informed consent, the lawyer must not reveal information relating to the representation. … This contributes to the trust that is the hallmark of the client–lawyer relationship" (Michmerhuizen, 2007, p. 1).

Private attorneys Represent those criminal defendants who can afford to pay for their own attorney and do not qualify as indigent. This involves a contract for a flat fee or an hourly rate.

Pro bono Work done for the public good, typically without financial compensation.

Public defenders Attorneys funded by the county, state, or federal government to provide representation to indigent defendants, as required by the US Constitution.

Reversible error A trial error that is so harmful to justice that it requires some or all of the elements of a conviction to be overturned; these reversals are submitted for reconsideration by the court, if not retrial.

Work-product Refers to any notes, observations, thoughts, or research produced by the attorney, and such material is protected from discovery processes.

Criminal defense attorneys encounter ethical dilemmas on a regular basis, as they are continuously trying to serve the competing interests of their clients, the law, and their own personal beliefs regarding justice. To make matters worse, not everyone agrees what these interests are, at least not precisely;

317

Ethical Justice. http://dx.doi.org/10.1016/B978-0-12-404597-2.00010-3

not everyone agrees which of these should win out when there is a direct contradiction; and not everyone agrees with the mission of the justice system in general. Each of these influences works to shape and guide the defense lawyer's response to an ethical dilemma. This results in decisions that are as much a reflection of a lawyer's personality and culture as they are of underlying ethics codes and the law.

The purpose of this chapter is to consider the major ethical issues and questions peculiar to criminal defense attorneys as they represent their clients. While it is not possible to consider or anticipate every dilemma faced by those advocating for criminal defendants, the authors will discuss the most significant issues as they have experienced them. For organizational purposes, specific ethical considerations are discussed across the following subjects: the *right to counsel*, the *presumption of innocence*, and ethical issues that occur *prior to and during trial*. This is preceded by a review of basic defense attorney types, their functions, and the defense attorney's often conflicted roles.

THE RIGHT TO COUNSEL

Criminal defendants have a constitutionally guaranteed right to legal representation. The Sixth Amendment to the US Constitution provides specifically that:

> In all criminal prosecutions, the accused shall enjoy the right to a speedy and public trial, by an impartial jury of the State and district wherein the crime shall have been committed, which district shall have been previously ascertained by law, and to be informed of the nature and cause of the accusation; to be confronted with the witnesses against him; to have compulsory process for obtaining witnesses in his favor, and to have the Assistance of Counsel for his defence.

The Sixth Amendment right to counsel is essential for due process in the criminal justice system, as everything else guaranteed to a criminal defendant relies upon it and fails without it. More than a requirement for a warm body, the defense attorney must also be competent, as explained in Gershman (2011, p. 560): "A defendant's right to counsel, guaranteed by the Sixth Amendment, has long been understood to include the right to the effective assistance of counsel." Thus, not only are criminal defendants entitled to legal counsel, counsel must also be effective; counsel may not be inadequate or incompetent.

When a criminal defendant cannot afford a legal representative, the state must provide one for them to ensure that they are receiving impartial legal advice. This was explained best in the US Supreme Court's ruling in *Gideon v. Wainwright* (1963):

> … in our adversary system of criminal justice, any person haled into court, who is too poor to hire a lawyer, cannot be assured a fair trial unless counsel is provided for him. This seems to us to be an obvious truth. Governments, both state and federal, quite properly spend vast sums of money to establish machinery to try defendants accused of crime. Lawyers to prosecute are everywhere deemed essential to protect the public's interest in an orderly society. Similarly, there are few defendants charged with crime, few indeed, who fail to hire the best lawyers they can get to prepare and present their defenses. That government hires lawyers to prosecute and defendants who have the money hire lawyers to defend are the strongest indications of the widespread belief that lawyers in criminal courts are necessities, not luxuries. The right of one charged with crime to counsel may not be deemed fundamental and essential to fair trials in some countries, but it is in ours. From the very beginning, our state and national constitutions and laws have laid great emphasis on procedural and substantive safeguards designed to assure fair trials before impartial tribunals in which every defendant stands equal before the law. This noble ideal cannot be realized if the poor man charged with crime has to face his accusers without a lawyer to assist him. A defendant's need for a lawyer is nowhere better stated than in the moving words of Mr Justice Sutherland in *Powell v. Alabama*: "The right to be heard would be, in many cases, of little avail if it did not comprehend the right to be heard by counsel. Even the intelligent and educated layman has small and sometimes no skill in the science of law. If charged with crime, he is incapable, generally, of determining for himself whether the indictment is good or bad. He is unfamiliar with the rules of evidence. Left without the aid of counsel, he may be put on trial without a proper charge, and convicted upon incompetent evidence, or evidence irrelevant to the issue or otherwise inadmissible. He lacks both the skill and knowledge adequately to prepare his defense, even though he have a perfect one. He requires the guiding hand of counsel at every step in the proceedings against him. Without it, though he be not guilty, he faces the danger of conviction because he does not know how to establish his innocence."

Further, the US Supreme Court has held that legal counsel must also be effective, in *Strickland v. Washington* (1984): "The Sixth Amendment right to counsel is the right to the effective assistance of counsel, and the benchmark for judging any claim of ineffectiveness must be whether counsel's conduct so undermined the proper functioning of the adversarial process that the trial cannot be relied on as having produced a just result." This was echoed is *Martinez v. Ryan* (2012), which explains that: "The right to the effective assistance of counsel at trial is a bedrock principle in our justice system."

However, this decision does not necessarily provide an immediate remedy for incompetent lawyering, as discussed in Freedman (2005, p. 918):

> ... under *Strickland*, even grossly incompetent lawyering is not enough to establish ineffective counsel. In addition, the lawyer's incompetence must have caused "prejudice" to his client, meaning that there must be a "reasonable *probability* that, but for counsel's unprofessional errors, the result of the proceeding *would* have been different." Thus, even a reasonable possibility that an innocent person might have been wrongly convicted because of his lawyer's established incompetence is not enough to justify a new trial.

Consequently, fulfillment of this obligation may rest entirely on the defense attorney's professional ethics. In any case, the ethical imperative is clear: the state must provide legal counsel for arrestees and the lawyers who represent them must be competent. Anything less risks derailing due process and subverts the cause of justice – without remedy in certain cases.

Those professionals that do not believe criminal defendants are entitled to, or even deserve, effective representation are at cross-purposes with one of the criminal justice system's most important pillars. Needless to say, such a belief has no place in it. Consequently, this issue is one of the most useful litmus tests for those considering work as a criminal defense attorney; they must be capable of, and willing to, represent anyone accused of a crime.

CRIMINAL DEFENSE ATTORNEYS: STRUCTURE AND FUNCTION

There are essentially four primary types of criminal defense attorneys in the United States: *legal aid, public defenders, appointed counsel,* and *private attorneys.* Each is differently employed, with varied budgetary constraints and access to resources. They will be discussed in turn.

Legal Aid

Although every criminal defendant is entitled to an attorney, not all can afford an attorney. For those who are *indigent,* justice is in fact quite different. The quality of indigent defense varies tremendously from region to region and it starts with access to legal aid.

Legal aid attorneys are those who volunteer to represent or assist indigent criminal defendants, usually as part of a non-profit organization (e.g., a legal aid society).

This is typically done at a very reduced rate, if not entirely *pro bono*.[1] Not every region has legal aid or even its equivalent.

In some states, legal aid attorneys are the first responders for indigent defendants that would otherwise have no representation prior to arraignment, as explained in Wilson (2007, pp. 30–31):

> Adults detained by the police have no right to speak to anyone other than an attorney while they undergo police interrogation. For people who can afford to hire an attorney to come to the police station and provide legal advice, this situation can be addressed quite easily by a phone call placed by either the detainee or his family to a private criminal defense attorney. Indigent people detained by the police in Illinois, however, have traditionally had no such recourse, because the law providing an indigent person accused of a crime with an attorney does not provide any representation until the person makes his first court appearance. Attorneys consider the time during which a person undergoes police interrogation a critical stage in a criminal defendant's case due to the potential for coerced statements. The founders of First Defense Legal Aid (FDLA) felt a gross inequity existed between those who could afford an attorney's advice during the investigation phase of a criminal prosecution and those who could not. Thus, a group of attorneys and laypeople created FDLA to fill the critical gap in indigent criminal representation that existed between the point that a CPD investigation began and the point that an Assistant Cook County Public Defender accepted the indigent defendant's case.

Legal aid groups around the nation work with local defense bars and law firms to coordinate volunteers, and solicit specialized expertise, to help ensure that indigent defendants are adequately represented throughout the legal process.

Public Defenders

Public defenders exist at the county, state, and federal level. As with the prosecutor's office, the public defender's office is held by a single individual who employs multiple assistant or deputy public defenders. Their mission is to provide zealous and effective representation to indigent defendants, in accordance with the US Constitution. They are funded by the county, state, or federal government.

Within a public defender's office there are generally different specialty units, such as child and family crimes, sex crimes, felony units, trial units, and civil

---

[1]*Pro bono* is short for *pro bono publico*, which is Latin for "the public good." *Pro bono* work is typically done without financial compensation.

mental health units. In jurisdictions with the death penalty, there will typically be a capital unit. In larger jurisdictions there will also be an alternate or conflict public defender, to handle cases where there is a conflict of interest (e.g., cases with multiple defendants).

While most public defenders make little money, there are advantages to working for a public defender agency. First, employees enjoy state or federal employment benefits (e.g., health insurance, life insurance, paid vacations, sick leave, and a pension). Second, they have access to other more experienced attorneys for information, advice, and even mentoring. This makes such employment ideal for those just starting out. Public defender agencies also generally have in-house administrative assistants, legal assistants, investigators, paralegals, interns, and access to legal databases such as Westlaw and LexisNexis. Given the expense, many private attorneys do not enjoy consistent access to these same resources – or their access is constrained by the budget of their client from case to case.

As explained in Freedman (2005), perhaps the biggest problem with both legal aid and public defenders is that they are seriously underfunded and overworked, often to the point of being ineffective (pp. 913–914):

> The other means of providing lawyers to poor people has been through public defender and legal aid offices. There, the problem has been not so much the incompetence of the lawyers, but the fact that the offices typically are seriously underfunded. This has produced overloading of the individual lawyers with far more clients than any lawyer could competently represent.

This concern is given statistical detail in Waxman (2013):

> In 2007, the last time the Bureau of Justice Statistics surveyed the nation's indigent defense services, there were 957 public defender offices employing 15,000 full-time staff. These offices handled about 80 percent of the country's criminal cases, on a combined budget of $2.3 billion. In that same year, 2,330 state prosecutor offices employed 78,000 full-time staff. Their budgets were falling, but with a total of $5.8 billion in the kitty, their means far outstripped that of their defender colleagues.
>
>   Faced with a larger and better-funded prosecution regime, defenders can't keep up. Twenty-two states operate public defender offices, and 17 reported full caseload information to the Bureau in 2007. Only four of those 17 states had enough attorneys to meet the government's caseload standards, guidelines for the maximum number of cases that should be assigned to an attorney. Where public defense operates at the county level, less than a third of offices had enough attorneys.

Other vital defense staff – investigators, paralegals, administrators – are similarly in short supply. It should come as no surprise, then, that you're more likely to wind up in jail if represented by a taxpayer-financed lawyer than by one you hire yourself.

The consequences of the defender resource shortfall are obvious in Detroit, to name just one example. In the Motor City, misdemeanor cases are handled by a low-bid private contractor. For $661,400, five part-time attorneys working for the Misdemeanor Defender Professional Corporation dispose of 12,000–14,000 cases per year. That comes to 32 minutes of attorney time spent on each case, according to the National Legal Aid & Defender Association.

The numbers point to a disconnect between the principle – that everyone has a right to effective counsel – and actual practice. That difference haunts the American justice system.

Budgets are so tight that attorneys in larger jurisdictions, like New York and Chicago, have started to make pre-trial ineffectiveness claims against themselves, knowing full well that they cannot possibly render adequate legal representation given their overwhelming caseloads, diminishing funds, and other limited resources.

Appointed Counsel

Appointed counsel are private defense attorneys appointed by the court to represent indigent defendants, often at a fixed or hourly rate. Appointed counsel tend to be one–lawyer shops or small law firms, operating with limited resources, and sometimes without access to paralegals, investigators, or expensive legal databases (e.g., LexisNexis and Westlaw). This is highly problematic and can result in the least competent representation, as explained in Freedman (2005, p. 912):

One way the states have purported to meet their constitutional obligation to provide counsel to poor people accused of crimes has been through court-appointed lawyers. However, the paltry compensation paid for these services has generally been inadequate to attract competent lawyers. In addition, judges have too often selected court appointed lawyers precisely because the lawyers are incompetent, and can be counted on to move the courts' calendars quickly by entering hasty guilty pleas in virtually all cases. In those few cases in which the accused insists on his right to trial by jury, the trials typically move rapidly because the court-appointed lawyers generally file no motions, conduct no investigations, and do little to impede the speedy disposal of the case from charge, to guilty verdict, to imprisonment.

Appointed counsel are used by the court to handle indigent cases under the following circumstances:

(1) The region does not have a public defender office or system.
(2) Both the public defender and the alternate public defender have conflicts of interest with a particular case.
(3) Neither the public defender nor the alternate public defender have the manpower available to handle a particular case – appointed counsel handle the overflow.
(4) Neither the public defender nor the alternate public defender have the expertise to handle the complexities of a particular case (e.g., a complex financial crime).

Private Attorneys

Private criminal defense attorneys work under a variety of circumstances. Some run a one-man practice out of a home office; others work for multi-partner law firms that occupy several floors of a downtown high-rise. Many are willing to accept *pro bono* and even appointed casework. However, they make their money by representing those criminal defendants who can afford to pay for their own attorney and do not qualify as indigent. This involves a contract for a flat fee or an hourly rate.

Often, private criminal defense attorneys will specialize their practices, representing primarily one type of case. Popular specialty areas include driving while intoxicated, sex crimes, or those involving the death penalty. Other attorneys specialize in white-collar crime, such as fraud and embezzlement. Private attorneys that are the most knowledgeable and effective are often more expensive; however, those that are expensive are not necessarily either.

In fact, the authors have encountered quite a few unethical private defense attorneys that will simply take a defendant's money up front, spend it, and have nothing left for trial expenses. For example, consider the case of New York criminal defense attorney Ivan Fisher. In 2013, he was barred from practicing law in Manhattan Federal Court for ethics violations related to the misappropriation of client funds, as reported in Ax (2013):

> The Committee on Grievances for the Southern District issued the order last week, calling Fisher's misappropriation of $50,000 from a client's funds "venal." "It was a breach of his most fundamental professional responsibilities," wrote US District Judge P. Kevin Castel in the three-page order.
>
> Fisher's client, Ebrahim Raphael, a cooperating defendant in an embezzlement case, agreed to pay $250,000 in restitution to his victim, according to the grievance committee. Raphael gave the money to Fisher in 2007. Rather than deposit all the funds into an escrow

account, Fisher spent $50,000 on personal expenses, according to the committee. Fisher had argued that the funds were a loan, rather than a payment intended for the victim.

Magistrate Judge Henry Pitman rejected that argument after presiding over an evidentiary hearing in the case last year. "Simply put, Respondent stole his client's money and has never repaid it," Pitman concluded. The 10-judge grievance committee had accepted Pitman's findings in December ....

The committee found that Fisher had committed numerous violations of professional ethics. Judge Lewis Stanton dissented in part, saying that there was sufficient evidence to support one of the violations, but otherwise agreed with the majority.

Fisher's history is colorful and includes representing Jack Henry Abbott, a prisoner whose jailhouse writings drew praise from Norman Mailer and others.

Mr Fisher was a high-profile criminal defense lawyer, known for his representation of such clients as Samarth Agrawal, a former Societe Generale trader convicted in 2010 of copying high-frequency trading code; Bashir Noorzia, an Afghan leader convicted in 2008 on heroin importing charges, identified as one of the world's most wanted drug traffickers; and a mafia crime boss involved charged with running a large-scale heroin importation ring.

Apart from the lack of resources and incredible expense that can accompany private defense attorneys, too many enter the criminal world blindly. That is to say, they accept cases outside their typical practice area without sufficient knowledge or experience. This often occurs when a family lawyer, perhaps accustomed to handling wills or tax matters, is asked to do a favor for a client or a friend of a friend.

The Role of Advocate

Regardless of their employment situation, the *criminal defense attorney* serves as an advocate for the criminal defendant. They must shepherd the defendant through the legal process; inform them of their rights and scrupulously protect them; and represent their will in the courtroom. They are, at best, a shield for the criminal defendant against what can be the relentless and overwhelming efforts of the state. Indeed, defense counsel's constitutional purpose is in fact to "test the prosecution's case to ensure that the proceedings serve the function of adjudicating guilt or innocence, while protecting the rights of the person charged" (*Martinez v. Ryan*, 2012).[2] Their representation must be both zealous and at the same time honorable.

---

[2] The previously discussed right to effective assistance of counsel, consequently, is "the right of the accused to require the prosecution's case to survive the crucible of meaningful adversarial testing" (*United States v. Cronic*, 1984).

As discussed at the beginning of this chapter, the criminal defense attorney's role is complex and suffers competing interests. This is described in Flowers (2010, p. 647):

> The Model Rules of Professional Conduct define the role of the attorney as threefold: "A lawyer, as a member of the legal profession, is a representative of clients, an officer of the legal system and a public citizen having special responsibility for the quality of justice." The language does not differentiate the roles based on the kind of law the lawyer practices nor does it prioritize the different roles. This lack of differentiation leads to the conclusion that all lawyers, no matter what area of law, have a responsibility that goes beyond merely advocating for the client. An attorney must act as an officer of the court, respecting the need for truth and truth-seeking within the confines of the adversary system and as an active participant of a system that places justice as a core value.

This multi-faceted capacity is not at all easy for the criminal defense attorney. At the very least, it requires a strong and informed sense of service to justice. The defense attorney must also care about the fate of their clients, about the rule of law, and be capable of doing so faithfully while subjected to the misunderstanding and general derision of just about everyone.

THE PRESUMPTION OF INNOCENCE

A fundamental virtue of the criminal justice system in the United States is that all criminal defendants are presumed innocent. Consequently, every aspect of a criminal trial is subordinate to this ideal. As explained in Nelson (2008, p. 713):

> Unlike the inquisitorial systems of Continental Europe, our adversarial system erects numerous protections for the accused. Indeed, "[n]o principle is more firmly established in our system of criminal justice than the presumption of innocence that is accorded to the defendant in every criminal trial."

The *presumption of innocence* places the burden of proving criminal guilt entirely on the government. In theory, the state must prove a defendant's guilt *beyond a reasonable doubt* in order to obtain a conviction. As explained in Hardaway (2008, pp. 271–272):

> The presumption of innocence does not automatically establish the burden of proof required to determine an accused's guilt or innocence. The presumption is an instrument of proof created by the law in favor of one accused, whereby his innocence is established until sufficient

evidence is introduced to overcome the proof which the law has created. The degree of proof required to overcome the presumption of innocence is defined by the prevailing burden of persuasion.

Conversely, the defense has an entirely lower evidentiary threshold. Ideally, they must only prove the existence of a *reasonable doubt* to obtain an acquittal. Although there are some clear interpretations regarding this standard, there has also been ongoing disagreement between courts regarding both the definition of reasonable doubt and whether that definition must actually be explained to the jury. As described in Hardaway (2008, pp. 272–273):

> In the American criminal justice system, the accused must be proven guilty beyond a reasonable doubt.
>
> ...
>
> *Commonwealth v. Webster* [1850] is representative of the time when American courts began applying the beyond a reasonable doubt standard "in its modern form in criminal cases." Writing for the majority, Chief Justice Shaw defined reasonable doubt as:
>
> [N]ot a mere possible doubt; because everything relating to human affairs, and depending on moral evidence, is open to some possible or imaginary doubt. It is that state of the case, which, after the entire comparison and consideration of all the evidence, leaves the minds of jurors in that condition that they cannot say they feel an abiding conviction, to a moral certainty, of the truth of the charge ... but the evidence must establish the truth of the fact to a reasonable and moral certainty; a certainty that convinces and directs the understanding, and satisfies the reason and judgment, of those who are bound to act conscientiously upon it.
>
> Many courts adopted Justice Shaw's definition of reasonable doubt in the nineteenth century, with one court characterizing the instruction as "probably the most satisfactory definition ever given to the words 'reasonable doubt' in any case known to criminal jurisprudence." [*People v. Strong*, 30 Cal. 151, 155 (1866)] However, while the Supreme Court has held that proof beyond a reasonable doubt is a constitutional requirement in every criminal trial and juries shall be instructed on the necessity of such proof, the Constitution does not require a definition of reasonable doubt as part of this instruction [*Jackson v. Virginia*, 443 U.S. 307, 320 n.14 (1979) (explaining that "failure to instruct a jury on the necessity of proof of guilt beyond a reasonable doubt can never be harmless error"); *Sullivan v. Louisiana*, 508 U.S. 275, 278 (1993) ("[T]he Fifth Amendment requirement of proof beyond a reasonable doubt and the Sixth Amendment requirement of a jury verdict are interrelated .... [T]he jury verdict required by the Sixth Amendment is a jury verdict of guilty beyond a reasonable doubt."]. The Supreme

Court's lack of guidance on the instruction of the reasonable doubt standard has given rise to confusion and a wide lack of uniformity in the treatment of its definition among federal and state courts. Not only does the definition of reasonable doubt vary between courts, but the jurisdictions also diverge on whether or not a jury is to be instructed on the definition.

This issue is an excellent reminder that the law is not a series of unequivocal "if–then" statements that are clearly understood, rationally interpreted, and consistently applied. Each judge in each courtroom in every country interprets and applies the law in their own way. On this particular matter, some believe in providing helpful definitions of key terms to juries; some believe in a "hands-off" policy to let jurors decide for themselves; and some can be found in-between. The result is a wide diversity with respect to understanding and application of the law by differing judges and courts, and frequent jury confusion.

However, the ethical imperative is clear: the presumption of innocence is a core value of the criminal justice system. The burden of proof is on the state, not the defense. Those professionals unwilling to embrace this concept have the potential to do more harm than good. This is especially true for defense counsel. They must believe in the presumption of innocence and they must act enthusiastically on their client's behalf to protect that belief.

ETHICAL ISSUES WITH CLIENTS

As advocates, criminal defense attorneys are obligated to protect their client's interests and can only act against them in extraordinary circumstances. This section will discuss conflicts of interest, confidentiality, attorney–client privilege, improper sexual relationships, and so-called "couch fees."

Avoiding Conflicts of Interest

As discussed in Chapter 9: "Ethical Issues for Criminal Prosecutors," a *conflict of interest* occurs when a person or an agency has competing or incongruent loyalties, because of their need to satisfy multiple roles, duties, or obligations. Just as with prosecutors, criminal defense attorneys are ethically bound to avoid conflicts of interest with respect to their representation. These conflicts generally occur when the interests of the attorney conflict directly with the client's interests. A discussion of examples can be found in Gershman (1997) and includes:

(1) Situations in which the defense attorney has important knowledge relating to the facts and evidence underlying the charges against their client, and is going to be called as a witness.

(2) When the defense attorney is implicated in criminal activity, either in relation to the charges against the client or by the same prosecutor's office.
(3) Representation of one co-defendant against the interests of another.

For example, consider Annette Morales-Rodriguez, a criminal defendant in a brutal double homicide case from Wisconsin. The prosecution moved to have both of her attorneys "conflicted out" of the case, arguing that each had a different conflict of interest that could bias the nature of their representation, as reported in Vielmetti (2012):

> As if the case of a woman charged with cutting an unborn child from a mother's womb in the hope of passing the child off as her own wasn't unusual enough, now prosecutors say her lawyers might have to be replaced because one faces criminal charges and the other is a victim in another criminal case.
>
> Defense counsel said Tuesday they were shocked by even the suggestion they might consider doing less for their client to serve their own interests.
>
> "I can't believe this," said lead defense attorney Robert D'Arruda. "I'm not going to get a waiver. I don't believe there's a conflict. This is a frivolous motion."
>
> Annette Morales-Rodriguez was charged in October with two counts of homicide. Her attorneys said they planned to challenge the admission of confessions she purportedly made to detectives, try to move the case to another county because of intense publicity and raise a possible not guilty by reason of mental disease or defect defense.
>
> A state psychiatrist has found Morales-Rodriguez, 33, was not suffering from mental disease when police say she befriended Maritza Ramirez-Cruz, 23, invited her into her south side home and killed her during a crude, botched Caesarean section procedure.
>
> The defense team hired an expert who worked in the Lorena Bobbitt case and is working on a new report.
>
> Now prosecutors have asked Circuit Judge David Borowski to make Morales-Rodriguez waive what they see as potential conflicts of interest among her lawyers.
>
> One of them, Patrick Rupich, has pending charges of third offense drunken driving, operating without a valid license and bail jumping. Assistant District Attorney Mark Williams said in a motion that Rupich theoretically might do less than his best in defending Morales-Rodriguez in order to try and win favor from the Milwaukee district attorney's office on his own cases.
>
> ...
>
> D'Arruda is the victim in a domestic case in which, according to a criminal complaint, an ex-girlfriend egged his car outside a Walker's

Point restaurant earlier this month, then chased him down National Ave. and confronted him at a gas station, where she struck him several times with her fist before getting back in her car, sideswiping his and running over his cellphone.

Williams says in his motion, D'Arruda might do less for Morales-Rodriguez in hopes of getting a better result in the misdemeanor prosecution of the woman who attacked him.

D'Arruda, a lawyer for 19 years, said he asked both police and the prosecutor that the woman just be ticketed, but they charged her anyway. "Is that a favor?" he asked.

"I'm not going to thank a client for a favor," he said. "I don't curry favors; I go to trial."

According to Williams, the case can't proceed until Morales-Rodriguez knowingly waives the concerns he raised in the motion. If she doesn't, or if Borowski thinks she can't fully appreciate and knowingly waive the possible conflicts, one or more of the lawyers could be ordered off the case.

Annette Morales-Rodriguez ultimately changed her legal team and her strategy. However, at the end of 2012, she was convicted of two counts of first-degree intentional homicide and sentenced to life in prison without parole.

Confidentiality and the Attorney–Client Privilege

Criminal defense attorneys are bound by both the principle of confidentiality and the attorney–client privilege. One is an ethical requirement, the other is a legal doctrine with related implications.

The *principle of confidentiality* is an ethical requirement, described in Michmerhuizen (2007, p. 1):

> The principle of confidentiality is set out in the legal ethics rules in each jurisdiction and in ABA Model Rule 1.6. Model Rule 1.6 Comment [2] states: "A fundamental principle in the client–lawyer relationship is that, in the absence of the client's informed consent, the lawyer must not reveal information relating to the representation. … This contributes to the trust that is the hallmark of the client–lawyer relationship." A violation of the ethics rule may lead to disciplinary sanctions.

This is a broad cloak and covers just about anything communicated to the client or from the client, regardless of whether it comes from another source. However, the attorney may be compelled to disclose these communications by the court at a later date.

The *attorney– client privilege* is legal entitlement intended to facilitate truthful communication and fully informed advocacy by a defendant's legal advisors. It protects the confidentiality of conversations and dealings between lawyers and their clients. As defined in *Black's Law Dictionary* (Black, 1990, p. 129):

> In law of evidence, client's privilege to disclose and to prevent any other person from disclosing confidential communication between him and his attorney. Such privilege protects communications between attorney and client made for the purpose of furnishing or obtaining legal advice or assistance.

The rationale is explained more thoroughly in Giesel (2011/2012, p. 481):

> The attorney–client privilege exists to encourage clients to make complete disclosure to their attorneys. The privilege protects communications between attorneys and clients from compelled disclosure and this protection encourages clients to make full disclosure to their counsel. Full disclosure allows lawyers to render the best and most apt legal advice. In a preventative view, clients may adapt their conduct to abide by the law in response to this superior advice. If clients, though not perfectly certain, are at least generally certain that the privilege protects their communications with counsel from disclosure in future proceedings, clients may disclose more fully.

The attorney–client privilege is held by the defendant, and may not be violated without their express knowledge and authorization. However, it is waived by the defendant when their communications occur in front of a third party that is not part of their legal team.

Work-Product

The privilege can also extend to the work-product of the attorney's agents, which includes defense investigators and expert consultants. *Work-product* refers to any notes, observations, thoughts, or research produced by the attorney and such material is protected from discovery processes. The privilege exists to facilitate full disclosure between attorney and client, to enable honest and informed representation (Aviel, 2011).

Physical Evidence

With respect to physical evidence, the issue is more complex. If the client provides their attorney with physical evidence, or information regarding how to find or retrieve it, that communication is protected under the privilege. However, the attorney may not take custody of the evidence to hide or destroy it, or instruct their client to do the same. This would be obstruction of justice and is a crime.

The ethical attorney has two options: immediately disclose the evidence to the authorities or seek to have it returned to its source, as explained in Uphoff (2011, p. 14):

> [American Bar Association] Standard 4-4.6 rightfully allows defense lawyers to seek to minimize harm to the client if they take possession of any piece of incriminating evidence by permitting counsel to return that evidence to the source instead of turning that evidence over to the authorities. It is not surprising that most defense lawyers would prefer this approach because they are not forced to betray their clients or to take action that is so contrary to their clients' best interests. Taking disloyal action is particularly difficult when counsel gained the client's trust through an unequivocal pledge of confidentiality.

Ultimately, defense attorneys take custody of physical evidence at the peril of their clients under such circumstances and can do so for only a brief interval before they must make a decision about what they are going to do with it.

Self-Incrimination and Testimony

If the client makes a self-incriminating statement, this does not raise an ethical issue by itself. However, it does if the client asks the attorney to put them on the stand and makes it clear that they intend to lie. If the client wishes to testify under these circumstances, involving false testimony, the attorney has an obligation to prevent it. As discussed in Chapter 9, specific criminal charges could actually include Subornation of Perjury or Conspiracy to Subornation of Perjury.

Improper Sexual Relationships and "Couch Fees"

Unless the attorney has a prior sexual relationship with an individual (e.g., a wife or a girlfriend), it does it is generally considered unethical to initiate or otherwise engage in a sexual relationship with a client. An enlightening discussion of the issues can be found in Moorman (2010), with respect to why some lawyers have opposed this issue (p. 1):

> Rule 1.13 [of the American Bar Association] prohibits a lawyer from having sex with a client that the lawyer is personally representing unless the lawyer and client are married to each other or are engaged in an "ongoing consensual sexual relationship that began before the representation." This rule prohibits what has been called a "couch fee." Under the Rule, a lawyer cannot solicit or accept sexual relations as payment of fees or condition the representation of a client or prospective client or the quality of such representation on the client having sex with the lawyer ....
>
> The exception to this rule is a lawyer's spouse or someone with whom the lawyer was engaged in an ongoing consensual sexual relationship that began before the representation.

There are lawyers who oppose this rule. It is my understanding that some lawyers who handle divorces are opposed to Rule 1.13. They contend that there are numerous instances in which a lawyer becomes involved with a client when they are representing that client in a divorce. They maintain that this rule would prohibit the lawyer from representing the person with whom they now have a consensual sexual relationship in any subsequent enforcement matters or contempt matters once the divorce is finalized. This is such an area of concern that the individuals responsible for promulgating these rules are worried that there may not be enough votes to pass these rules because of the existence of Rule 1.13. Truth remains stranger than fiction.

Although outlawed in many states, couch fees are alive and well in criminal defense work – especially among vulnerable defendant populations, such as those related to sex work (e.g., exotic dancers and prostitutes) and drug addicts. For example, in 2009 assistant public defender Matthew Swedick was found guilty of criminal charges related to engaging in sex with a client in exchange for promising to work harder on her case. The client, Latoya Gordon, was being represented for drug charges; she secretly recorded two of the encounters, which took place in Mr Swedick's office, and the recordings were used as evidence against him at his trial (Demare, 2009).

In a more complex example, involving a pattern of related misconduct, consider the case of attorney Michael Inglimo in Wisconsin. The facts are taken directly from the State Supreme Court record (*In Re: Inglimo*, 2007):

6 Attorney Inglimo was admitted to the practice of law in Wisconsin in September 1985. He practiced in the Superior area.

7 Counts 1 and 2 relate to Attorney Inglimo's representation of L.K. in a criminal case between April 2000 and January 2001. During this representation in October 2000, Attorney Inglimo had sexual relations with L.K.'s girlfriend in L.K.'s presence and with L.K. also engaging in sexual relations with his girlfriend during the sexual encounter. The referee further found, however, that there was no evidence that during the encounter there was any intimate physical contact between Attorney Inglimo and L.K.

8 Count 1 of the OLR's [Office of Lawyer Regulation's] complaint alleged that by having sexual relations with L.K.'s girlfriend in L.K.'s presence and with L.K. participating in the encounter, Attorney Inglimo had violated SCR 20:1.8(k)(2). Although the referee found that there had been a three-way sexual encounter involving L.K., his girlfriend and Attorney Inglimo, he concluded that there was no violation of SCR 20:1.8(k)(2) because there was no evidence that Attorney Inglimo and his client, L.K., had "sexual relations" as that term is defined in the rule. Specifically, there was no

evidence that Attorney Inglimo and L.K. engaged in sexual intercourse or intentionally touched each other's intimate parts.

9 One of the conditions of bail in L.K.'s criminal case was that he could not use or possess any controlled substances. In addition, Wis. Stat. § 969.03(2) (1999–2000) provided that "[a]s a condition of release in all cases, a person released under this section shall not commit any crime." Possession and use of marijuana were criminal acts in the State of Wisconsin. Wis. Stat. § 961.41(3g)(e). Beginning in 1998, Attorney Inglimo and L.K. regularly went out drinking at various taverns. In addition to drinking, Attorney Inglimo occasionally used marijuana with L.K. Specifically, in October 2000 while L.K. was out on bail, L.K. went to Attorney Inglimo's house, where the two of them used cocaine and smoked marijuana.

10 A couple of months later, a week or two before his criminal trial, L.K. returned to Attorney Inglimo's house to discuss the upcoming trial. L.K. testified that Attorney Inglimo was under the influence of drugs at the time, because his eyes were dilated, he could not focus, and he was "antsy." L.K. stated that he could tell when Attorney Inglimo had used drugs because he had previously used drugs with Attorney Inglimo on past occasions.

11 The referee found, based on L.K.'s testimony, that Attorney Inglimo had been high on drugs during L.K.'s trial, that Attorney Inglimo was not prepared, and that he had not represented L.K. adequately at the trial.

12 The referee concluded that this conduct by Attorney Inglimo constituted a violation of SCR 20:8.4(b). The referee acknowledged that using marijuana is a crime under Wisconsin law, but he did not believe that marijuana use, by itself, reflected adversely on a lawyer's honesty, trustworthiness or fitness as a lawyer in other respects. He believed that the OLR had to prove a nexus between Attorney Inglimo's criminal act of marijuana use and his provision of legal services to L.K. With respect to Count 2, the referee concluded that the evidence showed that Attorney Inglimo had been high during L.K.'s criminal trial and that Attorney Inglimo's performance as an attorney had been affected thereby. He did not base his legal conclusion of a violation of SCR 20:8.4(b) on the fact that Attorney Inglimo, by using marijuana with L.K., had aided and abetted L.K. to violate a condition of his bail. The referee stated that Count 2 was drafted as alleging a criminal act of using drugs, rather than as alleging a criminal act of aiding and abetting L.K. to violate his bail condition.

13 Counts 3 through 6 relate to Attorney Inglimo's use of his client trust account and his failure to maintain proper trust account records.

The referee's factual findings on these counts include that Attorney Inglimo wrote two checks out of his client trust account totaling $1,327 to purchase a car for himself. Attorney Inglimo claimed that these funds belonged to his mother, for whom he had previously handled a real estate matter, and that she gave the funds to him so that he could purchase the car. Based on the OLR's reconstruction of Attorney Inglimo's client trust account transactions, however, the referee found that Attorney Inglimo's trust account checks for the car had exceeded any trust account funds belonging to his mother by at least $150. Thus, Attorney Inglimo had drawn on funds belonging to other clients.

14 In addition, OLR's reconstruction demonstrated that as of December 31, 2001, several clients and Attorney Inglimo himself had negative balances in the trust account. Indeed, between January 1, 1999, and December 31, 2001, Attorney Inglimo used funds on deposit for clients with positive balances to cover at least $386.05 of disbursements for those with negative balances.

15 For many years Attorney Inglimo maintained personal funds in his client trust account to act as a "cushion" against overdrafts. Prior to May 2004, Attorney Inglimo kept no written records that would show what amounts of personal funds were in the client trust account. He made more than $1,500 in disbursements from his trust account for personal expenses when he had no way to determine whether he had sufficient personal funds in the trust account to cover those disbursements.

16 Attorney Inglimo also did not maintain subsidiary client ledgers for individual clients and did not keep a running balance of receipts, disbursements and the amount remaining in the trust account for each client. He did not record deposits in the trust account checkbook register and kept no other receipts journal showing the sources and dates of deposits. Attorney Inglimo did not keep a running balance for his trust account and did not perform monthly reconciliations between his trust account balance and the bank statements.

17 Despite his failure to keep the trust account records required by former SCR 20:1.15(e), Attorney Inglimo certified on his annual state bar dues statements for fiscal years 1999–2004 that he had complied with each of the trust account record-keeping requirements. Each of these certifications was false.

18 Based on these factual findings, the referee concluded that Attorney Inglimo had violated former SCR 20:1.15(a) 5 (Counts 3 and 4) by failing to hold in trust at least $386.05 in funds belonging to clients or third persons and by depositing and co-mingling his personal funds with client funds in his trust account. The referee also concluded that Attorney Inglimo had failed to keep the necessary trust account

records, in violation of former SCR 20:1.15(e) (Count 5). Further, the referee determined that Attorney Inglimo had violated former SCR 20:1.15(g) (Count 6) by falsely certifying on his state bar annual dues statements that he was in compliance with the trust account record-keeping requirements.

19 Count 7 related to improper trust account disbursements made by Attorney Inglimo between 1999 and 2001. Based on the OLR's reconstruction of the trust account transactions, during that time period Attorney Inglimo's disbursements to himself and to third parties on behalf of clients P.K. and K.K. exceeded the funds on deposit for them in Attorney Inglimo's trust account by at least $2,661.47. Attorney Inglimo also disbursed $33 for client T.P. when he knew there were no funds on deposit for her in his trust account. He likewise disbursed $94 to obtain a preliminary hearing transcript in L.K.'s criminal case when he knew that there were no funds on deposit for L.K. in the trust account.

20 The referee concluded that these facts demonstrated that Attorney Inglimo had engaged in conduct involving dishonesty and misrepresentation, in violation of SCR 20:8.4(c).

21 Count 8 involved Attorney Inglimo's representation of M.S. in a divorce matter between September 27, 2001, and August 7, 2002. M.S.'s wife, K.S., was not represented by counsel. The divorce proceeding was a fairly simple matter because the couple had been separated for several years, they had no children, they had very little property to divide, and apparently the only real dispute involved possession of a camper.

22 The referee found that during the course of the divorce case Attorney Inglimo developed at least a significant social relationship with K.S. Attorney Inglimo not only met with K.S. at the public library multiple times, but he went to K.S.'s residence on multiple occasions and she came to his house on multiple occasions. Specifically, the referee found that Attorney Inglimo went to a party at K.S.'s residence, that he asserted the Fifth Amendment when asked about using a controlled substance at the party, and that he did not tell his client about attending this party. The referee also found, based on the testimony of P.K. and K.K., who were living on Attorney Inglimo's property and were in his home watching a movie on the relevant date, that Attorney Inglimo and K.S. returned to Attorney Inglimo's home late one evening, immediately went into Attorney Inglimo's bedroom, and did not leave the bedroom until morning. The referee further found, based on Attorney Inglimo's admission, that he engaged in a three-way sexual encounter with K.S. and another woman within two weeks after M.S. fired him in August 2002. The cause of the firing was

M.S.'s belief that Attorney Inglimo and K.S. were seeing each other and that Attorney Inglimo was not being loyal to him.

23 The referee also found that M.S. had instructed Attorney Inglimo to provide copies of all communications between Attorney Inglimo and K.S. Attorney Inglimo admits that there were e-mails sent between him and K.S. that were not given to M.S. Attorney Inglimo claims that the e-mails were all business-related and that he deleted them immediately after they were sent or received. He asserted that M.S. never asked to receive copies of the e-mails until after they had been deleted.

24 The referee did not make a finding that Attorney Inglimo and K.S. were engaging in a sexual relationship during Attorney Inglimo's representation of M.S. because no one testified that they had personally witnessed the two engaging in sex. He did find, however, that Attorney Inglimo's admission of sex with K.S. within a few days after being fired by M.S. showed at least a substantial social relationship during Attorney Inglimo's representation of M.S. and a desire on Attorney Inglimo's part to pursue his own selfish interests.

25 Based on these factual findings, the referee concluded that Attorney Inglimo had violated SCR 20:1.7(b) because his representation of M.S. may have been materially limited by his own interests and because he never consulted with his client or obtained his client's written consent to his social relationship with K.S.

In sum, the Supreme Court held that Mr Inglimo, in his capacity as a criminal defense attorney and a divorce attorney, had engaged in improper sexual relationships with clients and their wives – sometimes in exchange for legal services; had improperly accessed client funds; and had participated in criminal activity with a client in violation of the client's parole. Accordingly, his license to practice law was suspended and it remains so as of this writing.

PRE-TRIAL ETHICAL ISSUES

Prior to trial, there are a number of ethical issues that a defense attorney must contend with, even before they accept the case. These include an evaluation of their resources, caseload, and professional competence with respect to the charges and issues involved in the case. This also involves requires reviewing the salient case facts and determining whether a plea deal is appropriate.

Reading the Case File

As with prosecutors in Chapter 9, and owing to an overwhelming caseload or lack of professional organization, it is not uncommon for some attorneys to refrain from learning the facts of their client's case until just before trial.

They might give the file a cursory look when initially assigned or they might just take a short briefing from a client, accept a retainer, and not look any further until the are compelled to by the trial schedule. Again, this means that important time-sensitive details can get missed, witnesses might not get interviewed or checked out, experts might not get hired in a timely fashion, and physical evidence favorable to the defense might not get recognized or tested.

Competence and Qualifications

As mentioned previously, criminal defense attorneys have an obligation to refrain from representing clients in cases that are outside of their general practice area. Divorce lawyers should not be representing defendants accused with homicide and malpractice attorneys have no business representing a defendant facing capital murder. Yet this happens in courtrooms every day, often at the instruction of an unsympathetic judge appointing counsel due to considerations like availability and personal relationships, as opposed to competent and qualifications.

The ethical criminal defense attorney will capably recognize those cases outside of their scope and competence, and decline to take them in the interest of justice for the defendant.

Resources and Caseload

Some cases are more complex than others, requiring tremendous resources to investigate, brief, and try. The ethical defense attorney has an obligation to determine, up front, whether they actually have the resources (e.g., investigators, paralegals, co-counsel) and the time to effectively represent the client all the way through trial. This issue is discussed thoroughly in Freedman (2005, pp. 920–921):

> In order to allow zealous investigation and research, defense counsel is forbidden to carry a workload that interferes with this minimum standard of competence, or one that might lead to the breach of other professional obligations. "The basic rule … is that the lawyer's total loyalty is due to *each* client in *each* case." This basic rule is violated whenever there is a significant *risk* that the lawyer's ability to consider, recommend or carry out an appropriate course of action for a client will be materially limited as a result of the lawyer's responsibilities to other clients. Thus, whenever a lawyer accepts one too many clients – to say nothing of 20, 50, or several hundred too many clients – she is involved in a conflict of interest, because total loyalty cannot be given to each client in each case. What follows from that is that any new client who presents a conflict of interest "must be declined."

Moreover, a lawyer is required to withdraw from a case if the representation will result in a violation of the rules of professional conduct or other law. Indeed, if a lawyer finds that she has failed to provide effective representation, she is required to explain her failure of competence to the defendant and to seek to withdraw from the case, with an explanation to the court of the reason for her motion for leave to withdraw.

These professional rules and standards make it clear that pattern representation, in which the lawyer hastily categorizes cases on the basis of insufficient information, is professionally unacceptable.

In short, if an attorney determines that they lack the time and resources to effectively represent a client, they have an ethical obligation to make this clear to the defendant and then decline the case.

Plea Deals

Many criminal cases are plead out or dismissed because of deals struck with the prosecution. In fact, the criminal justice system is generally structured to force plea deals – to leverage frightened defendants into a position where they feel compelled to plead guilty, in order to avoid more serious charges and increased ail time. Often this is the result of overcharging, as discussed in Chapter 9.

The question for the ethical defense attorney is whether to advise a client to accept a plea deal when they fully believe in their client's innocence. This, while at the same time, understanding that the prosecution has the capability of convicting a ham sandwich of just about anything in most cases. Such injustice is possible because the criminal justice system often places more value on procedural swiftness than accurate fact development and just adjudication. If the attorney advises their client to decline a plea deal that has been put on the table by the prosecution, the client may be exposed to additional charges and a significantly longer sentence. In other words, if they fight the charges then they risk losing – big.

The ethical defense attorney has an obligation to lay all of this out for their client, and not to encourage them to accept any plea deal without fully understanding the consequences. Ultimately, it must be the client's decision.

ETHICAL ISSUES AT TRIAL

In the courtroom, criminal defense attorneys have an obligation to conduct themselves in a professional and honorable fashion. This includes avoiding the following forms of misconduct (Gershman, 1997):

(1) Offering false evidence.
(2) Offering inadmissible evidence.

(3) Misstating the evidence.
(4) Questions in bad faith (questions that imply evidence exists when it actually does not).
(5) Disobeying an order from the judge.
(6) Rudeness and derogatory or offensive remarks directed at the court or the prosecution.
(7) Improper arguments to the jury.
(8) Failure to abide the rules of discovery.
(9) Obstructing access to evidence and witnesses.

The ethical defense attorney also has an obligation to avoid what is referred to as *ineffective assistance of counsel*. As discussed throughout this chapter, this refers to defense attorney conduct that undermines the proper functioning of the adversarial process to the extent that the trial cannot be relied on as having produced a just result (*Strickland v. Washington*, 1984). It includes things like (Gershman, 1997):

(1) Failing to investigate a potential defense.
(2) Failing to present crucial evidence.
(3) Failing to impeach a prosecution witness.
(4) Opening the door to damaging evidence.
(5) Failing to object to prosecutorial misconduct.
(6) Failing to object to discriminatory jury strikes.
(7) Failure to communicate a plea offer.
(8) Client abandonment (e.g., conceding reasonable doubt, or guilt, in closing arguments).

Ineffectiveness claims can also be based on what Gershman (1997) refers to as "deprivation of counsel" (p. 228). This can be demonstrated by the following conditions:

(1) The defense attorney's physical absence from the courtroom (e.g., missed court dates or absence from the courtroom for extended periods during the trial).
(2) Physical or mental impairment (e.g., physical illness, mental illness, alcohol abuse, or drug use and abuse during trial).
(3) Incompetence to the point of effective abandonment.
(4) Conflicted representation, as discussed previously in this chapter.

Deprivation of counsel will often result in the failure of defense counsel to recognize prosecutorial misconduct in the courtroom and then also to fail in their duty to object to it in order to preserve the issue on the record for appeal. In their research on prosecutorial misconduct, Ridolfi and Possley (2010) determined that this was a major failing on the part of the defense (pp. 40–41):

In the 78 waiver cases, appellate courts refused to consider the claims of prosecutorial misconduct because the defense attorneys failed to make a timely or proper objection at trial sufficient to preserve the matter for appellate review. To avoid waiving a claim of prosecutorial misconduct, defense attorneys must satisfy strict and formal requirements: they must object to the prosecutor's specific actions, cite the actions as prosecutorial misconduct and request that the trial judge specifically instruct the jury about the misconduct. Failure to satisfy any one of these requirements can result in the permanent loss of appellate review of the issue .... Courts refrained from making a ruling on the issue of prosecutorial misconduct and instead held that any error would have been harmless or refused to consider the issue because the defense failed to make a proper objection in 282 cases.

Such a failure on the part of the defense is, again, evidence of ineffective assistance.

Ineffective assistance of counsel, when it meets the requirements set forth in *Strickland*, can result in *reversible error* – which is a trial error that is so harmful to justice that it requires some or all of the elements of a conviction to be overturned; these reversals are submitted for reconsideration by the court, if not retrial.

For example, consider the case of 31-year-old Ronda Watts out of Pennsylvania. A criminal defendant, Ms Watts was convicted of one count of criminal homicide in the 2007 death of her 2-year-old daughter. She originally plead guilty in 2009, but her first lawyer failed utterly in his efforts to defend her. This had resulted in a first-degree murder verdict, as explained by the court in Ward (2013):

> What an Allegheny County Common Pleas Judge David R. Cashman called some of the "worst" lawyering he had ever seen meant the difference Friday between life in prison without parole and a sentence of six to 12 years.
>
> Ronda Watts, who suffered from postpartum psychosis when she killed her 2-year-old daughter in 2007, pleaded guilty to a general count of criminal homicide on Wednesday.
>
> ...
>
> Watts, 31, pleaded guilty in 2009 to the same general count of criminal homicide. Her then-defense attorney, James Sheets, who had postponed the case five times, failed to present any evidence on the woman's behalf, including a lengthy history of mental illness, featuring a previous bout of postpartum depression.

Based on that lack of evidence, Judge Cashman found Watts guilty at the time of first-degree murder, which carries a mandatory prison term of life with no chance for parole.

"It was probably one of the worst performances I've ever seen," Judge Cashman said of Watts' first hearing. "I had no picture of you other than a cold-blooded murderer who could suffocate her own daughter."

....

Watts obtained a new lawyer, Thomas N. Farrell, and quickly filed a request to withdraw her plea based on ineffective assistance of counsel.

According to investigators, Watts called police to report Bryonna missing on Jan. 11, 2007.

Officers searching the home found the girl in a cardboard box in a bedroom closet with a plastic bag over her head. Her body was still warm, but she was pronounced dead.

During a police interview, Watts first denied knowing how the girl died, but she later confessed.

She told detectives her daughter had complained of a sore throat and would not stop crying. Watts said she put her hand over Bryonna's mouth to quiet her and the girl passed out and fell to the floor.

The woman told detectives she suffered from postpartum depression after her then-4-month-old son was born.

On Friday, in a statement by Watts read by Mr Farrell, she said she had been taking medication at the time, but when she started to feel better, she stopped.

In that statement, Watts thanked Judge Cashman for giving her a second chance.

"My guilt and shame that I carry because of what happened on Jan. 11, 2007, can't even be described," she said. "If I would not have been so scared to tell my husband or family members about the voices, things would be different, and you would never know who I was."

...

After taking on the case, Mr Farrell had his client evaluated by a psychiatrist and submitted to the court voluminous medical records documenting the woman's struggles with postpartum depression, as well as sexual abuse she endured as a child.

Subsequent to a review of the full record as established and presented by the new defense attorney, Judge Cashman was compelled to find Ms Watts guilty of third-degree murder. This was because he found that there was no evidence of intent to kill, given the totality of the circumstances. Judge Cashman added that: "Any sentence I impose upon you is not going to bring your daughter back, and it won't change the knowledge that you are responsible for that death" (Ward, 2013). He sentenced Ms Watts to 6–12 years in prison. In accordance with this sentence, she was immediately eligible for parole.

SUMMARY

This chapter reviews the major ethical issues and questions peculiar to criminal defense attorneys as they represent their clients. While it is not possible to consider or anticipate every dilemma faced by those advocating for criminal defendants, the authors discuss the most significant issues as they have experienced them. Specific ethical considerations are discussed across the following subjects: the *right to counsel*, the *presumption of innocence*, and ethical issues that occur *prior to and during trial*. This is preceded by a review of basic defense attorney types, their functions, and the defense attorney's often conflicted roles.

Questions

1. Explain the significance of the US Supreme Court's ruling in *Gideon v. Wainwright*.
2. List the four primary types of criminal defense attorneys in the United States.
3. Criminal defense attorneys are obligated to protect their client's interests and can only act against them in extraordinary circumstances. Explain.
4. Define *ineffective assistance of counsel*. Provide three examples.
5. Does attorney–client privilege extend to *work-product*? Explain.
6. Explain what is meant by "couch fee." Are there exceptions to this rule?
7. List three pre-trial ethical issues.

References

Aviel, R., 2011. When the state demands disclosure. Cardozo Law Review 33 (2), 675–736.

Ax, J., 2013. Lawyer barred from federal court for stealing client funds. Thompson-Reuters News and Insight, March 18; url: http://newsandinsight.thomsonreuters.com/Legal/News/2013/03_-_March/Lawyer_barred_from_federal_court_for_stealing_client_funds/.

Black, H.C., 1990. Black's Law Dictionary, sixth ed. West Publishing, St Paul, MN.

Demare, C., 2009. Lawyer guilty of sex with client. Albany Times-Union, September 24; url: http://www.timesunion.com/local/article/Lawyer-guilty-of-sex-with-client-555084.php.

Flowers, R., 2010. The role of the defense attorney: not just an advocate. The Ohio State Journal of Criminal Law 7 (2), 647–652.

Freedman, M., 2005. An ethical manifesto for public defenders. Valpraiso University Law Review 39 (4), 911–923.

Gershman, B., 1997. Trial Error and Misconduct. Lexis Law, Charlottesville, VA.

Gershman, B., 2011. Judicial interference with effective assistance of counsel. Pace Law Review 31 (2), 560–582.

Gideon v. Wainwright, 1963. US Supreme Court, 372 US 335.

Giesel, G., 2011/2012. End the experiment: the attorney–client privilege should not protect communications in the allied lawyer setting. Marquette Law Review 95 (2), 475–561.

Hardaway, R., 2008. Beyond a conceivable doubt: the quest for a fair and constitutional standard of proof in death penalty cases. New England Journal on Criminal and Civil Confinement 34 (2), 221–289.

In Re: Inglimo, 2007. Disciplinary Proceedings, Wisconsin Supreme Court, No. 2005AP718-D, April 26.

Martinez v. Ryan, 2012. 132 S.Ct. 1309, 1317.

Michmerhuizen, S., 2007. Confidentiality, privilege: a basic value in two different applications. Center for Professional Responsibility, American Bar Association website, url: http://www.americanbar.org/content/dam/aba/administrative/professional_responsibility/confidentiality_or_attorney.authcheckdam.pdf.

Moorman, R.H., 2010. No sex, no lies: engagement agreements and other issues in light of the new/proposed disciplinary rules. State Bar of Texas 34th Annual Advanced Estate Planning and Probate Course, San Antonio, TX, 23–25 June; url: http://www.texasbarcle.com/Materials/Events/9183/121705_01.pdf.

Nelson, J., 2008. Facing up to wrongful convictions: broadly defining 'new' evidence at the actual innocence gateway. Hastings Law Journal 59 (3), 711–729.

Ridolfi, K., Possley, M., 2010. Preventable Error: A Report on Prosecutorial Misconduct in California 1997–2009. Northern California Innocence Project at Santa Clara University School of Law, Santa Clara, CA.

Strickland v. Washington, 1984. US Supreme Court, No. 82–1554, 466 US 668.

Uphoff, R., 2011. Handling physical evidence: guidance found in ABA Standard 4–4.6. Criminal Justice 26 (2), 1–14.

United States v. Cronic, 1984. US Supreme Court, 466 US 648, 656.

Vielmetti, B., 2012. Defense lawyers in fetus abduction case accused of conflict of interest. The Milwaukee Journal-Sentinel, February 21; url: http://www.jsonline.com/news/crime/defense-lawyers-in-fetus-abduction-case-accused-of-conflict-of-interest-nl49jcl-139932513.html.

Ward, P., 2013. Judge criticizes lawyer, reduces sentence: woman pleaded guilty to killing her daughter, 2, in 2007. Pittsburgh Post-Gazette, March 23; url: http://www.post-gazette.com/stories/local/neighborhoods-city/judge-criticizes-lawyer-reduces-sentence-680484/.

Waxman, S., 2013. Pleading out: America's broken public defense system. Los Angeles Review of Books, March 18; url: http://lareviewofbooks.org/article.php?id=1508.

Wilson, M., 2007. Due process for the past due: a legal aid attorney's account of the indigent experience in today's criminal justice system. DePaul Journal for Social Justice 1, 29–49, (Fall).

CHAPTER 11

Judicial Ethics

Ronald Miller and Brent E. Turvey

[handwritten annotation] — requsil — requsis themselves from case, I can't hear this, I may have a conflict of interest. Judge steps away bec they know someone in the case.

Key Terms

Admissibility "As applied to evidence ... means that the evidence introduced is of such character that the court or judge is bound to receive it; that is, allow it to be introduced at trial" (Black, 1990).

Conflict of interest Occurs when a person or an agency has competing loyalties, or loyalties that are at odds, because of their need to satisfy multiple roles, duties, or obligations.

Embroilment Occurs when a judge becomes so involved in a case that they actually take sides.

Evidence "Testimony, writing, material objects, or other things presented to the senses that are offered to prove the existence or non-existence of a fact" (Black, 1990).

Forensic expert An individual qualified to testify by virtue of "knowledge, skill, experience, training, or education" at the discretion of the judge.

Judge Presides, impartially, over trials and appeals as a legal arbiter.

Judicial dispassion The court's obligation to conduct itself without emotion or bias.

Judicial independence The promise that "any litigant or lawyer appearing before a judge can be certain that the judge will rule according to the applicable rules and precedents without any external influence" (Abramson,1997, p. 752).

Judiciary The pillar of the criminal justice system that deals with the adjudication or criminal defendants to include exoneration, punishment, treatment, and efforts to reform.

Jury A group of men and women lawfully selected, convened, and sworn to investigate a legal dispute and then render an impartial finding in accordance with the law (adapted from Black, 1990).

Sentence The terms of punishment decided by the trier of fact.

Trier of fact A judge or jury responsible for determining the legal guilt or innocence of a criminal defendant. The trier also decides the sentence.

While admittedly not jurists ourselves, the authors have accrued a collective multidisciplinary courtroom experience of about 60 years. This includes time spent working as forensic scientists and testifying as expert witnesses; employed by law enforcement and the prosecution; and employed by the defense in an exhaustive number of capital murder trials. So, while lacking the experience that accumulates in the service of the judiciary, the authors have had appreciable occasion to observe and become acquainted

Ethical Justice. http://dx.doi.org/10.1016/B978-0-12-404597-2.00011-5

with judicial misconduct. It is that experience upon which we draw for the present effort.[1]

With all due respect to the court, and in furtherance of its mission of fairness and integrity, this chapter is focused on judicial ethics. That is to say, it is not focused on the many competent and ethical jurists that currently populate the bench in any given county or legal region, or those evidencing an understanding of their ethical responsibilities and able to abide accordingly. Rather, it is a review of ethical issues arising from those that some refer to as "bad judges": those who are guided by principles that are "incompetent, self-indulgent, abusive, or corrupt" and ultimately "terrorize courtrooms, impair the functioning of the legal system, and undermine public confidence in the law" (Miller, 2004, p. 431).

THE ROLE OF THE JUDICIARY

The *judiciary* is the branch of the criminal justice system that deals with the adjudication and exoneration or punishment of criminal defendants.[2] This includes everything from arraignment to acquittal; from sentencing to appeals. A judge or jury, referred to as the *trier of fact*, determines the legal guilt or innocence of a criminal defendant. Subsequently, the trier also decides the terms of punishment, also referred to as the *sentence*. Some of these cases will be taken before the appellate court, whether a function of defendant preference or a legal requirement associated with the most serious crimes. A short list of those involved in the judiciary includes magistrates, judges, court clerks, court appointed investigators, paralegals, court reporters, court bailiffs, and the jury, which is drawn from the local citizenry.

Judges preside over trials and appeals as legal arbiters. Judges have two primary roles in the service of the criminal justice system. First, they have a responsibility to ensure due process (i.e., fairness) in criminal trials. This is accomplished by interpreting the law and ruling on any legal questions that are raised – like a moderator. This is further accomplished by assisting the jury with their efforts, and then ruling on sentencing once the jury has rendered its verdict. Upon appeal, this involves a review of cases presided by other judges to ensure that any legitimate issues raised by the defense are addressed.

The second part of their role is in service of the criminal justice system as a whole. Judges have an obligation to police the courtroom and the courts for bad actors, which includes unethical attorneys and judges. Useful language

---

[1]For a blunt discussion of judicial ethics by a seasoned trial judge in the appellate court, see Kozinski (2004).
[2]Some parts of this chapter have been adapted from Petherick and Turvey (2010).

describing this last duty is found in a decision by the Texas Court of Appeals (*In re: J.B.K.*, 1996):

> We recognize our obligation not only to ensure the proper administration of justice in this Court but also our duty to the system of justice as a whole. We hasten to add that we are not merely the gatekeepers who monitor and patrol the conduct of members of the Bar. While we owe a duty to the legal system as a whole and to the administration of justice, we are ever mindful that the judiciary also has a duty to the lawyers who appear before them, to the public at large which elects them, and even to other members of the judiciary to ensure that our democracy is preserved and protected and that professionalism reigns supreme. We take this duty seriously.

The ethical obligations of judges therefore transcend any personal relationships they may hold or any political concerns they may suffer.

Miller (2004) offers a list of general categories associated with judicial abuse, each suggestive of corresponding ethical obligations (pp. 432–433):

> Most examples of bad judging can be grouped into the following categories: (1) corrupt influence on judicial action; (2) questionable fiduciary appointments; (3) abuse of office for personal gain; (4) incompetence and neglect of duties; (5) overstepping of authority; (6) interpersonal abuse; (7) bias, prejudice, and insensitivity; (8) personal misconduct reflecting adversely on fitness for office; (9) conflict of interest; (10) inappropriate behavior in a judicial capacity; (11) lack of candor; and (12) electioneering and purchase of office.

Additionally, Miller (2004) explains that there are strong motivators for violating judicial ethics and engaging in judicial misconduct (pp. 434–435):

> Bad judges get various rewards for influencing cases: goods, sex, debt relief, cash, or the satisfaction of helping out family, friends, lovers, employees, elected officials, and colleagues. Judges also accept gratuities. Although gifts may not themselves constitute bribery or extortion, they smack of impropriety when offered by lawyers or litigants with cases that may come before the judge.

In addition, they may also be motivated by the desire to protect themselves from the legal process or legal consequences, or in the furtherance of seeking revenge against their enemies.

While this chapter will not cover each of these general areas in depth, it will provide sufficient discussion and examples of those that are of greatest concern to the authors.

Judicial Integrity: Independence, Dispassion, and Bias

The integrity of the court, and its ability to serve the criminal justice system, rests almost entirely in the notion of *judicial independence*. This is the promise that "any litigant or lawyer appearing before a judge can be certain that the judge will rule according to the applicable rules and precedents without any external influence" (Abramson, 1997, p. 752). In the absence of judicial independence, any rulings wielded by the court have an immense capacity to improperly affect the outcome of a trial.

Part of the equation for achieving judicial independence is the requirement of *judicial dispassion*, which refers to the court's obligation to conduct itself without emotion or bias. As reported in Maroney (2011, p. 630):

> Is it ever appropriate for emotions – anger, love, hatred, sadness, disgust, fear, joy – to affect judicial decision making? In contemporary Western jurisprudence, there is only one accepted answer: no. A good judge should feel no emotions; if she does, she should put them aside and insulate the decision-making process from their influence ....
>
> In 2009 ... then-Judge Sonia Sotomayor testified at her Supreme Court confirmation hearing that judges "apply law to facts. We don't apply feelings to facts." The idea that emotion might influence judging has been characterized as "radioactive." Then and now, to call a judge emotional is a stinging insult, signifying a failure of discipline, impartiality, and reason.

Maroney goes on to explain that (p. 633): "Indeed, judicial dispassion has come to be regarded as a core requirement of the rule of law, a key to moving beyond the perceived irrationality and partiality of our collective past."[3]

This is echoed in Irwin and Real (2010), who explain that (pp. 1–2):

> For members of the judiciary, the very notion of impartial decision-making is codified in the Judicial Code of Conduct. It is in the very nature of being a judge to be an impartial and unbiased arbiter of the cases presented to the court for disposition. Most judges expend significant energy and thought consciously avoiding personal biases and prejudices in the decision-making process.

Failure to remain objective abandons the judicial role, devolving into what may be referred to as *embroilment*, which is when a judge becomes so involved in a case that they actually take sides. When a judge becomes embroiled in a case, they usually do so in such a manner as to risk assuming the role of

---

[3]Maroney (2011) goes on to argue that judicial emotions exist, that they affect judging, and that this is not always a bad thing.

prosecutor. This becomes evident when a judge assists the prosecution by suggesting motions, working to selectively exclude defense witness, engaging in defense witness interrogations in front of the jury, and by making discourteous or disparaging comments intended to undermine defense witness credibility.

The harsh reality is that much of what happens in a courtroom, or what does not happen, is a reflection of attorney concern stemming from unchecked judicial bias. Lawyers on both sides of the courtroom know all too well which judges favor the prosecution (or are married to prosecutors); which favor police officers (or are married to police officers); which have a poor or quick temper; and which judges simply do not like them, for whatever reason. Consequently, they observe judicial temperament and biased decision making everyday. They understand that their ability to be effective in court is often less a function of the law and their legal skills, all of which can easily take a back seat to judicial personality, temperament, and animosity (Maroney, 2011). Experience quickly teaches them which battles they can fight in which courtrooms and when to keep their heads down altogether. It is wholly improper for attorneys to be under the judicial heel in such a fashion, as the law is ultimately intolerant of that kind of judicial immaturity.

Consider, for example, the case of Clark County Superior Court Judge Edwin Poyfair in Washington State. As reported by the Washington State Commission on Judicial Conduct (*In re: Poyfair*, 2012):

> From an agreed statement of facts, the Commission found that Clark County Superior Court Judge Edwin Poyfair violated Canon 1 (Rule 1.2) and Canon 2 (Rules 2.2, 2.3(A) and (B), and 2.8(B) of the Code of Judicial Conduct when he failed to order the return of a child to her biological mother, when that mother tried to revoke her consent to a voluntary adoption. The mother had learned that the proposed adoptive father had a history of molesting girls. Judge Poyfair stipulated that he failed to recognize the mother's legal right to revoke her consent, and that he failed to provide adequate information as to obtaining counsel to the child's biological parents despite recognizing they had an absolute right to same, and he injected the legally irrelevant issue of the father's immigration status in an intimidating fashion, and displayed an impatient, undignified and discourteous demeanor in that and in a separate matter involving a custody dispute. The Commission censured Judge Poyfair and, because he retired from office shortly after the acceptance of the stipulation, imposed no other conditions.

The ethical jurist does not engage in such conduct, treating all who come before them with the same respect and consideration, regardless of their personal prejudices, mood, or current bedmates. They understand that everyone is entitled to the same justice and they do their part to ensure that this is possible.

Conflicts of Interest

As already defined in Chapter 9: "Ethical Issues for Criminal Prosecutors," a *conflict of interest* occurs when a person or an agency has competing loyalties, or loyalties that are at odds, because of their need to satisfy multiple roles, duties, or obligations. Judges are similar to attorneys in this regard, in that they must avoid not only impropriety, but even the appearance of impropriety when none actually exists. For example, as explained in Kozinski (2004, p. 1095) "everyone agrees that a judge may not sit in judgment in a case where he participated as a party or a lawyer" and "a judge may not participate in a case where doing so would create the appearance of impropriety."

When there is a conflict of interest, the judge must *recuse* themselves, as described in Bam (2011, p. 943):

> Recusal, which in certain circumstances requires a judge to step aside from hearing a case, is a doctrine that protects (some would say is *crucial* to protecting) both judicial impartiality and the appearance of impartiality. That a judge must be disinterested, and must appear disinterested, is universally accepted in American legal culture.

Judges consequently have an obligation to recognize when it is necessary to recuse themselves and to consider recusal even when the conflict is merely perceived by others. Only by doing so faithfully can they "ensure judicial independence and impartiality and to protect the legitimacy of the courts as well as the reputation of the judiciary" (Bam, 2011, p. 1003). This in turn helps to preserve the overall legal requirement of due process.

However, there are judges unafraid, or unconcerned, with openly flouting existing rules and conventions associated with these issues.

Many of these judges sit at the local level. Consider retired Craighead Circuit Court Judge David Burnett of Arkansas. In 1994, he presided over the criminal trials of the so-called "West Memphis 3": Jessie Misskelley, Jason Baldwin, and Damien Echols. Subsequent to their convictions for the murder of three young boys, Judge Burnett (also a close friend of Mr Misskelley's court appointed attorney, Dan Stidham) continued to preside over the circuit court decisions in these cases – including subsequent hearings regarding newly discovered evidence, evidence testing, and ineffective assistance of counsel (IAC).[4] As of 1 January 2009, he retired; however, he continued to serve as a "special judge" on the case for any appeals. Judge Burnett indicated that he felt an obligation to preside over any attack on these convictions, or those that helped to achieve them, in order to preserve what he believed was justice already served. It was not until after Judge Burnett was replaced by Judge David Laser in December of 2010 that the state offered the West Memphis 3 an Alford Plea in exchange for their immediate release – which they accepted in 2011.

Some of these judges also sit higher up, even on the US Supreme Court, as described in Bam (2011, pp. 964–965):

> … in the last decade alone, five current Supreme Court Justices – Justice Scalia, along with Justices Thomas, Ginsburg, Roberts, and Alito – have been embroiled in recusal-related controversies. Justice Scalia's denial of plaintiffs' recusal request in *Cheney v. United States District Court* is perhaps the most controversial incident in the last decade. In the underlying action, plaintiffs sought discovery regarding an Energy Advisory Panel that was convened by then-Vice President Dick Cheney. When the issue reached the Supreme Court, one of the plaintiffs asked Justice Scalia to recuse himself because while the appeal was pending, Scalia and Cheney took a duck hunting trip together. Justice Scalia denied the recusal motion, concluding that his impartiality could not reasonably be questioned.

The reality of recusal is that judges vary on whether and when they remove themselves from a case, often leaving it to the appellate court to decide whether or not they have made the right decision.

Knowledge of the Law

It is, ultimately, unethical to practice in any area that one is ignorant of. As mentioned already, judges are required to interpret the law and rule on the many legal questions that naturally arise in relation to a criminal trial. In order to do this, they have an ethical responsibility to be knowledgeable of the law

---

[4]One of the authors (Turvey) served as an expert for the defense in the appeals related to these cases. He also testified as to his findings in a Rule 37 (IAC) hearing before Judge Burnett, back in 1998. During one of the lunch breaks over several days of testimony, all parties and the judge broke bread together. At that time, the author was handed a stack of crime scene and autopsy photos that had not been provided to the defense previously. The author remarked that this was a concern, given the *Brady Rule* (*Brady v. Maryland*, 1963; see Chapter 9). The room went quiet and Judge Burnett stated firmly: "Mr Turvey, Brady versus Maryland is a federal ruling and you are in the state of Arkansas." Apparently, Judge Burnett was of the opinion that the rules on timely discovery were his to ignore on behalf of the state, which had been more than delinquent. That experience was truly an education in Arkansas justice.

in general; to read up on areas of relevant law when they are not; and to read all motions put before them so that they know their own limitations when anticipating the necessity of a ruling.

Unfortunately, too many judges are ignorant of the laws and legal procedures related to the cases brought before them. A percentage of these subsequently fail to admit their limitations, let alone rectify the situation with the required study. As discussed in Miller (2004, pp. 439–440):

> Bad judges may lack even slight command of the law. They confuse elementary burdens of proof and persuasion, misunderstand fundamental rights, rule prematurely, and generally display egregious ignorance of the rules that supposedly govern their decisions.

As this would suggest, these same judges also tend to bristle at the suggestion that reading the motions before them is necessary; they may feel strongly that legal rulings can be made based on oral arguments alone, without the need for examining the strengths and weaknesses of the statutes and case law being relied upon. In other words, judges are too often found shooting from the hip with respect to their reasoning, relying on heuristic intuition rather than deliberation of the established facts and relevant legal precedent.[5]

Time Allotment and Caseload

Many judges are capable of realistically evaluating their caseload in order to establish pre-trial and trial schedules. This in turn allows them to keep track of their obligations in each case, and allot the appropriate amount of time required for the issues anticipated and raised by attorneys on both sides. They also re-evaluate these schedules in light of significant developments. This gives everyone the time they need to adequately prepare for court, and generally helps to ensure fairness in the process. When it comes to the jury, appropriate time is given as well, with respect to breaks, providing meals, and the lateness of court.

Some judges, however, do little or none of this. They may fail to set pre-trial schedules, skip out on court, fail to set aside enough time for complex issues, and push back court dates to advantage one side over the other. They may also keep juries until unreasonable hours of the night during the trial, or in sequester, in order to rush the trial or force a verdict. As discussed in Miller (2004, p. 440): "Bad judges also procrastinate. Whether because of physical or emotional problems or simple laziness, they fail to rule on motions, set cases for trial, or issue decisions." Additionally, Miller explains (p. 441):

---

[5]For a discussion of research related to how judges make decisions, see Guthrie *et al.* (2007) and Irwin and Real (2010).

Poor administration can also be an issue. Bad judges lose evidence, misplace files, mismanage staff, and fail to keep account of the court's financial registry. They neglect official responsibilities by delegating them to law clerks, prosecutors, court clerks, and even law students and law professors!

Whichever the case, judges have an ethical obligation to attend their caseload and budget their time appropriately. This helps to avoid delays, trial by ambush, and professional disorganization. Failure to do so is unfair to attorneys, unfair to defendants, and places improper strain on the jury.

Consider, for example, the misconduct of Clark County District Court Judge Valorie Vega of Las Vegas, Nevada (Figure 11.1). She was accused of keeping juries far too long in order to reach a verdict and interrupting court during the day for personal reasons, as reported in Toplikar (2012):

> The ethics charges partly stem from Vega keeping the jury overnight to reach a verdict in Fakoya's retrial. Juries are regularly dismissed at the end of a workday and asked to return the next morning to continue deliberations.
>
> According to the complaint, to accommodate her personal schedule, Vega kept the jury, the attorneys and staff to conduct proceedings for almost 18 hours – from 1:12 p.m. on Dec. 16, 2010, until the jury returned with its acquittal verdict at 6:57 a.m. Dec. 17, 2010.

Initially, Judge Vega stated publicly that she would fight the charges, as they lacked merit. However, she admitted wrongdoing a year later, as reported in Ryan (2013):

FIGURE 11.1
Clark County District Court Judge Valorie Vega, of Las Vegas, Nevada, accepted a public reprimand from the Nevada Commission on Judicial Discipline for misconduct related to abuses of the jury in a murder trial.

Vega presided over the retrial of Victor O. Fakoya who was accused of first degree murder. She kept the jury overnight until 6:57 a.m. to reach a verdict.

The charge against Vega said she "did so for various reasons, including but not limited to her personal schedule and thus Respondent (Vega) was not courteous to the individuals involved at trial."

...

In November and December 2010, she recessed a trial in the court in early afternoon six times to attend her daughter's soccer games, according to the charges.

Ultimately, Judge Vega agreed to accept a public reprimand and admitted that she improperly recessed a trial on six occasions for personal reasons.[6]

IMPROPER INFLUENCE OVER THE JURY

A *jury* is a group of men and women lawfully selected, convened, and sworn to investigate a legal dispute, and then render an impartial finding in accordance with the law (adapted from Black, 1990).[7] Trial by jury is the constitutional right of US citizens, preserved by the Sixth Amendment to the US Constitution (Starr and McCormick, 2001).

During trial, the presiding judge maintains perhaps the single greatest influence over the jury. They make the rules, decide when the rules have been broken, and dole out any sanctions for infractions. In doing so, the judge also dictates when jurors must arrive for court in the morning; where and when they must wait before entering; when they can take breaks to eat or use the restroom; whether and when they may have contact with friends and family; and how late they must stay in court every evening. Poor decision making in these areas can create pressure and stress for jurors in a situation that is already going to have too much of both from everyone else involved.

Shaping the Facts

In each case, a judge rules on the admissibility of facts, evidence, witness testimony, and permissible case theory. This gives them tremendous power to direct the narrative or "story" that either attorney may use when arguing their side of the case. The judge shapes both the character of the facts, and any fact

---

[6]Judge Vega also presided over the first-degree murder re-trial of Kirsten Lobato in 2006, for the death of a homeless man (see original Case Example in Chapter 9). As explained in McCarty (2012): "The jury in her case deliberated until midnight and later found her guilty of voluntary manslaughter." One of the authors (Turvey) testified as a forensic expert in that case.

[7]This section is adapted from writing originally published in Turvey and Freeman (2012).

patterns, that are available for a jury to consider in their deliberations. For those unfamiliar with this reality, some explanation will be helpful.

Evidence, as explained in Black (1990), is "testimony, writing, material objects, or other things presented to the senses that are offered to prove the existence or non-existence of a fact." This is consistent with Lilly (1987, p. 2), which provides that evidence is "any matter, verbal or physical, that can be used to support the existence of a factual proposition." Evidence in a courtroom context is not a scientific designation; rather, it is a legal construct.

Consider that any fact or finding gathered in relation to a legal proceeding is considered evidence until a judge says it is not. For instance, documentation of a factual event may exist, such as a taped interview or a written confession or an exclusionary test result. However, a judge may determine that it is not admissible, for whatever reason, and that fact and any related documentation may not be considered by the jury as evidence at trial.

As direct result of this legal reality, the sum of evidentiary facts under consideration by a judge or jury in a given case generally does not represent the entire picture of known facts or findings. It represents a judge's interpretation and reduction of the evidence based on their determination of what is and is not admissible. According to Black (1990) *admissibility* "as applied to evidence ... means that the evidence introduced is of such character that the court or judge is bound to receive it; that is, allow it to be introduced at trial." Trial judges have broad discretionary authority with respect to deciding the admissibility of any proposed evidence. It is in reality a complex and inconsistently applied legal heuristic whereby a judge determines which facts and circumstances may actually be introduced as evidence based on a "material relevance" standard. Such determinations may be standardized for certain kinds of proposed evidence, or they may require an evidentiary hearing.

In any event, by the time the jury hears arguments and testimony, and sees the evidence, all of this has been heavily edited by the judge. Judicial editing profoundly changes the character of the trial that the jury sees. As such, the court has an obligation to take great care when blinding the jury, to ensure that this is done lawfully and without prejudice.

Access to Notes and Exhibits
The judge further controls the jury by deciding whether they may take written notes and which evidence, records, or testimony they may take with them into their deliberations (referred to as "exhibits"). Human memory is frail and imprecise. In cases where jurors are not allowed to take notes, they must rely on that memory when deliberating on the verdict. In cases where note-taking is permitted, those jurors who prepared the most complete notes can have an inordinate sway over others. Jurors also tend to take more

notes in the beginning and less over time as the trial progresses. This issue becomes increasingly important in lengthy trials that involve complex fact patterns or require an understanding of how to interpret complex physical evidence. The judge ultimately controls whether and how the jury is allowed to recall what they have experienced during the trial and the mechanism by which they may refresh their memory when important details become a matter of dispute.

Telegraphing Bias

Apart from imposing many procedural influences over the jury that affect their capability and temperament, the judge also wields tremendous influence over the emotional content of the courtroom by virtue of their own professional conduct. The judge is the only person in court who can speak to anyone and everyone at any time and often in any manner that they see fit. A judge's manner and tone, intentional and otherwise, can improperly telegraph their personal agenda or preferences to the jury. This can be the result of general intolerance and impatience with attorneys resulting from a strained relationship, as they tend to see the same legal players playing the same legal games despite numerous advisements from the bench. This can also be the result of an improper pro-prosecution bias, as many judges are former prosecutors themselves.

Judges may conduct themselves improperly toward the defendant or defense witnesses. This includes assuming the role of the advocate (acting as a backup prosecutor), openly conveying skepticism or disbelief, active disinterest (such as sleeping through or otherwise ignoring testimony), disparaging remarks, and obvious character attacks. This also includes improper remarks that disparage witness credibility, the use of sarcasm and ridicule, and racial, ethnic, or other derogatory remarks (Gershman, 1997). When this kind of judicial behavior takes place in front of the jury, a prejudicial message is unavoidable. The jury will perceive that the judge believes the defense and their witnesses are deserving of the court's admonitions and hostility – and are therefore less credible. If the judge treats the defense and its case as less credible, then the jury is going to have a hard time to seeing them in any other light.

Favoritism and Vouching

The judge engages in improper conduct toward the prosecution and its witnesses by virtue of eliciting favorable proofs, acts of advocacy for the prosecution, vouching for character or testimony, or any other form of obvious favoritism (Gershman, 1997). If this type of judicial behavior takes place in front of the jury, the message, again, is all too clear: the prosecution is deserving of favor and therefore is deserving of preferential treatment, which equates to greater credibility. If the judge treats the prosecution as more credible, then it will likely be viewed by the jury in the same fashion because of the power structure inherent in their relationship.

ETHICAL ISSUES WITH EXPERTS

The court has unparalleled power with respect to expert witnesses. The trial court judge in particular decides whether a proffered witness is actually an expert and in which areas; they decide which areas of testimony are admissible in court (irrespective of expert qualification); they decide when an expert may testify; they decide the limits of cross-examination (if any); and they can intervene to interrupt or question experts at any point. All of this without the necessity of specialized education, training, or experience in the subject matter before them. Ethical judges are mindful of this limitation, and allow the expert to explain their knowledge, skills, and abilities in an unbiased fashion before the court in order to learn what they might not actually know. Impatient and otherwise biased judges believe themselves the final arbiter of all facts, legal and scientific alike, and will not be told otherwise by anyone.

Ideally, there are guidelines intended to help judges with decisions related to expert funding and qualification. However, they are only guidelines and are therefore often ignored.

Ake v. Oklahoma: Funding Parity with the Prosecution

In the United States, every defendant is entitled to an adequate defense, which includes reasonable access to scientific expert assistance should the need arise. This stems from the right of the accused to due process. This was explained by the US Supreme Court decision in *Ake v. Oklahoma* (1985):

> This Court has long recognized that when a State brings its judicial power to bear on an indigent defendant in a criminal proceeding, it must take steps to assure that the defendant has a fair opportunity to present his defense. This elementary principle, grounded in significant part on the Fourteenth Amendment's due process guarantee of fundamental fairness, derives from the belief that justice cannot be equal where, simply as a result of his poverty, a defendant is denied the opportunity to participate meaningfully in a judicial proceeding in which his liberty is at stake. In recognition of this right, this Court held almost 30 years ago that once a State offers to criminal defendants the opportunity to appeal their cases, it must provide a trial transcript to an indigent defendant if the transcript is necessary to a decision on the merits of the appeal. *Griffin v. Illinois*, 351 U.S. 12 (1956). Since then, this Court has held that an indigent defendant may not be required to pay a fee before filing a notice of appeal of his conviction,

Burns v. Ohio, 360 U.S. 252 (1959), that an indigent defendant is entitled to the assistance of counsel at trial, *Gideon v. Wainwright*, 372 U.S. 335 (1963), and on his first direct appeal as of right, *Douglas v. California*, 372 U.S. 353 (1963), and that such assistance must be effective. See *Evitts v. Lucey*, 469 U.S. 387 (1985); *Strickland v. Washington*, 466 U.S. 668 (1984); *McMann v. Richardson*, 397 U.S. 759, 771, n. 14 (1970). Indeed, in *Little v. Streater*, 452 U.S. 1 (1981), we extended this principle of meaningful participation to a "quasi-criminal" proceeding and held that, in a paternity action, the State cannot deny the putative father blood grouping tests, if he cannot otherwise afford them.

Meaningful access to justice has been the consistent theme of these cases. We recognized long ago that mere access to the courthouse doors does not by itself assure a proper functioning of the adversary process, and that a criminal trial is fundamentally unfair if the State proceeds against an indigent defendant without making certain that he has access to the raw materials integral to the building of an effective defense. Thus, while the Court has not held that a State must purchase for the indigent defendant all the assistance that his wealthier counterpart might buy, see *Ross v. Moffitt*, 417 U.S. 600 (1974), it has often reaffirmed that fundamental fairness entitles indigent defendants to "an adequate opportunity to present their claims fairly within the adversary system," *id.*, at 612. To implement this principle, we have focused on identifying the "basic tools of an adequate defense or appeal," *Britt v. North Carolina*, 404 U.S. 226, 227 (1971), and we have required that such tools be provided to those defendants who cannot afford to pay for them. To say that these basic tools must be provided is, of course, merely to begin our inquiry.

The Supreme Court's decision in *Ake* basically held that because the government has overwhelming access to manpower, money, and forensic experts, the defense must be given parity if the criminal justice system is to function equitably (recall Chapter 9, regarding prosecutorial budgets and expenditures). This ruling is of course an ideal. The reality is that not every judge and lawyer understands and invokes *Ake* appropriately or consistently, as explained in Findley (2008, pp. 929–931):

> … [T]he government has significantly greater access to forensic science services and experts than do most criminal defendants. Crime laboratories exist to provide such services to prosecutors; no corresponding institutions exist for defendants. And, because most defendants are indigent, their ability to hire experts is dependent on public funding of legal services to the indigent, which is abysmally inadequate in virtually every jurisdiction. Because funding for

indigent defense is so inadequate, defense services are rationed in ways that put innocents at risk; rationing disfavors expensive, substantive innocence claims (such as expensive litigation about the validity of forensic evidence), and instead favors more inexpensive procedural constitutional claims. While the Supreme Court in *Ake v. Oklahoma* recognized a constitutional right to publicly funded experts for the indigent, exercise of that right is dependent on the willingness of a local judge to order the expenditure of scarce local resources, and on a cumbersome case-by-case, expert-by-expert process for requesting funding. Any risk of failure of that case-by-case process to provide adequate expert services falls on the defendant, and courts have tended to apply *Ake* narrowly. That system comes nowhere close to providing the level of forensic sciences assistance that is needed, or that is available to the prosecution.

Without adequate access to independent scientific assistance in the examination of evidence, or even interpreting the government's findings, and set against the overwhelming resources of the government, due process cannot prevail. As explained in Giannelli (2005, p. 539):

In many criminal cases, securing the services of experts to examine evidence, to advise counsel, and to testify at trial is critical. As the commentary to the American Bar Association (ABA) Standards notes: "The quality of representation at trial ... may be excellent and yet unhelpful to the defendant if the defense requires the assistance of a psychiatrist or handwriting expert and no such services are available." As early as 1929, Justice Cardozo commented: "[U]pon the trial of certain issues, such as insanity or forgery, experts are often necessary both for the prosecution and for defense .... [A] defendant may be at an unfair disadvantage, if he is unable because of poverty to parry by his own witnesses the thrusts of those against him."

Similarly, Judge Jerome Frank observed in a 1956 opinion: "The best lawyer in the world cannot competently defend an accused person if the lawyer cannot obtain existing evidence crucial to the defense, e.g., if the defendant cannot pay the fee of an investigator to find a pivotal missing witness or a necessary document, or that of an expert accountant or mining engineer or chemist." He went on to observe: "In such circumstances, if the government does not supply the funds, justice is denied the poor – and represents but an upper-bracket privilege."

The ABA Standards require adequate access to experts for both the defense and prosecution, and there are some statutory provisions for defense experts. For example, the Criminal Justice Act provides for expert assistance for indigent defendants in federal trials. The Act, however, limits expenses for experts to $1,000.00 unless the court certifies that a greater amount is "necessary to provide fair compensation for services of an unusual character or duration." But, as Judge Weinstein has noted, "The Act's $1,000 limit for defense experts is far too low … and must be increased if due process is to be afforded defendants." Many states have comparable provisions, but the monetary limits are often incredibly low – until recently $250 maximum in capital cases in Illinois.

In *Ake v. Oklahoma*, [470 U.S. 68 (1985)] the Supreme Court recognized a due process right to a defense expert. The Court wrote: "[W]hen a State brings its judicial power to bear on an indigent in a criminal proceeding, it must take steps to assure that the defendant has a fair opportunity to present his defense." This fair opportunity mandates that an accused be provided with the "basic tools of an adequate defense." Nevertheless, some courts have attempted to limit this right to capital cases or to psychiatric experts. This narrow application fits the facts in *Ake* but not its rationale. Other courts have imposed demanding threshold standards for the appointment of defense experts. If the threshold standard is too high, the defendant faces a "catch-22" situation, in which the standard "demand[s] that the defendant possess already the expertise of the witness sought." A number of sources indicate that the lack of defense experts continues to be a problem for indigent defendants.

The bottom line is that criminal defendants are entitled to resources on par with the state when confronted by criminal charges from what is likely to be a well-funded prosecution. The judge has the authority, and the ethical obligation, to ensure that this happens. Otherwise, as is often the case, the state can more easily convict impoverished defendants – and being a poor defendant results in *de facto* guilt.[8]

Expert Qualification, Admissibility, and Treatment

A forensic *expert*, according to Federal Rule of Evidence (FRE) 702 (*Federal Rules of Evidence,* 2006), is qualified to testify by virtue of "knowledge, skill, experience, training, or education" at the discretion of the judge. The entire concept of forensic expertise is a legal one, unrelated to science or scientific practice. Judges are meant to invoke standards for the admissibility of experts, such as

---

[8]In the many miscarriages of justice that are overturned each month around the nation, few tend to involve wealthy defendants or those afforded due process in the form of adequate access to funding. In fact, the opposite is more likely to be true (see, generally, Garrett, 2011).

Frye, Daubert, or *Kumho,*[9] to screen out junk science or unproven methods of analysis. As already mentioned, these are guidelines only and not strict requirements; trial court judges have broad discretion with respect to admissibility of all things – to include experts and expert testimony.

In reality, judicial rulings on expert admissibility are partial to say the least, as discussed in Moreno (2004, pp. 3–4):

> Judges routinely admit expert testimony offered by prosecutors, but frequently exclude expert testimony offered by the defense. A review of federal criminal court cases reveals that 92% of prosecution experts survive defense challenges while only 33% of defense experts survive challenges by federal prosecutors. A recent study of federal appellate criminal cases found that more than 95% of prosecutors' experts are admitted at trial, while fewer than 8% of defense experts are allowed to testify. Why do judges consistently fail to scrutinize prosecution experts? Maybe it is the uniform. The most common prosecution expert witness is a police officer or a federal agent. In state and federal criminal trials, law enforcement experts are routinely permitted to testify to opinions and conclusions derived from their on-the-job experience and personal observations. Prosecutors rely on police officer experts most frequently in narcotics cases. In drug cases, law enforcement experts are often asked to interpret ambiguous words or phrases used by the defendant and/or his coconspirators. The purpose of, and problem with, this expert testimony is that it tells jurors precisely which inculpatory inferences they should draw from the factual evidence.

Judges have an ethical duty to refrain from pro-prosecution bias with respect to qualifying anything with a badge as an expert – as is too often the case. They must evaluate each expert on objective criteria having nothing to do with which side they work for or whether their decision will effect other cases (e.g., disqualifying a law enforcement expert can affect every case that they work on from that point forward).

For example, consider the case of Judge Ronald Himel from Cook County, Illinois. He was given a novel and creative punishment for what is generally reported as outrageous judicial conduct (conduct that is actually quite

---

[9]*Frye v. United States* (1923) requires that expert testimony be generally accepted by the relevant scientific community; in *Daubert v. Merrell Dow Pharmaceuticals, Inc.* (1993), the Supreme Court held that Rule 702 superseded *Frye,* requiring scientific testimony to be "not only relevant, but reliable;" in *Kumho Tire Co. v. Carmichael* (1999), the Supreme Court held that *Daubert* "applies not only to testimony based on 'scientific' knowledge, but also to testimony based on 'technical' and 'other specialized' knowledge." Each state has adopted its own guidelines related to some, all, or none of these rulings.

common in many courts). Judge Himel, who has a history of similar behavior, continuously interrupted a witness, argued with him, and then allowed him to be questioned by a group of visiting high-school students, as reported in Hanna (2002):

> For years, Himel's conduct has earned him a reputation of being a brash jurist with a tendency to speak his mind. But the criticisms have become particularly intense in recent months because of the way he handled the trial of three sheriff's officers accused of beating an inmate to death.
>
> ...
>
> Prosecutors in that case accused Himel of being biased, complaining about his frequent interruptions of their witnesses while constantly sparring with them during the bench trial. They took the unprecedented step of asking that the trial be started again before another judge, but the request was denied. Himel ultimately acquitted the three officers.
>
> Himel also was criticized for allowing high school students visiting his courtroom in March to question a witness who was testifying in a trial, a move legal experts said was improper, but one Cummins characterized as "innovative."
>
> Himel's supervisors suggested he take time off after the incident occurred, and Himel subsequently went on a three-week vacation beginning April 16.
>
> Judges are routinely provided legal training, and mentoring is often provided to those new to the bench. But some legal experts said it was unprecedented to ask a veteran judge to take a personal leave in order to submit to additional training and anger management classes.
>
> "I cannot recall any case where a judge was placed on, or agreed to go on personal leave or administrative leave in a situation where the judge was under scrutiny because of ill temperament," said Allan Sobel, executive vice president of the American Judicature Society.
>
> "I'm also not aware of a judge being placed on leave – voluntarily or involuntarily – because of using unorthodox procedures," Sobel said, referring to Himel's decision to allow the students to question the witness.
>
> The American Judicature Society is a non-profit organization of lawyers and judges that monitors the criminal justice system, including judicial ethics, throughout the country.
>
> Terrence Murphy, executive director of the Chicago Bar Association, called the response to the questions about Himel's conduct "a new approach."

"Given the publicity over what happened in Judge Himel's courtroom, for the chief judge to take a measure like this has to give the public confidence that the system is responsive," Murphy said.

...

Himel, 60, was appointed to the bench in 1984.

Even before the most recent controversy, Himel has been chastised by appeals courts for the way he handled cases.

He was once rebuked for interrupting a defense lawyer's closing arguments 45 times, and he was criticized for suggesting in one case that defense witnesses were "thieves, drug addicts," according to an appeals court ruling.

Despite suggestions that this kind of behavior is uncommon, defense counsel and non-law-enforcement experts called by the defense in criminal trials are acutely aware that such behavior from a sitting judge is not at all unusual. Hostility towards the defense and anyone seeking to help them is anticipated in the many less than professional courtrooms that exist. This is especially true when the judge is pro-law enforcement. In some instances, judges will actually bar the defense, or their experts, from saying anything that undermines law enforcement credibility – especially if it happens to be true.[10]

IMPROPER JUDICIAL BEHAVIOR

There are some judges that abuse their positions of authority by engaging in behavior that is improper for someone in their position of authority. Some of these are described in Miller (2004, p. 441):

Bad judges display poor judgment and inappropriate behaviors when acting in their judicial capacities. They curse in open court and in professional relationships. They visit pornographic web sites from chambers, leaf through lingerie catalogs in court, ask rape victims for dates, and have sex with bailiffs, secretaries, law clerks, court reporters, paroled felons, and spouses of defendants awaiting sentencing.

---

[10]In *Mississippi v. Robert Grant*, one of the authors (Turvey) was instructed by the judge to assume that the investigation conducted by law enforcement was competent and missed nothing in any expert testimony given. The author had discovered that key evidence in the case had been photographed and not collected (e.g., a weapon that had been used to strike the victim with blood on it and the bloody shoes of suspects at the scene). Also, the bullet that had killed the victim was missed by law enforcement crime scene efforts; the author re-examined the scene and collected the bullet himself. The judge forbid any mention of these facts and no criticism of the police was allowed. This is not an uncommon instruction from the trial judge to a defense expert.

Judges have further been caught "sexting" explicit photos to their court officers (Langlois, 2012) and trading jobs for sex (McDade, 2013). There are also a surprising number of established incidents that involve judges masturbating while court is in session. For example, consider the case of former Oklahoma District Judge Donald Thompson (Figure 11.2). He was accused of using a penis pump in court, lied about it, and ultimately paid the price, as reported by Associated Press (2006):

> A former judge convicted of exposing himself while presiding over jury trials by using a sexual device under his robe was sentenced Friday to four years in prison.
>
> Donald Thompson had spent almost 23 years on the bench and had served as a state legislator before retiring from the court in 2004. He showed no reaction when he was sentenced.
>
> At his trial this summer, his former court reporter, Lisa Foster, testified that she saw Thompson expose himself at least 15 times during trial between 2001 and 2003. Prosecutors said he also used a device known as a penis pump during at least four trials in the same period
>
> ...
>
> Thompson, a married father of three grown children, testified that the penis pump was given to him as a joke by a longtime hunting and fishing buddy.

FIGURE 11.2
In 2006, Oklahoma District Judge Donald Thompson was convicted of four counts of indecent exposure, after being caught using a penis pump to masturbate himself in court on multiple occasions.

"It wasn't something I was hiding," he said.

He said he may have absentmindedly squeezed the pump's handle during court cases but never used it to masturbate.

Foster told authorities that she saw Thompson use the device almost daily during the August 2003 murder trial of a man accused of shaking a toddler to death. A whooshing sound could be heard on Foster's audiotape of the trial. When jurors asked the judge about the sound, Thompson said he hadn't heard it but would listen for it.

Police built a case against the judge after a police officer testifying in a 2003 murder trial saw a piece of plastic tubing disappear under Thompson's robe. During a lunch break, officers took photographs of the pump under the desk.

Investigators later checked the carpet, Thompson's robes and the chair behind the bench and found semen, according to court records.

In 2006, former Judge Thomas was convicted of four counts of indecent exposure, with a sentence of 1 year in prison and $40 000 in fines. In 2008, he was disbarred by the state supreme court.

JUDICIAL ALERTNESS DURING TRIAL

Ruling competently and impartially on matters related to the facts and evidence presented during a criminal trial requires the undivided attention of the court. This means that judges have an obligation to be physically and mentally present when hearing evidence and arguments from either side.

Unfortunately, judges can routinely be observed in court engaged in the following activities, paying little or no attention to attorneys and witnesses: sleeping, reading, taking personal calls, texting, playing solitaire on their computer (or some other game), and surfing the Internet. Most do so unapologetically, as there is typically no one in the courtroom that would dare report them out of either friendship or fear of reprisal. However, consider the case of Special Education Judge Larry Craddock. The elder jurist resigned from his position after he fell asleep for an extended period during a crucial hearing and film of the incident was released by the media (*Daily Mail* Reporter, 2012). Former Judge Craddock blamed his drowsiness on the side-effects of his medication.

As stated in Chapter 9, those making decisions in court to determine the course of justice and influence its outcome have an ethical obligation to do so while wholly sober. This means that they should not be under the influence of controlled substances, such as illegal drugs or alcohol. Even high doses of prescription medications can be observed to cause problems. Indications of improper courtroom behavior from an impaired officer of the court would include slurred speech, impaired reasoning, sluggishness or stumbling, paranoia, physical aggressiveness, inappropriate yelling or threats, and falling asleep or passing out.

If a jurist has a medical condition or is taking medication that impairs their mental functions, especially to the point of unconsciousness, then they have an obligation to take leave until they are capable or resign from the bench entirely. Sitting on the bench while not fit to hear cases for lack of being physically or mentally capable is not acceptable for what should be obvious reasons related to judicial competence and the defendant's right to due process.

If a jurist has a full-blown drug addiction, then others have an obligation to report. Drug addictions, including alcoholism, are commonly found in association with both unethical and criminal activity. For a sitting judge, the temptation to abuse the bench in furtherance of their addiction is too much to ignore. Consider, for example, the case of former Criminal Court Judge Richard Baumgartner in Knox County, Tennessee (Figure 11.3). As result of his drug addiction and related misconduct, the question immediately arose as to his fitness to sit on the bench and preside over cases. One of his colleagues, another judge, has already tossed out convictions presided over by Judge Baumgartner, as reported in Burke (2012):

> ... Other defendants are hoping for a similar outcome, and bids
> for new trials from the many people convicted in Baumgartner's

FIGURE 11.3
In 2011, Criminal Court Judge Richard Baumgartner pled guilty to one count of misconduct related to his drug abuse, at least some of which occurred during criminal trials. Investigators determined that his addiction also led to a pattern of unethical and criminal pill-seeking behavior.

court could overwhelm the criminal justice system in Knox County, Tennessee's third-largest county with more than 400,000 residents. Baumgartner was one of three judges in the county who heard felony cases.

"We're getting pleadings almost daily now from people in the penitentiary filing habeas corpus saying, 'Let me out too.' It's raining over here," said Knox County District Attorney General Randy Nichols.

Baumgartner left the bench to seek drug treatment before pleading guilty to misconduct. A special judge handed Baumgartner a sentence that allowed him to wipe the felony conviction off his record if he stayed out of trouble. The sentence also allowed Baumgartner to avoid jail time and keep his pension.

The judge who sentenced Baumgartner has since said he would have come down harder on him had he known the full details of the criminal investigation. The U.S. attorney's office is also investigating.

Baumgartner, 64, could not be reached for comment and his attorney didn't return phone calls seeking comment.

Baumgartner, a criminal court judge in Knoxville since 1992, got addicted to painkillers he was prescribed for pancreatitis caused by chronic alcoholism, according to the Tennessee Bureau of Investigation file. His physician told authorities that Baumgartner acknowledged being a pill addict but disregarded the doctor's advice to retire.

The district attorney went to Baumgartner in 2010 because he was concerned about the judge's health. Nichols said it was widely known that Baumgartner suffered a variety of health issues. "I never suspected narcotics," the prosecutor said.

Although only a small portion of the investigative file on the former judge has been released to the public, it shows a man completely consumed by his addiction.

The judge looked around for multiple doctors who would prescribe him oxycodone, hydrocodone and generic Xanax and Valium. When the prescriptions weren't enough, he turned to convicts he had punished – and their friends.

One of his suppliers was Deena Castleman, a woman who graduated from Baumgartner's drug court. Castleman told authorities that she regularly supplied the married judge with pills and sex, sometimes during breaks from court. The woman, who is nearly half his age and has a history of arrests, told TBI agents that she and the judge even engaged in sexual activity several times in the judge's chambers.

Castleman's name appears frequently in the investigative file. She told agents the judge sometimes paid her bills and provided money for her to make bail after she got arrested. She also said the judge falsified the results of a drug test after she tested positive for drugs.

...

The judge's sole misconduct charge stemmed from his dealings with Chris Gibson, a felon on probation in Baumgartner's court. He said the judge would come by his house every two to three days to buy pills.

Gibson told agents that Baumgartner was fast depleting his retirement fund buying pills, and the judge would sometimes make a drug deal during court breaks. The felon said he gave the judge an extra supply of pills when Baumgartner had to travel to Nashville so that an out-of-town jury could be picked to hear the murder case now overturned.

The investigative file has raised but not fully answered questions about whether Knox County court system officials knew about Baumgartner's drug problem and failed to report him. It indicates some people attributed the judge's bizarre behavior to his illness.

Baumgartner's secretary told investigators that the judge was so out of on some days that she'd have to reschedule hearings. The secretary, Jennifer Judy ... told agents that Baumgartner had previously battled an alcohol addiction and was treated for it. As time progressed "Baumgartner became visibly worse to the point that he could not function or carry on a conversation at times," she said.

Prosecutors also noticed problems. Two of them revealed to agents that they saw him swerving while driving home from the jury selection in Nashville, 180 miles west of Knoxville. The prosecutors called the judge on his cell phone to try to get him to pull over ....

The Tennessee Supreme Court has recently adopted tougher ethics rules that require judges to "take appropriate action" if they believe that another judge or a lawyer is impaired by drugs or alcohol. A judge could face discipline for failing to report another judge for being impaired, but the rules don't say what that punishment would be.

In March 2011, Judge Baumgartner stepped down from the bench, agreed to be disbarred, and pleaded guilty to one count of official misconduct.

REPORTING ATTORNEY MISCONDUCT

By now it should be clear that the *judiciary* is not above the law and must abide their own set of ethical obligations or else risk sanction. As mentioned, they also have a related duty to remain alert for, and report, ethics violations and misconduct committed by those in their courtroom. For example, consider the findings of Superior Court Judge Anne-Christine Massullo in San Francisco, as described in Ridolfi and Possley (2010, p. 7):

> An estimated 700 to 1,000 drug prosecutions were dismissed or dropped because prosecutors in the San Francisco District Attorney's Office failed to disclose damaging information about a police drug lab technician. In May, Superior Court Judge Anne-Christine Massullo found that prosecutors violated the constitutional rights of a vast number of defendants by failing to tell defense attorneys about problems relating to the lab technician who was engaged in cocaine-skimming. The judge found that a memo written by deputy district attorney Sharon Woo, expressing concerns about the lab technician being a less than reliable witness, showed that prosecutors "at the highest levels of the District Attorney's Office" knew about the problems, but the information was never disclosed to attorneys for defendants whose cases involved the technician's work. The failure "to produce information *actually in its possession* regarding [the technician] and the crime lab is a violation of the defendants' constitutional rights," the judge declared. The judge was highly critical of the District Attorney's Office for failing to have in place procedures designed to obtain and produce information for defense attorneys. The San Francisco District Attorney's Office has since instituted policies regarding evidence disclosure.

The drug lab technician in this case was Deborah Madden. One of the authors (Turvey) experienced the misconduct of the prosecutor's office first hand when testifying as an expert for the defense in *California v. Culton*. The author was there, in part, to testify regarding crime scene processing efforts by Ms Madden – as she had been the criminalist on scene. The prosecution became furious when the author explained that he did not seek out information about the homicide scene directly from Ms Madden because she was in fact a known fraud – and therefore unreliable. The prosecutor had attempted to conceal Ms Madden's identity by listing her as a witness under her maiden name. This began a line of questioning in which the author was able to explain exactly why this was so. When the infuriated prosecutor asked that the author's remarks be stricken, the judge in that case rightly told the prosecutor "stop asking questions that you don't want the answers to".

Unfortunately, there are judges that fail in their requirement to report ethical breaches and misconduct, discussed Abramson (1997, pp. 779–780):

> ... A judge's protection of colleagues and friends is an honorable and valued character trait which extends beyond personal benefit and subordinates the judge's well-being for others. Undoubtedly, a judge's

decision to remain silent may be preferable to the alternative course of action: reporting others and then enduring their likely response to the judge's report. Moreover, when a judge reports another judge or a lawyer, even one widely regarded as acting unethically, others may "blame" the notifying judge, whose status may diminish more than that of the reported offender. Understandably, what judge would want the reputation of a snitch? ....

Indeed, the silent judge may have integrity, but consider the price of the judge's silence: the unreported offensive conduct will continue to infest the legal system. Judges should demonstrate the responsibility to take action and thereby protect the court system they serve. The duty to provide unsolicited information seems fitting when rectifying unethical behavior is central to the continued credibility of an increasingly disparaged legal system. Moreover, the responsibility to communicate unprofessional behavior becomes all the more compelling when one considers that judges comprise the one group that is most likely to observe or receive information regarding others' misconduct.

These concerns are echoed in McMorrow *et al.* (2004, pp. 1427–1428):

Penetrating judicial motivation when regulating attorney conduct can be particularly challenging. We can envision several possible motivations. Judges are likely to be very concerned about the limits of their power or other aspects of their institutional role. Efficiency concerns are likely to be a dominant factor. In states with an elected judiciary, election pressures are perceived to influence a judge's actions on the bench. Judges may be concerned about collegiality among the judges on their court and/or for one's reputation as a fair-minded judge. Judges may also be cognizant and protective of the reputation of the attorney whose conduct is being questioned. These concerns may be very hard to ascertain from written opinions, particularly since the very concerns of efficiency, collegiality and reputation may encourage a judge to be silent or do nothing.

In the State of California, the issue of reporting misconduct is muddled by legal requirements. As explained in Ridolfi and Possley (2010, p. 9): "where courts find strong evidence pointing to the defendant's guilt, a prosecutor's misconduct, no matter how egregious, will not lead to reversal of the case." Moreover, they explain that: "In California, unless a case is reversed, there is no requirement that the misconduct be reported to the State Bar." What this means is that prosecutors are actually emboldened to engage in misconduct by the appellate court's unwillingness to overturn convictions – which is the only circumstance under which reporting is required.

However, the courts in California appear to be failing even when required to report misconduct, as observed in Ridolfi and Possley (2010, pp. 14–15):

Despite these mandates, there remains little evidence that courts are meeting even this limited reporting obligation. The reporting statute for courts does not afford a court the discretion to choose not to report misconduct it deems not egregious: it specifically requires reporting "*[w]henever* a modification or reversal of a judgment in a judicial proceeding is based in whole or in part on the misconduct, incompetent representation, or willful misrepresentation of an attorney." The statute evidences recognition that *any* conduct on which a modification or reversal is based, even in part, is serious enough to require notification of the State Bar concerning potential disciplinary investigation.

From 1997 through 2010, the Veritas Initiative has found evidence that courts noted in public rulings their intent to report misconduct on only eight occasions, two of those in 2010 ....

From 1997 to date, seven prosecutors have been disciplined publicly in California for misconduct in handling of criminal cases. No prosecutors were disciplined publicly by the State Bar in 2010. Private reprimands are not considered public discipline.

The reality is that the court has an ethical obligation to report misconduct regardless of the letter of reporting requirements. Otherwise, they knowingly allow the community of professionals serving in their courts to rot with respect to the quality of their character and conduct. They also foment a courtroom culture that embraces *noble cause corruption*[11] when they believe that a defendant is otherwise guilty – which is likely to be much of the time.

POST-CONVICTION ISSUES

Those unfamiliar with the criminal justice system might assume that factually innocent defendants can get their day in court on appeal, especially in light of the highly publicized exonerations that continue to occur around the United States almost weekly. What is often missed is the fact that such exonerations are a hard-earned labor that can take years of work by attorneys, investigators, and forensic experts.

The authors have worked many hours, over the course of many years, on such cases. They have over that time assisted with earning the exoneration or release of numerous wrongfully convicted criminal defendants. This experience has

---

[11]*Noble cause corruption* "is the belief that a war against crime is currently being waged against particular evils or societal ills (e.g., drugs, terrorism, gang violence), and that those working for law enforcement are on the only good or moral side of the conflict. By extension, anyone not working with or supporting law enforcement is on the wrong side of the conflict, protecting or practicing evil." (Turvey, 2013, p. 49). It is used to justify law enforcement and prosecutorial misconduct or criminal activity in the service of getting bad guys off the street.

taught us that one of the greatest hurdles to be cleared by the defense in such cases is the bias of the judiciary, which can block all manner of remedy on a whim.

To help us identify the most concerning issues post-conviction, with respect to judicial ethics and responsibilities, we asked for some help from a learned colleague. Professor Tiffany Murphy, JD, of the Oklahoma City University School of Law, serves as Director of the Oklahoma Innocence Project.[12] Based on her case experience, the following judicial issues are paramount, in state post-conviction:[13]

(1) Failure to understand the legal process. As at trial, judges often do not know the law or the correct procedures to follow post-conviction. Each day can bring with it a new battle against the ignorance of the court.

(2) Failure to provide adequate assistance of counsel in state post-conviction. As at trial, if convicted defendants are not properly represented they cannot get justice. The judge has tremendous influence over whether this becomes a reality.

(3) Not providing inmates discovery for their claims. Inmates are lawfully entitled to certain discovery material, even though they may be convicted and sitting in prison. Depriving them of it is a violation of their rights.

(4) Not allowing evidentiary hearings. Judges can agree to hear about evidentiary issues post-conviction or not. By refusing to hear such arguments, judges can effectively blind themselves, and the public, to the basis for inmate claims.

(5) Providing no forensic testing on DNA motions. Given the relatively low expense of modern DNA tests, refusing to grant motions for DNA testing of evidence originally collected by the state is akin to sticking one's head in the sand. It evidences bias, indicating that the court does not want to know the results of such DNA testing because it would prefer not to know the outcome.

(6) Not making the state look for evidence. In the course of post-conviction efforts, evidence is often identified that was not originally tested for DNA. When asked about its disposition, the answer from the state can be something along the lines of "we don't know where that is" or "that item might have been lost when we moved it to a new location." The court can instruct the state to look for the evidence, to determine its current state and location. Failing to do so deprives the defendant of access to potentially exculpatory evidence and encourages the state to be sloppy with evidence storage post-conviction – lest they threaten their convictions with good record-keeping.

---

[12]One of the authors (Turvey) also works for Oklahoma City University as an Adjunct Professor in the School of Sociology and Justice Studies, as he has done so faithfully since 2003.

[13]Commentary on each item is provided by the authors.

(7) Believing a convicted defendant has a viable constitutional claim, or claim of innocence, but refusing to grant relief. If a judge is of the opinion that a defendant has a viable claim of any kind, then they have an ethical obligation, as an impartial jurist, to grant the defendant some measure of relief. This could be in the form of a hearing, or setting aside all or part of a verdict or a sentence. Doing nothing sends the message that incompetence, error, or misconduct is acceptable to the court, encouraging that behavior by the police and prosecution.

(8) Believing that the petitioner has viable claims but not allowing for further development of those claims. If a judge is of the opinion that a defendant has a viable claim of any kind, then they have an ethical obligation to allow the defendant to investigate those claims further. Denying them access to representation, investigators, and discovery material under such circumstances, again, encourages misconduct by others.

(9) Denying a convicted defendant access to court records, or their own trial transcripts, then arguing that it has been denied because there is no proof of what claims might be raised. This argument is essentially circular. The only way for a convicted defendant to know for certain what issues might be raised post-conviction is to allow them, and their legal counsel, access to court records and trial transcripts. Only then can the defendant learn what these records contain. Denying such a request is essentially punitive.

While certainly not a complete list of everything that the judiciary can do to fail with respect to its ethical duties towards a convicted defendant, this is certainly a good start. The bottom line is that convicted defendants do not lose their rights to representation, discovery, testing, or court records just because they have been convicted. They have the right to appeal and judges have an obligation to hear them out.

SUMMARY

The *judiciary* is the branch of the criminal justice system that deals with the adjudication and exoneration or punishment of criminal defendants. This chapter reviews the ethical issues arising from those that some refer to as "bad judges": those who are guided by principles that are "incompetent, self-indulgent, abusive, or corrupt" and ultimately "terrorize courtrooms, impair the functioning of the legal system, and undermine public confidence in the law" (Miller, 2004, p. 431).

This chapter discusses judicial integrity, conflicts of interest, knowledge of the law, time allotment and caseload, improper influence over the jury, ethical issues with experts, improper judicial behavior, judicial alertness during trial, reporting attorney misconduct, and post-conviction issues.

Questions

1. List the two primary roles of the judge in the service of the criminal justice system. Explain.
2. Explain the difference between *judicial dispassion* and *judicial independence*.
3. Define *embroilment*. Explain why this is an issue.
4. List three examples of judges, improper influence over the jury.
5. List five judicial issues that are paramount post-conviction.

References

Abramson, L., 1997. The judge's ethical duty to report misconduct by other judges and lawyers and its effect on judicial independence. Hofstra Law Review 25, 751–783.

Ake v. Oklahoma, 1985. US Supreme Court, 470 US 68, February 26.

Associated Press, 2006. Penis pump judge gets 4-year jail term. USA Today, August 18; url: http://usatoday30.usatoday.com/news/nation/2006-08-18-judge-sentenced_x.htm.

Bam, D., 2011. Making appearances matter: recusal and the appearance of bias. Brigham Young Law Review 943, 943–1003.

Black, H.C., 1990. Black's Law Dictionary, sixth ed. West Publishing, St Paul, MN.

Brady v. Maryland, 1963. US Supreme Court, 373 US 83, Case No. 490.

Burke, S., 2012. Ex-judge Richard Baumgartner's drug-addicted downfall makes national spotlight. Associated Press, April 4; url: http://www.knoxnews.com/news/2012/apr/04/investigators-tenn-judge-high-on-pills-in-court/.

California v. Dwight Culton, 2011. San Francisco Superior Court.

Daubert v. Merrell Dow Pharmaceuticals, Inc, 1993. US Supreme Court, 509 US 579.

Daily Mail Reporter, 2012. Judge resigns after he was caught on camera sleeping during testimony. Daily Mail, February 11; url: http://www.dailymail.co.uk/news/article-2099763/Judge-resigns-caught-camera-sleeping-testimony.html.

Federal Rules of Evidence, 2006. US Government Printing Office. , Washington DC: December 1; url: http://www.uscourts.gov/rules/Evidence_Rules_2007.pdf.

Findley, K., 2008. Innocents at risk: adversary imbalance, forensic science, and the search for truth. Seton Hall Law Review 38, 893–973.

Frye v. United States, 1923. 293 F. 1013, DC Cir.

Garrett, B., 2011. Convicting the Innocent: Where Criminal Prosecutions Go Wrong. Harvard University Press, Cambridge, MA.

Gershman, B., 1997. Trial Error and Misconduct. Lexis Law, Charlottesville, VA.

Giannelli, P., 2005. Forensic science. Journal of Law and Medical Ethics 33, 535–543, (Fall).

Giannelli, P., McMunigal, K., 2007. Prosecutors, ethics, and expert witnesses. Fordham Law Review 76, 1493–1537, (December).

Guthrie, C., Rachlinski, J., Wistrich, A., 2007. Blinking on the bench: how judges decide cases. Cornell Law Review 93, 1–43, (November).

Hanna, J., 2002. Outspoken judge will take class to curb anger. Chicago Tribune, May 9; url: http://articles.chicagotribune.com/2002-05-09/news/0205090402_1_allegations-of-judicial-misconduct-outspoken-judge-judge-evans.

In re: J.B.K, 1996. Texas Court of Appeals, 931 S.W.2d 581.

In re: Poyfair, 2012. CJC No. 6691-F-153, May 4.

Irwin, J., Real, D., 2010. Unconscious influences on judicial decision-making: the illusion of objectivity. McGeorge Law Review 42, 1–18.

Kozinski, A., 2004. The *real* issues of judicial ethics. Hofstra Law Review 32 (4), 1095–1106.

Kumho Tire Co. v. Carmichael, 1999. US Supreme Court, 526 US 137.

Langlois, J., 2012. Sexting judge sends shirtless photo to female court bailiff. The Global Post, April 24; url: http://www.globalpost.com/dispatches/globalpost-blogs/weird-wide-web/sexting-judge-sends-shirtless-photo-female-court-bailiff-video.

Lilly, G., 1987. An Introduction to the Law of Evidence, second ed. West Publishing, St Paul, MN.

McCarty, C., 2012. District court judge facing misconduct counts. KLAS-TV, June 8.

McDade, M., 2013. O.C. judge accused of trading job for sex. KTLA-Los Angeles, March 7.

McMorrow, J., Gardina, J., Ricciardone, S., 2004. Judicial attitudes toward confronting attorney misconduct: a view from the reported decisions. Hofstra Law Review 32, 1425–1473.

Miller, G., 2004. Bad judges. Texas Law Review 83, 431–487.

Mississippi v. Robert Grant, 2006. Pearl River County Circuit Court, NO. 2007-KA-00108-COA.

Moreno, J., 2004. What happens when Dirty Harry becomes an (expert) witness for the prosecution? Tulane Law Review 79, 1–54, (November).

Maroney, T., 2011. The persistent cultural script of judicial dispassion. California Law Review 99, 629–681.

Petherick, W., Turvey, B., 2010. Cognitive ethos of the forensic examiner. In: Turvey, B., Petherick, W., Ferguson, C. (Eds.), Forensic Criminology, Elsevier, San Diego, CA.

Ridolfi, K., Possley, M., 2010. Preventable Error: A Report on Prosecutorial Misconduct in California 1997–2009. Northern California Innocence Project at Santa Clara University School of Law, Santa Clara, CA.

Ryan, C., 2013. Judge Valorie Vega accepts public reprimand. Las Vegas Sun, February 6; url: http://www.lasvegassun.com/news/2013/feb/06/judge-vega-accepts-public-reprimand/.

Starr, V.H., McCormick, M., 2001. Jury Selection, third ed. Aspen Law & Business, New York.

Toplikar, D., 2012. Judge Valorie Vega says ethics charges lack merit. Las Vegas Sun, June 8; url: http://www.lasvegassun.com/news/2012/jun/08/judge-says-ethics-charge-against-her-lacks-merit/.

Turvey, B., Freeman, J., 2012. Jury psychology. In: Ramachandran, V. (Ed.), Encyclopedia of Human Behavior, second ed. Elsevier, London.

Turvey, B., Petherick, W., Ferguson, C., 2010. Forensic Criminology. Elsevier, San Diego, CA.

CHAPTER 12

Ethical Issues for Corrections Staff

Angela N. Torres and Brent E. Turvey

Key Terms

Compassion fatigue "… the formal caregiver's reduced capacity or interest in being empathic or 'bearing the suffering of clients' and is 'the natural consequent behaviors and emotions resulting from knowing about a traumatizing event experiences or suffered by a person'" (Adams *et al.*, 2006, p. 104).

Contraband With respect to corrections, material forbidden to be in the possession of inmates, such as drugs, alcohol, weapons, and cell phones.

Correctional officers Those tasked with maintaining order and security within prisons.

Corrections The pillar of the criminal justice system that deals with the probation, incarceration, management, rehabilitation, treatment, parole, and in extreme cases the execution of convicted criminals.

Duty of care With respect to corrections, the state's responsibility for what happens to inmates while in its custody.

Inmate An individual that has been arrested and detained by law enforcement, to be held in either a jail or a prison depending on their conviction status.

Jails Used to hold those who have been recently arrested prior to any court proceedings, such as an arraignment, in law enforcement custody.

Prisons Designed to facilitate the long-term sentences of convicted felons.

Corrections is the branch of the criminal justice system that deals with the probation, incarceration, management, rehabilitation, treatment, parole, and sometimes execution of convicted criminals.[1] It is attended by a wide range of professionals, including wardens, sheriffs, jail officers, prison guards, corrections investigators, probation/parole officers and administrative support staff.

Despite the violent or aggressive nature of some incarcerated offenders, the conditions of incarceration make prison inmates a particularly vulnerable population. That is to say, the vast majority are easily exploited and abused. Consequently, they are entirely dependent upon the ethics and professionalism of corrections staff for their day-to-day survival, let alone the protection of their rights and personal safety.

CONTENTS

---

[1]Sections of this chapter have been adapted from material originally presented in Turvey and Torres (2010).

Ethical Justice. http://dx.doi.org/10.1016/B978-0-12-404597-2.00012-7

This chapter will focus on the responsibilities of front-line corrections staff, specifically those working directly with the incarcerated, exercising supervision and control of detainees, prisoners, or convicts. Its purpose is to contextualize the role of corrections and corrections officers, and then provide an overview of related professional ethical obligations.

TYPES OF FACILITIES

Depending on the nature of their offense, where it took place, and whether or not they have been convicted, inmates may be held in a local *jail* or incarcerated in one of several different types of *prisons*. Defendants convicted of felonies against the state will be sentenced to serve time in *state prisons*. Those convicted of felonies that violate federal law will be sentenced to serve time in *federal prisons*.

It is important to understand that while the courts may dictate sentencing requirements, any decisions about inmate security, housing, and privileges are made by the prison staff employed within the walls of a given facility. They have the authority to extend or revoke inmate privileges, alter or reassign inmate housing, and change both the level and duration of contact that inmates have with other inmates or those in the outside world (e.g., friends, family, and legal counsel). It is not an exaggeration to say that this gives corrections staff a tremendous amount of power over the inmates in their custody.

Jails

Most local (county and municipal) law enforcement agencies and courthouses have on-site jail facilities. *Jails* are used to hold those who have been recently arrested prior to any court proceedings, such as an arraignment, in law enforcement custody. They are also available for the short-term incarceration of offenders convicted of non-felonies. Further still, they are used to accommodate the local court appointments of felons "visiting" from other jails and correctional institutions.

Jail is vastly different from prison. Jails can be smaller, with only a few holding cells to accommodate a small community, or they can be much larger, intended to serve the needs of a heavily populated metropolitan area.

Jails also tend to have fewer amenities because incarceration is meant to be brief and they are in a constant state of turnover with respect to population. Inmates may only stay in a jail for a few hours, a few days, or a few weeks – which means that on any given day new inmates may be processed in and other inmates may be getting processed out. It also means that jail staff have a very short period of time in which to evaluate new inmates, determine their conditions and needs, and then respond in a way that keeps everyone safe and healthy.

Making matters much worse, those sent to jail are more likely to be in custody while severely intoxicated, heavily under the influence of controlled substances, or suffering from an exigent mental health crisis than are those in prison. In fact, it is violent and/or criminal behavior associated with such episodes that lands many in jail to begin with. This makes jail a strained and explosive environment with respect to the ever-present threat of inmate aggression and physical violence.

Prisons

Federal and state penitentiaries are designed to facilitate the long-term sentences of convicted felons. Generally speaking, state prisons are operated by the state government, usually through a Department of Corrections. Federal prisons, on the other hand, are operated by the Federal Bureau of Prisons, which is an agency within the US Department of Justice. Prisons tend to have more amenities than jails because they accommodate inmates with longer sentences, but they also suffer from less inmate population turnover.

According to information from the Federal Bureau of Prisons website, there are many federal prison facilities around the United States, each operating at one of five different security levels (http://www.bop.gov/locations/institutions):

> The Bureau operates institutions at five different security levels in order to confine offenders in an appropriate manner. Security levels are based on such features as the presence of external patrols, towers, security barriers, or detection devices; the type of housing within the institution; internal security features; and the staff-to-inmate ratio. Each facility is designated as either minimum, low, medium, high, or administrative.

As a result of the long-term incarcerations that are facilitated by prisons, prison staff have more time to get to know individual inmates. They can become familiar with individual criminal histories, affiliations, addictions, medical or mental health needs, and general inmate dispositions. They will deal with fewer unknowns during an inmate's stay and have the luxury of considering any challenges over a period of months or years.

Private Correctional Facilities

Throughout the United States it has become common for the government to contract out the administration responsibilities of its correctional facilities. This is done because of increased inmate populations and escalating costs, to streamline the budgets and management of often-declined state prison systems, and to reduce the overall size of government in response to taxpayer demands. It is also done with the notion that private companies competing for government contracts may achieve a higher quality of service, and a swifter responsiveness to correctional dynamics, than a state bureaucracy is capable of.

Despite the proliferation of privately run correctional facilities, there is little research to suggest that they are necessarily better or more cost-effective than the institutions they are meant to replace. The available research is in fact mixed on the issue. However, we are unlikely to abandon the privatized prison model, as discussed in Pozen (2003, pp. 255–256):

> It has been quite a debate: since their beginnings in the mid-1980s and the early 1990s, respectively, the prison privatization movements of the United States and the United Kingdom have provoked several rounds of congressional and parliamentary hearings and hundreds of articles discussing their philosophical, organizational, economic, and legal implications. Yet while there remains a contingent of vocal critics of private prisons in both countries today, the debate over privatization has lost much of its early ardor and prominence as the industry has reached a level of maturity over the course of the past decade. After the initial flurry of academic and popular commentary on American private prisons in the 1980s, public discussion had largely died down by 1990.
>
> However, even as prison privatization has entered the criminological mainstream and the controversy has largely faded from the public eye, nothing resembling consensus has emerged regarding the desirability or even the performance of private prisons.

Given current contractual obligations that would need to extend well into the future, and the logistical headaches that accompany the search for alternative facilities, there seems to be little incentive for pulling out of the privatized prison approach. That is to say, the United States is so heavily entrenched in this model, with so many stakeholders, that going back seems unlikely.

THE ROLE OF CORRECTIONS

Ideally, the role of corrections is to securely detain those convicted of crimes; to protect them from themselves and any others detained in the same facility; and to provide essential medical and mental healthcare. This includes treatment for physical injuries, medical conditions, and any drug or alcohol addictions. It can also include treatment for various mental health conditions.[2]

---

[2]See Chapter 13: "Ethical Issues for Treatment Staff in Forensic Settings."

With respect to society, the role of corrections is to provide protection. Historically, this has meant protection in the immediate sense by virtue of separating dangerous felons from regular citizens. However, it also requires a role in inmate rehabilitation – to ensure that what comes out is not worse, and better organized, than what went in.

As society has become less tolerant of crime and criminality, legislators and courts have felt the push to deliver sometimes appropriate but sometimes inflated "tough on crime" sentences. Additionally, they have felt great pressure from voters to cut prison costs and amenities, so as not to "coddle" inmates and reward their crimes with above-standard living conditions. However, ongoing economic crisis has forced many of those involved with the criminal justice system to rethink political motivations for tougher sentencing in favor of financial ones, as explained in Johnson (2009):

> ... [A]cross the nation, the deepening financial crisis is forcing dramatic changes in the hard-line, punishment-based philosophy that has dominated the USA's criminal justice system for nearly two decades. As 31 states report budget gaps that the National Governor's Association says totaled nearly $30 billion last year, criminal justice officials and lawmakers are proposing and enacting cost-cutting changes across the public safety spectrum, with uncertain ramifications for the public.
>
> There is no dispute that the fiscal crisis is driving the changes, but the potential risks of pursuing such policies is the subject of growing debate. While some analysts believe the philosophical shift is long overdue, others fear it could undermine public safety.
>
> Ryan King of The Sentencing Project, a group that advocates for alternatives to incarceration, says the financial crisis has created enough "political cover" to fuel a new look at the realities of incarcerating more than 2 million people and supervising 5 million others on probation and parole. "It's clear that locking up hundreds of thousands of people does not guarantee public safety," he says.
>
> Joshua Marquis, a past vice president of the National District Attorneys Association, agrees the economy is prompting an overhaul of justice policy but reaches a very different conclusion about its impact on public safety. "State after state after state appears to be waiting for the opportunity to wind back some of the most intelligent sentencing policy we have," Marquis says. "If we do this, we will pay a price. No question."
>
> Among recent state actions:
> - Kansas officials closed two detention facilities last month to save about $3.5 million. A third will be shuttered by April 1, says Roger

Werholtz, chief of the state prison system. Inmates housed in the closed units will be moved to other facilities in the state.

- A California panel of federal judges recommended last month that the cash-strapped state release up to 57,000 non-violent inmates from the overcrowded system to help save $800 million.
- Kentucky officials last year allowed for the early release of non-violent offenders up to six months before their sentences end to serve the balance of their time at home.
- New Mexico and Colorado are among seven states where some lawmakers are calling for an end to the death penalty, arguing capital cases have become too costly to prosecute, reports the Death Penalty Information Center, which tracks death penalty law and supports abolition of the death penalty.

"State governments operated on the principle that if you built it, they would come," King says of prison construction during the economic boom. Since 1990, corrections spending has increased by an average of 7.5% annually, reports the National Association of State Budget Officers. "As soon as they built those prisons, they filled them," King says. "They were never able to keep up with it. There is certainly a different atmosphere now."

Despite economic hardships and the need for fiscal belt-tightening, government agencies retain a dual duty to both society and those that they take into custody. This means that they have an obligation to release offenders only once their time has been served and make efforts to enable their safe re-integration into society. It also means that they have a corresponding obligation to adequately and safely house those that cannot be released – as will be discussed later in this chapter.

THE ROLE OF CORRECTIONAL OFFICERS

Correctional officers are tasked with maintaining order and security within prisons. They are also required to enforce institutional rules while modeling appropriate behavior to inmates. Far from being mere guards, they are further obligated to help support and even facilitate the rehabilitation efforts being made by other prison staff. This requires a careful professional balance. For example, providing security and maintaining order can necessitate forceful intervention (e.g., physical violence) that should not be tolerated from inmates, hinders offender vocational initiatives (e.g., solitary confinement, or removal from the general population), and is ultimately counterproductive to medical and mental health treatment. This means being well-trained in the use of appropriate penalties and force, and when to exercise restraint.

Complicating matters are the conditions under which correctional officers must work, as explained in Appelbaum *et al.* (2001, p. 1345):

> Correctional officers face significant job-related pressure. In many states they must cope with understaffing, mandatory overtime, rotating shift work, and low pay. However, correctional officers identify the threat of violence by inmates as their most frequent source of stress.

As further described in Peak (2007, pp. 276–277):

> In most assignments, correctional officers experience stimulus overload, are assailed with the sounds of "doors clanging, inmates talking or shouting, radios and televisions playing, and food trays banging … [and odors] representing an institutional blend of food, urine, paint, disinfectant, and sweat." Correctional officers are not allowed to provide informal counseling or to aid in the rehabilitative effort. Due process rights for prisoners have made corrections jobs even more difficult. Therein lies what Hawkins and Alpert referred to as "the big bitch" of correctional officers: They are losing power and influence while inmates are gaining them as they are accorded more due process rights. This frustration can be vented in physical ways. Although certainly not frequent today, beatings and even sexual attacks by some officers have been documented.

Despite hostile working conditions and being "the other prisoners" – essentially locked in with the inmates that they are responsible for – corrections staff are expected to maintain a professional attitude as well as a strict code of professional ethics. It should come as no surprise that trying to function every day in such a strained environment can result in staff burn-out. Specific working conditions that induce stress, and their consequences, are described more thoroughly in Finn (2000, p. 2):

> There are many sources of stress for correctional officers, including –
> - Organization-related conditions, such as understaffing, overtime, shift work, and unreasonable supervisor demands.
> - Work related sources of stress, including the threat of inmate violence, actual inmate violence, inmate demands and manipulation, and problems with coworkers.
> - A poor public image and low pay.
>
> A few facts illustrate the stressful nature of correctional work:
>
> - Many officers do not answer their home telephones because it might be the institution calling for overtime. Some officers get a second, unlisted telephone number that they keep secret from the department.

- Between 1990 and 1995, the number of attacks on correctional officers in State and Federal prisons jumped by nearly one-third, from 10,731 to 14,165, at a time when the number of correctional officers increased by only 14 percent.
- Except for police officers, the number of workplace nonfatal violent incidents is higher per 1,000 employees for correctional officers than for any other profession, including taxi drivers, convenience store staff, mental health workers, and teachers. From 1992 to 1996, there were nearly 218 incidents for every 1,000 correctional officers, for a total of 58,300 incidents.
- One officer said, "The public hasn't a clue as to what correctional officers do. Someone asked me just the other day if I beat inmates all the time." Another officer reported she routinely tells other people, "I work for the State," refusing to specify her precise job. The end result is some officers come to feel isolated and estranged from friends and family.

As this suggests, on the job stress from "role ambiguity and conflict" can also result in health problems for officers such as "cardiac difficulties, substance abuse, hypertension problems, and an increase in sick leave" (Peak, 2007, p. 283).

The job stress experienced by correctional officers can also result in general apathy, or what has been referred to as *compassion fatigue*, which is defined as (Adams *et al.*, 2006, p. 104): "the formal caregiver's reduced capacity or interest in being empathic or bearing the suffering of clients and is the natural consequent behaviors and emotions resulting from knowing about a traumatizing event experienced or suffered by a person." Those suffering from *compassion fatigue* essentially stop caring about their professional and ethical obligations with respect to inmates, co-workers, and even the law. This increases the likelihood that they will resign, get someone hurt on the job, or start crossing legal and ethical lines.

Ultimately, correctional officers are expected to live with daily threats, intimidation, manipulation, and violent behavior from inmates that require their constant attention and protection. Often this must be accomplished under employment conditions that involve scarce resources, suffer poor leadership, create low morale, induce health problems, and can eventually alienate the officer from friends and family. The result of this harsh reality is that not everyone can serve faithfully as a correctional officer: some will wash-out with only days on the job, while others run a high risk of becoming inured and apathetic.

INMATE DUTY OF CARE

When the state deprives a citizen of their liberty and confines them to a prison, it takes on the responsibility for their health, safety, and general welfare. That is to say, the state has a *duty of care*. The government cannot simply throw an inmate into confinement with other inmates, many of whom are violent, and forget about them; the government is responsible for what happens to those in its custody. This is discussed in Tartaro (2005, p. 113): "When police or corrections personnel take custody of an alleged offender, the government becomes responsible for that person's safety and general well-being (*Estelle v. Gamble*, 1976)."

When the state or one of its agents breaches its duty of care to an inmate by allowing or encouraging adverse conditions, the state is civilly liable for any harm that is suffered. This liability forms the basis for a number of the ethical responsibilities that must be embraced by corrections professionals. However, precisely what constitutes an acceptable standard of care for inmates is a matter of continuous debate and litigation.

Civil Rights: Section 1983

The basic duty of care that exists between a correctional facility and its inmates is found in the understanding that the state must refrain from violating an inmate's civil rights. In the United States, all citizens are guaranteed protection of their civil rights by Title 42, Section 1983 of the US Code titled "Civil action for deprivation of rights." Section 1983 explains that:

> Every person who, under color of any statute, ordinance, regulation, custom, or usage, of any State or Territory or the District of Columbia, subjects, or causes to be subjected, any citizen of the United States or other person within the jurisdiction thereof to the deprivation of any rights, privileges, or immunities secured by the Constitution and laws, shall be liable to the party injured in an action at law, suit in equity, or other proper proceeding for redress, except that in any action brought against a judicial officer for an act or omission taken in such officer's judicial capacity, injunctive relief shall not be granted unless a declaratory decree was violated or declaratory relief was unavailable. For the purposes of this section, any Act of Congress applicable exclusively to the District of Columbia shall be considered to be a statute of the District of Columbia.

The nature, intent, and usage of Section 1983 protections are explained in Rigby (2008, p. 419):

> Title 42, Section 1983 of the United States Code prohibits public officials from violating individuals' civil rights and liberties guaranteed by the Constitution and federal law. The Act seeks to accomplish its objective by providing a civil cause of action for plaintiffs whose civil rights and liberties are infringed by government actors. Section 1983 is frequently employed to sue state and local law enforcement and corrections officers. Although the legal elements of Section 1983 apply

equally throughout the United States, the effect of Section 1983 may vary depending on each jurisdiction studied. For instance, individuals in some areas of the nation seem to be particularly at risk of having their individual constitutional rights violated. In other jurisdictions, however, the government appears to be burdened by an unusual amount of frivolous Section 1983 claims.

Section 1983 is meant to provide citizens, even incarcerated ones, with the ability to hold the government accountable for violations of their civil rights. It is one of the only safeguards that citizens have against abuses by law enforcement and corrections officers because of its power and deterrent effect. It serves the important function of reminding government agents, and those who would abuse their positions of authority, that they are subordinate to the law just like everyone else.

Ironically, Section 1983 lawsuits are often filed by prison inmates without the benefit of legal counsel, many of which are successful. This is because reasonable access to legal resources is considered an inmate right. As described in the American Bar Association Standards for Criminal Justice (American Bar Association, 2011, pp. 315–316):

> A correctional facility should provide prisoners reasonable access to updated legal research resources relevant to prisoners' common legal needs, including an appropriate collection of primary legal materials, secondary resources such as treatises and self-help manuals, applicable court rules, and legal forms. Access to these legal resources should be provided either in a law library or in electronic form, and should be available even to those prisoners who have access to legal services. Correctional authorities should be permitted to regulate the time, place, and manner of prisoners' access to these resources for purposes of facility security and scheduling, but prisoners should have regular and sufficient access, without interference with the prisoners' ability to eat meals, work, receive health care, receive visits, or attend required treatment or educational programming. Prisoners who are unable to access library resources because of housing restrictions, language or reading skills, or for other reasons, should have access to an effective alternative to such access, including the provision of counsel, or of prisoners or non-prisoners trained in the law.

Consequently, depriving prisoners of this right, or interfering with it, can be considered a breach of professional ethics, if not a violation of institutional policy and the law.

Inmate Lawsuits

As suggested in the previous section, inmates are able to bring suit against correctional facilities for a broad spectrum of issues related to the circumstances of their incarceration – often successfully. Common problems raised in inmate lawsuits include complaints regarding conditions of confinement such as the following:

- *Cruel and unusual punishment.* This requires demonstrating that the deprivation of a basic human need was sufficiently serious and that prison staff acted with a "sufficiently culpable state of mind" (*Williams v. Ozmint,* 2008).
- *Excessive use of force by prison staff.* This requires establishing whether the force applied was "in a good faith effort to maintain or restore discipline, or maliciously and sadistically to cause harm" (*Williams v. Ozmint,* 2008).
- *Inadequate medical care.* This requires establishing whether prison staff were deliberately indifferent to the inmate's serious medical needs. As explained in *Miltier v. Beorn* (1990): "To establish that a health care provider's actions constitute deliberate indifference to a serious medical need, the treatment must be so grossly incompetent, inadequate, or excessive as to shock the conscience or to be intolerable to fundamental fairness."
- *Access to courts.* Inmates have a right to fair access to the courts, and must be provided with the means to present appeals and complaints. According to *Bounds v. Smith* (1977), inmate access must be "adequate, effective and meaningful." As discussed earlier, this means that the prison must either provide inmates with access to a law library or with some form of legal counsel. To prove such claims, the inmates must demonstrate that their right to access has been interfered with in some way, if not entirely infringed upon.

While sometimes frivolous and retaliatory, the ability of inmates to make these kinds of legal complaints is an important part of acknowledging their civil rights, as well as providing an important check against institutional corruption and inmate abuse.

CASE EXAMPLE

Stephen Slevin, 59, Dona Ana County Jail, New Mexico

Stephen Slevin was subjected to inhumane treatment while incarcerated at the Dona Ana County Jail in New Mexico; he was initially jailed for a driving while intoxicated (DWI) and suspected automobile theft. He was incarcerated there from 2005 until 2007, as reported in Chuck (2013):

Slevin's mistreatment by Dona Ana County started the moment he was arrested back in August of 2005, his attorney told NBC News. "He was driving through New Mexico and arrested for a DWI, and he allegedly was in

CASE EXAMPLE *CONTINUED*

a stolen vehicle. Well, it was a car he had borrowed from a friend; a friend had given him a car to drive across the country," [Matt] Coyte [Slevin's Albuquerque-based attorney] said in an interview last January.

Slevin was depressed at the time, Coyte explained, and wanted to get out of New Mexico. Instead, he found himself in jail. "When he gets put in the jail, they think he's suicidal, and they put him in a padded cell for three days, but never give him any treatment."

Nor did they give him a trial, Coyte said. Slevin said he never saw a judge during his time in confinement. After three days in the padded cell, jail guards transferred Slevin into solitary confinement with no explanation. "Their policy is to then just put them in solitary" if they appear to have mental health issues, Coyte told NBC News.

While in solitary confinement, a prisoner is entitled to one hour per day out of the cell, but often times, Slevin wasn't even granted that,

Coyte said. "Your insanity builds. Some people holler or throw feces out their cell doors," he said. "Others rock back and forth under a blanket for a year or more, which is what my client did."

By the time Slevin got out of jail, his hair was shaggy and overgrown, his beard long, and his face pale and sunken, a drastic contrast from the clean-shaven booking photo taken of him when he was arrested 2 years prior.

Further still, Mr Slevin was denied access to a dentist and forced to pull one of his own teeth; and his toenails grew "so long that they curled around his foot, and fungus festering on his skin because he was deprived of showers" (Chuck, 2013). According to Mr Slevin (Chuck, 2012): "[Jail guards were] walking by me every day, watching me deteriorate .... Day after day after day, they did nothing, nothing at all, to get me any help."

Mr Slevin eventually gained his freedom and filed a lawsuit against Dona Ana County. In March 2013 he agreed to a settlement of $15.5 million, which is one of largest civil rights judgments awarded to a prisoner in US history. The Dona Ana County public information office has stated that jail personnel were fired in relation to this incident (Chuck, 2013).

Health Care

One of the key duties of care held by the state with respect to prison inmates involves providing adequate access to health care. As explained by the court in their decision in *Estelle v. Gamble* (1976):

An inmate must rely on prison authorities to treat his medical needs; if the authorities fail to do so, those needs will not be met. In the worst cases, such a failure may actually produce physical "torture or a lingering death,".... The infliction of such unnecessary suffering is inconsistent with contemporary standards of decency as manifested in modern legislation codifying the common law view that "it is but just that the public be required to care for the prisoner, who cannot, by reason of the deprivation of his liberty, care for himself." We therefore conclude that deliberate indifference to serious medical needs of prisoners constitutes the "unnecessary and wanton infliction of pain," *Gregg v. Georgia, supra*, at 173 (joint opinion), proscribed by the Eighth Amendment. This is true whether the indifference is manifested by prison doctors in their response to the prisoner's needs or by prison guards in intentionally denying or delaying access to medical [p105] care or intentionally interfering with the treatment once prescribed. Regardless of how evidenced, deliberate indifference to a prisoner's serious illness or injury states a cause of action under § 1983.

This obligation is significant because inmate populations are on the rise, and rates of inmate illness are much higher than those found on the outside. The situation is described in Jones (2008, p.181):

> The prison population in America is not only vast and rapidly expanding, but also "the prevalence of chronic illness, communicable diseases, and severe mental disorders among people in jail and prison is far greater than among other people of comparable ages." Specifically, the "[s]ignificant illnesses afflicting corrections populations include coronary artery disease, hypertension, diabetes, asthma, chronic lung diseases, HIV infection, hepatitis B and C, other sexually transmitted diseases, tuberculosis, chronic renal failure, physical disabilities and many types of cancer." While physical illness is prevalent in inmate populations, so too is mental illness.

Add in the reality of inmate violence and the necessity of force that may be required as a response from corrections staff, and the likelihood of inmate injury compounds. Appelbaum *et al.* (2001) provide a useful discussion that explains how to approach the problem in order to achieve at least some success (p. 1343):

> Prisons have become the homes of thousands of inmates who have mental disorders. The stress of incarceration can cause morbidity among these individuals, resulting in more severe symptoms and more disruptive behavior. Effective treatment for such inmates often involves services provided by a multidisciplinary treatment team that includes correctional officers. Correctional officers can assist in observations and interventions, and they play a unique role on specialized housing units. Successful collaboration between correctional officers and treatment teams requires a foundation of mutual respect, shared training, and ongoing communication and cooperation. With these elements in place, correctional officers can assist the treatment team and make important and constructive contributions to the assessment and management of offenders who have mental disorders.

This discussion suggests adopting one standard of care that involves all prison staff working together for the betterment of the inmate. It is an ideal that looks great on paper, but ignores the strain suffered by corrections staff, mentioned previously in this chapter.

Additionally, required standards of care vary widely from region to region. For example, in US federal institutions prisoners have a right to the standard of care that exists in the community where the facility is located. As a result, inmates at the Federal Medical Clinic in Rochester, Minnesota, are entitled to treatment at the Mayo Clinic because this is the local standard of care. In communities with smaller hospitals and fewer trained medical personnel, the prison's standard of care can be much lower.

When prison staff or administrators are aware of medical conditions that go untreated, or of treatment conditions that are beneath the ascribed standard of care, both the state and the individual may be held responsible. This is explained in a discussion regarding the dangers of outsourcing prison health care to private for-profit corporations in Jones (2008, pp. 201–202):

> The practice of outsourcing health care in prisons and jails to for profit corporations is fundamentally broken. The level of care these corporations provide inmates is dangerously inadequate and considering the race to the bottom that occurs when several of these corporations compete for the same contract, the level of care can only get worse. Because prison officials know of the substantial risk to inmate health that outsourcing prison health care can cause, when a prison official chooses to implement a prison health care system that is outsourced to a for-profit corporation, that prison official is deliberately indifferent to the health care rights of inmates. Therefore, that prison official could be held liable for violating the Constitutional rights of inmates by implementing a prison health care system that is the equivalent of cruel and unusual punishment.

As an example of what administrators are and are not aware of with respect to offender treatment, consider the following: to cut down on the high costs of prisoner mental health care, many facilities no longer have a psychiatrist on staff. In these locations, consultations may be performed through tele-psychiatry rather than by an on-site psychiatrist. Furthermore, many inmate psychological services are also provided for by master's degree-level counselors or practicum students who are supervised by a few doctoral-level psychologists. In any other counseling or treatment environment, such practices would likely be unacceptable.

MISCONDUCT AND UNETHICAL BEHAVIORS

Throughout this chapter we have discussed how the tremendous authority wielded by correctional officers, combined with the stress of their jobs and the vulnerability of inmates, can lead to unethical choices and even staff misconduct. These tend to involve inmate mistreatment and abuse, providing inmates with contraband, and sexual exploitation. Some of these breaches result in penalties, like demotions or suspension. Others rise to the level of requiring staff termination, and even criminal charges. In this section, we will discuss these general issues with respect to ethics and misconduct; and we will provide examples of how related cases have been disposed.

Use of Force

The use of force in a correctional facility involves multiple considerations. The inmate has a right to be free from harm, and to be free of the fear of harm (e.g., threats of injury or death), with respect to correctional officers and other inmates. However, correctional officers have an obligation to intervene against inmates with "reasonable force", in order to protect themselves, their co-workers, or other inmates. They may also use "reasonable force" in order to get inmates to comply with institutional policy, to prevent escape, or to facilitate recapture. As explained in Hemmens and Stohr (2001, p. 27):

> Incarceration, by its nature, involves forcing an individual to do something against his or her will. Not surprisingly, these individuals are at times uncooperative, occasionally to the point of physical resistance. Corrections officers have the right and responsibility to use reasonable force to protect themselves and others, and to ensure compliance with institutional policies (Smith, 2000). At the same time, courts have repeatedly held that inmates retain a right to be free from excessive force (*Hudson v. McMillan*, 1992).

The obligation to protect inmates from harm using force extends to that which is foreseeable by corrections staff; in fact staff members that fail to protect inmates can be held accountable for what the courts refer to as "deliberate indifference" (Hemmens and Stohr, 2001, p. 30):

> Correctional personnel have a duty to the inmates they supervise to prevent them from foreseeable harm. Failure to do so may constitute "deliberate indifference" and subject the officer to liability (*Farmer v. Brennan*, 1994). This duty to prevent harm includes preventing criminal activity within the prison. This criminal activity may take the form of direct harm to an inmate (as in an assault), or it may take the form of an indirect harm to an inmate (as in criminal activity such as drug sales or extortion). Correctional staff are justified in using reasonable force to prevent criminal activity and to apprehend those who commit crimes within prison.

Correctional officers are therefore required to be properly trained in the *use of force* policies adopted by their institution, as well as receiving training on any related techniques, protective gear, or weaponry. In addition, they are required to be aware of the potential threats to the inmates in their care, and they must not place them in harm's way – whether intentionally or through dereliction of their duties. Officers without such training, and incapable of such awareness, are a liability for all concerned.

CASE EXAMPLE

Theresa L. Daniel, 60, Ohio Department of Rehabilitation and Correction

In January 2013, Corrections Officer Theresa L. Daniel, of the Ohio Department of Rehabilitation and Correction, was placed on administrative leave without pay. She is believed by Highway Patrol investigators to have locked a handcuffed prisoner in a cell with an inmate who proceeded to beat and rape him. As reported in Johnson (2013):

> A report says investigators are considering the possibility of charges against both the officer and the inmate who committed the alleged assault. The officer could be charged with dereliction of duty, a second-degree misdemeanor, while the offending inmate could be hit with a felony charge of rape by sodomy. The patrol's brief initial report said Daniel (who was not named in the report) "has been

accused to leaving handcuffs on the victim/inmate while in his cell in segregation. The victim/inmate alleged that he was assaulted while he was still handcuffed."

The alleged attack occurred at the Allen Oakwood Correctional Facility in Lima, Ohio which maintains around 1600 inmates; Officer Daniel has been employed in the prison system since 1996. Immediate issues of concern would include establishing why the first inmate needed to be cuffed; whether staff was aware of the presence of the other inmate and his propensity for violence; and whether placing the cuffed inmate in with him was appropriate or the result of somebody putting him in the wrong place, getting distracted, and then forgetting that he was in there.

Professional Boundaries

Corrections staff have a professional obligation to set and maintain consistent boundaries between themselves and the inmates in their charge. As explained in Blackburn *et al.* (2011, p. 352):

> Boundaries in prison can be blurred due to the proximity in which officers and inmates interact and by the staff's need to control inmates. Sykes (1958) introduced the norm of reciprocity where officers reward inmates with privileges, assignments, or with unnoticed minor violations in exchange for good behavior. In turn, the inmate will not cause trouble and may even assist in keeping other inmates in line. While reciprocity certainly assists officers in keeping order, it serves to further blur the professional boundary set by prison policy.

Consequently, inmates are not to be considered potential friends, confidantes, sexual partners, or romantic interests. First, there are the ethical and legal ramifications – violations of which can have serious penalties. However, there is much more. Some inmates have learned to survive as predators in their institutional environment – looking to create any opportunity to induce corrections officers into doing something unethical or illegal. The inmate can then use the threat of exposing that one incident, no matter how small a breach, to get the officer even deeper in their pocket. The problem, and how to identify it, is discussed thoroughly in Hicks (2011):

> The need for setting boundaries is especially important in a corrections setting because of the innate power imbalance. Not only is there

a power imbalance between employees and staff, but there is also a power hierarchy among inmates, and of course, between any correctional staff member and the inmate.

"You have power and authority over offenders," Fleming said. "When you choose not to own your power, that's when boundaries get crossed and problems occur." According to Fleming, here are the characteristics of collapsed boundaries for a [correctional officer]:

- Unable to say no due to fear or rejection
- Exhibits a high tolerance for abuse or disrespect
- Absorbs the feelings of others
- Shares too much information before establishing mutual trust in a relationship
- Avoids conflict at all costs
- Possesses no clear identity or sense of self

"This is the definition of a dependent person and they can be very dangerous in a correctional setting," said Fleming.

If an officer does not set clear professional boundaries, then they put themselves at risk of developing an inappropriate relationship with an inmate that can result in boundary violations, described in Hicks (2011):

While it's common for people to have a down day, COs [correctional officers] must be especially careful not to let boundaries slip with inmates. Vulnerabilities like low self-esteem, job dissatisfaction, personal problems at home and/or personal isolation can lead to a CO getting too personal with an inmate.

Boundary violations for COs can include:
- Deviation from the traditional
- Self-disclosure
- Bending the rules
- Taking gifts from inmates
- Giving information to inmates
- Joking around
- Receiving help or information for self-gain

"A boundary violation occurs when you place your needs above the needs of an inmate and gain emotionally or personally at their expense," said Fleming. "Saying 'here are two Benadryls' at night can turn into something bigger down the road."

Inappropriate relationships with inmates generally start out small and can be completely innocent – lacking any apparent seriousness. However, this can change quickly, and lead to ethical violations and serious misconduct.

Inappropriate Relationships

Because of the power imbalance that exists between corrections staff and inmates, and because of staff access to contraband and the outside world, any personal relationship between the two is inherently inappropriate. Everyone understands this going in. With inmates, staff need to act professional and keep their emotional distance, or risk penalties, loss of their career, or the loss of someone's life.

However, there are inmates who seek to violate the personal boundaries of staff members in order to get what they want. As described in Worley *et al.* (2003), an inmate typology was developed back in 1981:

> Allen and Bosta (1981) suggest five varieties of offenders that attempt to form inappropriate relationships with correctional staff members: "observers," "contacts," "runners," "point-men," and "turners." Observers were inmates who watched (e.g., personal mannerisms, body language, facial expressions) and listened to staff members to determine which employees might be susceptible to manipulation. These offenders in turn provided crucial information to other inmates who actually initiated the manipulation. "Contacts" were prisoners that ascertained personal details about an employee's life and passed on this "intelligence" to other inmates. "Runners" tested staff members by purposely violating the rules (e.g., asking the officer for a candy bar) to gauge the employee's reaction and willingness to enforce the rules or use discretion. "Point-men" functioned as lookouts to alert other inmates who were attempting to manipulate staff. Finally, these researchers stated that some offenders acted as "turners," or inmates who befriended employees and used that friendship to ultimately coerce employees into rule infractions. "Runners" also went to great lengths to gain an employee's trust, which was used later to corrupt the staff member. This typology illustrates that inmates can be the aggressor or the initiator of an inappropriate relationship with a staff member.

Worley *et al.* (2003) report the findings of an independent study, which identifies three types of "turners" – *Heartbreakers*, *Exploiters*, and *Hell-raisers*.

Heartbreakers were found to have "initiated a relationship with a security officer to establish a long-term romantic relationship" and "typically formed strong emotional bonds with prison employees, and it was not uncommon for a lengthy courtship to unfold prior to any romantic involvement. It was also not usual for ex-staff members to reside with the family or close friends of heart breakers" (Worley *et al.*, 2003, pp. 182–183). These illicit courtships tended be private, not shared by the inmate with anyone inside the prison. Also, they were often initiated by the inmate with innocent but intentional touching of the staff member, designed to appear incidental but lead towards intimacy over time.

Exploiters were found to have "aggressively forged inappropriate relationship with staff members to make illicit profits in the underground prison economy" and would "obtain contraband" by developing "a lever or hold over security officers. Levers … were ploys that offenders use to manipulate staff members into violating organizational policies and procedures" (Worley *et al.*, 2003, p. 185). These "levers" and "holds" include things like reporting minor infractions by staff, such as smoking or using chewing tobacco, but could also include threats of filing of grievances with superiors involving fabricated misconduct. In the most serious cases, the exploiter might threaten to harm the staff member's family upon release. However, most instances were not this severe and the entrapment of staff was accomplished by relatively simple means, as described in Worley *et al.* (2003, p. 185):

> Interestingly enough, the most common entrapment technique among exploiters involved the exchange of small items with prison staff members, like food or reading materials. Exchange of these minor items was used to establish an inappropriate relationship. One interviewee, for example, stated:
>
>> Here a boss may go a whole shift and not get a lunch break. We can take advantage of them because of this. You know, we might offer a boss a candy bar or a soda on a hot day. Sometimes we might offer them a sandwich or something, and this can lead to all kinds of things. Sometimes they take it and sometimes they don't. When they do, it's like a fish on a hook. You just got to reel them in slow. It takes patience. Hey all I got is time, man, so time is on my side.
>
> Other exploiters claimed to provide staff members with newspaper or "jack books" (pornography) to develop a unique type of rapport. Interestingly, both female exploiters stated that it was not unusual for inmates to solicit staff members to put money in their trust funds.

In some cases, exploiters were found to have used their leverage over staff members to extort sexual favors from them – especially if the staff member was a female supplying them with contraband. In any case, once the staff member broke institutional rules or the law, it would be almost impossible for them get out from underneath the exploiter's influence without serious professional consequences.

Consider the following Case Example of staff exploitation and whether this involves behavior associated with a *heartbreaker* or an *exploiter*.

CASE EXAMPLE

Amber Stanley, 25, Southeast Ohio Correctional Institution

In the Fall of 2012, Corrections Officer Amber Stanley, was working at the Southeast Ohio Correctional Institution when the Ohio State Highway Patrol accused her of engaging in phone sex with an inmate and of supplying coworkers with illegal drugs. An investigation revealed that she also provided the inmate with contraband (e.g., photos of herself), as reported in Sacco (2013):

> The Patrol began investigating Stanley after a tip that an inmate was bragging about having a relationship with a corrections officer, including phone sex, according to an Ohio Highway Patrol report included in court documents.
>
> After troopers began listening to phone conversations, Stanley was arrested in October. Initially, she faced charges of illegal conveyance of drugs onto a detention faculty, a third-degree felony, and complicity, a third-degree felony, in addition to her dereliction of duty charge.
>
> Phone records showed that between Sept. 2 and Oct. 10, the inmate made more than 300 calls to Stanley, the report said.
>
> During those calls, Stanley discussed using and buying drugs and buying drugs for co-workers, the report said. Court documents also indicated Stanley provided the inmate with narcotics on at least one occasion. The records also said Stanley was recorded talking about using drugs herself and that Stanley once was recorded saying she still was high and needed to come down before reporting to work in two hours.
>
> Stanley admitted she was receiving calls from an inmate, and that she photographed herself and sent the inmate the pictures, the report said.
>
> Karrie Hupka, the warden's assistant, said Stanley still was in her probationary period and was removed without the prison launching an investigation of its own.

In early March 2013, Ms. Stanley pleaded guilty to dereliction of duty, was sentenced to 180 days in the Fairfield County Jail, and was ordered to pay a fine and court costs (the jail sentence was suspended in favor of 2 years of house arrest).

Of course, trading food for sex can go both ways in prison. Consider the following case example.

CASE EXAMPLE

Abner Canda, 58, Snohomish County Jail, Washington State

Abner Canda was a Deputy Corrections Officer that used to work for the Snohomish County Jail in Washington State – until he was put on leave for trading homemade chocolate chip cookies for sex with a female inmate, as reported in Harthorne (2013):

> According to charging documents, Abner Canda, who was placed on paid administrative leave in January, provided food to a 22-year-old female inmate in exchange for sexual favors on a number of occasions between November 2012 and January 2013.According to documents, video surveillance appears to corroborate the inmate's story. And, at least two other inmates have suggested they had sexual contact with Canda as well, including one who claims she was dating him while incarcerated in the jail, according to documents.
>
> The 22-year-old inmate brought the allegations against Canda in January, telling police she felt guilty for what she had done.

CASE EXAMPLE *CONTINUED*

"I'm sorry," she told police. "I'm trying to change and be a better person now. I'm ashamed for my actions. That's why I'm saying something."

The Snohomish County Prosecuting Attorney's Office filed first-degree custodial sexual misconduct charges against Canda on March 5 after an investigation from the

Snohomish County Sheriff's Office Special Investigations Unit.

Of concern in this case is the allegation that the activity took place over a period of months, was easily corroborated with video surveillance from the facility and uncovered other potential victims. It speaks to a lack of supervision, a lack of accountability, and an absence of professional ethics.

Hell-raisers were inmates that "engaged in a unique kind of psychological warfare. As many of these offenders admitted, they simply wanted to cause trouble and create hell for the prison system. These 'rebels with a cause' were consumed with the idea of creating havoc and trouble for an institution for the sake of it" (Worley *et al.*, 2003, pp. 189). Additionally, hell-raisers "thrived on putting staff members into situations that compromised their jobs as well as the facility's security" and "aimed to embarrass correctional administrators, and many claimed they enjoyed the notoriety that followed after their relationship was exposed. As one offender explained, having an inappropriate relationship with a prison staff member was the 'ultimate way to out-con the law'" (p. 190).

The Introduction of Contraband

As already mentioned, poor employment screening and low pay can be a problem in corrections, as correctional officers account for much of the contraband that ends up in a given facility. This includes obvious items, such as drugs, alcohol, weapons, and cell phones. However, it can also include other forbidden material, such outside food items, jewelry, metal, money, maps, and officer uniforms.

Cell phones are the most frequently seized item; as reported in Blackburn *et al.* (2011, p. 352) "cell phones have become the 'new prison cash' not only because they can be used to keep in contact with the outside world but also because officers and inmates alike can generate revenue by 'selling' minutes." They are also among the most dangerous, as it allows inmates to organize criminal activity from inside the prison.

Unfortunately, the smuggling of contraband by prison staff is not always a terminal offense, as reported in a study conducted by Sandberg and Stiles (2009):

> Knives and drugs, cell phones and smokeless tobacco. Even McDonald's hamburgers. Texas prisons are a virtual bazaar of prohibited and illicit goods smuggled in by guards and correctional employees who have rarely faced harsh punishment when caught, according to a *Houston Chronicle* review.

Nearly 300 employees, many lowly paid correctional officers, were reprimanded for possessing prohibited items at 20 prison units with the most pervasive contraband problem between 2003 and 2008, records show. Of the 263 employees disciplined solely for contraband, about three fourths were given probation, where they were placed under special scrutiny for specified periods. Thirty-five were fired; 26 received no punishment at all. One of the 263 was criminally prosecuted for the contraband, but served no prison time.

Contraband trafficking gained national attention ... when a Texas death row inmate used a smuggled cell phone to threaten a prominent lawmaker. The phone was used by fellow death row inmates to place 3,000 other calls.

John Moriarty, the prison system's inspector general, called contraband "the biggest security problem the prisons face." Until recently, guards found introducing contraband into the system were more likely to be handed minimal penalties rather than be fired, and the punishment varied widely, a newspaper review of five years of disciplinary records shows. In 47 cases in which an employee attempted to deliver contraband to an offender, only seven cases resulted in dismissals, according to the analysis ....

Top prison officials have called for zero tolerance in stamping out prison contraband, though it "doesn't mean someone is terminated," said the prison system's spokeswoman, Michelle Lyons. "It means it's addressed and is dealt with accordingly. In some cases, depending on the contraband, the fitting punishment is probation or suspension," she said. "In more serious cases, where the facts support that the person intended to introduce contraband to an offender, then it's dealt with possibly by termination."

But in 2003 a correctional officer at the Estelle Unit was given 10 months probation and suspended for four days without pay after his backpack turned up an assortment of knives, prescription drugs, a cell phone, two electric razors, a box blade, a lighter, a set of portable radios, cigarettes and cigars.

Another correctional officer with an otherwise clean record at the Beto Unit got six months' probation, simply for walking through a metal detector with an unopened can of chewing tobacco.

A retired Estelle Unit prison guard said getting cigarettes into the prisons was never a problem. "I used to walk behind the cellblocks every night and would find cigarette ashes out there behind maybe a third of the cellblocks," said the former guard, who was once placed on probation for being found on prison grounds with a bag containing a paring knife, a spoon, scissors, an alarm clock, a deck of playing cards and an ashtray.

Not all contraband is intended for inmates. "A lot of it is personal use stuff," Moriarty said. Officials must try to figure out whether a guard simply forgot to unload his cell phone before entering a prison, or intended to deliver it to an inmate, and pocket as much as $2,000 for one destined for death row, he said.

Lyons said changes made after the death row cell phone scandal, such as pat-downs of everyone entering the prisons, have made it harder for contraband to get in. Still, more than 200 cell phones have been confiscated systemwide since a lockdown for illicit items ended ..., including eight seized from death row.

... Whitmire said ... that few inside the system would acknowledge the problem until he found himself on the line with a death row prisoner. Now, the lawmaker is calling for a no-tolerance policy regarding contraband. He said staffing shortages have forced prison administrators to compromise in both discipline and hiring practices, adding, "There are instances where they are hiring people with matters in their background who normally wouldn't be hired."

He said rank-and-file officers' salaries – their base pay is capped at $34,000 annually – contribute to the problem. "The low pay certainly would make those who are susceptible to being dishonest cross the line." One legislative proposal would give correctional officers as much as a 20 percent raise – at a two-year cost of at least $400 million.

Brian Olsen, executive director of the Texas branch of the American Federation of State, County and Municipal Employees, a union that represents prison workers, said the contraband problem could persist unless guards receive professional wages. Still, he said most officers follow the rules, and others get into trouble for "trafficking" in seemingly harmless items, such as candy and soft drinks. "There are going to be bad officers," Olsen said. "I don't think it's as rampant a problem as everyone says."

This line of argumentation is important to note, as low pay and shrinking budgets are repeatedly cited throughout the criminal justice system as the primary reason for hiring and retaining the unqualified, or even those with criminal records, by law enforcement and corrections agencies. Such decisions would seem to lack any basis in professional ethics and would in fact seem to work directly against them.

SUMMARY

Corrections is the branch of the criminal justice system that deals with the probation, incarceration, management, rehabilitation, treatment, parole, and sometimes execution of convicted criminals. It is attended to by a wide range of professionals, including wardens, sheriffs, jail officers, prison guards, corrections investigators, probation/parole officers, and administrative support staff. This chapter focuses on the responsibilities of front-line corrections staff, specifically those working directly with the incarcerated, exercising supervision and control of detainees, prisoners, or convicts. Unethical behaviors of corrections staff include inmate mistreatment and abuse, providing inmates with contraband, and sexual exploitation.

Questions

1. What is the role of a corrections officer?
2. Explain the difference between a jail and a prison.
3. List and explain two common problems raised in inmate lawsuits.
4. Explain the significance of the court decision in *Estelle v. Gamble* (1976).
5. Discuss three unethical behaviors of correctional officers.
6. What is the most commonly seized item in a correctional facility?

References

Adams, R.E., Boscarino, J.A., Figley, C.R., 2006. Compassion fatigue and psychological distress among social workers: a validation study. American Journal of Orthopsychiatry 76 (1), 103–108.

Allen, B., Bosta, D., 1981. Games Criminals Play. Rae John, Susanville, CA.

American Bar Association, 2011. ABA Standards for Criminal Justice: Treatment of Prisoners, third ed. American Bar Association, Washington, DC.

Appelbaum, K., Hickey, J., Packer, I., 2001. The role of correctional officers in multidisciplinary mental health care in prisons. Psychiatric Services 52, 1343–1347, (October).

Blackburn, A., Fowler, S., Mullings, J., Marquart, J., 2011. When boundaries are broken: inmate perceptions of correctional staff boundary violations. Deviant Behavior: An Interdisciplinary Journal 32 (4), 351–378.

Bounds v. Smith, 1977. US Supreme Court, 430 US 817 (825), 97, S.Ct. 1491, 52 L.Ed.2d 72.

Chuck, E., 2012. Man spends 2 years in solitary after DWI arrest, NBC News, January 25; url: http://usnews.nbcnews.com/_news/2012/01/25/10233835-man-spends-2-years-in-solitary-after-dwi-arrest.

Chuck, E., 2013. Man left in solitary confinement for 2 years gets $15.5 million settlement, NBC News, March 6; url: http://usnews.nbcnews.com/_news/2013/03/06/17212442-man-left-in-solitary-confinement-for-2-years-gets-155-million-settlement.

Estelle v. Gamble, 1976. US Supreme Court, 429 US 97, Case No. 75–929, November 30.

Finn, P., 2000. Addressing Correctional Officer Stress: Programs and Strategies. National Institute of Justice, Washington DC, NCJ 183474.

Harthorne, M., 2013. Corrections deputy charged with trading cookies for sex with inmate, KOMO News, March 6; url: http://www.komonews.com/news/local/Corrections-deputy-charged-with-trading-cookies-for-sex-with-inmate-195686511.html.

Hemmens, C., Stohr, M., 2001. Correctional staff attitudes regarding the use of force in corrections. Corrections Management Quarterly 5 (2), 27–40.

Hicks, E., 2011. Professional boundaries in corrections: how to set and keep them. CorrectionsOne, August 9; url: http://www.correctionsone.com/correctional-psychology/articles/4190920-Professional-boundaries-in-corrections-How-to-set-and-keep-them/.

Hudson v. McMillan, 1992. US Supreme Court, 503 US 1, No. 90–6531 February 25.

Johnson, A., 2013. Handcuffed inmate raped by prisoner, corrections officer investigated. The Columbus Dispatch, February 12; url: http://www.dispatch.com/content/stories/local/2013/02/12/Handcuffed-prisoner.html.

Johnson, K., 2009. To save money on prisons, states take a softer stance. USA Today, March 17.

Peak, K., 2007. Justice Administration: Police, Courts, and Corrections Management, fifth ed. Prentice Hall, Upper Saddle River, NJ.

Miltier v. Beorn, 1990. 896 F.2d 848, 851 (4th Cir.1990).

Pozen, D., 2003. Managing a correctional marketplace: prison privatization in the United States and the United Kingdom. Journal of Law and Politics 19, 253–284, (Summer).

Rigby, J., 2008. Section 1983 actions in North Dakota: an empirical study of agency policies and law enforcement and correctional officers. North Dakota Law Review 84, 419–451.

Sacco, F., 2013. Patrol still investigating former SCI guard: former corrections officer found guilty of dereliction of duty. The Eagle-Gazette, March 5; url: http://www.lancastereaglegazette.com/article/20130304/NEWS01/303040005/Former-corrections-officer-found-guilty-dereliction-duty.

Sandberg, L., Stiles, M., 2009. Illicit goods keep flowing into prisons: workers caught with contraband rarely get fired. Houston Chronicle, March 15.

Tartaro, C., 2005. Section 1983 Liability and Custodial Suicide: a look at what plaintiffs face in court. Californian Journal of Health Promotion 3 (2), 113–124.

Turvey, B., Torres, A., 2010. Forensic criminology in correctional settings. In: Turvey, B., Petherick, W., Ferguson, C. (Eds.), Forensic Criminology, Elsevier, San Diego, CA.

Williams v. Ozmint, 2008. US District Court, D. South Carolina, Charleston Division, C/A No. 6:07–2409-DCN-WMC, September 22.

Worley, R., Marquart, J., Mullings, J., 2003. Prison guard predators: an analysis of inmates who established inappropriate relationships with prison staff, 1995–1998. Deviant Behavior: An Interdisciplinary Journal 24, 175–194.

CHAPTER 13

Ethical Issues for Treatment Staff in Forensic Settings

Michael McGrath and Brent Turvey

Key Terms

Competency to stand trial evaluations Examinations that address the inmate's current mental state, and whether they are able to understand their charges and assist their attorney in their defense.

Criminal responsibility evaluations Examinations that deal with the mental state of an offender at the time of a crime.

Dual agency Occurs when the same provider is expected to both treat an inmate and perform a forensic evaluation for the court.

Malingering Feigning illness, often for medication, attention, or as the result of personal crises.

Correctional settings are visited by mental health practitioners under a variety of different employment circumstances, providing inmate evaluations and treatment.[1] Some work as employees of the correctional agency, some are employed by a company contracted to the correctional agency, and others can be private practitioners that are contracted to a specific county or corrections system.

The purpose of this chapter is to present an overview of the ethical issues encountered by those mental health practitioners employed directly by a correctional facility. Such professionals generally provide a range of mental health counseling and educational programs, including those related to stress management, anger management, and addiction. However, they may also perform forensic evaluations in order to address legal issues. In any case, it can be dangerous work that is performed under strained conditions in which a number of significant ethical issues arise. These must be recognized and properly managed in order to avoid what can be quite serious consequences.

PRACTITIONER COMPETENCE

Mental health practitioners have an obligation to be competent when providing their services in general. This means they must not accept casework or seek

---

[1]For a general overview of mental health practitioners in forensic settings, see McGrath and Torres (2010).

403

Ethical Justice. http://dx.doi.org/10.1016/B978-0-12-404597-2.00013-9

employment placing them beyond their professional abilities. This is particularly important when providing specialized services to inmate populations, such as those requiring sex offender or substance abuse treatment. For example, those unfamiliar with the complexities of mental health practice, or simply looking to fill a position, may be willing to employ a practitioner despite the absence of sufficient background or credentials. An employer's willingness to hire should not be taken as evidence of the practitioner's competence; rather, the practitioner has a responsibility to be aware of their qualifications and limitations.

In addition, practitioners have an obligation to seek education and credentialing from legitimate institutions, and to avoid diploma mills where credentials can be purchased without the completion of a formal academic program or coursework. Consider the following examples out of Washington State, which include health care providers that worked for the prison system (Department of Health, 2009):

> The Department of Health has charged three health care providers with unprofessional conduct for using bogus degrees from diploma mills in their practice:
>
> - Michael Strub (LW00004263), a licensed social worker, allegedly bought a Doctor of Philosophy in Psychology (PhD) diploma and transcript in March 2004. He got it from Hamilton University, an online diploma mill. Charges say Strub misrepresented his education and training to clients and insurance companies.
> - David Larsen (RC00021390, CP00000530), a registered counselor and chemical dependency professional, bought a Doctor of Psychology (PsyD) degree in October 2002. He purchased it from St Regis University, another online diploma mill. Larsen didn't complete an academic program or course work through St Regis. He allegedly misrepresented his education and training on a resume he submitted for a counselor position in August 2004. Larsen was known as "Dr Larsen" at that agency by staff and clients.
> - Taylor Danard (RC00013399), registered counselor, purchased a Doctor of Philosophy in Psychology (PhD) degree from St Regis University in January 2003. From 2003 to July 2008, Danard allegedly misrepresented her education and training by referring to herself as a PhD in her practice. Danard did not complete an academic program or course work from St Regis. Charging papers say she provided false information to a Department of Health investigator.

Mental health practitioners have a responsibility to avoid unaccredited programs and outright diploma mills, as using credentials from such institutions amounts to fraud; as demonstrated, this can result in both loss of licensure and criminal charges.

ROLE OF FORENSIC UNITS

In correctional settings, behavioral health care is provided in a local county jail, a state or federal prison, or a detention facility. Federal and state correctional systems have access to forensic units where inmates requiring an inpatient level of behavioral health care will be sent. In these units, there are two types of evaluations that occur. One is an evaluation for the legal system and the other is an evaluation for the purpose of providing treatment. Unfortunately, sometimes the two overlap.

Dual Agency

Forensic mental health (FMH) practitioners who are assessing an inmate for a strictly legal (i.e., forensic) issue, such as criminal responsibility or competency to stand trial, should advise the inmate that they are not there to treat them. They should further advise that the information obtained in the course of the evaluation is not confidential. Failure to do so may confuse the inmate about the nature and purpose of the evaluation, and it may also compromise the legal integrity of the results.

In some units, due to either staffing constraints or lack of understanding, the same provider is expected to both treat an inmate and perform a forensic evaluation for the court. Referred to as *dual agency*, this is an unfortunate feature in many systems. Dual agency is not inherently unethical or always avoidable. If an inmate is in a unit for treatment and refuses needed medication, the treating physician will be required to appear in court in some states and the federal system to override the inmate's refusal, regardless of the physician's role. What is important is for the treating physician to make it clear to the inmate what role they will be playing in the treatment and/or evaluation paradigm.

Further still, behavioral health staff should not allow themselves to be placed in the position of performing any non-medical functions. For example, they should never conduct physical searches or escort inmates. The only exception is in an emergency where life and limb is threatened, such as during an ongoing fight, hostage situation, or riot (Bonner and Vandecreek, 2006).

Access to an Attorney

When assessing recently arrested inmates, FMH examiners should inquire as to whether the inmate has had access to an attorney. If not, they have an ethical obligation to advise the arrestee that a decision must be made as to whether they want to proceed. Alternatively, they may want to consult with an attorney first. It should be made clear to the inmate that simply requesting an attorney prior to being evaluated will not influence the examiner's future opinion or reflect negatively in the evaluation. If the examiner believes the inmate feels pressured to proceed without consulting an attorney, then they should not proceed with the evaluation; they should postpone it until the inmate has had access to an attorney.

CORRECTIONAL CULTURE

It is important for behavioral health care providers in the correctional setting to understand the culture in which they will be administering care. They must understand that the correctional setting belongs to the law enforcement personnel mandated with maintaining the security of both inmates and non-inmates. Providers who are used to getting their way in the community setting are in for a rude awakening if they bring that mindset into a jail or prison.

Jail staff will generally not compromise security to meet the needs of others. They understand that security lapses in prison can result in serious injury and even death. For example, consider a 2012 incident at the Tennessee Department of Corrections Riverbend Maximum Security Institution, as reported in Johnson (2012):

> A state prison counselor was beaten so severely he had to be rushed to Vanderbilt University Medical Center with possible life-threatening injuries.
>
> It was a surprise attack from an inmate who should have been locked up.
>
> While the Tennessee Department of Correction confirmed an employee was struck and injured, it came just over a week after the commissioner gave Channel 4 News a tour of the same prison facility to show how safe it is.
>
> ...
>
> Channel 4 has learned that last Saturday, an inmate counselor not in uniform or protective gear was left to man an entire unit by himself.
>
> The cells were supposed to be locked, but an inmate opened his, jumped the counselor from behind and beat him until a unit manager finally noticed what was happening.
>
> "It seems to indicate that there are systemic problems in the prison system that are not being adequately addressed," said Alex Friedmann, with the Human Rights Defense Center.
>
> Despite a statement from prison officials saying the counselor was simply "hit by an inmate," the beating was so severe it took 38 stitches to repair the damage. Also, the counselor sustained a concussion, and friends say his speech is now slurred from time to time.

"People are getting hurt and injured, and we need to know what's going on in the system. The public deserves to know, and the correctional system needs to acknowledge the problems that are happening so they can fix them," Friedmann said.

...

A source inside the prison told Channel 4 that the locking mechanisms in this particular unit had been malfunctioning in the prior week, and maintenance workers had been trying to fix the problem.

The Department of Correction did not respond to questions about that claim and also rejected our request to view video surveillance of the assault.

In addition, the department declined our request to interview the prison counselor who was injured.

Owing to their competing goals, there is often a tension between health care providers and jail security staff. There are different rules in a correctional setting and varying levels of danger. If that bothers a FMH provider, then they should not seek to work in that environment.

EVALUATIONS

As mentioned at the beginning of this chapter, there are a number of different kinds of inmate evaluations. Each has their own related ethical issues. In this section, we will provide a general overview of these evaluations with some discussion of each.

Treatment Evaluations

Inmates with mental health needs can be treated in general population, in specialized settings, in a jail set aside for mentally ill inmates, or in a forensic unit – all of which is an inpatient level of care.

Treatment evaluations will be conducted in the same manner as in the community, with a heightened sensitivity to issues related to contraband, risk of suicide in the jail setting, predation in the correctional setting, as well as other security and treatment concerns. While some correctional settings are well designed for medical and behavioral health treatment, many are not. Often providers are forced to speak with inmates through cell doors, in corridors, and often in small rooms not designed or even intended for use as treatment settings.

Confidentiality is at times honored in the breach. It is not uncommon for a mental health worker to go to a unit or pod and ask to see an inmate, with the guard announcing loudly, "Smith, mental health is here to see you." Staff must determine if it is reasonable for them to provide treatment in a particular milieu. If not, they need to make it clear to jail or prison administration that conditions are not acceptable. The same issues found in evaluations will be present in ongoing treatment.

Malingering mental illness in correctional settings is problematic. Practitioners must be aware of this, as inmates will feign illness to get medication that they will then sell. Also problematic is the targeting of truly mentally ill inmates by others to get medication appropriately prescribed to them.

Competency to Stand Trial

Competency to stand trial evaluations are conducted in the community and in correctional settings. These examinations address the inmate's current mental state, and whether they are able to understand their charges and assist their attorney in their defense. In a jail they can done on someone in general population or on a forensic unit. When done in general population, usually a forensic psychiatrist who contracts with a county will perform the evaluation and there will be no treatment relationship.

It is possible that a psychiatrist providing treatment in the jail setting could be asked by the court to perform a competency to stand trial evaluation. As these are two fundamentally different roles, the provider should ask that a separate clinician be asked to perform the second role. Unfortunately, in some areas, due to a lack of competent evaluators, this may not be possible. As previously mentioned, the inmate must be made aware of this, as it affects the treatment alliance and expectations around confidentiality. The attorney representing the inmate should also be aware that the same person who is treating the inmate is involved in completing a separate forensic evaluation.

When an inmate has been found incompetent to proceed, the rules vary by state. In some states misdemeanor charges will be dropped. Regardless of the state, incompetence related to felony charges almost always results in commitment to a forensic unit for the purpose of restoring competency. In this context the treating psychiatrist is almost always involved in evaluating the inmate's competency.

Criminal Responsibility

Criminal responsibility evaluations deal with the mental state of an offender at the time of a crime. They were referred to as *Insanity Pleas* in the past. This evaluation should not be done by a treating behavioral health provider. It is not unheard of for a practitioner in a jail setting to evaluate for treatment, competency to stand trial and criminal responsibility at the same time. Such situations belie ignorance of both ethical concerns and lack of formal forensic training. Treating someone is so fundamentally different from assessing criminal responsibility that a practitioner ought to refuse to participate in such a situation.

Dangerousness

Once found not responsible due to mental disease or defect, the acquittee[2] will undergo an evaluation to determine if they need to be transferred to a forensic unit (i.e., a secure setting), a civil psychiatric unit in the community, or outpatient treatment. Periodic evaluations will be conducted to determine the level required. These evaluations are characteristically done by psychiatrists employed by a state or the federal government and who work in a forensic unit, although there is no requirement that they be. Although it would be best for these evaluations to be done by non-treating clinicians, usually the treating provider is involved in, if not doing, the examination. This presents problems in the context of juggling forensic and treatment roles. It is unfortunate, but not unethical so long as the client is fully aware of the role issues.

ONGOING TREATMENT

While there are inherent tensions between those providing mental health care and those providing security, mental health care can complement the security functions by engendering responsibility, respect for authority, and pro-social behavior (Dignam, 2003). The American Correctional Health Services Association (ACHSA) is an organization composed of providers from many disciplines, including nurses, physicians, psychiatrists, psychologists, social workers, etc. ACHSA has developed a code of ethics to deal with the complicated interplay between promoting healing, autonomy, dignity, and maintaining safety in a correctional setting. This code attempts to allow provision of health care, while maintaining role separation. For example:[3] "Honor custody functions but not participate in such activities as escorting inmates, forced transfers, security supervision, strip searches or witnessing use of force."

The International Association for Correctional and Forensic Psychology[4] (IACFP) (formerly the American Association for Correctional and Forensic Psychiatry) has developed a code of ethics (International Association for Correctional and Forensic Psychology, 2010) that highlights attempts to provide care and respect the inmate's dignity and minimize harm, while resisting pressure to provide substandard care. Good communication between behavioral health providers and other correctional staff is important. Non-behaviorally trained correctional staff often see attempts at treatment and intervention as coddling

---

[2]A successful "Not Responsible" plea results in an acquittal. Any further legal issues regarding retention, release, etc., are now technically civil in nature.
[3]http://www.achsa.org/mission-ethics-statement/;last accessed on 6 March 2013.
[4]While the IACFP is an organization of psychologists, the ethical guidelines offered would seem apply to any behavioral health discipline.

inmates. It is important to educate correctional staff that properly treated mental illnesses will make their job easier. Engaging them in suicide prevention strategies (no correctional facility likes a completed suicide) is often a way to begin breaking down some cultural barriers.

INFORMED CONSENT/CONFIDENTIALITY

As noted by Bonner and Vandecreek (2006), correctional behavioral health providers juggle responsibility to their inmate clients, other correctional staff, and to society. Their first duty is to the inmate client, but this must be tempered by legitimate concerns for security and safety, not all that different from in the larger community in some ways. Inmate clients, as well as clients outside of correctional facilities, should be informed of the benefits and risks of any treatment and of any limits on confidentiality (e.g., when there is legitimate concern about imminent danger to self or others). At times assessments are made for another client (jail or prison), such as evaluations for segregation, lethality risk, parole board, so that correctional staff can have professional input into decision making. Inmate clients should have to consent for protected health information being shared, the same as in the community.

When lethality issues are forefront, breaching confidentiality is an easy decision. However, what is the ethical route when the stakes are significantly lower (e.g., when inmates disclose in a mental health treatment context that they violated facility rules)? It is hard to imagine feeling compelled to notify authorities of transgressions such as masturbating or having consensual sexual contact with another inmate. Other things may be different, however, and there is no clear place to draw the line. It must be kept in mind that some transgressions are crimes, even felonies. What about an inmate revealing he had sex with a correctional staff member?

There is a treatment–security dichotomy that is not always amenable to easy resolution. One approach is four-pronged (Pinta, 2009). First, one must be aware of the ethical issues or concerns. Second, one must have an ethics-based priority paradigm. This includes strict self-honesty to weigh whether a decision is based on self-interest (e.g., personal needs, fear of litigation, loss of employment, etc.) or the best interest of the client (inmate) and/or a professional code of ethics. Third, there is hopefully a period of deliberation, even if brief, possibly including input from another professional. This phase should include being aware of any applicable laws. The fourth phase is making a decision and taking responsibility for it. There will be many times when withholding knowledge of rule violations can backfire on the professional. This is not an easy pool to swim in. (See the discussion of transgressions by staff in "Sexual Relationships" below.)

DISCIPLINARY HEARINGS

The role of behavioral health staff in disciplinary hearings varies by state, if at all. Behavioral health professionals may be asked to opine on competency to proceed with a disciplinary hearing, responsibility of the offender and/or input on disposition of the violation. Divergent opinions exist regarding these issues, with the responsibility piece most contested. The consensus appears to be that behavioral health professionals should not participate in assessing the responsibility of inmates for violations of correctional regulations (Krelstein, 2002).

Solitary Confinement

Usually called segregation, isolating inmates from others can be problematic, especially when the inmate suffers from a major mental disorder. The ensuing sensory deprivation can lead to depression, psychosis, and/or suicide (Sanzhez, 2013). Bonner and Vandecreek (2006) report that it is unethical for mental health clinicians to participate in any administrative proceeding regarding the placement of non-violent inmates in segregation unless lethality concerns override. Inmates in segregation should have the same access to mental health care as those in general population (see "Physical and Sexual Assault Victims" below).

Restraint

There are times when an inmate is placed in restraints by correctional staff due to self-injurious or other directed violence. Behavioral health staff should assess the mental health needs of such individuals at and during the time of restraint. This means attending the inmate in person, documenting the condition and circumstances of their restraint, and monitoring for any developments of consequence or concern.

SEX OFFENDERS

Treatment of sex offenders in prison is ethical, although there are some issues that arise, such as true voluntariness and confidentiality of the treatment. A thorough exploration of the ethical issues related to sex offender treatment in correctional facilities is beyond the scope of this chapter. It is, however, interesting that the Association for the Treatment of Sexual Abusers' Professional Code of Conduct (Association for the Treatment of Sexual Abusers, 2001) offers no specific guidance to practitioners working in correctional settings.

The authors will make the following commentary regarding *civil commitment* of sex offenders at the end of their sentence. Due to political considerations, behavioral health professionals have been given the task of housing sex offenders past the expiration of their sentence through so-called civil commitment for dangerous sexual predators. This is a misuse of the behavioral health field professions. Behavioral health practitioners should avoid allowing their professional skills to be subverted to this end. The problem is at the sentencing end, not the end of the sentence.

PHYSICAL AND SEXUAL ASSAULT VICTIMS

Behavioral health staff should cooperate in assessing the mental health needs of physical and sexual assault victims, and help ascertain the need for protective custody, special cell arrangements, and even transfer to another correctional facility (International Association for Correctional and Forensic Psychology, 2010).

SEXUAL RELATIONSHIPS

When providing behavioral health care in the community, sexual contact with patients is considered unethical because of the context and the power differential. In the very same way, sexual contact with inmates is also unethical and even more so as the power differential in a forensic unit or jail is much greater. In fact, even apparent consensual sex with an inmate by a prison guard is considered rape.

It is also good to keep in mind that inappropriate sexual behavior by professional staff is not limited to males (Faulkner, 2011). For example, consider the case of Dr Madalena Sanchez, as reported in Marzulli (2008):

> An inmate who had sex with a prison psychologist is suing federal prosecutors for intercepting their phone chats, the *Daily News* has learned.
>
> Demetrius Hill, 29, contends that not only were his civil rights violated, but someone might think he consented to the monitoring – which would make him a rat.
>
> "To be known in [Hill's] community or in the prison system as has having worked as an informant, has proved fatal(!)" Hill wrote in the complaint scrawled in longhand from a federal prison, where he is serving a 20-year sentence on gun-related charges.
>
> The suit was filed in Long Island Federal Court – the same day ex-prison psychologist Magdalena Sanchez pleaded guilty this month in Brooklyn to lying about her sex romps with the inmate.
>
> Sanchez, 35, is married, has a PhD and worked for the NYPD before landing a job with the Bureau of Prisons. She admitted she lied to investigators when she originally denied having sex with the inmate.
>
> Prosecutors came up empty for DNA evidence at the scene of the crime in Sanchez's office at the Metropolitan Detention Center in

Brooklyn, but were ready to play jailhouse tapes of the sexy shrink having steamy telephone conversations with Hill, a reputed Bloods gang member.

As this case demonstrates, such unethical conduct not only has potential civil consequences, but can also result in criminal charges.

Consider also the case of an Ex-Counsel in the Augusta State Medical Prison, which involves her alleged rape and unreported threats by an inmate in her care, as reported in Gardner (2009):

An Augusta State Medical Prison employee was fired after she and an inmate allegedly sex. Now, weeks later, she says it was rape. But the Department of Corrections says their investigation tells a much different story.

It's an alleged relationship that the Department of Corrections states may have been criminal on the counselor's part. It also cost her her job and she says her ten-year career ....

Could an Augusta State Medical Prison mental health counselor have been having sex with a convicted murderer? The counselor admits she did, but alleges Marcus West raped her two times while she counseled him in mid-January.

The woman has since been fired. After that, she filed a report with the Richmond County Sheriff's Office. It says she was raped by murder inmate Marcus West.

News 12: "Why didn't you come forward sooner with rape allegations?"

Ex-Counselor: "Because he told me he would kill my children and my family if I did."

But the Department of Corrections has a different story in the same report. The Augusta State Medical Prison says the woman confessed she had sexual intercourse multiple times with West and that she may soon face criminal charges.

That's something this woman claims could have been stopped if someone listened to her sooner. She began working with the prison in November and says over the next few weeks, West had become obsessed with her. She says she took her concerns to her Deputy Warden, but her counseling sessions with West continued, and that's when she says she was forced to have sex with him out of fear.

"He (West) told me he planned this from the very beginning when he saw me come in, that I was young and naive and that was going to be part of his plan to sue the Department of Mental Health. Told me he paid guards to spread rumors we were having a relationship. He fabricated a journal to that effect."

After she heard this, she says she went to her Deputy Warden again to tell him everything. "He (Deputy Warden) was the one that informed me then that what I had done was illegal, by having inappropriate relations with the inmate, which is absurd. He said he believed me and would do whatever it took to protect me."

Now that she's out of a job and her career, she says she hopes justice will be done. But the Department of Corrections says it's pursuing its own justice as well.

All behavioral health providers in correctional settings need to be vigilant for attempts to entice them to engage in minor boundary violations by inmates. As mentioned in Chapter 12: "Ethical Issues for Corrections Staff," even minor transgressions can be used against staff with threats to report the violations unless preferential treatment is afforded, even including sex. Inmates can be deft manipulators and professional staff need to be alert to attempts to compromise them. This is a dangerous slippery slope. Self-reporting a significant breach of facility rules and not allowing it to be used against oneself is preferable to being pressured into criminal conduct (e.g., bringing in contraband), even at the risk of losing one's job, as such breaches can result in a prison sentence for the provider.

DEATH PENALTY

Ethical issues pertaining to the death penalty are myriad, and best addressed by the ethical codes and guidelines of a discipline's professional organization. Ultimately, the mental health community appears divided on the specifics. It is generally held that it is unethical for behavioral health care workers to directly participate in the implementation of the death penalty. However, what constitutes "directly" is hotly debated. Some providers, for example, believe that it is unethical to provide treatment for an inmate in order to get them well enough to be tried for capital murder or to get them well enough to simply have their death sentence carried out. Others see no ethical issues whatsoever and regard the administration of the death penalty as an issue that is separate from their role or professional concern. It is, however, permissible to treat a death row inmate who accepts treatment voluntarily.

RESEARCH

Any psychological research conducted in a correctional setting must comply with the ethical standards of the National Commission for the Protection of Human Subjects of Biomedical and Behavioral Research (1976) as well as the most recent standards available from the Office for Human Research Protections (2003) of the US Department of Health and Human Services and any applicable research standards of professional associations such as the American

Psychological Association and/or the American Psychiatric Association and any applicable international human rights agreements. (International Association for Correctional and Forensic Psychology, 2010)

RELEASE TO THE COMMUNITY

Behavioral health care workers should actively ensure that mentally ill inmates are not released without appropriate follow up arranged in the community. Failure in this regard constitute negligence. This can result in harm to the former inmate, as well as causing a threat to the community.

ADMINISTRATIVE EDUCATION

Behavioral health staff in correctional settings have an ethical obligation to educate and/or alert correctional staff and administration to issues interfering with the delivery of appropriate behavioral health care to inmates (International Association for Correctional and Forensic Psychology, 2010). This can refer to housing conditions, food, or treatment by prison staff. Whatever the issue, it must be put in writing in order to ensure that the situation is communicated to and then addressed by the administration in the appropriate manner.

SUMMARY

Providing mental health care in correctional settings is a challenging endeavor (Daniel, 2007).The FMH professional must navigate the tension between providing humane treatment to incarcerated individuals with dignity and confidentiality, while helping the facility maintain a safe milieu. The landscape is fraught with many ethical dilemmas. The best protection is to be prepared and to be honest. One must also have professional ethical codes to rely on and ethical colleagues to turn to when needed. Most importantly, one must have or develop the courage to stand up for what one believes to be ethical conduct and practice.

Questions

1. List two examples of programs that are generally provided by mental health practitioners employed by a correctional facility.
2. Forensic mental health practitioners who are assessing an inmate for a forensic issue are bound by confidentiality. True or False?
3. Define dual agency. Explain why this is an issue.
4. List the two types of evaluations that occur in forensic units.
5. Explain the difference between competency to stand trial evaluations and criminal responsibility evaluations.
6. Explain why solitary confinement may be problematic.

References

Association for the Treatment of Sexual Abusers, 2001. Professional Code of Conduct. Association for the Treatment of Sexual Abusers, Beaverton, OR, url: http://www.atsa.com/pdfs/COE.pdf.

Bonner, R., Vandecreek, L.D., 2006. Ethical decision making for correctional mental health providers. Criminal Justice and Behavior 33 (4), 542–564.

Daniel, A.E., 2007. Care of the mentally ill in prisons: challenges and solutions. Journal of the American Academy of Psychiatry and Law 35, 406–410.

Dignam, J., 2003. Correctional mental health ethics revisited. In: Fagan, T., Ax, R. (Eds.), Correctional and Mental Health Handbook, Sage, Thousand Oaks, CA.

Department of Health, 2009. Diploma mill: phony degrees lead to charges for three health care providers; bogus degrees purchased online. New Release, Washington State Department of Health, May 28; url: http://www.doh.wa.gov/Portals/1/Documents/1500/NewsReleases/2009/09-094DiplomaMillCharges.pdf.

Gardner, L., 2009. Prison counselor fired for sex with inmate claims rape. WRDW-TV Augusta, February 5; url: http://www.wrdw.com/news/crimeteam12/headlines/39109032.html.

International Association for Correctional and Forensic Psychology, 2010. Standards for psychology services in jails, prisons, correctional facilities, and agencies, third ed. Criminal Justice and Behavior 37, 749–808.

Johnson, J., 2012. Prison counselor attacked as inmates rebel against new policies. WSVM-TV Nashville, November 9; url: http://www.wsmv.com/story/20059359/prison-counselor-attacked-as-inmates-rebel-against-new-policies.

Faulkner, C., 2011. Sexual boundary violations committed by female forensic workers. Journal of the American Academy of Psychiatry and Law 39, 154–163.

Krelstein, M.S., 2002. The role of mental health in the inmate disciplinary process: a national survey. Journal of the American Academy of Psychiatry and Law 30, 488–496.

Marzulli, J., 2008. Inmate who had sex with prison psychologist files civil rights suit. New York Daily News, March 18; url: http://www.nydailynews.com/news/crime/inmate-sex-prison-psychologist-files-civil-rights-suit-article-1.288842.

McGrath, M., Torres, A., 2010. Forensic mental health experts. In: Turvey, B., Petherick, W., Ferguson, C. (Eds.), Forensic Criminology, Elsevier, San Diego, CA.

National Commission for the Protection of Human Subjects of Biomedical and Behavioral Research, 1976. Research Involving Prisoners (DHEW No. (OS) 76-131). National Commission for the Protection of Human Subjects of Biomedical and Behavioral Research, Bethesda, MD.

Office for Human Research Protections, 2003. OHRP Guidance on the Involvement of Prisoners in Research. US Department of Health and Human Services, Washington, DC, url: http://archive.hhs.gov/ohrp/humansubjects/guidance/prisoner.htm.

Pinta, E.R., 2009. Decisions to breach confidentiality when prisoners report violations of institutional rules. Journal of the American Academy of Psychiatry and Law 37, 150–154.

CHAPTER 14

Professional Organizations in the Criminal Justice System

Stan Crowder and Brent E. Turvey

Key Terms

Credential mill Refers to organizations that sell credentials to members for a fee, without a background check or the verified demonstration of knowledge, skills, and ability. In other words, members of such organizations are not required to earn credentials in any meaningful or demonstrable fashion.

General knowledge exam An exam that is intended to help guide members early in their careers through a valid course of study, covering broadly the basic knowledge and principles held in one or more fields of study.

Practice standards Fundamental rules that set the limits of evidentiary interpretation, offering a standard for evaluating acceptable work habits and application of methods.

Profession Defined by its ability to set a basic standard for competent workmanship and compel its members to conform.

Professional certification The process of establishing that a practitioner has achieved a particular level of knowledge, skill, and ability as demonstrated by coursework, instruction, and/or supervised experience.

Professional organization A group with clear membership guidelines that establishes terms of professionalization and pledges sanction or expulsion for those unable or unwilling to meet those terms.

Professionalization The process by which any trade or vocation becomes professional, characterized by a high degree of competence with respect to domain-specific knowledge, skills, and abilities.

Social club An organization that serves a group of like-minded individuals within a profession, without actual member accountability and without advancing the profession as a whole.

A *profession* is defined by its ability to set a basic standard for competent workmanship and compel its members to conform. This requires a uniform set of terms, definitions, practice standards, and ethical guidelines. Generally, this is accomplished by the formation of a *professional organization* – a group with clear membership guidelines that establishes terms of professionalization and pledges sanction or expulsion for those unable or unwilling to meet those terms.

In many licensed professions, certifications are mandated by state law, and are often accompanied by continuing education and recertification requirements.

CONTENTS

Ethical Justice. http://dx.doi.org/10.1016/B978-0-12-404597-2.00014-0

As will be discussed in this chapter, such legal stipulations make individual membership in a professional organization a necessity for survival. This is in part because they serve to coordinate and facilitate professional requirements for certifications and continuing education – like those in the medical and legal professions.

In the criminal justice system, however, only certain professionals are legally mandated to be licensed or certified by the state. Criminal justice "professions" that do not require state licensure or certification include college and university professors, forensic scientists, and some law enforcement officers.[1] For these unlicensed criminal justice professionals, membership in a professional organization is obviously not a strict requirement. However, it can be beneficial.

The purpose of this chapter is to discuss the role of professional organizations in the regulation and maintenance of the criminal justice professions. This will include a general discussion of their intended role; their obligation to set requirements, practice standards, and ethical guidelines; and their responsibility towards unethical practitioners. This chapter will close with a discussion of successes and failures with respect to this regulatory role. Case examples are provided throughout.

THE ROLE OF PROFESSIONAL ORGANIZATIONS IN CRIMINAL JUSTICE

Professionalization is the process by which any trade or vocation becomes professional, characterized by a high degree of competence with respect to domain-specific knowledge, skills, and abilities. Ideally, professional societies, associations, and organizations are intended to assist with the professionalization of the fields they serve. This generally involves the education, support, and oversight of a given membership.

In fulfillment of this broad-ranging responsibility, everything that a professional organization does should generally contribute to the guidance and mentoring of students, and the professional maintenance or advancement of regular members. When managed responsibly, these efforts also serve another equally important function. They provide a level of protection for the discipline, and the rest of society, from unqualified, unethical, and incompetent practitioners.

Consider how the following efforts can be served by membership in a professional organization.

---

[1]Some states require certain types of law enforcement officers to acquire and maintain general or job specific certifications, and some do not.

Student Support
Professional organizations can help support students in a number of ways essential to their entry into a particular discipline. First, they let students know the basic educational pathways and requirements for entering a particular field. This helps them make better choices as they decide where to attend school and what coursework to study. They also provide students with a set of guidelines, to help them make good professional decisions and avoid conduct that might serve as exclusionary criteria for some employers.

Professional organizations can also provide discounted training opportunities to students through annual meetings, workshops, and practicums. These can allow students to see professional behavior modeled by those already at work in the field. They can also provide important networking opportunities that can lead to internships, mentorships, and even entry-level employment.

In short, professional organizations can help usher students into a particular discipline by providing them with the ability to make good decisions about critical aspects of their career choices; by supporting them with a safe professional environment that encourages structured guidance; and by providing them with access to those working professionals that are best situated to help them.

Professional Development and Advancement
Professional organizations provide members with a means of professional development and advancement. This is partially accomplished with a tiered membership structure in which advancement is based on a combination of education, training, experience, and testing. It is also accomplished by offering the development of consistent terminology and uniform practice standards, continuing education and training, and, in some instances, professional certifications.

Informing the Criminal Justice System
The ability to sustain active membership in a legitimate professional organization is an important credential. It signals an ethical disposition, as well as a commitment to competence and professional betterment. It also lets those in the criminal justice system know that there is some measure of accountability at work in the member's life outside of the workplace.

Regulating the Criminal Justice Professions
Professional organizations help regulate their respective disciplines by setting basic standards that members are expected to meet or abide. These include requirements for membership, practice standards, general knowledge exams, professional certifications, continuing education, and a strong code of ethics. Each of these will be discussed in turn.

Requirements for Membership

When a professional organization sets their basic requirements for membership, they are setting the low-water mark for entry into a given discipline. The lower these requirements, the lower the quality of applicants, members, and other practitioners in the community. The obligation here is to ensure that new applicants have the appropriate background, and that they have the opportunity to advance in membership as they gain education, training, and experience.

Education

No matter the discipline, criminal justice professional organizations have a duty to require that non-student applicants have at least a 4-year college degree from an accredited institution. This ensures that the applicant is in fact on a professional path, with a basic core level of knowledge. It further demonstrates that they can commit to a lengthy course of study to its full completion. Professional organizations that do not have an educational requirement serve only to keep the professional water mark low and prevent the development or advancement of their membership community.

Criminal History

As discussed at multiple points throughout this text, employment in the criminal justice system requires a trustworthy character – for the most part. Criminal justice work, it must be clear by now, is fraught with report writing, and the taking of pledges and oaths, upon which considerable decisions rest. Those with a dishonest character cannot be relied upon by their employers, their co-workers, or the courts to provide believable reports or sworn affidavits and testimony.

In particular, those convicted of criminal activity have proven their lack of integrity. Consequently, professional organizations associated with the criminal justice professions have a duty to refrain from credentialing criminals. For instance, they have an obligation to screen applicants (and expel members) that have a felony conviction or a conviction of a misdemeanor based on a felony charge. Similarly, they must screen applicants (and expel members) that have a conviction related to perjury, false statements or testimony, or moral turpitude.

To be clear, there is no reasonable justification for a criminal justice organization to accept an application from anyone convicted as described above or for retaining them as a member. Such individuals are generally unemployable in the justice system, except as educators at certain institutions or at unprofessional law enforcement agencies. As such, these individuals have little if any ability to mentor students or to write them letters of recommendation for employment, and can actually harm their student's future employment prospects by association.

Practice Standards

Professional organizations must establish *practice standards* to help ensure the competent work-product of their members. These are basic foundations and precepts that enable accurate and reliable results. As discussed in Chisum and Turvey (2011, p. 104):

> Practice standards define a minimum threshold of competency.
> They also help define a practitioner's role and outline a mechanism
> for demonstrating their facility. They are a compass for diligent
> practitioners to follow and a screen against which those who have lost
> their way can be delayed and educated. As this suggests, the purpose
> of defining practice standards is not only to help professionals achieve
> a level of competency but also to provide independent reviewers
> with a basis for checking work that purports to be competent.
> Practice standards set the bar and are a safeguard against ignorance,
> incapacity, and incomprehension

As explained in the National Academy of Sciences Committee on Science, Engineering, and Public Policy report *Strengthening Forensic Science in the United States: A Path Forward* (the *NAS Report*; National Academy of Sciences, 2009), the development of practice standards is a threshold requirement for the facilitation of professionalism because they provide a mechanism for *auditing* (i.e., external integrity assessment, p. 194):

> Standards and best practices create a professional environment
> that allows organizations and professions to create quality systems,
> policies, and procedures and maintain autonomy from vested interest
> groups. Standards ensure desirable characteristics of services and
> techniques such as quality, reliability, efficiency, and consistency
> among practitioners. Typically standards are enforced through
> systems of accreditation and certification, wherein independent
> examiners and auditors test and audit the performance, policies, and
> procedures of both laboratories and service providers. In addition,
> requirements for quality control can be imposed on entities receiving
> federal funds, and professional groups can develop codes of ethics
> and conduct to serve as measures against which performance can be
> assessed.

Practice standards generally encompass the establishment of a basic duty of care, the reliability of methodologies, standardized terminology, and the requirements of report writing and expressing findings.

General Knowledge Exams

Professional organizations will offer a *general knowledge exam* to help guide members early in their careers through a valid course of study. The exam will cover the basic subjects related to the field. The required study materials will be explicit and in some cases produced by the organization itself to ensure quality. While not a certification, successfully passing a general knowledge exam typically signals that the member has achieved a fundamental level of knowledge and insight. This is used to separate those with only a passing interest from those who are committed to their own long-term professional development.

In order to achieve and maintain integrity, a general knowledge exam or any other kind of testing must be proctored in person. It cannot be something that is done online or without direct supervision. Otherwise it is difficult to confirm the true identity of the person taking the exam, and it is impossible to ensure the absence of cheating.

Professional Certification

Professional certification refers to the process of establishing that a practitioner has achieved a particular level of knowledge, skill, and ability as demonstrated by coursework, instruction, and/or supervised experience. This fact is attested by a signed document from the organization facilitating or providing the certification.

A discussion regarding the value of professional certification, and its absence in the forensic sciences, is provided in the *NAS Report* (National Academy of Sciences, 2009, p. 208):

> The certification of individuals complements the accreditation of laboratories for a total quality assurance program. In other realms of science and technology, professionals, including nurses, physicians, professional engineers, and some laboratorians, typically must be certified before they can practice. The same should be true for forensic scientists who practice and testify. Although the accreditation process primarily addresses the management system, technical methods, and quality of the work of a laboratory (which includes the education and training of staff), certification is a process specifically designed to ensure the competency of the individual examiner.

However, as discussed in Giannelli (2007), not every organization cares about quality or competence; many care only about the ability of members to pay fees and dues (p. 227):

> A number of organizations offer examiner certification programs. Some certifying organizations, however, appear to lack stringent

requirements. Instead, they issue what are reported to be "checkbook credentials." Rigorous certification standards should be instituted for examiners in order to ensure competence. Demanding written examinations, proficiency testing, continuing education, recertification procedures, an ethical code, and effective disciplinary procedures should form the basis of such a program.

In the criminal justice community, for example, many states require their law enforcement agents to be certified by a state agency, much like teachers. In this way, their law enforcement credentials can be suspended or revoked should they engage in unethical behavior, misconduct, or criminal activity. However, the value of such credentialing is equal only to the character of those that offer it.

For example, recall in Chapter 5: "Ethical Issues in Police Administration" that an investigation of State records revealed 1384 Officers with arrests and convictions for serious offenses that also remained certified to practice law enforcement with the Georgia Peace Officer Standards and Training Council (POST); many were also still on active duty with police agencies (Moore, 2008).

See also the final section of this chapter on "Credential Mills."

Continuing Education

Some professional organizations offer continuing education courses. In the criminal justice community, this may be a legal requirement, as with certain state law enforcement credentials. However, it may also be an organizational requirement, intended to address the ever-shifting knowledge of an association that is linked to legal statutes and rulings. For example, bar associations offer the legal community seminars and short courses in order to satisfy *continuing legal education* requirements.

Without a continuing education requirement, members do not need to keep up with changes or developments in the profession. Also, they may not keep up with refinements to vital methodology and related legal precedent. This can result in a professional community whose youngest members are the most knowledgeable, but least experienced, and whose eldest members are experienced, but essentially out of touch with contemporary thinking. Such circumstances are anathema to professional growth and development.

Code of Ethics

Professional organizations have an obligation to prescribe codes of conduct that promote ethical behavior among its membership. At the very least, they should include specific requirements and prohibitions regarding member professionalism, abuses of authority, universal honesty, casework, and sworn testimony. In this way, a professional code of ethics serves two functions: first, it educates the membership; second, it serves as a mechanism for member sanction and expulsion.

Member sanctions for ethical violations should generally be tiered (e.g., advisement, written warning, and then expulsion). The purpose of such sanctions is not necessarily to simply punish those responsible for unethical behavior, but to educate them and give them an opportunity to make changes before more serious sanctions are levied. This provides a mechanism for identifying well-intentioned individuals who err in judgment, as opposed to those whose professional ethics are at odds with those of the organization.

In service of these goals, professional organizations must maintain an ethics committee that is responsible for receiving and investigating complaints made against members. Subsequent to a fair hearing, the committee is then responsible for assigning the appropriate sanction. The problem with most professional organizations with respect to ethics is that they do not have a code of ethics, they do not have a relevant code of ethics (i.e., it protects the organization and does nothing to regulate other member behavior), or they do not enforce their code of ethics. As discussed in *NAS Report* (National Academy of Sciences, 2009, p. 26):

> A number of forensic science organizations – such as AAFS, the Midwestern Association of Forensic Scientists, ASCLD, and NAME – have adopted codes of ethics. The codes that exist are sometimes comprehensive, but they vary in content. While there is no reason to doubt that many forensic scientists understand their ethical obligations and practice in an ethical way, there are no consistent mechanisms for enforcing any of the existing codes of ethics. Many jurisdictions do not require certification in the same way that, for example, states require lawyers to be licensed. Therefore, few forensic science practitioners face the threat of official sanctions or loss of certification for serious ethical violations. And it is unclear whether and to what extent forensic science practitioners are required to adhere to ethics standards as a condition of employment.

This lack of accountability exists because many criminal justice professionals do not like the conflict that comes with reporting or sanctioning those responsible for ethics violations, no matter how severe. In addition, they risk workplace retaliation and professional blacklisting if they do (see, generally, Turvey, 2013). Rather, many would rather protect their colleagues, and the organizations that they represent, from the bad press that accompanies scandal.

For example, the major finding of a study of prosecutorial misconduct in the State of California found that (Ridolfi and Possley, 2010, p. 3): "those empowered to address the problem – California state and federal courts, prosecutors and the California State Bar – repeatedly fail to take meaningful action." Specifically, Ridolfi and Possley (2010) reported that the failure to hold prosecutors accountable for misconduct was widespread, typically denied, and rarely sanctioned (p. 3):

> ... Courts fail to report prosecutorial misconduct (despite having a statutory obligation to do so), prosecutors deny that it occurred, and the California State Bar almost never disciplines it.
>
> Significantly, of the 4,741 public disciplinary actions reported in the *California State Bar Journal* from January 1997 to September 2009, only *10* involved prosecutors, and only *six* of these were for conduct in the handling of a criminal case. *That means that the State Bar publicly disciplined only one percent of the prosecutors in the 600 cases in which the courts found prosecutorial misconduct and NCIP researchers identified the prosecutor* [emphasis in original].
>
> Further, some prosecutors have committed misconduct repeatedly. In the subset of the 707 cases in which NCIP was able to identify the prosecutor involved (600 cases), 67 prosecutors – 11.2 percent – committed misconduct in more than one case. Three prosecutors committed misconduct in four cases, and two did so in five.

A similar pattern exists in the forensic sciences as well. Consider the following Case Examples of the track record of the American Academy of Forensic Sciences (AAFS), arguably among the largest and most politically influential professional organization servicing that professional community.

CASE EXAMPLE

Enrico Togneri, Past President of the AAFS

In 1998, former Washoe County Sheriff's Captain Enrico Togneri, also a former president of the American Society of Crime Lab Directors (ASCLD), was granted parole after serving approximately 40 months of his sentence related to a drunk driving death that he caused. As reported in Associated Press (1998):

> Togneri, 51, was sentenced to 12 years in prison after pleading guilty in the 1994 death of Gunter Paschkowiak, 55. The former head of the Washoe County Crime Lab was returning from having dinner with a friend in Carson City when he rammed Paschkowiak's vehicle that was stopped at a traffic light at U.S. Highway 395.
>
> Togneri was charged with causing a death while driving with a blood-alcohol level of more than 0.10 percent. According to police reports, his blood-alcohol level was placed as high as 0.182 percent.
>
> He served more than a year in prison before being allowed to continue serving his sentence under house arrest.

Continued

CASE EXAMPLE *CONTINUED*

The friend that Mr Togneri was visiting was in fact his mistress and he was racing home drunk to his wife. In 1994, at the time of the homicide, Mr Togneri was also the President of the AAFS (Bashinski, 2004). On his resume, right up until the time of his death in 2003, he was involved in forensic casework and listed full membership in the AAFS. Both the AAFS and the California Association of Criminalists (CAC)

gave what amounted to a hero's send-off when Mr Togneri died, with no mention of the homicide he had been convicted of causing in either obituary (American Academy of Forensic Sciences, 2004; Bashinski, 2004). Ironically, one of these reported that "He could always be counted on to 'do the right thing' and for the right reasons" (Bashinski, 2004, p. 4). Mr Togneri was not expelled from any of these or other professional organization for his crimes and in fact was heralded with great fondness upon his death 10 years later.

CASE EXAMPLE

Rod Englert, AAFS Fellow

In 2004, an ethics complaint was filed against AAFS Fellow Rod Englert, a well-known law enforcement bloodstain expert with no formal scientific credentials who testifies almost exclusively for the prosecution. The complaint documented instances of inconsistent testimony regarding bloodstain interpretations across multiple cases, misrepresentations of science, and misrepresentations of training on his professional resume. Then President of the AAFS, Ronald Singer, wrote a memo in response to an ethics complaint against Mr Englert, in which no action was taken by the AAFS Ethics Committee. It reads in part (Singer, 2004):

> [The AAFS] did receive a more detailed response from Hon. Haskell Pitluck, Chair of the Ethics Committee, which was distributed to the members of the executive Committee prior to our meeting last month. The matter was thoroughly discussed (in Executive Session) at our recently completed meeting, and after considerable debate, it was decided that no further action on the part of the Executive Committee or the Board of Directors was warranted.
>
> The Executive Committee saw two major issues in this case – one involving entries on the C.V. of the accused, and the other involving testimony given by the accused. Both issues hinged on whether or not the actions on the part of the accused could be proven to be deliberate. In the first case, the accused agreed to correct the offending portions of their C.V. while claiming no impropriety. The Ethics Committee was subsequently provided with

> a copy of the corrected version. Obviously, should the accused continue to provide uncorrected copies of their C.V., or make the same representation as before the hearing, there would no longer be an issue of intent.
>
> The second issue is a somewhat different matter. After having reviewed the materials provided to me, I was also troubled by some of the testimony given. However, as you know, this is basically opinion testimony, and under our current Bylaws, it is not unethical to be ignorant. Also, as Haskell pointed out in his memo these issues were subject to cross-examination at the time of trial. Barring any positive proof that the testimony was deliberately intended to misrepresent the facts of the case, there is really nothing that the Ethics Committee can do at this time.

As discussed in Cooley (2011), the AAFS ethics committee's final ruling in this matter appears at odds with their own Code of Ethics and Conduct (CEC). Under the AAFS CEC, "Every member … shall refrain from providing any material misrepresentation of education, training, experience, or area of expertise. Misrepresentation of one or more criteria for membership in the AAFS shall constitute a violation of this section of the code." Stating that one was the instructor of a course and not a student, as was the case in this compliant, would seem to fall in this category. It is also untenable to assert that it is not unethical to be ignorant while continuing to professionally credential the ignorant party without sanction.

CASE EXAMPLE

Barry Logan, AAFS President (2013)[2] and Ann Marie Gordon, AAFS

According to his professional resume, which lists a PhD in Forensic Toxicology, Dr Barry Logan became the Washington State Forensic Toxicologist in 1990. In 1999, he was hired to be the Director of the Washington State Patrol Forensic Laboratory Services Bureau – responsible for overseeing four full-service crime labs, two satellite labs, two latent print labs, and all of their combined 160 employees. He served in both positions simultaneously until he resigned in 2008 (Johnson, 2008).

According to her professional resume, Ann Marie Gordon holds a BA in "Genetics" and an MS in "Microbiology and Immunology," both from the University of California at Berkeley. She was hired as a forensic toxicologist for the Washington State Toxicology Laboratory (WSTL) in 1998 and promoted to Laboratory Manager in 2000. She served in that position until 2007, when she resigned while still under investigation for laboratory fraud (Johnson and Lathrop, 2007).

Based on anonymous tips regarding fraudulent certifications of blood-alcohol-related tests from inside the WSTL, an investigation was launched that ultimately led to the dismissal of at least 100 criminal cases and harm to the credibility of thousands more. According to a joint three-judge-panel decision granting an "Order of Suppression" across multiple criminal cases (*Washington v. Amach et al.*, 2008; Judge David Steiner, Judge Darrell Phillipson, and Judge Mark Chow), the findings of fact regarding accusations of fraud and misconduct by Ann Marie Gordon and Dr Barry Logan are as follows, detailed in the section of the decision labeled "False Certifications" (pp. 3–4):

1. Ann Marie Gordon [AMG] became lab Manager at WSTL by appointment of Dr Logan.
2. [In 2000] AMG informed Dr Logan that her predecessor as lab manager had engaged in a practice of having other toxicologists prepare and test simulator solutions for him and yet certify that he had prepared and tested the simulator solutions.
3. AMG told Dr Logan that she did not approve of this procedure and was then also informed by Dr Logan that it was not acceptable for a toxicologist to engage in this practice.
4. Nonetheless, AMG did engage in this practice beginning in 2003. Ed Formoso was a lab supervisor; he prepared and tested simulator solutions for AMG from 2003–2007. This involved 56 simulator solution tests.

5. Each test was accompanied by a CrRLJ 6.13 certification that AMG had performed the test and that the test was accurate and correct.[3]
6. Melissa Pemberton was the quality control manager at the WSTL during a part of this time, and knew that AMG was not performing tests but was certifying them.
7. This deception was uncovered after two anonymous tips received by the Chief of the Washington State Patrol.
8. The first was received on March 15, 2007. Dr Logan was directed by Assistant Chief Beckley to investigate this complaint.
9. Dr Logan directed AMG and Formoso to investigate the complaint.[4]
10. AMG and Formoso discussed the procedure and agreed that Formoso would no longer perform tests on behalf of AMG.
11. AMG informed Dr Logan that she did not perform the tests of the solutions but that she signed the forms indicating that she did.
12. AMG and Formoso prepared a report stating that there was no problem with the certifications and that no solution had left the lab with an incorrect solution in 20 years.
13. Dr Logan, AMG, and Formoso knew, or should have known, that this report was incorrect and misleading, but took no steps to correct it provide for another investigation.
14. Melissa Pemberton had run vials prepared for AMG by Formoso through the gas chromatograph along with her own sample, knowing that these were to be attributed to AMG, and that AMG would sign certificates alleging that she did this.
15. Dr Logan was aware of this by August of 2007.
16. Dr Logan and Pemberton both testified under oath that no one other that Formoso ever ran test for AMG.[5]

The three-judge-panel decision (*Washington v. Amach et al.*, 2008) goes on to describe other significant problems with the WSTL under the direction of Dr Barry Logan and the management of Ann Marie Gordon, including: various "Defective and Erroneous Certification Procedures;" numerous detailed instances of "Software Failure, Human Error, Equipment Malfunction, and Violation of Protocols"; the ongoing use of

Continued

CASE EXAMPLE *CONTINUED*

"Improper Evidentiary Procedures"; the persistence of "Inadequate and Erroneous Protocols and Training"; the overall "Impact on Tests Conducted in the Field"; the WSTL's intentional "Nondisclosure of Machine Bias" to defendants, attorneys, or the public; and the WSTL's "Systematic Inaccuracy, Negligence, and Violation of Scientific Protocols" – all of which affected "Thousands of Tests." The judicial panel determined that all of this misconduct combined to create a "culture of compromise" in the WSTL. Furthermore, the panel explained that ongoing "ethical compromises" and "fraud" committed by Ann Marie Gordon and her colleagues must have been known to others in their immediate work environment.

Aside from describing false testimony, the judicial panel also made it clear that Dr Barry Logan was responsible for allowing a "culture of compromise" to develop. Additionally, the panel elicited inconsistent testimony from Dr Logan in which he stated that he was not aware of the specific certifications that were being provided by his lab personnel in toxicology cases. However, the manual of laboratory protocols explaining these certifications in detail bears his signature on each protocol. Subsequently, and in accordance with other findings of fraud, negligence, incompetence, and error already mentioned, the judicial panel determined that Dr Logan's ignorance, incompetence, and negligence as Director prevented these problems from being identified, revealed, and corrected (*Washington v. Amach et al.*, 2008, pp. 22–23).

Ann Marie Gordon resigned on 20 July 2007, only a few days after the investigation into her misconduct was initiated (Johnson and Lathrop, 2007). In 2008, the Office of the Medical Examiner for the County of San Francisco hired her as a forensic toxicologist. She worked in that system for 2 years, testifying under oath, before her history of fraud in Washington State was made known to local prosecutors and defense attorneys (Van Der Beken, 2010). She has since asserted her Fifth Amendment right to remain silent and not self-incriminate in subsequent court proceedings. She remains a member of the AAFS in good standing and as recently as 2011 hosted the Annual Meeting for The International Association of Forensic Toxicologists (TIAFT) in San Francisco, where she apparently enjoys the continued support of her peers (Verstraete, 2011).

Dr Barry Logan resigned from the Washington State Patrol Forensic Laboratory in 2008, 1 year after the resignation of Ann Marie Gordon. Dr Logan's resignation was necessary for "restoring public and judicial confidence," according to Washington State Patrol Chief John R. Batiste (Batiste, 2008). However, Dr Logan himself strongly disagrees with the findings of the judicial panel in *Washington v. Amach et al.* (2008) and takes only some responsibility for the problems that occurred under his management; he believes that the problems with the WSTL were "dramatically overstated" by defense attorneys (Johnson, 2008).[6]

Dr Barry Logan remains a Fellow of the AAFS in good standing; became Vice-President of the AAFS subsequent to his resignation from the WSTL; and in early 2012, he was voted in as their President-Elect. In 2013, he began serving as President of the AAFS. Ironically, at the same meeting where he took office, the AAFS also presented him with an award for his contributions to the field of forensic toxicology and for his leadership in the forensic science community (Press Release, 2013).

He also remains a member in good standing of TIAFT, the Society of Forensic Toxicologists, and the American Society of Crime Laboratory Directors. He is currently the National Director of Forensic Services for National Medical Services Labs, and continues to testify in major cases throughout the United States (Longo, 2011).

---

[2]*All documents, exhibits, and testimony referenced in this case example can be found archived online at: "KING COUNTY, 3 JUDGE PANEL RULING;" url: http://www.waduicenter.com/?page_id=470. Cited as Washington v. Amach et al. (2008); this example has been adapted with minor edits and additions from Turvey (2013).*
[3]*The record is clear that the forms signed by Ann Marie Gordon indicate they are signed "under penalty of perjury" (McEachran, 2008; O'Brien, 2007; Washington v. Amach et al., 2008, p. 20).*
[4]*The wrongness of directing those committing fraud to investigate themselves was not lost on the panel, which they referred to as (Washington v. Amach et al., 2008, p. 23): "a situation screaming with irony."*
[5]*Dr Logan testified before the three-judge panel in Washington v. Amach et al. (2008) from 7 to 9 January 2008.*
[6]*In April 2008, the Washington State Forensic Investigations Council (FIC) wrote a report condemning fraud among Dr Logan's subordinates at the crime lab. However, it did not hold Dr Logan himself accountable (McEachran, 2008). Comprised of appointees from the law enforcement community with a mandate to preserve and protect the lab system, the FIC ignored the court's findings of fraud in Washington v. Amach et al. (2008). It also did not appear to hold Dr Logan accountable for the negligence it agrees occurred under his supervision – failing to adequately supervise Ann Marie Gordon and others, failing to know what certifications were being provided by lab employees to the courts, and failing to be aware of ongoing fraud and error despite the fact that everyone else in the lab was aware of it.*

According to the *NAS Report* (see Chapter 8: "Ethical Issues in Forensic Examination") the forensic science community is in fact fragmented and broken, without a single voice or purpose; it cannot identify, let alone fix, its own problems. Nor has the adversarial process been adequate to the task. As explained in the *NAS Report* (National Academy of Sciences, 2009, p. 16):

> The forensic science enterprise lacks the necessary governance structure to pull itself up from its current weaknesses. Of the many professional societies that serve the enterprise, none is dominant, and none has clearly articulated the need for change or presented a vision for accomplishing it.

The authors concur that this is the case throughout the criminal justice system, and it will continue to be so until such time as the professional organizations that are associated with it seek to develop, maintain, and enforce rigorous codes of professional ethics.

PROFESSIONAL ORGANIZATIONS *v.* SOCIAL CLUBS

An important distinction must be drawn between actual professional organizations and mere social clubs. In this context, a *social club* is an organization that serves a group of like-minded individuals within a profession, without actual member accountability and without advancing the profession as a whole. It generally serves its members by providing the appearance of legitimate professional achievement or credentials to those outside the organization. Although, in reality, they have simply paid a fee, are friends with the right people, or work for the appropriate agency or agencies.

Indicators that a criminal justice organization is a social club, and not a legitimate professional association, include one or more of the following:

(1) The organization does not have clearly defined educational requirements for the admission of new members.
(2) The organization does not have established practice standards for members.
(3) The organization does not have an established code of conduct for members.
(4) The organization does not publish its code of member conduct publicly.
(5) The organization does not have a mechanism for submitting complaints against members for misconduct (e.g., an ethics committee).
(6) The organization does not enforce, or selectively enforces, its code of conduct.
(7) The organization only allows law enforcement, retired law enforcement, or those aligned with law enforcement to join.

(8) The organization does NOT allow those in law enforcement, or those aligned with law enforcement, to join.

(9) The organization allows convicted felons to join or retain membership.

(10) The organization allows non-professionals to join (e.g., spouses, members of the media).

Consider The Vidocq Society (http://www.vidocq.org), which is an organization that appears dedicated to solving cold cases. On their website, they explain that: "the process leading to membership is neither automatic nor open to members of the public. New Vidocq Society Members must be sponsored by existing members." Vidocq Society members, however, are known to include true crime authors and publicists – among others. In any case, several testifying members place the letters "VSM" after their names on professional resumes, as though this is a degree or a professional credential.

Of note is the fact that one of their founding members, Richard Walter, a retired prison therapist with an MA in counseling, was found by the courts to have committed perjury. In a 1982 case, the defense discovered and a federal appeals court agreed that Mr Walter perjured himself in regard to his qualifications during sworn expert testimony in a double homicide shooting case. According to the record in *Drake v. Portuondo* (2003):

> … The prosecution informed defense counsel on the Thursday evening that it intended to call a psychologist named Richard D. Walter to testify about psychological profiling. On the Friday, the prosecution successfully moved to add Walter as a witness, and Walter mounted the stand. …
>
> …
>
> It is now apparent that Walter's testimony concerning his qualifications was perjurious. He claimed extensive experience in the field of psychological profiling, including: work on 5000 to 7500 cases over several years in the Los Angeles County Medical Examiner's Office; an adjunct professorship at Northern Michigan University; more than four years as a prison psychologist with the Michigan Department of Corrections; and expert testimony given at hundreds of criminal trials in Los Angeles and Michigan.
>
> …
>
> Years after exhausting his direct appeals, Drake discovered evidence, through his own research in prison, that Walter had lied about his credentials. Although Walter is a prison psychologist with the Michigan Department of Corrections, Drake found suggestive evidence that Walter lied about his other credentials. As the prosecution now concedes, Walter performed no criminal profiling in the Los Angeles County Medical Examiner's Office. According to Walter's supervisors

there, he was employed as a lab assistant responsible for cleaning and maintaining the forensic lab. There seems to be no record that Walter was ever on the payroll of Northern Michigan University, where he claimed to be an adjunct professor. The Los Angeles County District Attorney's office has found no record of Walter testifying as an expert witness in a criminal proceeding between October 1975 through May 1978.

Federal judge John T. Elfvin ultimately concluded, based on Mr Walter's testimony and its context, that it was reasonable to presume that he had indeed given false testimony with regard to his qualifications. Moreover, Judge Elfvin found that he had made additional false and misleading statements about his credentials while under oath. This is detailed in *Drake v. Portuondo* (2006). Mr Walter, also a fellow of the AAFS, was not expelled from either organization despite the court's incontrovertible rulings and subsequent ethics complaints.

CREDENTIAL MILLS

A distinction must be also drawn between legitimate professional organizations and credential mills. Courts rely heavily on practitioner involvement in professional organizations, and subsequent professional credentialing, with respect to determinations of expert fitness and admissibility. Consequently, some schools and organizations have appeared that are simply in the business of selling credentials in just about anything to anyone.

For example, consider this early critique regarding the origins and motives of the American College of Forensic Examiners[7] from the American Bar Association (Hansen, 2000, pp. 44–45):

> Robert O'Block has come a long way since 1994, when he made $40,000 a year as a professor at the College of the Ozarks in Point Lookout, Mo.
>
> Now he's making a six-figure income as the executive director of the American College of Forensic Examiners, a Springfield, Mo.-based nonprofit organization that credentials forensic experts.
>
> O'Block started in 1992 with $500 of his own money and in the beginning ran a credentialing service single-handedly out of a spare room in his home. It has since grown into a 13,000-member organization with more than $2.2 million in annual revenue.
>
> He was paid nearly $190,000 for his efforts in 1997, according to the most recent federal tax return available for the organization.

---

[7]Currently referred to as the American College of Forensic Examiners International (ACFEI).

But O'Block, 48, apparently has made few friends and admirers along the way. One former associate calls him a con artist. And more than one describes his organization's credentialing process as a complete scam.

"He basically takes people's money and gives them a worthless piece of paper," says Robert Phillips, an Audubon, N.J., document examiner. "He's just in it for the money."

Phillips claims he has reason to know. He says he resigned as chair of the organization's certification committee in 1993 after discovering that O'Block was issuing credentials to unqualified candidates behind the committee's back.

Many of the nation's leading forensic scientists don't seem to have much use for O'Block or his organization either.

James Starrs, a professor of law and forensic sciences at George Washington University, says the organization's certification process lacks objectivity. "It's driven by the felt needs of the people in charge," he says. "If they want you in, you're in, even if they have to break all of the rules to do it."

Andre Moenssens, a law school professor at the University of Missouri-Kansas City and an expert on scientific evidence, goes even further. He says O'Block's organization is basically a certification mill. "For the right amount of money, he will certify just about anybody as an expert in anything," Moenssens says.

Indicators that a criminal justice organization is a credential mill, and not a legitimate professional association, include one or more of the following:

(1) An emphasis on organizational marketing over practitioner competence.
(2) The promise of receiving professional credentials in a short period of time or in no time at all.
(3) The ability to receive professional credentials based on life experience, without coursework, training, or subsequent examination.
(4) Little or no information is available regarding established credentialing curricula.
(5) Little or no information is available regarding instructors.
(6) Little or no interaction with instructors or those signing off on credentials.
(7) Little or no information regarding other members.
(8) No request for applicant resumes or places of employment.
(9) Little or no background check into member applications.

Legitimate professional organizations require applicants to prove their backgrounds; they conduct scrupulous investigations into the qualifications listed on the applicant's professional resume; and they require hard work and verifiable accomplishment to achieve full membership.

SUMMARY

A *professional organization* is a group with clear membership guidelines that establishes terms of professionalization and pledges sanction or expulsion for those unable or unwilling to meet those terms. This chapter discusses the role of professional organizations in the regulation and maintenance of the criminal justice professions. This includes a general discussion of their intended role; their obligation to set requirements, practice standards, and ethical guidelines; and their responsibility towards unethical practitioners.

Questions

1. All criminal justice professions require state licensure or certification. True or False?
2. Explain how professional organizations help regulate their respective disciplines.
3. Define practice standards. Explain why they are important.
4. List the two functions of a professional code of ethics.
5. Explain the difference between professional organizations and social clubs.
6. List three differences between professional organizations and credential mills.

References

American Academy of Forensic Sciences, 2004. Remembering Enrico. Academy News: AAFS Newsletter 34 (1), 3.

Associated Press, 1998. Former sheriff's captain paroled in fatal accident. Las Vegas Review-Journal, November 7.

Bashinski, J., 2004. Farewell to *Enrico Togneri*. CAC News, 10, Second Quarter.

Batiste, J., 2008. Logan resigns as head of WSP forensic laboratory Bureau. Office of Chief John R. Batiste, Washington State Patrol Media Release February 14.

Chisum, W.J., Turvey, B., 2011. Crime Reconstruction, second ed. Elsevier, San Diego, CA.

Cooley, C., 2011. Reconstructionists in a post-Daubert and post-DNA courtroom. In: Chisum, W.J., Turvey, B. (Eds.), Crime Reconstruction, second ed. Elsevier, San Diego, CA.

Drake v. Portuondo., 2003. Docket No. 01–2217, January 31 (321 F.3d 338); argued. September 9, 2002; decided: 31 January 2003.

Drake v. Portuondo., 2006. United States District Court, Western District of New York, 99-CV-0681E(Sr). Memorandum and Order, March 16.

Giannelli, P., 2007. Wrongful convictions and forensic science: the need to regulate crime labs. North Carolina Law Review 86, 163–236.

Hansen, M., 2000. Expertise to go. American Bar Association Journal (No. 86), 44–52.

Johnson, T., 2008. State crime lab chief resigns after problems raised on DUI evidence. Seattle Post-Intelligencer, February 14.

Johnson, T., Lathrop, D., 2007. State lab manager quits after she's accused of signing false statements. Seattle Post Intelligencer, July 31.

Longo, A., 2011. Can Oak Ridge science be trusted in Casey Anthony case? Bay News 9, March 23; url: http://www.baynews9.com/article/news/2011/march/221903/.

McEachran, D., 2008. Forensic Investigations Council Report on the Washington State Toxicology Laboratory and the Washington State Crime Laboratory. Washington State Forensic Investigations Council, April 17; url: http://www.governor.wa.gov/boards/profiles/1000219.asp.

Moore, J., 2008. Channel 2 finds nearly 1,400 certified officers with criminal records. Action News 2, December 8; url: http://www.wsbtv.com/videos/news/channel-2-finds-nearly-1400-certified-officers/vCLXw/.

National Academy of Sciences, 2009. Strengthening Forensic Science in the United States: A Path Forward, National Academy of Sciences Committee on Identifying the Needs of the Forensic Sciences Community. National Academies Press, Washington, DC.

Press Release, 2013. AAFS Recognizes award-winning forensic toxicologists of NMS labs. Business Wire, February 19.

Ridolfi, K., Possley, M., 2010. Preventable Error: A Report on Prosecutorial Misconduct in California 1997–2009. Northern California Innocence Project at Santa Clara University School of Law, Santa Clara, CA.

Singer, R., 2004. Memo to Ms Patricia S. Lough, San Diego Police Department, re: ethics complaint filed with AAFS Ethics Committee against Rod Englert. November 10.

Turvey, B., 2013. Forensic Fraud. Elsevier, San Diego, CA.

Van Der Beken, J., 2010. Problems of S.F. toxicologist not disclosed. San Francisco Chronicle, May 26.

Verstraete, A., 2011. President's message. The International Association of Forensic Toxicologists, October 21; url: http://www.tiaft.org/president_message.

Washington v. Amach, et al., 2008. District Court of King County, Case No. C00627921 et al., Decided January 30.

CHAPTER 15

Whistleblowers in the Criminal Justice System

Stan Crowder and Brent E. Turvey

Key Terms

Code of Silence (a.k.a. Blue Wall of Silence) An unwritten rule in most police departments that prohibits reporting of perjury or other misconduct by fellow officers; it also forbids officers from testifying truthfully if the facts would implicate the conduct of a fellow officer.

Whistleblower Describes someone that reports misconduct within their own agency or institution.

Whistleblower Protection Enhancement Act of 2012 Signed into law in 2012, this legislation is intended to reform protections for federal employees seeking to report misconduct, fraud, and illegality.

Perhaps the greatest dilemma faced by an ethical professional working in the criminal justice system is whether to report the misconduct of others.[1] That is why the authors saved this particular chapter for last. Informing on colleagues and co-workers is a decision that requires an informed awareness of the conflicted politics, policies, and laws that govern employment in the criminal justice community. By now the reader is terribly acquainted with these. The decision to become a whistleblower also requires serious deliberation, because there are a number of ways to err and misunderstand the consequences.

Whistleblower is a generic term used to describe someone that reports misconduct within their own agency or institution, or, as described in Miethe (1999, p. 11), "an employee or former employee who reports misconduct to persons who have power to take action." This includes reporting breaches of administrative policy, professional ethics, professional responsibilities, and also violations of the law. The label of "whistleblower" is sometimes used in reference to those that report such violations internally (e.g., to a supervisor, to human resources, to internal affairs, or to an office of professional responsibility). However, it is more appropriately associated with those making such disclosures to external government agencies or to the public via the media.

In this chapter, we present a discussion of the ethical obligations, policies, and laws associated with reporting misconduct by employees within the

CONTENTS

---

[1]Some few sections of this chapter have been adapted from material written for Turvey (2013).

Ethical Justice. http://dx.doi.org/10.1016/B978-0-12-404597-2.00015-2

criminal justice system. This includes mention of the protections that are ostensibly afforded to those with the courage to come forward under such circumstances. These ideals are counter-balanced with discussions regarding the potential consequences to whistleblowers – personal, professional, and legal. This chapter closes with some hard-earned advice regarding the steps that a would-be whistleblower can take in order to achieve the best possible professional outcomes, as well as likely repercussions.

THE PROFESSIONAL OBLIGATION TO REPORT

Many criminal justice practitioners have an explicit obligation to report any misconduct they have direct knowledge of. As discussed in prior chapters, these obligations may be a function of professional ethics, agency policy, or the law. For example, attorneys have an duty to report misconduct mandated by their respective state bar associations (Ridolfi and Possley, 2010; Badgerow, 2013). In law enforcement, corrections, and the military, failure to report knowledge of wrongdoing up the chain of command may be considered a form of *professional misconduct*, if not utter *dereliction of duty* – both of which are criminal charges. Even the judiciary is not entirely immune. Judges are required to report misconduct by other judges and attorneys to ensure the integrity of the court, in comportment with state codes of judicial ethics and the law (McMorrow *et al.*, 2004; and see also Abrahamson, 1997; Ridolfi and Possley, 2010). All of this in the name of preserving due process – which again is equal parts justice, fairness, and personal liberty.

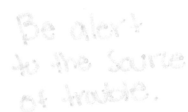

However, for the ethical criminal justice practitioner, the obligation to report misconduct exists whether there is a specific mandate or not. They understand that the stakes are high in the criminal justice system. As actors in the criminal justice community, they observe daily that the failure to report misconduct is likely to result in someone losing their life, their job, and their family, along with their basic liberties. As we have learned, harm from misconduct can befall victims, suspects, and even co-workers. The ethical criminal justice practitioner also understands that doing nothing makes them complicit in whatever results and even responsible to a varying degree. Consequently, they do not shirk their professional duties with respect to seeking to weed out the inept, the unethical, and the criminal. As described in the Whistleblower Protection Enhancement Act (WPEA) of 2012 (Whistleblower Protection Enhancement Act, 2012, p. 1):

> Whistleblowers play a critical role in keeping our government honest and efficient. Moreover, in a post-9/11 world, we must do our utmost to ensure that those with knowledge of problems at our nation's airports, borders, law enforcement agencies, and nuclear facilities are able to reveal those problems without fear of retaliation or harassment.

Therein lies the dilemma. Reporting misconduct is vital to institutional and government integrity. However, the personal, financial and professional repercussions for reporting misconduct are not generally favorable to the reporter. In fact, as we have learned through this text most do not survive the ordeal, at least not professionally (see the Case Example of Senator Ted Stevens, revealed in part by former FBI Agent and whistleblower Chad Joy, in Chapter 9: "Ethical Issues for Criminal Prosecutors").

EMPLOYMENT CONTRACTS

The majority of practitioners in the criminal justice system work for agencies and institutions that require them to sign employment contracts. These contracts are likely to contain confidentiality agreements, and non-disclosure clauses, that preclude communication of any kind about active casework, internal matters, or employee activities. Restrictions are also placed on the dissemination of information that reflects negatively on the employer – as would allegations of misconduct, especially if true.

For example, government (i.e., public) institutions, including prosecutor's offices, law enforcement agencies and their respective crime laboratories, and correctional facilities, generally have written policies and rules of conduct that severely limit the speech of their employees. These are generally binding both in and outside of the workplace. Consider that law enforcement policies are adapted from, or draw heavily on, the "Model policy on standards of conduct" developed by the International Association of Chiefs of Police, which states (International Association of Chiefs of Police, 2012):

1. Officers shall not, under color of authority,
   a. make any public statement that could be reasonably interpreted as having an adverse effect upon department morale, discipline, operation of the agency, or perception of the public;
   b. divulge or willfully permit to have divulged, any information gained by reason of their position, for anything other than its official, authorized purpose; or
   c. unless expressly authorized, make any statements, speeches, or appearances that could reasonably be considered to represent the views of this agency

An example of an adapted standard comes from the Seattle Police Department's *Policy and Procedure Manual* (Seattle Police Department, 2013):

IV. Communication and Confidentiality
   A. Through Chain of Command
      1. Employees shall direct communications through their chain of command unless directed otherwise. If an employee believes they have information of such a sensitive nature as to

require communication outside the chain of command, the employee may communicate directly with any higher-ranking officer, including the Chief of Police, and at that point the responsibility for any further dissemination of that information lies with the higher-ranking officer.

B. Representation of the Department

1. Responsibility for management of the Department and dissemination of policy and budget rests with the Chief of Police.

2. Employees shall not disseminate information concerning their personal interpretations of Department policy, investigations, crime patterns, budget, deployment or other opinions that could be construed as representing the Department or the Chief of Police. Subordinate employees may be granted authority to represent Department issues on a case-by-case basis, but only following delegation by their chain of command. Specific employees (e.g., Public Affairs Unit personnel) may be granted broad authority to represent Department issues outside their chain of command, or on behalf of the Chief of Police (or his/her designee).

This is similar to the restrictions placed on complaints of misconduct that can be made by military personnel (i.e., Department of Defense), which requires them to report up the chain of command and not outside it.[2] Whistleblowers unable to report within their chain of command are required to file complaints of misconduct, in writing, to the Inspector General, in accordance with Army Regulation 20-1, which provides that (Inspector General, 2012, pp. 1–2):

1–4. Responsibilities

a. *The Inspector General.* TIG will—

...

(10) Oversee Army IG investigations and special investigations by—

(a) Performing investigations and investigative inquiries directed by the SA and CSA and submitting the relevant reports of investigation (ROIs) and reports of investigative inquiry (ROIIs) to the respective directing authority.

(b) Assessing or investigating alleged violations of the Army's professional ethic (see AR 600–100).

(c) Processing DOD whistleblower reprisal investigations related to Army activities.

---

[2]Those unfamiliar with the military may be unaware of its role in populating the criminal justice system with personnel or that it has a criminal justice system entirely its own.

This kind of language is a part of most government employee contracts, intended to maintain the confidentiality of sensitive issues, to provide for operational authority, and to help maintain overall agency effectiveness.

A careful read of these sample regulations makes it clear that government employees with concerns or grievances regarding co-workers, supervisors, or other internal matters must report them only within the institutional chain of command. Having done this, they are forbidden from pursuing such matters themselves or speaking out about them publicly – lest they harm the "operation of the agency, or perception of the public." Consequently, unless a matter of public interest is involved (which is a subjective standard at best), government employees can be punished, and even terminated, for violating these and related administrative policies (Ronald, 2007).

For example, the courts held that the Atlanta Police Department did not violate the free speech rights of a police officer who was denied promotion because she was under investigation for posting an allegation of police department corruption on her personal Facebook page. Officer Maria Gresham claimed retaliation in violation of her First Amendment right to free speech after a posting on her Facebook newsfeed. A complaint was filed against Officer Gresham for violating *Atlanta Police Department Work Rule 4.1.06, Criticism*, which states: "Employees will not publicly criticize any employee or any order, action, or policy of the Department except as officially required. Criticism, when required, will be directed only through official Department channels, to correct any deficiency, and will not be used to the disadvantage of the reputation or operation of the department or any employees." As a result of the Office of Professional Standards investigation against Officer Gresham, she was denied promotion to the position of "investigator." A federal district court in Georgia upheld the decision on reconsideration, once again granting summary judgment in the department's favor on the officer's First Amendment retaliation claim (*Gresham v City of Atlanta*, 2011).

GARCETTI et al. v. *CEBALLOS*

Restrictions on employee speech have a longstanding tradition within government agencies and currently enjoy coverage from the US Supreme Court, which holds that (*Garcetti et al. v. Ceballos*, 2006): "When public employees make statements pursuant to their official duties, they are not speaking as citizens for First Amendment purposes, and the Constitution does not insulate their communications from employer discipline."

The failure of these and related court decisions were recognized by Congress, and then the Office of the President of the United States, in the WPEA of 2012 (Whistleblower Protection Enhancement Act, 2012, pp. 1–2):

> Unfortunately, federal whistleblowers have seen their protections
> diminish in recent years, largely as a result of a series of decisions by

the United States Court of Appeals for the Federal Circuit, which has exclusive jurisdiction over many cases brought under the Whistleblower accorded a narrow definition to the type of disclosure that qualifies for whistleblower protection. Additionally, the lack of remedies under current law for most whistleblowers in the intelligence community and for whistleblowers who face retaliation in the form of withdrawal of the employee's security clearance leaves unprotected those who are in a position to disclose wrongdoing that directly affects our national security.

In a work environment where punishment, termination, and loss of employee benefits (e.g., wages, medical coverage, and pensions) can result from sharing internal matters outside the chain of command, institutional secrecy regarding misconduct is all but assured except in perhaps the most extreme cases (Papandrea, 2010; Diehl, 2011; Wright, 2011).

Again, what this means is that government employees who are in a position to have direct knowledge, and an applied understanding, of misconduct do not generally enjoy unfettered freedom of speech. They are contractually bound to report such violations strictly within their chain of command. They are also contractually bound to refrain from speech that harms the image or effectiveness of their agency. By abiding with their employment contracts and keeping agency secrets, they preserve its image to the public, their professional reputation within the community, and their continued employment prospects. When they fail to abide, and disclose misconduct publicly, the courts have not been on a government employee's side.

WHISTLEBLOWER PROTECTIONS

There are various forms of protection available to whistleblowers. Some are a matter of policy, and some are a matter of state and federal law. Consider the following examples.

OSHA

The US Department of Labor's Department of Occupational and Safety and Health Administration (OSHA) currently maintains a Whistleblower Protection Program. As explained on their government website (Department of Occupational and Safety and Health Administration, 2013):

OSHA's Whistleblower Protection Program enforces the whistleblower provisions of more than twenty whistleblower statutes protecting employees who report violations of various workplace safety, airline, commercial motor carrier, consumer product, environmental, financial reform, food safety, health insurance reform, motor vehicle safety, nuclear, pipeline, public transportation agency, railroad, maritime, and securities laws. Rights afforded by these whistleblower acts include, but are not limited to, worker participation in safety and health activities, reporting a work related injury, illness or fatality, or reporting a violation of the statutes.

Government-Funded Research

The US government employs a disproportionate number of scientists and funds a significant amount of scientific research worldwide.[3] It also requires any organization that receives government funding to have policies and procedures in place for the reporting, investigation, and identification of any questionable research practices. As mandated by the Office of Research Integrity (2009b, p. 4):

> All institutions receiving research funds from Public Health Service (PHS) agencies must have on file an assurance form with the Office of Research Integrity (ORI). This assurance is to ensure that the institution has in place policies and procedures for dealing with allegations of research misconduct, has provided ORI with contact information for its assurance official, and will submit an annual report to ORI identifying any activity from the previous year requiring inquiries and investigations into allegations of possible research misconduct involving research supported by PHS funds.

This means that all researchers that are employed or funded by the federal government must have a formal mechanism in place with respect to responding to whistleblower complaints. If they do not, or if they fail to comply, they can theoretically lose their funding.

Paul Coverdell Forensic Science Improvement Grant Program

To alleviate the tendency to maintain institutional secrecy, forensic examiners working for crime labs or law enforcement agencies that receive federal funding are meant to enjoy immunity from employer retaliation when acting as a whistleblower (Giannelli, 1997). As explained in a report from the Innocence Project (2009, p. 4):

> In 2004, Congress established an oversight mechanism within the Paul Coverdell Forensic Science Improvement Grant Program, which

---

[3]In 2003, as reported in Sovacool (2008, p. 271): "between six and eight million scientists were employed in research and development in the United States. Their activities – roughly 40% of the world's R&D effort – constituted a $300 billion industry, accounting for roughly 3.2% of the entire country's gross domestic product."

provides federal funds to help improve the quality and efficiency of state and local crime labs and other forensic facilities. In order to receive the federal funds, applicants are required to designate independent external government entities to handle allegations of serious negligence or misconduct affecting the quality of forensic analysis in facilities that receive Coverdell grants, and those oversight entities must also have a process for handling such allegations.

This is similar to the kinds of protections ostensibly afforded all federally funded scientific endeavor, as explained in the previous section.

Varied Coverage

The protections offered at the state and federal level vary on the precise definition of whistleblower, requiring that different conditions be met depending on the jurisdiction. As explained in Sinzdak (2008, p. 1637):

> Some statutes, for instance, protect an employee only if the employee reports an actual violation of the law. By contrast, some statutes protect employees who are mistaken about an employer's wrongdoing, so long as the employee reasonably believed that wrongdoing had occurred. Many statutes offer protection for a report of any violation of a law, statute, or regulation. Others protect only those employees who report legal violations that pose "a substantial and specific danger to the public health or safety." Some statutes cover only public employees, while others apply to both public and private employees.

In other words, each state protects defines its whistleblowers differently and affords them different conditions of protection. Questions also arise for whistleblowers with respect to the appropriate agency, or the proper recipients, of their formal complaints (Sinzdak, 2008, p. 1637):

> Most lawmakers agree that whistleblowers should not receive protection for reporting to just anyone. However, significant disagreement exists as to who should qualify as an appropriate recipient. At the moment, three alternatives predominate. These are: (1) protecting only those employees who report externally to a government agency, (2) protecting only those employees who report internally to a supervisor or senior executive, and (3) protecting employees who report *either* externally to a government agency *or* internally to a supervisor or senior executive.

What is clear is that going to the media first, or perhaps ever, is strictly forbidden. In fact, according to the literature: "Virtually no states protect those who choose to report to the media or other non-governmental third parties" (Sinzdak, 2008, p. 1634).

WPEA of 2012

In November 2012, President Barack Obama signed S.743, the WPEA of 2012 (Whistleblower Protection Enhancement Act, 2012), into law. It was intended to fund and broaden protections for federal employees seeking to report misconduct, fraud and illegality. In addition, as reported in Reubenfeld (2012): "It clarifies the scope of protected disclosures, tightens requirements for nondisclosure agreements, expands penalties for violating protections and adds to the staff of some federal agencies an ombudsman whose job will be to educate agency employees of their rights."

As of this writing, it is unclear whether this legislation will have its intended reformative effect. Its language seems to grasp at least some of the problems facing whistleblowers. However, whether prosecutors and the courts will simply choose to ignore it is another matter.

However, the first of many high-profile post-WPEA whistleblower cases has already been concluded. Relevant to this text, it arose from within a criminal justice organization: the case of former CIA Agent John Kiriakou. As reported in Chamberlain (2013):

> In October [2012], Kiriakou was charged by the DoJ for violating the Intelligence Identities Protection Act (IIPA) for releasing the name of an officer implicated in a CIA torture program to the media. Federal prosecutors had originally charged Kiriakou for violations against the Espionage Act – which held a sentence of up to 35 years – but a plea agreement saw those charges lessened.
>
> Kiriakou was the first employee of the CIA to publicly acknowledge and describe details of the torture program that thrived under the Bush administration.

According to Mr Kiriakou, he was a whistleblower and critics say that the charges against him were contrived as punishment. He is also the author of *Reluctant Spy: My Secret Life in the CIA's War on Terror* (Kiriakou, 2012). In January 2013, he was sentenced to 30 months in prison.

WHISTLEBLOWER PROTECTION IS THEORETICAL

Seasoned criminal justice professionals understand that the notion of whistleblower protection is entirely theoretical. This is because agencies and institutions do not always understand, abide, or enforce required whistleblower protections. This is done by publicly denying the claims of the whistleblower, refusing to investigate those claims and thereby preventing any additional corroboration, and then taking action to harm the complainant and starve them of further access. This can result in a whistleblower who is initially terminated or otherwise sanctioned, who must then personally bear any legal costs of proving their status and asserting related protections. For example, as reported in Maier (2003):

> ... forensic scientists who levy charges of incompetence or corruption against their labs often find themselves unemployed. Former FBI forensic expert Whitehurst was suspended, then fired, before settling in 1997 for a $1.46 million payment in a lawsuit for wrongful discharge. Elizabeth Johnson, former director of a DNA lab in the Harris County Medical Examiner's Office in Texas, now often works as a consultant for criminal-defense teams, but she found herself unemployed in 1997 after failing to be a "team player" and link a murder suspect's blood to the scene of a crime. She was vindicated in a jury trial and settled for $375,000. When DNA lab worker Laura Schile called attention to serious problems in Oklahoma, she found herself under investigation and resigned in 2001 because of a "hostile work situation."

This is consistent with Johnson (2005), explaining that criminal justice agencies and organizations will actually go out of their way to make whistleblowing difficult for the rank and file – especially those affiliated or identifying with law enforcement. In reality, whistleblowers with the criminal justice community are commonly viewed, or characterized, as disloyal trouble makers against whom retaliation is not only acceptable, but encouraged.

Loyalty

Those who work in the criminal justice system do not generally applaud whistleblowers as heroes, despite the difficulties they must endure (Johnson, 2005; Rich, 2012). Generally, those who inform on their colleagues, co-workers, supervisors, and employers are regarded in a negative fashion. They are more often referred to internally with pejoratives, such as snitch, rat, weasel, turncoat, stool-pigeon, and squealer. In other words, they are regarded as being disloyal (Pershing, 2002; Rich, 2012).

Loyalty is a quality that is highly regarded by many criminal justice employment cultures, whether it is within a law enforcement agency, a correctional facility, or a crime lab. In particular, law enforcement culture is defined by the requirement of utter loyalty to not only an agency, but to brother officers in blue everywhere – referred as the "Code of Silence." This is significant because it is an aggressive and domineering culture, whose attitudes both pervade and shape the criminal justice system as a whole (Turvey, 2013).

Of great concern, then, is the law enforcement "Code of Silence" (a.k.a. "Blue Wall of Silence"), which has long been a feature of the literature related to law enforcement corruption, even as an international phenomenon (Knapp Commission, 1972; Mollen, 1994; Chin and Wells, 1998; Rothwell and Baldwin, 2007; Cooper, 2009; Shockley-Eckles, 2011; Wolfe and Piquero, 2011). It is described as (Chin and Wells, 1998, p. 238): "an unwritten code in many departments which prohibits disclosing perjury or other misconduct by fellow officers, or even testifying truthfully if the facts would implicate the conduct of a fellow officer." As explained further in Cooper (2009, p. 7): "what many people know as the 'Code of Silence' or 'Blue Wall of Silence' merits concern. The police subculture is dominated by the Cop Code. Its foundational norm dictates that 'cops protect cops.'"

Inevitably, the culture in most criminal justice environments (which tends to be dominated by law enforcement attitudes if not personnel) becomes inhabited by "workplace conditions" that "create an atmosphere where the repercussions of blowing the whistle outweigh the motivations for doing so …. Repercussions can include social ostracism by coworkers as well as retaliation from management in the form of blacklisting, demotion, and sometimes dismissal" (Pershing, 2002, p. 152).

As this suggests, the problem extends to failed leadership, wherein supervisors often have no interest in dealing with the message brought to them by the whistleblower; rather, leaders prefer to punish the messenger (Uys, 2010). Viewed as disloyal, whistleblower subordinates are often not supported by their supervisors because of perceived damage to their own professional reputation (e.g., lack of competence, lack of leadership skills) or because of potential damage to organizational standing in the professional community. Supervisors are subsequently willing to turn a blind eye towards, or actively participate in, whistleblower retaliation.

Whistleblower Retaliation

Whistleblowers take decisive ethical action by disclosing misconduct to the appropriate authorities, but often at their own peril, as described in Johnson (2005, p. 74): "There are almost always dire consequences to whistleblowers, to their careers, and to their personal lives as a result of their actions." To be clear, retaliation from co-workers and supervisors can be extreme, resulting in social and professional abandonment by those normally relied upon for support.

Dehaven-Smith (2011) is even more blunt, observing that retaliation against whistleblowers tends to have the following characteristics: "It often originates at the very highest levels of government" (p. 212); "Officials are often willing to commit felonies in an effort to retaliate against whistleblowers;" "Retaliation is sometimes designed to place people's lives at risk;" "Retaliation is usually devastating for the victims," resulting in ruined careers; and "When retaliation has been exposed, the laws protecting whistleblowers are not strengthened, nor are the retaliators usually punished" (p. 215).

This is consistent with the experiences of the authors, observing that retaliation for whistleblowing can include personnel actions, such as poor performance ratings, transfers that involve undesirable working conditions and less pay, withheld promotions, suspension, and dismissal. It can also result in personal harassment, such as separation from peers or long-time work mates, the fabrication of sexual rumors, threats of violence, and the theft, vandalism, or destruction of personal property. Whatever the bosses can dream up to make the whistleblower miserable and reconsider their complaint, very little is off the table, as reported Johnson (2005, p. 80): "the full force of the agency, formal and informal, is brought to bear on the 'snitcher' ... Rats are scorned, shunned, excluded, condemned, harassed, and almost invariably, cast out."

Consider the case of NYPD Police Officer Adrian Schoolcraft. When Officer Schoolcraft threatened to blow the whistle on falsified crime stats, his supervisors had him committed to a mental hospital, as reported in Parascandola (2010):

> A whistleblower cop vowed Monday night never to settle his $50 million federal lawsuit against the NYPD.
>
> "This is not about money," Police Officer Adrian Schoolcraft told the *Daily News*.
>
> Although Schoolcraft said he's flat-broke and living on Ramen noodles, he said that "There's not enough money in the state to get me to settle this suit. It's going to trial and there's no way around that – the truth has to come out."
>
> Schoolcraft, an eight-year veteran from the 81st Precinct in Bedford-Stuyvesant, Brooklyn, has been suspended without pay since last Halloween, when, he says, the NYPD forced him against his will into a mental ward at Jamaica Hospital in Queens.
>
> He said in his suit that the NYPD cast him as a lunatic because he blew the whistle on supervisors who fudged crime stats, enforced illegal quotas and badgered victims trying to report felonies.
>
> Many of his allegations are supported by secret audiotapes he made of the precinct commander, Deputy Inspector Steven Mauriello, and other supervisors.
>
> He has a website – schoolcraftjustice.com – that he and his lawyer Jon Norinsberg said has led to more tips and evidence about how police brass cook the books.
>
> ...

He is glad other officers have come forward with similar charges – most notably Adhyl Polanco, a cop at the 41st Precinct in the Bronx – but said he is not surprised most officers turn a blind eye when forced to meet summons quotas or downgrade felonies to misdemeanors.

In 2013, Schoolcraft's legal team was joined by the notorious whistleblower Frank Serpico, who became famous for suffering nearly fatal on the job retaliation while exposing corruption inside the NYPD in the 1970s. As reported in Parascandola (2013):

> "This is the way they do it," Serpico told *The News*. "They make you a psycho and everything you do gets discounted. But I told Adrian just to tell the truth as he knows it and to be himself. When you tell the truth, they can't do a damn thing to you."
>
> Serpico, 76, was credited with exposing corruption inside the NYPD. He testified in front of the Knapp Commission in 1971 and retired the following year. His career was captured on the big screen in the 1973 movie "Serpico," starring Al Pacino as the Brooklyn-born cop.

As a direct result of the Schoolcraft scandal, the resulting media coverage, and his impending lawsuit, NYPD Police Commissioner Raymond Kelly announced that a committee of former federal prosecutors would be appointed to look into allegations that the NYPD has been inappropriately downgrading criminal complaints.

SUGGESTED REFORMS

Initially, the authors thought to include many high-minded reforms that might assist the would-be whistleblower or at the very least could serve to deter and penalize those obstructing them. However, after much deliberation, it was concluded that no state or federal law could be written that would have the desired effect.

The reality is that reforms must take place in criminal justice leadership and culture. This means the hiring and retention of ethical employees, and the sanction or expulsion of anyone contrary. That is a leadership issue, and until there are better and more ethical criminal justice leaders in place there will continue to be scandals in the system.

The rules and laws already on the books tend serve honest men well. In contrast, they teach the dishonest how to hide what they have done and when to lie about it. Better and more laws would simply change the way that liars must lie; laws are incapable of changing fundamental professional character.

HARD-EARNED ADVICE

If an ethical criminal justice professional has knowledge of misconduct and wants to report it, what is the appropriate course of action? This is a question that the authors have been faced with time and time again, from students, colleagues, and even from themselves. Supervisors are often no help, if not the actual problem. Co-workers will not want to rock the boat and may even retaliate. Often, there seems no good answer. As explained in Sullivan (2012):

> Make sure you understand what you are getting into.
> "It's a life-changing experience," said John R. Phillips, founder of the law firm Phillips & Cohen and the man credited with devising the amendments that strengthened the government antifraud law, the False Claims Act, in 1986. "If you look at the field of whistle-blowers, you see a high degree of bankruptcies. You may find yourself unemployable. Home foreclosures, divorce, suicide and depression all go with this territory."

This grim sentiment is echoed in Johnson (2013):

> Whistle-blower lawyer Neil Getnick says the people in those tales usually came to a sad end. "Unfortunately, all the stories had pretty much the same plot line," Getnick says. "Something bad happened with an organization. A person stood up to do something about it. That person changed things for the better. And their life was changed for the worse."

The authors' best advice for those ethical souls who find themselves jammed up in the bowels of whistleblowing challenges, having already decided to file a complaint, includes the following:

(1) *Employment contracts.* Your employment contract may contain clauses the prevent you from disclosing certain kinds of information. Read it carefully, to the point of actual understanding. If you do not understand something, ask someone about (e.g., supervisor, union representative, or a lawyer). There may be certain conditions that the employer is not allowed to violate.

(2) *P&Ps.* Agency/institutional policies and procedures (P&Ps) should be part of an employee handbook. This will generally instruct on the appropriate filing of internal complaints. Again, read it carefully, to the point of actual understanding. Once things start happening, you may be the only one that has read it, which provides a significant advantage – especially if your employer is violating these policies and acting in bad faith.

(3) *State laws.* Every state has its own laws regarding what constitutes whistleblowing and what is required of the whistleblower. Again, read them carefully, to the point of actual understanding. If you do not understand something, contact those that produced or are mandated to enforce the legislation, or a knowledgeable attorney. Your state may require a very specific set of circumstances, and a very specific path of reporting, for related protections to kick in.

(4) *Federal laws.* If you work for a federal agency, or your agency receives federal money, federal guidelines for reporting misconduct likely apply. If so, find out whether your agency or institution is in compliance with these federal guidelines, and whether there is the required local mechanism in place for making such complaints. Also, read the WPEA of 2012. Again, if you do not understand something, contact those mandated to enforce the legislation – or a knowledgeable attorney.

(5) *Mentors and "rabbis."* Find a trusted mentor and seek advice. In law enforcement, this person may be your training officer and is sometimes referred to as a "rabbi" – as they offer not only advice, but perhaps even political protection. They may not have all the answers, but they can be a confidential sounding board and help to determine the most ethical path.

(6) *Documentation.* Document everything related to your concerns in order to back up your complaint. Take notes, save emails and text messages, and create a journal record of your related actions, supervisory responses, and any retaliation.

(7) *Put it in writing.* Many agencys and institutions are not required to respond to any complaint unless it is written down. If you are unwilling to do that, it speaks to the seriousness and logic of your complaint. Once a written complaint has been received, they are on the hook for a response.

(8) *CC the complaint.* Unless it is a violation of policy, do not send the complaint to just one person. Copy it to multiple supervisors, or your supervisor's supervisor, to create transparency and accountability. Your supervisor might be less inclined to act unless they are aware that others know and are paying attention.

(9) *Unions.* As already suggested, unions may be an option for some whistleblowers. The ethics of those leading the union will be tested and some unions may help, but in reality some may hurt. Unions are political, so be careful. Involve them when there is a breakdown between yourself and your supervisor, but not before.

(10) *Determine who has oversight.* Seek the "eyes and ears" of your supervisor, commander, or agency head. In the military, the Inspector General Corps serves as the eyes and ears of the commander. They exist to

serve the commander and the soldiers in resolving problems. Many states now have an Inspector General tasked to resolve state issues of fraud, waste and abuse. Employees must be able to go to an Inspector General without going through a supervisor first. The Inspector General must report to the head of the agency or unit only – there can be no middleman.

(11) *Take it up a level.* If the issue is at a local level, take it to a state agency; from the a state level, take it to a federal agency. This is for when there is an internal failure to act on your original complaint.

(12) *Hiring a lawyer.* Before taking any legal action, it is always best to seek out advice from a qualified legal professional. However, bear in mind that talk is cheap until you hire a lawyer. Then it drains financial resources like pulling the plug in a bathtub – sometimes faster. Choose legal counsel carefully and make certain that they understand your concerns. Sometimes a lawsuit is necessary, sometimes not.

(13) *Politicians.* Contacting a local politician is an option, but their individual ethics must be considered in such a decision. Most cannot be trusted, and will defer tough decisions to the prevailing winds. There are, however, cases of politicians assisting and even standing beside whistleblowers.

(14) *The media.* Contacting the news media should be the whistleblower's tool of last resort. Be aware of whether doing so voids legal protections. Also, understand that doing so will have an immediate impact on your professional reputation. There are no confidentiality rules in media and be prepared for them to spin the story in their own way. The only upside to reporting misconduct in such a public fashion is public attention and accountability.

(15) *Civil litigation.* Some agencys and supervisors will not respond to a complaint unless they think they have to, and getting the media involved can be a powerful motivator. Most people do not want to be seen in public doing the wrong thing. However, there are those who do not care what others think or who have a lot to hide because of their complicity in misconduct. In such cases, a formal external investigation is the best option for revealing the truth and holding wrongdoers accountable. Sometimes this can be accomplished through state or federal authorities. Once the administrative and criminal investigations are complete, the results may dictate a civil action. In other cases, a civil action is the only way to conduct an investigation, with subpoenas, discovery requests, and sworn depositions. Again, this is a lengthy and expensive process that should only be undertaken by the most serious of whistleblowers capable of enduring the loss of everything they once cared about, professionally.

Ultimately, the whistleblower in the criminal justice system must be prepared to be alone. They must accept the reality that as a result of their willingness to report ethical violations and other forms of misconduct, they may lose their job, and their professional identity, and may also be forced to change careers. It is unlikely that they will be considered heroic by anyone, and it is unlikely that they will experience success in their complaint other than that which is expensive, long-term, and hard-fought. Not everyone has the financial resources or stamina to survive that kind of experience.

Whistleblowers, being vital to the integrity of the criminal justice system and public safety, must be free to expose misconduct without the fear of reprisal or sanction. They must also be free to do so without fear of losing their livelihood. Currently, as demonstrated by the examples adduced throughout this text, this is not the case. Until such time as whistleblowers are free to act, ethical professionals will continue to remain silent and keep their heads down while others act in naked self-interest, against the cause of justice.

SUMMARY

Whistleblower is a generic term used to describe someone that reports misconduct within their own agency or institution or, as described in Miethe (1999, p. 11): "an employee or former employee who reports misconduct to persons who have power to take action." This includes reporting breaches of administrative policy, professional ethics, professional responsibilities, and also violations of the law.

This chapter presents a discussion of the ethical obligations, policies, and laws associated with reporting misconduct by employees within the criminal justice system. This includes mention of the protections that are ostensibly afforded to those with the courage to come forward under such circumstances. These ideals are counter-balanced with discussions regarding the potential consequences to whistleblowers – personal, professional, and legal. This chapter closes with some hard-earned advice regarding the steps that a would-be whistleblower can take in order to achieve the best possible professional outcomes, as well as likely repercussions.

Questions

1. Define the term whistleblower. List three consequences of reporting misconduct.
2. For the ethical criminal justice practitioner, the obligation to report misconduct exists whether there is a specific mandate or not. True or False?
3. List two forms of protection available to whistleblowers.
4. Explain the significance of the Whistleblower Protection Enhancement Act of 2012.
5. Provide three examples of whistleblower retaliation.

References

Abrahamson, L., 1997. The judge's ethical duty to report misconduct by other judges and lawyers and its effect on judicial independence. Hofstra Law Review 25 (751), 751–783.

Badgerow, J., 2013. The beam and the mote: a review of the lawyer's duty to report. Journal of the Kansas Bar Association 82 (February), 20–29.

Chamberlain, J., 2013. CIA torture whistleblower sentenced to 30 months. Common Dreams, January 25; url: https://www.commondreams.org/headline/2013/01/25-3.

Chin, G., Wells, S., 1998. The "blue wall of silence" as evidence of bias and motive to lie: a new approach to police perjury. University of Pittsburgh Law Review 59 (Winter), 233–299.

Cooper, C., 2009. Yes Virginia, there is a police code of silence: prosecuting police officers and the police subculture. Criminal Law Bulletin 45 (2), 4–20.

Dehaven-Smith, L., 2011. Myth and reality of whistleblower protections: official behavior at the top. Public Integrity 13 (3), 207–220.

Department of Occupational and Safety and Health Administration, 2013. Whistleblower protection program. Department of Occupational and Safety and Health Administration website, US Department of Labor, url: http://www.whistleblowers.gov.

Diehl, C., 2011. Open meetings and closed mouths: elected officials' free speech rights after Garcetti v. Ceballos. Case Western Reserve Law Review 61 (2), 551–602.

Garcetti et al. v. Ceballos, 2006. US Supreme Court No. 04, 473, May 30.

Giannelli, P., 1997. The abuse of scientific evidence in criminal cases: the need for independent crime laboratories. Virginia Journal of Social Policy and Law 4, 439–470.

Gresham v. City of Atlanta, 2011. US District Court, NDGa, September 29.

Innocence Project, 2009. Investigating Forensic Problems in the United States. The Innocence Project, New York, url: http://www.innocenceproject.org/docs/CoverdellReport.pdf.

Inspector General, 2012. Army Regulation 20-1: Inspections, Assistance, and Investigations, Inspector General Activities and Procedures, Rapid Action Revision (RAR) Issue Date: 3 July 2012. Headquarters, Department of the Army, Washington, DC.

International Association of Chiefs of Police, 2012. Model policy on standards of conduct. The International Association of Chiefs of Police website, url: http://www.theiacp.org/PoliceServices/ProfessionalAssistance/Ethics/ModelPolicyonStandardsofConduct/tabid/196/Default.aspx.

Johnson, R., 2005. Whistleblowing and the police. Rutgers Journal of Law and Urban Policy 3 (1; Fall), 74–83.

Johnson, C., 2013. Government slowly changes approach to whistle-blowers. National Public Radio, February 18; url: http://www.npr.org/blogs/itsallpolitics/2013/02/18/172099026/government-slowly-changes-approach-to-whistle-blowers.

Kiriakou, J., 2012. Reluctant Spy: My Secret Life in the CIA's War on Terror. Skyhorse, New York.

Knapp Commission, 1972. Report of the New York City Commission to Investigate Allegations of Police Corruption and the City's Anti-Corruption Procedures. Bar Press, New York.

Maier, T., 2003. Inside the DNA labs. UPI Insight Magazine, June 23.

McMorrow, J., Gardina, J., Ricciardone, S., 2004. Judicial attitudes toward confronting attorney misconduct: a view from the reported decisions. Hofstra Law Review 32, 1425–1473.

Miethe, T.D., 1999. Whistleblowing at Work: Tough Choices in Exposing Fraud, Waste, and Abuse on the Job. Westview Press, Boulder, CO.

Mollen, M., 1994. Commission Report, The City of New York: Commission to Investigate Allegations of Police Corruption and the Anti-Corruption Procedures of the Police Department.

Office of Research Integrity, 2009b. The Office of Research Integrity Annual Report 2009. US Department of Health and Human Services, Washington, DC, url: http://ori.hhs.gov/documents/annual_reports/ori_annual_report_2009.pdf.

Papandrea, M., 2010. The free speech rights of off-duty government employees. Brigham Young University Law Review 6, 2117–2174.

Parascandola, R., 2010. Whistleblower cop Adrian Schoolcraft on lawsuit against NYPD: 'This is not about money'. New York Daily News, September 28.

Parascandola, R., 2013. Frank Serpico joins forces with whistleblower suing NYPD for $50 million. New York Daily News, February 4.

Pershing, J., 2002. Whom to betray? Self-regulation of occupational misconduct at the United States Naval Academy. Deviant Behavior: An Interdisciplinary Journal 23, 149–175.

Rich, M., 2012. Lessons of disloyalty in the world of criminal informants. American Criminal Law Review 49 (Summer), 1493–1539.

Ridolfi, K., Possley, M., 2010. Preventable Error: A Report on Prosecutorial Misconduct in California 1997–2009. Northern California Innocence Project at Santa Clara University School of Law, Santa Clara, CA.

Reubenfeld, S., 2012. Obama signs whistleblower protection bill into law. The Wall Street Journal, November 27; url: http://blogs.wsj.com/corruption-currents/2012/11/27/obama-signs-whistleblower-protection-bill-into-law/.

Ronald, K., 2007. Garcetti v. Ceballos: the battle over what it means has just begun. Urban Lawyer 39 (4), 983–1015.

Rothwell, G., Baldwin, J., 2007. Whistle-blowing and the code of silence in police agencies: policy and structural predictors. Crime and Delinquency 53 (4), 605–632.

Shockley-Eckles, M., 2011. Police culture and the perpetuation of the officer shuffle: the paradox of life behind 'the blue wall'. Humanity and Society 35 (August), 290–309.

Sinzdak, G., 2008. An analysis of current whistleblower laws: defending a more flexible approach to reporting requirements. California Law Review 96 (6), 1633–1669.

Sovacool, B., 2008. Exploring scientific misconduct: isolated individuals, impure institutions, or an inevitable idiom of modern science? Bioethical Inquiry 5 (4), 271–282.

Seattle Police Department, 2013. Policy and Procedure Manual, Seattle Police Department. , March 28; url: http://www.seattle.gov/police/publications/manual/05_001_standards_duties.html.

Sullivan, P., 2012. The price whistle-blowers pay for secrets. The New York Times, September 21; url: http://www.nytimes.com/2012/09/22/your-money/for-whistle-blowers-consider-the-risks-wealth-matters.html.

Turvey, B., 2013. Forensic Fraud. Elsevier, San Diego, CA.

Uys, T., 2010. Speaking truth to power: the whistleblower as organizational citizen in South Africa. In: Lewis, D. (Ed.), A Global Approach to Public Interest Disclosure: What Can We Learn from Existing Whistleblowing Legislation and Research, Edward Elgar, Northampton, MA.

Whistleblower Protection Enhancement Act, 2012. Whistleblower Protection Enhancement Act of 2012, 112th Congress, 2d Session, Senate Report 112-155, to accompany S. 743. April 19.

Wolfe, S., Piquero, A., 2011. Organizational justice and police misconduct. Criminal Justice and Behavior 38 (4), 332–353.

Wright, R.G., 2011. Retaliation and the rule of law in today's workplace. Creighton Law Review 44 (3), 749–768.

Glossary

Academia The pillar of the criminal justice system comprised of those criminal justice researchers and educators working in colleges, universities, academics, and institutions around the world.

Academic misconduct A specific type of student misconduct, referring to any action that is intended to create an unfair academic advantage for oneself or that unfairly impacts the advantages of other members in the academic community.

Administrative investigations Fact-finding inquiries conducted by an agency or government regarding its own management and performance, generally in relation to internal violations of policy and procedure.

Admissibility "As applied to evidence … means that the evidence introduced is of such character that the court or judge is bound to receive it; that is, allow it to be introduced at trial" (Black, 1990).

Adversarial system A "jurisprudential network of laws, rules and procedures characterized by opposing parties who contend against each other for a result favorable to themselves. In such a system, the judge acts as an independent magistrate rather than prosecutor; distinguished from an inquisitorial system" (Black, 1990).

Appointed counsel Private defense attorneys appointed by the court to represent indigent defendants, often at a fixed or hourly rate.

Attorney–client privilege Legal entitlement to privacy intended to facilitate truthful communication and fully informed advocacy by a defendant's legal advisors.

Bias Prejudice in favor of, or against, something. Generally used to suggest an unfair advantage or disadvantage.

Brady v. Maryland A legal ruling from the US Supreme Court that holds, "the suppression by the prosecution of evidence favorable to an accused upon request violates due process where the evidence is material either to guilt or to punishment, irrespective of the good faith or bad faith of the prosecution" (*Brady v. Maryland*, 1963) It requires timely disclosure of exculpatory evidence by the prosecution to the defense.

Capability Possessing adequate resources for completing a particular task or serving in a particular appointment.

Cheating Any dishonest behavior that is intended to secure an unfair advantage – especially during an examination or an assessment of some kind.

Circular reasoning Using data to prove something that was used to develop the hypothesis; a proof that essential restates the question.

City/Municipal Attorneys Elected or appointed officials, serving to represent and advise local governments (e.g., assemblies, boards, administrators, and department heads in villages, townships, and cities) in criminal prosecutions, civil disputes, and other legal matters.

Code of Silence (a.k.a. Blue Wall of Silence) An unwritten rule in most police departments that prohibits reporting of perjury or other misconduct by fellow officers; it also forbids officers from testifying truthfully if the facts would implicate the conduct of a fellow officer.

Coercion   The use of force, threats, or intimidation to gain someone's compliance.

Compassion fatigue   "... the formal caregiver's reduced capacity or interest in being empathic or 'bearing the suffering of clients' and is 'the natural consequent behaviors and emotions resulting from knowing about a traumatizing event experiences or suffered by a person'" (Adams *et al.*, 2006, p. 104).

Competence   Possession of the knowledge, skills, and abilities required in order to do something effectively.

Competency to stand trial evaluations   Examinations that address the inmate's current mental state, and whether they are able to understand their charges and assist their attorney in their defense.

Conduct unbecoming   A charge used by police agencies to discipline its officers for any behavior that violates department rules and virtues.

Confession   A voluntary statement, written or recorded, by a criminal suspect that acknowledges guilt for a particular crime.

Conflict of interest   Occurs when a person or an agency has competing loyalties, or loyalties that are at odds, because of their need to satisfy multiple roles, duties, or obligations.

Consent   The act of giving permission with an awareness of the consequences.

Contingency fee agreements   Agreements in which experts are paid based on outcomes, which arguably guarantee findings or testimony favorable to their employer.

Contraband   With respect to corrections, material forbidden to be in the possession of inmates, such as drugs, alcohol, weapons, and cell phones.

Correctional officers   Those tasked with maintaining order and security within prisons.

Corrections   The pillar of the criminal justice system that deals with the probation, incarceration, management, rehabilitation, treatment, parole, and in extreme cases the execution of convicted criminals.

Credential mill   Refers to organizations that sell credentials to members for a fee, without a background check or the verified demonstration of knowledge, skills, and ability. In other words, members of such organizations are not required to earn credentials in any meaningful or demonstrable fashion.

Criminal defense attorney   Serves as the legal representative and advocate for the criminal defendant.

Criminal justice system   The network of government and private agencies intended to manage accused and convicted criminals.

Criminal responsibility evaluations   Examinations that deal with the mental state of an offender at the time of a crime.

Date and information fabrication   "Making up data or results and recording or reporting them" (Office of Research Integrity, 2009, p. 5).

Direct plagiarism   The exact reproduction of published work without any attribution of its original source.

Dishonesty   Any deliberate misrepresentation of fact by an act or an omission.

Dissemblers   Examiners who exaggerate, embellish, lie about, or otherwise misrepresent findings.

District Attorneys (DAs)   Elected officials that operate at the borough or country level to represent local government in the prosecution of criminal defendants.

Doyle Error   As held in *Doyle v. Ohio* (1976), "after an arrested person is formally advised by an officer of the law that he has a right to remain silent, the unfairness occurs when the prosecution, in the presence of the jury, is allowed to undertake impeachment on the basis of what may be the exercise of that right."

Dual agency   Occurs when the same provider is expected to both treat an inmate and perform a forensic evaluation for the court.

Due process   The preservation of federal and state constitutional rights; the rights of citizens as described in these constitutions may not be violated or taken away without strict adherence to the law.

Duty of care   The professional and legal obligation to be competent custodians of any victims that are encountered; any criminal investigations that are initiated; and any evidence that supports or refutes allegations of criminal activity against accused suspects. With respect to corrections, the state's responsibility for what happens to inmates while in its custody.

Embroilment   Occurs when a judge becomes so involved in a case that they actually take sides.

Enforcement-oriented policing   An approach to policing where there is a clear separation between members of an agency or department and the citizens they police.

Entrapment   A general term that refers to law enforcement inducing a person to commit criminal acts, specifically one that they would not have otherwise been likely to commit.

Employment disqualifiers   Are past and present activities or affiliations that evidence, or even appear to evidence, criminality, a propensity for dishonesty, or poor character.

Ethical dilemma   A type of ethical issue that arises when the available choices and obligations in a specific situation do not allow for an ethical outcome.

Ethics   The specific institutional rules of conduct constructed from morality and other elements of character (e.g., motivation, libido, courage, loyalty, integrity, and empathy); they are, consequently, the result of reflection and deliberation.

Evidence   "Testimony, writing, material objects, or other things presented to the senses that are offered to prove the existence or non-existence of a fact" (Black, 1990).

False confession   An admission of guilt that is untrue, often involuntary, made under duress, and as the result of coercion.

Falsification   Refers to subjecting a theory to repeated attacks in order to disprove it – testing it against the case facts or alternative theories.

Forensic examiner   Any professional who examines and interprets physical evidence with the expectation of courtroom testimony.

Forensic expert   An individual qualified to testify by virtue of "knowledge, skill, experience, training, or education" at the discretion of the judge.

Forensic fraud   Occurs when forensic examiners provide sworn testimony, opinions, or documents (e.g., affidavits, reports, or professional resumes) bound for court that contain deceptive or misleading information, findings, opinions, or conclusions, deliberately offered in order to secure an unfair or unlawful gain.

Forensic services   The pillar of the criminal justice system that deals with the examination and interpretation of evidence – physical, behavioral, and testimonial alike.

Garrity Rule   Refers to the US Supreme Court's decision in *Garrity v. New Jersey* (1967). It provides that during an administrative investigation, a police officer or other public employee may be compelled to provide statements under threat of discipline or discharge, but those statements may not be used to prosecute him/her criminally.

General knowledge exam   An exam that is intended to help guide members early in their careers through a valid course of study, covering broadly the basic knowledge and principles held in one or more fields of study.

Ghost authorship   "Ghost authorship occurs when the person whose name appears on the publication was not involved either in doing the research, framing the ideas behind the articles, or in writing the article. Alternatively, it can occur when an individual who has made substantial contributions to the manuscript is not named as an author or whose contributions are not cited in the acknowledgements" (Krimsky, 2007, p. 450).

Grand jury   Used to determine whether or not there is probable cause to believe that specific crimes have been committed by those named in any indictment – this instead of relying solely on the discretion of law enforcement.

Harmless error   An error that is not egregious enough to require a criminal conviction to be set aside or overturned.

Hazing   A particular kind of initiation ritual that involves physical pain or mental distress coupled with humiliating, intimidating, and demeaning treatment.

Hired guns   Private forensic experts who will testify to any opinion for a fee.

Inappropriate relationships   Any relationships that cause or promote ethical dilemmas.

Inculpatory statement   A voluntary statement, written or recorded, by a criminal suspect, acknowledging a particular decision or activity associated with a crime.

Ineffective assistance of counsel   Refers to defense attorney conduct that undermines the proper functioning of the adversarial process to the extent that the trial cannot be relied on as having produced a just result (*Strickland v. Washington*, 1984).

Inmate   An individual that has been arrested and detained by law enforcement, to be held in either a jail or a prison depending on their conviction status.

Intelligence-oriented policing   An approach to policing that is driven by gathering intelligence and analyzing it for crime patterns and trends.

Jails   Used to hold those who have been recently arrested prior to any court proceedings, such as an arraignment, in law enforcement custody.

Judge   Presides, impartially, over trials and appeals as a legal arbiter.

Judicial dispassion   The court's obligation to conduct itself without emotion or bias.

Judicial independence   The promise that "any litigant or lawyer appearing before a judge can be certain that the judge will rule according to the applicable rules and precedents without any external influence" (Abramson,1997, p. 752).

Judiciary   The pillar of the criminal justice system that deals with the adjudication or criminal defendants to include exoneration, punishment, treatment, and efforts to reform.

Jury   A group of men and women lawfully selected, convened, and sworn to investigate a legal dispute and then render an impartial finding in accordance with the law.

Justice   Fair and impartial treatment during the resolution of conflict.

Law enforcement   The branch of the criminal justice system that is legally commissioned to respond to crime.

Leadership   A set of traits and abilities that compel others to follow.

Legal aid attorneys   Those who volunteer to represent or assist indigent criminal defendants, usually as part of a non-profit organization (e.g., a legal aid society).

Legal justice   The result of forging the rights of individuals with the government's corresponding duty to ensure and protect those rights.

Logical fallacies   Errors in reasoning that essentially deceived those whom they are intended to convince. They are brought about by the acceptance of faulty premises, bias, ignorance, and intellectual laziness.

Malingering   Feigning illness, often for medication, attention, or as the result of personal crises.

Mandatory arrest laws   Requires law enforcement to make an arrest at the scene if there is probable cause that a crime has been committed.

Material witness   A witness that has information that is material to a criminal proceeding (the material nature of which is largely at the discretion of the prosecutor).

Material witness warrant   Used to detain a witness until their testimony is complete if the prosecutor believes that the witness would not respond to a subpoena to appear.

Mere suspicion   A level of confidence that is sometimes considered a gut feeling, or a hunch, that leads the individual to question a particular circumstance.

Moral dilemma   Exists when available choices and obligations do not allow for moral outcomes.

Morality   A significant contributor to the development of ethics and is most commonly associated with individual feelings or beliefs regarding actions.

NAS Report   Presents the findings of a Congressionally funded system-wide investigation and review of the forensic science disciplines and related crime lab practice.

Noble cause corruption   Corrupt or illegal acts committed by law enforcement in order to secure or maintain an arrest or conviction, or some other worthy end.

Observer effects   Any form of bias that occurs when the results of a forensic examination are distorted or influenced by the context (e.g., environment, culture) and mental state of the forensic scientist, to include subconscious expectations and desires.

Overcharging   The practice of charging a defendant with every conceivable criminal act committed or with the most serious form of a crime with the steepest penalty.

Overgeneralization   Making general statements to a broad population based on insufficient data.

Paraphrasing   A form of plagiarism that involves reproducing the work of others while changing the precise language of the original source only slightly and then failing to acknowledge the original source.

Patrol officers   Uniformed police assigned to move in a pattern within designated areas of a community (a.k.a. "beats") by foot, horse, bicycle, motorcycle, or more commonly a marked patrol car.

Peacekeeper-oriented policing   An approach to policing where officers are often integrated with the community they serve, viewing themselves as an important part of it.

Peer review   The process of subjecting an author's work, research, or ideas to the scrutiny of others who are experts in the same field.

Perjury   The act of lying or making verifiably false statements on a material matter under oath or affirmation in a court of law or in any sworn statements in writing.

Plagiarism   Involves the use of intellectual property (e.g., words, constructs, inventions, or ideas) without proper acknowledgement, giving others the false impression that it is original work.

Plagiarism of authorship   Involves placing one's own name on the completed work of another without significant alteration.

Police administration   The control and operation of law enforcement agencies, and the subsequent discharge of policies that keep the peace, increase public safety, and prevent crime.

Practice standards   Fundamental rules that set the limits of evidentiary interpretation, offering a standard for evaluating acceptable work habits and application of methods.

Presumption of innocence   The premise that all criminal defendants are considered innocent until proven guilty and that the burden of proving criminal guilt rests entirely on the government.

Principle of confidentiality   "A fundamental principle in the client–lawyer relationship is that, in the absence of the client's informed consent, the lawyer must not reveal information relating to the representation. … This contributes to the trust that is the hallmark of the client–lawyer relationship" (Michmerhuizen, 2007, p. 1).

Prisons   Designed to facilitate the long-term sentences of convicted felons.

Private attorneys   Represent those criminal defendants who can afford to pay for their own attorney and do not qualify as indigent. This involves a contract for a flat fee or an hourly rate.

Probable cause   Exists when the known facts and circumstances, of a reasonably trustworthy nature, are sufficient to justify a person of reasonable caution or prudence to believe that a crime has been or is being committed by the person being arrested. A reasonable belief that an individual has, is, or will commit a crime.

Pro bono   Work done for the public good, typically without financial compensation.

Profession   Defined by its ability to set a basic standard for competent workmanship and compel its members to conform.

Professional certification The process of establishing that a practitioner has achieved a particular level of knowledge, skill, and ability as demonstrated by coursework, instruction, and/or supervised experience.

Professional ethics The specific ideals, principles, values, and constraints imposed on practitioners by the mandates of their profession and workplace.

Professional organization A group with clear membership guidelines that establishes terms of professionalization and pledges sanction or expulsion for those unable or unwilling to meet those terms.

Professionalization The process by which any trade or vocation becomes professional, characterized by a high degree of competence with respect to domain-specific knowledge, skills, and abilities.

Prosecutorial misconduct "… the use of deceptive or reprehensible methods to attempt to persuade either the court or the jury" (*California v Hill*, 1998; *California v. Espinosa*, 1992; *California v. Price*, 1991; *California v. Pitts*, 1990).

Pseudoexperts Examiners who fabricate or misrepresent their credentials.

Public defenders Attorneys funded by the county, state, or federal government to provide representation to indigent defendants, as required by the US Constitution.

Quality control Monitoring and evaluating the environment, methods, and work-product for scientific integrity.

Racial profiling Discrimination against an ethical racial group based on the presumption that all members share criminal traits or tendencies.

Reasonable suspicion A level of confidence that is intended to describe facts and circumstances that may lead an officer to believe that a person will be involved in a crime, or was involved in a crime.

Reliability A test is reliable if it consistently yields the same result within whatever margin or error we are willing to accept.

Reversible error A trial error that is so harmful to justice that it requires some or all of the elements of a conviction to be overturned; these reversals are submitted for reconsideration by the court, if not retrial.

Role strain Provides that individual strain increases when "demands associated with one role interfere directly with one's ability to satisfy the demands of another role" (Hecht, 201, p. 112).

Scholarship A broad term that refers to academic study or achievement.

Scientific integrity Refers to consistency with the scientific method and established scientific guidelines, as well as the absence of corruption by other influences. A level of trustworthiness that must be earned and must not be assumed.

Scientific method A way to investigative how or why something works, or how something happened, through the development of hypotheses and subsequent attempts at falsification through testing and other accepted means.

Scientist "Someone who possesses an academic and clinical understanding of the scientific method, and the analytical dexterity to construct experiments that will generate the empirical reality that science mandates" (Chisum and Turvey, 2011).

Search and seizure laws The laws surrounding police authority to stop and search persons and their property for evidence related to a crime, as long as they have probable cause to believe that a crime has occurred and that the person being stopped is the one responsible.

Selective enforcement The arbitrary punishment of certain individuals or groups for legal violations or crimes, rather than the equal punishment of all known offenders.

Self-plagiarism (a.k.a "double dipping") The practice of submitting the same work product or one that is only slightly altered, to satisfy the requirements of multiple separate courses.

Sentence   The terms of punishment decided by the trier of fact.

Sexual coercion   The psychological, emotional, chemical, or physical manipulation of one person by another for sexual purposes – and can occur in an otherwise consenting relationship.

Sexual misconduct   Any sexually oriented behavior that violates established codes of conduct.

Simulators   Examiners who physically manipulate physical evidence or related forensic testing.

Social club   An organization that serves a group of like-minded individuals within a profession, without actual member accountability and without advancing the profession as a whole.

Stalking   Repeated and persistent unwanted communication or contact that creates fear in the target.

Student code of honor (a.k.a student code of ethics or student code of conduct)   A mandate that spells out the values, virtues, and behaviors that are expected of all confirmed registrants and their guests.

Student misconduct   Any violation of institutional rules, regulations, or codes of conduct by a student.

Theft or damage of intellectual property   Intentionally stealing or destroying the work of another.

Trier of fact   A judge or jury responsible for determining the legal guilt or innocence of a criminal defendant. The trier also decides the sentence.

Ultimate facts   "Facts which are necessary to determine issues in cases, as distinguished from evidentiary facts supporting them" (Black, 1990).

Ultimate issue   The legal question before the trier of fact (a.k.a. the judge or the jury).

Ultimate Issue Doctrine   Holds that witnesses are prohibited "from giving an opinion on the ultimate issues in the case. The rationale underpinning the ultimate issue rule is that expert opinion should not be permitted to invade the province of the jury" (Moenssens *et al.*, 1995, p. 75).

US Attorneys   Operate at the Federal level, working directly for the US Attorney General and representing the US government.

Validity   In reference to testing, when the results are reliable and accurate.

Whistleblower   Describes someone that reports misconduct within their own agency or institution.

Whistleblower Protection Enhancement Act of 2012   Signed into law in 2012, this legislation is intended to reform protections for federal employees seeking to report misconduct, fraud, and illegality.

Work-product   Refers to any notes, observations, thoughts, or research produced by the attorney, and such material is protected from discovery processes.

Index